NAFTA in the New Millennium

Contributors

Carlos Alba Vega
Leigh Anderson
Graciela Bensusán
Robert Brym
Edward J. Chambers
Wayne A. Cornelius
Debra J. Davidson
James B. Gerber
Raúl Hinojosa-Ojeda
Ryan Hoskins
Steven Kull
Robert K. McCleery
Rolf Mirus
Ross E. Mitchell
Alejandro Moreno
Neil Nevitte
Kenneth Norrie
Mark Ojah
Antonio Ortiz Mena L.N.
Douglas Owram
Robert A. Pastor
Barry E. Prentice
Linda C. Reif
Nataliya Rylska
Constance Smith
Peter H. Smith
José Luis Valdés Ugalde
Michele M. Veeman
Terrence S. Veeman
Phillip S. Warf

NAFTA

IN THE NEW MILLENNIUM

edited by

Edward J. Chambers and

Peter H. Smith

LA JOLLA

EDMONTON

Center for U.S.-Mexican Studies
University of California,
San Diego

The University of Alberta Press

30.00

Co-published by

Center for U.S.–Mexican Studies
University of California, San Diego
La Jolla, CA USA 92093-0510

ISBN 1-878367-41-1 (CUSMS

The University of Alberta Press
Ring House 2
Edmonton, Alberta, Canada T6G 2E1

ISBN 0-88864-386-1 (UAP)

Library of Congress Cataloguing-in-Publication Data

NAFTA in the new millennium / edited by Edward J. Chambers and Peter H. Smith
  p.cm.
  Papers selected from a conference.
  Includes bibliographical references.
  ISBN 1-878367-47-1 (paper)
    1. Free trade—North America—Congresses. 2. Canada. Treaties, etc. 1992 Oct. 7. 3. North America—Economic integration—Congresses. 4. North America—Foreign economic relations—Congresses. I. Chambers, Edward J. II. Smith, Peter H. III. University of California, San Diego. Center for U.S.-Mexican Studies.

  HF1746.N3352 2002   382'.917—dc21   2002074014

National Library of Canada Cataloguing in Publication Data

Main entry under title:
NAFTA in the new millennium
  Includes bibliographical references.
  ISBN 0–88864–386–1
    1. Free trade—North America. 2. Free trade—Economic aspects—Canada. 3. Free trade—Economic aspects—United States. 4. Free trade—Economic aspects—Mexico. 5. North America—Economic integration. I. Chambers, Edward J. II. Smith, Peter H.

  HF1746.N3428 2002   382'.917   C2002–910972–8

    The Center for U.S.-Mexican Studies acknowledges the generous support provided to its publications program by the William and Flora Hewlett Foundation.

    The University of Alberta Press gratefully acknowledges the support received for its publishing program from The Canada Council for the Arts. In addition, we also gratefully acknowledge the financial support of the Government of Canada through the Book Publishing Industry Development Program for our publishing activities.

Canadä

Contents

SECTION 3 — Economic Integration and Public Opinion

SECTION 4 — NAFTA in the Next Ten Years: Issues and Challenges

SECTION 5 — NAFTA in the Longer Term: Prospects for Institutional Development

Acknowledgments

It started at lunch. It moved on to a workshop and expanded into a conference. Then it turned into this book.

The idea of reassessing NAFTA took on a life of its own.

Brian Stevenson first provoked that seemingly innocuous lunchtime conversation. Two centers at the University of Alberta—the Western Centre for Economic Research and the Centre for International Business Studies—and two programs at the University of California, San Diego—the Center for Iberian and Latin American Studies and the Center for U.S.-Mexican Studies—provided institutional sponsorship for a multiyear study of NAFTA. Outstanding institutions from Mexico—the Centro de Investigación y Docencia Económicas (CIDE), El Colegio de México, the Instituto Tecnológico Autónomo de México (ITAM), and the Universidad Nacional Autónoma de México (UNAM)—formed an informal consortium in support of this project. In letter and spirit, this has become a truly trilateral endeavor.

We received financial support from the Chancellor's Associates and the Project on International Security Affairs (PISA) at UCSD, from the George M. Cormie Endowment and the Offices of the Vice President Research and the Vice President Academic at the University of Alberta, and from the Government of Alberta's Department of International and Intergovernmental Relations.

Graduate students made vital contributions. From UCSD, Kati Suominen served as rapporteur for the workshop and the conference, translated one of the papers, and offered insightful comments on successive drafts of papers. Chrisje Aardening and Alise Garni of UCSD and Ronald Volpi and research associate Stephen Janzen of the University of Alberta provided valuable research assistance.

We are grateful to Guy Stanley and Van Whiting for their editorial suggestions and substantive advice. We thank Linda Cameron of The University of Alberta Press for her patience and persistence. We appreciate the talents of Sandra del Castillo, who oversaw production of this volume at the Center for U.S.-Mexican Studies. For their administrative skill and constant good humor, we thank Nora Bodrian of UCSD and Jean Frost of the University of Alberta.

Finally, we thank our contributors—for their professionalism, their collegiality, and their commitment to the project.

Acronyms

ACN	Action Canada Network
AFL-CIO	American Federation of Labor–Congress of Industrial Organizations
ASEAN	Association of South East Asian Nations
ASERCA	Apoyos y Servicios a la Comercialización Agropecuaria / Support Services for the Marketing of Agricultural and Livestock Products
BECC	Border Environment Cooperation Commission
BIT	bilateral investment treaty
BNSF	Burlington Northern–Santa Fe
CADELEC	Cadena Productiva de la Industria Electrónica, A.C. / Production Chain of the Electronics Industry
CANIETI	Cámara Nacional de la Industria Electrónica, Tele-comunicaciones e Informática / National Chamber of the Electronics, Telecommunications, and Informatics Industry
CAP	Common Agricultural Policy
CARICOM	Caribbean Community
CEA	cumulative effects assessment
CEJALDI	Centro Jalisciense de Diseño / Jalisco Design Center
CEM	contract electronics manufacturer
CEPE	Consejo Estatal de Promoción Económica / State Board for Economic Development
CET	common external tariff
CGE	computable general equilibrium model
CLC	Canadian Labour Congress
CM	common market
CN	Canadian National
COECYTJal	Consejo Estatal de Ciencia y Tecnología de Jalisco / Jalisco State Council for Science and Technology
CONASUPO	Compañía Nacional de Subsistencias Populares / National Basic Foods Company

CONCAMIN	Confederación Nacional de Cámaras Industriales / National Confederation of Chambers of Industry
CPR	Canadian Pacific Railway
CRTC	Canadian Radio-television and Telecommunications Commission
CSA	Customs Self-Assessment system
CT	Congreso del Trabajo / Labor Congress
CU	customs union
CUSFTA	Canada–United States Free Trade Agreement
DRIE	Department of Regional Industrial Expansion
DSB	Dispute Settlement Body
DSM	dispute settlement mechanism
DSU	Dispute Settlement Understanding
EC	European Community
ECE	Evaluation Committee of Experts
ECLAC	Economic Commission for Latin America and the Caribbean
ECU	European currency unit
EFTA	European Free Trade Association
EIB	European Investment Bank
EMO	environmental movement organization
EOS	economies of scale
ERDF	European Regional Development Fund
ESF	European Social Fund
EU	European Union
FAT	Frente Auténtico del Trabajo / Authentic Labor Front
FDI	foreign direct investment
FESEBS	Federación de Sindicatos de Empresas de Bienes y Servicios / Federation of Goods and Services Unions
FIRA	Foreign Investment Review Agency
FOBAPROA	Fondo Bancario de Protección al Ahorro / Bank Savings Protection Fund
FOJAL	Fondo Jalisco de Fomento Industrial / Jalisco Industrial Promotion Fund
FTA	free trade area
FTAA	Free Trade Area of the Americas
GATS	General Agreement on Trade in Services

GATT	General Agreement on Tariffs and Trade
GCC	global climate change
GCC	Gulf Co-operation Council
GDP	gross domestic product
GMZ	Guadalajara Metropolitan Zone
GNP	gross national product
GST	Goods and Services Tax
HFCS	high-fructose corn syrup
HOS	Heckscher-Ohlin-Samuelson framework
ICSID	International Centre for Settlement of Investment Disputes
IDB	Inter-American Development Bank
ILO	International Labour Organization
IMF	International Monetary Fund
IMSS	Instituto Mexicano del Seguro Social / Mexican Social Security Institute
INEGI	Instituto Nacional de Estadística, Geografía e Informática / National Institute of Statistics, Geography, and Informatics
ISI	import-substitution industrialization
IT	information technology
ITA	International Trade Administration
ITS	intelligent transportation systems
JIT	just-in-time
JPAC	Joint Public Advisory Committee
MERCOSUR	Common Market of the South
MFN	most favored nation
NAAEC	North American Agreement on Environmental Cooperation
NAALC	North American Agreement on Labor Cooperation
NACEC	North American Commission for Environmental Cooperation
NACU	North American Customs Union
NADBank	North American Development Bank
NAFTA	North American Free Trade Agreement, North American Free Trade Area
NAFTA-TAA	North American Free Trade Agreement–Transitional Adjustment Assistance

NAO	National Administrative Office
NATAP	North American Trade Automation Prototype
NATO	North Atlantic Treaty Organization
NCC	negative cumulative causation
NDP	New Democratic Party
NTB	nontariff barrier
OECD	Organisation for Economic Co-operation and Development
OEM	original equipment manufacturer
ORIT	Organización Regional Interamericana de Trabajadores / Inter-American Regional Organization of Workers
PAN	Partido Acción Nacional / National Action Party
PCC	positive cumulative causation
PDI	private disposable income
PIPA	Program on International Policy Attitudes
PRD	Partido de la Revolución Democrática / Party of the Democratic Revolution
PRI	Partido Revolucionario Institucional / Institutional Revolutionary Party
Procampo	Programa para el Campo
PRODER	Programa de Desarrollo Empesarial Regional / Regional Business Development Program
PTA	Preferential Trade Arrangement/Agreement
RMALC	Red Mexicana de Acción frente al Libre Comercio / Mexican Free Trade Action Network
ROO	rules of origin
SAFTA	South American Free Trade Area
SECOFI	Secretaría de Comercio y Fomento Industrial / Ministry of Trade and Industrial Development
SEIJAL	Sistema Estatal de Información de Jalisco / Jalisco State Information System
SEPROE	Secretaría de Promoción Económica / Secretariat for Economic Promotion
SMEs	small and medium-sized enterprises
SPS	sanitary and phytosanitary
SS	specialized supplier
STRM	Sindicato de Telefonistas de la República Mexicana / Mexican Telephone Workers Union

TEU	twenty-foot equivalent unit
TFM	Transportación Ferroviaria Mexicana
TFP	total factor productivity
TMM	Transportación Marítima Mexicana
TOFC	trailer-on-flatcar
TPA	trade promotion authority
TRIMS	trade-related investment measures
TRIP	trade-related intellectual property
TRQ	tariff rate quota
UNCITRAL	United Nations Commission on International Trade Law
UNT	Unión de Trabajadores de Mexico / Union of Mexican Workers
UR	Uruguay Round
WIIT	Women in International Trade
WTO	World Trade Organization
WVS	World Values Survey

NAFTA in the New Millennium: Questions and Contexts

Edward J. Chambers and Peter H. Smith

NAFTA is ready for change. It seems like a long time ago, and in a different world, that Canada, Mexico, and the United States joined together in a free trade area. Once a much-feared superpower, Russia plunged into a downward spiral for most of the 1990s. Despite the appalling disintegration of Yugoslavia, the European Union (EU) reached out toward Eastern Europe, renewed its sense of purpose, and launched a common currency. A decade-long recession substantially diminished the economic and political standing of Japan, and by the late 1990s much of Asia was mired in the aftermath of a regional currency crisis; yet China, always an exception to the rule, pushed forward with economic opening and vigorous growth. The United States in the meantime enjoyed a remarkable burst of prosperity, one that began to slow down only by the century's turn.

Things also changed at home. The upstart Democrat Bill Clinton defeated Republican George H.W. Bush in the U.S. presidential election of 1992, won a second term in 1996, and was succeeded in 2000 by George W. Bush (the former president's son). In 1993 Canadian voters ousted the Progressive Conservatives, long regarded as the champions of free trade, and awarded the prime ministership to Jean Chrétien of the Liberal Party. The most stunning shift occurred in Mexico, where opposition candidate Vicente Fox broke the ruling party's 71-year stranglehold on power by sweeping the presidential vote in July 2000 and ushering in a new era of democratic contestation.

The new millennium thus dawned in an atmosphere of cautious optimism—until September 11, 2001, when terrorist teams hijacked commercial airliners and slammed them into the World Trade Center in New York City and the Pentagon in Washington, D.C. The horrendous attacks led to the loss of more than three thousand lives, billions of dollars in property damage, and a single-minded campaign by the

U.S. government to punish the perpetrators. Newly focused and de-termined, President Bush declared war on global terrorism, formed a broad international coalition in support of his goal, and launched mili-tary action in Afghanistan—whose Taliban rulers were said to be har-boring Osama bin Laden, the mysterious head of the Al Qaeda net-work assumed to be responsible for the September 11 assaults. For the United States, the fight against terrorism became an all-consuming mission.

Yet other issues have persisted, and they will have profound effects on the shape of the twenty-first century. In November 2001, represen-tatives from more than 140 countries met in the secluded setting of Doha, Qatar, and pledged to undertake a "millennium round" of nego-tiations designed to liberalize trade and stimulate the faltering global economy. Moreover, the People's Republic of China and Taiwan (deli-cately referred to as Chinese Taipei) were both admitted to the World Trade Organization (WTO), an institution that consequently gained a new lease on life. These decisions not only underlined the self-evident importance of economic factors in shaping the global arena; they also drew attention to the need for reviewing and reassessing trade ar-rangements at the regional level.

This brings us to the North American Free Trade Agreement. We now have eight years of experience with NAFTA. Leaders and citizens in member countries have a sense of what the agreement is and is not, what it can and cannot do. NAFTA has perhaps resolved some prob-lems but revealed (or created) others. The net result is (or ought to be) a process of collective learning, as reflection on the past leads to con-templation of the future: Should NAFTA be altered or reformed? How and why? Might it become the foundation for a Free Trade Area of the Americas (FTAA)?

To assess these possibilities, this book raises key questions:

- How has NAFTA performed thus far? How has it affected the member countries?

- Is there popular support for NAFTA? What do people in the member countries see as important or unimportant, effective or ineffective, successful or unsuccessful?

- What are the prospects for change? What are the foreseeable chal-lenges ahead? What are the longer-term issues? Should NAFTA be either "broadened" (by adding more members) or "deepened" (by extending levels of economic integration)? Or both?

- And how does NAFTA fit into the still-evolving world economy? How does it relate to initiatives for hemispheric economic integration—and for multilateral connections on a global scale?

Chapters in this volume respond directly to these queries.

In exploring such issues, we do not contemplate the possibility of renegotiating the NAFTA treaty itself. That would be counterproductive in political, economic, and bureaucratic terms. What we imagine instead is the possibility of a series of trilateral agreements on specific issues—such as migration, currency coordination, or financial support for regional development—that could eventually form a network or "web" of NAFTA-related agreements. The idea would be to supplement and strengthen existing accords, rather than to revise them. In this way, NAFTA could become a keystone for the creation of a constantly evolving North American community and, perhaps, for a hemispheric community of the Americas.

NAFTA: PROVISIONS AND CHARACTERISTICS

The North American Free Trade Agreement binds Canada, Mexico, and the United States together in an ambitious and far-reaching experiment in regional economic integration. It took shape in several stages. First was the negotiation of a bilateral free trade accord between Canada and the United States—approved in 1988 and initiated January 1989. Mexico began discussions with the United States in 1990, and Canada soon entered these deliberations. The text for a trilateral agreement was unveiled in August 1992 and signed that October by the leaders of the three countries. In the heat of the U.S. presidential campaign, Bill Clinton pledged to support NAFTA only on the condition that it include effective safeguards for environmental protection and worker rights; shortly after his inauguration, the governments reached "supplemental" or side agreements on both these matters. After ratification by legislatures of all three governments, NAFTA took effect in January 1994.

The treaty promotes the free flow of goods between member countries by eliminating duties, tariffs, and trade barriers over a period of up to fifteen years. Sixty-five percent of U.S. goods gained duty-free status immediately or within the first five years; half of U.S. farm goods exported to Mexico immediately became duty-free. There are special exceptions for certain "highly sensitive" products in agriculture, typically one of the sectors most resistant to economic integration; phase-outs on tariffs for corn and dry beans in Mexico and orange juice and sugar in the United States extend to the year 2009. Tariffs on all automobiles within North America are to be phased out over ten years, but rules of origin stipulate that local content would have to be substantial (62.5 percent of engines and transmissions, 50 percent of other parts) for vehicles to qualify. Not surprisingly, Asian governments regarded this clause as a transparently protectionist effort to exclude their industries and products from the North American market.

NAFTA opens Mexico to U.S. and Canadian investments in various ways. Under the treaty Canadian and U.S. banks and securities firms could establish branch offices in Mexico, and their citizens could invest in Mexico's banking and insurance industries. While Mexico continued to prohibit foreign ownership of oil fields, in accordance with its Constitution, U.S. and Canadian firms became eligible to compete for contracts with Petróleos Mexicanos (PEMEX) and to operate, in general, under the same provisions as Mexican companies.

NAFTA creates a free trade area (FTA), the most limited form of regional integration. It provides for the reduction and eventual elimination of barriers to the exchange of goods and to the flow of capital. It also permits the free exchange of selected services, particularly producer services, and it provides for the temporary movement of corporate executives and selected professionals.

NAFTA is not a customs union, in which participants apply a uniform external tariff schedule. All three members retain their own external tariffs. Neither does NAFTA envision a free flow of labor and financial services, as a common market does. As an FTA, NAFTA does not make any provision for the migration of labor. As a result, the continuing large-scale flow of "undocumented workers" from Mexico to the United States has remained a major source of contention and concern in the bilateral relationship. And unlike the European Union, NAFTA does not establish supranational regulatory agencies, a centralized bureaucracy, or parliamentary institutions. At face value, NAFTA appears to establish a fairly modest degree of economic integration.

NAFTA brings together very different countries. As shown in table I.1, the United States has the greatest number of people, with more than two-thirds of the free trade area's total population, Mexico has almost one-quarter of the total, and Canada—with the largest land surface of all—has well under one-tenth. And as illustrated in figure I.1,

Mexico has by far the greatest density of population, Canada has the least, and the United States stands in between. In fact these variations helped provide one of the underlying rationales for NAFTA in the first place: Canada had the land, it was said, Mexico had the people, and the United States had the money and technology.

Table I.1. Canada, Mexico, and the United States: Basic Profiles ca. 2000

	Canada	Mexico	United States
Population (millions)	30.7	98.0	281.6
Surface (million sq. km)	10.0	2.0	9.4
Population density[1]	3.3	51.3	30.7
Gross domestic product[2]	689.5	498.0	9,900.0
Per capita income[3]	21,050.0	5,080.0	34,260.0
Income/highest 20 percent[4]	39.3	58.2	46.4
Infant mortality[5]	6.0	36.0	8.0
Secondary school ratio[6]	95	66	96
Personal computers/000	360.8	44.2	510.5

Source: World Bank Web site, www.worldbank.org/data/. And see World Development Report 2000/2001: Attacking Poverty (New York: Oxford University Press, 2000), tables 1, 2, and 19.

[1] Persons per square kilometer.

[2] Billions of current U.S. dollars.

[3] Gross national income (GNI) per capita, Atlas method; U.S. dollars.

[4] Proportion of wealth held by top 20 percent of population.

[5] Mortality per thousand live births (through age 5).

[6] Proportion of school-age children enrolled, as percent of total.

In addition, NAFTA embraces partners at disparate levels of development—that is, one developing country (Mexico) and two developed nations (Canada and the United States). This situation creates profound asymmetries. According to table I.1, Canada's gross domestic product (GDP) (US$690 billion in 2000) is 35 to 40 percent larger than that of Mexico ($498 billion)—but both are overwhelmed by the United States ($9.9 trillion). Similarly, per capita income in Canada is over $21,000 per year—compared with $5,080 in Mexico and more than $34,000 in the United States. Moreover, Mexico displays typical

Figure I.1. Population Densities of NAFTA Countries

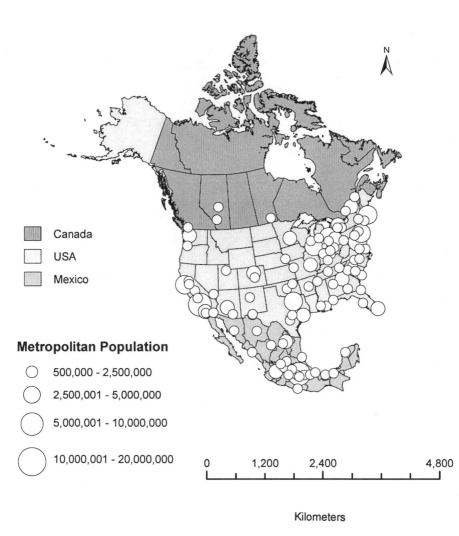

features of developing societies—highly uneven distribution of income, persisting infant mortality, modest school enrollment rates, and technological backwardness. (Note that the United States has more than ten times as many personal computers per thousand inhabitants as does Mexico, while Canada as eight times as many.) These disparities would present continuing challenges to NAFTA.

There are also major differences in economic performance. Figure I.2 displays data on economic growth in Mexico, Canada, and the United States from 1980 through 2000. Canada's rate underwent sharp oscillations during the 1980s and early 1990s, exceeding 5 percent in the mid-1980s but dropping below zero in 1982 and 1991, then showing steady growth from 1992 onward. The United States followed a similar pattern, with negative years in 1980, 1982, and 1991, then strong and steady expansion throughout the 1990s. Within this comparison, Mexico stands out for its volatility—having by far the worst years (1983, 1986, 1995) and also some of the best (1997 and 2000).

Political differences add even more complexity. Some differences derive from variations in cultural tradition—Hispanic, French, Anglo-Saxon, indigenous. Others relate to power in the world arena. Institutional considerations seem especially pertinent to NAFTA. One concerns electoral systems—parliamentary in Canada, presidentialist (with separately elected legislatures) in Mexico and the United States. Another concerns levels of "federalism" or provincial/state autonomy—which tend to be relatively high in Canada, low (although possibly changing) in Mexico, and intermediate in the United States. What this means is that local or provincial jurisdictions can have significant impacts on NAFTA's implementation. And in effect, the number of jurisdictions varies among the three countries—with ten provinces and three territories in Canada, fifty states plus the District of Columbia in the United States, and thirty-one states and one federal district in Mexico (where authority nonetheless remains highly concentrated in the central government).

Viewed in comparative context, NAFTA has three outstanding characteristics. First is its commitment to economic integration. Despite its title, NAFTA is not merely concerned with "free trade." By 1990 tariff and even nontariff barriers to North American commerce were already low. NAFTA is concerned with investment as well. By obtaining preferential access to U.S. and Canadian markets and a formal "seal of approval" through NAFTA, Mexico has been hoping to attract sizable flows of foreign direct investment (FDI)—from Japan and Europe as well as from its NAFTA partners. By obtaining un-

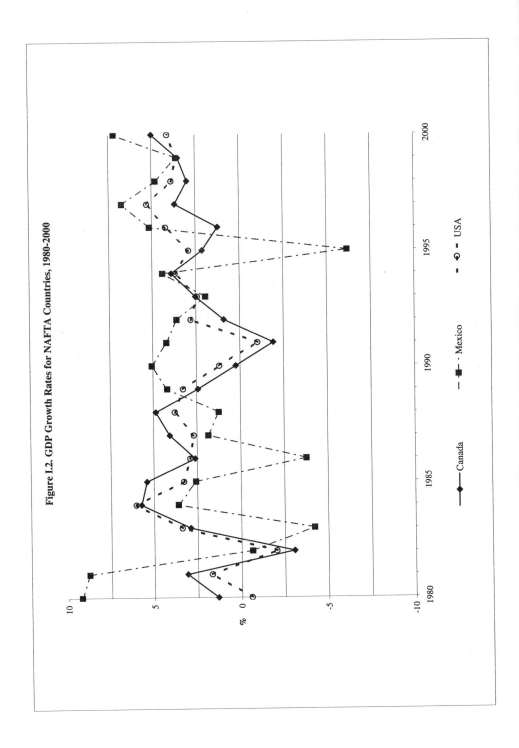

Figure I.2. GDP Growth Rates for NAFTA Countries, 1980-2000

trammeled access to low-wage (but skilled) Mexican labor, the United States was hoping to create an export platform for manufactured goods to improve its competitive position in the global economy. For these reasons the NAFTA treaty contains extensive chapters about investment, competition, telecommunications, and financial services. Commerce was only one part of the picture. Implicitly, NAFTA envisions a substantially more profound form of integration than its label suggests.

Second, NAFTA is essentially an intergovernmental accord. Unlike the European Union, with its elaborate structure for governance with genuine supranational authority, NAFTA relies mainly on negotiations and presumed consensus between national governments. As revealed by its provisions for dispute resolution, NAFTA does not entail any "pooling" or "sharing" or "delegation" of political sovereignty along European lines. The result might be inconsistency between the relatively "deep" level of economic integration envisioned by NAFTA—much of it already achieved—and its distinctly "shallow" level of political integration. To illustrate this point, table I.2 presents intra-regional trade as a share of all international trade for the three NAFTA members and draws comparisons with other integration schemes. NAFTA's intra-regional share has grown sharply, from 33 percent in 1980 and 37 percent in 1990 (before the treaty existed) to 47 percent in 1999—by which time it was fairly close to the EU proportion of 61 percent. Other regional groupings show much lower levels of commercial integration.

Table I.2. Intra-regional Trade as Share of World Trade

	1980 (%)	1990 (%)	1999 (%)
European Union	57	66	61
NAFTA	33	37	47
MERCOSUR	13	14	22
Andean	4	5	10
ASEAN	14	14	18

Source: International Monetary Fund, *Direction of Trade Statistics*, various years.

Third, NAFTA possesses an underlying political rationale. In this respect it shares a defining characteristic of all enduring integration schemes.[1] The political interests of the signatory countries were not identical, but they proved to be compatible.

- The United States was seeking, first, to preserve stability along its southern border; the idea was that NAFTA would stimulate economic growth in Mexico, ease social pressure, and sustain the prevailing regime. Second, Washington wanted a bargaining chip for its trade negotiations with Europe, Japan, and the General Agreement on Tariffs and Trade (GATT), now the World Trade Organization (WTO). Third, the United States wanted to assure access to petroleum from Mexico. Finally, the United States wanted to consolidate diplomatic support from Mexico on foreign policy in general; with NAFTA in place, Mexico became unlikely to express serious disagreement with the United States on major issues of international diplomacy.

- Mexico was seeking, first and foremost, preservation of its social peace. The hope was that NAFTA would attract investment, stimulate employment, alleviate poverty, reduce social tension, and perpetuate the country's political regime. Moreover, NAFTA offered President Carlos Salinas de Gortari an opportunity to institutionalize and perpetuate his neoliberal economic reforms. At the same time, Mexico was seeking international benediction for its not-quite-democratic political regime; such acceptance was especially important because—in comparison with Argentina, Chile, Brazil, and other countries undergoing processes of "democratization"—Mexico no longer looked like a paragon of political civility. Finally, Mexico believed that NAFTA would provide it with diplomatic leverage vis-à-vis the rest of Latin America and, by extension, the developing world as a whole.

- Political concerns were somewhat less salient for Canada, which had just reached its own FTA with the United States and was unhappy to learn in mid-1990 about ongoing discussions between Mexico City and Washington. Although reluctant, Ottawa eventually decided to join the NAFTA negotiations for defensive reasons: to prevent Mexico and the United States from devising a bilateral accord of their own that would damage Canadian interests. Economically, Canada appeared to have little to gain (and something to lose) from the inclusion of Mexico in an expanded North American market. Politically, however, Ottawa was in the process of elevating its profile in hemispheric affairs—and NAFTA membership eventually became an unanticipated source of diplomatic strength.

The convergence of political interests among the three countries was thus a driving force behind the conception of NAFTA. Maintenance of a political consensus will also be essential for continuing support of the agreement and its possible modification.

NAFTA: ISSUES, ASSESSMENTS, DEBATES

NAFTA has generated a good deal of controversy. That comes as no surprise. What is surprising is that academic and research communities across the three member countries have failed to reach agreement on NAFTA's accomplishments and impacts. Using disparate methodologies and parameters, analysts and commentators have forged a broad range of opinions about the treaty's function and future.

One thing is indisputably clear: trade among member countries has increased substantially since NAFTA went into effect. As shown in figure I.3, there has been growth in two-way trade between all pairs of partners: U.S.-Canada, U.S.-Mexico, and Canada-Mexico. Expressed in constant U.S. dollars (of 1996), total intra-NAFTA trade has expanded sharply, from just over $300 billion in 1993 to $500 billion in 1998 and more than $600 billion in 2000. By the end of the century, the United States was exporting more to Mexico than to China, Korea, and Singapore combined, and Mexico displaced Japan as the second largest trading partner of the United States; Canada remained in first place.

The data reveal a stark reality. Up to the present at least, NAFTA has not created a truly trilateral economic community. Instead it incorporates two bilateral relationships—one between Canada and the United States, the other between Mexico and the United States. The Canada-Mexico axis is conspicuously underdeveloped (and accounts for just a tiny fraction of intra-NAFTA trade). In effect, the United States is now the hub of NAFTA, while Canada and Mexico are spokes—and, partly as a result, their own economic performance is highly dependent upon the performance of the U.S. economy. This might or might not change in the future.

In general, there is no serious dispute about the existence of these commercial trends in NAFTA. Controversies focus on the causes, consequences, and implications of these trends. Legitimate questions arise:

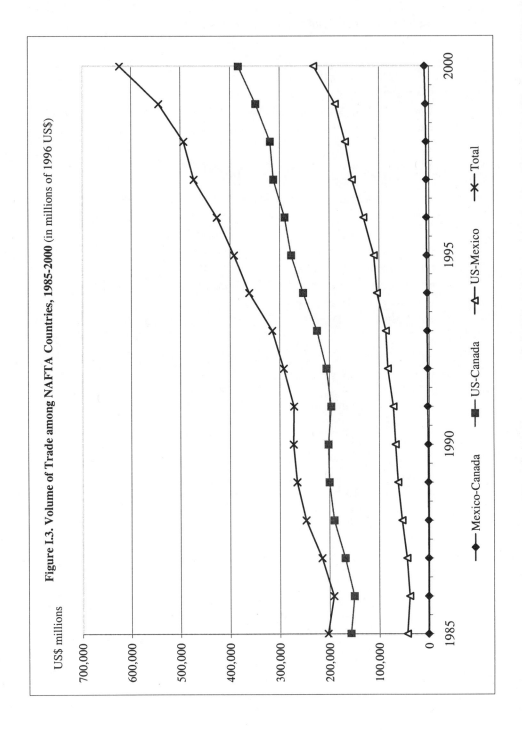

Figure I.3. Volume of Trade among NAFTA Countries, 1985-2000 (in millions of 1996 US$)

- How much of the expansion in trade is due to NAFTA? Supporters attribute virtually all this growth to NAFTA (as the *New York Times* editorial page said recently, NAFTA "has tripled commerce between Mexico and the United States in less than a decade").[2] Skeptics note that trends were generally upward throughout the 1980s and early 1990s—as can be seen in figure I.3—and they assert that (a) these increases would have occurred on their own, and/or (b) they result more from Mexico's 1986 entry into GATT and to conclusion of the GATT Uruguay Round than from NAFTA itself. Methodologists and econometricians insist that, whatever the outcome, it is essential to separate the "NAFTA effect" from other causal factors.

- Has NAFTA resulted predominantly in trade creation or trade diversion? Resolution of this question requires analysis of trade not only among the member countries but also, and more importantly, between member and nonmember countries. There is some evidence, for instance, that countries of the Caribbean have lost shares of the U.S. market to Mexico.[3] It remains possible that "created" trade still exceeds "diverted" trade—an issue that leads to an assessment of net welfare for non-NAFTA countries as well as its three members.[4]

- What impact has NAFTA had on employment? Has it created more new jobs than it has displaced? Are jobs moving rapidly from high-wage areas (Canada and the United States) to low-wage areas (Mexico)? Politicians in all countries have had a field day with unsubstantiated assertions on these subjects. Analysts worry about problems of measurement and attribution: according to an understated report from the White House in mid-1997, NAFTA resulted in "a modest increase in U.S. net exports, controlling for other factors," and boosted jobs in the export sector by 90,000 to 160,000.[5]

- What about wages and working conditions? Has NAFTA protected the interests of workers? Have wages been rising in Mexico? And is NAFTA having any effect on undocumented migration from Mexico to the United States (and Canada)?

- How has NAFTA affected the distribution of economic power? Proponents have argued that economic liberalization promotes efficiency and competition and, by definition, makes it possible for new contenders to enter the marketplace. Critics maintain that only the largest and strongest corporations are able to withstand the forces of international economic competition, and that, as a consequence, NAFTA has inflicted devastating blows to small and midsize businesses and to start-up ventures. Both camps cite Mexico as their principal case in point.

- What have been NAFTA's political effects? As supporters claim, has NAFTA promoted the process of democratization in Mexico? And has it led to any observable redistribution of political power in Canada and the United States?

- Has NAFTA established a "level" playing field for its member countries? Or is it really a tool for U.S. domination? Advocates insist that NAFTA's regulations, especially those pertaining to dispute resolution, mean that all three countries have to abide by uniform rules. Skeptics maintain that NAFTA provides just one more disguise for the naked assertion of U.S. hegemony throughout North America and, by extension, the entire Western Hemisphere.

Questions of this kind have prompted considerable discussion and controversy. On an analytical level, such questions also pose complex issues of causality. How much of any given phenomenon is a *direct consequence* of NAFTA? What might be accurately regarded as an *indirect consequence* of NAFTA? And how much just happens to be *coincidentally concurrent* with NAFTA?

Naturally enough, NAFTA debates about and within the member countries have varied sharply from nation to nation. Here follow some samples.

Canada

The most wrenching debates in Canada focused not on NAFTA but on the Canada–United States Free Trade Agreement (CUSFTA). In this context, NAFTA symbolized the streamlining of a process that had already begun in the late 1980s. The question is whether this free trade policy has improved the well-being of Canadian citizens.

Predictably enough, NAFTA proponents focus principally on the expansion of exports. In its 1999 report, the Canadian Ministry for

International Trade cited increases in exports of nearly 80 percent to the United States and 63 percent to Mexico over the five-year period from 1994 through 1998. Foreign direct investment in Canada also increased by 68 percent. The official stance, therefore, is that NAFTA was boosting the Canadian economy while creating additional jobs (one million or more) and stabilizing inflation rates.[6] Pro-NAFTA analysts concede that specific sectors of Canadian industry—energy, banking, transportation, and telecommunications—have gained the most thus far. Fundamentally, they assume that increased competition may be difficult for firms initially, but that it yields greater productivity and efficiency in the long term.[7]

Critics point to the distributional effects of NAFTA and free trade. Daniel Drache and others argue that competition and restructuring have led to the downsizing and dislocation of many Canadian firms—costing many workers their jobs or reducing their salaries. And as the social safety net has weakened, Canadian laborers are finding themselves "punished" by NAFTA in particular and by globalization in general.[8]

Skeptics also contend that increases in exports need to be assessed in relation to imports—which have been rising as well. During the 1990s, they observe, Canada was running a negative balance of trade with Mexico—which suggests that NAFTA, in contrast to CUSFTA, has actually diminished Canada's net position. More specifically, Mexico's expansion in the automobile and textile industries is seen as a threat to Canada's long-standing corner on the export market in these sectors. Having become a *low-cost* producer of autos, auto parts, and textiles, Mexico may begin to eliminate higher-cost competitors from Canada.[9]

Asymmetry has further shaped Canadian debates. As noted in table I.1, the U.S. GDP is fourteen times the size of Canada's and twenty times the size of Mexico's. This is not an equal relationship. As a result, critics have voiced a number of alarms:

- The size of the U.S. market makes the balance of the agreement (as a whole) increasingly dependent upon the performance of the U.S. economy.

- Disproportionate bargaining strength in the treaty negotiations allowed the United States to extract unfair concessions from Mexico and Canada, which could no longer protect themselves from foreign penetration.

- NAFTA's regulatory institutions are largely based on U.S. laws and precedents.

- The more generalized agreements under NAFTA (versus specific ones under CUSFTA) may exacerbate the United States' already disparate influence within the trade relationship.[10]

- Mechanisms for dispute resolution favor big business, not the public interest.

As an illustration of this last point, Canadian journalist Linda McQuaig cites cases under Chapter 11 of NAFTA in which large corporations have successfully sued governments for compensation. "What makes this new set of corporate rights particularly startling," she has written, "is that corporations get to make their claims to NAFTA tribunals operating in secret.... [N]o member of the public is allowed to attend these tribunal hearings, no transcripts are released, and no reasons are given for the decisions."[11]

More broadly speaking, academics in Canada often maintain that NAFTA's regulatory institutions are weak and ineffective. In fact, they insist, guidelines for NAFTA implementation and oversight are conspicuously vague—thus opening loopholes for the United States to resort to disguised protectionism. (Examples: the United States might refuse to import Mexican tomatoes that were not "grown according to NAFTA health and safety standards" or, as shown by recent events, might refuse to abide by the ruling on Mexican trucks on U.S. highways.)[12]

U.S. economists Gary Hufbauer and Jeffrey Schott have contested the claim that Canada's economy is excessively dependent on that of the United States. Acknowledging that the two economies tend to "move in tandem," they argue that that "the degree of correspondence is greatest in the money markets"—whereas inflation and unemployment rates between Canada and the United States do not show strong correlations.[13] With regard to institutional structures, the Canadian Ministry for International Trade suggests that NAFTA's regulatory mechanisms will develop and become increasingly effective over time.[14]

In terms of inter-American affairs, Ottawa has espoused the official view that NAFTA is improving relations among American nations and encouraging greater cooperation among North American trading partners. To this extent it has also strengthened Canada's diplomatic role throughout the hemisphere. The unstated assumption is that Canada's interests are essentially convergent with those of the United States.

Mexico

NAFTA proponents and critics tend to be one and the same in Mexico. Most are apt to cite both pros and cons on the issues. (It is indicative that, in the electoral campaigns of 1994 and 2000, left-wing presidential candidate Cuauhtémoc Cárdenas called not for the rejection of NAFTA but instead for its revision.) Overall, even those who are critical are, ultimately, largely optimistic that the agreement will boost the Mexican economy and provide benefits to broad sectors of the national society.

Interestingly enough, NAFTA has *not* been widely held responsible for two of Mexico's most traumatic events in the 1990s: the peasant rebellion in Chiapas, and the 1994–1995 peso crisis. Although Subcomandante Marcos specifically denounced the free trade accord at the time of the uprising (January 1, 1994, the same day that NAFTA went into effect), most observers attribute the rebellion to local and historic causes. Similarly, NAFTA has escaped widespread blame for causing the precipitous plunge of the peso in December 1994 (even though the accord might have encouraged "overshooting" by investors and excess optimism within official circles). Instead, the principal charge is that NAFTA failed to prevent the peso crisis. At the same time, it is often conceded that NAFTA helped assure that the United States would provide a substantial rescue package in early 1995.

Foreign investment under NAFTA has nonetheless provoked concern in Mexico. Analysts agree that NAFTA prompted a surge in investment—not to mention the repatriation of Mexican capital from abroad. Yet while proponents assert that FDI has raised wages and skills among workers (via employment training programs), opponents contend that labor is gradually replaced by technology and that regional concentrations of foreign capital provide benefits only to certain areas and not to those most in need.

Uneven growth among industries creates regional disparities. While observers acknowledge that exports are on the rise, they simultaneously contend that there are only a few Mexican companies—large and powerful ones—that are capable of exploiting opportunities under NAFTA. Firms in electronics, autos or auto parts, and textiles will realize advantages—but only at the expense of workers' benefits and salaries. Mining, lumber, and agriculture have fallen on hard times and have little hope for support or protection from the Mexican government. As in Canada's case, NAFTA optimists argue that, following an initial adjustment period, increased competition among multinational companies will eventually improve employment and living standards for most Mexicans.[15]

Regarding NAFTA's impact on labor, U.S. expert Harley Shaiken has pointed to a glaring inconsistency: "between 1993 and first quarter 1997," he has written, "productivity in Mexican manufacturing rose by over 38 percent while real hourly wages for production workers plummeted by 21 percent." The disparity in wage versus productivity trends is traceable to the 1980s, when organized labor began cooperating with the Mexican government to contain wages, and also to the lack of enforceable labor rights. Overall, the minimum wage in Mexico has dropped to one-third of its 1980 level (in real terms),[16] and NAFTA has provided little effective support for members of the working class. Whereas wage ratios between Mexico and the United States were 8 to 1 before NAFTA's implementation, they are now 10 to 1.[17]

Mexican President Vicente Fox has expressed acute displeasure with this downward trend. It is largely for this reason, in fact, that he has proposed transformation of NAFTA from an FTA into a common market. As he declared in July 2000, "we want to move upward from the trade agreement to a community of nations agreement or a North American common market."[18] This would eventually require such radical measures as opening North American borders to "free flows of labor and capital"[19] and implementing a common currency ("20, 30, or 40 years from now").[20] Ultimately, Fox has proclaimed, "we think NAFTA can do much better.... [It] has to go to the level of small and medium-sized companies which, up to today, have not yet benefited from the agreement."

Not everyone agrees with this position. Some analysts argue that while NAFTA is not ideal, it is providing jobs that were previously unavailable to most Mexicans. Due to NAFTA-related increases in trade, they add, workers in the *maquiladora* (in-bond processing) sector are earning higher wages than they formerly did as agricultural or seasonal workers. Lastly, the concentration of *colonias* surrounding the maquiladoras along the U.S.-Mexico border promotes the development of informal sectors, which provide additional opportunities for the sale of personal goods and services.[21]

Politically, most observers agree that the treaty is helping the United States and Mexico to overcome their historic differences and thus improving North American relations. One problem, however, is that Mexico's judicial system is not sufficiently developed to expeditiously mediate NAFTA-related disputes. As a result, the United States might continue to exploit Mexico by exerting an asymmetrically powerful influence through loosely structured and inadequately endowed trilateral institutions.

United States

Debates over NAFTA are, perhaps, fiercest in the United States. The official line expresses unwavering praise for the agreement. Politicians insist that NAFTA will provide U.S. firms with access to an increasingly affluent consumer market in Mexico, and that it will enhance existing trade advantages with Canada. Policymakers, moreover, assert that NAFTA can help to insulate the U.S. economy from external shocks—such as the Asian crisis of 1997–1998.[22] All recent presidents—Bush the Elder, Clinton, and Bush the Younger—have consistently expressed their faith in NAFTA and in the benefits it brings to the United States. As Bill Clinton once proclaimed, "NAFTA is an integral part of a broader growth strategy that has produced the strongest U.S. economy in a generation."[23]

Opponents are vocal, organized, and ambitious. To counter the claim that NAFTA creates new opportunities for U.S. exports, they point to the rise in imports—and to the nation's swelling trade deficit. In fact, NAFTA critics tend to attribute virtually all growth in the trade deficit (an average of −$16 billion per year) directly to the treaty itself.[24] Others claim that U.S. export data are misleading, since they include goods that are actually produced abroad and merely routed through the United States.[25] They point with apprehension to the exportation of U.S. technology—especially for electronics, autos, and auto parts—that threatens American jobs and production bases.[26] Charles McMillion has gone so far as to assert that NAFTA will ultimately eliminate the nation's historic comparative advantages, noting, for example, that the United States now pays more for technology and autos than it sells abroad.[27]

Critics also focus on exchange rates and currency instability. As shown by the Mexican peso crisis of 1994–1995, sharp devaluations can place U.S. goods at a marked disadvantage because imported products become less expensive in dollar terms, while U.S. goods increase their price in foreign markets.[28] Without increased wages and purchasing power, Canadians and Mexicans can afford fewer U.S. goods.

Often representing organized labor, critics further contend that NAFTA serves the interests of large-scale corporations—while average

American workers feel the squeeze of competition from cheap overseas labor. They also insist that the availability of inexpensive (and underrepresented) labor will ultimately draw U.S. manufacturing into Mexico and lead, in effect, to the exportation of American jobs.[29] (This is what erstwhile presidential candidate Ross Perot derisively referred to as "that giant sucking sound.")

At its core, much of the debate turns upon a simple question: whether NAFTA will drag U.S. and Canadian wage (and employment) rates down to the current level of Mexico, or whether NAFTA will bring Mexican standards up to prevailing levels in Canada and the United States. The same concern holds true for environmental practices. Proponents maintain that NAFTA's side agreement will enforce environmental regulations and encourage the public to demand effective implementation. Opponents insist that large multinationals will use the agreement to circumvent regulations and, in particular, pressure Mexico to relax environmental standards as a means of attracting foreign investment.

Politically, the debate over NAFTA focuses on domestic versus international interests. Advocates assert that the agreement will improve U.S. living standards and thereby encourage greater political participation. Opponents argue that the use of fast track authority for trade agreements, such as NAFTA, inherently threatens U.S. democratic institutions since it prohibits congressional amendment to negotiated treaties. In this sense, NAFTA imposes severe costs on American citizens who simultaneously lose their jobs, their safety nets, and their access to responsible political representation.[30] On the international level, proponents assert that NAFTA serves national security interests by increasing the incentives for U.S. trading partners to cooperate with Washington. They also see NAFTA as a bulwark for democracy in Mexico and as a keystone for a Free Trade Area of the Americas. Critics regard these claims as vacuous and denounce FTAA as an additional threat to American workers.

UNCERTAINTY ABOUT UNCERTAINTY

Debates and deliberations about NAFTA take place in a changed and changing world. One of the terrible tolls of the September 11 attacks is widespread uncertainty—about personal safety, about the transregional reach of terrorist organizations, about the efficacy of antiterrorist measures, about the relationship between individual freedom and collective security, about international alignments and the structure of global power. Some observers have expressed fear of a "clash of civilizations," a deep-rooted and long-lasting conflict between the West and Islam; others have confidently predicted the dawn of a "new world order." For leaders and citizens within North America, three major scenarios loom large:

- One concerns the prospect that the United States will adopt an essentially isolationist posture, seeking safety and security by closing itself off (as much as possible) from the outside world—including Mexico and even Canada. Hints of this possibility come from efforts to tighten security at U.S. borders, both north and south, wreaking havoc on commerce, travel, and other legitimate forms of social and economic integration. A prolonged American stance of this kind would have a directly negative impact on NAFTA and stifle prospects for its future development.

- A second scenario imagines that the Bush administration will continue the suddenly and surprisingly internationalist tack that it adopted in the wake of the September 11 attacks—but will concentrate virtually all its energy and resources on the regions directly involved (that is, the Middle East and South and Central Asia). That certainly describes the situation during the last several months of 2001 and the first half of 2002. Under these circumstances, the United States will aspire to international leadership—but contrary to President Bush's initial inclinations, NAFTA might be reduced to a minor role in U.S. global policy.

- A third scenario, by far the most positive, assumes a restoration of "balance" about world affairs—on the part of America's allies as well as the United States itself. An increasingly multilateral anti-terrorist campaign will focus not only on justice (or revenge) but also on the root causes of anger, resentment, and hysteria. Equity and development will receive as much attention as military and para-military exploits. NAFTA will come to be viewed by all its members as a key element in global strategy: as a source of prosperity and security for the citizens of North America, as a demonstration of the geopolitical importance of economic cooperation, and as an example of productive relationships between the developed and the developing world.

It is entirely possible that all three tendencies will coexist with one another and, in combination, give simultaneous shape to the global and hemispheric order. Along with uncertainty, contradiction and complexity seem likely to mark the foreseeable future. This panorama poses yet another fundamental challenge to NAFTA and its potential evolution.

Notes

1. The European Union provides a case in point. From the time of its foundation in the late 1950s, the idea of regional integration had two major political goals: placing constraints on Germany, in order to preserve postwar stability, and strengthening Western Europe against the Soviet bloc, in order to contain communism.

2. *New York Times*, August 6, 2001, p. A16.

3. Jamaica's minister of foreign affairs and foreign trade has bluntly stated: "the stark reality is that Mexico can now export its products to the United States free of duty, which makes it more profitable for producers to operate from there.... Putting it very simply, if that is not stemmed, it could do untold damage to our manufacturing sector and economy as a whole," *New York Times,* January 30, 1997, pp. A1–2.

4. See Anne O. Krueger, "Trade Creation and Trade Diversion under NAFTA," National Bureau of Economic Research Working Paper 7429 (Cambridge, Mass.: NBER, 1999).

5. *Study on the Operation and Effects of the North American Free Trade Agreement* (Washington, D.C.: The White House, 1997), p. iii.

6. Canadian Ministry for International Trade, 1999 report.

7. Gary C. Hufbauer and Jeffrey J. Schott, *North American Economic Integration: 25 Years Backward and Forward* (Ottawa: Industry Canada Research Publications Program, 1998), p. 36. See also Hufbauer and Schott, *NAFTA: An Assessment* (Washington, D.C.: Institute for International Economics, 1993).

8. Daniel Drache, "Pensar desde afuera de la caja: una perspectiva crítica del quinto aniversario del TLCAN," in *Para evaluar al TLCAN*, ed. Arturo Borja Tamayo (Mexico City: Porrúa, 2001); Teresa Gutiérrez Haces, "Canadá y el libre comercio," in *Nuevas dimensiones de la integración: del TLCAN al regionalismo hemisférico*, ed. Germán de la Reza and Raúl Conde Hernández (Mexico City: Plaza y Valdés, 1999); Bruce Campbell, "'Free Trade': Destroyer of Jobs" (Ottawa: Canadian Center for Policy Alternatives, 1993); and Mel Clark, "Restoring the Balance: Why Canada Should Reject the North American Free Trade Agreement, Terminate the FTA and Return to GATT" (Ontario: Council of Canadians, 1993).

9. See Jon R. Johnson, "NAFTA and the Trade in Automotive Goods," in *Assessing NAFTA: A Trinational Analysis*, ed. Steven Globerman and Michael Walker (Vancouver, B.C.: Fraser Institute, 1993).

10. See essays by Daniel Drache and A. Imitaz Hussain in *Para evaluar al TLCAN*, ed. Borja Tamayo; Campbell, "'Free Trade'"; and Clark, "Restoring the Balance."

11. "Free Trade Face Off: Counterpoint," *Canadian Business* April 30, 2001, pp. 107–109. It should be observed, however, that NAFTA tribunals do not really operate "in secret"—as is common in commercial arbitration, proceedings are confidential (to protect proprietary information) unless the parties to the dispute agree otherwise, and most interim and final decisions under NAFTA have in fact been made publicly available by consent. Transparency is still a legitimate concern, however, and the governments have recently agreed to promote greater openness in the arbitration process.

12. Joseph A. McKinney, *Created from NAFTA: The Structure, Function, and Significance of the Treaty's Related Institutions* (New York: M.S. Sharpe, 2000); and chapters by Drache and Hussain in *Para evaluar al TLCAN*, ed. Borja Tamayo.

13. Hufbauer and Schott, *North American Economic Integration*, p. 19.

14. See also Beatriz Leycegui and Rafael Fernández de Castro, eds., *¿Socios naturales? Cinco años del Tratado de Libre Comercio de América del Norte* (Mexico City: Instituto Tecnológico Autónomo de México, 2000).

15. See Leycegui and Fernández de Castro, *¿Socios naturales?*; Borja Tamayo, *Para evaluar al TLCAN*; and José Luis Valdés-Ugalde, *Análisis de los efectos del Tratado de Libre Comercio de América del Norte en la economía mexicana: una visión sectorial a cinco años de distancia*, 2 vols. (Mexico City: Miguel Ángel Porrúa/ Senado, 2000).

16. Harley Shaiken, "China, Mexico: Same Depressing Tale on Labor Rights," *Los Angeles Times*, May 16, 2000.

17. Robert Manning, "Five Years after NAFTA: Rhetoric and Reality of Mexican Immigration in the 21st Century" (Washington, D.C.: Center for Immigration Studies, 2000).

18. Linda Dieble, "Mexico's Fox Makes Free Trade a Priority for Talks with Canada," *Toronto Star*, July 5, 2000.

19. Quoted on CNN, August 24, 2000.

20. Dieble, "Mexico's Fox," p. 2.

21. Leycegui and Fernández de Castro, *¿Socios naturales?* and Borja Tamayo, *Para evaluar al TLCAN*.

22. *Study on the Operation*; and *NAFTA Works for America: Administration Update on the North American Free Trade Agreement* (Washington, D.C.: U.S. Government Printing Office, July 1999).

23. *Study on the Operation*, p. i.

24. Robert E. Scott, "NAFTA's Pain Deepens: Job Destruction Accelerates in 1999 with Losses in Every State," Briefing Paper (Washington, D.C.:

Economic Policy Institute, 1999); John R. MacArthur, *The Selling of Free Trade: NAFTA, Washington, and the Subversion of American Democracy* (New York: Hill and Wang 2000); Manning, "Five Years after NAFTA."

25. See especially MacArthur, *The Selling of Free Trade.*

26. With characteristic hyperbole, columnist Patrick Buchanan testified to Congress in April 1999 that 70 percent of American jobs in electronics manufacturing have been lost because of NAFTA.

27. Charles McMillion, testimony before the Committee on Foreign Relations, April 13, 1999.

28. Ibid.

29. MacArthur, *The Selling of Free Trade*; Scott, "NAFTA's Pain."

30. MacArthur, *The Selling of Free Trade.* For dispassionate academic analyses, see Maxwell Cameron and Brian Tomlin, *The Making of NAFTA: How the Deal Was Done* (Ithaca, N.Y.: Cornell University Press, 2000); and Maryse Robert, *Negotiating NAFTA: Explaining the Outcome in Culture, Textiles, Autos, and Pharmaceuticals* (Toronto: University of Toronto Press, 2000).

Section 1

The Political Economy of North American Economic Integration

What has been the impact of the North American Free Trade Agreement (NAFTA) on member economies? Essays in Section 1 of this volume provide empirical and up-to-date assessments of NAFTA's consequences for the United States, Mexico, and Canada.

Raúl Hinojosa-Ojeda and Robert McCleery argue that, from the standpoint of the United States, the political and economic significance of NAFTA has been global as well as regional. They maintain that the domestic debate over NAFTA could have provided—and could still provide—important lessons for future policies regarding regional and global integration, but that it has become much too highly polarized to serve this purpose. As for the impacts of NAFTA, they stress the importance not only of trade but also of labor and capital flows. They subject a series of prominent hypotheses in the economics literature to empirical tests. And they utilize the concept of cumulative causation, which stipulates that conditions and processes at an initial point lead to path-dependent developments which may be either positive, in which case integration leads to closing of productivity and income gaps (convergence), or negative, in which these gaps widen (divergence). While Hinojosa-Ojeda and McCleery find evidence of both positive and negative cumulative causation in the NAFTA experience for Mexico and the United States, they see no fundamental shift in pre- and post-NAFTA patterns of trade, investment, and production.

In chapter 2, José Luis Valdés-Ugalde evaluates the impacts of NAFTA on Mexico and emphasizes the need to conduct a sector-by-sector analysis. Valdés-Ugalde notes that important trade liberalization came well before NAFTA, most notably through the accession to the General Agreement on Tariffs and Trade (GATT) in the mid-1980s. Under these conditions, NAFTA provided some Mexican producers with guaranteed access to the U.S. market. The treaty also encouraged foreign investment in Mexico. But at the same time, the North American accord has promoted concentration in Mexico's export sector, reduced levels of integration in domestic manufacturing, and led to negligible adaptation of technology. Unemployment has risen and wages have declined. All in all, Valdés-Ugalde concludes that NAFTA is only one of many factors affecting the Mexican economy—and that, in his words, "the relative weight of the other factors was more decisive than that of NAFTA."

Kenneth Norrie and Doug Owram offer a Canadian perspective in chapter 3. They begin by asking why continental trade liberalization should have happened at all, considering Canada's long-standing resistance to free trade with the United States. They then assess the impact of the Canada–United States Free Trade Agreement (CUSFTA) and of NAFTA on Canada's economic performance. They find that liberalization had pretty much the predicted results in terms of resource allocation within and among industrial sectors, but that free trade effects were overwhelmed by the impacts of macroeconomic policies and low productivity growth. Finally, they examine the emerging role of free trade as an "idea," an organizing concept that shapes Canadian attitudes toward economic policy, regional relations (with Mexico as well as the United States), and patterns of globalization.

Put succinctly, the relative impact of NAFTA has thus far proven to be greatest in Mexico and least in the United States—with Canada somewhere in the middle, but where observable effects are perhaps more due to CUSFTA than to NAFTA itself. A general rule thus holds: the larger the economy, the less the impact of the free trade area.

And while these chapters marshal a great deal of evidence in support of their claims, it also seems too early to render definitive judgments on NAFTA. As with other integration schemes, short-term effects are concentrated and sometimes negative; longer-term effects are more diffuse and often more positive, and they have not all begun to appear.

1

NAFTA as Metaphor: The Search for Regional and Global Lessons for the United States

Raúl Hinojosa-Ojeda and Robert K. McCleery

The political-economic significance of the North American Free Trade Agreement (NAFTA) for the United States has always been global as well as regional. It was within a global perspective of national security concerns and the stalled Uruguay Round of world trade negotiations that U.S. policymakers in 1990 first decided to move ahead with NAFTA.[1] And it was within a global perspective that most critics of NAFTA focused their apprehensions, sensing it as a commitment to a dubious "neoliberal" global agenda. Indeed, the dividing lines in ensuing controversies about "globalization"—and, in fact, the widespread use of the term itself—were rooted in the NAFTA debate and the lack of closure in its aftermath.[2]

The U.S. debate on NAFTA in the early 1990s continues to have a profound effect, not only on North American policy discussions but also on broader debates about globalization. The NAFTA issue came at a crucial time, as trade between the developed and developing world was growing more rapidly than ever before. NAFTA was the first free trade agreement between the United States and a developing country, and it was the most ambitious anywhere in the world between countries with such extreme differences in income and development. NAFTA promised to provide an important opportunity to ask perhaps the most significant question of the current era in international political economy: What is the impact of accelerating economic integration between countries at very different levels of development? Exploration of this question yields insights into the relationship between efficiency impacts on sectoral output and employment, the growth rates of national income and productivity, and the distribution of income within and between countries. A well-reasoned analysis of NAFTA could provide important lessons for the United States in formulating future regional and global integration policies.[3]

THE PUBLIC CONTROVERSIES

Unfortunately, the NAFTA debate quickly became highly politicized and starkly polarized into uncompromising "pro" and "anti" positions. Supporters and critics both sought to use NAFTA as a metaphor for focusing on the benefits or the costs of expanded global economic integration. As the debate began, many U.S. interest groups were only beginning to develop a theoretical understanding and policy position on the relationship among globalization, economic efficiency, and the convergence or divergence of national and international income levels. NAFTA proponents suggested that trade liberalization would produce a boom in U.S. export jobs and a "win-win" growth prospect for North America, with job growth expanding in export industries, pulling up wages, and absorbing the unemployed on both sides of the border. NAFTA opponents focused on fears that trade liberalization would produce a "race to the bottom" in wages, working conditions, and environmental standards, with the United States on the losing end while investment flowed out to Mexico as multinationals exploited Mexican labor. An evaluation, or even a critical discussion, of these metaphors became very restricted, in part because the research agendas of think tanks and some academics began to mirror what was necessary to support one or another faction in the political debate. What was similar is that both sides used simple linear models of causality with overly simple methodologies, supporting similarly simplistic policy responses.

An alternative "third way" position—acknowledging the benefits of integration while emphasizing the need to address income disparities—was drowned out in a polarized political debate. A small number of analysts and policymakers began forging an alternative perspective that simultaneously recognized the costs and benefits and developed a policy framework for "upward convergence" of productivity and incomes. (Ironically, after being eclipsed by partisan views during the Clinton administration, this idea reappeared in the February 2001 "Guanajuato Proposal" of Presidents George W. Bush and Vicente Fox, who declared their intent to "consolidate a North American economic community whose benefits reach the lesser-developed areas of the region and extend to the most vulnerable social groups in our countries.")

Such an approach, however, requires a more complex theoretical framework, improved methodologies for analysis, and a more flexible and varied set of policy strategies.

The conceptual and policy challenges of North American integration require an analytical framework that simultaneously analyzes trade, foreign investment, migration, and remittances. This framework must also account for two major dynamics that are extremely important in the real world but which are only beginning to be understood theoretically and empirically: (1) the dynamics that produce enhanced productivity growth (through economies of scale, innovation, agglomeration, and so on); and (2) the political and institutional dynamics across borders that engender complementary strategies by social actors (through improved international conditions for long-term capital investment, distribution of gains to workers, a new vision for the state's international role in providing social investment, proper safety nets, and enhancing investments in innovation and lagging regions).

This chapter reexamines debates about NAFTA and globalization in the light of data before and after NAFTA. We try to set the record straight on what NAFTA did or did not do for the U.S. economy. We also address the larger problem of the underlying evolution of uneven development in North America, driven by what we will define as both positive and negative dynamics of cumulative causation. We show that NAFTA did not create these dynamics, but neither did it significantly alter them. We argue that it is crucial for the United States to understand its national and collective interest in moving beyond NAFTA to foster regional and global economic integration with upward convergence of income and development patterns across countries.

The remainder of our essay has four parts. In the first of these we review the NAFTA debate and analytically deconstruct the various theoretical propositions that policymakers, think tanks, and academics used. This review indicates serious problems in the way trade and integration have been analyzed in the U.S. policy debate and, more importantly, provides insight into the important issues that North Americans need to focus upon as they compare dynamics of integration in different parts of the world and "globalization" in general. The following section offers a brief overview of the U.S. economy in the post-NAFTA period, evaluating the usefulness of the principal economic models that influenced the NAFTA debate and comparing their predictions to the empirical outcomes observed thus far. We seek to help refocus the terms of the NAFTA debate toward more important factors that should have been, and still need to be, the core of research and policy analysis. We next turn to an empirical review of the major dynamics driving convergence and divergence in North American integration. Our analysis seeks to incorporate a wide range of integration processes and to explain how freeing trade and facilitating investment in the context of labor market distortions can create both positive and negative dynamics across sectors and regions in the United States and Mexico. We conclude with a brief recapitulation of what we have learned from the NAFTA debate, NAFTA-related modeling efforts, and the economic performance of the U.S. economy after NAFTA. We then postulate questions and possible approaches for further research, along with the outline of a discussion of policy implications.

THE ANALYTICAL DEBATES

The NAFTA debate presaged and continues to mirror a still underdeveloped globalization debate; indeed, the evolution of these debates provided a condensed look at three hundred years of trade theory. Rather than illuminating key issues for policymakers, much of the published research too often tried to reinforce stark positions in the U.S. political debate. Hence much of the "expert testimony" either focused on the wrong issues or finessed difficult conceptual issues to come up with simplistic and quantitatively significant numbers in support of a particular position. Paradoxically, the search for large numbers did lead some researchers into previously neglected but empirically important areas, such as the impact of economies of scale, migration, and investment flows.

Table 1.1 displays four major analytical approaches that emerged in the NAFTA debates: what we call the "mercantilist" approach, the standard trade model (also known as the Heckscher-Ohlin-Samuelson model), the economies of scale model, and a framework stressing factor mobility. Unfortunately, the early stages of the debate were dominated by the "mercantilist" approach, which focused on highly dubious criteria for measuring the impact of economic integration—changes in trade balance and, presumably, corresponding changes in production and employment levels. NAFTA proponents argued that free trade with Mexico would improve the U.S. trade balance, increasing U.S. production and creating American jobs. The underlying implication was that trade is a zero-sum game. Such a position had been forcefully discredited by the critical insights of Adam Smith and David Ricardo, who argued that nations become wealthy through trade due to increased production specialization based on their comparative advantage.

Table 1.1. Analytical Approaches and Methodologies

Approach	Predictions	Methodology Used
Mercantilist	Pre-Smithian/Ricardian Trade Surplus = Job Gain Trade Deficit = Job Loss	NAID Armington methodology (a measure of the limited net relationship between trade and employment)
Heckscher-Ohlin-Samuelson (HOS)	Small Efficiency Gains (and adjustments) from trade based on Ricardian comparative advantage	HOS computable general equilibrium (CGE) models measuring comparative static gains from trade
	Small Factor Price Equalization	CGE models testing for income inequality impacts
Economies of scale	Larger gains based on efficiency + trade-facilitated increased scale economies	CGE models incorporating variables from the new international economics
Factor mobility	Large gains/adjustments based on FDI and labor migration/remittances dynamics	CGE models incorporating factor mobility and variables from the new economics of labor migration

Within the mercantilist vein, researchers at the Institute for International Economics repeatedly used a methodology, cited by many U.S. officials, that made the U.S. net gain of jobs a linear function of the U.S. trade surplus with Mexico in the early 1990s, which these researchers predicted would continue to grow at rates similar to the recent past.[4] Although NAFTA proponents would soon find their mercantilist argument discredited by academics' analytical critiques and ensuing macroeconomic events, a major position for the NAFTA debate had been established. All future studies would have to mention changes in the trade balance and employment levels. In an ironic twist, anti-NAFTA think tanks such as the Economic Policy Institute gleefully utilized the same "pro-NAFTA methodology" following Mexico's 1994–1995 peso crisis to proclaim the damage to the U.S. economy from NAFTA.[5] Simply reversing the dubious proposition that trade surplus produces "net job gains," they argued that a large fall in the U.S. balance of trade with Mexico would generate a huge "net job loss." Furthermore, the United States' trade deficit *with the world*, clearly a result of macroeconomic factors, was cited as a cost to society and a source of "unnecessary" unemployment—as if all imported goods, from autos to coffee, and diamonds to zinc—could and would be domestically produced in the absence of trade. Challenging this simplistic assumption, Raúl Hinojosa-Ojeda and associates, applying a partial equilibrium test to the mercantilist proposition with empirical data on the nonsubstitutability of domestic for imported goods, found a significantly lower relationship between trade and employment levels.[6]

In a compelling testament to the fluctuating role of ideas in the policy process, the concepts of comparative advantage and gains from trade had to be reintroduced to the policy debate centuries after their initial development. Trade, it had to be argued again, is not a zero-sum game, and imports (even in consumer goods, which account for only a third of total U.S. imports) do not necessarily displace American production. It became necessary to reemphasize notions of efficiency and competitiveness. If trade with Mexico reduces the cost of auto parts for U.S. auto makers, for instance, more cars could be produced and sold; this could lower total imports and increase exports to Europe or other third markets. Such ideas seemed difficult to grasp in comparison with images of textile workers, garment workers, or steelworkers standing unemployed outside closed factories, blaming "unfair" foreign competition that was "sucking" jobs away.

The standard model used to make the traditional pro-trade arguments through the early 1980s was the Heckscher-Ohlin-Samuelson (HOS) framework, based on Ricardian comparative advantage. A number of mostly academic researchers employed sophisticated empirical tests of this framework with the use of computable general equilibrium (CGE) models. These CGE models, however, yielded predictions of fairly minor changes in trade flows and production levels when applied to the modest tariff reductions associated with NAFTA. These results were derisively termed "positive zero" and were politically rather ineffective; in effect, researchers were emphasizing the likely yet unglamorous fact that NAFTA's impacts on the U.S. economy would be positive but economically insignificant.

A further problem for NAFTA proponents derived from a key implication of the HOS model called the factor-price equalization theorem, which states that a country's abundant factor(s) of production will benefit from trade liberalization, but its scarce factors will be hurt. Because unskilled labor is scarce in the United States relative to Mexico, the HOS model predicted a rise in unskilled wages in Mexico combined with a corresponding fall in the United States. Supporters of

NAFTA could then be characterized as insensitive to distribution problems in the U.S. economy, however weak their relationship to NAFTA. Recall that, at the time of this debate, the Reagan-Bush policies of the 1980s had substantially widened the gap between rich and poor in the United States.

A further feature of the HOS model is that gains from trade result from abandoning production of goods in which you have a comparative disadvantage to specialize in products in which you have a comparative advantage. These dislocations, or adjustment costs, were generally finessed or ignored by the pro-NAFTA modelers themselves, but they were examined very carefully by NAFTA opponents. Thus NAFTA proponents using the HOS model faced an insoluble dilemma. Either the potential gains from NAFTA—and the adjustment costs—were trivial, or the gains were substantial but the adjustment costs were substantial as well.

Fortunately for economic modelers seeking evidence of potential gains from NAFTA, the theory they needed had been introduced by Paul Krugman and others in the early 1980s and adapted to computable general equilibrium models in the mid-1980s by Canadians Richard Harris and David Cox.[7] This new international economics, based on economies of scale (EOS), seemed to be just the thing. According to this framework, gains from trade come from two sources: (1) falling average costs, as firms increase their scale of production in response to increased export demand, and (2) gains from increased competition reducing inefficiency due to collusion within an industry. These gains potentially dwarfed those predicted by HOS models. Cox and Harris reported potential gains on the order of 8 percent of Canada's gross domestic product (GDP) from unilateral liberalization with the world. Similarly, Raúl Hinojosa-Ojeda and Sherman Robinson analyzed the impact of NAFTA on the Mexican economy and found order-of-magnitude differences using EOS versus HOS specifications, without the large displacement effects of pure HOS specifications.[8]

There are two further attractive features of these EOS models. First, there is so little empirical evidence on the extent and magnitude of scale economies by sector that there can be little grounds for criticism, whatever parameter values are selected.[9] Second, adjustment costs can be interpreted differently in EOS models. In HOS models, adjustment costs mean that textile workers in North Carolina who are displaced through international trade must relocate and retrain to make software in Silicon Valley or aircraft in Washington. In EOS models, in contrast, mergers and acquisitions "rationalize" the industry, so the same workers do the same jobs in the same industry, maybe even in the same factory, but perhaps under a different corporate logo. This type of adjustment seems much smoother and less costly, for both individuals and society.

One critical problem remained. The way was now clear to predict substantial gains for Mexico and Canada from integration with the larger U.S. market, but it was still difficult to make the case that integration with Mexico and Canada would substantially affect either the scale of U.S. production or the level of competition within American markets.

Meanwhile, other researchers were taking alternative tacks. Both HOS and EOS models generally focus on the movement of *goods* rather than *factors of production*. Yet both investment flows and labor flows have historically been very important in North America, especially in U.S.-Mexico economic relations. Understanding adjustments in these flows was seen as crucial to predicting the economic impacts of NAFTA. To the extent that mainstream modelers thought about these issues at all, it was generally to say that rising wages for unskilled workers in Mexico would lead to lower levels of undocumented immigration from Mexico. In contrast, NAFTA opponents seized on the possibility of investment flows from the United States to Mexico to focus on the danger of plant relocation and job loss.

Yet the real insights to be gained from the study of international factor movements involved the growing cross-border dynamics in labor markets and production sharing. Sherman Robinson and others were the first to note that economic dislocations in Mexican agriculture could easily lead to an increase, rather than a decrease, in undocumented immigration to the United States.[10] Their conclusion—that increased migration could be mitigated by long tariff phase-ins and direct economic transfers to the rural sector—has been substantiated by empirically based micro CGE modeling of the village-level relationships between migration, price liberalization, and the impacts of new Mexican rural policies (such as Procampo income transfers).[11] Robert McCleery was the first to predict changes in foreign direct investment (FDI) flows to Mexico and to estimate their impact on wages and employment in the United States.[12] Others introduced international coordination of production, pricing, and sales by multinational enterprises, with the North American auto industry as a case study.[13] As an example of complex positive cumulative causation, a dynamic can emerge whereby international investment flows are increased to take strategic competitive advantage of sectors with scale economies. Indeed, it is possible that the post-NAFTA pattern of trade has been less determined by tariff liberalization than by the pattern of FDI.

NAFTA PREDICTIONS AND POST-NAFTA PERFORMANCE OF THE U.S. ECONOMY

We now evaluate the "pro-" and "anti-" NAFTA positions in light of the actual post-NAFTA experience, specifically testing the validity of the major predictions. This exercise is crucial in order to discuss how the economic literature must evolve in order to provide insights into the impact of future initiatives for integration and globalization.

Empirical evidence shows that the theoretical-predicative case against NAFTA was clearly oversold with respect to the U.S. economy as a whole. The claim that NAFTA would lead to a "giant sucking sound," as investment and jobs left the country for Mexico or as the U.S. developed a trade deficit with Mexico, does not seem to be borne out by the data. The post-NAFTA period in the United States corresponds with the longest continuous economic expansion since World War II. By almost any measure (real income growth, productivity growth, unemployment rate, inflation, and so on), U.S. economic performance was substantially better after than before NAFTA. The unemployment rate fell from nearly 8 percent in mid-1992 to under 4 percent in 2000, before rising to 6 percent in the 2001–2002 recession. FDI into Mexico did increase, but that inflow was dwarfed by the increase of foreign investment into the United States. While Mexico attracted a total of US$48 billion in new FDI cumulatively from its NAFTA partners from 1994 through the first quarter of 2000, the United States garnered $276 billion in gross FDI (and $125 billion net) from abroad in 1999 alone.[14]

Yet the U.S. current account has clearly deteriorated over the past decade. Is the worsening of the trade balance a result of NAFTA? The U.S. current account deteriorated steadily and dramatically through the first quarter of 2001, before beginning to improve as a result of the recession. Similarly, the deterioration was the result of rapid growth (outstripping that of U.S. trading partners) combined with massive capital inflows, particularly from Europe and Asia. Additionally, the dollar strengthened against an average of major foreign currencies during this time, making imports cheaper and U.S. exports more expensive. While these macroeconomic changes may well be driving the deficits with Mexico and Canada, NAFTA and those deficits have had a minimal impact on the U.S. current account deficit with the world.

Granting more rapid income, productivity, and job growth, has NAFTA led to a worsening of income distribution in the United States? On the one hand, income growth rates were similar for the rich and the poor, worsening absolute inequality. The poorest 20 percent of the U.S. population saw income growth of 15 percent from 1993 to 1999, compared with 14.2 percent for the richest 20 percent. The economic performance in the post-NAFTA period, however, was also much *better* with respect to income distribution than in the Reagan-Bush years. For instance, the proportion living in poverty fell from 15.1 percent in 1993 to 11.8 percent in 1999, although that figure still exceeds the level recorded in 1979.

Perhaps the only clear area of decline, and the one point stressed by anti-NAFTA groups today, is manufacturing employment. This has nourished a public perception that the expansion of trade shifts workers from well-paid manufacturing jobs to low-paying service-sector jobs. Although it is true that employment growth in manufacturing lagged well behind overall employment growth in the economy—0.4 percent to 2.3 percent per year—growth has nonetheless been positive, and the primary reason for the slower growth has been increased labor productivity, not trade.

But as we shall see below, the overzealous pro-NAFTA predictions are not particularly accurate either. While the NAFTA opponents' worst fears clearly have not materialized, only a tiny share of the improvement in economic conditions in the United States can be directly linked to NAFTA. The Clinton administration credited the improved economic performance from 1993 to 2000 to "three interrelated factors ... technological innovation, organizational changes in businesses, and public policy."[15] "Opening markets at home and abroad" is listed as the third of four important policy initiatives. NAFTA, one of several such openings, can thus be given perhaps one-fourth of one-fourth of one-third, or about 2 percent, of the credit—unless we can also link it to technological innovation and/or organizational changes.

Assessing the Analyses

Keeping in mind that some of the proposed NAFTA liberalizations are still being phased in (for corn, banking, and others) and that others are being held up by legal disputes (Mexican trucks' access to the United States, relaxation of the U.S. sugar quota, and so on), what have we learned? The short answer is that the ability of economic models and modelers to anticipate the complex interactions between the United States and Mexico, not to mention other global and regional events that color perceptions of those interactions, has been limited. Special features of the U.S.-Mexico economic relationship made any trade theory–based approach incomplete, and thus necessarily incorrect from the point of view of predicting aggregate and macroeconomic trends. Indeed, it would have been surprising if that were *not* true.

But we have enough of a track record with NAFTA to reach preliminary judgments about what *types* of models are appropriate for predicting and measuring economic interdependence between countries with complex cross-border linkages and at very different levels of development. We shall do this below, concluding with some thoughts on how to improve those economic models in light of what we are learning about interdependence from NAFTA.

At the macro level, few bold predictions were made. One study predicted improvements in the U.S. trade balance with Mexico,[16] while another predicted a worsening.[17] Comparing the 1993 through 1999 bilateral trade balance reveals that the U.S. trade balance with Mexico improved only in the first year of NAFTA. In every year thereafter, the United States has recorded bilateral deficits in excess of $14 billion, in contrast to surpluses in each year from 1991 to 1994.

Only two studies have focused on income distribution. Both predicted that the distribution of income in the United States would worsen, as trade (and additional migration, according to one of the analyses) hurts unskilled workers and helps skilled workers and capital owners. This prediction has been weakly supported by recent experience, although, again, rapid technological change within the U.S. economy—rather than trade itself—no doubt accounts for most of the worsening of income distribution.

Next we consider sectoral impacts. Suppose we consider predicted sectoral increases or decreases of less than 1 percent to be approximately zero. Looking at predicted changes of more than 1 percent, we need to remember what they suggest. These are the predicted partial impacts of NAFTA on the United States, holding everything else constant. We interpret this to refer to the sectors and social groups that will do particularly well or poorly in the post-NAFTA world, relative to the averages in the economy as a whole. For instance, estimated parameters of −4.2 percent for urban unskilled wages and +5.17 percent for food corn output are treated as predictions that wages for urban unskilled workers would rise by 4.2 percent *less than average* wages post-NAFTA (1994–1998) while food corn production would grow 5.2 percent *faster* than average output.[18]

One standard econometric study considers the impact of phasing in reductions in tariff and nontariff barriers (NTBs) between Mexico and the United States over a period of ten years. Only one bold prediction emerges—that electronic appliance employment (and production) would increase. Thanks in part to quality adjustments that are disputed in other industrialized countries, the production of electrical goods (code 506 in the National Income and Product Accounts of the United States, the closest match we could find) leaped by 70 percent, 50 percentage points more than the U.S. economy. We cannot rule out the basic conclusions of this study, that NAFTA would have little impact on the pattern of U.S. economic growth and employment. Massive increases in two-way apparel trade were also predicted as a result of NAFTA (exports up 42 percent and imports up 59 percent relative to the baseline without NAFTA), and this prediction is roughly confirmed in the data.[19]

In a study commissioned by KPMG Peat Marwick (a pro-NAFTA group), Carlos Bachrach and Lorris Mazrahi employed a HOS-type CGE model, modified to allow a net capital inflow to Mexico of US$25 billion. Since all of the additional investment in Mexico is assumed to come from other regions or from a reshuffling of U.S. foreign direct investment, the capital inflow in Mexico has no impact on the United States. Two of its predictions cross the 1 percent threshold: a projected decline in sugar, and growth in miscellaneous manufactures. In fact, sugar production did lag behind overall U.S. growth for 1994–1998, although it exceeded average growth in 1999 and 2000.[20] But miscellaneous manufactures grew slower than average. Thus we could say that this CGE model helped identify sugar as a contentious sector worthy of more detailed study, but it was incorrect regarding miscellaneous manufactures.

A third estimation of sectoral results for the United States simulates the elimination of tariffs and NTBs along with a 10 percent increase in real investment in Mexico (again, with no projected impact on the U.S. capital stock).[21] The model identifies textiles and miscellaneous manufactures as key growth sectors, and glass, nonferrous metals, and electrical machinery as sectors that could be hurt by NAFTA. From 1994 to 1998, in fact, textile production grew 26 percent *slower* than the U.S. economy, and miscellaneous manufactures also failed to match the overall U.S. growth rate; in the meantime, glass, nonferrous metals, and electrical machinery all grew at least 15 percent *faster* than the U.S. average. Indeed, electrical machinery was the fastest-growing sector of the U.S. economy over that period. With a zero-for-five prediction record and large margins of error, this model was clearly not helpful.

Focusing primarily on agriculture, yet another analysis predicted production gains for the United States in food corn and program crops. Changes in price supports and guarantees, particularly the reduction in support as part of the "freedom to farm" act of 1996, have had a greater, negative impact on these sectors than the projected positive impact of NAFTA. Thus we evaluate these predictions as incorrect in aggregate terms due to events not related to NAFTA. The predictions seemed valid at the time; in fact, policymakers implementing the agricultural reforms widely believed that increasing export opportunities, not just to Mexico but to China and East Asia as well, would more than offset the income losses to American farmers from the decline in subsidies.[22] An analogous study concentrated exclusively on auto and auto parts production and trade.[23] It predicted a negative impact on production, but during the post-NAFTA years U.S. auto production actually grew slightly *faster* than average.

With the possible exception of some agricultural subsectors, therefore, CGE models apparently did not adequately identify any significant production shifts resulting from NAFTA. Two explanations come to mind. One is that these models failed to capture the key elements of U.S.-Mexico economic interdependence. The other is that the impact of NAFTA itself was negligible and was overshadowed by technological, international, and other economic developments affecting the United States.

Our recent research tests these assertions with regressions.[24] Traditional CGE models showed that tariff liberalization impacts were bound to be tiny and could not greatly affect economic disparities in North America. Our post-1994 regression results show that NAFTA tariff liberalization did not significantly predict the composition of trade at a detailed sectoral level, as basic neoclassical theory would predict. In other words, the sectors that grew most rapidly in the United States following the implementation of NAFTA had little correlation with the sectors in which significant trade barriers were reduced. Hence the HOS focus on the impact of reduced trade barriers on trade flows—and, thus, on production levels—seems to have little explanatory power in the NAFTA case.

But EOS models, while doing somewhat better, still explain only about half of the variance in changes in sectoral production. Unbelievably, predictions based on both HOS and EOS models do slightly worse than the prediction asserting that the sectors that would grow the fastest after NAFTA would be precisely those that grew the fastest in the period immediately preceding NAFTA. That hypothesis yields a simple correlation of nearly two-thirds. Should we not do better than this? Probably not, since NAFTA liberalizations had a modest impact on a rapidly evolving economy that was also beset by technological change, policy changes, and multilateral liberalization from the Uruguay Round agreement.

CONVERGENCE AND DIVERGENCE

The NAFTA debates in general have lacked the theoretical discussion and empirical testing of key dynamics that gave rise to divergent predictions of positive or negative outcomes. Perhaps more importantly, the debates failed to identify the possibility of more complex outcomes when rich and poor countries engage in economic integration. To rectify this shortcoming, we need a framework to analyze empirically what the post-NAFTA experience has taught us about the potential costs and benefits of integration between high- and low-income countries.

In this section, we turn from previous NAFTA debates to an empirical review of the major dynamics necessary to understand convergence and divergence in North American integration. The focus is on the process of uneven development in North America. This we take to be driven by "dynamics of cumulative causation" in which relative incomes can evolve along either positive (convergent) or negative (divergent) paths. The evidence clearly shows that NAFTA did not create these North American dynamics of inequality, but neither did it significantly alter them. If anything, NAFTA appears to have only slightly accelerated both the positive and the negative dynamics of cumulative causation.

Our argument is that what should have been, and what continue to be, the crucial issues for U.S. policymakers are the factors and policies that can transform the pattern of North American integration toward greater growth, development, and income convergence on both sides of the border. The fundamental issue will continue to be the factors driving alternative paths of cumulative evolution in two major areas: (1) investment-production-trade dynamics, and (2) employment-wages-migration-remittance dynamics. Taken together, these are the major drivers of regional income convergence and divergence.

While patterns of positive cumulative causation are clearly evident in sectors throughout North America, these dynamics are neither necessarily sustainable (in terms of incentives for innovation and future productivity growth) nor expanding rapidly enough to be a major source of employment absorption, particularly in Mexico. Negative cumulative causation dynamics linked across national economies continue to produce a drag on low-wage labor markets, reducing incentives for productivity-enhancing investments in low-wage sectors as well as in the entire regional economy. Our analysis points to the need for major policy development efforts directed at both the investment-production-trade dynamics and the employment-wages-migration-remittance dynamics.

Cumulative Causation in Integration Theory

A number of authors have recently explored the theoretical conditions, and offered empirical examples, of very different patterns of integration and development. Masahisa Fujita and others have developed theoretical/numerical simulation frameworks showing that different conditions of initial inequality and factor mobility, combined with differential scale economies and transaction costs, can produce highly divergent dynamic paths of core-periphery integration and development.[25] CGE modelers have also developed alternative scenarios of North American integration and development. Both approaches are based on notions of positive and negative cumulative causation (derived from Gunnar Myrdal)[26] with sets of conditions and processes at an initial point setting off path-dependent developments which, in turn, create constraints on conditions and processes in the future.

The theoretical possibility exists that economic integration can generate a process of positive cumulative causation (PCC). The story goes roughly as follows: (1) integration itself can open wider markets (for both goods and capital); (2) this brings about the possibility of resource reallocation for specialized production to take root in regions of comparative advantage; (3) producers can then take advantage of increased economies of scales; (4) the results are rapid output and employment growth; (5) this then opens the possibility for enhanced growth of both profit and wage income; (6) this facilitates improved productivity and further innovation for both trading partners; (7) this allows for sustained growth of investment and consumption; and (8) the outcome is sustained income growth and upward income convergence on both sides of the border. Further, the process creates the possibility of the transnational region gaining in competitiveness relative to other regions around the world. Integration with PCC can generate relative productivity growth and a regional specialization in joint production for increased exports to third markets, attracting investment from outside the region. The potential is for substantial trade creation that would dwarf trade diversion.

Theoretically, it is also possible that integration between rich and poor regions will produce a number of dynamics of negative cumulative causation (NCC). One scenario—the richer country gets richer—can operate via the following kind of sequence: (1) highly unequal initial conditions in resources and economies of scale favor the rich country; (2) this makes the absolute competitive position of the rich region so high that poor regions cannot develop sufficient scale to make investment viable in order to compete; and (3) resources (labor, capital) are drawn from the poorer region to the richer, widening the gap between rich and poor. This argument is strengthened by the new institutionalists, who would claim that the higher quality of institutions and bureaucracy in the United States raises the productivity and lowers the risk of investment, outweighing the advantage of low-cost Mexican labor in most economic sectors.[27]

Yet another NCC theoretical possibility exists—the classic "race to the bottom" scenario, in which sufficiently large differences in "surplus" labor endowments are combined with low differences in productivity and scale economies. Here the following occurs: (1) poorer countries can draw capital resources from the rich country (or the rich country can draw abundant labor from the poor countries) in order to produce at a more labor-intensive yet less productive choice of technique or in ways that are privately profitable yet socially costly in terms of pollution and other externalities; and (2) the result is a negative impact on both rich and poor countries from reduced overall intra-regional income potential and extra-regional competitiveness.

Empirical Analyses of Cumulative Causation

We want now to consider the extent of cumulative causation, positive or negative, in the process of North American integration. To do so, we use a specially constructed database. This includes (1) macro data at the economy-wide level; (2) eleven subsectors (based on U.S. definitions of end-use categories); and (3) a more detailed 39-subsector analysis (constructed at the most disaggregated level of concordance between published data in the three NAFTA countries). We begin with a review of cumulative causation dynamics at the macro-national level in North America, turning to a discussion of regional dynamics at the sectoral level.

In the case of North America, what can be said is that elements of an integration process with PCC, as well as NCC, had been operating across parts of the United States, Canada, and Mexico both before and after NAFTA. Economic integration between the United States and Mexico can be shown to have exhibited a similar dynamic of PCC beginning with Mexico's unilateral opening in the mid-1980s, as well as between the United States and Canada since the mid-1970s. There is clearly a common cluster of industrial subsectors in all three countries that are undergoing a very rapid process of transnational industrial restructuring. This has resulted in all three countries experiencing similar characteristics of higher growth in trade, employment, productivity, and wages in specific linked sectors on both sides of the border. The dynamics are led by high growth of foreign direct investment associated with an expansion of intermediate-goods trade for the purposes of transnational co-production of final goods exported throughout North America and the world.

Particularly in light of the exaggerated expectations that the NAFTA debate generated on both sides of the issue, one of the most important findings from the ongoing tracking of North American integration is the lack of fundamental shift in pre- and post-NAFTA patterns of trade, investment, and production. Whereas NAFTA became operational only in January 1994, trade relations within North America had already begun a dramatic transformation in the mid-1980s. Years before NAFTA was contemplated, Mexico underwent a major opening to international trade and investment, which ushered in a period of rapid trade growth, large trade and current account deficits, and substantial capital inflows. The period surrounding the implementation of NAFTA was characterized by a quick acceleration of these previously initiated trends, but there has been a maturation and deceleration of these trends in recent years.

FDI began rising around the start of the NAFTA negotiations, and that rise accelerated post-NAFTA. Yet this FDI level represented a declining share of both U.S. and Mexican GDP. Foreign investment, more broadly defined to include speculative portfolio investments and loans, contributed to the overheating of the Mexican stock market in 1993–1994. Thus, although NAFTA may have created the unrealistic expectations that led to Mexico's dramatic crash, it also seems to have had an effect on Mexico's ability to mount its most rapid macroeconomic recovery (via exports and FDI), indicating the significant power of the NAFTA "policy fix."

In general, however, NAFTA does not seem to have significantly altered preexisting differences in Mexico and the United States at the macro and sectoral level both before and after 1994. In terms of the Mexican economy, the pre- and post-NAFTA period represents an export boom (with growth of net imports and capital inflow), modest employment growth, relatively flat productivity growth, and declining real wages, resulting in a net improvement in per-unit labor cost and in Mexico's relative global competitiveness position. The correlation between productivity growth and wage growth in Mexico, though still weaker than expected, is greater than in the United States. Similarly, rapid technological progress has an even stronger tendency to lead to employment losses in Mexico. But in contrast to the United States, we can see a distinct negative relationship between wage growth and employment growth. This implies that Mexico will have a difficult time moving beyond its role as a low-wage complement to U.S. industry while employing its rapidly growing labor force.

In overall terms, the U.S. economy in the post-NAFTA period did very well, actually better than Mexico and Canada in output, real wages, and even employment and productivity. Meanwhile, sectors in which U.S. exports to Mexico and Canada rose had very strong performance in terms of employment. For the United States, it is important to note that in more than two-thirds of the sectors where U.S. imports from Mexico are growing, U.S. employment grew as well. Yet we note that there is a very weak positive correlation in general between productivity growth and wage growth before and after NAFTA. While it is true that this relationship between productivity and wages is more likely to hold in the long run than over the short term, the positive relationship is extremely weak even if we look at the entire 1988–2000 period. We observe no correlation between wage growth and employment growth (but a moderate negative correlation between productivity growth and employment growth). In other words, the strongest relationship between these three variables is that rapid technological progress in a sector tends to lead to a reduction in employment levels.

Similarly in Canada, the defining issue during this period was not NAFTA but the U.S. recession and recovery, which precipitated and accentuated the 1990–1992 recession and inhibited recovery north of the border. The Canadian recession and accompanying manufacturing-sector job decline coincided with the implementation of the Canada–

United States Free Trade Agreement (CUSFTA) and contributed to the fall of the Conservative government. Once in power, the Liberals reversed their electoral position on free trade and embraced the negotiations that led to the inclusion of Mexico in the 1994 agreement. Post-NAFTA data show a continuation of the 1992–1993 Canadian recovery, and by 1998 GDP growth had regained rates similar to the mid-1980s. After rapidly falling during the 1990–1992 recession, Canadian employment levels rose sharply in 1995. They have since grown at moderate levels, slower than during the 1980s and, except for 1995, slower than GDP growth in the post-NAFTA period. After strong growth in 1991 and 1992, Canadian average productivity levels slowed during the mid-1990s and, much like Mexico, sharply decreased in 1995. They have since recovered, weaker than during the early 1990s but generally higher than the second half of the 1980s. After surpassing U.S. and Mexican levels between 1991 and 1994, Canadian average productivity rates have since grown more slowly than in the United States and have exceeded Mexican levels only since 1998. Average earnings lagged during the 1991–1995 period and then recovered during the second half of the 1990s, although not to the same level as in the second half of the 1980s. Canadian international competitiveness was strong during the 1990s (with a positive trade balance throughout the decade) and particularly strong in 1995–1996 and again in 1999–2000. With the exception of 1995, growth in wages consistently exceeded employment growth during all of the 1990s.

Patterns of Positive Cumulative Causation

We examined our 39-sector database (with 25 traded sectors) for evidence of strong or moderate positive cumulative causation (see table 1.2). Note that if the five key variables (output, employment, productivity, wages, and trade) were unrelated, then statistically there should be only one or two instances in which all grew faster than average. Instead, four "strong PCC" sectors have most variables at or above the average annual growth rate.[28] A second group of sectors is presented in which growth in these variables was mostly positive, although not necessarily greater than average for the economy. This group of sectors is said to exhibit moderate positive cumulative causation. While many of these PCC dynamics are shared by all three countries, in this essay we will focus on the import and export dynamics between Mexico and the United States given that much of the NAFTA discussion in the United States has concerned trade with Mexico.

Table 1.2. Positive Cumulative Causation Sectors in the United States (average compound growth, 1994–2000)

	Output (%)	Employment (%)	Productivity (%)	Wages (%)	Exports (%)	Imports (%)
U.S. Average[1]	**5.0**	**0.5**	**4.5**	**1.4**	**14.9**	**20.2**
Electronic and other electric equipment	21.3	1.6	19.3	3.8	16.7	21.1
Industrial machinery and equipment	13.6	1.3	12.1	2.4	14.4	29.0
Nonmetallic minerals, except fuels	7.0	1.3	5.6	0.8	11.2	13.2
Rubber and miscellaneous plastic products	5.5	1.6	3.9	0.6	20.1	21.8
Farms	5.0	0.5	4.4	2.1	11.5	7.1
Chemicals and allied products	4.9	-0.5	5.4	2.9	15.2	17.7
Motor vehicles and equipment	4.6	2.8	1.7	-1.2	15.5	23.9
Stone, clay, and glass products	4.5	1.6	2.8	1.0	16.6	16.3
Fabricated metal products	4.0	2.0	1.9	0.1	15.0	23.5
Miscellaneous manufacturing industries	3.8	0.5	3.3	1.7	8.9	10.6

Source: NAID Center Database.
[1] Average of the twenty-five traded sectors.

Thus positive cumulative causation is clearly observable in certain key sectors of the U.S. economy. But there are additional elements, beyond the variables listed above, that are particularly relevant to the NAFTA debate. It should be no surprise that all leading PCC sectors are in the fastest-growing quarter of the thirty-nine U.S. sectors. But it may come as quite a surprise to NAFTA opponents that most of the sectors listed above have also experienced faster-than-average *import* growth from Mexico. Hence we observe positive cross-border linkages in the PCC sectors, contributing to industrial development on both sides of the border. A final point, equally illustrative of the potential for positive cross-border linkages, is that the leading PCC sectors from the United States have been responsible for more than a quarter of all U.S. FDI in Mexico since 1994.[29]

To summarize the clear but limited pattern of PCC since NAFTA, we see that the agreement has led to production-sharing relationships across the Mexican border. Parts and components are fabricated in Mexico, integrated with knowledge-intensive U.S. components into U.S. designs, and marketed around the world. Thus we observe output, employment, productivity, and wage gains in the very sectors that attract U.S. investment in Mexico and exhibit an expansion in two-way trade. While these PCC sectors account for nearly 43 percent of U.S. exports to Mexico, they employ just 4 percent of the total U.S. labor force. When we further consider the moderate PCC sectors, we still only account for 7 percent of U.S. employment and 11 percent of total output. We turn now to consider the possibility that negative cumulative causality is potentially more important, quantitatively, for the U.S. economy.

Patterns of Negative Cumulative Causation

Eight U.S. sectors display the spirit, if not the letter, of negative cumulative causality, again more than should occur by chance. They are identified as those sectors displaying below-average growth in output, employment, wages, and productivity, with an absolute decline in at least one variable. All qualify in every respect except that five of the eight have wage growth rates higher than the national average. One hypothesis to explain this pattern is that seniority-based raises in union contracts left layoffs as the only way to adjust the labor market in these sectors when demand slumped and/or productivity declined. However, these are not highly unionized sectors overall. Hence the more likely explanation may be that management has elected to trim pro-

Table 1.3. Negative Cumulative Causation Sectors in the United States (average compound growth, 1994–2000)

	Output (%)	Employment (%)	Productivity (%)	Wages (%)	Exports (%)	Imports (%)
U.S. Average[1]	**5.0**	**0.5**	**4.5**	**1.4**	**14.9**	**20.2**
Food and kindred products	0.4	0.2	0.3	0.8	8.6	16.4
Printing and publishing	-0.6	0.3	-0.9	1.7	10.7	22.1
Textile mill products	-1.0	-3.4	2.5	1.1	26.8	34.1
Other transportation equipment and instruments	-1.6	-1.1	-0.5	1.6	8.5	22.4
Paper and allied products	-2.7	-0.8	-2.0	0.7	12.4	22.8
Apparel and other textile products	-2.9	-6.1	3.4	2.1	13.5	22.6
Leather and leather products	-3.2	-7.1	4.2	2.8	24.8	23.2
Tobacco products	-5.6	-3.5	-2.2	3.0	-14.2	0.3

Source: NAID Center Database.
[1] Average of the twenty-five traded sectors.

duction workers while keeping white-collar jobs. This could explain the fall in employment while average wages climbed and productivity stagnated. Apparel and leather are the two sectors that record the largest percentage employment declines since NAFTA's inception while simultaneously exhibiting increases in relative wages (above national averages) (see table 1.3).

GDP and employment in these NCC sectors have generally experienced moderate to strong declines, contrasted with U.S. average growth rates of 5.0 and 0.5 percent, respectively. Imports from Mexico may have been a factor in a few sectors,[30] but import growth in all NCC sectors combined was close to the economy average of 20.2 percent. Imports grew much more slowly than average in the food and tobacco sectors. Imports grew faster in textiles than in any other sector, yet job losses here were not the highest. Also suggesting a lack of correspondence between imports and economic performance is the fact that both the NCC and PCC sectors exhibited similar import growth. Meanwhile, collectively we see that export growth was not much below average—with the exception of textile mill products and leather and leather products. Furthermore, these NCC sectors contributed 22 percent of U.S. FDI in Mexico—less than the share drawn by the sectors showing PCC characteristics—despite representing a larger share of U.S. output and employment. Hence the negative dynamic in the United States cannot be attributed to either a large surge in imports or an outflow of investment.

The dynamic becomes even more interesting if we consider non-traded sectors such as construction. Boosted by increasing demand in the U.S. economy and a ready supply of low-wage immigrant labor, the construction sector expanded by 4.5 percent per year—slightly exceeding the average growth rate of the U.S. economy, despite falling productivity. The boom in employment (5.4 percent annual growth) may have been caused by a crowding-in of immigrant labor as blue-collar manufacturing jobs contracted in the above eight sectors, excluding the food sector.

This observation regarding the construction industry raises a serious question. Construction is a cyclically sensitive sector, subject to slowdowns when the economy moves into recession and resulting in significant impact on low-skill and immigrant workers in the United States. This expectation seems to be confirmed by a recent study conducted by the Pew Hispanic Center.[31] The study's authors cite unemployment levels for operators, fabricators, and laborers that are higher than national levels (8.7 percent, compared to 5.4 percent for the nation, in October 2001), as well as a higher rate for Latinos (7.9 percent versus a national rate of 5.8 percent in December 2001). At least a portion of this greater vulnerability to recession can be attributed to NCC, enhanced by NAFTA.

Observations on North American Cumulative Causality

Contrary to the pro-NAFTA metaphor, many of the current PCC patterns are not necessarily sustainable in terms of expanding technological innovation and productivity growth throughout the North American economies. Nor are PCC sectors expanding fast enough to be a major employment creator for the low-wage labor markets in the United States and Mexico. Low-wage manufacturing, meanwhile, cannot be a lasting basis for growth given increasing global competition, from which NAFTA has given Mexico (and parts of the United States) a temporary exemption. Mexico must very soon address its ability to find a comparative advantage position based on innovation and productivity growth (product and process innovation), given its present "assembly" role in the industrial integration process. This transition is complicated by the fact that export growth has not extended to small and midsize enterprises, often key sources of innovation. Exports remain dominated by large firms dependent on external financing.

Lack of productivity and income growth in Mexico and its skewed regional concentration can also be a drag on U.S. productivity and income growth. If China and Southeast Asia exhibit stronger productivity and income growth, Northeast Asian producers will benefit in terms of their global competitiveness. Similarly, if Southern, Central, and Eastern European countries enhance their role as complementary producers and trade partners with the European Union core, overall European productivity and competitiveness are enhanced. The United States has gained much from the integration of a select group of PCC sectors across North American economies, but it must recognize that its long-term interests are tied to expanding PCC dynamics on a much wider basis throughout North America.

The United States must also acknowledge that the current pattern of North American integration clearly exhibits NCC dynamics, although it is not based on the simplistic "race to the bottom" anti-NAFTA metaphor. As in the case of PCC, there is evidence of a common cluster of sectors on both sides of the border that share similar characteristics and linked dynamics. These exhibit slower growth in trade, employment, productivity, and wages. They also share immigrant labor markets, linking migrant-sending regions in Mexico with immigrant-receiving and heavily Latino regions in the United States.

This low-wage binational labor market also makes up the bulk of employment-displacing effects from NAFTA, including trade realignment and plant relocation. These sectors include, for example, corn production in Mexico and garment production in the United States. Not only are negative employment impacts highest in these sectors, but these low-wage binational labor markets also exhibit the lowest levels of education and training spending. Finding employment to even sustain similar low-wage levels after layoffs is very difficult, let alone attaining a transition to higher-skilled export jobs. The negative pressures on these migration-linked labor markets are compounded by a lack of productivity-enhancing capital outlays, exacerbated by low levels of human and social capital investment. Demographic growth is also highest in rural and urban low-skilled sectors with low social investments, on both sides of the border. Adding to negative causality is that this binational labor market has access to only very limited labor, migration, and political rights, compounding these individuals' inability to demand higher wages and increased social investments for their communities on either side of the border.

Remittance transfers are very substantial for Mexico (nearly matching FDI), but their current role is to maintain basic consumption levels among large segments of that country's poorest communities and to perpetuate external dependence on their family networks in the poorest communities in the United States. Low-wage migration is thus functionally maintained and reproduced, yielding a shortsighted subsidy to the U.S. consumers of low-wage goods and services. Over the long run, this maintains communities in poverty on both sides of the border, as well as high levels of inequality in both countries. The United States must recognize its long-term stake in leveraging the migration-remittance dynamic toward increased financing of productive savings and investments in immigrant-sending and immigrant-receiving regions.

CONCLUSIONS

We believe this chapter highlights what should and should not be the focus of debate between pro- and anti-NAFTA groups, as perhaps between pro- and anti-globalization groups in general. Short-run effects on jobs and bilateral trade balances are irrelevant to the countries involved. The key question should be how to enhance cross-border complementarities that can lead to mutual productivity growth, specialization, and trade—which, in turn, will lead to income growth and improvements in the quality of life across rich and poor countries. Trade flows and their impacts must be assessed as just one dimension of complex economic relationships, including investment and capital flows, labor flows, and social and institutional strengths and constraints on both sides of the border.

We demonstrate that the NAFTA debate in general displayed a dearth of theoretical frameworks focused on the dynamics of cumulative causation, either positive or negative. One example of complex positive cumulative causation is a dynamic involving increased investment flows to take strategic competitive advantage of sectors with scale economies. One dynamic we reveal is that the post-NAFTA pattern of trade has been less determined by tariff liberalization than by the pattern of FDI. An example of negative cumulative causation, on the other hand, is the dynamic between trade liberalization and increased displacement in migrant-sending sectors in Mexico (agriculture) and low-wage, immigrant-receiving sectors in the United States (garments).

Competition from the rest of the world means low-wage manufacturing cannot be a lasting basis for North America's economic growth, despite the temporary advantage from NAFTA. This directly affects linked producers and suppliers in the United States. For instance, if the garment industry in Latin America is swamped by a wave of imports from Asia after the implementation of multilateral liberalization already agreed to in the Uruguay Round, the exports and output of the U.S. textile sector will plummet. Mexico will soon face a test of its ability to adapt its comparative advantage based on innovation and productivity growth (product and process innovation), moving beyond its current "assembly" róle in the regional industrial integration process.

North American integration also exhibits NCC dynamics, but not based on the simplistic "race to the bottom" anti-NAFTA metaphor. A low-wage, binational labor market is absorbing the bulk of employment-displacing effects from NAFTA and increased trade and plant relocation. The negative pressures on these migration-linked labor markets are compounded by a lack of productivity-enhancing physical capital investment, as well as low levels of human and social capital investment. Adding to negative causality is limited access in this binational labor market to labor, migration, and political rights, hindering the ability to secure higher wages and increased social investments in communities on either side of the border.

A slowdown in the U.S. economy would bring to the fore this weakness in the pattern of integration that NAFTA enhanced but did not initiate. The U.S. service sector (primarily construction, personal services, and wholesale and retail trade) might not expand rapidly enough to absorb labor from contracting manufacturing subsectors on both sides of the border, along with offering options to Mexican corn farmers. With this safety value threatened, the unsustainability of the current pattern of integration and growth may be painfully revealed.

Whether proposed integration is regional or global, the same fundamental questions are presented to the United States. What integration scenario is in the best interest of U.S. output and income growth? Can the existing pattern of regional integration be improved to extend the positive and minimize the negative cross-border externalities?

We have merely scratched the surface of these important issues. While we can claim a much better understanding of the key questions and issues than has been exhibited by either pro- or anti-globalization forces in the recent debates, we are still struggling to understand the many interrelated aspects of the economic relationships in North America as modified by NAFTA. Identifying sectors that exhibit PCC and NCC across countries is an important first step toward detailed sectoral studies that dig deeper into the economic, social, and institutional causes of these dynamics.[32] A next step is to design macroeconomic models that reflect these added dimensions of interdependence and can better anticipate the results of economic integration between countries at vastly different levels of development. Such models would be valuable in assessing the impact of Chile's accession to NAFTA and the formation of a Free Trade Area of the Americas. The final challenge will be to design economic and social policies that harness the gains from economic integration while also providing both safety nets and social infrastructure spending to boost wages and productivity levels in the region. Since an economic slowdown would threaten a substantial portion of the income gains of the post-NAFTA period, particularly for the transnational migrant class, the design and implementation of such policies should be a priority. The irony is that years before the Guanajuato Proposal, the NAFTA debate did result in the creation of a $3 billion institution (the North American Development Bank, or NADBank) that was originally crafted to address these issues but which has failed to be properly implemented by the U.S. and Mexican governments.[33]

Although beyond the scope of this chapter, we believe that a policy framework that could promote positive dynamics would have to harness the potential productivity and income benefits of integration, and at the same time address the adjustment costs of increased integration. Most importantly, this requires broadening the participation of a wide range of economic actors into an emerging integrated economy. Specifically, that will require the support of small and midsize enterprises, together with new private and public investment into low-wage labor markets and marginalized regions. In this way, integration can lead to productivity, income, and consumption expansion. Concerted institutional changes have to be encouraged in support of new accords on productivity, income distribution, and social investment across borders. These will be necessary to sustain integration with both political and economic convergence.

Notes

1. NAFTA proponents embraced the accord almost reluctantly, as a substitute for more multilateral liberalization and reforms. For example, see the chapter that asks "Should Free Traders Support NAFTA?" in A.R. Riggs and Tom Velk, eds., *Beyond NAFTA: An Economic, Political and Sociological Perspective* (Vancouver, B.C.: Fraser Institute, 1993), pp. 68–73.

2. Specific recent examples of the ongoing controversy include the debates surrounding Permanent Normal Trade Relations for China and its WTO accession, progress or lack thereof on FTAA (Free Trade Area of the Americas), inclusion of labor and environmental issues in the U.S.-Jordan FTA, Seattle and Doha WTO ministerial meetings, and so on.

3. For a review of the NAFTA debate at the time, see Raúl Hinojosa-Ojeda and Sherman Robinson, "Labor Issues in a North American Free Trade Area," in *North American Free Trade: Assessing the Impact*, ed. Nora Lustig, Barry Bosworth, and Robert Lawrence (Washington, D.C.: The Brookings Institution. 1992). On popular debates, see also Mary E. Burfisher, Sherman Robinson, and Karen Thierfelder, "The Impact of NAFTA on the United States," *Journal of Economic Perspectives* 15, no. 1 (Winter 2001): 125–44.

4. Gary Hufbauer and Jeffery Schott, *North American Free Trade: Issues and Recommendations* (Washington, D.C.: Institute for International Economics, 1992).

5. Robert E. Scott, "Fast Track to Lost Jobs: Trade Deficits and Manufacturing Decline are the Legacies of NAFTA and the WTO" (Washington, D.C.: Institute for International Economics, 2001), at http://epinet.org/briefingpapers/bp118.html.

6. Raúl Hinojosa-Ojeda, David Runsten, Fernando De Paolis, and Nabil Kamel, "The US Employment Impacts of North American Integration after NAFTA: A Partial Equilibrium Approach" (Los Angeles: NAID Center, University of California, Los Angeles, 2000), at http://naid.sppsr.ucla.edu.

7. Paul Krugman, "Increasing Returns, Monopolistic Competition and International Trade," *Journal of International Economics* 9 (November 1979): 469–79; Elhanan Helpman and Paul Krugman, *Market Structure and Foreign Trade* (Cambridge, Mass.: MIT Press, 1985); Richard Harris, "Applied General Equilibrium Analysis of Small Open Economies with Scale Economies and Imperfect Competition," *American Economic Review*, December 1984, pp. 1016–32; and David Cox and Richard Harris, "Trade Liberalization and Industrial Organization: Some Estimates for Canada," *Journal of Political Economy* 93 (February 1985): 115–45.

8. Raúl Hinojosa-Ojeda and Sherman Robinson, "Diversos escenarios de la integración de los Estados Unidos y México: enfoque de equilibrio general computable," *Economía Mexicana* 1, no. 1 (1992): 71–144.

9. John Whalley, "'Trade, Industrial Policy and Canadian Manufacturing' by Richard Harris (with the assistance of David Cox): A Review Article," *Canadian Journal of Economics* 17 (May 1984): 1–13.

10. Sherman Robinson, Mary Burfisher, Raúl Hinojosa, and Karen Thierfelder, "Agricultural Policies and Migration in a U.S.-Mexico Free Trade Area: A Computable General Equilibrium Analysis," *Journal of Policy Modeling* 15, nos. 5–6 (1993): 673–701, also published in *Economy-Wide Modeling of the Economic Implications of a FTA with Mexico and a NAFTA with Canada and Mexico*, USITC Publication 2508 (Washington D.C.: USITC, May 1992); Santiago Levy and Sweder van Wijnbergen, "Transition Problems in Economic Reform: Agriculture in the Mexico-U.S. Free Trade Agreement," also in *Economy-Wide Modeling*.

11. Edward Taylor and Antonio Yúnez-Naude, "Agricultural Policy Reforms and Village Economies: A CGE Analysis from Mexico," *Journal of Policy Modeling* 21, no.4 (1999): 453–80.

12. Robert McCleery, "An Intertemporal, Linked, Macroeconomic CGE Model of the United States and Mexico Focussing on Demographic Change and Factor Flows," in *Economy-Wide Modeling of the Economic Implications of a FTA with Mexico and a NAFTA with Canada and Mexico*, USITC Publication 2508 (Washington D.C.: USITC, May 1992).

13. Linda Hunter, James Markusen, and Thomas Rutherford, "Trade Liberalization in a Multinational-Dominated Industry: A Theoretical and Applied General Equilibrium Analysis," in *Economy-Wide Modeling of the Economic Implications of a FTA with Mexico and a NAFTA with Canada and Mexico*, USITC Publication 2508 (Washington D.C.: USITC, May 1992).

14. Data on U.S. international transactions and the dollar from Bureau of Economic Analysis, Survey of Current Business, January 2002 and selected April issues, available on-line at http://www.bea.doc.gov/bea/pubs.htm.

15. Council of Economic Advisors, *Economic Report of the President, 2001* (Washington D.C.: U.S. Government Printing Office, 2001).

16. INFORUM, "Industrial Effects of a Free Trade Agreement between Mexico and the USA," report prepared for the Department of Labor (College Park: University of Maryland, 1990).

17. Carlos Bachrach and Lorris Mizrahi, "The Economic Impact of a Free Trade Agreement between the United States and Mexico: A CGE Analysis," KPMG Peat Marwick (Washington, D.C., February 1992).

18. Robinson, Burfisher, Hinojosa, and Thierfelder, "Agricultural Policies and Migration."

19. INFORUM, "Industrial Effects."

20. GAO, "Supporting Sugar Prices Has Increased Users' Costs While Benefiting Producers," GAO/RCED-00-126, June 2000.

21. Drusilla K. Brown, Alan V. Deardorff, and Robert M. Stern, "A North American Free Trade Agreement: Analytical Issues and a Computational Assessment," *World Economy* 15 (January 1992): 11–30.

22. Incidentally, the decline in subsidies was designed to seize the moral high ground for further subsidy reduction negotiations with the European Union.

23. Hunter, Markusen, and Rutherford, "Trade Liberalization in a Multinational-Dominated Industry."

24. Hinojosa-Ojeda, Runsten, De Paolis, and Kamel, "The US Employment Impacts of North American Integration after NAFTA."

25. Masahisa Fujita, Paul Krugman, and Anthony Venables, "Core and Periphery," in *The Spatial Economy: Cities, Regions, and International Trade,* by Masahisa Fujita, Paul Krugman, and Anthony Venables (Cambridge, Mass.: MIT Press, 2000).

26. Gunner Myrdal, *Economic Theory and Underdeveloped Regions* (London: Duckworth, 1957).

27. Robert Hall and Charles Jones, "Why Do Some Countries Produce So Much More Output per Worker than Others?" CEPR Working Paper (Palo Alto, Calif.: Stanford University, 2000).

28. Note that the average growth rate of employment used is that of industrial employment. The share of manufacturing employment continued to shrink relative to service sectors over this period.

29. While beyond the scope of the present essay, a similar analysis for Mexico highlights electronics as the only sector meeting the strict requirements for strong PCC, while industrial machinery, rubber, and motor vehicles all display moderate PCC. Hence these four sectors show the possibility of binational PCC. No other sectors in Mexico show even moderate PCC. Thus we can postulate that PCC can be developed in Mexico through a "pull" effect from PCC in the United States, and perhaps *only* in conjunction with PCC in the United States. An important question is whether PCC in the United States, both strong and weak, can successfully exist without corresponding sectors in Mexico. A further step to our research concerns the economic dynamic in Canada in sectors exhibiting PCC in the United States.

30. Hinojosa-Ojeda, Runsten, De Paolis, and Kamel, "The US Employment Impacts of North American Integration after NAFTA."

31. http://www.pewtrusts.com/pdf/vf_pew_hispanic_recession.pdf.

32. These studies are being coordinated by the NAID Center at the University of California, Los Angeles, with the support of the Ford Foundation and the MacArthur Foundation.

33. For the original vision of the NADBank and reasons for its bureaucratic-political stalemate, see Raúl Hinojosa-Ojeda, "The North American Development Bank: Forging in New Directions in Regional Integration Policy," *Journal of the American Planning Association* 60, no. 3 (Summer, 1994): 301–304; and Raúl Hinojosa-Ojeda, "North American Integration Policy Formation from the Grassroots Up: Transnational Implications of Latino, Labor, and Environmental NGO Strategies," in Jonathan Fox and David Brooks, eds. *Cross-Border Learning: Lessons from Mexico-U.S. Social Movement Dialogues* (La Jolla: Center for U.S.-Mexican Studies, University of California, San Diego, forthcoming 2002).

2

NAFTA and Mexico: A Sectoral Analysis

José Luis Valdés Ugalde

> *Did the United States succeed in nation-building and in forcible nation-restoration because it was virtuous, or because it had Canadians and Mexicans as its neighbors rather than Russians and Germans?*
> —C.S. Gray

Globalization, economic reform, and trade integration are the central components of today's global village. These components also played a key role in post–Cold War foreign policies around the world, leading nations to alter their view of themselves and of the international arena as they strove to cope with emerging paradigmatic challenges. The end of bipolarity is giving way to an evolving new economic world order. Besides concerns about national sovereignty, one key question regarding the new economic order is how to distribute financial and material resources in ways that lead to national and global progress and modernity. As Ricardo Pozas Horcasitas suggests, "today, the global era defines the terms of international integration. This takes place through a new distribution of the world into regions, blocs, and communities, forms of organization that imply constant and mandatory points of reference for defining political behaviors and actors' actions in societies and nation-states."[1] Globalization is not, then, an abstraction, but rather a cultural, economic, and political space that redefines geopolitics.[2]

Confronted by new global dynamics, nation-states have to redefine their economic, political, and social aspirations. Most countries have set out to search for new regional and global alliances. Many have joined regional trading arrangements in an attempt to make their domestic economic reforms compatible with the economic realities of the new world order. To be sure, this was not done without risking a head-on collision with the challenges posed by progress and modernity.

Economic integration is a fact in today's world. It is a complex and heterogeneous process, as well as an inevitable and possibly irreversible one. In short, "the articulation among globalization, regional integration processes, and diverse cultures is becoming a key issue both in study agendas and in negotiations."[3] The specific manifestations of integration cannot be understood without reference to some of the challenges that accompany it. Among these are progress and modernity—something Octavio Paz called "elusive ghosts"—and their convergence with U.S. interests.[4] The ties between Mexico and the United States indicate that local leaderships, by virtue of their legitimate quest for external and internal conditions of economic development, will collaborate on transferring modernizing elements to the periphery. However, they will do so only as long as conditions are consistent with the interests of the established local powers.[5]

This formulation leads to an evaluation of the position that Mexico and its multiple economic, social, and political actors hold in today's unprecedented, potentially modernizing, sociopolitical context. This study focuses not only on Mexico's position as an actor in the global arena but, more importantly, on the *nature* of Mexico's insertion into the U.S.-dominated regional sphere. This insertion crystallized with the 1994 implementation of NAFTA, one of the most significant trade integration schemes in Mexico's history. Understanding Mexico's entry into the global economy is a prerequisite to analyzing Mexico's future prospects in the face of regionalism and globalism—a reality that is as extraordinary as it is filled with contradictions and ambiguities.

This study involves a sectoral analysis of the Mexican economy in the NAFTA years, dissecting the logic of each economic sector in hopes of drawing useful inferences. Each sector is defined broadly, incorporating its preexisting characteristics and dynamics in order to produce a comprehensive analytical framework. Thus the sectoral analysis of NAFTA's impacts depends not only on the agreement's effects but also on the attributes of the specific sector in question.[6]

BACKGROUND AND APPROACH

Since the early 1980s, Latin American policymakers have embraced the concept of market liberalization. An export-oriented industrialization policy, along with deregulation and liberalization, came to be seen as imperative for developing countries trying to restructure their productive systems and to enter the globalizing marketplace. The "Asian tigers" set the example with their huge success in export-oriented microelectronics and their rapid GDP growth. In Latin America, including Mexico, liberalization has played a central role in both the theoretical and the political realms.

Mexico's Economic Opening

The process of reducing state participation in the Mexican economy began in the 1980s with the sale of parastatal companies. On a more general level, the 1980s marked a dramatic turning point in Mexico's subsidy, trade, and regulatory policies. One immediate consequence of the new policy framework was export-oriented production—production geared to foreign markets. Moreover, the import-substitution industrialization (ISI) model had run its course in Mexico by 1985, and economic opening became a prerequisite for the country's integration into the global economy. However, economic opening did not always achieve the desired modernization.

Economic opening and trade liberalization can both be traced to Mexico's adhesion to the General Agreement on Tariffs and Trade (GATT) in 1986.[7] However, Mexico's efforts to gain access to the global economic stage actually go back even further, to the country's unilateral tariff reductions initiated in 1982. By early 1988, Mexico's average tariff (100 percent in 1982) had dropped to 20 percent across most sectors (one exception was the automotive industry). There were further cuts between 1988 and NAFTA's implementation in 1994. Thus, when NAFTA negotiations began in 1989–1990, the Mexican economy was already relatively open; the few exceptions included the automotive and telecommunications industries. Even so, Mexico saw economic integration with the United States as its most ambitious endeavor; by providing access to the world's largest market, NAFTA was expected to boost Mexico's trade and attract investment.

NAFTA can be seen as a regional effort to maximize the benefits from international flows of goods and services. However, it is also a highly innovative and ambitious trade agreement because it went beyond trade to incorporate investment issues and other economic considerations. NAFTA's provisions significantly altered the norms regulating trade in North America. Moreover, in some areas NAFTA eclipsed other trade agreements, including the Canada–United States Free Trade Agreement (CUSFTA) and the rules governing the GATT and, subsequently, the World Trade Organization (WTO). Although NAFTA also gave rise to regionwide agreements in noncommercial spheres—such as labor and the environment—goals in these areas have yet to be fully realized. Further, NAFTA does not specify the macroeconomic policies that each member country should implement. If NAFTA negotiators had included such matters in their discussions—as did the negotiators of the European Union, which represents a much deeper level of integration—NAFTA probably would not have been viable.

Evaluating Sectoral Performance

An analysis of NAFTA's effects by productive sector allows us to differentiate between impacts produced by the agreement and those spurred by other factors. A sectoral approach also ensures that impacts are not attributed to NAFTA that are the result of Mexico's late economic development. Indeed, sectoral performance is shaped by many variables, including domestic and international economic dynamics, the preexisting organization of economic activity, macroeconomic policies, and significant economic and trade matters not touched on in the NAFTA agreement. In short, both NAFTA and the overall economic scenario influence the expectations and decision-making of economic agents in Mexico and abroad.

Given the heterogeneity of Mexico's economic sectors, NAFTA's performance in achieving its objectives in Mexico is uneven. For this reason, a macroeconomic, quantitative analysis may not be a suitable tool with which to evaluate NAFTA. Rather, what is required is a qualitative examination of individual industrial sectors, their infrastructural context, and the laws and regulations that guide the behavior of their economic agents.

The theory of industrial organization contains elements that are useful for understanding the market structure of any given industry, and these can be used to detect and assess the impact of NAFTA on an industry's development. Industrial market structure comprises four key elements: concentration, barriers to entry, product differentiation, and market demand.[8]

Industry concentration is probably the most decisive feature in market structure. Several indices—the Herfindhal Index, the Absolute Concentration Index, the Entropy Index, and the antilogarithm—have been developed to measure concentration. All indicate the degree of market power that firms in a given sector exercise.[9]

Entry barriers are the comparative advantages—and, hence, market power—that established firms hold over firms that are seeking to enter their market. There are four types of entry barriers. The first is economies of scale; these can be real economies of scale, which determine a sector's technological characteristics, or financial/economic, which means that firms already established in the sector can obtain their inputs at lower prices if they increase production. The second entry barrier involves preestablished firms' access to capital, generally through credit, as well as their behavior in areas such as patents or dumping. The third barrier is the experience of established firms, which gives them advantages over aspiring entrants to any given sector. These advantages include knowledge gained by a prolonged process of "learning by doing," access to the fruits of research and development, and exclusive contracts with suppliers. The fourth and final barrier lies in the legal framework; each industry operates under laws that are the product of negotiations between sectoral representatives and officials and policymakers. For example, constitutional restrictions regulate entry into the Mexican energy sector, and the textile sector is governed by the Multi-Fiber Arrangement reached during the Uruguay Round of the GATT. These norms influence the course of sectoral development—be it for better or for worse.

Product differentiation is one of the key strategies that firms employ to establish "institutional" monopolies.[10] Differentiation implies the production of a good or service that is functionally similar to other products in the market yet different, for example, in terms of appearance or marketing. If firms producing differentiated goods gain market power, markets become imperfect. However, the development of a monopoly is unlikely; this would require that the consumer's choices be limited by a single brand's domination of the market or by agreements among producers to curb competition between them.

Market demand, the final element in market structure, can vary drastically from one industry to the next for a number of reasons. Some products, because of their elasticity coefficients, display a fairly constant demand curve. However, the demand curve for others can behave in a highly unpredictable manner over time. Moreover, shocks can occur that are not accounted for in initial predictions.

One such shock was Mexico's 1994–1995 peso crisis. Although exchange rate policy questions were not central to NAFTA, the currency crisis had repercussions for the agreement. In December 1994, the Mexican peso began a downward spiral, ultimately losing more than 50 percent of its value. Tariffs, meanwhile, dropped by an average of only 12 percent and had a lesser impact on trade in 1995 than did the currency depreciation.[11] The peso crisis also exposed the fact that trade integration cannot correct deep-seated flaws in any country's macroeconomic and structural policies. Strong domestic economic growth depends on industrial and technological policies, which until recently in Mexico were inconsistent and ineffective. Yet such policies hold the key to generating the necessary conditions for achieving sustainable development. In this sense, NAFTA could be placed on a firmer ground through a strategy aimed at reducing Mexico's dependence on the United States and Canada for modern technology, particularly in the manufacturing sector.

Principal Concerns

This analysis aims to discover the degree to which Mexico's economic adjustment process in key areas is consistent with the characteristics and requirements of the domestic market, and also to identify the needs of the Mexican economy vis-à-vis the U.S. and the Canadian markets. In sum, the analysis will reveal the benefits that trade opening has brought to various sectors of the Mexican economy. This is particularly relevant given the fact that several regulatory measures were excluded from NAFTA, including measures affecting foreign investment, intellectual property, textiles, and telecommunications. Moreover, NAFTA's core text, excluding the parallel agreements, does not establish any supranational mechanism to address questions such as subsidies or environmental, labor, and consumer protections. The absence of such features from the agreement raises questions about the degree to which the virtuous circles that trade liberalization promised can be achieved.

A further concern is the domestic market. The classical principles of Adam Smith's economic liberalism remain largely absent from the Mexican reality. These involve the principle of converting a selfish society into one capable of meeting the general public interest; the principle of perfect competition, whereby economic actors (including foreign ones) interact in symmetrical relations and those breaching the principle will be punished; and access by all economic actors to *all* information in the market, which would result in rational decisions and the establishment of clear priorities. This analysis seeks to uncover how well these principles work in Mexico's liberalized economy in general, and in the context of NAFTA in particular.

THE ADVANTAGES OF NAFTA

NAFTA has given Mexican exports unfettered access to the U.S. market, providing a huge boost to Mexico's volume of exports. NAFTA has also fostered the liberalization strategy that Mexico adopted in 1988 to promote exports. The country's openness index (exports plus imports as a percentage of gross national product [GNP]) has risen markedly since the beginning of 1990 (see figure 2.1). Exports represented 11.5 percent of Mexico's GNP in 1988; they had risen to 28.7 percent by 1998, making the export sector the main engine of Mexico's economic growth.[12]

Figure 2.1. Trade Liberalization Index (exports + imports as % of GNP)

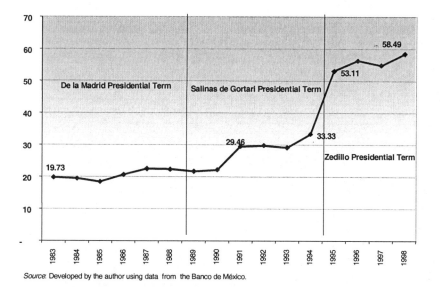

Source: Developed by the author using data from the Banco de México.

Eduardo Loría provides a thoughtful analysis of Mexico's export performance relative to other major Latin America economies. "By 1985 ... Argentine, Brazilian, Chilean, and Mexican total exports were $8.396, $25.693, $3.823, and $21.664 billion, respectively. In short, Mexico's total exports were 2.6 times higher than those of Argentina, 0.8 those of Brazil, and 5.7 times those of Chile."[13] This performance, Loría notes, is even more impressive if we consider three additional factors:

(1) the notable growth of the Chilean and, to a lesser extent,
Argentine economies; (2) Brazil's high manufacturing exports since the 1960s; and (3) the multiplication of Mexico's
manufacturing exports against the backdrop of an unfavorable domestic context. Domestic demand grew substantially
in Mexico between 1989 and 1994, and the real exchange
rate was systematically overvalued. These factors imply that
some other variables affecting Mexico's international competitiveness must have evolved spectacularly in order for
the Mexican economy to weather the adverse economic effects.... This paradox would support—in principle—the
economic dualism hypothesis, which postulates the coexistence of an extremely dynamic modern sector ... with a traditional [lagging] sector.[14]

Exports to the U.S. market grew to 80.83 percent of Mexico's total
exports in 1998. Since 1990, Mexico has been the third most important
exporter to the U.S. market. If current trends continue, Mexico is likely
to overtake Japan in the medium term as the second most important
exporter to the United States.

The automotive industry offers a useful illustration of the positive
repercussions of NAFTA. By establishing clear rules guaranteeing access within the North American market, NAFTA ensured continuity in
investment flows to Mexico's automotive sector, despite declining domestic demand following the 1994–1995 peso crisis. These investments boosted the sector's modernization which, along with free access to the U.S. market, enabled the automotive sector to gain a
foothold in the United States. M.I. Studer summarizes it as follows:

> We must underscore NAFTA's fundamental role in guaran-
> teeing access to the U.S. and Canadian markets. Absent the
> treaty, there would have been a very real risk in 1995 that
> the U.S. government—under pressure from unions and
> auto parts producers—would have taken measures to avoid
> trade deficits due to substantial increases in Mexican car
> imports. In fact, several historical antecedents attest to the
> natural tendency of the United States to protect industries
> in sectors that face substantial trade deficits.[15]

For this sector, at least, NAFTA provided essential market guarantees.

Also because of NAFTA, Mexico has come to be viewed as a relatively attractive target for foreign investment. In 1994, the stock of
foreign direct investment (FDI) in Mexico was $42.37 billion. Between

1994 and 1998, total inflows were $41.22 billion (see table 2.1). This means that Mexico's stock of FDI doubled in just a few years. The evolution of investment coming from the United States shows similar trends: inflows of U.S. investment in 1994–1998 were $24.7 billion, nearly equal to the total stock of U.S. investment in 1993 ($26 billion).

Table 2.1. Foreign Direct Investment in Mexico, by Country of Origin, 1993 and 1994–1998 (billions of U.S. dollars)

	United States	Canada	Other	Total
1993	$26.62	$0.65	$15.10	$42.37
1994–1998	24.67	1.71	14.84	41.22

Source: Author's calculations based on data from the Banco de México.

Changes in the laws that regulate foreign investment, property rights, trade, and privatization have consolidated the increase in investment inflows. However, the key has been the credibility that NAFTA provides. Foreign investors do not only look for changes in legislation; they also look for guarantees that the changes will be enforced.

NAFTA also played a significant role during the 1994–1995 peso crisis by ensuring Mexico's access to Canadian commodity markets and, more importantly, to the U.S. market. As such, the agreement helped prevent an even deeper recession in Mexico. Moreover, the credibility that NAFTA accorded helped Mexico weather the crisis. For example, the entry of foreign capital to Mexico's financial sector reduced the vulnerability of the banking system by allowing for the recapitalization of domestic banks. This lowered the fiscal costs of the bank rescue, and it ameliorated the impact of the deep sectoral crisis. Employment and production levels declined less than expected. NAFTA also contributed to the modernization of the legal framework as it applies to various issue areas and economic sectors, including the property rights regime and the financial sector. As such, the agreement helped the economy adapt to international standards.

Questions of Cause and Effect

Mexico's trade opening has been accompanied by structural changes that have had repercussions on the composition of Mexico's exports. Oil has ceased to be the main source of export revenue. Loría notes that crude oil and natural gas accounted for 72 percent of all exports in 1981–1983, whereas manufacturing contributed just 19 percent. By 1998, however, manufacturing's share had climbed to 90.2 percent, while oil had dropped to 6.1 percent. Despite fallout from financial crises in Asia and Russia in 1998—"the worst global financial crisis since the 1930s," in Loría's estimation—"the value of Mexican non-oil exports increased 11.3 percent, one of the highest rates in the world."[16]

A clarification is in order. When analyzing Mexico's economic performance from 1994 forward, several problems emerge that cannot, with the exception of the proliferation of dumping practices, be directly or exclusively attributed to NAFTA. Most of the post-1994 problems stem from the outward-oriented industrialization traceable to Mexico's entry into the GATT in 1986, not from NAFTA per se. Thus the consequences of Mexico's 1994–1995 economic crisis need to be examined carefully in order not to confuse the impacts of NAFTA with those of other variables that affect the Mexican economy. Indeed, the crisis inhibits efforts to analyze trends in the Mexican economy since mid-1995.

In other words, NAFTA should be understood as only one element in Mexico's model of economic integration and opening. Francisco Zapata argues that:

> An evaluation of NAFTA's effects cannot be derived by examining the period 1994 to 1999.... Such an analysis necessarily must be inserted within a much broader time frame.... The process of trade opening, negotiation of a free trade agreement, privatization of parastatals, and labor market restructuring all began before NAFTA was enacted.[17]

Thus, C. Salas asserts, "NAFTA should be seen as one of the elements in Mexico's economic integration.... NAFTA is a natural outcome of a policy implemented in Mexico since 1982, whose aim is to go from a model centered on the domestic market to one centered on the foreign market."[18] Taking this point further, H. Juárez argues that in the automotive industry,

> The position of Mexican production, and even of U.S. production, was already defined before the end of the 1980s.... Mexican production as a share of North American production, and North American production as a share of world production, have not, in fact, varied [since then]. That is, we

do not find 1994, the year of NAFTA's implementation, to be a turning point.[19]

Jorge Máttar, a petrochemical-sector analyst at the Economic Commission for Latin America and the Caribbean (ECLAC), adds:

> One of the elements [having a bearing on the Mexican economy] is precisely NAFTA, but it should be noted that ... it is practically impossible to isolate the different determinants that influence industry performance.... We cannot ascribe to NAFTA either all of the benefits or all the drawbacks in this industry.[20]

Even so, there are setbacks in the Mexican economy that can be traced to NAFTA. Yet even in this context, NAFTA should be seen as only one factor contributing to the negative trends discernible since the mid-1980s. Indeed, the relative weight of other factors was more decisive. For example, the deterioration of the financial sector had its origins in the privatization process that took place during the administration of Carlos Salinas de Gortari (1988–1994). The 1994–1995 crisis signaled that privatizations geared to maximizing revenue in the short term, at the cost of creating a clear regulatory framework for the long term, were hurting the economy. Consequently NAFTA had to confront a severe banking crisis, which was exacerbated by poor management, inexperience, and the absence of a strong regulatory framework. Fallout from these problems led to the establishment of emergency programs such as the FOBAPROA deposits protection fund. Similarly, the decline of metal prices undercut the mining sector, but this trend cannot be attributed to NAFTA alone; rather, it was due to fluctuations in global commodity markets. Similarly, world grain prices would have continued to fall with or without NAFTA.

NAFTA'S DRAWBACKS

The Mexican export sectors most strongly stimulated by NAFTA have become increasingly concentrated. From 1993 through 1997, some three hundred firms supplied, on average, 54.6 percent of Mexico's total exports, and the share of the *maquiladora* (in-bond processing) sector was 40.4 percent. By contrast, the rest of Mexico's economy—more than 2.1 million firms—exported less than 5 percent of the total, and their share declined during the period. Furthermore, firms producing for the domestic market and small firms in general have not been part of the export boom.

The concentration of export sectors is mirrored in employment. Between 1988 and 1998, the share of micro, small, and midsize enterprises in total manufacturing-sector employment dropped from 49.8 to 42.8 percent. This trend has allowed for the polarization of industrial organization in Mexico, and it obviously has not helped resolve the structural problems afflicting the Mexican economy.

Several productive sectors have been unable to withstand the competition spurred by economic opening. This has generated a systematic increase in imported contents included in goods destined for both the domestic and export markets; what we are witnessing is growth of the maquiladora sector amid a process of de-industrialization.

In other words, NAFTA has not produced favorable results in terms of establishing structural links between foreign and domestic producers in Mexico. At the same time, zones with important local production have been eroded.[21] Today, maquiladora production represents about 50 percent of Mexican exports, and it is the large multinational companies that play a central role in defining the main characteristics of the sector—trade flows, investment, and employment.[22]

Many Mexican firms that previously operated in traditional manufacturing industries have moved to the maquiladora sector and now import most of their inputs. From 1994 to 2000, fixed gross investment rose 3.6 percent at the domestic level, while domestic investment in the maquiladora sector rose 30.4 percent. This clearly indicates a new industrialization process along the border, which, in turn, has paved the way for the creation of one million new jobs. This trend has accentuated the regional concentration of manufacturing in Mexico's northern frontier states. Nevertheless, the maquiladora sector has branched out under NAFTA to other parts of the country, such as the states of Puebla and Oaxaca, as foreign direct investment has sought new productive spaces.

It should be noted that Mexico's manufacturing industry has long faced de-industrialization, bankruptcy, and the disappearance of poorly performing companies. Ruiz Nápoles provides a lucid explanation:

> A recent issue of a business magazine affirmed that our destiny is to become a maquiladora country.... If we subtract current maquiladora operations from manufacturing exports and imports, the resulting trade deficit for the decade is between $20 and $30 billion. Except during 1995 and

> 1996 [years of the peso crisis] ... a policy to integrate the
> maquiladora industry into domestic industry did not ex-
> ist.... It is not that the maquiladora industry becomes full
> industry; rather, export industry tends to become maqui-
> ladora.[23]

According to this view, then, Mexico has faced two structural problems since the 1950s: endemic trade deficits, which have been particularly notable since 1986, and the decline of the manufacturing sector—
which helps explain the trade deficit.

Equally problematic, employment elasticity is decreasing in relation
to income, confirming the weaknesses of the manufacturing sector.
Table 2.2 illustrates the substantial share of intermediate and capital
goods in Mexico's import basket. Together, these imports have represented more than 90 percent of total imports since 1995. As Ruiz Nápoles
explains,

> Liberalization produced ... a substantial reduction in the
> degree of integration in the domestic economy.... This
> seems to imply that the degree of integration lost in internal
> productive branches was gained by the import sector....
> The manufacturing sector clearly shows a strong trend to-
> ward a replacement of national inputs with imported inputs
> since the beginning of the process of trade liberalization.[24]

These features are also discernible in the meager technological
spillovers to domestic productive sectors. The technology gap between
U.S. and Mexican firms remains so wide that innovative processes are
essentially imported. This is vividly illustrated by trends in patent applications in Mexico. J. Aboites argues that,

> There is a clear predominance of patent applications from
> residents and nonresidents, both before and after the trade
> opening process began.... Changes in the intellectual prop-
> erty rights framework produced a deep breach between
> these two flows.... For the OECD [Organisation for Eco-
> nomic Co-operation and Development] countries, two
> groups can be discerned ... [first] those where there is no
> correlation between the flow of foreign firm applications
> and that of national firms [Mexico, for instance] ... and
> [second] the group in which arriving technology and tech-
> nology created domestically are correlated.[25]

Table 2.2. Mexico's Imports by Sector and Type of Good, 1985–1998 (millions of U.S. dollars)

	1985 (%)	1990 (%)	1994 (%)	1995 (%)	1996 (%)	1997 (%)	1998 (%)
By Sector							
Maquiladora	3,826.0 (20.8)	10,321.4 (24.8)	20,466.2 (25.8)	26,178.8 (36.1)	30,504.7 (34.1)	36,332.0 (33.1)	42,557.0 (34.0)
Non-maquiladora	14,533.1 (79.2)	31,271.9 (75.2)	58,879.7 (74.2)	46,274.3 (63.9)	58,964.1 (65.9)	73,476.0 (66.9)	82,685.0 (66.0)
Total	18,359.1 (100)	41,593.3 (100)	79,345.9 (100)	72,453.1 (100)	89,468.8 (100)	109,808.0 (100)	125,242.0 (100)
By Type of Good							
Consumer goods	1,081.7 (5.9)	5,098.5 (12.3)	9,510.4 (12.0)	5,334.7 (7.4)	6,656.8 (7.4)	9,326.0 (8.5)	11,108.0 (8.87)
Intermediate goods							
—Maquiladora	3,826.0 (20.8)	10,321.4 (24.8)	20,466.2 (25.8)	26,178.8 (36.1)	30,504.7 (34.1)	36,332.0 (33.1)	42,557.0 (34.0)
—Non-maquiladora	10,286.6 (56.0)	19,383.7 (46.6)	36,047.5 (45.4)	32,242.3 (44.5)	41,384.9 (46.2)	49,034.0 (44.6)	54,248.0 (43.3)
—Total intermediate goods	14,112.6 (76.9)	29,705.1 (71.4)	56,513.7 (71.2)	58,421.1 (80.6)	71,889.6 (80.3)	85,366.0 (77.7)	96,805.0 (77.3)
Capital goods	3,164.8 (17.2)	6,789.7 (16.3)	13,321.7 (16.8)	8,697.3 (12.0)	10,922.4 (12.2)	15,116.0 (13.8)	17,329.0 (13.8)

Sources: *Comercio Exterior* (1997); Banco de México (1997), at http://www.banxico.org.mx.

Thus we can conclude that Mexico has yet to exploit the access to foreign technology that NAFTA provides. Foreign technology has not been disseminated to Mexican firms, and Mexico continues to be a *technology follower*. This is antithetical to the idea of a nation boasting "a strong relationship between foreign technology and domestic technology" or a nation "with solid technological capacity, learning mechanisms, and well-developed relationships and networks for the diffusion of technological information." Aboites concludes that forces are operating in the opposite direction in countries like Mexico, "whose framework of technological capabilities is at a formative stage (and, therefore, fragile), countries in which patent flows do not affect domestic activity." Over the past ten years, Mexico and countries facing similar circumstances, such as South Korea and Taiwan, have derived huge advantages from foreign technologies. The challenge for Mexico is to design an industrial policy that will allow technological information from abroad to filter into domestic technological processes.[26]

Mexico is extremely dependent on the performance of the U.S. economy. In fact, U.S. economic performance has been a stronger factor in Mexico's export success than have, for example, fluctuations in the dollar-peso exchange rate. Mexico's total exports increase only by some 2.9 percent in response to a 10 percent currency devaluation (see table 2.3), but the demand for Mexican non-oil exports increases 18 percent in response to a 10 percent increase in U.S. GNP.[27] Maquiladora exports show an even weaker response to exchange rate fluctuations because the sector's production strategies are set by headquarters located abroad.

Surprisingly, total imports also increase—although very slightly—when the peso loses strength vis-à-vis the dollar. The fact that a more expensive dollar does not discourage imports seems to reflect Mexico's dependence on imported inputs: 80 percent of imports are intermediate goods geared to domestic production. Even in the face of a depreciating peso, therefore, the Mexican economy continues to depend on import flows. The exception lies with imported consumer goods, which have proved to be extremely sensitive to exchange rate fluctuations and national income (see table 2.3).

What is the explanation for this pattern? Enrique Dussel offers the following interpretation:

> On the one hand, manufacturing has generally been extremely successful in promoting growth and productivity, and particularly so in the area of exports. NAFTA, in this

view, has allowed a deep integration between Mexico and
the United States in terms of intra-firm trade and the maquiladora industry. On the other hand, these firms generate
a minimum amount of employment, and, surprisingly, their
salaries have shown a downward trend when compared to
the rest of the manufacturing sector's salaries from 1998
onward. The most relevant characteristics, however, are the
new industrial organization generated by the maquiladora
sector and the fact that, in order to grow in GNP terms, the
economy requires more and more imports.[28]

Table 2.3. Determinants of Mexican Exports and Imports

Dependent Variable	Independent Variable: 10 Percent Increase In:			
	Exchange Rate	*Mexican GNP*	*U.S. GNP*	*Oil Price*
Exports	(%)		(%)	(%)
Total	2.9	—	18.4	—
Manufacturing	1.2	—	18.3	—
Maquiladora	—	—	19.5	—
Petroleum	—	—	4.6	8.9
Imports	(%)	(%)		
Total	1.1	3.3	—	—
Intermediate goods	0.8	2.3	—	—
Consumer goods	−9.3	8.9	—	—
Capital goods	0.8	3.9	—	—

Source: Author's calculations based on data from the Banco de México.

NAFTA has not eliminated all practices that run counter to free
trade. For example, U.S. antidumping actions against Mexican cement
run counter to the spirit of the agreement. Carlos Villareal, of the Vil-
lacero Financial Group in Michoacán, argues that the United States has
erected protectionist barriers at the same time that it requires key inputs from abroad. Kansas and Missouri have applied entrance restrictions to products used in the construction industry, such as wire and
reinforcing bar (rebar), an action that Villareal considers both absurd
and contrary to the basic principles of NAFTA.[29]

Similar problems have emerged in the agriculture and livestock sectors. Mexico's sugar producers fault NAFTA for their economic problems; the agreement opened the Mexican market to corn syrup, a
sweetener that can be purchased for a lower price than the country's
domestically produced sugar. In 1994, Mexico's Cattlemen's Associa-

tion filed an antidumping suit to halt beef imports. Of the 12,000 tons of beef imported into Mexico each month in 1994, approximately 35 percent entered at dumping prices. In 1997, of the 28,000 tons of beef that entered Mexico each month, some 18,000 tons (77 percent) were dumped. Not only had the volume of imported beef increased, but so had the margin of price discrimination. These discriminatory practices continued even after the affected parties had reached a settlement.[30]

Representatives of the Cattlemen's Association are deeply concerned about rising imports of U.S. beef. Their efforts to have a special tariff imposed on beef imports have been largely unsuccessful, and there have been no national proposals for improving the competitiveness of Mexican beef—although some cattlemen are working privately to strengthen the country's livestock sector. One such private-sector project, supported by ASERCA (Support Services for the Marketing of Agricultural and Livestock Products), involves developing a bulk purchasing system for grain. But unlike large-scale, multinational producers, which can buy inputs directly and obtain the ASERCA benefits, small and midsize egg and dairy farmers, for example, do not have access to such supports. Another private project aims to halt or reduce Mexican exports of yearlings and bull calves so as to prevent interruptions in the domestic production chain and to reduce Mexico's imports of packaged beef. Importantly, this effort incorporates clear technical outlines to ensure production efficiency and long-term economic viability in Mexico's beef-producing sector. A third project involves establishing a center for technological research and development efforts with application for the livestock sector.[31]

How has Mexican labor fared under NAFTA? The rising levels of Mexican exports, foreign investment inflows to Mexico, and the burgeoning maquiladora sector together have helped create a total of roughly 1.5 million new jobs. However, the employment situation remains precarious in several economic sectors. One indication of the lack of employment options is the continuing out-migration of Mexican workers to the United States. Another is the evolution of wages; even though the productivity of Mexican workers vis-à-vis their U.S. and Canadian counterparts has increased, average wages declined by more than 25 percent between 1994 and 1998 (see table 2.4).

Unemployment tells another part of the story. Annual unemployment averaged 3.12 percent from 1987 through 1993, but it rose to 4.1 percent from 1994 to 1999 (see figure 2.2). Even if we exclude 1995, a year of severe economic crisis, the average rate of unemployment would be 3.7 percent. This indicates that employment generation was better prior to NAFTA than after the agreement's implementation. As noted previously, the NAFTA negotiators, unlike those who shaped the rules of the European Union, failed to resolve the issue of the free movement of labor. Indeed, the United States has sought to halt the entry of Mexican workers, and Mexico, as a major exporter of labor, will need to deal forcefully with this issue in the future.[32]

Table 2.4. Trends in Labor Productivity: Mexico, Canada, and the United States, 1994–1998 (average annual increase)

	1994 (%)	1995 (%)	1996 (%)	1997 (%)	1998 (%)	1994– 1998 (%)
Mexico	9.9	4.9	9.0	4.1	3.8	6.3
United States	3.1	5.2	5.2	5.3	3.7	4.5
Canada	4.5	3.3	−0.7	0.4	1.7	1.8

Source: Author's calculations based on data from the Banco de México and the Instituto Nacional de Estadística, Geografía e Informática (INEGI).

Figure 2.2. Unemployment in Mexico, 1987–1999 (percentages)

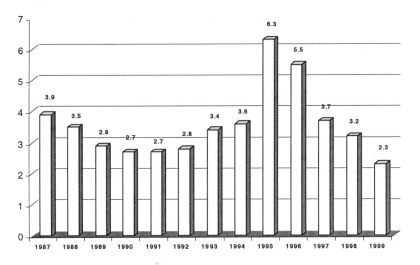

Source: Author's calculations based on data from the Banco de México and the Instituto Nacional de Estadística, Geografía e Informática (INEGI).

What of the agricultural sector? Except for 1997, neither import quotas nor tariff schedules have been respected. According to U.S. government data, U.S. corn exports to Mexico have risen to 3,054,000 tons since NAFTA entered into effect, surpassing the 2.5-million-ton corn import quota specified in the trade agreement.[33] Moreover, corn importers have not paid the required tariffs. In short, Mexico's corn producers have been fully exposed to the impacts of corn imports, even though, under NAFTA, they are to be protected—with levels of protection decreasing year by year—for fifteen years in order to give them time to adjust to international competition.[34] In the case of live-stock, the United States' share in Mexico's imports hovers above 98 percent. U.S. producers have maintained their preeminent position through a domestic price control policy, management of surpluses, and a variety of market penetration strategies.

CONCLUSION

NAFTA can be assessed from several different angles. First, Mexican exports have become an important engine driving the country's economic growth. The main destination for these exports is the U.S. market. Second, NAFTA has reinforced Mexico's liberalization strategies, but it has not necessarily represented a turning point for Mexico's industrial sectors. Third, NAFTA has enhanced Mexico's attractiveness as a destination for foreign investment—even though the country's weak domestic regulatory framework continues to hamper long-term prospects for economic industrial development.

Our analysis has revealed that exports are highly concentrated in a few sectors, including the increasingly important maquiladora sector. Meanwhile, the performance of non-exporting economic sectors has been lackluster and inconsistent. At the same time, imports have shot up—not because of increased domestic consumption but because of the lack of value-added in the export sector. NAFTA is not the central cause behind these trends, however, although it has exacerbated the asymmetrical industrial organization of the Mexican economy.

Notes

I am grateful to Jimena Otero, Rosalva Miguel, and Fernanda Paredes for their valuable research assistance in the preparation of this essay.

1. See his statement in J.L. Valdés-Ugalde, *Análisis de los efectos del Tratado de Libre Comercio de América del Norte en la economía mexicana: una visión sectorial a cinco años de distancia* (Mexico City: Miguel Ángel Porrúa/Senado, 2000), vol. 1, p. 697.

2. Although it is common to refer to globalization as a relatively recent phenomenon, I believe that the current phase represents the third major stage of capitalist reorganization—the first and the second stages having occurred during the postindustrial era and World War II. See James Mittelman, ed., *Globalization: Critical Reflections* (Boulder, Colo.: Lynne Rienner, 1996). For other perspectives, see Christos C. Paraskevopoulos, ed., *Global Trading Arrangements in Transition* (Cheltenham: Edward Elgar, 1998); Octavio Ianni, *La era del globalismo* (Mexico City: Siglo Veintiuno, 1999); Néstor García Canclini, *La globalización imaginada* (Mexico City: Paidós, 2000); and Eleonore Kofman and Gillian Youngs, *Globalization: Theory and Practice* (London: Pinter, 1996).

3. Valdés-Ugalde, *Análisis*, vol. 1, p. 625.

4. Octavio Paz, *One Earth, Four or Five Worlds: Reflections on Contemporary History* (London: Carcanet, 1985), p. 22.

5. Robert W. Cox, "Gramsci, Hegemony and International Relations: An Essay in Method," *Millenium* 12, no. 2 (Summer 1983): 173.

6. Valdés-Ugalde, *Análisis*. In its full book-length form, the analysis comprises fifteen sectors of the economy. Since these are the key sectors under NAFTA, the study serves to uncover the central dynamics of the agreement.

7. See J.L. Valdés-Ugalde, "The Mirror of the Hemispheric Past: The United States and Latin America," *International Journal of Politics, Culture and Society* 9, no. 1 (Fall 1995).

8. Limitations of space make it impossible to present sector-by-sector results in this chapter. For the full analysis, see Valdés-Ugalde, *Análisis*.

9. The Herfindhal index is calculated by the following formula: $H = \Sigma^{n}_{i=1} (s_i)^2$, where $s_i = q_i/Q$, q_i is the enterprise i sales level, Q are the industry's total sales, and n is the number of enterprises in the market. Elevating each term times square, we weight large firms over small firms. If we had perfect competition, H would be equal to $1/n$, so that this index is found between 1 and $1/n$ depending on whether we are dealing with monopoly or with perfect competition. The Absolute Concentration Index is calculated by the sum of the market shares of the m largest firms. Thus this index's limits are found between 1 and m/n for monopoly and competition, respectively. Depending on the competition degree, different zones that explain market conditions are established. The Entropy Index is defined as $E = \Sigma\, S_i \log (1/s_i)$, with the same interpretation as physics with regard to the existing disorder degree.

10. I understand institutional monopolies as those that result from firms' efforts to distinguish their goods with a commercial brand protected by law, by which they *ensure* a particular position in the market.

11. See Colleen Morton, "Efectos del TLC en el comercio y la inversión," in *Elaboración del marco de trabajo para evaluar efectos ambientales del TLC* (1996).

12. Pablo Ruiz Nápoles argues that the share of exports shot up from 18.7 to 31.1 percent of GNP during the period; see Ruiz Nápoles, "Liberalización, crecimiento económico y divisas: un análisis preliminar del TLCAN" (October 20, 1999). Even when their figures differ, both show an upward trend. For comparative purposes, see Enrique Dussel Peters, "Los impactos causados por el TLCAN al sector eléctrico y computación," in Valdés-Ugalde, *Análisis*, vol. 2.

13. See Eduardo Loría, "Efectos de la apertura comercial en la manufactura mexicana 1980–1998," presented at the XIII Congreso Nacional de Economistas, Mexico City, February 8–10, 2000, pp. 3–4.

14. Ibid.

15. See María Isabel Studer Noguez, "Los efectos del Tratado de Libre Comercio en la industria automotriz," in Valdés-Ugalde, *Análisis*, vol. 2.

16. See Loría, "Efectos de la apertura comercial," p. 3.

17. See Valdés-Ugalde, *Análisis*, vol. 2, p. 580.

18. Ibid., p. 584.

19. Ibid., p. 27.

20. Ibid., p. 160.

21. Gerardo Mendiola offers the example of Oaxaca and Puebla, "where wooden furniture has been produced for years, and there is a maquiladora furniture industry that is totally unrelated to it in any way; much of these states' experience and input capacity could have been used." Ibid., p. 66.

22. The sector is highly concentrated; according to a recent study, the national integration level in the maquiladora industry was only 2.5 percent. Ibid., p. 64, and Gerardo Mendiola, "Mexico, empresas maquiladoras de exportación en los noventa" (ECLAC, 1998), mimeo. By contrast, data provided by SECOFI (Mexico's Ministry of Trade and Industrial Development) indicate a national input usage above 20 percent. Reports from the U.S. Department of Trade give a high percentage of national input (close to 44 percent), although it is not clear how these figures were calculated.

23. Ruiz Nápoles, "Liberalización, crecimiento económico y divisas," pp. 7–9. Loría ("Efectos de la apertura comercial," pp. 8–9) reaches similar conclusions. He proposed a model where a coefficient (T) is calculated; this captures the impact of a percentage of the product (Y) over trade balance (TB). Thus he found that, from 1991 to 1994, this coefficient reached a −1.48 value, and that from 1995 to 1998 it was only −0.6. This means that, for the former period: "the sector's growth progressively increased its import demand, so that it is plausible to consider that manufacture raised its capital-work relationship.

This is how several studies explain the rise in total factor productivity (even at the expense of employment), even though these studies use very different methodologies and theoretical focuses." Coefficient reduction during the last period could indicate structural changes, although it is too soon to make such an assertion. "In the whole of this development we find that there has been an important change in the composition of employment … given that, even if the manufacturing sector's total employment did not grow between 1985 and 1995, employment tripled in the maquiladora subsector while falling by almost 40 percent in the non-maquila subsector."

24. Ruiz Nápoles, "Liberalización, crecimiento económico y divisas," p. 4.

25. Valdés-Ugalde, *Análisis*, vol. 2, p. 547.

26. Aboites adds, "South Korea was chosen as a reference point as there are certain symmetries between its economy and the Mexican economy. Moreover, South Korea has been a paradigm in the design of Mexico's economic policy, and the workings of its manufacturing exports are largely parallel and symmetrical to those of Mexico," in Valdés-Ugalde, *Análisis*, p. 546.

27. These figures were derived from the author's observations.

28. See Dussel Peters, "Los impactos causados por el TLCAN," p. 7.

29. Valdés-Ugalde, *Análisis*, vol. 2, pp. 285–319.

30. Beatriz Cavalloti, Hermilio Suárez Domínguez, and Víctor H. Palacio Muñoz, *El impacto del TLCAN en la ganadería de bovinos de carne (1994–1998)* (Mexico: Departamento de Zootecnia, Universidad de Chapingo).

31. This information is based on the following document: "Rancho el 17," at –rancho17@prodigy.net.mx, July 13th, 1999 (email). Also see jbarrio@compac.net.mx.

32. Apparently this is starting to change, and it is possible that Mexico and the United States may reach agreement on migration within the foreseeable future.

33. USDA/FAS, *Grain: World Markets and Trade; NAFTA, Year Two and Beyond* (USDA, February 1997) (hyperlink).

34. Valdés-Ugalde, *Análisis*, vol. 2, pp. 319–71.

3

NAFTA and Canada: Economic Policy and National Symbolism

Kenneth Norrie and Douglas Owram

Viewing the North American Free Trade Agreement (NAFTA) from a Canadian perspective raises three natural, perhaps inevitable, questions. First, why did continental trade liberalization happen at all? For more than a century the issue of Canada-U.S. free trade had been raised in various forms only to be rejected each time, either by wary Canadian politicians or by fearful Canadian voters. This reluctance ended suddenly and dramatically beginning in the late 1980s as Canadians experienced in quick succession the FTA, NAFTA, bilateral deals with Chile and Costa Rica, and official interest in bringing about a Free Trade Area of the Americas (FTAA).

Second, what effects have these free trade arrangements had on Canada's economic performance? All sorts of promises and warnings were uttered in the run-up to the Canada–United States Free Trade Agreement (CUSFTA) and, to a much lesser extent, the subsequent NAFTA agreement. With more than a decade of experience behind us, we can begin to provide some answers as to who was right.

Third, how will their experiences with the FTA and NAFTA affect Canadians' attitudes about future economic liberalization efforts?[1] The "battle of Seattle" and the events in Quebec City amply illustrate that free trade has become a powerful symbol of issues that transcend simple potential real income gains. Free trade is part of globalization, which is a liberating force to some and a limiting force for others.

This analysis is thus created as a triumvirate, linking the historical issue of North American trade, the actual impact of the trade agreements to date, and the degree to which free trade has become a symbol to be battled over, condemned, or supported as a flash point for broad issues of public policy and national identity.

CANADA-U.S. ECONOMIC RELATIONS IN HISTORICAL PERSPECTIVE

The Canada–United States Free Trade Agreement was, in historical terms, a remarkable event. To come to such an arrangement required overthrowing more than a century of Canadian political tradition, the realignment of political ideology, and an unusual coalition between regions. It is a clear example of the way in which economic theory, public policy, and political opportunity interact.

From the time of the American Revolution, the British colonies in North America defined both identity and policy against the shadow of the two greater powers in the North Atlantic triangle—Britain and the United States. The pulls between the powers began violently in the Revolution, the Loyalist exodus, and the War of 1812. Even after the violence ended, however, border disputes, internal rebellion, and even the framing of the Confederation itself played out against those who distrusted American intentions and those who strained against British colonial policy.[2] Was Canada to be a British or an American nation?

There was no doubt where Goldwin Smith stood. The Manchester Liberal and Oxford professor had migrated to Canada, only to argue that his new country made little sense. In 1891 he penned the classic *Canada and the Canadian Question*, in which he argued that the future of Canada lay with the United States as a matter of necessity and geography. "Whoever wishes to know what Canada is, and to understand the Canadian question, should begin by turning from the political to the natural map." For each revealed something quite different. The political map displays a vast and unbroken area of territory extending from the boundary of the United States up to the north pole. On the other hand, the physical map displays four separate geographic regions projecting upward "into arctic waste." Then Smith came to the heart of the issue; Canada was not linked east to west at all but only with its neighbor to the south. These "blocks are not contiguous, but are divided from each other by great barriers of nature, wide and irreclaimable wildernesses or manifold chains of mountains."[3]

Smith's pessimistic diatribe against Canada's existence struck at the heart of Canadian insecurities. People roundly condemned the book at the time, yet the fear that Smith might be right shaped Canadian economic policy for more than a century.

The principle was simple. If there were north-south pulls due the growing U.S economy and the realities of geography, policy must be used to turn the axis from north-south to east-west. An east-west axis linked the regions of the country and, best of all to a nineteenth-century observer, had an ultimate eastern metropolitan destination in Great Britain.

By the time Smith wrote, the basics of the policy were already in place. In the late 1870s, the Conservative Party had developed what was known as the "National Policy." Using tariff barriers and the energetic construction of the Canadian Pacific railway, the national policy sought to develop a flow of people and goods on an east-west axis. Immigrants were to go west, grow crops, and then ship them east by the same railway. Manufacturers, protected by tariffs, would develop in the St. Lawrence–Lower Great Lakes heartland and ship goods west to the rising immigrant population. It is important to note that, in Canada, tariffs were first and foremost a nationalist instrument rather than a sop to big business (though big business appreciated them nonetheless). The idea though was that Canada would be made whole, ties to Britain would be reinforced, and the pull of the large American economy would be mitigated.

The Liberal Party, in contrast, distrusted the whole idea. They were much influenced by British liberal doctrines of free trade; and besides, they were the opposition. Thus they directly challenged the principles of the national policy and called for "unrestricted reciprocity," or total free trade with the United States. In 1887 and again in 1891 they took on the Conservatives on the issue, but both times they lost, in large part because of Canadian distrust of the United States. John A. Macdonald's accusation that "there is a deliberate conspiracy by force, by fraud, or by both to force Canada into the American Union" during the 1891 election typified the sort of nationalist appeal that kept the Liberals in opposition.[4]

Unrestricted reciprocity quietly faded from the Liberal platform in the interval to the next election. The election was fought on other issues, and the Liberals, under Wilfrid Laurier, emerged with a comfortable majority. The implication was not missed. Though the Liberals still talked of lower tariffs and freer trade, their policy in government was fundamentally a continuation of the principles of the national policy. Over the next fifteen years, the Liberals continued a set of tariff and developmental policies that sought to overcome Goldwin Smith. New railway lines were pushed west. Britain was given preferential tariff treatment. The St. Lawrence system was improved and the east-west flow of goods generally encouraged. On balance, the Liberals were still more "North" American and the Conservatives more "British," but nobody, it seemed, wanted to get too close to the United States. This was true even as, by this time, Canadians imported more from the United States than from Britain.

Then, with a growing number of western seats, which are normally free trade in orientation, and a U.S. Congress unusually amenable to open borders, the Liberals forgot the earlier lessons and entered the 1911 election on the issue of free trade. The Conservatives countered with the phrase, "no truck nor trade with the Yankees," won the election, and once again reminded politicians of the dangers of getting too close to the neighbors to the south.

The subsequent years made it clear that the lesson was learned. The Liberals talked of freer trade but stayed away from any notion of sweeping trade deals with the Americans. The Conservatives tended to higher tariffs and emphasized ties to Britain. The reality was, though, that neither party strayed far from the basic principle. Canadian economic policy was, to a greater or lesser degree, shaped around national obsessions with the balance within the North Atlantic triangle. This was as true in 1921, when the Liberals returned to power on a program that equivocated about lower tariffs for the West, as in 1930 when the Conservatives won on the unusual notion that higher tariffs were the route to special preferential arrangements. Those arrangements were, as usual, aimed at Britain and the Commonwealth and not at the United States.

By 1945, though, changes in economic circumstances once again forced a reassessment of the whole issue of trade policy and nationalism. Specifically, three forces came to bear. First, during the Depression, the nations of the world had hidden behind tariff barriers in order to protect what they could of local production. The result had been to further constrict trade flows and prolong the economic collapse. By 1945 the international economic community and many politicians had reacted against such attitudes and stressed freer economic interplay between nations. The horrors of nationalism evident in World War II reinforced the direction that led to such bodies as the International Monetary Fund and the General Agreement on Tariffs and Trade (GATT).

Second, World War II had removed a significant incentive to the use of tariffs—revenue. Until the war the Canadian government had depended on tariffs for a significant portion of its income. The war, however, had shifted the revenue base from indirect to direct taxes and from tariffs to income and corporate taxation. This was not by itself a reason to turn away from tariffs, but it did remove one barrier to any change in policy.

Third, the North Atlantic triangle was not what it used to be. The war had completed two longer-term trends. First, the United States was now much more powerful politically and economically than Great Britain. Indeed, with the creation of the North Atlantic Treaty Organization (NATO) in 1949, both Canada and Britain were in reality partners in the U.S.-dominated western alliance. Most pertinent to this essay, the imbalance within the North Atlantic triangle was now clearly visible in trade patterns. Through the earlier part of the century, Canadian reliance on U.S. imports had been, to some extent, countered by a significant volume of exports to Britain as well as by British direct investment in Canada. By the early 1950s, Americans dominated import, export, and foreign investment flows.

These trends changed the axis upon which Canadian economic policy turned. The North Atlantic triangle was more myth than reality. High tariff and nontariff barriers were under increasing fire. Canadian prosperity was increasingly dependent upon American trade. Yet the cultural resistance to Americanization and political memories of what might happen if one was seen as "too American" had a significant residual influence. For nearly twenty years after the war, Canadians wrestled between old assumptions and new realities.

On the one side was a continued and growing concern with the American influence over Canada. Thus in 1948, when Canadian and American civil servants proposed a sweeping free trade agreement, it was Canada's cautious prime minister who killed the idea. As he confided in his diary, it reminded him too much of Laurier's ill-fated 1911 proposal.[5] Nor was such caution unjustified. When, in 1956, the Liberal government proposed an oil pipeline arrangement with a strong American influence, it became an issue of national controversy and helped in the defeat of the government at the polls. The subsequent Conservative government under John Diefenbaker was soon proposing a diversion of trade away from the United States to the amount of 15 percent.

All of this seems to be in accord with the pattern that had been established decades earlier. The Liberals tended to be more favorable to pro-American arrangements but nervous lest they pay a price politically. The Conservatives tended to be more anti-American and look to the British as a counterweight. However, there were new forces at work as well.

Liberal distrust of colonialism and the pro-British, anti-American stance of the Conservatives were confronting changing circumstances. The Liberals had always been a mildly nationalist party. That was why they had tended to resist pulls that tied Canada more tightly to British imperial notions. Yet by the 1950s the threat of British influence was hardly meaningful. In the postwar years, they dutifully tidied up remnants of an earlier era. There was a new citizenship act and a new flag. At the same time, though, elements of the party were becoming increasingly concerned that the real threat to Canada's independence lay south of the border.

This showed most clearly in the conclusions of the Royal Commission on Canada's Economic Prospects, appointed by the St. Laurent government in the mid-1950s. Headed by prominent Liberal Walter Gordon, the Commission was designed to assess likely economic trends now that the immediate postwar adjustments had occurred. In so doing, it headed in an unexpected direction. "Until a few years after the end of the War," wrote the Commission, "the pattern of Canada's trade was triangular." However, while "vestiges of the trading pattern are still discernible ... our trade is now concentrated so preponderantly on the United States that for most purposes it has ceased to be useful to think of it as being triangular."[6] In addition, U.S. direct investment in Canada had reached unprecedented proportions, while the British had largely withdrawn from the field.

Finally, the Commission turned explicitly to the link between Canadian economic policy and nationalism. Tariffs with the United States, it noted, probably cost the Canadian consumer in terms of higher prices. It also noted, though, that "no generation of Canadians has been prepared to reverse the basic decision taken in the era of Confederation." While there may be arguments about specific tariffs, generally "Canadians have been willing to pay the price the tariff exacts in lower average incomes, regarding it as part of the legitimate cost of nationhood."[7] There was no doubt that the commissioners included themselves in this statement.

The Gordon Commission's mild nationalist undertones signaled a growing division within the Liberal Party. New nationalist voices would push the party to preserve the new threat to Canadian nationalism by resisting the lure of the United States. As minister of finance (1963–1965) and minister without portfolio (1965–1968) in subsequent Liberal governments, Walter Gordon would be influential in beginning the reorientation of the party in a more nationalist direction. By the time Pierre Trudeau came in as prime minister in 1968, his concern that Canada was a mouse sleeping next to an elephant seemed fully in keeping with the emergent outlook of the Liberal Party. Over the next years, mildly nationalist programs such as the Foreign Investment Review Agency (FIRA), Canadian Radio-television and Telecommunications Commission (CRTC) regulations, and other measures testified to the way in which the Liberal Party had reassessed its own nationalism. By the time the free trade debate came in 1988, it was no surprise that the old continentalist party stood against free trade.

The Liberal shift caused some internal turmoil. The Conservative shift almost tore the party apart. John Diefenbaker was a prairie populist and thus at odds with the party's urban Ontario core support. However, he was also a nationalist with at least a modicum of affection for Britain and perhaps more than a modicum of distrust for the United States. In his impractical proposal to divert 15 percent of trade from the United States to Britain, in his decision to sell wheat to China despite American displeasure, and in his enthusiasm for the Canadian monarchy, Diefenbaker seemed very much within the traditional Conservative national framework.[8]

Then, amidst controversy and the most anti-American campaign since 1911, John Diefenbaker went down to defeat in 1963. For many within his party, the vision of a pro-British Canadian nationalism seemed anachronistic. It alienated Quebec because of its adherence to old imperial ideals, and it harmed business because its anti-American attitude deterred investment. In 1967 John Diefenbaker was dumped as leader of the Conservative Party, and the party turned toward a mildly pro-business, pro-American, and pragmatic interpretation of Canada. The old rhetoric of the pro-British nationalism now had no political home in Canada.

Thus the stage was set for the free trade debate almost a generation before it actually occurred.[9] The old vision of Canada as integrally linked to Britain no longer had a political voice. With that and with the reality that Canada-U.S. trade was more than nine times Canada-British trade, the old notion of balance within the triangle was not even an issue by the end of the 1960s. Conversely, the Liberal Party had shed its old free trade–North American orientation in favor of a mildly nationalist and interventionist approach to economic policy.

Many issues decide an election. Nonetheless, when the Conservatives went to the public in 1988, free trade was at the forefront of the differences between parties. Stephen Lewis, leader of the New Democratic Party (NDP) and very much opposed to free trade, tried to summon the spirit that had served so well in 1887, 1891, and 1911. "This isn't so much about free trade as it is about the heart and the soul of this country. It is about the definition of Canada."[10] For the first time in Canadian history, though, the appeal failed. Canada entered into a new and unknown era of free trade with the elephant to the south.

HOW THE ECONOMY FARED

With the FTA in place, attention turned to the economy. Pierre Fortin's masterful C.D. Howe Institute Benefactors Lecture[11] indicates why the 1980s and 1990s will be remembered as two of the more interesting decades in Canadian economic history. At one point in his paper, Fortin plots the purchasing power of total real national income per adult in Canada as a percentage of that in the United States from 1970 to 1998. Canada's relative standard of living improved significantly during the 1970s, rising from about 72 percent of that in the United States in 1970 to nearly 84 percent by 1980. This trend flattened in the 1980s and then declined precipitously in the following decade. By 1998 the Canadian figure had fallen below 74 percent of the U.S. figure, putting Canadians back where they were, in a relative sense, three decades earlier.

Fortin's finding is intriguing because the FTA was expected by its supporters to improve Canada's macroeconomic performance. At the very least, allowing for economic fluctuations and recognizing that Canada-U.S. business cycles are tightly linked, it was expected to raise Canadian living standards relative to those in the United States. Yet the reverse apparently happened. After 1990, Canada lost whatever ground it had gained in the previous two decades.

Free Trade and Canadian Living Standards

Recent work by Daniel Trefler adds to the puzzle.[12] Trefler first compares growth in Canadian and American total factor productivity (TFP)[13] since 1980. He shows that whatever gap in TPF there was in 1980 became substantially worse during the 1980s and widened further to 1996. Further, he illustrates that TFP growth in Canadian manufacturing was lower between 1988 and 1996 than it was in the period 1980–1988, and lower still from what it had been between 1961 and 1980.

Trefler's results indicate the challenge facing policy analysts. Whatever was happening to Canadian manufacturing productivity and relative living standards had its roots in the 1980s, before the FTA was in place. Yet the FTA obviously had an impact on the Canadian economy as well. Trefler notes that there were nearly 400,000 fewer jobs in manufacturing in 1993 than there had been in 1988, and that real gross domestic product (GDP) in manufacturing fell over the same period as well. Both series turned the other way after 1993. Employment in manufacturing in 1998 was still down by about 6 percent from its 1988 levels, while real GDP was nearly 25 percent higher. Further, Canadian exports and imports rose in the 1990s, to nearly 40 percent of GDP, with an increasing concentration in trade with the United States.

What exactly was the contribution of the free trade agreement to Canada's aggregate economic performance? At an aggregate level, the pre-FTA tariffs appear too small for their removal to have had much effect on subsequent economic performance. But aggregate data hide differences among industries. Some manufacturing sectors were largely or completely unaffected by the agreement, while others experienced significant losses in protection. Trefler uses a highly disaggregated industry data set, identifies changes in Canadian tariffs directly attributable to CUSFTA (as opposed to reductions through simultaneous multilateral agreements), controls for other factors that affect trade flows between the two countries, and is left with an estimate of the effects of FTA tariff reductions on the manufacturing sector.

Table 3.1 presents his results. The first column lists the manufacturing variables of interest. Column 2 shows the changes in these variables for all manufacturing industries between the pre- and the post-FTA period, while column 3 shows the changes attributed to the FTA. Columns 4 and 5 do the same for those manufacturing industries most affected by the FTA, defined as ones where the change in the Canadian tariff was greater than 8 percent.

Table 3.1. Estimated Impact of FTA on Canadian Manufacturing

Variable	All Industries		Most Impacted	
	Total Change (%)	Due to FTA (%)	Total Change (%)	Due to FTA (%)
Employment	−16	−4	−36	−18
Output	9	−2	−20	−12
Labor productivity	20	5	28	26

Source: Derived from Daniel Trefler, *The Long and Short of the Canada-U.S. Free Trade Agreement*, Paper No. 6 (Ottawa: Industry Canada Research Publications Program 1999), table 8, p. 36.

Table 3.1 indicates that employment in all 213 industries fell by 16 percent in the post-FTA period, with one-quarter of those losses attributable to the free trade agreement. The situation is quite different in the most impacted industries, however. Employment fell by 36 percent, with half of this loss coming from FTA effects. Output for all industries rose by 9 percent in the post-FTA period, even though the FTA acted to reduce output by 2 percent. Output in the most affected industries fell by 20 percent in the post-FTA period, with more than half of this shift coming from FTA effects. Labor productivity rose by 20 percent in all industries, with one-quarter of the rise attributable to the FTA. Productivity gains were higher in the impacted industries, with the FTA accounting for nearly all of the gain.

It seems clear from these results that the agreement had the predicted impact on the Canadian economy. Trefler summarizes his findings as follows: "Dramatically higher productivity in low-end manufactures and resource reallocation to high-end manufactures are the key gains from the FTA."[14]

If the CUSFTA had the expected positive effect on manufacturing productivity, how can one account for the apparent relative decline in Canadian living standards in the 1980s and 1990s? Pierre Fortin addressed this question by observing, first, that real private disposable income (PDI) per adult grew by 3.19 percent per annum on average between 1970 and 1979, by 1.77 percent on average between 1979 and 1989, and by only 0.05 percent between 1989 and 1998. For whatever reasons, Canadian economic growth rates slowed dramatically in the final two decades of the century, the 1990s in particular. Further, Fortin noted that changes in real private disposable income per adult can be resolved into four components: changes in the terms of trade, changes in the private income retention rate, changes in labor productivity, and changes in the employment rate. He used this identity to estimate the contributions of each to the slowdown of growth in real PDI per adult between 1970 and 1979 and 1979 and 1989, between 1979 and 1989 and 1989 and 1998, and for the whole period. Table 3.2 reproduces his results.

Table 3.2 indicates that for the period as a whole, the first three components each accounted for about one-fifth of the decline in the growth rate of real disposable income per adult, while changes in the employment rate accounted for just over two-fifths. There is considerable variation by decade, however. The terms of trade effect is the most constant of the components, contributing 15 percent to the decline in income growth in the 1980s compared to the 1970s and 20 percent in the 1990s compared to the 1980s. Changes in the private income retention rate were a somewhat larger factor in the 1980s than they were in the 1990s. The final two rows contain the interesting story, however. Slower labor productivity growth rates accounted for nearly 40 percent of the decline in the growth rate of real private disposable income per adult in the 1980s, making this the most significant factor by far. By contrast, declining labor productivity accounted for only 5 percent of the decline in the 1990s, by far the least significant factor.

Table 3.2. Contributions to the Decline in the Growth Rate of Real Disposable Income per Adult

Component	1970–79 to 1979–89 (%)	1979–89 to 1989–98 (%)	1970–79 to 1989–98 (%)
Terms of trade effect	15	20	18
P. I. retention rate	25	16	20
Labor productivity	37	5	19
Employment rate	23	59	43

Source: Derived from Pierre Fortin, *The Canadian Standard of Living: Is There a Way Up?* (C.D. Howe Benefactors Lecture, 1999), p. 28.

The final row of table 3.2 shows the contributions of changes in the employment rate to the decline in the growth rate of real personal disposable income per capita. This factor is twice as important as the other three over the three decades, as already noted, accounting for 40 percent of the decline in growth rates. The pattern between decades is the mirror image of that for labor productivity. Declining employment rates were an important factor in the decline in the 1980s, explaining nearly one-quarter of the fall. But they were by far the major factor explaining the trend in the 1990s, at nearly 60 percent.

Explaining the decline in the rate of growth of Canadian living standards thus comes down to explaining why labor productivity growth lagged in the 1980s compared to the 1970s, and why employment rate growth lagged in the 1990s compared to the 1980s. The latter question is easier to answer. The Canadian economy went into a recession in 1990 because a recession in the United States reduced demand for Canadian exports, because anti-inflationary monetary policy in Canada raised short-term interest rates significantly, and because the Canadian dollar appreciated relative to the U.S. dollar. The real question, Fortin notes, is explaining why the Canadian economy remained in a slump until 1997 when the U.S. economy was experiencing a sustained boom. His answer lies in what he terms "the damaging interaction between high accumulated public debt and high real interest rates."[15] The details of his argument, however fascinating, are not important for purposes of this chapter. Suffice it to say that they rest on a combination of bad luck and poor policy decisions by monetary and fiscal policy authorities.

The productivity quandary is of direct concern to our topic. Table 3.3 shows estimates of total factor productivity growth for Canada and the United States for three periods: 1970–1979, 1979–1989, and 1989–1996. They are given separately for the total business sector and for the manufacturing sector.

Table 3.3. Average Annual Labor Productivity Growth in Canada and the United States (real output per hour of work)

	Canada	United States
Business sector	(%)	(%)
1970–1979	2.4	2.0
1979–1989	0.9	1.2
1989–1996	1.2	1.3
Manufacturing sector	(%)	(%)
1970–1979	3.2	2.9
1979–1989	1.7	2.6
1989–1996	2.1	3.6

Source: Derived from Fortin, *Canadian Standard of Living*, table 7, p. 70.

Table 3.3 reveals that labor productivity in the Canadian business sector (75 percent of the economy) grew faster than that in the United States in the 1970s, somewhat slower in the 1980s, and at about the same rate in the 1990s. The picture in the manufacturing sector is very different, however. There, Canadian labor productivity grew faster than that in the United States in the 1970s, but it lagged significantly in the 1980s and 1990s. The implication of these two results is that labor productivity in non-manufacturing sectors in Canada has grown faster than in the United States.

Closer analysis shows that virtually all of the difference in productivity growth in Canadian and American manufacturing between 1989 and 1997 is accounted for by two industry groupings: electrical and electronic machinery, and commercial and industrial machinery.[16] Canada has done well relative to the United States in other manufacturing sectors, particularly those that experienced the largest FTA tariff changes. Indeed, if electrical and electronic machinery and commercial and industrial machinery are stripped from the data, Canada's labor productivity growth in manufacturing exceeds that in the United States by a significant margin.

If this analysis is correct, it suggests that Canada's competitiveness problems in manufacturing lie elsewhere than with the FTA. One intriguing possibility is that the United States is in the early stages of the much-anticipated "new economy" revolution, but that this revolution has yet to spread to Canada and other industrial nations. The term "new economy" is still not well defined, but most analysts take it to mean an acceleration in the rate of technical advance in information technology (IT), bringing about, in the words of Alan Greenspan, "a more deep-seated, still developing, shift in our economic landscape."[17] To some observers, the arrival of the new economy explains the miracle of U.S. economic performance in the late 1990s. Others are more skeptical of this claim.[18] One influential research organization, the Centre for the Study of Living Standards, is predicting that Canada will see a significant pickup in productivity growth in the next decade.

The 1980s and 1990s are clearly exceptional decades from an aggregate economic performance perspective; future economic historians will certainly find much to write about. The FTA is not likely to be a major part of the story, however. The long delay in recovering from the 1990–1992 recession is likely to be the main theme for the first two-thirds of the 1990s. More intriguing is the possibility that future scholars will be dating the onset of a third industrial revolution in the 1980s and 1990s.

How Thick Is the Border?

One of the deliberate aims of Canadian commercial policy, as noted above, was to foster east-west trade. Tariffs, along with transcontinental railways, were intended to make the Canada-U.S. border an economic factor as well as a political one. This historical setting raises two interesting questions. First, how successful were Macdonald and successors in creating a national economy? Second, what impact has the FTA had on this creation?

Some recent work provides at least partial answers. John McCallum began his analysis by asking how important the national border was in explaining the trading patterns of Canadian provinces. To answer this question, he used what he termed a "gravity model" of trade flows. To illustrate, consider the pattern of Alberta's exports. These products go to other provinces in Canada, to states in the United States, and to overseas destinations. The challenge is to explain the magnitudes of the export flows.

The gravity model postulates that exports will be greater (a) the larger the economy of the destination market, and (b) the closer the destination market is to Alberta geographically. Thus Alberta will export more to California than to British Columbia (BC), ignoring geography, because California is a larger economy than BC. At the same time, Alberta will export more to BC than to California, ignoring market size, because geographical distances are less. If the market size effect dominates the distance effect, Alberta will export more to California than to British Columbia. Conversely, if the distance effect dominates, BC will be the more significant destination.

There is a third factor that affects trade flows, however—the national border. Exports from Alberta to California must cross an international border, while those to British Columbia only cross a provincial one. One can think of several reasons why national borders might affect trade flows: tariffs, nontariff barriers, the need to deal in foreign currencies, and so forth. To the extent that these matter, the simple predictions of the gravity model will be altered. Thus Alberta will export relatively more to British Columbia, and relatively less to California, than market size and distance alone would predict: the larger this differential, one can then conclude, the "thicker" is the border.

McCallum's results using this simple model were startling. Merchandise trade among Canadian provinces in 1988, just prior to the FTA, was about 20 times what one would predict on the basis of market size and distance alone. To continue the example above, the results indicated that Alberta's exports to British Columbia were twenty times greater than those to a U.S. state of equivalent size and distance. The model does not tell us why inter-provincial trade flows are so large, but it is certainly a result that would have gladdened the hearts of John A. Macdonald and subsequent nation builders.[19]

John Helliwell uses a methodology similar to McCallum's, with more recent data, to assess the impacts of the CUSFTA. He finds that the border effect declined by about one-third after the agreement was introduced. There was little impact until 1990, a sharp increase in north-south trade from 1991 to 1993, and a rough constancy to 1996 when the data end. He concludes that in 1996, "the typical Canadian province traded twelve times as much with another Canadian province as with a U.S. state of similar size and distance."[20]

There are two ways to view these results. One is to conclude that border effects, while less than they were prior to the FTA, are still very significant. The challenge in this case is to explain their persistence, which Helliwell does by interpreting them as reflections of national tastes and networks. However unnatural the Canadian economic union might have been in Goldwin Smith's time, a century and a half of Canadian provinces trading with each other have created the national bonds that Macdonald and others sought.

One might equally be struck, however, by the *decline* in the border effect in such a short time. The questions, then, are how much thinner the border will become as new north-south networks develop, and if so, what the impact would be on Canadian social and political life.

FREE TRADE AS AN IDEA

In light of our analysis thus far, one might expect the trade pacts to be viewed with indifference or disappointment by politicians and public. At best, the CUSFTA and NAFTA do not appear to be the main economic stories for the past two decades. The main theme in the 1990s was the sluggish recovery from the 1990–1992 recession, and a plausible case can be made that the roots lie in debts and monetary and fiscal policies. Declining productivity growth is the other main theme running through the two decades, and here there is reason to think the experience reflects adjustments to the new information economy. The border, while noticeably thinner, is still a significant determinant of provincial trade patterns.

In fact, hemispheric free trade has been the central focus of economic policymakers and commentators since the initiation of CUSFTA. The agreement was extended to include Mexico in 1992, with the FTA expanding to NAFTA on January 1, 1994. Once in office, the Liberals were active in extending free trade to Chile and in pushing for an expanded Free Trade Area of the Americas. In the last federal election, no major party campaigned to halt North American trade liberalization.

How can we explain the salience of CUSFTA and NAFTA in political and public discourse given their relative lack of impact? Economic history provides one possible answer. Some time ago, Robert Fogel set out to estimate the contribution of railroads to American economic growth.[21] His sophisticated and detailed analysis produced a surprising conclusion: railroads were apparently not that important. Fogel defined the impact of railroads in two ways. The primary effect was the impact of railways on the cost of transporting commodities, which he termed social savings. The derived consequences included changes in the location of economic activity and the mix of products. He concluded that the social savings from railroads in 1890 added a couple of percentage points to U.S. GDP. The derived consequences were likewise relatively small.

These quantitative results did not sit well with other scholars, historians in particular. Even if the estimates are correct, some argued, they ignored the most significant impact of railroads, one that likely can never be quantified. They spoke of the railway as an "idea." The new transport medium encouraged new ways of thinking about economic progress and the geographic reach of social and business activity. The results were products, processes, institutions, and attitudes that could never have developed incrementally from old transportation technologies.

The same point is evident in writing on Canadian railways as well. As early as 1849, before there was a significant Canadian railway system, engineer Thomas Keefer published a tract with the grand title *The Philosophy of Railroads*. For Keefer, the steel and steam technology of railways was an almost mystical means to free Canadians from the tyranny of nature.[22] As Keefer put it, with the arrival of the railway a spirit is engendered in the village that "is not confined to dress or equipage, but is rapidly extended to agriculture, roads, and instructive societies, and finally exerts its most powerful influence where it is most needed—in the improved character it gives to the exercise of the franchise."[23]

In this interpretation, the railway in North America has been transformed into a mythical force, converting the psychology of the community, breaking down localism, and even changing the basic values of the community. If the total impact of the railway is to be understood, then one must consider it not just as a superior transportation medium but also as a mythic force, shaping public policy, community debate, and social outlook.

The idea of free trade has similar characteristics in some ways. The psychological impact of free trade makes it something far more than an economic arrangement. On the positive side, the acceptance of free trade was a statement by Canadians that they felt they could compete with the "big guys." Canadians did not need protection to survive but were ready, as Prime Minister Mulroney said at the time, to take on the world. Free trade and the subsequent NAFTA agreement also closed the door on the remnants of the North Atlantic triangle. The British Commonwealth had long lost its force in Canadian trade and Canadian policy. Nonetheless, the decision to cast Canada's lot within North America was an important break. There was to be no "third option" such as had been sought in Canadian foreign policy as late as the 1970s.[24]

Recent discussions among Canadian political economists about North America as a collection of regional city-states and controversial arguments for and against a common currency reflect just how far the notion of free trade and the North American market have affected the framework of the Canadian national debate.

Further, NAFTA contained an important "idea" in its own right. Canadians had not considered Mexico as an important trade partner. In a world where the United States, Asia, and the European Union dominated our thoughts, Mexico had always seemed far away and important mainly as a place to escape our winters. However, NAFTA opened the mind of Canadians to Mexico as an important and somewhat special market. Compared to the United States or other major trading partners, the Canadian-Mexican market remains miniscule. It may not remain that way for long, however. Between 1997 and 2000, Canadian-Mexican exports increased by more than 50 percent. In the year 2000, Canada imported more from Mexico than it did from Japan.

NAFTA has raised more than economic interest in Mexico and Central and South America, however. In the 1990–1991 academic year, total student registrations in Spanish at the University of Alberta were about 20 percent of those in French. Since then, registrations in Spanish have risen more or less continuously, while those in French have fallen. Thus by academic year 2000–2001, total Spanish registrations stood at nearly 90 percent of those in French. And at the introductory level, registrations in Spanish passed those in French in 1997–1998, and the gap has continued to grow since.

Free trade is not a universally positive symbol, however. As government leaders convened in Seattle and Quebec City to discuss further economic liberalization, thousands took to the streets to protest what they view as the evils of globalization. More recently, the emergence of recession and the tragic events of September 11 have opened new questions about the nature of globalization and future directions of internationalism. However these protests and events may affect the specific timing or details around trade, the broad issues of scale, technology, and interdependence will remain as forces creating interdependence within the North American and global contexts. The genie will not be put back in the bottle.

CONCLUSION

We have addressed three questions in this chapter. First, why did Canadians suddenly embrace continental trade liberalization in the 1980s, after vigorously opposing it for more than a century? Second, who was more correct in predicting the consequences of free trade on Canada's economic performance, the proponents or the opponents? Third, how will our experience with free trade affect Canadians' attitudes about future liberalization efforts?

The answer to the first question is found in a complex mix of economic determinism and practical politics. Since at least 1867, Canada has been increasingly and irreversibly drawn into the American economic orbit—and out of the British one. It was inevitable that some political party, in this case Brian Mulroney's Tories, would recognize that there was electoral support for a continental economic union. The old economic and political securities were giving way to a belief that Canadians could compete economically with the world's most powerful economy, and do so without sacrificing political independence. Canadians were, in Donald Macdonald's words, ready for "a leap of faith."

Answers to the other two questions are found in the concept of free trade as an idea. The CUSFTA and NAFTA have not been either the panacea or the evil in economic terms that proponents and opponents of trade liberalization were predicting. The evidence suggests that trade liberalization had pretty much the predicted economic impacts with respect to resource reallocations within and among industrial groups. But from a macro viewpoint, these free trade effects were swamped by the impacts of macroeconomic policies and low productivity growth.

Nonetheless, CUSFTA and NAFTA have been a powerful, almost mythic force. They have challenged and perhaps overthrown old nationalist assumptions. They have raised our awareness of the "other" North American country and have begun to distinguish Mexico from the rest of Latin America. They have helped raise new protest movements and reawaken old ones. NAFTA thus is likely to remain the single most important public policy issue in trade in the foreseeable future.

Notes

1. Acronyms for the Canada-U.S. Free Trade Agreement are either FTA or CUSFTA, the latter form being adopted to distinguish it from NAFTA. Both forms are used in this chapter.

2. S.F. Wise and R.C. Brown, *Canada Views the United States* (Toronto: Macmillan of Canada, 1967).

3. Goldwin Smith, *Canada and the Canadian Question* (London: Macmillan, 1891).

4. Cited in J.M. Beck, *Pendulum of Power* (Scarborough, Ont.: Prentice-Hall, 1968), p. 64.

5. R. Bothwell, J. English, and I. Drummond, *Canada since 1945*, rev. ed. (Toronto: University of Toronto Press, 1989), p. 72.

6. Canada, *Royal Commission on Canada's Economic Prospects. Final Report*, p. 37.

7. Ibid., pp. 50–51.

8. Diefenbaker's administration provoked strong feelings. For a critical assessment of Diefenbaker's foreign policy, see Peter Newman's acerbic *Renegade in Power* (Toronto: McClelland and Stewart, 1965). For the argument that Diefenbaker marked the last gasp of Canadian nationalism, see George Grant, *Lament for a Nation: The Defeat of Canadian Nationalism* (Toronto: McClelland and Stewart, 1965).

9. See Duncan McDowall, "The Trade Policies of Canada's Grits and Tories," in *The NAFTA Puzzle: Political Parties and Trade in North America*, ed. Charles Doran and Gregory Marchildon (Boulder, Colo.: Westview, 1994).

10. Doug Owram, "The NDP and Free Trade," in *The NAFTA Puzzle*, ed. Charles Doran and Gregory Marchildon (Boulder, Colo.: Westview, 1994).

11. Pierre Fortin, *The Canadian Standard of Living: Is There a Way UP?* (Toronto: C.D. Howe Benefactors Lecture, 1999).

12. Daniel Trefler, *The Long and Short of the Canada-U.S. Free Trade Agreement*, Paper No. 6 (Ottawa: Industry Canada Research Publications Program, 1999).

13. Roughly, the growth in GDP after allowing for contributions made by growth in the labor force and the stock of capital.

14. Trefler, *Long and Short*, p. 35.

15. Fortin, *Canadian Standard of Living*, p. 35.

16. Ibid., table 8, p. 74.

17. Cited in Robert J. Gordon, "Does the 'New Economy' Measure Up to the Great Inventions of the Past?" (Chicago: Northwestern University, May 2000), manuscript, p. 3.

18. See insert on the new economy in the September 23, 2000, edition of *The Economist* for a very readable survey of this debate.

19. John McCallum, "National Borders Matter: Canada-U.S. Regional Trade Patterns," *American Economic Review* 85 (June 1995): 615–23.

20. John F. Helliwell, *Globalization: Myths, Facts and Consequences* (Toronto: C.D. Howe Benefactors Lecture, 2000), p. 3.

21. Robert William Fogel, *Railroads and American Economic Growth: Essays in Econometric History* (Baltimore, Md.: Johns Hopkins University Press, 1964).

22. Doug Owram, *Promise of Eden: The Canadian Expansionist Movement and the Idea of the West, 1856–1900*, 2d ed. (Toronto: University of Toronto Press, 1993), p. 18.

23. Thomas Keefer, *The Philosophy of Railroads, and Other Essays,* ed. H.V. Nelles (Toronto: University of Toronto Press, 1972).

24. Bothwell et al., *Canada since 1945*, p. 425.

Section 2

NAFTA and Subregional Economies

Discussions of NAFTA have placed relatively little emphasis on sub-national experiences, despite abundant evidence of substantial variance in the spatial impacts of liberalization. Section 2 provides a corrective by examining NAFTA's impacts upon provincial and state-level economies in the three countries.

Edward Chambers begins with an examination of the effects of CUSFTA and NAFTA on two Canadian provinces—Alberta and British Columbia. These westernmost provinces offer a stunning contrast in economic performance during the 1990s. Chambers attributes this difference to a variety of factors: initial conditions (Alberta's core industry was energy, liberalized under free trade, while British Columbia specialized in forest products, still highly restricted in terms of trade), dissimilar experience with external shocks, and contrasting provincial trade policy stances. As a result, Alberta gained substantial benefits from the changing North American trade environment while British Columbia did not. In short, this chapter presents a suggestive analysis of the provincial impacts of free trade and, conspicuously, of unfree trade.

In a case study of the Mexican state of Jalisco, Carlos Alba Vega starts by tracing the rise to local power of an opposition party, the National Action Party (PAN), in response to the economic crisis of the early 1990s. With the implementation of NAFTA, the PAN government fostered public-private cooperation to provide information services, to establish industrial parks, to create a design center, and to foster economic stimulation in other ways. Taking advantage of a low-wage cost structure and strong educational and cultural institutions, these policies led to a veritable boom in the electronics industry in Guadalajara. (In 1999, electronics exports from Jalisco alone exceeded $9 billion, more than petroleum exports from all of Mexico that year.) In this way, NAFTA-related opportunities allowed a strong and dynamic recovery from the crisis of 1994–1995. Future advances, in Alba's view, will depend on the continuation and extension of training, modernized management, and technical know-how.

For the United States, James Gerber offers an analysis of California and Texas, the two most populous states in the nation. Prior to NAFTA the Texas economy had endured declines in oil and cattle, its former mainstays, while California had suffered from the slowdown in aerospace, the closing of military bases, a bursting real estate bubble, and the collapse of financial institutions. But in both states, Gerber argues, "the crises led to positive economic changes that enabled them to reinvent themselves in a more competitive, international context." In both California and Texas, export growth was led by electronics (as was true for Jalisco). Gerber also takes note of domestic conflicts that can arise between states and the federal government in areas related to, but not directly caused by, NAFTA—such as trucking and migration. As with softwood lumber, the problems stem not from provisions of the NAFTA agreement but from what was left out of it.

Taken together, these studies underscore the ideas that NAFTA (or any free trade area) offers uneven opportunities to different localities, that it can heighten (or reduce) regional disparities, and that the acquisition of benefits depends significantly upon the consistency and quality of local leadership. Clearly, subnational policies can make a crucial difference.

4

Canadian Provinces under Free Trade: Alberta and British Columbia

Edward J. Chambers

The increasing liberalization of trade during the past half-century, culminating in the Canada–United States Free Trade Agreement (CUSFTA) and its later incorporation into the North American Free Trade Agreement (NAFTA), was among the most important events in Canadian economic policy during the twentieth century. Much of the analysis of the impacts of globalization in Canada, as elsewhere, considers increased trade, immigration, and investment flows with the nation-state as the unit of study. Following on the CUSFTA and NAFTA and also the most recent Uruguay Round of the General Agreement on Tariffs and Trade (GATT) (now the World Trade Organization, or WTO), real Canadian exports of goods and services grew at an annual rate of 8.4 percent between 1993 and 1999. This trend, which emphasizes the export side of globalization, is well known. In any country, however, the degree to which globalization occurs consistently, let alone uniformly, across regions is less well understood.

One can ask why there has been less focus on the experience of state and provincial entities. An important reason is that regional analysis of impacts is more difficult and the conclusions more tenuous. In the case of subnational jurisdictions, merchandise and service import data are either of poor quality or unavailable. As a result, merchandise exports that are available for these jurisdictions become a proxy for globalization. In Canada, evaluation is further complicated by the fact that there are no published series on provincial inflows and outflows of foreign direct investment (FDI).

Table 4.1 contains a distribution of the annual rate of growth in state and provincial merchandise exports during the 1990s. The range of export experience among subnational jurisdictions in the two countries is substantial. At one end of the spectrum, ten states and one province recorded annual growth in excess of 10 percent, while at the other, fifteen states and one province experienced export growth of less than 5 percent. The results suggest the uneven diffusion of global forces that enhances the desirability of knowing avenues of engagement with the rest of the world, and the degree of adaptation by subjurisdictions to the opportunity set presented by globalization. In sum, the spatial dimensions of globalization within the national state may bear further attention.

Table 4.1. Average Rates of Growth in Merchandise Exports: U.S. States and Canadian Provinces, 1990s

Annual Rate of Growth in Exports	Number of U.S. States	Number of Canadian Provinces
Over 10%	10	1
7.1 to 10%	17	5
5.1 to 7%	8	3
5% and less	15	1

Sources: Statistics Canada, CANSIM, and the Canadian Trade Analyser; United States Census Bureau, Exporter Location.

This essay considers the response of two provincial economies in Canada—Alberta and British Columbia—to CUSFTA and NAFTA. Alberta (AB) and British Columbia (BC) have a current combined population equal to about 23 percent of the national and 75 percent of the Western Canadian total. In mid-2000 there were approximately 4 million people living in BC and 3 million in AB. The provinces are neighbors with numerous social, economic, and trading ties, and their respective per capita incomes have exceeded the national average for many years. In Canadian parlance, they are both "have" provinces. Each possesses a strong natural resource base that, historically, has been the foundation of their international trading relationships; forestry and minerals have dominated in BC, and energy and agriculture in Alberta. Both also have a strong human resource base, ranking at the top nationally in levels of educational attainment. However, there are differences in their respective demographic profiles. Most notably, in BC, the population has a higher median age—a fact reflected in the labor force participation rate, which, at about 65 percent, is some 7 points lower than AB's 72 percent.

For the past century, the international ties of the two provinces—like those of Canada as a whole—have been very strongly reflected not only in trade flows but also in international investment and in the role of immigration in their settlement patterns. With the coming of CUSFTA/NAFTA, both provinces experienced an increase in the importance of the U.S. market as an export destination. For AB, the share rose steadily from 69.5 percent in 1988 to 80.7 percent in 1996 and to 84.5 percent in 1999. BC's U.S. export share also rose steadily from the lower level of 42.7 percent in 1988 to 54.8 percent in 1996 and 68.2 percent in 1999. The question is: what happened within the two provincial economies?

RESTRUCTURING

In considering the response of states or provinces to trade liberalization, one approach—the approach adopted in this analysis—is to distinguish the tradable from the nontradable sector of the economy. The separation is not a hard and fast one given that modern technology has reduced the scope of the nontradable sector and widened that of the tradable. However, the concept remains a useful one for our purposes. The tradable sector is identified by product mobility leading to workable competition between domestic and foreign producers, while in the nontradable sector, the product is immobile and the demand must be satisfied through local suppliers. Goods production—reaching all the way up the value chain from raw materials to technologically advanced value-added manufactures, together with business/producer services—is at the heart of the tradable sector. The dominant activities in the nontradable sector are housing and a wide range of personal services, together with other activities such as community services, health care, and primary and secondary education. The direct impacts of trade liberalization are on those activities that make up the tradable sector of the economy. From a provincial perspective, the CUSFTA, and subsequently the NAFTA, amounted to a policy initiative that was two-edged, creating both new market opportunities for the tradable sector and exposing its existing structure to increased competition. In terms of opportunity, the agreements increased access, either totally or in substantially greater measure, to markets orders of magnitude greater than the domestic, putting in place the demand conditions for structural change.

By way of background, for raw material–producing industries in AB and BC, the meaning of access to the U.S. market is situational. In the case of crude oil and natural gas, the northern tier of U.S. states contains no major energy producers, and even more importantly, the depletion of U.S. reserves in the lower forty-eight states led to the adoption in the CUSFTA of a continental energy policy implying unfettered market access. Alberta energy exports dominate provincial foreign shipment values. They accounted for 52.5, 57.6, and 54.3 percent, respectively, of shipments in 1988, 1996, and 1999, virtually all of which went to the American market.

For agricultural products, the situation is entirely different. This is the case not only because grain and livestock are important products in contiguous western states, but also because agricultural support programs in Canada and the United States differ in their composition, and conflict is endemic over subsidy size and its measurement.

Forest product exports—sawn lumber, wood pulp, and paper—dominate BC's export trade, amounting to 47.6, 50.0, and 44.4 percent of the value of shipments in 1988, 1996, and 1999, respectively. The United States grew as a market, with shares increasing from 43.4 percent in 1988 to 62.4 percent in 1999. For forest products, access problems center on softwood lumber (more than one-half of the Canadian total is produced in BC). Conflicts go back to the beginning of the twentieth century to the failed Canada-U.S. Reciprocity Treaty of 1911 which was vigorously opposed by the U.S. lumber industry. Softwood lumber remains today the significant nonagricultural sector where there is no free trade.[1]

Access for producers of higher value-added goods and business services has largely been a matter of tariffs, standards, mutual recognition agreements, and the search for appropriate networks that facilitate trade. That is why the CUSFTA/NAFTA was so important to AB and BC; it provided substantially greater assurance of a more open American market right next door. It presented to businesses in many sectors a relatively benign environment for acquiring knowledge and experience as exporters—even for an initial venture into exporting. Empirically, for the two provinces this is apparent in the share of manufactured output going to international markets. For AB, some 36 percent of manufactured product was marketed internationally in 1996, compared with 21 percent in 1988. In the case of BC, 53 percent went to international markets in 1996, compared with 48 percent in 1988.

Changes in the Composition of the Goods Sector

What is the evidence of trade liberalization's impact on manufacturing? More open trading arrangements should be an instrument of both development and restructuring in the tradable sector. At the core in an advanced economy is manufacturing. A more open economy will demand a more competitive cost structure, but also the opportunity for greater revenues from a wider and deeper market. Generally, these altered conditions for market access should increase the efficiency and profitability of firms in the tradable sector. I attempt below to provide an overview of the changes that have taken place in the goods-producing sectors of the two provincial economies.

Table 4.2 shows the average size of the goods sector for three periods: 1984–1990, 1990–1996, and 1996–1999. These periods roughly coincide with the pre-CUSFTA period, the transition years from the CUSFTA to NAFTA, and the years when NAFTA was fully operative. In Alberta, there was an increase from 0.404 to 0.415 in the goods-sector share of GDP between the first and second period and a further increase in the third period. The growth in the goods sector was more than accounted for by the expansion in manufacturing.

Table 4.2. Goods and Manufacturing as Share of GDP: Alberta and British Columbia, 1984–1999

	Goods Sector in GDP		Manufacturing in Goods Sector		Manufacturing in GDP	
	AB	BC	AB	BC	AB	BC
1984–1990	0.404	0.308	0.187	0.402	0.076	0.124
1990–1996	0.415	0.277	0.207	0.376	0.086	0.104
1996–1999	0.417	0.257	0.233	0.379	0.097	0.097

Source: Statistics Canada, CANSIM.

In British Columbia, the goods sector as a whole over the entire period accounted for a consistently smaller share of output compared with Alberta, and it also declined in importance. BC manufacturing, which was absolutely larger and also larger as a share of GDP compared with AB, declined over the period both as a share of the goods sector and as a share of GDP. The result was that, in the latter part of the 1990s, the shares of manufacturing in GDP were identical in AB and BC. The table reveals the rising importance of manufacturing in Alberta and its declining importance in British Columbia.

Provincial Manufacturing Sectors

For further information on the provincial manufacturing sectors based upon the 1980 Canadian SIC classifications, table 4.3 shows the relative importance of the durable and nondurable components in two periods: 1984–1990 and 1991–1999. There was a slight increase in the share of durable manufacturing in both provinces, with the durable component in BC about 10 points larger than in AB.

Table 4.3. Shares of Durable and Nondurable Components of Manufacturing Output: Alberta and British Columbia, 1984–90 and 1991–99

	Durable Manufacturing		Nondurable Manufacturing	
	AB	BC	AB	BC
1984–1990	0.445	0.554	0.555	0.446
1991–1999	0.455	0.565	0.545	0.435

Source: Statistics Canada, CANSIM.

More detail on the manufacturing sector allows better understanding of how well components have responded to the dual challenges of trade openings: seizing the opportunity of access to a market ten times greater than the inter-provincial, and restructuring sectors to secure resource rationalization. This more micro view of the provincial sectors is found in tables 4.4 and 4.5. The tables show the comparative growth performance of the more important manufacturing activities. Growth trends in other segments of the tradable sector, including business services and primary activities, are included for comparative purposes in the tables. Log linear trends were fitted to the real GDP in each component for the periods 1984–1990 and 1991–1999.

The data reveal the sharp differences in the provincial records. In Alberta, the annual rate of growth in manufacturing output rose from 3.8 percent in the pre-CUSFTA period to 7.1 percent in 1991–1999, an increase displayed in both the durable and nondurable components. In British Columbia, by contrast, the rate of growth in manufacturing output fell from 3.7 percent in the first period to 1.5 percent in the second, a decline experienced in both durable and nondurable components. During the 1984–1990 period in Alberta, there were six manufacturing sectors that recorded negative growth, while in the later period positive growth was achieved in all sectors. In BC, two sectors recorded negative growth in the first period and three in the 1991–1999 years. For AB, growth rates in 1991–1999 exceeded—or were equal to, in the case of chemicals—those in the pre-CUSFTA years for all but five of seventeen manufacturing activities. The rates themselves exceeded 5 percent annually in thirteen sectors. In BC, growth rates in the second period were either negative or lower in ten instances, and in only four sectors did the rate exceed 5 percent. It can be noted also that AB manufacturing remains more diversified than that in BC. In British Columbia, wood, paper, and allied products in the 1991–1999 period still made up 37 percent of manufacturing output, though somewhat down from 43 percent in 1984–1990. The largest of the manufacturing sectors in AB is chemical products, with output maintained at approximately 17 percent of manufacturing activity over both periods. Overall, the rather startling fact is that BC real manufacturing GDP was 65 percent larger than AB's in 1984, 83 percent larger in 1988 (as shown in the tables), but only 3 percent greater in 1999 (C\$9.145 billion vs. C\$8.876 billion).

Trends in employment growth in these sectors generally coincide with trends in GDP growth, showing strength in the durable and nondurable sectors in AB and weakness in BC.

"Business services" are certainly part of the tradable economy, yet hard evidence on cross-border business service activities is wanting. We can only speculate about the significance of the CUSFTA/NAFTA in fostering a more international outlook for this sector. Those in business services move back and forth across borders, and this enlarges the opportunity for network linkages so dominant in this activity. There is considerable anecdotal evidence of provincial firms acquiring, or being acquired by, foreign firms, and of joint venturing and strategic alliances with U.S. and Mexican firms. What we can say is that in AB the real output of the sector grew at a rate of 9.0 percent in the CUSFTA/NAFTA period, compared with 2.1 percent in 1984–1990, while in BC the rate of output fell from 8.2 percent in the first period to 5.2 percent in the second.

In primary activities, growth rates in Alberta were positive but lower in the second period for agriculture and logging/forestry; they rose from 1.1 percent to 2.2 percent for mining/drilling. In BC, fishing/trapping output moved from growth to decline, while other primary sectors displayed higher rates in the CUSFTA/NAFTA years.

Table 4.4. Alberta GDP Growth Rates by Selected Sectors

	1988 GDP at Factor Cost (millions C$92)	Trend Growth Rate, 1984–1990 (%)	Trend Growth Rate, 1991–1999 (%)
MANUFACTURING	**$4,839.8**	**3.8**	**7.1**
DURABLE MANUFACTURING	2,288.5	4.7	8.7
Machinery	406.8	–2.1	8.2
Metal fabricated products	379.2	4.4	8.6
Wood products	378.0	8.9	5.9
Non-metallic mineral products	257.3	2.3	5.8
Primary metals	227.8	2.0	1.5
Electrical equipment	179.0	12.4	15.4
Transportation equipment	155.3	8.8	7.0
Other manufactures	115.7	2.4	8.1
Furniture	99.2	12.9	16.5
NONDURABLE MANUFACTURING	2,645.3	3.0	5.9
Chemical products	769.7	6.3	6.3
Food industries	667.4	–2.5	5.6
Printing and publishing	518.6	–0.6	0.7
Beverages	197.6	–0.9	2.8
Paper and allied products	161.1	–1.8	7.6
Refined petroleum products	155.3	11.2	4.2
Plastics	100.2	–0.3	15.0
Clothing	75.4	5.4	3.1
BUSINESS SERVICES	2,702.7	2.1	9.0
AGRICULTURE and SERVICES	1,977.7	8.6	4.0
LOGGING and FORESTRY	166.7	4.9	4.4
MINING and DRILLING	12,052.8	7.7	2.2

Table 4.5. British Columbia GDP Growth Rates by Selected Sectors

	1988 GDP at Factor Cost (millionsC$92)	Trend Growth Rate, 1984–1990 (%)	Trend Growth Rate, 1991–1999 (%)
MANUFACTURING	**$8,851.7**	3.7	1.5
DURABLE MANUFACTURING	4,897.7	4.9	1.9
Wood products	2,536.0	5.3	−2.3
Metal fabricated products	546.9	5.5	1.6
Machinery	491.6	6.3	3.6
Transportation equipment	375.1	1.0	7.1
Primary metals	293.0	1.3	1.5
Non-metallic mineral products	264.7	5.2	1.4
Electrical equipment	164.8	13.0	14.8
Other manufactures	135.5	0.6	9.1
Furniture	90.1	7.6	5.5
NONDURABLE MANUFACTURING	3,954.0	2.2	1.0
Paper and allied products	1,374.9	1.8	0.2
Food industries	1,019.5	−0.1	0.4
Printing & publishing	639.6	3.4	−0.3
Chemical products	334.1	1.1	4.0
Beverages	181.7	−6.1	3.5
Plastics	169.1	9.7	4.8
Refined petroleum products	117.7	6.4	−4.5
Clothing	114.5	9.1	2.3
BUSINESS SERVICES	3,157.0	8.2	5.2
AGRICULTURE and SERVICES	777.7	3.5	3.9
LOGGING and FORESTRY	2,503.8	1.7	2.0
MINING and DRILLING	1,937.8	3.3	4.1
FISHING and TRAPPING	257.4	8.1	−6.9

The conclusion is that AB secured a substantial restructuring of its tradable sector to accommodate changes brought by more open access to a much larger market and to realize the opportunities created. The same cannot be said for the BC economy; we need to turn to other forces that may aid our understanding of these observed differences.

POPULATION GROWTH: IMMIGRATION AND DOMESTIC MIGRATION

The demographic experience of the two provinces during the 1990s is remarkably different. BC experienced a population surge—a shock. This type of shock to an economy generates demands for absolute and relative growth in the nontradable sector. The most obvious demand impact is on the key nontradable—housing. But the demands also fall on other elements of the nontradable sector—education, health care, personal services, and community and social services. Demographic shocks alter the ratio between prices in the tradable and nontradable sectors, with nontradable prices appreciating relative to those of tradables, and, through this altered price ratio, accommodation to the shock occurs. The result is greater market opportunity and higher expected returns in the nontradable sector, leading to heightened entrepreneurial activity and increased capital flows. Because nontradable prices are inputs in most sectors, increases put upward pressure on the regional cost structure. This can have disastrous consequences for the competitive position of traditional export- and import-competing sectors. In terms of employment and production, these sectors will decline in relative terms and, at worst, in absolute terms.

The demographic shock in BC came from both foreign immigration and domestic migration. Figure 4.1 shows the annual immigration flows to Canada and to BC for the years 1980–2000; flows to BC are on the left axis, and those to Canada are on the right axis. In the first half of the 1980s, immigration flows declined, but then, commencing in 1986, they increased steadily both nationally and in BC. In 1993, Canadian flows reached a peak. However, immigrant landings in BC continued to increase, reaching 53,100 in 1997, almost one-quarter (23.6 percent) of the national total. Much of the immigration to the province in these years was from East Asia, and most specifically Hong Kong. It was of the "push" variety, set in motion by uncertainty over the future relationship with China once jurisdiction over the territory was transferred from the United Kingdom to China.[2]

High levels of immigration coincided with high levels of net in-migration from other parts of Canada. Some of that appears to have been of the social "pull" variety—belief that the quality of life in BC was higher. Other factors in the net in-migration were associated with business restructuring in central Canada reflecting the recession of 1991–1992 and the sluggish recovery experienced in Ontario and Quebec; with an opting for early retirement; and with the "pull" of a strong BC provincial economy in the mid-1990s primarily driven by the performance of the nontradable sector. Between 1993 and 1995, for example, one of every five new full-time jobs in the country was created in BC. The peak in net domestic in-migration was 40,000 in 1993 and averaged over 36,000 annually between 1990 and 1995.

Figure 4.1. Number of Immigrants: Canada and British Columbia, 1980–2000

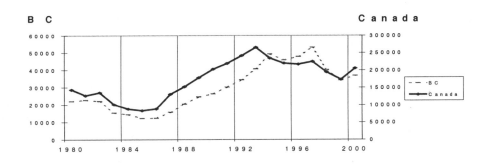

Evidence on the markedly different demographic experience of the two provinces appears in figure 4.2, which expresses the annual sum of domestic in-migration and immigration as a percent of the population in the prior year. The differing provincial experience is evident in al-most every year. In the period between 1990 and 1995—one that was particularly relevant for tradable-sector accommodation to trade agreement opportunities—net domestic and foreign migration to BC reached an annual average of 2.2 percent of the previous year's popula-tion level. Foreign and domestic migration shared about equally in this number. These inflows to British Columbia compare with a 1990–1995 average of 0.8 percent for Alberta. Arguably, these years were a critical interval for tradable-sector adaptation to the new CUSFTA/NAFTA trade policy framework.

Figure 4.2. Immigration and Net Domestic Migration as a Percent of Population in the Prior Year: Alberta and British Columbia, 1985-2000

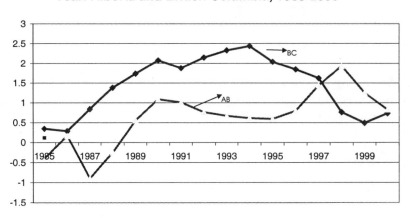

Housing Impacts

Shocks to the nontradable sector cannot be mitigated by increased imports. The core nontradable is housing, and price change should be reflected in housing prices. This was indeed the case. Price increases ration existing supply and provide the incentive to expand stocks over the longer term. Table 4.6 shows the average selling price for detached dwellings in the Vancouver metro area between 1990 and 1995, with comparisons for Calgary and Edmonton. In Vancouver, which received a substantial portion of the in-migration, the average selling price of a detached dwelling rose from $270,000 (Canadian dollars) in 1990 to $410,000 in 1995, an increase of 52 percent. This compares with an average detached house price in Calgary of $128,000 in 1990 and $132,000 in 1995 (an increase of merely 3 percent), while in Edmonton the average price rose by 10 percent.

We would expect the sharp increase in Vancouver housing prices to be reflected in capital investment in new residential quarters. It was. From 1990 to 1995, these expenditures amounted on average to one-quarter of the national total. Alberta residential capital expenditures were 10 percent, a ratio about equal to the province's share of Canada's population.[3]

Table 4.6. Average Selling Price of Detached Dwellings, Vancouver, Calgary, and Edmonton, 1990–1995 (thousands of C$)

	Vancouver	Calgary	Edmonton
1990	270	128	101
1991	275	127	107
1992	300	128	109
1993	350	132	111
1994	375	133	112
1995	410	132	110

Sources: Communications from the Real Estate Board of Greater Vancouver, the Calgary Real Estate Board Co-operative Ltd, and the Edmonton Real Estate Board.

Labor Market Impacts

Cost pressures in the BC economy induced by the housing market are apparent. Is there any evidence that cost pressures were diffused more widely in the provincial cost-price structure, thereby adding to the difficulties of restructuring in the tradable sector? Labor costs are the important case in point. Wage levels in British Columbia are generally higher than those in Alberta. In the mid-1980s, for example, before the CUSFTA came into effect, hourly earnings in BC manufacturing averaged about 18 percent higher than in AB, while in the service sector the difference was 19 percent. Figure 4.3 reports the BC to AB ratio of average hourly earnings (excluding overtime) during the last decade for manufacturing and for the service sector as a whole, employing these as proxies for the tradable and nontradable sectors. The figure shows that, commencing in 1992, the ratio for the service sector started to increase, reaching a peak ratio of 1.28 in 1995 and then retreating. The ratio of hourly wages in manufacturing lagged by one year, displaying an initial increase in 1993 and reaching a maximum differential of 1.32, or 32 percent, in 1996. The increase in these ratios arises from increases in the numerator (BC hourly earnings) and not from a decline in the denominator (AB hourly earnings).

The data suggest that demographic shocks—both foreign and domestic in origin—greatly expanded opportunities in the nontradable sector, attracted capital flows, inflated the cost-price structure of the BC economy, and generally magnified difficulties in the way of restructuring the tradable sector.

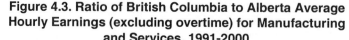

Figure 4.3. Ratio of British Columbia to Alberta Average Hourly Earnings (excluding overtime) for Manufacturing and Services, 1991-2000

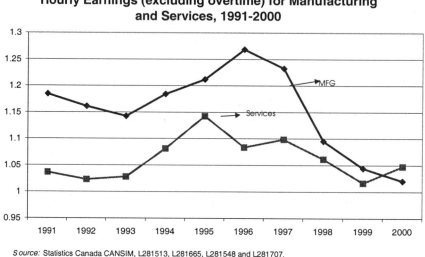

Source: Statistics Canada CANSIM, L281513, L281665, L281548 and L281707.

FOREIGN DIRECT INVESTMENT

In Canada, there are no provincial data on the amount, let alone the source, of FDI.[4] The best information available on the topic is found in an internal document of Statistics Canada.[5] The paper suggests that estimates might be derived using three allocators—provincial taxable income of corporations, payroll deductions by province, and capital expenditure surveys of establishments by province. Allocators are derived from three separate sources: returns under the Corporate and Labour Unions Returns Act, which requires data reports on the assets, revenues, and profits of foreign-owned enterprises; the Survey of Employment, Payroll and Hours; and the Survey of Capital Expenditures.

No time series of FDI by province has ever been published by Statistics Canada, which provides a snapshot of the three allocators only for a single year, 1994. Giving equal weight to each of the three, Rolf Mirus estimates on this basis that AB received about 14 percent of FDI inflows (an amount equal to that of Quebec), while BC received about 8 percent.[6] Based on this evidence, AB attracted, at least in that year, a higher—and BC a lower—proportion of FDI relative to their respective shares of the labor force.

DOES PROVINCIAL PUBLIC POLICY MATTER?

Canada is often described as one of the world's most decentralized federations. The Constitution assigns provincial governments substantial economic responsibilities in inter-provincial trade and commerce, in regulatory matters, and, of particular importance to AB and BC, in the stewardship of natural resources arising from ownership of subsurface mineral rights and the vast share of forested areas. The result is that the economic strategies formulated by provincial governments can play a significant role in shaping the direction of their respective economies. In foreign economic policy, the realities of constitutional power sharing has led the federal government over the past generation to put in place a process of extensive consultation, not simply with the private sector but also with provincial governments, about international trade policy, and, specifically, on negotiations preceding the CUSFTA, NAFTA, and the multilateral Uruguay Round. Therefore, positions on trade policy publicly enunciated by a provincial government are recognized as inputs to a consultation process and are likely to influence private-sector perceptions about the kind of provincial economic environment within which strategic planning alternatives evolve. The evidence indicates that, first with the FTA and subsequently with NAFTA, there were clear differences between the international trade policy stance of the two provincial governments.

The positions of the AB government on CUSFTA and on NAFTA were unequivocal. The government was consistently supportive of the two agreements, both prior and subsequent to their signing. Further, the AB government engaged in outreach to market the agreement throughout the continent. The chief spokesperson was a senior cabinet minister, the Hon. James Horsman. In a 1986 address, he stated:

> Quite simply, we produce well in excess of what we can ever consume given our comparatively small population.... Obviously, we rely heavily on exports to foreign markets to sustain our standard of living, to generate employment and to stimulate our private sector. Exports are our lifeblood. We see a free trade agreement as vital to the maintenance of a healthy economy.[7]

In Alberta, the fact of an open trade orientation, strongly espoused and extensively marketed long before the signing of the FTA, provided the basis for dialogue with the business community about the coverage of a prospective agreement and its potential benefits. The private sector was encouraged and given every opportunity to consider and assess the market opportunities that an agreement could offer. This position carried through to pre-NAFTA negotiations. In 1992 Horsman declared that: "With respect to the North American Agreement, our government strongly supports the negotiations under way. From our perspective, the North American Free Trade Agreement represents the best chance at succeeding in an increasingly complex and competitive international marketplace."[8]

It is also likely that the province saw the trade agreements as a market opening that could be instrumental in facilitating economic diversification. This was a priority issue in Alberta, which was severely affected by the energy market weaknesses of the early 1980s and the subsequent crude oil price collapse in 1986.

The province of British Columbia has a long history of deep political divisions. In the past fifteen years these differences have yielded different policy configurations toward globalization. One source of what could be characterized as policy ambiguity is undoubtedly the ongoing trade dispute between Canada and the United States over softwood lumber, the product that has been throughout the twentieth century—and remains today—BC's ranking export. More than half of exports go to the U.S. market. This unresolved dispute existed prior to the CUSFTA, and it is likely to continue to be met with accommodations outside of NAFTA.

The spokesperson for a right-of-center administration, a senior cabinet minister, the Hon. Grace McCarthy, stated that the BC government:

> recognizes the tremendous opportunities that come with greater and freer access to the markets of our American neighbour.
>
> At the same time, we understand that along with the new trade agreement come changes that will mean additional competition for certain BC products and services. Nevertheless, opening the door to markets many times larger than ours presents British Columbia with unlimited job-creating opportunities.[9]

This statement epitomizes the more cautious approach to the CUSFTA (also FTA) taken by the then BC provincial government, one that could be compared with AB's strong endorsement. A statement on the signing of the agreement is supportive, but it also asserts that

future provincial efforts will be devoted to liberalizing trade relationships with other countries:

> The British Columbia government believes that the FTA is
> a sound and beneficial agreement for British Columbians.
> Accordingly, the Province will continue to give the FTA its
> fullest support and will work to ensure that both Canada
> and the U.S. implement the agreement and build on the
> momentum created by the FTA. Future efforts will be
> aimed at further liberalizing our trade relationships with
> other countries and creating even greater opportunities for
> the province.[10]

In 1991 a left-of-center party become the BC government. The new
government expressed concern about the potential impact of a
NAFTA on its trade relations and market opportunities in Southeast
Asia. Its policy stance also reflected the softwood lumber dispute.
Speaking in the Legislature on June 25, 1992, the Hon. David Miller
stated:

> I'm assuming, of course, that Canada will refer the issue to a
> bi-national panel under the free trade agreement. It certainly
> supports the position that this government has taken: that
> it's right and proper for British Columbia to question the
> value of the free trade agreement, given the kind of harass-
> ment we've seen from the United States; and it's right and
> proper for British Columbia to question the wisdom of
> proceeding with NAFTA, considering the abuse that we
> have been subjected to by the United States.[11]

On June 4, 1992, the premier, the Hon. Michael Harcourt, wrote to
the prime minister requesting that Canada withdraw from negotiations
over NAFTA. He outlined his action and stated his position in the
Legislature on June 25:

> Our decision [was] to write to the Prime Minister and say
> that we should withdraw from the North American free
> trade agreement because it's part of a severely flawed trade
> philosophy.... That trade philosophy is tied to being a
> branch plant to the American hub-and-spoke theory of
> trade in the Americas. I and our government are much
> more firmly committed to a more egalitarian and fairer
> form of trade that goes from the tip of Chile to the top of

Canada on the Arctic Ocean—a hemispheric trade relationship rather than one that's dominated by one particular nation. That decision was made before the board was appointed. It was made by the government after looking at the text of the proposed North American free trade agreement, which we unfortunately couldn't make available to the people of British Columbia to have a look at because of the secrecy requirements of the federal government.[12]

The Board to which Mr. Harcourt refers was an Advisory Board of business and industry leaders which was appointed only after the provincial government had requested the Canadian government to withdraw from NAFTA negotiations.

To reiterate, assessment of respective provincial trade policies clearly indicates that there were sharp differences between the two provinces regarding the agreements.

CONCLUSION

Alberta's economy has benefited substantially from CUSFTA/NAFTA. The CUSFTA put in place an energy policy that was positive for the most important sector of the provincial economy. Change took place from that starting point. It is reasonable to conclude that the CUSFTA and NAFTA are essential to understanding the change that occurred. That should not be interpreted, however, as attributing observed changes in the political economy over the past decade exclusively to the agreements. It is obvious that a correct measure of the impact requires a weighing of a factual condition against a counterfactual. Changes would have taken place in structure and in export markets absent CUSFTA/NAFTA.

The British Columbia case can be seen as a failure to adapt to expanded trade opportunities. There are several reasons. The core industry with the province's largest export product was one which, in practical terms, even now remains outside the CUSFTA/NAFTA. The forest products industry was caught on the demand side by restricted access to its most important market, and on the supply side by environmental concerns and forest constraints. The situation was compounded by the importance of the industry as an economic base for smaller communities outside the lower mainland area. Adjustments in the tradable sector facilitated by CUSFTA/NAFTA—and necessary for reduced dependence on the lumber industry—were inhibited by a population surge that produced market disincentives for restructuring and directed resources into the nontradable sector. Finally, the province lacked a set of coherent public policies that provided direction and priorities in reorienting the economy. Coherence in public policy follows from a clear sense of direction about required transformations. Lacking a broadly supported vision, public policy is paralyzed at worst and sends mixed messages at best.

Notes

1. Lumber disputes in the contemporary period go back twenty years. In 1982 a petition from U.S. lumber companies charged the Canadian government with subsidizing its softwood lumber industry. This petition was rejected, but a second identical petition, filed four years later, was accepted by the Department of Commerce. This led to negotiations that resulted in an agreement under which the Canadian government would impose an export tax on softwood lumber exports and attempt to have the provinces (who own virtually all public timber land) transform their forestry programs. In September 1991 Canada terminated the tax, claiming it was no longer needed. One month later, the U.S. Department of Commerce self-initiated the case, claiming the subsidy still existed, and it added a second allegation claiming that the BC government prohibited the export of logs only when the needs of the domestic industry had been met, thus providing preferential treatment for a specific industry. Between 1991 and 1996, the question came before FTA dispute settlement panels, resulting in judgments favorable to Canada. However, in 1996 the two countries reached an agreement assigning a sawn lumber quota to producers in British Columbia, Alberta, Ontario, and Quebec. Softwood lumber shipments exceeding the quota were subject to duty. The agreement expired in March 2001. Since then, the softwood dispute has escalated as negotiations over a new agreement have so far failed. As of May 2002, the United States imposed a 29 percent tariff on lumber imports sourced from provinces other than those in the Maritimes, while Canada has referred the dispute to both NAFTA and the WTO for resolution.

2. In the 1993–1997 period, a significant share of the "business class" category of immigration came to BC. The province's share during these years averaged 38.9 percent of the Canadian total. Business-class immigrants consisted of "entrepreneurs," "investors," and the "self-employed." The "investor" group averaged about 57 percent of business-class immigrants to BC during these years. Investors had to have operated, managed, or controlled a business abroad and accumulated a net worth of at least C$800,000. They were required to remit C$400,000 allocated to the province of landing, to be refunded without interest after five years. In BC about 30 percent were in the

"entrepreneurial" subclass, who were required to establish and actively manage a business within two years of their arrival in the province. On average, from 1993 to 1997, 18.8 percent of the immigrants landing in BC were "business class," a share greater than that of any other province.

3. Statistics Canada, CANSIM Series D845012, D849421, and D849410.

4. This section relies heavily on Rolf Mirus, *The Trade and Investment Impact of NAFTA on Canada,* Joint Series on Competitiveness (Centre for International Business Studies, University of Alberta, October 2000).

5. Rosemary Bender, "Issues in Provincialising Foreign Direct Investment" (Statistics Canada, Balance of Payment Division, April 1998).

6. Mirus, *The Trade and Investment Impact of NAFTA,* p.13.

7. Speech to the Foreign Trade Association of Southern California, November 1986.

8. Remarks to the University of California at San Diego–COLEF Rosarito conference, Tijuana, January 1992.

9. Grace McCarthy in Ministry of Economic Development, *Building Future Opportunities: British Columbia and the Canada/United States Bilateral Negotiations* (Victoria: Ministry, 1987).

10. Ministry of Economic Development, *The Free Trade Agreement: Impact on British Columbia* (Victoria: Ministry, 1988), p. 6.

11. British Columbia Hansard, June 25, 1992.

12. Ibid.

5

Regional Policy under NAFTA: The Case of Jalisco

Carlos Alba Vega

The Mexican state of Jalisco has undergone profound economic and political change since NAFTA went into effect. In the mid-1990s a severe economic and political crisis led to a serious deterioration in the living conditions of the population and to a loss of political legitimacy for the prevailing regime. The aftermath witnessed a change of political rule at the regional level and a reactivation of the economy in some exporting sectors; in 1995 the National Action Party (PAN) took over the state government,[1] which had been in the hands of the Institutional Revolutionary Party (PRI) since 1929, while in the economic sphere sizable investments began to arrive from abroad, mainly channeled into the electronics industry. People began to refer locally to the capital city of Guadalajara as Mexico's "Silicon Valley." By the end of the decade, much of the employment lost as a result of the crisis had been recovered, and in 2000 the PAN again won the elections for the state governorship and for the most important municipal presidencies.

This chapter aims to present the initial results of an investigation of the economic, social, and political consequences for Jalisco of the economic reforms, Mexico's insertion into the global economy, and NAFTA, in order then to establish comparisons with other regions in the United States and Canada. I also examine public policies of the state government and the initiatives of other actors, such as local entrepreneurs and the transnational corporations established in Jalisco, as they attempted to adapt and respond to the challenges and opportunities offered by the new context of NAFTA. In so doing, I address several principal questions: What are the effects of the economic reforms, Mexico's reinsertion in the global economy, the 1994–1995 financial crisis, and NAFTA on economy and politics in Jalisco from 1990 to 2000? What impact is the arrival of new foreign direct investment (FDI) in the electronics industry having on the economy and society of Jalisco? And what roles are governmental actors and public policies playing in the context of economic, social, and political transformations?

SETTING AND CONTEXT: REGIONAL ECONOMIC AND POLITICAL DECLINE

One of the effects of the expropriation of the banks in 1982 was the politicization of Mexican entrepreneurs; it galvanized them into adopting a greater autonomy vis-à-vis the state and transformed them into new political actors. Within the space of two decades, representatives of the business sector triumphed in elections for municipal presidencies (mayorships), captured seats in the federal Chamber of Deputies and Senate, won several state governorships, and, finally, in 2000 won the presidency of the republic.[2] But each region had its particular characteristics. The businessmen of Guadalajara offer an interesting contrast with other regions. They were less affected by the bank expropriation and the economic crisis of the early 1980s than were their counterparts in other areas of the country. Nearly all the local and regional banks created in Guadalajara had already lost their autonomy on being absorbed by large private institutions. Nevertheless, many businesspeople in Jalisco remained close to the state government and the PRI until the mid-1980s.[3] At that point things started to change: in 1988 Manuel Clouthier, as the PAN's candidate for the presidency, obtained the adherence and sympathy of many small and midsize entrepreneurs, some of whom would later attain high elected posts. In the February 1995 election for the governor of Jalisco, some of the most prominent businessmen continued openly and directly to support the PRI's candidate, as had been the custom for many decades; nevertheless, the PRI lost.

From the mid-1980s onward, widespread discontent was generated—in rural and urban environments—by both economic reforms and political factors. In the countryside, the withdrawal of agricultural subsidies, the commercial opening to the exterior (which resulted in the flooding of the market with very low priced agricultural imports), and high interest rates critically affected both subsistence and commercial farmers and stockbreeders. It was in this context that the creditors' movement known as El Barzón was born in Jalisco, later spreading to the rest of Mexico. In the towns, and especially in the city of Guadalajara, nonconformity arose in response to both economic and political factors. On the one hand, several of the economic reforms, especially the opening of the market to foreign competition, had a drastic impact on small and midsize industries producing end-consumer goods for the regional and national markets. These industries had previously been afforded strong protection and been supported by a variety of subsidies. They simply could not compete with cheap imports from the Far East, where—although wage levels were more or less equivalent, or even a little higher than those in Mexico—production methods were more efficient, financial costs lower, and experience in international trade much greater.

Politically, dissatisfaction resulted from an apparent inability to govern in the face of an alarming increase in crime rates associated with the narcotics trade (Enrique Camarena, a DEA agent, was murdered in Guadalajara in 1985), an activity that also sowed corruption at various levels of the public administration. The increase in public insecurity also manifested itself in a number of extreme and highly symbolic events. These include explosions of industrial gases in Guadalajara's drainage system on April 22, 1992, which killed more than two hundred people, something an efficient administration could have avoided; the murder of Cardinal Juan Jesús Posadas at the Guadalajara airport on May 24, 1993; and various kidnappings, acts of terrorism, and drugs-related violence occurring in public places. The crisis of regional governability was accentuated by conflicts between the governor (Guillermo Cosío Vidaurri) and the Guadalajara economic elite, especially real estate developers, and also between the governor and President Carlos Salinas de Gortari (the governor did not agree with the president's policies, nor did he identify with his project to modernize Mexico).

The political crisis culminated in the removal of the governor. He was not, however, replaced by means of the constitutional mechanism that allows the Senate (with the dominant party, the PRI, in the majority, and subject to the president's control) to withdraw recognition of a state government. Instead, Cosío Vidaurri was subjected to a campaign of destabilization until he was obliged to request a temporary leave, which ultimately became permanent. Finally, the financial crisis and consequent devaluation of 1994, which occurred two months before state and local elections in Jalisco, had severe repercussions on economic activities as a whole. Its effects were especially strong in the job market, where large sections of the population were thrown out of work or shifted into the informal sector. According to official data, over 2,700 (mainly small) establishments were obliged to shut down, and more than 37,000 jobs were lost in 1995.[4]

The PAN capitalized on the regional economic and political crisis to achieve victory in the elections for state governor and the presidencies of the most important municipalities. It also won a majority in the state legislature and in local representation to the federal legislature, thus bringing an end to sixty-six years of unbroken control by the PRI.

NEW LEADERSHIP, NEW PRIORITIES

The new governor, Alberto Cárdenas Jiménez, surrounded himself with a team of individuals with experience in small and midsize businesses, naming them to head the main secretariats involved in the economy. The secretary for economic promotion, who enjoyed strong support from the governor and the business community, was responsible for designing a new and truly innovative model of regional development. The new administration took over a state with a serious unemployment problem, and one of its priorities was the recuperation of the local productive plant and employment through the reconversion of firms in traditional sectors. This was to be accomplished by redirecting products and services toward more profitable sectors and markets, and by aggressively promoting investment and job creation in sectors with a greater technological base, added value, and market growth. Foreign investment was sought, along with more geographic dispersion of productive activities, which since 1930 had become ever more concentrated in Guadalajara—to the detriment of the rest of the state. The state government also set out to stimulate a recovery of the internal market through employment generation and increased wages and salaries.

To attain these objectives, mechanisms were designed to provide incentives for productive investment, job creation, and exports. Programs were also set in motion to promote a more competitive entrepreneurial culture, while financial support was given to stimulate midsize and small-scale industry and microenterprises. Prior to 1995, by contrast, there had been no active promotion of the economy.

Institutional Promotion of Development

One of the most important phenomena to appear in Jalisco in recent years is the proliferation of all types of organizations. The new gov-

ernment promoted development through a variety of institutions, programs, and associations, almost all of recent creation; a full evaluation
of the results is still to be seen. The secretary for economic promotion
became the leading figure in the development of a new model and the
drive to attract investment. The main responsibility for promoting investment previously had rested with the federal government. State
governments have little, and municipal governments even less, margin
for action, as well as scarce incentives to offer investors.

In view of the changing economic and political context at the
global, national, and regional levels, the Secretariat for Economic
Promotion (SEPROE) underwent a thoroughgoing reorganization and
modernization; it acquired a new status within the government, broadened its relations, and acquired greater powers. The institutional life of
this government agency (previously known as the Departamento de
Economía and as the Departamento de Programación y de Desarrollo)
has varied depending on the director's power and ability and the governor's goodwill and support. After 1995 SEPROE's importance was
enhanced further by the strong backing of foreign corporations and
regional businessmen, and it had ample economic, human, and technical resources at its disposal. Its budget rose from Mex$6,626,386 in
1995 to $122,382,000 in 2000; its direct staff grew from 105 to 128,
and its indirect employees (people in subsidiary agencies) increased
from 60 to 117. Starting with only 10 staff computers, the agency and
its subsidiaries soon had 224; office space expanded from 1,100 to
2,887 square meters; and the number of subsidiary agencies—
established to meet specific SEPROE needs—rose from three to
seven.

Some activities are of special interest. To generate and disseminate
information, an existing division of SEPROE was reorganized in 1997
and given a new name—the Jalisco State Information System (SEI-
JAL). This agency took advantage of new information and communications technologies to embark on a process of modernization, achieving high degrees of efficiency in gathering, processing, formulating,
and disseminating socioeconomic statistical information (made available on the Internet since 1998).

The State Board for Economic Development (CEPE) was set up in
1995 and, in coordination with SEPROE, became responsible for
promoting investment and implementing Jalisco's new Law for Economic Promotion. This law grants incentives based on a formula that
includes factors such as the number and quality of new jobs generated,
salaries offered, company size, investment, commitment to remain in

Jalisco, project location, funding offered for projects outside the Guadalajara Metropolitan Zone (GMZ), support offered to small firms and microenterprises, and the volume of exports.[5]

The state government has promoted the planning and construction of a number of industrial parks over the years. A total of twenty-three industrial parks are currently envisioned for the GMZ.[6] Six of these were in existence before 1995, some are currently under construction,[7] and four are at the project stage.[8] Since 1995 twelve parks have been constructed elsewhere in the state (there were none previously), and four more are projected.[9]

SEPROE has achieved a remarkable degree of cooperation with the federal government (even under President Ernesto Zedillo's PRI administration, 1994–2000), as well as with the regional private sector and public and private universities. The agency has sought to attract foreign investment using as a starting point the experience, contacts, and interests of the large companies already established in Jalisco (principally in the GMZ). With the assistance of Mexico's embassies, tours were arranged for representatives of foreign firms interested in investing in Jalisco. SEPROE also designed promotional materials, cultivated potential investors, participated in international fairs and exhibitions, and published announcements in economic and business journals. The American Chamber of Commerce has played an active role as host to potential investors.

SEPROE also supported the launching of new programs and projects. The Regional Business Development Program (PRODER) delivered courses and arranged conferences aimed at training personnel interested in setting up their own firms or improving an existing company. A program for establishing entrepreneurial groups was developed, its aim being to enhance the position of small businesses through network development. Another innovation was FIDERAZA, a trust founded with both public and private funds and designed to reduce the transaction costs that Jalisco migrants in the United States incurred when remitting money to their families, while simultaneously directing a proportion of the savings to social infrastructure. The Jalisco Industrial Promotion Fund (FOJAL), a government financing institution for small firms and microenterprises which provided support for businesses affected by the April 1992 gas explosions, went into bankruptcy in 1995; the new administration rescued and restructured it. The Institute for Promoting Foreign Trade (Instituto de Fomento del Comercio Exterior; also known as JALTRADE) was created after 1995 by the state government, in cooperation with the private sector, to promote Jalisco's exports, advise on exporting, foment an "export-ing culture," and attract direct investment from abroad. The Jalisco Design Center (CEJALDI) was created to develop products for small and medium-scale industry and microenterprises in areas such as handicrafts, agroindustry, leather and footwear, textiles and clothing, jewelry, furniture, and metal-mechanics.

In 1998, the Production Chain of the Electronics Industry (CADE-LEC) was established in cooperation with the National Chamber of the Electronics, Telecommunications, and Informatics Industry (CANIETI). Also involved were several electronics companies (includ-ing IBM, HP, Natsteel, and Jabil Circuit), the Industrial Integration Program (Programa de Integración Industrial), and the state govern-ment, which supports the project through SEPROE.[10] CADELEC's objective is to integrate suppliers to the region's electronics industry. In addition, the Jalisco State Council for Science and Technology (COECYTJal) was set up to promote and coordinate public and pri-vate initiatives aimed at scientific and technological development.

THE STATE GOVERNMENT AND TRANSNATIONAL ELECTRONICS FIRMS

Foreign investment has been crucial for economic recovery, for em-ployment growth, and for the legitimacy of the state's new political leadership. The government, therefore, has directed a considerable part of its efforts toward attracting outside capital.[11]

The electronics industry has experienced an extraordinary boom in Jalisco as miniaturization of electronic components and drastic price reductions have ensured the application of microprocessors on a mas-sive scale in all areas of everyday life, from homes to transportation, from computers to satellite communications, from individual personal appliances to the information systems of large companies. This revolu-tion in information and communications technologies has provided a significant impetus toward the global integration of financial markets and the segmented articulation of production and world trade. It was also crucial to the process of economic restructuring that began in many parts of the world in the 1980s.[12] The annual growth rate in the global electronics industry ranges around 12 to 14 percent, with trade in its products totaling about US$1 trillion, or 18.5 percent of all world trade.[13] This sector's importance as a key element in the process of globalization is even greater because of its application to systems of

production and communication. These affect national states and regional territories, the division of labor and labor relations, methods of
production, and distribution and consumption. They also influence
collective identities and daily domestic life, and they foster the tendency to separate economics from the realms of politics and culture.

The electronics industry is of prime importance for Mexico. Its annual exports have already reached Mex$35 billion, and it has been re-
sponsible for the creation of 600,000 jobs.[14] It affects labor competen-
cies and has transformed the regions in which electronics production
has located. Mexico's northern border zone is highly specialized in au-
dio and video equipment and, particularly, televisions. By 1999 this
region had reached an annual output of 25 million television sets, was
supplying 80 percent of the North American market, and was employing some 90,000 workers, including more than 10,000 technicians and
engineers.[15]

Ciudad Juárez, Chihuahua, and Matamoros are strategically located
in terms of the distances between capital-intensive parent companies in
the United States, labor-intensive assembly plants in Mexico, and the
U.S. market. Tijuana is best situated as a base for Japanese *maquiladora*
(in-bond processing) plants that were originally conceived as articulated stages of a segmented process also involving factories in California, the birthplace of the "third industrial revolution."

Mexico's 1994–1995 financial crisis and peso devaluation (and the
resulting cheapening of wages and salaries) had a much greater impact
in Guadalajara than in northern Mexico. One immediate consequence
was a conspicuous rush into a newly specialized branch of the electronics industry—the manufacture or assembly of printed circuits,
electronic circuit boards, and silicon chips and wafers. The movement
toward these basic components, which are inputs for other manufactured products, also responded to the stimulus and pressures of
NAFTA; Article 303 of the agreement states that inputs originating in
nonmember countries would be taxed starting in 2001, a strong reason
for Asian companies to relocate within Mexico.[16] The nature of work
in this specialization has led to the hiring of a largely female workforce
(around 85 percent) for soldering and assembly. Leading companies in
the sector are IBM, which began manufacturing typewriters in Guadalajara in 1975 and now has its main personal computer plant in this
city;[17] Hewlett-Packard, with Guadalajara serving as its worldwide distribution center; and Motorola (now the Motorola Semiconductor
Products Sector), which began making radios in the 1960s and now
makes silicon wafers for computer hard drives. This sector is so
important that, according to official statistics, Jalisco's electronics

portant that, according to official statistics, Jalisco's electronics exports in 1999 (US$9.33 billion) exceeded the value of national crude petroleum (US$8.86 billion).[18]

This process was the result of several factors. Restructured industrial concerns already established in the Guadalajara area, such as Kodak, IBM, Hewlett-Packard, and Siemens, or new ones like Marvill Electronics, NEC, and Quest Systems[19] availed themselves of incentives that NAFTA offered. With the help and encouragement of the new PAN administration, which had entered office in a context of severe unemployment, these companies succeeded in relocating many of their suppliers from Asia (then in crisis) and the United States and increasing their companies' use of just-in-time (JIT) systems to raise productivity.[20] Several assembly firms transformed into manufacturers. Thus an industrial structure was generated by original equipment manufacturers (OEMs) who ordered parts from contract electronics manufacturers (CEMs), who were supplied, in turn, by specialized suppliers (SSs).[21] In addition, there are suppliers of raw materials. An important portion of this group of some 125 companies with around 45,000 workers operates as a network and is located in Guadalajara and surrounding areas.

There has been a remarkable boom in capital investment in Jalisco since 1995, peaking in 1997. Between 1995 and 2000, there was an overall direct investment of slightly over $5.62 billion. Of this total sum, 52 percent was foreign investment, 38 percent domestic, and the remainder joint foreign and domestic. The importance of U.S. investment is considerable, representing 42 percent of the total, though this percentage is less than at the national level. European investment from Germany, Great Britain, Spain, and Switzerland is also of great importance. There is Asian investment from Singapore, Japan, Taiwan, and China. Canada has also been a significant source of investment capital. The sectors receiving the largest investments are electronics and telecommunications (38.8 percent of the total), restaurants and hotels (13.3 percent, mainly in Puerto Vallarta and Guadalajara), services in telecommunications (9.8 percent), foods and beverages (8.9 percent), automotive and parts (3.4 percent), educational services (3.4 percent), and textiles and clothing (3 percent).

Capital spending data reveal how Jalisco's transformation was associated with increased export orientation. Sectors linked to exports included tourism (hotels and food services), the industrial sector producing both for domestic consumption and for export, and finally, but possibly the biggest, investment in maquiladora plants. Traditional sectors such as foods and beverages, together with textile and clothing industries, also grew, but activities oriented to intermediate consumption and capital goods, such as electronics and telecommunications, and the automotive and parts industries, were key growth sectors.

POPULATION AND JOBS

The population of the Guadalajara Metropolitan Zone (which includes the municipalities of Guadalajara, Zapopan, Tlaquepaque, and Tonalá) amounted, in the year 2000, to 3,461,540 inhabitants, representing 54.8 percent of Jalisco's 6,321,278 inhabitants. The lure of Guadalajara appears to have fallen off somewhat in recent years, however, and the state's annual rate of demographic growth has also fallen (by decades, it was 3.4 percent in 1950–1960, 3.2 percent in 1960–1970, 2.8 percent in 1970–1980, 2.0 percent in 1980–1990, and 1.8 percent in 1990–2000, similar to the overall national rate). Between 1990 and 1995, population growth in the municipality of Guadalajara was almost zero (average annual inter-census growth rate of 0.2 percent); the remaining three municipalities of the Metropolitan Zone did, however, experience rapid growth: Zapopan, 4.7 percent; Tlaquepaque, 5.1 percent; and Tonalá, 8.8 percent. This means that the locus of growth in the Metropolitan Zone has shifted from the center to the periphery, where fewer restrictions exist on economic and demographic expansion.

Nearly all investments in the electronics industry are situated in this peripheral zone, while those in the clothing industry have moved out to small towns and villages and even to rural areas. Some clothing maquiladoras that were poised to set up in Jalisco ultimately decided to locate in Honduras or the Dominican Republic. The location strategy of the electronics industry oriented toward informatics is highly complex; in the case of Guadalajara, it responds to a number of factors, including the higher wage levels prevailing in Mexico's northern border region. It would be unwise to overlook these differentials. Executives associated with the electronics industry acknowledge that the boom in investments since 1995 is closely linked to the financial crisis, peso devaluation, and cheapening of labor costs. Nonetheless, the dynamism of the new investments has brought almost full employment to Guadalajara, so that for the first time in living memory, companies have placed advertisements as a means of attracting workers. The recent slowdown in the growth of the U.S. economy has, however, had marked repercussions on Jalisco's exporting sectors. In contrast to the approximately 60,000 new jobs that were being generated annually in

Jalisco, the first four months of 2001 saw a loss of 20,000 jobs. Nevertheless, demand for labor remains strong, and this has induced electronics industries and other local enterprises to hire transportation services to bring in workers daily[22] from villages and towns in the central and southern portions of the state, at distances of up to 150 kilometers. This seems paradoxical if we consider the large number of people working in Guadalajara's informal sector. In the opinion of some local government officials and maquiladora administrators, many people who work in the informal sector are not prepared to accept the discipline, intensity, and modest wages found in the electronics sector, preferring the independence and higher incomes available through self-employment. By February 2001, the daily wage for unskilled workers directly involved in production processes was between 70 and 90 pesos (US$7.50–$9.50) plus benefits (themselves equivalent to about 40 percent of the basic wage).[23] At the same time, wages in Monterrey ranged between 100 and 120 pesos, and in Tijuana, between 150 and 200 pesos.

An important aspect in these firms is worker turnover. Although very high by local standards, turnover in Guadalajara is only about half what it is on the northern border—where historically it has remained around 10 percent per month.[24] The Staff Turnover Index for the electronics industry in Jalisco averages 5 percent a month. However, the numbers vary depending on the type of personnel, the season, and the kind of industry. Direct personnel (staff directly involved in productive processes, such as factory workers, technicians, and engineers) have a monthly turnover rate of 6.6 percent, while indirect personnel (those not involved in production, such as administrative or desk staff) show a turnover rate of only 3.5 percent.

There are a number of clear differences between industries in Guadalajara and those on the northern border. Even though foreign investment is important in Guadalajara, particularly with respect to the export sector, domestic investment still predominates. With regard to human resources, Guadalajara firms register much lower rates of staff turnover, and they also have a lower proportion of migrants and, probably, a better-educated and higher-skilled workforce (according to administrative staff at maquiladoras that have plants in both Guadalajara and the border zone). Many Guadalajara electronics firms have their own engineering and technology development departments. At Hewlett-Packard, for example, research and development is carried out by Mexican engineers. Another difference is that logistics channels have been developed in Guadalajara, where companies send merchan-

dise directly to clients, something that does not occur on the border.
There is also a perception that processes are less complex in the border zone and that workers in Jalisco have a stronger sense of regional
identity, which translates into a stronger identification with their work.
And, although they lack border workers' access to employment alternatives in the United States, workers in Guadalajara have greater access
to higher education.

Another assumption that merits examination is that border maquiladoras provide fewer benefits—such as health insurance, paid vaca-
tion, and Christmas bonuses—than electronics firms in Guadalajara. A
further difference involves training; in Guadalajara it is mandatory that
each worker receive between twenty-five and forty hours of training
per annum, conducted during working hours and helping employees
qualify for bonuses or promotion.[25] It should also be remembered that
the basic benefits packages in Guadalajara maquiladoras lack the relative homogeneity seen across different sectors and cities on Mexico's
northern border.[26] It appears that large, capital-intensive companies—
"second-generation" maquiladoras—are making increased, though se-
lective, use of beefed-up benefits packages as an important inducement
for retaining some kinds of qualified workers. By contrast, "first-
generation" firms located in smaller cities and towns in central and
western Mexico appear to be offering only the benefits required by law.

Since the implementation of NAFTA in 1994, many electronics
firms in Guadalajara, both maquiladoras and non-maquiladoras, have
been contracting temporary workers through other companies, both
foreign and domestic. Some firms satisfy nearly 50 percent of their
staff requirements through this method, which also enables large companies to minimize their legal commitments to employees, diminish
labor union pressures, and reduce benefits, although they are required
to meet basic wage and benefit levels. There are also set minimum
contributions that employers pay to the Mexican Social Security Institute (IMSS, the national health insurance administrator) for these temporary workers. Likewise, under this system of "staff rental," companies avoid the legal obligation to train personnel, and firms sidestep the
distribution of dividends specified by law.[27] And finally, because the
"boss" is a third party, and not the firm where staff actually work,
workers' identification with the firm is also lessened. The use of external contracts has become common, in both maquiladoras and other
companies, for services such as cleaning, security, meal service, and
staff and freight transportation, but it has not been extended to that
portion of the workforce involved directly in the production process.

Domestic sourcing of inputs to Guadalajara electronics firms is still very low, nearly as low as it is for the country as a whole. It has been possible to develop domestic suppliers in only two areas: materials for packaging and for plastic injection molding. Notwithstanding, a very wide range of the services alluded to above have been subcontracted. Also, many new sources of employment have appeared at higher levels; these include, for example, openings for advisers on legal, fiscal, and foreign trade matters. Notably, between 1995 and 2000, nearly 50,000 new technical and professional jobs were created within the service sector.

On the positive side, new firms have introduced a new culture of work. They have raised product quality; promoted teamwork, order, ability to work under pressure, and cleanliness; and developed links with technical institutes and institutions of higher learning that now offer curricula that meet firms' needs and incorporate hands-on workplace experience. One negative effect is Guadalajara's soaring living costs, especially housing costs, which have risen nearly 20 percent in the last five years. In a context where firms operate three shifts a day, seven days a week, it is also likely that crime and insecurity may increase.

These transformations in Guadalajara and elsewhere in Jalisco affect the structure of employment and wages. For example, managerial and executive personnel at large local companies assert that foreign investments are causing labor scarcity and a "distortion" of wages and salaries, leading to pay levels that local firms cannot afford. In particular, they mention the shortage of traditional tradesmen such as welders, carpenters, and plumbers. Some businessmen would like to call a halt to foreign investment. As they put it: "We've had enough of this foreign money; they'll end up buying us all out." This view is shared by middle-class households who note that it is becoming more difficult to find domestic help because everyone is working in the maquiladoras.

CHANGES IN EMPLOYMENT AND INCOME STRUCTURES

The 1994–1995 financial crisis adversely affected many companies, such as the midsize and large firms that had made substantial capital expenditures. However, the ensuing peso devaluation gave a boost to labor-intensive industrial sectors, both local and foreign-owned, and it set off the sharp upturn in employment. NAFTA itself significantly improved the confidence of many businessmen who, during the previous ten years, had begun to doubt the benefits of an open economy. The implementation of NAFTA brought about a change in regional businessmen. They became interested in training. Credit shortages compelled them to keep their firms financially healthy (a common adage in the past was that firms were poor but their owners were rich). They began to look for applicable new technology and struggled to find ways of networking. Likewise, losing their fear of exporting, they began to incorporate exports into their business plans and to acquire a more international culture.

Nearly 400,000 new jobs were created in Jalisco between 1994 and the end of 2000 (see figure 5.1). This brought about a progressive reduction in the open unemployment rate of the Guadalajara Metropolitan Zone from 6.4 percent in 1995 to 5.0 percent in 1997 and 1.9 percent in 2000.[28]

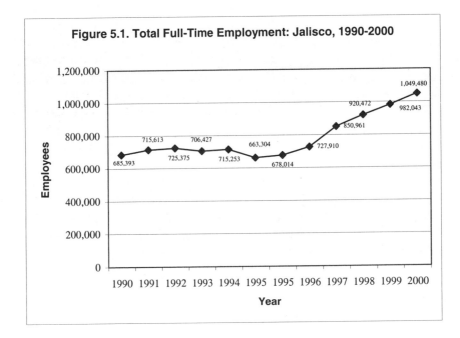

Figure 5.1. Total Full-Time Employment: Jalisco, 1990-2000

Job creation has been highly differentiated by sector. The largest number of jobs was created in manufacturing (136,055)—mainly in electronics, followed by clothing and transportation equipment (automotive sector)—that is, in sectors connected with the maquiladora industry, which absorbed some of the workers shed by firms as a result of the crisis. Yet employment growth was also significant in industries such as foodstuffs, furniture (which has shown an upturn), rubber and plastics (suppliers to the electrical and motor industries), and metal products. Even sectors badly hit by liberalization were able to grow, albeit at a slower rate; such sectors include footwear and apparel, the latter becoming a subcontractor to U.S.-based firms.

The service sector created just under 95,000 jobs. In this sector, overall expansion took place despite job loss in the financial and insurance subsector, which suffered a severe crisis and restructuring (this was the only subsector that reduced its personnel in absolute terms). In contrast, an impressive expansion took place in professional and technical services, which created almost 50,000 new jobs between 1995 and 2000. The growth in professional and technical services is undoubtedly related to the export growth that drove economic activity in Jalisco.

The building industry, which provides a highly sensitive gauge of the general performance of the regional economy, ranked third in job growth (54,585). Industrial construction accounted for much of this growth. Commerce generated some 50,000 jobs. The principal sources of employment growth in this sector were firms buying and selling food and beverages, articles of clothing, and raw materials. Lesser employment growth occurred in seasonal rural employment (16,686), transport and communications (12,966), agriculture (7,265), electrical and water services (1,368), mining and quarrying (428), and other groups (7,870).

Turning to income, the 1994–1995 financial crisis had a very deleterious impact in Jalisco. If we examine the changes that took place between 1994 and 2000 in Guadalajara, we notice that two social sectors were particularly affected. The first was the extremely poor population, which received an income below a single minimum wage. This sector, which in 1994 represented 6.7 percent of the population, grew to 12.4 percent in 1996. The relative size of this population began to decrease in 1998, falling to 7.8 percent (yearly average) in 2000. The other badly affected sector comprised workers receiving incomes equivalent to between two and five minimum wages, a stratum including wage earners in the modern sector. It represented 38.1 percent of the employed population in 1994, fell to 27.8 percent in 1997, then rose to 42 percent of the employed population in 2000.

THE FUTURE OF REGIONAL INDUSTRY

The local industry that previously produced consumer goods for the regional and national markets needs to undergo a profound transformation in several directions if it is to develop and survive. In the case of management, the preparation of businessmen (who are generally self-taught) needs to be professionalized—in the senses both of separating ownership from management and of strengthening managerial qualifications. Employees require upgrading as well, including the knowledge of how to apply management information systems. In the new competition, knowledge counts for much more than low labor rates. In the open market, making and implementing decisions requires a continuous analysis of changing conditions and events at local, national, and world levels, based on reliable information. Such information needs to address a broad range of issues, from strictly economic and commercial factors (competitors, suppliers, customers) to technological considerations (new technologies, processes, or products) and human resources. In other words, profound change is necessary in the fields of business organization, leadership and administration, technology, and staff training. Businessmen and businesses require radical transformation in order to make a virtue out of necessity.

Small-scale industry, the basis of the whole model of regional industrial development, needs to become more dynamic, with capacity for orientation toward flexible specialization. One of this region's advantages over other parts of Mexico is a broad base of workers and technicians with a certain degree of training. This situation evolved through several decades of experience in the formal educational system and in the world of work itself. This labor force needs to incorporate the new knowledge and skills of a globalized economy. If products from Jalisco are to compete in their own territory—and, even more so, in the export market—the challenge is to improve quality and add value.

CONCLUSIONS

Changes at global and national levels over the last ten years have had a profound impact on economics and politics in Jalisco. The crisis of the early 1980s (with a protected market) had fewer negative effects than in other regions of the country because of the diversification of the local economy—with its productive industrial base constituted by small companies producing for the national market—and the cushion provided by the financial resources emanating from the drugs trade. From the late 1980s onward, the economic situation worsened, however, when the economic opening to international trade widened.

Many Asian products flooded in, to the detriment of both small- and large-scale industries in the region.

During the first half of the 1990s, difficulties increased when the regional political regime failed to address growing threats of public insecurity and political violence, creating problems that were exacerbated by conflicts within the regional economic elite and with the national political leadership. The 1994–1995 financial crisis accelerated economic deterioration and highlighted the lack of political legitimacy. The PAN was able to capitalize on this situation, winning the 1995 elections for the state government, gaining a majority in the local legislature and some representation in the federal chambers, and capturing the state's principal municipalities.

The new administration gave a fresh orientation to the regional development model by addressing high unemployment and responding to the challenges and opportunities derived from the opening of the economy and membership in NAFTA. It created, in collaboration with private business and foreign corporations, an institutional fabric for promoting development. It succeeded in forming a coalition with new allies who were key elements in this scenario. These included local businessmen and, even more important, foreign investors attracted by the opportunities inherent in the changed world and regional contexts—economic distress in Mexico resulting in devaluation, unemployment, and hence cheaper relative costs; the Asian crisis; and the incentives offered by NAFTA and pro-entrepreneurial administrations at national and local levels. Thus large-scale investments began to arrive from abroad, directed in particular toward the electronics industry, both maquiladora and otherwise. These circumstances facilitated a strong recovery in employment (nearly 60,000 jobs a year) and a moderate improvement in wages. The global, national, and regional contexts made it possible for multinational companies and local actors to participate in the development of a cluster of established firms in the electronics industry oriented toward high-technology informatics. Part of this cluster—consisting of original equipment manufacturers, contract electronics manufacturers, and specialized suppliers—involves a high degree of technological content and, taken as a whole, has been the most, though not the only, successful sector in the NAFTA context.

Aside from its specialization in high-technology electronics, the industrial process in Guadalajara shows several important differences from the northern border region. First, Guadalajara is less dependent on migrant workers. This means that the labor force is better skilled and educated and turnover is lower, not because wages are better but, on the contrary, because of considerations such as the scarcity of viable alternatives. Second, the system of technical and higher education is more extensive in Guadalajara, and more of the jobs available have a high-technology profile. This city does, however, share with the north a low level of productive linkages within the regional economy and a sharp differentiation between highly qualified and unskilled personnel. Productive restructuring in response to economic and political change led to an abrupt fall-off in employment but also to a rapid recovery. Between 1995 and 2000, nearly 400,000 new jobs were generated, mainly in manufacturing (electronics, clothing, and automotive industries linked to the maquiladora sector, but also foodstuffs, furniture, rubber and plastics, and metal products). Services were second in job growth thanks to the impressive volume of employment generated for technicians and professionals linked to the exporting sector (50,000 in the 1995–2000 period), which more than compensated for the severe adjustment imposed by the financial subsector—the only component of services that did not grow during the period. The building industry and commerce were the other two sectors creating significant numbers of jobs.

The 1994–1995 financial crisis brought about a steep fall in employees' incomes. In Guadalajara the proportion of workers receiving lower incomes increased, while that of middle-income workers declined. During the subsequent years of employment expansion, however, a recovery took place at both levels, especially at the middle income range.

Leaving aside the dynamic sector formed by the large foreign exporting companies and some domestic midsize and large firms that have successfully reconverted, Jalisco's economy still faces a serious challenge. Its specialty has been the production of end-consumer goods for the regional and national markets, including farm products such as cereals (maize), sugarcane, cattle for dairy and meat production, hogs, poultry, and eggs. All these sectors display high production costs and low productivity and, therefore, are highly sensitive to the opening of the economy and to NAFTA. The industrial sector in Jalisco grew under the protection of the import-substitution model for production of traditional end-consumer goods such as foodstuffs, beverages, leather goods and footwear, textiles, and clothing. It underwent a substantial restructuring in the 1980s and 1990s and has probably touched bottom. Nevertheless, severe problems can still be glimpsed on the horizon. Regional businessmen need to undertake thoroughgoing changes in order to adapt their firms to the new environment and draw full advantage from NAFTA.

The fundamental challenge is to ensure that the new dynamism—which has been evident in specific sectors and regions of Jalisco since the 1995 financial crisis, the ensuring devaluation, and the implementation of NAFTA—can be extended to the entire state economy and to society as a whole.

Notes

1. Jorge Alonso, *El cambio en Jalisco: las elecciones de 1994 y 1995* (Guadalajara: Centro Universitario de Ciencias Sociales y Humanidades, Universidad de Guadalajara, 1995).

2. Ricardo Tirado and Matilde Luna, "La politización de los empresarios mexicanos (1970–1982)," in *Grupos económicos y organizaciones empresariales en México*, ed. Julio Labastida (Mexico City: Alianza Editorial Mexicana/UNAM, 1986); and Francisco Valdés Ugalde, *Autonomía y legitimidad: los empresarios, la política y el estado en México* (Mexico City: Siglo Veintiuno, 1997).

3. Fernando M. González and Carlos Alba, *Cúpulas empresariales y poderes regionales en Jalisco* (Guadalajara: Universidad de Guadalajara, 1989).

4. SEPROE (Secretaría de Promoción Económica), "Evolución en el modelo de desarrollo económico" (Guadalajara, February 2001), p. 12.

5. The incentives offered are: temporary 2 percent reduction in payroll tax, access to land that is under the control of the state or municipalities, support for land purchases (outside the GMZ), personnel training at both technical and professional levels, and infrastructure construction. The first PAN administration (1995–2000) allocated nearly 165 million pesos to promote investment by national and foreign companies. The bulk of these resources went to developing infrastructure (electricity, water, highway construction, fiber optics, and so on) in municipalities outside the Guadalajara Metropolitan Zone. The incentives offered to companies in Guadalajara mainly involved training the workforce employed at the technical level and above. Although most of the resources were devoted to Guadalajara in the first years, a balance was later maintained with the other municipalities. Seventy percent of the resources went to micro, small, and midsize firms, and the remaining 30 percent went to large companies.

6. The industrial parks currently in operation are Vallarta, Ferrán, Electronic Technologic "Flextronics," Ecopark Technology and Business Park, El Salto, San Jorge, Guadalajara, El Bosque 1, El Bosque 2, Parque Industrial Tecnológico, San Agustín, the Southern Industrial Zone, El Álamo, Los Belenes, Eastern Industrial Zones 1 and 2, and Zapopan North.

7. The industrial parks under construction are San Ángel, CIMEG, and La Azucena.

8. The projected industrial parks are Guadalajara Technology Park, El Tigre Industrial Park, and Equus Industrial Park.

9. The industrial parks in the municipalities outside the Guadalajara Metropolitan Zone are the following: (in operation) Arandas Santa María, San Miguel El Alto, Villa Hidalgo, Yahualica, Lagos de Moreno, Ciudad Guzmán, Zapotlán 2000; (under construction) Zapotlanejo, Kin Wei (Tala), Ocotlán (San Andrés), La Barca, San Diego de Alejandría; (projected) Acatlán de Juárez, Ameca, Ocotlán (AFAMO), and Zapotlanejo (Careintra).

10. Interview with Emigdio Franco Preciado, general manager of the National Chamber of the Electronics, Telecommunications, and Informatics Industry (CANIETI), August 2001.

11. The principal arguments used by the government of Jalisco in support of the region's competitive advantages are: lower turnover rate than that for the border area; abundant and trainable workforce (the country's second most important center as regards education); well-established support services; access to NAFTA countries and other markets; industrial clustering (Mexico's "Silicon Valley"); an international airport with daily air freight services; bonded warehouses; supplier base; a quality of life among the highest in Mexico; industrial parks and buildings; supportive government; one-stop processing; incentive packages; shopping centers and sports clubs; and hospitals of the first rank. Likewise, the government lays stress on Jalisco's strategic location, noting that over 50 percent of Mexico's population is situated within a radius of 563 kilometers (350 miles) of Guadalajara. Although the government does not say so, investors are well aware that in Jalisco labor costs are some 20 percent lower than those on the northern border. Nonetheless, the scenario for making comparisons is by no means limited by national frontiers. Nowadays, Guadalajara compares itself not so much with Monterrey as with Singapore and other Asian cities.

The government also offers a list of the principal high-profit production areas available for investment: acoustics, power adapters, antennas, antistatics, wires and harnesses, electronic components, connectors, clean rooms, packaging, tooling, plastic injection, rubber parts, metal parts, PCBs, semiconductors, switches, LCD monitors, microchips, sheet metal stamping, and logistics.

12. Manuel Castells, *The Rise of the Network Society* (Malden, Mass.: Blackwell, 1996).

13. Interview with Marco Gordillo and Federico G. Lepe (public relations manager), Hewlett-Packard, February 2001.

14. CANIETI-Jalisco, *Propuestas para la nueva administración del gobierno federal* (Mexico, November 2000, p. 4).

15. Óscar Contreras, *Empresas globales, actores locales: producción flexible y aprendizaje industrial en las maquiladoras* (Mexico City: El Colegio de México, 2000).

16. The problem consists in the fact that many of the maquiladoras use inputs of Asian origin that cannot be produced in the United States or Mexico at the same cost or to the same quality. Importing them from Asia, however, would entail a cost in tariffs of between 5 and 15 percent.

17. Interview with Alfonso Alva Rosano, director of manufacturing and technology programs at IMB México, August 2001.

18. SEPROE, "Evolución en el modelo de desarrollo económico," p. 11.

19. Besides these companies, the following are also present: LTCP de México, Vtech Communications, BTC, Xerox, Telec, GPI Mexicana de Alta Tecnología, Resser, ATR, Advantra, Marvill Electronics, and Computadoras Garco.

20. The most important companies in this group are: SCI Systems, Flextronics, Solectron, Jabil Circuit, Natsteel, Pemstar, Omni Electronics, Micro Technologies International, Benchmark, Copuworld, Mexikor, Pentex, Universal Scientific Industrial, Radio Servicio Espacial, and Manelec.

21. The main ones are: On Semiconductor, H&T Technologies, Interplexico, Laser Stencil, Micron Engineering, Tecnologías Acumen, Tral, Multek, Alta Calidad en Inyección, DTM Products, High Precision Moulding, Kemex, Trend Technologies, Triquest, Yamaver, Puget Plastic, KRS International, Lo Dan West, Ureblock, SPM Dynacast, Competitive Manufacturing, Grupo Ferrau, Peosa, CIMME, Redwood Systems, Usco Santander, Maquiser Industrial, Acoustic Control, Estatec, Grupo Gollet, JPM Pantera, Molex, Clare Remtech, Coilcraft Electrónica, and Cherokee Electrónica.

22. This involves approximately 15 percent of workers, according to Ernesto Íñiguez González, chairman of the Western Mexico Maquiladora Industry Chamber (Asociación de la Industria Maquiladora de Occidente); interview, February 2001. A similar situation can be seen in Aguascalientes.

23. Interview with Hanón Quijas, head of the Jalisco government's Department of Labor, February 2001.

24. CADELEC/SEIJAL, "Rotación de personal en la industria electrónica de Jalisco" (Guadalajara, 2000).

25. Interview with Ernesto Íñiguez González, April 2001.

26. Contreras, *Empresas globales, actores locales.*

27. Interview with Jorge Guevara Rubio, Conciliation and Arbitration Board, February 2001.

28. Open unemployment rate in the Guadalajara Metropolitan Zone (1994–2000), in *Indicadores Económicos de Jalisco*, vol. 6; Secretaría de Promoción Económica/SEIJAL, based on data provided by the Instituto Nacional de Estadística, Geografía e Informática (INEGI); Dirección de Estadísticas, Gobierno de Jalisco, 2001, p. 37.

6

Different States, Similar Responses: California, Texas, and NAFTA

James B. Gerber

California and Texas are the two most populous states in the United States. Given their size, their common borders with Mexico, and the fact that both states are more export oriented than the national average, it is not surprising that they collectively account for nearly 35 percent of U.S. merchandise exports to Mexico. Locational factors also help explain their relatively smaller share of U.S.-Canada trade, although Canada is the second most important market for both states, and in the case of California, the dollar value actually exceeded trade with Mexico in 2000 (Japan is California's largest market).

The purpose of this chapter is to explain the impact of North American Free Trade Agreement (NAFTA) on the state economies of California and Texas and, in particular, to show how they used the increasing openness of the world economy to their advantage. NAFTA represented one major element of the new openness both states confronted; it came into being approximately simultaneously with the ratification of the Uruguay Round, the creation of the Single Market in Western Europe, and the collapse of communism, which opened Central and Eastern Europe to world commerce.

After a period of crisis and restructuring in the 1980s and early 1990s, both states were ready for a global market. In Texas, the crisis of the 1980s was severe. The sudden decline in oil prices in 1982, following a decade of price hikes and predictions of further increases as far into the future as anyone could see, was a dramatic shock to the state economy, yet one that ultimately led to greater diversification and a stronger manufacturing base. California experienced a milder shock in the early 1980s, when its semiconductor memory chip manufacturers lost out to more efficient, high-volume Japanese producers and Silicon Valley teetered on the edge of technological obsolescence.[1] The challenge of foreign competition hit the state's private technology sector hard, in much the same way that it hit the rest of the nation's auto, steel, shipbuilding, and consumer electronics industries.

These technological challenges were compounded by the overvalued dollar of the mid-1980s and a flood of imports into U.S. domestic markets. In 1985, the Plaza Agreement among the G-7 nations was implemented to bring down the value of the U.S. dollar, followed in 1986 by the opening of negotiations between the United States and Canada to form a free trade area, and Mexico's joining of the General Agreement on Tariffs and Trade (GATT). It was becoming increasingly harder to ignore the global market.

By the time of the U.S. recession of 1990–1991, the Texas economy was prepared to enter global markets with goods other than oil and cattle and, in particular, to take advantage of Mexico's recovery and growing U.S.-Mexico economic ties. In California's case, the national recession of 1990–1991 lingered until 1994, as the end of the Cold War and the downsizing of the aerospace industry coincided with the bursting of a statewide real estate bubble and the collapse of a number of financial institutions. Ultimately, foreign markets proved crucial to the state's strong recovery after 1994.

The next section of this chapter looks at state-level per capita income over the last two decades and provides background information on the sectoral changes that have accompanied the long-run trends. This is followed by a discussion of the role of trade and the changing international environment, both of which have been significantly positive developments. After the discussion of income and trade, two lingering NAFTA problems—migration and trucking—are examined in demographic and political context. History, geography, and politics make NAFTA more than a simple economic arrangement, and it is not surprising, then, that the agreement has created opportunities but also posed challenges for both states. Trucking and migration illustrate how individual states struggle to shift the burden and benefits of U.S. international commitments.

INCOME AND POPULATION

California is the most populous state in the nation, and Texas ranks second. Table 6.1 shows population and income in 2000.[2] California's

2000 census count of nearly 34 million is about 62 percent larger than Texas's population of just under 21 million. The large populations of these states lend credence to the belief that each is a world unto itself, a belief reinforced by state income levels. Total personal income in California is nearly US$1.1 trillion, or about one-eighth (13 percent) of the nation's and not far behind that of Italy or the United Kingdom. Both states would be moderately large by world standards if they were independent nations.[3]

Table 6.1. Population and Income, 2000

	California	Texas
Population	33,871,648	20,851,820
Percent of U.S.	12.0	7.4
Personal income (billions US$)	1,093.2	581.2
Percent of U.S.	13.1	7.0

Sources: U.S. Bureau of Economic Analysis; U.S. Census Bureau.

Figure 6.1 illustrates the trend in each state's per capita personal income since 1970. Income is measured as a share of the U.S. average, and a value of 100 indicates that the state's income is equal to the national average. Figure 6.1 is divided into three periods: (1) the oil boom of the 1970s and early 1980s, (2) the oil collapse and adjustment, 1982–1990, and (3) recession and global expansion, 1990–1999.

Throughout the period 1970–1982, California's income was about 15 percent higher than national income and showed no trend up or down. By contrast, Texas's income was about 90 percent of the U.S. average in 1970, but that decade's oil boom caused incomes to converge to the national average by the end of the period. This was followed by the oil price collapse in 1982, a deteriorating Texas real estate market, and declines in the construction and financial sectors which spread recession through the state economy. The period of decline lasted until 1989, by which time Texas's per capita income was slightly less than 90 percent of the U.S. level.

California's story during the 1980s was one of continual convergence toward U.S. per capita income levels. Because wages and salaries make up the largest component of income, their relatively slower growth in real terms was responsible for most of the observed convergence.[4] The trend toward convergence with average U.S. values is weak through the 1980s, but it strengthens during the third period with the

onset of the 1990–1991 recession. The simultaneous beginning of a
national recession—together with layoffs in California's aerospace industry and the closing of a number of military bases at the end of the
Cold War—were contractionary economic events, and they were reinforced by the impact of a bursting real estate bubble and the collapse
of a number of financial institutions. As a consequence, the national
recession of 1990–1991 lasted until 1994 in California. By 1994, with
the onset of NAFTA, a much more robust, diversified, and globally
competitive economy had emerged, thanks in no small degree to the
development of information technologies and Silicon Valley's reemer-
gence as a world center of technology and innovation.

**Figure 6.1. Percent of Average U.S. Per Capita
Personal Income, 1970-1999**

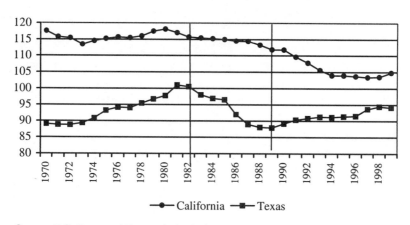

Source: U.S. Bureau of Economic Analysis.

The common thread in the experiences of the two states is that
both were severely affected by world events that originated outside the
United States. For Texas, as in the case of Mexico and the Canadian
province of Alberta, it was the collapse of oil prices and the deep recession that ensued. California's greatest challenge came somewhat
later, with the collapse of communism and the end of the Cold War
military budgets, but in both states the crises led to positive economic
changes that enabled them to reinvent themselves in a more competitive, international context.

INTERNATIONAL TRADE AND STATE ECONOMIES

It is easy to spot the impact of international trade on the Texas economy in the 1990s. Table 6.2 shows the growth in real sectoral output during 1990–1999. Given that the restructuring of the Texas economy began in the 1980s, by the early 1990s it was farther along than California in making the changes necessary to restore growth. Over the course of the decade, not only has Texas outperformed California, but it has grown about 50 percent more than the overall U.S. average (52 percent versus 35 percent). Most notable is the growth in construction, manufacturing, transportation and utilities, and wholesale trade sectors. Three of these sectors—manufacturing, transportation and utilities, and wholesale trade—are directly related to international trade, while the fourth sector—construction—is indirectly related.

Table 6.2. Change in Real Gross Product, by Sector, 1990–1999

Industry	United States (%)	California (%)	Texas (%)
Total gross product	35	28	52
Agriculture, forestry, fish	27	41	52
Mining	15	27	8
Construction	24	-2	60
Manufacturing	39	61	69
Transportation and utilities	43	43	75
Wholesale trade	80	66	117
Retail trade	51	41	73
F.I.R.E.	35	15	42
Services	30	23	46
Government	9	1	20

Source: Bureau of Economic Analysis.

In both California and Texas, the growth of manufacturing output during the 1990s stands in marked contrast to its growth in the nation as a whole and to the growth of overall state product in both states. The California case is remarkable given its loss of aerospace industry jobs in the early 1990s, which resulted in a net loss of over 168,000 jobs in the manufacturing sector between 1990 and 1999.[5] While manufacturing jobs fell, manufacturing output rose, particularly after

1994. The state increased its specialization in the production of industrial machinery and electronic equipment and, especially, the new information technologies related to personal computers and peripheral equipment such as hard drives, printers, and memory devices. Much of this new, non-defense manufacturing was centered in Silicon Valley, but it also reflected the extremely large and diversified manufacturing base of the Los Angeles basin. A significant share of the production of parts and equipment for information technology was for the domestic U.S. market, but an ever-increasing amount was targeted on foreign markets, as San Jose joined Seattle and Detroit in a race to become the nation's largest metropolitan area exporter.[6]

The growth of manufacturing in Texas is equally remarkable and stands in marked contrast to California and the rest of the nation. While output rose in California and the nation (table 6.3), employment fell as productivity increases led to fewer workers producing more output. Nationally, 630,000 manufacturing jobs were lost between 1990 and 1999 (168,600 in California), while Texas gained 109,848 jobs. The increase in manufacturing jobs actually began a few years earlier, in 1987, and between that year and 1999 more than 166,000 manufacturing jobs were added to the state economy.[7]

The causes of this remarkable performance are varied and can be divided into state, national, and foreign elements. At the state level, Texas used its revenue from the 1970s oil boom to attract firms, particularly high-tech firms. The University of Texas at Austin played a role similar to the one played by Stanford University in building Silicon Valley, where land, industrial park infrastructure, and public-private partnerships came together to foster a growing information technology sector. The University of Texas was able to play this role as a result of its multi-billion-dollar endowment stemming from the discovery of oil on university land in 1923. Through the 1970s there was a stream of high-technology firms that grew up or moved to the Austin area, including Motorola, Texas Instruments, Lockheed, and Advanced Micro Devices. The migration continued through the 1980s with the Microelectronics and Computer Technology Corporation (MCC), 3M, and, in 1988, an important new private-public joint venture, Sematech.[8] The latter is a consortium that began with fourteen of the leading U.S.-based semiconductor firms and is half-funded by the U.S. government (originally, by the Defense Advanced Research Projects Administration) with an explicit mission to regain and maintain U.S. leadership in semiconductor design and manufacturing.[9]

Not all of the expansion in Texas's manufacturing throughout the 1990s was in high technology. In addition to electronic equipment, instruments, and industrial machinery, several relatively low-technology sectors experienced rapid growth. Among these were the building materials sector, leather products, and lumber and wood products. Building materials and lumber and wood products responded to a construction boom that continues to be fueled by the national movement of population toward the Sun Belt. Housing prices remain relatively modest in Texas by comparison to California, and the economy's robust job creation makes it a desirable place to live.

In addition to state policies and national demographic trends, international forces are important. In particular, an unknown share of the growth of manufacturing in Texas is related to the rapid industrial development of Mexico's northern border region. For example, three of the five cities that collectively contain more than 50 percent of the firms and workers in U.S.-origin Mexican *maquiladora* firms are directly on the border with Texas (Ciudad Juárez, Matamoros, and Reynosa).[10] Gordon Hanson estimates that growth in the border maquiladora has a positive impact on manufacturing employment in the adjacent U.S. border cities—despite well-publicized cases such as El Paso, which lost apparel assembly jobs to Ciudad Juárez.[11]

Although manufacturing is a beneficiary of Texas's proximity to Mexico, the growth of international trade—both of goods that originate in the state and of goods that pass through the state—has strongly positive effects on a number of other sectors. As noted in table 6.2, transportation and wholesale trade added jobs and income at a much more rapid pace than in the rest of the nation.

Trade Patterns

In 1993, California and Texas traded slightly more than the United States as a whole, relative to their total state product.[12] Table 6.3 shows measures of merchandise exports divided by gross state product or gross national product. Note also that the gap between the U.S. average and each state widened between 1993 and 1999, implying that trade grew in importance more rapidly at the state level than it did for the nation overall. In particular, exports from Texas grew very rapidly during the first six NAFTA years and by comparison to California and the nation.

NAFTA encouraged trade growth in both California and Texas, but in a very uneven manner. Table 6.4 shows the dollar value of each state's trade with its most important markets during the year 2000, along with a measure of the state's trade as a share of total U.S. trade with the selected markets. Canada, Mexico, and Japan are the top three markets for both states, although not in that order. In California, Japan is number one, followed by Canada and Mexico, and all three are of the same magnitude. In Texas, Mexico clearly dominates, followed by Canada (with less than half the value of Mexico) and Japan (with less than one-third the value of Canada). Texas trade is so focused on Mexico that its share of other major markets is well below its share of overall U.S. trade.

Table 6.3. Merchandise Trade as Share of Gross Product, 1999

	1993 (%)	1999 (%)	Difference
California	8.0	8.4	+0.4
Texas	7.8	9.0	+1.2
United States	7.1	7.4	+0.3

Sources: U.S. Bureau of Economic Analysis; U.S. International Trade Administration.

Table 6.4. Trade Patterns: California and Texas, 2000

	California		Texas	
Merchandise exports to:	*Millions US$*	*% of U.S. trade*	*Millions US$*	*% of U.S. trade*
World	129,939	16.6	68,746	8.8
Top 3 markets				
Canada	15,162	8.4	10,461	5.9
Mexico	14,404	12.9	24,623	22.0
Japan	17,976	27.5	2,938	4.5
Other leading markets				
China	3,620	22.3	1,124	6.9
European Union	28,492	17.3	7,233	4.4
Korea	9,238	33.1	2,076	7.4
Taiwan	9,360	38.4	1,934	7.9

Source: U.S. International Trade Administration.

California, by contrast, is more oriented toward the Pacific Basin, with a disproportionately large share of total U.S. trade in that region.[13] The state's Pacific orientation is not a new phenomenon. From the earliest years of the American period in California, trade and immigration were disproportionately oriented toward Pacific Basin countries, including Australia, China, South America, and Japan.[14]

The sectoral composition of California and Texas trade with Canada and Mexico is easy to summarize. Table 6.5 shows the top three exporting sectors. Number one in every category, reflecting the competitiveness of both states in information technology, is computers and electronic products. In every one of the four cases (California to Mexico, Texas to Mexico, California to Canada, Texas to Canada), the second most important item is less than one-half the value of the number one, computers and electronic products. Given the high levels of research and development in each state, together with the regional agglomerations of high-technology firms, the importance of computers and electronic products is not surprising. In the number two and three items in each case, exports reflect natural resource endowments (agriculture, petroleum), the rationalization and integration of the automotive industries in all three countries (transportation equipment), and capital-intensive production (chemicals, machinery).

NAFTA: THE CONFLUENCE OF POLITICS AND ECONOMICS

NAFTA's status as an international agreement between three sovereign nations, together with the fact that commercial policy in the United States is exclusively a federal matter, implies that individual states are relatively impotent in their ability to change the terms of the agreement. Even large states such as California and Texas have a very limited range of actions they can take to try to influence specific provisions of the agreement. When states do take action, the rules of international relations require them to act through their national governments, and hence the perception of an uneven distribution of benefits and costs becomes a domestic dispute between subnational and national governments.

In addition to sharing over one-third of U.S.-Mexico merchandise trade, California and Texas also share the distinction of having some of the most intense conflicts between state and federal governments over NAFTA-related issues. To date, the two most contentious disputes have been over trucking and migration. These issues are not entirely parallel: migration is largely outside the formal agreement while trucking is specifically included, and migration issues cut deeper and are more difficult to resolve in a mutually satisfactory manner. Never-

Table 6.5. Top Three Exports from California and Texas to Canada and Mexico, 2000

Top Three Sectors	Share (%)	Top Three Sectors	Share (%)
California Exports to Canada		*Texas Exports to Canada*	
Computers and electronic products	50.1	Computers and electronic products	34.7
Transportation equipment	11.5	Transportation equipment	16.7
Crop production	5.3	Chemical manufactures	14.7
Total, top three	66.9	Total, top three	66.1
California Exports to Mexico		*Texas Exports to Mexico*	
Computers and electronic products	40.8	Computers and electronic products	24.3
Machinery manufactures	7.6	Petroleum and coal products	9.1
Transportation equipment	5.4	Chemical manufactures	8.5
Total, top three	53.8	Total, top three	41.9

Source: U.S. International Trade Administration.

theless, trucking and migration are alike in one respect—they are sources of conflict between states, which have no direct control over national policy, and the federal government, which has no formal requirement to provide resources for states to implement federal policies. Migration and trucking issues have boiled over in the public debate, largely as a result of California's and Texas's position that the federal government has not provided them with financial reimbursement for the state-level costs of the federal policies. Politics in the narrow sense also plays an important role.

Migration and Politics in California

The ratification of NAFTA in 1993 and its implementation in 1994 coincided with the heating up of gubernatorial politics in California. An unpopular governor, Pete Wilson, was fighting for his political life against the daughter of one of the state's leading political families. Kathleen Brown would have been the third member of her immediate family to serve as governor, after father Pat Brown and brother Jerry Brown. Wilson's first term was filled with a number of man-made and nature-caused disasters, and a year before the fall 1994 election it seemed unlikely he could win. The state had suffered a prolonged recession from 1990 to 1994, a drought in the agriculturally rich Central Valley, the collapse of the state's financial sector with the bursting of a real estate bubble, and the loss of a significant share of its high-tech defense industries with the end of the Cold War. These events all took their toll on state finances, and as governor, Wilson was forced to make deep cuts in order to achieve the constitutionally mandated balanced state budget. In political terms, he appeared extremely vulnerable.

Wilson's constant refrain throughout his first term was that the state's poor economic performance was a result of its unfriendly business climate. His criticism of the state's business climate went only so far, however, as it failed to explain the politically difficult problem of the unprecedented state budget deficit—$14 billion at the start of 1992. Wilson was handed an explanation for the budget deficits and, simultaneously, a path to electoral victory by the qualification of Proposition 187 for placement on the November 1994 ballot. Proposition 187 was a statewide initiative that, among other things, eliminated all public services for undocumented immigrants, including public education for immigrant children and medical services for those too poor to purchase private services. Proposition 187 enabled Wilson to harness frustration over the state's poor economic performance by presenting the public with two scapegoats—undocumented migrants who used services paid for by the state, and the federal government which allowed them to enter but which refused to reimburse the state for the cost of their education and other services.

In a fit of anger, the voters of California chose to ignore public problems such as illiteracy and tuberculosis, and voted in favor of Proposition 187. A court-ordered injunction delayed its implementation while its constitutionality was determined, and ultimately the courts threw it out. Nevertheless, it consumed much of the statewide civic debate during late 1993 and 1994, and it enabled an unpopular governor to polarize and divide the electorate in a successful bid for reelection.

The immediate consequences of Proposition 187 for California's relations with Mexico were dramatically negative but mostly symbolic. Mexicans were understandably offended by having been blamed for the state's economic problems, but there was little they could do to register their displeasure. Trade shows in Mexico City, organized by the state's commerce department, suddenly had no attendees, and Mexico blocked the state's bid to host such NAFTA institutions as the North American Development Bank (NADBank) or the Border Environment Cooperation Commission (BECC). At the local level, discussions between Mexico and San Diego County over the joint use of the airport in Tijuana were suddenly terminated. In the long run, however, businesspeople make deals where there are opportunities, regardless of what they think about their trading partner's government (witness U.S. firms wanting to go into Cuba and China), and the NAFTA institutions have minuscule economic development impacts where they locate.

Between 1990 and 1999, California received three out of every ten migrants to the United States. New York received the second greatest number but half as many as California.[15] There is little consensus among economists over the costs and benefits of undocumented immigration; as a consequence, much of the debate in California reflected previously held convictions which were reinforced by various interpretations of statistical analysis.[16] The one point of agreement, however, seems to be that "immigration studies reveal a distribution problem: the federal government gains net revenue, and the states lose it."[17]

In the case of California, the political struggle over the costs and benefits from immigration was intensified by an opportunistic politician, a prolonged economic downturn, and a highly visible concentration of immigrants. In one sense, it had nothing to do with NAFTA, but in another sense it raises concerns about the potential mischief that can result from NAFTA's failure to resolve the issue of migration. Recessions will come again, and opportunistic politicians are not in short supply. While it is true that NAFTA is not a common market allowing for the free movement of labor, as is the European Union, it is equally true that forces will continue to generate large numbers of migrants. Mexico's ongoing economic changes, the United States' desire for relatively inexpensive unskilled labor, the broad expanse of social networks among immigrants currently residing in California and elsewhere, and the large income differentials between Mexican and U.S. residents all guarantee a continued inflow of families and workers. Mexican emigration may be less with NAFTA than it would be without it, but that is far different than saying that the numbers are small.

Trucking in Texas

On the surface, the issue of trucking is light-years from the issue of immigration. Oddly enough, however, it ballooned into a front-page news story partly because of the conflict between a large state—Texas—and the federal government over the distribution of NAFTA-related costs and benefits.

Barry Prentice and Mark Ojah's chapter in this volume details the NAFTA institutional arrangements and trends in transportation. By 1995, each country's truckers were expected to have access to each other's border states, and by 2000, reciprocal nationwide access was required. The United States blocked implementation of the 1995 step on the basis that it believed Mexican trucks to be unsafe. Mexico appealed, and in February 2001 a NAFTA arbitration panel ruled that the United States was in violation of its NAFTA obligations, in response to which the U.S. president promised to open the U.S. market to Mexican trucks by January 2002.

Once again, the distribution of functional responsibilities between U.S. states and the federal government came into play. The U.S. system of trucking relies on state-level regulations and state-level enforcement of safety standards. In the case of Texas, the policy response of its government since the implementation of NAFTA has been to argue that it is a federal responsibility to ensure the safety of Mexican trucks carrying goods in Texas. Their reasoning is based on the simple observation that NAFTA is a federal agreement. Hence, if the cost of its implementation is shifted to the states, it constitutes an unfunded federal mandate and upsets the balance of powers between states and the federal government. This argument ignores the fact that federal involvement in regulation and inspection activities could potentially reduce state autonomy, but it is essentially the same argument made by the government of California in its dispute over immigration policy.

Table 6.6. Truck Crossings into the United States from Mexico

Port of Entry	Truck Crossings from Mexico, 1997 (%)	Out-of-Service Rate for Mexican Trucks, 2000[1] (%)
Texas	67	40
New Mexico	1	32
Arizona	10	40
California	22	26

Source: U.S. Department of Transportation, 2001.

[1] Out-of-service rate is the percent of trucks failing the Commercial Vehicle Safety Alliance's Level-1 inspection. The overall failure rate for U.S. trucks is 24 percent, although there is very wide state-level variation.

Most of the trucks entering the United States from Mexico do so by way of Texas. Table 6.6 shows the percentage of truck crossings into the United States from Mexico by state of entry, along with the state-specific safety inspection failure rates (called "out-of-service rates"). Two-thirds of Mexican trucks entering the United States cross in Texas, which also has the highest out-of-service rate. In a February 2001 report on the implementation of NAFTA's trucking provisions, the inspector general of the U.S. Department of Transportation noted, "A direct correlation exists between the condition of Mexican commercial trucks entering the United States and the level of inspection resources at the border."[18] California built two inspection stations at its two main border crossings (Otay Mesa in San Diego, and Calexico, next to Mexicali) and inspects every truck without the requisite Commercial Vehicle Safety Alliance sticker.[19] The out-of-service rate for Mexican trucks crossing in California is no different from the nationwide average of U.S.-based trucks.

Unlike the case of California and immigration, the mix of factors leading to Texas's resistance to hiring inspectors and building inspection stations does not include an embattled governor struggling to stay alive politically, but it does include the powerful Teamsters labor union and the politicians who depend on its support. And the role of the xenophobes in California that supported Proposition 187 is taken in Texas by conservatives who favor the rights of states over the federal government and who oppose federal measures that generate additional fiscal costs for states.

Is Federalism a Trade Barrier?

Many scholars have pointed out that as tariffs and quotas are eliminated, through either multilateral or regional agreements, domestic policies become more serious barriers, often unintentionally. Examples include national competition policies, labor market policies, and government procurement policies, among others. In the cases of trucking and immigration, it is not domestic U.S. policy per se that has the potential to stymie further integration, but rather the way that U.S. federalism distributes the costs and benefits of federal policies and the way it settles disputes among states over the resulting distribution. It is easy to believe that most commercial disputes, such as the one over trucking, will be settled, perhaps after an initial period of conflict. Immigration issues are more contentious, but even in this area the United States and Mexico have finally begun to discuss the issue. Federalism is a permanent feature of the U.S. political landscape, however, and it seems highly likely that the incentives for states to try to shift the costs and burdens of federal policies will not disappear. What the next issues might be is anyone's guess.[20]

CONCLUSION

Foreign trade has been both a bright spot and a source of conflict in the recent economic histories of California and Texas. Both engage in international trade relatively more than the United States as a whole, and foreign markets have been essential to the growth of their high-technology sectors which, in turn, have been important generators of wealth. Additionally, it seems likely that they have collectively received disproportionate shares of the benefits accruing to the United States from trade with Mexico. Texas's position next to Mexico and just south of the traditional U.S. industrial belt is a very favorable location. But California, as well as Texas, has been able to expand the export of information technology products and services. At the same time, Canada is the number two trading partner of both, and although each has a smaller share of U.S. exports to Canada than its share of overall U.S. trade, the absolute value of exports is large.

It is customary to think about economic policy reform in the context of Mexico and other Latin American economies or the transition economies of Central and Eastern Europe. Less obvious but critical to their growth, both California and Texas have turned toward outward-oriented economic strategies over the last fifteen years. Both states continue to foster their high-technology industries, and both created trade promotion agencies (the Office of International Business in Texas and the Technology, Commerce, and Trade Agency in California) which sponsor trade shows around the globe and maintain foreign offices to follow trade leads.

One of the key differences in their global activities is that, despite picking up a significant amount of trade with the United States' NAFTA partners, California's geographical location and industrial mix have supported the continuation of historical trade patterns heavily focused on Pacific Rim countries, including not only Canada and Mexico but also Japan and the rest of East Asia. By contrast, Texas's trade is primarily concentrated on Mexico and, to a lesser extent, Canada.

This chapter has not addressed the likely effects of an expanded hemispheric agreement or Free Trade Area of the Americas (FTAA). If such an expansion of an American trade area comes to pass, it is nonetheless easy to imagine that—given existing patterns of trade and preparedness for international competition—California and Texas will capture a significant share of the United States' gains from trade, just as they have under NAFTA.

Notes

1. Annalee Saxenian, *Regional Advantage: Culture and Competition in Silicon Valley and Route 128* (Cambridge, Mass.: Harvard University Press, 1996), pp. 2–4.

2. Note that income is measured as personal income. Personal income includes all forms of pretax income received by households, including wages and salaries, dividends, interest, rents, proprietor's income, and transfers.

3. This is not meant to imply that they should be analyzed as independent nations. The U.S. Constitution places trade policy in the hands of Congress, which implies that U.S. states lack one of the basic tools that independent nations use to engage the world economy. In addition, and perhaps too obvi-

ously, they also lack independent foreign, monetary, and exchange rate poli-cies, regardless of how large they might be. While obvious, it is a point that the economic boosters in both states seem often to forget.

4. G. Andrew Bernat, Jr., "Convergence in State Per Capita Personal In-come, 1950–99." *Survey of Current Business* 81, no. 6 (June 2001): 36–48.

5. U.S. Department of Commerce, "Regional Economic Information Sys-tem," at http://fisher.lib.virginia.edu/reis/ (July 2001).

6. San Jose was the leading U.S. metropolitan export area in 1996 and 1997. It was third behind Seattle and Detroit in 1998, and second behind Se-attle in 1999. Caution is warranted in interpreting metropolitan area export statistics given that the Department of Commerce's method for tabulating metropolitan area exports is not an accurate measure of the production of export goods. Nevertheless, the general point about the growth of production in San Jose and Silicon Valley is valid.

7. U.S. Department of Commerce, "Regional Economic Information."

8. Elizabeth Whitnew, "Austin a City of Big Plans, Empty Offices," *St. Petersburg Times*, July 3, 1988.

9. Laura D'Andrea Tyson, *Who's Bashing Whom? Trade Conflict in High-Technology Industries* (Washington, D.C.: Institute for International Economics, 1992).

10. The other two cities—Mexicali and Tijuana—are directly on the Cali-fornia border. See Solunet Info-Mex, Inc., *The Complete Twin Plant Guide* (El Paso, Tex.: Solunet Info-Mex, Inc., 2001).

11. Gordon H. Hanson, *U.S.-Mexico Integration and Regional Economies: Evidence from Border-City Pairs* (Cambridge, Mass.: National Bureau of Economic Research, 1996), and "The Effects of Offshore Assembly on Industry Loca-tion: Evidence from U.S. Border Cities," in *The Effects of U.S. Trade Protection and Promotion Policies*, ed. Robert C. Feenstra (Chicago: University of Chicago Press, 1997). Despite the loss of some apparel jobs, El Paso continues to have a larger nondurables manufacturing sector than the U.S. average, relative to the size of its economy: James Gerber and Serge Rey, "The Employment Dynamics of Regional Economies on the U.S.-Mexico Border," San Diego Dialogue Working Paper (San Diego: San Diego Dialogue, University of Cali-fornia, San Diego, 1999).

12. State and city trade data include merchandise goods only. Services, which include items such as royalties that are important to R&D, entertain-ment, and software industries, are only measured at the national level. State-level merchandise export data are from the Origin of Movement (OM) series derived from the U.S. Customs form called the Shipper's Export Declaration (SED). This series is also known as the MISER series since it is tabulated and reported by the Massachusetts Institute for Social and Economic Research (MISER) under contract with the Census Bureau. The OM series uses the SED form to identify the state where the product began its movement to-

wards a U.S. port, which is not necessarily the state in which the good is pr o-
duced. According to the Census Bureau, the OM series tends to understat e
exports from farm states (producers of bulk commodities) and overstate e x-
ports from states such as Louisiana with large numbers of trade intermedia r-
ies that move bulk products. For manufactured goods, however, it is relatively
accurate.

13. If services were counted, it is likely that California's share of U.S. –
Pacific Basin trade would increase, given the state's large software, tourism,
and entertainment industries, all of which pr oduce service exports.

14. James Gerber, "Gold Rushes and the Trans -Pacific Wheat Trade:
California and Australia, 1848–1857," in *Pacific Centuries: Pacific and Pacific Rim
Economic History since the Sixteenth Century*, ed. Dennis O. Flynn, Lionel Frost,
and A.J.H. Latham (London: Routledge, 1999).

15. Texas was the third state of c hoice for migrants, with slightly less than
one in ten immigrants choosing to locate there. U.S. Census Bureau, "State
Population Estimates and Demographic Components of Population Change:
April 1, 1990 to July 1, 1999," ST -99-2, at http://www.census.gov/
population/estimates/state/st-99-2.txt (December 1999).

16. For the two poles of the debate, see George Borjas, *Heaven's Door: Im-
migration Policy and the American Economy* (Princeton, N.J.: Princeton University
Press, 1999) and Jagdish Bhagwati, "Illegals in Our Midst: Getting Policy
Wrong" and "Why Borjas Fails to Persuade," *The Wind of the Hundred Days:
How Washington Mismanaged Globalization* (Cambridge, Mass.: MIT Press, 2000).

17. Bhagwati, *Wind of the Hundred Days*, p. 295.

18. U.S. Department of Transporta tion, "Interim Report on Status of I m-
plementing the North American Free Trade Agreement's Cross -Border
Trucking Provisions," Report number MH -2001-059 (Office of Inspector
General, May 2001).

19. The Commercial Vehicle Safety Alliance is a NAFTA standards -setting
body that has harmonized truck inspection proc edures.

20. Several possibilities come to mind: softwood lumber, environmental
enforcement, genetically modified foods, and taxes on e -commerce, among
them.

Section 3

Economic Integration and Public Opinion

The third section moves into the political realm and explores levels of popular support for NAFTA in the member countries. How have public attitudes evolved since the passage of NAFTA? Focusing on each of the NAFTA countries, chapters 7 through 9 offer novel insights and comparisons on shapes and determinants of public opinion.

Alejandro Moreno offers an analysis of Mexican perceptions with respect to free trade in general, to NAFTA in particular, and to prospects for a Free Trade Area of the Americas (FTAA). Surveys indicate that a strong majority of Mexicans—especially young and educated members of the middle class—support free trade in principle. But there are widespread apprehensions about NAFTA's impact on Mexico, especially among professionals and managers. Most believe that NAFTA has affected the national identity, but in unclear ways, and most support preservation of the state oil monopoly. There is considerable support for FTAA, partly in hopes that it might diminish Mexico's dependence on the United States, but most Mexicans would nonetheless prefer to have the United States as the country's leading trading partner rather than Brazil or any other nation in the hemisphere.

In chapter 8 Neil Nevitte, Leigh Anderson, and Robert Brym examine Canadian attitudes toward continental integration, including CUS-FTA as well as NAFTA. Has Canadian support for free trade increased or decreased over the course of the last ten years? Using data from World Values Surveys, the authors find considerable skepticism about NAFTA—but a continuing belief in the value of closer economic ties with both Mexico and the United States. Interestingly enough, high levels of Canadian national pride were positively associated with closer ties with the United States; and while ideological orientation became increasingly important in regard to closer ties with the United States, it had almost no bearing on prospective ties with Mexico. By the end of the 1990s, nearly one-third of Canadians favored "doing away with the border" with the United States, and a substantial share of the populace—especially the young and socioeconomically marginalized—favored outright political integration with the United States. High levels of pride in nation and culture nonetheless prevail among most sectors of the population.

In chapter 9 Phillip Warf and Steven Kull examine U.S. public attitudes on free trade. The overall assessment of NAFTA is positive but only mildly so: despite notable fluctuations, a plurality (40 to 47 percent) of the American public regarded NAFTA as a positive development. Skepticism was especially strong during the early years of the agreement. In broader perspective, a strong majority of Americans support free trade in general. (Higher levels of education, negatively associated with support for free trade in Mexico, are positively associated with pro–free trade opinions in the United States.) Many Americans perceive that free trade is good for the country and good for business but believe that it might have negative impacts on workers. There is strong support—and potentially stronger support—for extending free trade to other countries, especially if there were adequate safeguards for displaced workers and meaningful standards for environmental protection and labor regulation.

The chapters reveal that public opinions in the three countries are generally favorable toward NAFTA but that, somewhat surprisingly, they are not very intense. Paradoxically, this state of public indifference might facilitate reform and/or modification of NAFTA, since change would be unlikely to generate much strident opposition. Indeed, there seems to be a broad consensus that NAFTA could well be improved.

Opinion toward NAFTA and

...eremonies for the signing of the North
...greement (NAFTA) took place in different
cities. In Ottawa, Prime Minister Brian Mulroney of Canada signed the
trade agreement arguing that it was the best and most direct way to
have a more prosperous country. In Washington, U.S. President
George Bush (the father) signed the document announcing that it was
just the beginning of a greater package of U.S. policies toward the rest
of the Americas. In Mexico City, President Carlos Salinas de Gortari
signed the agreement saying that the treaty was good for Mexicans as
well as for its northern neighbors.

On November 21, 1993, NAFTA was approved by the United
States Congress. Two hundred and thirty-four votes in favor and 200
votes against marked the end of a chapter and the beginning of another for one of the most heated issues in the region. Voices of dissent
were common among citizen organizations, consumers, ecologists,
workers, farmers, and politicians in the United States and Canada, but
little opposition was visible in Mexico. A free trade agreement with
Canadians and Americans appeared, as Salinas put it, to be something
good for Mexicans. The few that contested such optimism at the time
were unable to express their dissent in the still state-controlled media.

Seven years after NAFTA went into effect, what do Mexicans think
of it? How do they evaluate it—as something good or bad? As Mexico
and its northern partners enter a new discussion over free trade, this
time about expanding it to the rest of the continent and creating a Free
Trade Area of the Americas (FTAA), what is the state of Mexican public opinion on free trade? Are Mexicans supportive of an FTAA? Evi-

dence from recent opinion surveys shows that most Mexicans are supportive of free trade and the idea of expanding their North American agreement to the south. However, Mexicans do not support an FTAA because NAFTA has been remarkable; on the contrary, they support an FTAA because NAFTA has failed to produce the expected benefits.

This chapter has a twofold task. First, it illustrates how Mexicans evaluate free trade in general and NAFTA in particular. Since NAFTA, Mexico has signed other trade agreements with new partners in the hemisphere and beyond, including one with the European Union that went into effect in 2000. Opinion surveys indicate that most Mexicans hold quite favorable opinions about free trade, but they are more critical when they evaluate NAFTA.

Second, this chapter shows Mexicans' attitudes and expectations toward the expansion of a free trade area to the rest of the Americas. Interviewed by Toronto's *Financial Post* while visiting Ottawa in April 1995, President Ernesto Zedillo of Mexico said that his country was dealing successfully with financial difficulties thanks to NAFTA. In December 1994, the "peso crisis" stormed the country as no other financial crisis had since the early 1980s. The Clinton administration acted rapidly through its "bailout" of the Mexican economy. "We have been very successful mostly because we were in a unique position," President Zedillo said in the interview. "I don't even want to think about what would have happened with a crisis like this to another country that was not in NAFTA and did not have this type of relationship with the U.S."[1]

Undoubtedly, Zedillo's remarks revealed his confidence in the trade agreement. However, they also confirmed Mexico's privileged position in the trade area, vis-à-vis other Latin American countries. Common sense indicates that such a privileged position would be hard to share and that Mexicans should oppose the admission of other Latin American or Caribbean nations to their exclusive partnership with the United States and Canada. But that is not the case. Mexicans are open to new membership. At the same time, they acknowledge that the U.S. economy should lead an expanded free trade area. The public mood toward an FTAA reflects the combination of a majority position in favor of free trade but also critical of NAFTA. Thus, why not just go further in this enterprise? Why not keep searching for greener pastures? The Mexican economy was characterized by protectionist policies for decades. Believing that a more open economy would bring better jobs and more wealth is like believing that pastures are greener beyond the fence. For most Mexicans, indeed they are.

This chapter explores how the Mexican public views free trade and why a policy of expansion finds support in that country, despite a "privileged" position with its northern partners. On the basis of public opinion surveys, it presents a number of key findings:

- The majority of Mexicans support free trade.

- A smaller proportion, although still a majority, thinks that joining NAFTA was the right decision for Mexico.

- Fewer than half of Mexicans consider that NAFTA has been good for Mexico.

- Mexicans are divided on how NAFTA has affected their national identity: some believe that it has strengthened it, while others think it has weakened it.

- Despite their support of free trade, Mexicans favor the protection of strategic industries, such as energy.

- The majority of Mexicans support a Free Trade Area of the Americas.

- In a scenario of expansion, Mexicans would rather have the United States as their primary trade partner over any other major economy in the hemisphere, such as Brazil.

- A plurality of Mexicans rejects the idea that democracy be required for admission to an FTAA.

The analysis relies on three nationwide opinion polls based on probability samples conducted by the polling unit at the newspaper *Reforma* between January and July 2001. About 1,200 interviews with Mexican adults were administered face to face around the country in each poll. The general results were published in *Reforma*, but breakdowns by variables such as age, education, and occupation were specifically prepared for this chapter.

MEXICAN ATTITUDES TOWARD FREE TRADE

To most Mexicans, as to most Americans and Canadians, the terms of a free trade agreement are not easily understandable. Liberalization, tariffs, accounting norms, and legal and financial jargon are definitely not the type of elements that the public would take into account when expressing an opinion. Instead, jobs, salaries, goods, services, and other aspects of everyday life make a better field for opinion formation and expression. The political discourse carried in the media may influence public opinion as long as it provides some cues of whether free trade and its international agreements are good or bad.

How do Mexicans evaluate free trade in general and NAFTA in particular? Opinion polls indicate that the majority supports free trade, but only a plurality considers that NAFTA has been good for Mexico. According to survey data gathered in July 2001 and displayed in table 7.1, six out of ten Mexicans favor free trade, and two out of ten oppose it, resulting in a 3 to 1 ratio in favor of free trade. This level of support is quite noticeable in a society where the economy was relatively closed for most of the second half of the twentieth century. It was not until the mid-1980s, when Mexico finally entered the General Agreement on Tariffs and Trade (GATT), that the economy began to open. However, it is NAFTA that has had the greatest impact on Mexicans, from the creation of new jobs to changes in the patterns of consumption.

The "NAFTA generation"—those Mexicans whose adult life has been accompanied by the free trade agreement since its starting talks— is generally more supportive of free trade than their elder counterparts. As shown in Table 7.1, 67 percent of respondents between 18 and 29 years of age favor free trade. That proportion is reduced to 60 percent among Mexicans between 30 and 49 years of age, and to 53 percent among those who are at least 50 years old. It is striking that those who lived their youth during the "Mexican Miracle" of the 1950s and 1960s, a period of substantial economic growth based on an import-substitution strategy, are mostly supportive of free trade. The proportion of individuals that opposes free trade is the same among all age cohorts, which means that the lower level of support registered among older Mexicans is not due to a higher level of opposition, but to a higher level of "don't know" responses: almost a third of those who are 50 or older have no clear opinion about free trade. Although important, age has a lesser influence in explaining the differences of opinion about free trade than do other sociodemographic variables.

Education makes a very significant impact on views of free trade. As shown in table 7.1, as many as 78 percent of respondents who have a higher education said they are in favor of free trade. That proportion is reduced to 47 percent among those who have an elementary education. That makes a 31-point difference in support for free trade be-

Table 7.1. Mexican Attitudes toward Free Trade

	Favor (%)	Oppose (%)	Neither (%)	Don't Know (%)	N (%)
Question: In general, do you favor or oppose free trade?					
Total Sample	61	19	8	12	1,196
Breakdown by:					
Age					
18–29	67	19	5	9	461
30–49	60	19	10	11	478
50 or more	53	18	12	17	242
Education					
Elementary	47	20	12	22	497
Middle/High school	70	17	8	5	500
Higher	78	17	4	1	194
Social class					
Urban middle class	71	17	8	4	499
Urban working class	56	21	11	12	324
Rural upper class	57	21	8	14	89
Rural lower class	49	18	6	26	259
Occupation					
Managerial	78	6	6	6	32
Professional	81	10	6	3	80
White-collar worker	81	13	4	2	91
Skilled manual worker	54	26	14	5	57
Semi-skilled manual	70	14	8	9	195
Unskilled manual	63	21	9	7	89
Farmer/*Ejidatario*	48	23	8	20	85
Unpaid work					
Housewife	49	20	9	21	365
Student	62	27	4	7	73
Retired	70	16	8	5	37
Unemployed	59	19	12	9	42

Source: *Reforma*, national face-to-face survey of 1,196 adults, July 2001.

tween the highest and lowest education categories used in the survey, as compared to the 14-point difference between the highest and lowest age categories.

Why is there such a large difference between the more and the less educated Mexicans? One possible explanation is that higher levels of education allow individuals to cope with a more competitive environment and be more supportive of it, assuming free trade increases competition in several areas, particularly in better-paid jobs. Another is that respondents with lower levels of education tend to have less information and express higher levels of "don't know" responses, thereby reducing the proportion of support and, perhaps, of opposition. The data in table 7.1 provide evidence for both explanations: less educated Mexicans are more likely to answer "don't know," and they are also more likely to oppose free trade. The net percent of favorable attitudes toward free trade (percent favoring, minus percent opposing) among the less educated is 27 points, compared to 61 points among the more educated Mexicans. The result is clear: the higher the level of education, the greater the support for free trade.

Class also makes a significant difference. According to table 7.1, urban middle classes are the most supportive of free trade and the rural poor are the least supportive. The data indicate that 71 percent of respondents classified as urban middle class—according to place of residence and level of income—said they favor free trade, but only 49 percent of those classified as rural lower class did too. The levels of support among the urban working class and the rural upper class were 56 percent and 57 percent, respectively. The differences according to class and urban-rural conditions are confirmed by occupational categories: professionals, managers, and white-collar workers are much more likely to support free trade than are farmers and skilled and unskilled blue-collar workers. However, it is noticeable that semi-skilled manual workers express a much higher level of support for free trade than skilled or unskilled ones do. Perhaps respondents in that category have greater expectations about the job opportunities that free trade brings. In the United States, by contrast, blue-collar workers tend to be more resistant to competition, given the lower wages that Mexican labor represents. One of the most common arguments raised by politicians and representatives of American workers is their potential disadvantage in competing with a cheaper workforce.

In sum, the majority of Mexicans (61 percent) express a favorable attitude toward free trade. This view is more likely among younger and better-educated Mexicans, and also among those who belong to the urban middle class and have professional, managerial, or white-collar occupations. Although these social categories are more supportive of free trade, however, not all of them believe that entering NAFTA was the right decision or that NAFTA has been good for Mexicans.

EVALUATIONS OF NAFTA

Seven years after the NAFTA went into effect, Mexicans may have a better perspective to evaluate it than in the years when it was starting to materialize. What do they think about it now? Evidence in this section suggests that the proportion of Mexicans who are convinced about the benefits of the accord is lower than the proportion that favors free trade. At the same time, some of the core supporters of free trade are, in fact, the harshest critics of NAFTA.

According to a Reforma national poll conducted in January 2001, 56 percent of respondents said that joining NAFTA was the right decision for Mexico, while 27 percent said it was the wrong decision. As revealed by table 7.2, younger Mexicans are more convinced than their elders that the trade agreement was right, confirming their general stand on free trade. Unlike Mexico's youth, some occupational categories that support free trade regard NAFTA with skepticism. For example, respondents with managerial or professional occupations do not seem as pleased with NAFTA as they were with free trade in general. Only 47 percent of managers and 57 percent of professionals think that joining NAFTA was the right decision, in comparison to the 71 percent and 81 percent, respectively, who support free trade in those categories (as shown in table 7.1). This depicts a critical view of NAFTA among those individuals who are generally supportive of free trade.

The proportion of respondents who believe NAFTA was a wrong decision is higher among managers and professionals than among blue-collar workers of any skill level: about four out of ten managers and almost four out of ten professionals think that joining NAFTA was the wrong decision, while about two out of ten manual workers—skilled, semi-skilled, and unskilled—also think that. This suggests that managers and professionals have not really seen the "wonders" that NAFTA promised to bring them. Farmers and housewives also share that skepticism. As much as 46 percent of farmers and 48 percent of housewives see NAFTA as the right policy, less than other Mexicans do.

Critical views of NAFTA observed among managers and professionals are confirmed by the fact that very few of them consider that the trade agreement has been good for Mexicans. As summarized in

Table 7.2. Mexican Public Opinion on the Decision to Join NAFTA

	Question: Do you think that entering NAFTA was the right decision or the wrong decision for Mexico?			
	Right (%)	Wrong (%)	Don't Know (%)	N (%)
Total Sample	56	27	17	1,200
Breakdown by:				
Age				
18–29	64	23	13	467
30–49	52	31	17	473
50 or older	51	24	25	244
Education				
Elementary	50	27	23	464
Middle/High school	71	22	7	531
Higher	62	31	7	191
Social class				
Urban middle class	65	25	10	480
Urban working class	56	25	19	351
Rural upper class	49	27	24	99
Rural lower class	42	32	26	246
Occupation				
Managerial	47	40	13	30
Professional	57	36	7	85
White-collar worker	72	19	9	99
Skilled manual worker	67	19	14	80
Semi-skilled manual	60	25	15	114
Unskilled manual	57	25	19	122
Farmer/ *Ejidatario*	46	32	22	95
Unpaid work				
Housewife	48	27	25	383
Student	67	24	9	80
Retired	68	23	9	44
Unemployed	63	24	13	38

Source: *Reforma*, national face-to-face survey of 1,200 adults, January 2001.

table 7.3, the January 2001 Reforma poll shows that only 44 percent of all respondents think that the free trade agreement between Canada, the United States, and Mexico has been very good or fairly good for Mexicans. This compares with the 56 percent who said in the same poll that joining NAFTA was the right decision, and with 61 percent who said in July that they were in favor of free trade. The belief in NAFTA's benefits for Mexicans is even lower among managers and professionals: 30 percent and 38 percent, respectively, think that NAFTA has been very good or fairly good, while 53 percent and 40 percent say that it has been fairly bad or very bad. In other words, evaluations of the free trade agreement are predominantly negative among managers and ambiguous among professionals.

In contrast, NAFTA has a positive balance in terms of evaluations among white- and blue-collar workers, housewives, students, and farmers. Retired and unemployed respondents also think NAFTA has brought Mexicans more good than harm. Young Mexicans speak favorably of NAFTA, but highly educated respondents are more critical of it. Why do managers and professionals evaluate NAFTA more negatively than do other Mexicans? Was this negative evaluation captured by polls conducted when the U.S. economy began to give signals of a slump? Unfortunately, there are no comparable data gathered in previous years to reveal whether evaluations of NAFTA have become more negative over time or have remained negative since it went into effect, especially among the managerial and professional categories analyzed here. Despite these limitations, the evidence suggests that professionals' experience with the free trade pact has not been as beneficial as they expected, either for themselves or for the country.

TRADE AND NATIONAL IDENTITY

Mexicans use the term *malinchismo* to refer to a preference for the foreign over the national, and they speak with disdain of a *malinchista*, a person who holds such preferences. The word—which comes from the figure of La Malinche, a native who served as both mistress and translator for Hernán Cortés, the Spanish conquistador—evokes the image of a "traitor." This discourse underlines the extent to which nationalism and national sovereignty were important concerns in the process of reaching a trade agreement with the United States. If some groups were worried about Mexican companies' lack of competitiveness, others were concerned about culture, identity, and threats to

Table 7.3. Mexican Evaluations of NAFTA

	Very Good/ Fairly Good (%)	Neither Good nor Bad (%)	Fairly Bad/ Very Bad (%)	Don't Know (%)	N (%)
Question: Since it started seven years ago, do you think that the North American Free Trade Agreement between Mexico, the United States, and Canada, has been very good, fairly good, fairly bad or very bad for Mexicans?					
Total Sample	44	18	26	12	1,200
Breakdown by:					
Age					
18–29	52	15	23	10	467
30–49	40	19	30	11	473
50 or more	35	22	25	18	244
Education					
Elementary	34	19	26	21	464
Middle/High school	52	17	23	8	531
Higher	45	17	36	2	191
Social class					
Urban middle class	48	18	28	6	480
Urban working class	45	19	25	11	351
Rural upper class	38	23	22	17	99
Rural lower class	37	15	25	23	246
Occupation					
Managerial	30	13	53	4	30
Professional	38	20	40	2	85
White-collar worker	54	16	22	8	99
Skilled manual worker	47	20	29	4	80
Semi-skilled manual	48	19	25	8	114
Unskilled manual	47	17	24	12	122
Farmer/ *Ejidatario*	34	22	25	19	95
Unpaid work					
Housewife	41	18	22	19	383
Student	58	12	24	6	80
Retired	48	18	23	11	44
Unemployed	45	18	29	8	38

Source: *Reforma*, national face-to-face survey of 1,200 adults, January 2001.

mexicanidad. Without entering a deep discussion, it is essential to include this theme in a meaningful assessment of public evaluations of NAFTA. A thorough analysis of nationalism and the cultural influence of trade would require a different research project. Even so, an overview of recently expressed opinions may illustrate how divided the Mexican public is on the subject.

The Reforma polls show that eight out of ten Mexicans believe that a trade partnership with the United States has affected their national identity. As shown by table 7.4, some of them think that such a partnership strengthens the national identity, and slightly fewer think that it weakens it. Asked whether they felt that a close trade relationship with the United States "makes our national identity much stronger, somewhat stronger, somewhat weaker, or much weaker," 46 percent of respondents in January 2001 said that the partnership had strengthened Mexican identity, while 34 percent thought the opposite. If "strong" and "weak" identity can be interpreted as more and less nationalist, respectively, then those who are more likely to believe that the U.S.-Mexico partnership has increased Mexican nationalism are the youth, as well as those with a medium level of education, white- and blue-collar workers, those with a self-described rightist ideological orientation, and those who identify with the currently governing National Action Party (PAN). Apparently, there is a marked tendency for conservative young Mexicans to hold strongly nationalist sentiments.

In contrast, those who believe that the trade partnership with the United States weakens the Mexican national identity are also likely to be young. But unlike their previous description, these young Mexicans have higher levels of education, hold managerial and professional occupations, are more likely to describe themselves as ideologically leftist, and tend to identify slightly more with the left-wing Party of the Democratic Revolution (PRD) or be independent. This suggests that young liberals in Mexico have weak nationalist sentiments.

A single survey question does not offer definite or conclusive information to assess the effects of trade on cultural and nationalist sentiments. Nonetheless, the data in table 7.4 indicate that almost all Mexicans think that doing business with their northern neighbor has some effects on their national identity. Leftists think it weakens nationalism, while rightists believe it strengthens it, and young Mexicans seem more aware of these effects than older ones. However, although left-right self identifications are related to assessments of national identity, they do not seem to account for differences of opinion in regard to nationalist—or protectionist—policies. One case in point is energy.

Table 7.4. U. S.–Mexico Partnership and Mexican National Identity

	Question: Do you feel that having the United States as Mexico's main trade partner makes our national identity much stronger, somewhat stronger, somewhat weaker, or much weaker?				
	Much or Somewhat Stronger (%)	Neither Stronger nor Weaker (%)	Much or Somewhat Weaker (%)	Don't Know (%)	N (%)
Total Sample	46	6	44	14	1,200
Breakdown by:					
Age					
18–29	48	5	38	9	467
30–49	46	6	34	14	473
50 or more	40	11	27	22	244
Education					
Elementary	46	6	28	20	464
Middle/High school	51	3	41	5	531
Higher	36	14	48	2	191
Social class					
Urban middle class	47	7	40	6	480
Urban working class	45	6	36	13	351
Rural upper class	45	5	25	25	99
Rural lower class	43	7	26	24	246
Occupation					
Managerial	43	6	47	4	30
Professional	36	13	47	4	85
White-collar worker	51	9	38	2	99
Skilled manual worker	57	4	30	9	80
Semi-skilled manual	54	10	29	6	114
Unskilled manual	40	9	36	15	122
Farmer/*Ejidatario*	50	7	23	20	95
Unpaid work					
Housewife	40	4	33	23	383
Student	53	2	44	1	80
Retired	61	5	23	11	44
Unemployed	37	5	42	16	38
Left-right self-placement					
Left	44	5	43	8	133
Center	50	8	35	7	282
Right	56	5	33	6	442
No placement	29	8	32	31	331
Party identification					
PAN	54	6	31	9	434
PRI	48	5	33	14	225
PRD	39	4	38	19	112
Independent	37	9	39	15	383

Source: Reforma, national face-to-face survey of 1,200 adults, January 2001.

ENERGY: A MATTER OF STATE

Despite their general support for free trade, Mexicans of all ideological tendencies are convinced that strategic industries should remain in the hands of the Mexican government. Oil is simply untouchable, and politicians do not dare open the subject for discussion. When President Vicente Fox named three prominent Mexican businessmen to the PEMEX (Petróleos Mexicanos) advisory council in early 2001, in the belief that this parastatal would benefit from a new entrepreneurial vision, their appointments did not last even a week. The message was plain: the political costs of keeping them on the council would have been higher for Mr. Fox than the embarrassment of their immediate removal. Private capital can enter the oil industry in Mexico, but it is limited for now to refining and basic petrochemicals, not extraction.

Although oil is out of the equation for the moment, the opening of the electric power industry to private investment was proposed more directly in the legislative session beginning in late 2001. What do Mexicans think about opening their second-largest domestic industry to private investment? Table 7.5 provides some answers. Asked about their preferences in a national poll conducted in July 2001, 66 percent said the "electric power industry should remain owned and managed by the Mexican government," as opposed to 18 percent who thought it "should be opened to investment of private capital." That is, the ratio of opposition over support for the opening of the electric power industry is slightly higher than 3 to 1.

In the spring of 2001, President George W. Bush and his Mexican counterpart, Vicente Fox, discussed the possibility of the United States providing Mexico with energy-generating technology, which Mexico would use to produce energy to be sold to the United States. Two nationwide Reforma polls, conducted in April and July 2001, indicate that Mexicans were not supportive of the idea. Only 21 percent of respondents in each poll agreed that "Mexico should sell energy to the United States and Canada if they provide the technology to produce it." In contrast, 66 percent in April and 68 percent in July thought that "Mexico should save its energy reserves for future domestic consumption instead of selling them now." Once again, the ratio was slightly higher than 3 to 1.

Despite their broad support for free trade, in sum, Mexicans do not want to open their strategic industries to private investment. They would rather have the electric power industry in government hands than under private management. At the same time, most Mexicans are willing to reject short-term benefits from trading electricity (even with technological means and know-how supplied by the United States) in order to protect future domestic consumption of energy.

Table 7.5. Public Opinion and the Energy Issue

Question	April 2001	July 2001
What would you prefer?	(%)	(%)
The electric power industry should remain owned and managed by the Mexican government.	N.A.	66
The electric power industry should be opened to investment of private capital.	N.A.	18
Don't know.	N.A.	16
With which statement do you most agree?	(%)	(%)
Mexico should trade energy with the United States and Canada in exchange for technology to produce them.	21	21
Mexico should save its energy reserves for future consumption instead of trading them.	66	68
Don't know.	13	11

Source: *Reforma*, national face-to-face surveys of 1,195 adults in April 2001 and 1,196 in July 2001.
N.A. = Not available.

SUPPORT FOR A FREE TRADE AREA OF THE AMERICAS

Mexico's apparently privileged position as the only Latin American member of NAFTA has not resulted in a very favorable evaluation of the trade agreement. Mexicans who are most supportive of free trade in general are the most critical of NAFTA. Nonetheless, public support for the idea of a Free Trade Area of the Americas is high, not low. This can be interpreted as a confirmation of support for free trade and the idea that NAFTA has not solved all of Mexico's problems. This last section shows one more side of Mexican views of free trade: support for an FTAA, support for the idea that the United States should be Mexico's primary partner even under a new agreement involving more nations, and a mild rejection that democracy should be a condition for FTAA membership.

By a ratio of 3 to 1, as revealed by table 7.6, Mexicans prefer a free trade area embracing all countries of the Americas over an exclusively North American arrangement. Reforma polls indicate that, in January 2001, 66 percent of respondents expressed their preference for an inclusive, hemispheric scheme, as opposed to 16 percent who preferred the restricted NAFTA formula. Similarly, an April poll found a 3 to 1 ratio favoring something closer to FTAA than to NAFTA. One difference between the two polls lies in the fact that the April questionnaire included the names of Brazil and Argentina as examples of partners in a free trade area of the Americas. This methodological difference probably accounts for the decrease from 66 to 59 percent in support for an all-Americas free trade area over NAFTA. Nonetheless, both polls show that Mexicans are inclusive, not exclusive, when they think of trade membership.

Does this attitude of inclusiveness respond to self-interest or principle?[2] If Mexicans are not closed to the possibility of expanding the free trade zone in spite of their apparently privileged position, one could argue that they respond to a matter of principle, perhaps the principle of solidarity. Given the unfavorable evaluations that many Mexicans grant NAFTA, however, it seems that agreeing with an expanded free trade area reflects high expectations about its results and is based, thus, on self-interest.

One more piece of evidence about a self-interested base of public opinion is a realistic view of FTAA (see part "b" of table 7.6). In January 2001, seven out of ten Mexicans reported they would rather have the United States as primary trade partner in an all-Americas free trade area than Brazil, which represents the largest Latin American economy (but is still much smaller than the United States). Only one out of ten respondents said they preferred Brazil over the United States, perhaps reflecting their anti-American attitudes more than their economic realism.

But not everything responds to self-interest. A plurality of Mexicans rejects the idea that membership in a trade area should be limited to democratic countries. Part "c" of table 7.6 shows that merely 31 percent of respondents in April 2001 agreed with the following statement:

Table 7.6. Mexican Opinion about a Free Trade Area of the Americas

Question	January 2001	April 2001
a. What would you prefer?[1]	(%)	(%)
A free trade zone that only includes Mexico, the United States, and Canada.	16	18
A free trade zone that includes all countries from the Americas that wish to be members.	66	59
Don't know.	18	23
b. Whom would you rather be Mexico's main trade partner, the United States or Brazil?	(%)	(%)
United States	69	N.A.
Brazil	11	N.A.
Some other country	2	N.A.
Don't know	18	N.A.
c. "A free trade area of the Americas should admit only democratic countries, and exclude the nondemocratic ones"	(%)	(%)
Agree	N.A.	31
Disagree	N.A.	42
No opinion	N.A.	27

Source: Reforma, national face-to-face surveys of 1,200 adults in January, and 1,195 in April 2001.
[1] In April 2001, the questionnaire added the phrase "including Brazil and Argentina."
N.A. = Not available.

"A free trade area of the Americas should only admit democratic countries, and exclude nondemocratic ones." By contrast, a plurality of 42 percent disagreed with such a requirement for admission. Opposition to this idea is not based on fear that they will themselves be excluded, since Mexicans do not think of themselves (or their nation) as undemocratic. Indeed, a nationwide poll conducted and published by *Reforma* in August 2000, shortly after the presidential election that ended seventy-one years of continuous rule by the Institutional Revolutionary Party (PRI), showed that over 60 percent of respondents think of Mexico as a democracy. It is a matter of principle that Mexicans reject the idea of exclusion from free trade.

CONCLUSIONS

This chapter has illustrated the state of Mexican public opinion in regard to free trade. As survey data indicate, the majority of Mexicans support free trade, but only a plurality believes that NAFTA has been good to them. The segments of Mexican society that are most supportive of free trade are also the harshest critics of NAFTA. Individuals engaged in managerial and professional activities express less favorable evaluations of the trade agreement than occupational categories that are less supportive of free trade in general, such as blue-collar workers. A paradox in Mexican public opinion is the coexistence of a taste for free trade and a preference for keeping strategic industries in government hands.

Mexicans are moved by self-interest, but principles matter as well. Most Mexicans support an FTAA, not because NAFTA has been good, but precisely because it has not been good enough. Despite this, Mexicans acknowledge the leading role of the U.S. economy and reject the idea that democracy should be a condition for membership in an FTAA. Whether it is a matter of self-interest or of principle, free trade uncovers Mexicans' position toward a term that is paradoxical in itself: freedom as a principle, and trade as a matter of self-interest. The two often confront each other. As long as the debate goes on, young generations of Mexicans show themselves supportive of free trade, but they are also deeply divided on how it affects their national identity: some believe that NAFTA has, so far, strengthened it and some are convinced that the agreement has weakened it.

Notes

1. *Reforma*, April 24, 1995.

2. Donald Kinder and Lynn Sanders argue that the primary ingredients in the formation of public opinion toward policy include self-interest and principles, which are often contradictory. In addition to those elements, the authors refer to group reference as another ingredient of opinion. See Kinder and Sanders, *Divided by Color* (Chicago: University of Chicago Press, 1996).

8

Ten Years After: Canadian Attitudes toward Continentalism

Neil Nevitte, Leigh Anderson, and Robert Brym

The 1988 Canadian federal election was an important turning point in Canada's continental relations. The Progressive Conservative Party, a party with a long-standing policy of resisting closer economic ties with the United States, called the election on the issue of free trade with the United States. The issue dominated the campaign. Voters supported the Progressive Conservatives, and the party returned to office with a mandate to pursue free trade. The expansion of the Canada–United States Free Trade Agreement (CUSFTA) to include Mexico signified a consolidation of that new direction.

Why did Canadians turn to support free trade when they did? A variety of possible explanations has been supplied. One is that Canada's pursuit of a formal free trade agreement with the United States was a defensive economic strategy designed to secure access to the domestic market of its largest trading partner. The emergence of trading blocs in other parts of the world in the 1970s and 1980s, and the threat that a "trade dependent" Canada might be shut out, made the matter more urgent.

Another line of speculation was that CUSFTA, and then NAFTA, simply represented a logical stage in the evolution of long-standing continental dynamics: the Canadian economy and society had become more closely entwined with those of the United States for decades. Cross-border trade flows, financial transactions, media flows, and cross-border travel had all been steadily rising since at least the early 1960s, and the cumulative effects of these transactions, some theorize, amount to de facto greater integration.[1] From that vantage point,

CUSFTA and NAFTA signified formal recognition of continental integration.

Then there is the ideological line of speculation. Here the argument is that the timing of NAFTA was attributable to a shift in the prevailing ideological winds, a change of direction experienced in many advanced industrial states in the 1980s.[2] The ideology of a resurgent right had champions in both Canada and the United States at about the same time. President Ronald Reagan promoted the cause of free enterprise with considerable enthusiasm, and Prime Minister Brian Mulroney did much the same. In effect, the two leaders had congenial outlooks, and both declared that their countries were "open for business." To the extent that free trade qualifies as an international face of free enterprise, then, the timing of NAFTA might well be seen as the product of these shifting ideological tides.

Each of these purported explanations is plausible, and they are not mutually exclusive. Moreover, each perspective contains within it somewhat different expectations about what might drive contemporary Canadian support for, and opposition to, the expansion of continental trade.

This chapter examines the public opinion underpinnings of Canadian views about continental free trade in a cross-time perspective. Has Canadian support for free trade increased or decreased since the signing of the free trade agreements? Have the bases of support for, or opposition to, free trade changed, or have they remained the same? And have public views about political integration changed over the course of the last decade?

THE DATA

The analysis relies on World Values Survey (WVS) data. These data, which come from hour-long, face-to-face interviews with random samples of respondents, have been collected for the Canadian public in three waves—1981, 1990, and 2000. The data meet conventional standards of comparability. The same core items using the same question wordings have been repeatedly tested in Canada and other national settings. The same protocols were followed in the design of the samples, and the same data collection procedures were followed in the 1981, 1990, and 2000 surveys.[3]

More important for the purposes of this chapter, the 1990 Canadian WVS contained a special module of questions specifically designed to explore citizens' views about free trade with the United

States and Mexico. The 2000 Canadian WVS replicated the same module of questions; taken together, these data sets provide the foundations of a useful cross-sectional research design for analyzing cross-time changes. The 1990 survey provides a fundamental benchmark, as its timing stands at the juncture of Canada's free trade agreement first with the United States (CUSFTA, 1989), and then with the United States and Mexico (NAFTA, 1994). The replication of the NAFTA module of questions within the 2000 WVS (Canada) survey means that it is possible not only to systematically explore cross-time changes in Canadian views toward continental trade, but also to explore a variety of orientations that could well shape those views toward NAFTA.

INITIAL FINDINGS

The 1990 WVS (Canada) asked respondents to indicate whether they supported or opposed CUSFTA. Canadians were divided on the matter: 57 percent said they supported free trade with the United States, whereas 43 percent were opposed. The Canadian public's experience with free trade in 1990 would have to be regarded as limited at best. But by 2000 Canadians had accumulated a decade's worth of experience with NAFTA upon which to draw and from which to form opinions about free trade. When Canadians were asked in 2000 how much confidence they had in NAFTA, the evidence shows that public opinion was still divided—57 percent indicated that they had little or no confidence in NAFTA. The 1990 and 2000 questions about support for free trade with the United States and confidence in NAFTA are not directly comparable, but at the very least they indicate that Canadians have not been wholeheartedly won over by their experience with NAFTA over the course of the 1990s.

For more reliable analyses we need to turn to directly comparable indicators of public opinion. Both the 1990 and the 2000 Canadian World Values surveys asked respondents their views about closer, or more distant, economic ties with both the United States and Mexico. The basic cross-time results, reported in figure 8.1, indicate aggregate stability in Canadians' views about closer ties with Mexico (71 percent), but there have been significant shifts in comparable orientations toward the United States. In 2000, support for closer economic ties with the United States increased by a substantial 8 percent from 71 percent in 1990.[4] While a majority of Canadians express limited confidence in NAFTA, there is no indication that Canadians have abandoned support for closer economic ties with either Mexico or the United States.

Figure 8.1. Canadian Preferences for Closer or More Distant Economic Ties with the United States and Mexico, 1990 and 2000

> **Question**: "In your opinion, should Canada have closer or more distant economic ties with the US/Mexico? Much closer, somewhat closer, somewhat distant or much more distant."

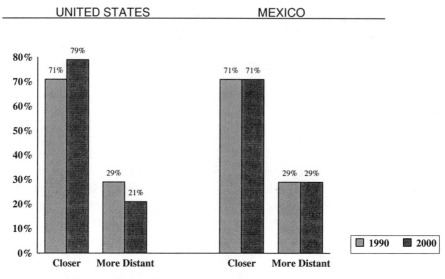

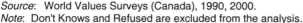

Source: World Values Surveys (Canada), 1990, 2000.
Note: Don't Knows and Refused are excluded from the analysis.

It is useful and important to determine whether there have been significant shifts in the levels of aggregate support for closer economic ties. But a more central analytical question is whether there have been any detectable shifts in the underlying structure of attitudes that lie behind these orientations. To answer that question requires a far more detailed examination of what factors drive the Canadian public's support for closer economic ties with both the United States and Mexico.

Table 8.1 reports the results of a multivariate analysis of the determinants of Canadian support for closer economic ties with the United States in 1990 and 2000. It employs a successive block entry variable logistic regression setup that examines the impact of three different kinds of variables, each of which might plausibly be related to support for closer economic ties. The first block contains the standard set of socioeconomic variables: age, gender, education, income, and occupation. If people's views about closer economic ties are shaped by their socioeconomic situation, then we should be able to detect systematic variations in support for expanding trade. Expanding trade environments can produce new sets of "winners" and "losers," redirecting domestic cleavages.[5] There is no reason to suppose a priori that socioeconomic factors would necessarily have the same impact on attitudes toward closer economic ties at both time points for which we have data. In 1990 it might well have been difficult for Canadians to ascertain just what impact freer trade might have, not least of all because the CUSFTA was so novel. But with nearly ten years of continental free trade experience under their belts, Canadians would certainly be better positioned to determine whether they had "won" or "lost" as a result of the expanded trade environment.

The second and third blocks of items in the multivariate setup contain a variety of attitudinal variables that might be more or less closely linked to support for closer economic ties. These include "identities": national pride, parochial-cosmopolitan orientations, and how much Canadians trust Americans. Given historical experience, the expectation might be that Canadians with high levels of national pride would be more likely to resist closer economic ties with the United States. Alternatively, Canadians who are more cosmopolitan, and more trusting of their American counterparts, might be expected to be more inclined to support closer economic ties. The third block of variables taps basic political and economic orientations, and these correspond to the ideological outlooks explanation for support for expanded trade: left-right self-location, support for the ideals of free enterprise, and concern for material security. Here the expectation might be that those who see themselves as "on the right," those who support free enterprise principles, and those who are more concerned with material security might be correspondingly more inclined than their left-leaning, big-state, postmaterial counterparts to support closer economic ties with the United States.

It comes as no surprise whatsoever to discover that a number of these variables are correlated (see appendix A). Education level, for example, is correlated with income ($r = .41$), and outlooks toward free enterprise are correlated with left-right self-placement ($r = .2$). Because of these inter-item correlations, it is useful to resort to a multivariate strategy to determine which variables emerge as significant predictors of support for closer economic ties net other factors—that is, after all of the other variables in the model are controlled.

Table 8.1. Predictors of Canadian Support for Closer Economic Ties with the United States, 1990 and 2000

Question: "In your opinion, should Canada have closer or more distant economic ties with the United States? Much closer; somewhat closer; a bit more distant; much more distant."

	1990			2000		
	Model 1	Model 2	Model 3	Model 1	Model 2	Model 3
Constant	.87**	.39	-.48	1.60***	.46	-1.30***
SES						
Age (old)	.07 (1.1)	-.22 (.80)	-.32 (.72)	.09 (1.1)	-.13 (.88)	-.31 (.74)
Gender (male)	.44 (1.6)***	.51 (1.7)***	.55 (1.7)***	.18 (1.2)	.19 (1.2)	.19 (1.2)
Education (high)	-.07 (.93)	-.15 (.86)	-.05 (.95)	-1.2 (.29)***	-1.1 (.32)***	-.67 (.51)*
Income (high)	.08 (1.1)	-.00 (.99)	-.07 (.93)	-.05 (.95)	-.26 (.77)	-.72 (.49)**
Occupation (white-collar)	-.43 (.65)	-.33 (.72)	-.34 (.71)	.45 (1.6)	.48 (1.6)	.37 (1.4)
Identities/Attitudes						
National pride (yes)		.26 (1.3)	.01 (1.0)		1.1 (2.9)***	.74 (2.1)**
Cosmopolitanism (yes)		-.18 (.84)	-.09 (.91)		.03 (1.0)	.19 (1.2)
Trust Americans (yes)		.89 (2.4)***	.86 (2.4)***		.73 (2.1)***	.72 (2.1)***
Orientations						
Left-Right (Right)			1.2 (3.2)***			1.3 (3.7)***
Capitalism/Free enterprise (agree)			.26 (1.3)			1.7 (5.3)***
Materialist concerns (yes)			.74 (2.1)***			.80 (2.2)***
Nagelkerke R^2	.021	.075	.102	.022	.069	.160

***$p < .01$; **$p < .05$; *$p < .1$

Source: World Values Surveys (Canada), 1990, 2000.

Coding: The dependent variable was recoded into a dichotomous variable: Much closer or somewhat closer (1), more distant or much more distant (0).

Notes: Entries are unstandardized logistic regression coefficients, with odds ratios in parentheses. Don't knows and refusals were excluded from the analysis.

Three basic findings emerge from the estimates in table 8.1. First, there are significant cross-time variations in the impact that socioeconomic factors have on views about closer economic ties. In 1990, there is evidence of a substantial gender gap after identities and ideological orientations are taken into account; men were significantly more likely than women to support closer economic ties with the United States. By 2000 that gender gap disappeared, but other socioeconomic factors— education and income—became significant predictors. Those with low levels of formal education and low income were significantly more likely to support closer economic ties with the United States than those with high levels of formal education and high income. That said, it is clear that socioeconomic factors, by themselves, were not very powerful predictors of Canadian attitudes to closer economic ties with the United States in either 1990 or 2000, as indicated by the modest R^2 values.

The second finding concerns attitudes and identities. In this regard, there is a significant and somewhat counterintuitive nonfinding. Given nationalists' long-standing concern that closer economic integration with the United States would undermine Canada's autonomy, there are reasons to suppose that high levels of national pride might be associated with opposition to closer economic ties with the United States. But the evidence points in the opposite direction. In both 1990 and 2000, higher levels of Canadian national pride turn out to be positively associated with support for closer economic ties. Moreover, national pride emerged as a significant predictor of support for closer economic ties in 2000. Trust in Americans turns out to be an even more powerful predictor of support for closer economic ties, a finding that also holds for both 1990 and 2000.

The third finding—and, in some respects, the most striking one— concerns ideological orientations. Left-right self-placement and materialism are both significantly related to support for closer economic ties in 1990 and in 2000. Capitalist orientations became a significant predictor in 2000. The pattern is consistent. What is even more intriguing is the clear evidence indicating that these ideological orientations became far more powerful predictors of support for closer economic ties with the United States in 2000 than in 1990. Ideology was a significant predictor of support for closer U.S. economic ties in 1990, but these same ideological variables explained more than twice as much variance in 2000.

One possibility is that the rising level of Canadian support for closer economic ties with the United States is part of a larger sea change: living in an export-driven economy, Canadians might have become increasingly sensitive to the need to develop "closer economic ties" with all major trading partners. The WVS evidence, however, provides no foundation for that kind of broad-gauge interpretation. It turns out that Canadian support for "closer economic ties" with Western Europe dropped by 3 percent between 1990 and 2000, and it fell by 6 percent for Eastern Europe over the same period. Aside from the United States, Canadian support for closer economic ties increased from 1990 to 2000 for only one other country or region—namely, Japan. In this particular case the increase was a modest 4 percent.

Figure 8.1 clearly shows that Canadian support for closer economic ties with its other NAFTA partner—Mexico—remained unchanged across the 1990–2000 decade. But stability in aggregate levels of support can mask underlying changes in the structure of that support. To explore this possibility, table 8.2 presents exactly the same kind of multivariate setup as that used in table 8.1 for the analysis of Canadian views about closer economic ties with the United States. But this time the focus is on Canadian attitudes toward closer economic ties with Mexico.

Once again, there are three significant findings that emerge from the data. First, and in sharp contrast with the case of the United States, socioeconomic factors are consistently significant predictors of Canadian support for closer economic ties with Mexico. Those predictors remain statistically significant even after the other blocks of variables are brought into the analysis. Not only do these socioeconomic factors explain more variance in the Mexican case, but these predictors also operate in the opposite direction than in the U.S. case. Notice in table 8.1 that support for closer economic ties with the United States comes from the young (not statistically significant), those with low levels of formal education, and those with low income. By contrast, Canadian support for closer economic ties with Mexico is found among older Canadians, males, and those with higher income and educational levels (not statistically significant).

The second significant finding concerns identifications. As in the case of the United States, the strongest predictor in this block of variables is "trust": the more trust Canadians have in their Mexican counterparts, the more likely they are to support the idea of having closer economic ties with that country. The other variables in model 2 also work in the same way for Mexico; both national pride and cosmopolitanism are positively and significantly related to support for closer economic ties with Mexico.

In some respects the third set of findings is the most intriguing. In striking contrast with the results for the United States (table 8.1), ideological orientations, such as left-right self-placement, capitalist views, and materialist orientations, appear to have no bearing whatsoever on Canadian support for closer economic ties with Mexico. Recall that in the case of Canadian support for closer economic ties with the United States, ideological orientations emerged as the most powerful predictors; they account for more than half of the explained variance in Canadian support for closer economic ties with the United States. Not only do these same ideological orientations provide virtually no additional explanation of variance in the Mexican case, but the directions of these relationships also work in the opposite way. Furthermore, these findings are consistent across both time points; there has been no detectable change in the basic structure of Canadian attitudes that shape support for closer economic ties with Mexico.

CROSS-NATIONAL TRUST

The preceding analysis indicates that trust emerges as a uniformly significant predictor of Canadian support for closer economic ties with both the United States and Mexico. These results are stable; they hold for both time points, which suggests the possibility that trust mediates these orientations. The implication is that rising, or falling, levels of trust could be responsible for the variations in levels of Canadian support for closer economic ties with both countries. As it happens, Canadian levels of trust in Americans and Mexicans are strongly correlated (r = .65; appendix A). The WVS data indicate that Canadian levels of trust in Americans and Mexicans have not changed substantially over the course of the decade for which we have data. As figure 8.2 shows, more than half of all Canadians reported that they "trusted" Americans in 1990 and 2000, and the changes between 1990 and 2000 are imperceptible. The same holds at the other end of the spectrum; just 15 percent of Canadians said they "distrusted" Americans in 1990, and that proportion remained virtually the same for 2000.

There is some indication that Canadians have less sharply formed evaluations when it comes to trusting Mexicans; a significantly larger proportion of Canadians indicates that they neither trust nor distrust Mexicans than is the case for Americans. The greater ambiguity might simply be attributable to the fact that Canadians have far fewer contacts with Mexico than the United States. Between 1990 and 2000, however, there was a small but statistically significant increase (4 percent) in the proportion of Canadians saying that they trust Mexicans.

Table 8.2. Predictors of Canadian Support for Closer Economic Ties with Mexico, 1990 and 2000

Question: "In your opinion, should Canada have closer or more distant economic ties with Mexico? Much closer; somewhat closer; a bit more distant; much more distant."

	1990			2000		
	Model 1	Model 2	Model 3	Model 1	Model 2	Model 3
Constant	−.74**	−.73	.63	−.65***	−1.61***	−1.36***
SES						
Age (old)	.56 (1.7)**	.50 (1.6)*	.48 (1.6)*	.61 (1.8)***	.52 (1.7)**	.57 (1.8)***
Gender (male)	.44 (1.5)***	.44 (1.5)***	.53 (1.5)***	.55 (1.7)***	.57 (1.8)***	.58 (1.8)***
Education (high)	.57 (1.8)*	.54 (1.7)	.52 (1.7)	.64 (1.9)*	.63 (1.9)*	.57 (1.8)
Income (high)	.94 (2.6)***	9.7 (2.6)***	.96 (2.6)***	.40 (1.6)*	.25 (1.3)	.31 (1.4)
Occupation (white-collar)	.31 (1.4)	.30 (1.4)	.30 (1.3)	.64 (1.9)**	.65 (1.9)**	.67 (1.9)**
Identities/Attitudes						
National pride (yes)		−.58 (.56)	−.56 (.57)		.53 (1.7)*	.58 (1.8)*
Cosmopolitanism (yes)		.30 (1.3)	.29 (1.3)		.57 (1.8)**	.54 (1.6)**
Trust Mexicans (yes)		1.1 (3.1)***	1.1 (3.1)***		1.1 (2.9)***	1.1 (2.9)***
Orientations						
Left-Right (Right)			.09 (1.1)			−.50 (.61)
Capitalism/Free enterprise (agree)			−.03 (.97)			−.00 (.98)
Materialist concerns (yes)			−.26 (.77)			−.15 (.86)
Nagelkerke R²	.057	.136	.137	.044	.099	.101

***p < .01; **p < .05; *p < .1

Source: World Values Surveys (Canada), 1990, 2000.

Coding. The dependent variable was recoded into a dichotomous variable: Much closer or somewhat closer (1), more distant or much more distant (0).

Notes: Entries are unstandardized logistic regression coefficients, with odds ratios in parentheses. Don't knows and refusals were excluded for all variables from the analysis.

Figure 8.2. Canadian Levels of Trust in Americans and Mexicans, 1990 and 2000

Question: "How much do you trust Americans/Mexicans? Trust them completely, trust them a little, neither trust nor distrust them, do not trust them very much, do not trust them at all."

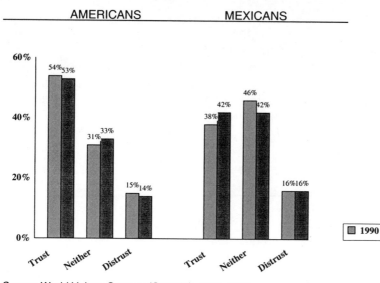

Source: World Values Surveys (Canada), 1990, 2000.
Note: Don't Knows and Refused are excluded from the analysis.

These results reinforce evidence from other research, which indicates that trust is a stable attribute.[6] Given the high correlation between trust in Americans and trust in Mexicans, we would expect to find cross-time and cross-national stability in those factors that are associated with levels of trust. The WVS data are consistent with that expectation. The results of multivariate analysis of the predictors of Canadians' trust of Americans and Mexicans (appendices B and C) show that most of the variance in trust is explained by the same set of individual socioeconomic background factors. Age is consistently a predictor of greater trust in Americans and Mexicans; older Canadians are significantly more likely to trust both of Canada's NAFTA partners. And in the 2000 WVS data, income is significant; those in higher income groups are significantly more likely to express trust in Americans and Canadians. The only other predictor to consistently emerge as significant is national pride: Canadians with higher levels of national pride are more trusting of Americans and Mexicans. Ideological orientations have almost no bearing on cross-national trust.[7]

A SLIPPERY SLOPE?

One reason why CUSFTA was so contentious was that some Canadians worried that formalizing closer economic ties with the United States would amount to a slippery slope. Some expressed the concern that harmonizing trade arrangements and economies would reduce Canada's policy autonomy and place at risk those social policy differences—such as Medicare and social welfare—about which Canadians, historically, had clearly made very different collective choices. Others pondered even more radical implications. Would knitting the economies together through trade agreements such as CUSFTA and NAFTA amount to taking an irretrievable step toward political integration?

In addition to tapping public views about various economic facets of expanding trade, the North American WVS also contained a special subset of questions designed to probe citizens' views about political integration. These included questions measuring support for full political integration as well as a set of experimental scenarios that make it possible to gauge how mobile attitudes toward political integration might be. Canadians were asked: "All things considered, do you think we should do away with the border between the United States and Canada?" That question goes far beyond any proposal that governments on either side of the border have discussed. Even so, the evidence from the 1990 WVS is truly striking: nearly one in four Canadians indicated that they would support such a proposal. That level of support is much higher than a projection based on past history would predict.[8]

After ten years of free trade, and substantial increases in Canada-U.S. transborder transactions, have levels of support for political integration changed among the Canadian public? The aggregate evidence, presented in figure 8.3, clearly suggests that they have. Support for "doing away with the border" climbed from one in four Canadians in 1990 to one in three by the year 2000.

The increase is both striking and significant. A comparison of correlations among a number of variables suggests that there might be some variations in the dynamics of support for doing away with borders within the Canadian public (see appendix A). For example, the correlation between age and these orientations became stronger ($r =$

.03 in 1990; r = .08 in 2000). Opposition to doing away with borders also became more strongly correlated with levels of national pride (r = -.06 in 1990; r = -.11 in 2000). And there is evidence indicating that support for "closer economic ties" is consistently associated with support for "doing away with borders" (r = .17 in 1990; r = .16 in 2000). Notice also that support for the American dollarization of the Canadian monetary system is powerfully related both to support for "doing away with borders" (r = .34, 2000) and to support for closer economic ties with the United States (r = .14), and even to "materialist" orientations (r = .09). These attitudes appear to be bundled in coherent ways. But correlations are not very revealing when it comes to determining precisely which factors drive support for, and opposition to, "doing away with borders." Once again, a multivariate setup is useful in that it can isolate the independent effects of each variable while controlling for others. Furthermore, a comparison of the results of replicated analyses for 1990 and 2000 should be able to clarify if, and how, support for "doing away with borders" might have changed.

Figure 8.3. Support among Canadians for "Doing Away with the Border," 1990 and 2000

Question: "All things considered, do you think we should do away with the border between the United States and Canada? Favor or Oppose."

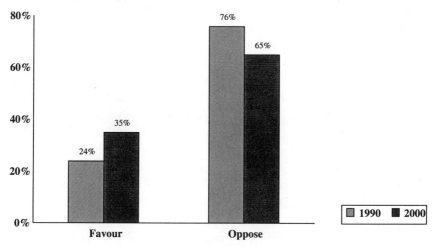

Source: World Values Surveys (Canada), 1990, 2000.
Note: Don't Knows and Refused are excluded from the analysis.

Table 8.3 reports the results of the multivariate analysis that identifies predictors of support for "doing away with the border" for 1990 and 2000. Here the first point to note is that none of the models for 1990 emerges as significant; the standard blocks of predictors used to estimate support for "doing away with borders" exhibit very little structure. But the results for 2000 are quite different; they are statistically significant. Among the socioeconomic predictors, age emerges as a significant predictor of support for doing away with borders; older Canadians are slightly more likely to favor that option. Much more explanatory leverage is provided by the other two blocks of variables, those that tap identities and ideological orientations. Support for the American dollarization of the Canadian monetary system and trust in Americans are predictors of support for doing away with borders, while high levels of national pride inhibit support for "doing away with borders." When it comes to political and economic outlooks, both right-wing self-identification and concern with material security are significant predictors of support for doing away with borders. But support for capitalist values is insignificant.

How should these results be interpreted? Certainly there has been a significant increase in the proportion of the Canadian public that is prepared to countenance doing away with the border, and those orientations were more sharply structured in 2000 than they were in 1990. Even though those supporting closer economic ties with the United States are somewhat more inclined to support "doing away with borders," it is not at all clear that there is any attitudinal slippery slope at work. There are three reasons for arriving at that conclusion. First, as a comparison of the analyses of support for closer economic ties (table 8.1) and doing away with borders (table 8.3) shows, there are significant differences in the socioeconomic bases of these orientations. Education (low) and income (low) are significant predictors of support for closer economic ties (table 8.1). But neither factor turns out to be a significant predictor of doing away with borders (table 8.3). And while age (older) is a significant predictor of support for doing away with borders (table 8.3), age is not a significant predictor of support for closer economic ties (table 8.1). To the extent that age is relevant at all, in fact, it is the young, not the old, who are more likely to support closer economic ties with the United States. The socioeconomic bases of support for these two sets of views, in short, come from different segments of the Canadian population.

Second, a parallel argument can be made with respect to the evidence concerning attitudes and identities. Both trust in Americans and national pride are significant predictors in the estimations of support for closer economic ties and doing away with borders. Trust in Americans works in the same way in both estimations (tables 8.1 and 8.3); it is positively associated with support for closer economic ties and for doing away with borders. But the impact of national pride on both outlooks is completely different; higher levels of national pride among Canadians encourage closer economic ties, but they are a deterrent to support for doing away with borders.

Finally, there is the evidence that comes from ideological orientations. All three ideological outlooks are powerful predictors of support for closer economic ties with the United States; it is this dimension that mostly explains support for closer economic ties. As to support for doing away with borders, materialist outlooks are relevant, and to a much lesser extent so too is right-wing self-placement. But support for capitalist values is not significant at all. A comparison of the relative impact of identities and ideological outlooks makes the point with emphasis: it is ideological outlooks that determine most of the support for closer economic ties, whereas it is identities that explain most of the variance in support for doing away with borders.

HOW DOES CANADIAN PUBLIC OPINION MOVE?

Both the 1990 and 2000 WVS incorporated experiments to allow us to explore how robust, or fragile, Canadian attitudes are to the prospects of "forming one country" with the United States. The scenarios entail probes that encourage respondents to take into account different considerations; the probes make the idea of forming one country less abstract by encouraging respondents to think about the possible outcomes, or consequences, that might be associated with such an arrangement. The idea of "forming one country" serves as an unambiguous analogue of the question asking respondents about "doing away with the border." Given this benchmark, the postulation of differential outcomes makes it possible to detect how public opinion moves in reaction to practical rather than abstract considerations.

Respondents were presented with the same five scenarios in 1990 and 2000, and the order of presentation of the scenarios was rotated to mitigate question order effects. The results, summarized in figure 8.4, indicate that Canadians in 2000 responded to these scenarios in very much the same way as they had in 1990. The same scenarios boost, or dampen, support for the idea of "forming one country" to about the

Table 8.3. Predictors of Canadian Support for "Doing Away with the Border," 1990 and 2000

Question: "All things considered, do you think that we should do away with the border between Canada and the United States? Favor or Oppose."

	1990			2000		
	Model 1	Model 2	Model 3	Model 1	Model 2	Model 3
Constant	.01	.38	−.08	−.59***	−.34	−1.3***
SES						
Age (old)	−.34 (.71)	−.40 (.67)	−.43 (.65)	.49 (1.6)**	.54 (1.7)**	.50 (1.6)**
Gender (male)	.26 (1.3)	.18 (1.2)	.21 (1.2)	.28 (1.3)**	.19 (1.2)	.19 (1.2)
Education (high)	−1.0 (.35)***	−1.2 (.29)***	−1.2 (.21)***	−.45 (.63)	−.46 (.63)	−.30 (.74)
Income (high)	−.72 (.49)**	−.80 (.45)***	−.83 (.44)***	−.29 (.74)	−.26 (.77)	−.30 (.74)
Occupation (white-collar)	.03 (1.0)	−.08 (.92)	−.06 (.94)	−.06 (.94)	−.23 (.79)	−.21 (.81)
Identities/Attitudes						
National pride (yes)		−.78 (.46)**	−.93 (.40)***		−1.2 (.30)***	−1.2 (.30)***
Cosmopolitanism (yes)		.19 (1.2)	.23 (1.3)		−.31 (.73)	−.27 (.76)
Trust Mexicans (yes)		.29 (1.3)*	.29 (1.3)*		.35 (1.5)**	.35 (1.4)**
Support US$ (yes)		--	--		1.4 (4.1)***	1.4 (3.9)***
Free trade (positive)		.57 (1.7)***	.54 (1.7)***		.19 (1.2)	.15 (1.2)
Orientations						
Left-Right (Right)			.30 (1.3)			.67 (1.9)*
Capitalism/Free enterprise (agree)			.15 (1.2)			−.40 (.67)
Materialist concerns (yes)			.68 (2.0)**			.50 (1.6)***
Nagelkerke R^2	.042	.077	.088	.017	.137	.147

***$p < .01$; **$p < .05$; *$p < .1$

Source: World Values Surveys (Canada), 1990, 2000.

Notes: Entries are unstandardized logistic regression coefficients, with odds ratios in parentheses. Don't knows and refusals were excluded for all variables from the analysis.

same extent. The promise of a "better quality of life" produces a significant increase in support for forming one country, over and above the 35 percent threshold response suggested by responses to the question of "doing away with borders." Under that scenario, half of all respondents in 1990 would "form one country," and that proportion climbed to 54 percent in 2000. Having a "higher standard of living" has about the same impact on support for political integration in 1990 as in 2000. And the impact of the scenario that has Canada becoming "twelve new states" is stable across the two time points. The shifts in responses to the other scenarios were statistically marginal.

Figure 8.4. Scenarios of Moving Public Opinion in Canada, 1990 and 2000

> **Questions***:* "Would you favor or oppose Canada and the United States forming one country if…
> (a) it meant a better quality of life
> (b) it meant you would enjoy a higher standard of living
> (c) it meant that Canada would form twelve new states in the United States
> (d) it meant slightly lower taxes but fewer government services
> (e) it meant losing Canada's cultural identity"

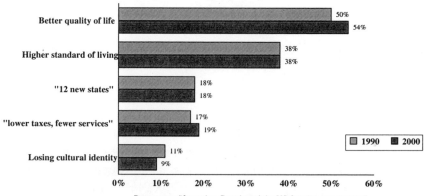

Sources: World Values Surveys (Canada) 1990, 2000.
Note: Don't Knows and Refused are excluded from the analysis.

A more detailed multivariate analysis of responses to each of these scenarios (not shown) reveals a similar pattern for both the 1990 and 2000 scenarios; the results for the "forming one country" dependent variable are somewhat sharper than those emerging from the analysis of "doing away with borders." The consistent finding is that it is the young and the socioeconomically marginalized that are most inclined to support the idea of Canada forming one country with the United States. More specifically, it is the young, males, those with low levels of formal education and income, workers in blue-collar occupations, and persons who exhibit low levels of national pride and materialist concerns and who see themselves as being "on the right" who are the most inclined to support the idea of "forming one country."

FINAL REMARKS

We began by suggesting that the 1990 and 2000 WVS provide a useful set of Canadian public opinion data for exploring how Canadian views about expanding trade environments over the course of that decade have changed. Are they stable? There is much evidence to suggest that Canadians and other publics generally care little about "foreign affairs," at least during tranquil times.[9] The debate surrounding the 1988 Canadian federal election, however, demonstrated that Canadians did care about continental free trade. Moreover, the 1990 and 2000 WVS evidence supports the view that continental trade remains relevant. Canadian opinion about expanded trade does not lack structure; it is structured in meaningful ways.

The investigation explored opinion change and stability from two vantage points. The first investigated stability and change in the aggregate levels of support for, and opposition to, closer economic ties with the United States and Mexico. The basic finding suggests both stability and change. Canadian attitudes to closer economic ties with Mexico remained the same, while support for closer economic ties with the United States increased from 1990 to 2000. The second vantage point examined evidence of stability and change in the structure of Canadian public opinion about closer economic ties with both countries.

This latter line of investigation supposed that Canadian public opinion about continental trade might be structured by at least three different kinds of considerations. First, public views might plausibly be shaped by calculations as to whether people were winners or losers in the expanding trade environment. To the extent that expanding trade redistributes the balance of domestic advantages and disadvantages, and that these would show up differentially in different sectors of society, there are reasons to suppose that public opinion about continental trade might be structured around the sociodemographic characteristics of respondents in the WVS surveys. Second, there were considerations concerning identities. While continental trade opened up new economic opportunities, public concern was also expressed about the possibility that this pursuit of continental trade might challenge and undermine long-standing identities. A third possibility explored was the notion that expanding continental free trade could reflect a changing ideological environment in which publics had become more inclined than in the past to embrace capitalist values.

The empirical evidence presented here shows that each one of these considerations did play a role in shaping Canadian public opinion about trade and closer ties with both the United States and Mexico. What is more significant, however, is that they worked in different combinations at different points in time depending on which country—the United States or Mexico—was the object of concern. Canadians do not respond to the idea of "closer economic ties" in some abstract, generalizable way. In the case of the United States, Canadian opinion about closer economic ties is driven more by ideology than by other considerations. To the extent that socioeconomic status matters, it is those Canadians with low levels of education and income who are attracted to the idea of closer economic ties with the United States. In the case of Mexico, Canadian views about closer economic ties are driven by socioeconomic status, not ideological considerations. Moreover, support for closer ties with Mexico comes from those with high income and education. To the extent that ideological considerations play any discernible role in structuring Canadian opinions about closer ties with Mexico, those considerations operate in ways that are the opposite of those that come into play in views about the United States.

Identities clearly play a secondary role in structuring Canadian opinion about the economic features of continental trade. But identities become of primary significance when political considerations come to the fore. Only a minority of Canadians holds to the view that closer economic ties represent a slippery slope toward greater political integration. After ten years of free trade with the United States, the idea of doing away with borders between Canada and the United States has become more popular. That finding is clear, and it is tempting to extrapolate that evidence into the future. But in addition to a variety of value differences that make Canadians distinct from their American counterparts,[10] it is the relatively high levels of national pride and concerns about culture that presently stand in the way of a broader Canadian enthusiasm for doing away with borders between the two countries.

Notes

1. Ronald Inglehart, Neil Nevitte, and Miguel Basáñez, *The North American Trajectory: Cultural, Economic, and Political Ties among the United States, Canada and Mexico* (New York: Aldine de Gruyter, 1996), p. 135.

2. Desmond King, *The New Right: Politics, Markets and Citizenship* (Chicago: Dorsey, 1987), p. 7.

3. The sample sizes for the Canadian surveys are as follow: 1981 N = 1,254; 1990 N = 1,730; 2000 N = 1,931.

4. The closer economic ties variable is correlated with support for the Free Trade Agreement (1990) (r = .16) and with Confidence in NAFTA (2000) (r = 0.2).

5. Ronald Rogowski, *Commerce and Coalitions: How Trade Affects Domestic Political Alignments* (Princeton, N.J.: Princeton University Press, 1989), p. 7.

6. Karl Deutsch et al., *Political Community and the North Atlantic Area* (Princeton, N.J.: Princeton University Press, 1957).

7. The single exception to that pattern is trust toward Mexicans. Canadians who support capitalist values are somewhat more likely to trust Mexicans, but the relationship is weak and it barely crosses the threshold of statistical significance.

8. Inglehart, Nevitte, and Basáñez, *North American Trajectory*, p. 139.

9. Neil Nevitte and Roger Gibbins, "Foreign Policy Debates and Sleeping Dogs," *Canadian Public Policy* 12, no. 3 (1986): 402.

10. Neil Nevitte, *The Decline of Deference* (Peterborough, Ontario: Broadview, 1996).

Appendix A. Inter-item Correlations, World Values Surveys (Canada), 1990 and 2000

Variables	Age	Education	Income	National Pride	Parochialism-Cosmopolitanism	Trust Americans	Trust Mexico
Age	1.0						
Education	-.18 / -.30	1.0					
Income	-.10 / -.14	.41 / .35	1.0				
National Pride	.09 / .09	-.06 / -.09	.06 / -.04	1.0			
Parochialism-Cosmopolitanism	-.06 / -.01	.10 / .08	.07 / .04	.02 / .03	1.0		
Trust Americans	.18 / .15	-.03 / -.00	.02 / .02	.08 / .10	-.02 / .04	1.0	
Trust Mexicans	.06 / .05	.04 / .02	.04 / .03	.07 / .04	-.01 / .11	.65 / .61	1.0
Left-Right dimension	.11 / .15	-.07 / -.02	.05 / .04	.13 / .14	-.02 / -.02	.09 / .10	.05 / .01
Capitalism/Free enterprise	.07 / .14	-.03 / -.03	.16 / .12	.12 / .04	-.04 / -.07	.07 / .14	.06 / .08
Materialism	.11 / .02	-.13 / -.15	.01 / -.08	.01 / .12	-.09 / -.10	.02 / -.02	-.02 / -.06
Closer economic ties with United States	.05 / .04	-.11 / -.02	-.04 / -.00	.09 / .05	-.00 / -.03	.16 / .19	.07 / .08
Closer economic ties with Mexico	.06 / .02	.10 / .09	.09 / .15	.04 / -.05	.09 / .07	.11 / .09	.23 / .24
Attitude toward NAFTA	-.06 / -.04	.08 / .12	.07 / .14	.01 / -.09	.05 / -.04	.11 / .13	.07 / .06
Doing away with the border	.08 / .03	-.10 / -.10	-.06 / -.10	-.11 / -.06	-.03 / .00	.08 / .09	-.03 / .02
Support adoption of US$ in Canada	.00	-.04	-.02	-.09	.03	.05	-.03

Appendix A (continued)

Variables	Left-Right	Capitalism/ Free Enterprise	Materialism	Closer Economic Ties with United States	Closer Economic Ties with Mexico	Attitude toward NAFTA	Doing Away with the Border	Support Adoption of US$
Age								
Education								
Income								
National Pride								
Parochialism-Cosmopolitanism								
Trust Americans								
Trust Mexicans								
Left-Right dimension	1.0							
Capitalism/ Free enterprise	**.20** .16	1.0						
Materialism	**.05** .11	**.11** .05	1.0					
Closer economic ties with United States	**.15** .12	**.18** .05	**.15** .12	1.0				
Closer economic ties with Mexico	**-.03** -.01	**.03** -.01	**-.06** -.06	**.20** .16	1.0			
Attitude toward NAFTA	**.12** .11	**.06** .16	**.05** .00	**.18** .27	**.16** .07	1.0		
Doing away with the border	**.04** .02	**-.01** .02	**.11** .05	**.16** .17	**-.00** -.02	**.08** .10	1.0	
Support adoption of US$ in Canada	**.03**	**-.01**	**.09**	**.14**	**.03**	**.08**	**.34**	1.0

Source: World Values Surveys (Canada) 1990, 2000.
Notes: Estimates in bold are results from the 2000 wave, with the 1990 results underneath. Reported measures of correlation are Pearson's r.

Appendix B. Predictors of Canadian Levels of Trust in Americans, 1990 and 2000

Question: "I now want to ask you how much you trust the following groups of people. Using the responses on this card, could you tell me how much you trust: Americans. Trust them completely; trust them a little; neither trust nor distrust them; do not trust them very much or do not trust them at all."

	1990			2000		
	Model 1	Model 2	Model 3	Model 1	Model 2	Model 3
Constant	−.42	−1.4***	−1.9***	−.55***	−1.1***	−1.3***
SES						
Age (old)	1.3 (3.6)***	1.2 (3.5)***	1.1 (3.1)***	.99 (2.7)***	.96 (2.6)***	.93 (2.5)***
Gender (male)	−.23 (.79)*	−.18 (.83)	−.20 (.81)	.19 (1.2)*	.20 (1.2)*	.18 (1.2)*
Education (high)	.42 (1.5)	.47 (1.6)	.44 (1.5)	−.14 (.87)	−.08 (.92)	−.05 (.95)
Income (high)	.36 (1.4)	.34 (1.4)	.23 (1.3)	.48 (1.6)**	.43 (1.5)**	.38 (1.5)*
Occupation (white-collar)	−.37 (.69)	−.32 (.72)	−.34 (.71)	.04 (1.0)	.04 (1.0)	.03 (1.0)
Identities/Attitudes						
National pride (yes)		.96 (2.6)***	.88 (2.4)***		.61 (1.8)**	.52 (1.7)**
Cosmopolitanism (yes)		.23 (1.3)	.28 (1.3)		−.06 (.94)	−.05 (.95)
Orientations						
Left-Right (Right)			.79 (2.2)**			.44 (1.5)
Capitalism/Free enterprise (agree)			.61 (1.8)**			.25 (1.3)
Materialist concerns (yes)			−.11 (.89)			−.06 (.94)
Nagelkerke R^2	.050	.066	.080	.029	.033	.036

***p < .01; **p < .05; *p < .1

Source: World Values Surveys (Canada), 1990, 2000.

Coding: The dependent variable was recoded into a dichotomous variable: trust them completely and trust them a little (1); do not trust them very much and do not trust them at all (0).

Notes: Entries are unstandardized logistic regression coefficients, with odds ratios in parentheses. Don't knows and refusals were excluded for all variables from the analysis.

Appendix C. Predictors of Canadian Levels of Trust in Mexicans, 1990 and 2000

Question: "I now want to ask you how much you trust the following groups of people. Using the responses on this card, could you tell me how much you trust: Mexicans. Trust them completely; trust them a little; neither trust nor distrust them; do not trust them very much or do not trust them at all."

	1990			2000		
	Model 1	Model 2	Model 3	Model 1	Model 2	Model 3
Constant	-.89***	-1.3***	-1.3***	-.98***	-1.6***	-1.7***
SES						
Age (old)	.50 (1.6)**	.47 (1.6)**	.45 (1.6)**	.40 (1.5)**	.37 (1.4)**	.37 (1.4)**
Gender (male)	-.03 (.97)	-.02 (.98)	-.03 (.97)	.01 (1.0)	.02 (1.0)	.00 (1.0)
Education (high)	.18 (1.2)	.16 (1.2)	.13 (1.1)	.06 (1.0)	.11 (1.1)	.09 (1.1)
Income (high)	.25 (1.3)	.26 (1.3)	.24 (1.3)	.44 (1.5)**	.39 (1.5)*	36 (1.4)*
Occupation (white-collar)	-.00 (.99)	-.02 (.97)	-.02 (.97)	.30 (1.4)	.31 (1.4)	.30 (1.3)
Identities/Attitudes						
National pride (yes)		.25 (1.3)	.30 (1.3)		.69 (2.0)**	.61 (1.8)**
Cosmopolitanism (yes)		.66 (1.9)***	.65 (1.9)***		.05 (1.0)	.04 (1.0)
Orientations						
Left-Right (Right)			-.18 (.83)			.08 (1.1)
Capitalism/Free enterprise (agree)			.18 (1.2)			.42 (1.5)*
Materialist concerns (yes)			-.21 (.81)			-.19 (.82)
Nagelkerke R²	.009	.023	.025	.012	.017	.020

***p < .01;**p < .05; *p < .1

Source: World Values Surveys (Canada), 1990, 2000.

Coding: The dependent variable was recoded into a dichotomous variable: trust them completely and trust them a little (1); do not trust them very much and do not trust them at all (0).

Notes: Entries are unstandardized logistic regression coefficients, with odds ratios in parentheses.
Don't knows and refusals were excluded for all variables from the analysis.

Appendix D. Variables and Coding

Unless otherwise indicated all "Don't Know" and "Refuse" responses were declared as missing.

Unless otherwise indicated assigned values are regression recodes.

Age
18–29 years (0); 30–39 (0.25); 40–49 (0.5); 50–69 (0.75); 70+ (1)

Education (WVS1990)
At what age did you or will you complete your full time education, either at school or at an institution of higher education? Please exclude apprenticeships.
< 12 years (0); 13–14 years (0.2); 15–16 years (0.4); 17–18 years (0.6); 19–20 years (0.8); 21 years or older (1).

Education (WVS2000)
No formal education (0); Incomplete Primary, Complete Primary (0.2); Incomplete Secondary, Complete Secondary (0.4); Incomplete College, Complete College (0.6); Some University-level education (0.8); Complete University-level education (1).

Gender
Male (1); Female (0).

Income
Up to $12,500 (0); $12,501–$20,000 (0.11); $20,000–$27,500 (0.22); $27,500–$35,000 (0.33); $35,000–$42,500 (0.44); $42,500–$50,000 (0.55); $50,000–$62,500 (0.66); $62,500–$75,000 (0.77); $75,000–$100,000 (0.88); $100,000 or more (1).

Occupation
Employer/Manager, Professional Worker (1); Mid-level non-manual, Junior-level non-manual (0.8); Foreman and Supervisor, Skilled Manual Worker, Member of the Armed Forces (0.6); Semi-Skilled Manual Worker, Unskilled Manual Worker (0.4); Farmer, Agricultural Worker (0.2); Never Worked (0).

National Pride

"How proud are you to be Canadian?"
Very proud (1); Quite Proud (0.66); Not Very Proud (0.33); Not At All
Proud (0); Not Canadian (missing).

Left-Right

"In political matters, people talk of the left and the right. How would
you place your views on this scale, generally speaking?"

Left										Right
0	.1	.2	.3	.4	.5	.6	.7	.8	.9	1

National/Geographical Identity

"Which of these geographical groups would you say you belong to first
of all?" Locality or town where you live (0); Region of country where
you live (0.25); Your country as a whole (0.5); North America (0.75);
The world as a whole (1).

Trust Americans/Mexicans

"I now want to ask you how much you trust the following groups of
people. Using the responses on this card, could you tell me how much
you trust: Americans; Mexicans." Trust them completely (1); Trust
them a little (0.75); Neither trust nor distrust them (0.5); Do not trust
them very much (0.25); Do not trust them at all (0). [Recoded into a
dummy variable for the logistic regression: Trust them completely and
Trust them a little (1); Neither trust nor distrust them, Do not trust
them very much and Do not trust them at all (0).

Closer Economic Ties with the U.S./Mexico

"In your opinion, should Canada have closer, or more distant economic ties with the United States, Mexico?" Much closer (1); Somewhat closer (0.66); A bit more distant (0.33); Much more distant (0).
[Recoded into a dummy variable for the logistic regression: Much
closer and somewhat closer (1); A bit more distant and much more
distant (0).]

NAFTA (WVS 1990)

"More than a year ago, Canada signed a Free Trade Agreement with
the United States. Thinking about the agreement today, which phrase
best describes your opinion?" I am a strong supporter of the FTA (1);

On balance, I support the FTA (0.66); On balance, I oppose the FTA (0.33); I absolutely oppose the FTA (0). [Recoded into a dummy variable for the logistic regression: I am a strong supporter and I support the FTA (1); I oppose and I absolutely oppose the FTA (0)].

NAFTA (WVS 2000)
"Please look at this card and tell me, for each item listed, how much confidence you have in them; is it a great deal, quite a lot, not very much or none at all?: NAFTA." A great deal (1); Quite a lot (0.66); Not very much (0.33); None at all (0). [Recoded into a dummy variable for the logistic regression: A great deal and quite a lot (1); not very much and none at all (0).]

Capitalism/Free Enterprise Index
Respondents strongly agreeing with free enterprise and capitalist values (1); Respondents agreeing (0.66); disagreeing (0.33); strongly disagreeing (0).

The Index is based upon the following variables and has been tested with factor analyses:

- "There is a lot of discussion about how business and industry should be managed. Which of these four statements comes closest to your opinion?" The owners should run their business or appoint managers (1); The owners and employees should participate in the selection of managers (0.66); The government should be the owner and appoint the managers (0.33); The employees should own the business and should elect the managers (0).

- "Now I'd like you to tell me your views on various issues. How would you place your views on this scale? Each card I show you has two contradicting statements on it. Using the scale listed, could you tell me where you would place your own view? 1 means agree completely with the statement on the left, 10 means you completely agree with the statement on the right, or you can choose any number in between."

    —Private Ownership of business and industry should be increased OR Government ownership of business and industry should be increased.

—Individuals should take more responsibility for providing for themselves OR Government should take more responsibility to ensure that everyone is provided for.

Scenarios

"Would you favor or oppose Canada and the United States forming one country if..."
(a) it meant that you would enjoy a higher standard of living?
(b) it meant losing Canada's cultural identity?
(c) it meant that Canada would form twelve new states in the United States?
(d) it meant slightly lower taxes but fewer government services?
(e) it meant a better quality of life?

Strongly favor (1); Favor (0.75); Neither favor nor oppose (0.5); Oppose (0.25); Strongly oppose (0).

Doing away with the border between Canada and the United States

"All things considered, do you think that we should do away with the border between Canada and the United States?" Favor (1); Oppose (0).

9

Tepid Traders: U.S. Public Attitudes on NAFTA and Free Trade Expansion

Phillip S. Warf and Steven Kull

In April 2001, leaders from every nation in the Western Hemisphere except Cuba met in Quebec City at the third Summit of the Americas. As the meeting drew to a close, they announced their collective commitment to seek a Free Trade Area of the Americas (FTAA) by 2005. President George W. Bush has since reaffirmed his desire to meet this goal, but given the complex and bitter national debate over trade expansion over the last few years, the road to FTAA is unlikely to be a smooth one. Many Democrats oppose further trade expansion unless they get assurances that labor and environmental standards will be included in future agreements. Most Republicans want to keep trade moving forward without linkage to such standards, as has been the case traditionally, but they are feeling pressure from businesses that could suffer from further reductions in trade barriers. At the same time, anti-globalization activists will probably continue to take to the streets demanding an end to further trade liberalization. This is a healthy debate, and one in which public opinion ought to play a large role. The question arises, then, as to where the broad majority of the public stands.

In answering this question, it is important to assess existing public attitudes on NAFTA as well as to capture a sense of how those views fit in with broader, more fundamental public attitudes about trade policy. Polls show that Americans give NAFTA modest support, but they also have serious reservations about its impact: a plurality thinks the trade agreement has been good for the United States overall, but a majority is also concerned about its impact on the jobs and wages of vulnerable workers. This is consistent with attitudes about trade more generally. As Benjamin Page and Robert Shapiro have pointed out, "most Americans like the idea of free trade (and cheap imports) in principle, but over many years large majorities have favored some measure of protectionism to safeguard American jobs."[1]

Attitudes about trade expansion are also complex, but they do present a picture of what kind of trade policies the public prefers. The few poll questions asked about a Free Trade Area of the Americas have revealed general support, but these questions are vague and not very recent. Attitudes on trade promotion authority (TPA) do not show majority support. (Formerly called fast track trade negotiating authority, TPA gives the executive the power to negotiate trade deals that Congress can vote up or down in their entirety, but not amend.) Instead, Americans are looking for assurances that any growth of trade will be accompanied by greater efforts to assist U.S. workers who are hurt by trade, and by the inclusion of labor and environmental standards in future trade agreements.

PUBLIC MILDLY POSITIVE ON NAFTA AND TRADE

Over the last few years, several polls have attempted to measure attitudes about NAFTA, in most cases asking whether it has been good or bad for the United States. Since late 1997, these polls have found a modest plurality expressing a positive view of NAFTA's impact. Most recently, a May 2000 Gallup poll found 47 percent saying NAFTA has been good for the United States, while 39 percent said it has been bad. Similarly, in an October 1999 poll by the Program on International Policy Attitudes (PIPA), a plurality of 44 percent viewed NAFTA as good for the United States, and just 30 percent saw it as bad. As figure 9.1 shows, these results are largely consistent with the results of other polls in recent years.

A high percentage of respondents—usually 15 to 25 percent—do not offer an opinion in these results. This is not surprising: whether NAFTA has been good or bad for the United States is a fairly technical question over which even many experts disagree. Indeed, when an August 1999 poll by the *Washington Post*, Kaiser Family Foundation, and Harvard University explicitly offered the option—"or haven't you heard enough to say?"—51 percent chose that option, while 24 percent said NAFTA had been good and 20 percent thought it had been bad.

When asked whether the United States should withdraw from NAFTA, only a small minority favors doing so. Since 1998, Epic-MRA polls for Women in International Trade (WIIT) have asked whether the United States should continue in NAFTA. In the latest survey, taken in May 2000, just 15 percent wanted to "pull out of NAFTA." In early 1996, when attitudes about NAFTA were less favorable, three Time/CNN polls found about a third of the public in favor of "withdrawing," while roughly half were opposed and the remainder unsure.

Figure 9.1. U.S. Perceptions of NAFTA, 1997–2000

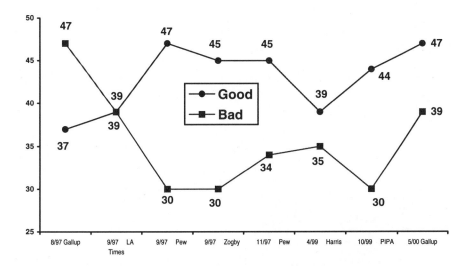

Attitudes about NAFTA have gone through a complex evolution. In 1991, Gallup polls found support for the North American free trade idea to be quite high; in two polls that year, over 70 percent said it would be "good for the U.S." But support had dropped dramatically by late 1992—to 54 percent in a September Gallup poll, and then to 46 percent in an October Newsweek survey. The high-profile debate of 1993 engendered even more uncertainty, and the public became quite divided by the fall of 1993. The rise to prominence of Ross Perot during the 1992 campaign and his strong opposition to further trade agreements, as well as the modest recession of 1991–1992, may well have contributed to dampening support for the expansion of free trade, especially in light of concerns that U.S. workers would be forced to compete with low-wage workers in Mexico.

At the time of NAFTA's passage, several polls found the public virtually evenly split on whether it favored or opposed the trade pact. In early November 1993, a Time/CNN poll found that 41 percent supported the agreement to "eliminate all trade barriers" between the United States, Canada, and Mexico. An almost equal number were opposed (39 percent), with 20 percent undecided. At the same time, ABC News found the public divided as to whether "Congress should approve or reject NAFTA": 42 percent said they should, and 42 percent said they should not. Also, a CBS/New York Times poll in November 1993 found 37 percent in favor and 41 percent opposed—a difference that falls within the margin of error. Again, polls that allowed respondents to say they were not familiar enough with the issue usually found pluralities giving such a response; still, those that did offer an opinion remained divided. As illustrated by figure 9.2, the response to NAFTA was very mixed, in what seems to have been a reasonable reaction to the intensity of the public debate and the complexity of the issues involved.

Figure 9.2. Final Pre-Vote NAFTA Polls, November 1993

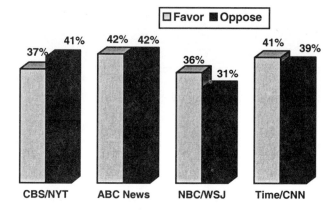

After the U.S. Congress approved the trade deal, however, the public expressed stronger support. An NBC/Wall Street Journal poll in December found that 53 percent of Americans said it was a "step in the right direction," and just 33 percent said it was a "step in the wrong direction." In other contexts, research has shown that public support for a contested policy increases once U.S. leadership resolves its internal differences enough that action is taken. And as already noted, Americans came into the debate with an initial positive orientation to the idea of NAFTA.

Between 1994 and 1997, as NAFTA went into effect, a plurality of Americans felt that the net results of NAFTA for the United States were initially more negative than positive. Between July 1994 and July 1997, for example, four NBC/Wall Street Journal polls asked the public for an assessment of NAFTA's "impact" on the nation "so far." In every case, a modest plurality, ranging from 35 to 48 percent, said they believed NAFTA had "more of a negative impact" on the United States. Those saying it had a more positive impact ranged from 21 to 32 percent. Very large percentages continued to express uncertainty.

Other polls taken during this period by CBS News, Times Mirror, and Harris found a slim plurality expressing support for the trade pact more generally, indicating that these negative views probably hinged on an interim assessment of impact, not attitudes about NAFTA overall. For example, Times Mirror found 43 percent in favor, 38 percent opposed (March 1995), and Harris found 48 percent in favor, 39 percent opposed (April 1995). A CBS News question found in October 1996 that about half preferred to say they did not know enough to make a judgment, but of the remainder, those who favored NAFTA outnumbered those who opposed it by about three to two.

As noted, in late 1997 support increased and has stayed relatively steady since. Recent questions about NAFTA have been asked in a period of remarkable economic performance in the United States, when large majorities rated the overall economy positively. When attitudes about the state of the U.S. economy grow more pessimistic in a period of economic slowdown, such as mid-2001, support for NAFTA and trade expansion may decline.

Views on Trade in General

Attitudes about NAFTA reflect the public's views of trade more broadly. A majority has consistently expressed a belief in the general proposition that free trade has a positive impact on the country and its economy. In February 2000, Pew found 64 percent felt free trade is "good for the United States," while just 27 percent said it was bad. As Kenneth Scheve and Matthew Slaughter have argued in their work on attitudes toward globalization, "the strongest support for international trade appears in response to questions that describe trade in broad terms."[2]

When the question is posed in a way that highlights the costs as well as the benefits of trade, a modest majority expresses support for free trade. Over the past decade, Gallup has asked whether Americans view "foreign trade" as "an opportunity for economic growth through increased U.S. exports or a threat to the economy from foreign imports." In four consecutive polls since 1994, as summarized in table 9.1, a modest majority has seen trade as an opportunity rather than a threat, most recently 51 percent to 37 percent in February 2001.

Table 9.1. Views of Foreign Trade as Opportunity or Threat, 1994–2000

Question: What do you think foreign trade means for America? Do you see foreign trade more as an opportunity for economic growth through increased U.S. exports or a threat to the economy from foreign imports? (Gallup)

	Opportunity (%)	Threat (%)	Both/Neither (%)
February 2001	51	37	9
May 2000	56	36	5
January 2000	54	35	5
November 1994	53	38	5

In PIPA's October 1999 poll, respondents were presented with two arguments. Fifty-one percent favored the statement, "Free trade is a good idea, because it can lead to lower prices and the long-term growth of the economy," while 44 percent endorsed the one that made the case, "Free trade is a bad idea, because it can lead to lower wages and people losing their jobs." These findings are very consistent with the Gallup results.

A strong belief in the theoretical economic benefits of trade undergirds this general support for freer trade. Scheve and Slaughter have noted that "large majorities of Americans think that trade generates the benefits predicted by economists," including reducing prices and expanding the selection of goods for consumers, spurring greater innovation and competitiveness among U.S. companies, and creating import-related jobs in other domestic industries. Several such poll results are detailed in their work.[3]

In addition, a majority of Americans supports the growth of trade in principle. In the October 1999 PIPA survey, for example, respondents were asked about the pace of lowering trade barriers. Only 30 percent said it was going too fast, while 62 percent said it was going the right speed (39 percent) or too slowly (23 percent). Asked what the U.S. government's goal should be for international trade, just 39 percent favored trying to "slow it down" (31 percent) or to "stop or reverse it" (8 percent), while 58 percent favored trying to "actively promote it" (32 percent) or to "allow it to continue" (26 percent). In the same survey, respondents were asked to rate "the growth of international trade" on a scale from 0 to 10, with 0 meaning completely negative, 10 meaning completely positive, and 5 meaning equally positive and negative. Forty-one percent gave trade a positive rating, 35 percent rated it as neutral, and just 21 percent scored it as negative.

Further, a majority supports free trade agreements. Over the years, other polls also have found support for agreements to liberalize trade. In three Epic-MRA polls conducted from 1998 to 2000, as shown in figure 9.3, about three-fifths of respondents said they approved of "free trade agreements with other countries." In an NBC News/Wall Street Journal poll from December 1997, 55 percent considered "more free trade agreements" to be a "step in the right direction"; just 22 percent said they were a step in the wrong direction, and 13 percent said they did not make any difference. In July 1994, Times Mirror found 62 percent support for "free trade agreements between the United States and other countries, such as NAFTA and GATT"; just 28 percent were opposed.

Figure 9.3. Support for Free Trade Agreements, 1998–2000

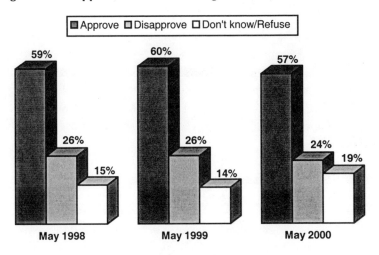

It seems likely that much of the support for trade agreements rests on the public's strong backing of reciprocal trade liberalization. In the 1999 PIPA survey, 64 percent said that "in general, if another country is willing to lower its barriers to products from the U.S. if we will lower our barriers to their products," the United States should comply. Just 29 percent disagreed. Support for reciprocal lowering of barriers is driven by the perceived strategic need to reduce American trade barriers only in order to put pressure on other countries to reduce theirs. In addition, Americans want reciprocity because they believe that other countries benefit more from trade than the United States, due to its more open economy, and that other countries often have unfair trade practices.[4]

DEMOGRAPHIC DIFFERENCES ON NAFTA AND TRADE

Analysis of key responses by demographic characteristics in the October 1999 PIPA poll and a February 2000 Gallup survey indicates that three variables—education level, age, and gender—appeared to have the most impact on attitudes about NAFTA and free trade. Other demographics revealed weak or inconsistent relationships. Even where significant differences were found, they were primarily matters of degree of support, rather than support for competing policies.

Education

There is a good deal of evidence in the PIPA survey that higher educational levels correlate with more positive views on NAFTA. As revealed by table 9.2, a majority of those with advanced degrees and college degrees thought NAFTA had been good for the United States. However, only pluralities of those with some college, a high school diploma, or less than a high school education considered NAFTA to have been good. In the February 2000 Gallup poll, solid majorities of post-graduates and college graduates felt NAFTA had been good for the United States, but those with some college or no college were far less sanguine.

A similar trend was evident on attitudes about free trade more generally. While a bare majority of all respondents in the PIPA poll said that free trade was a good idea, a strong majority of those with advanced degrees (69 percent) felt this way. High school graduates split (47 to 48 percent) on whether free trade is a good or a bad idea; just 37 percent of respondents without a high school diploma thought free trade was a good idea, while 57 percent said it was a bad idea. A similar dynamic emerges from the February 2000 Gallup survey. In that poll, a whopping 84 percent of those with advanced degrees viewed foreign trade as an opportunity for the United States, and nearly two-thirds of college graduates (64 percent) felt the same way. In contrast, those with just a high school education or less were divided as to whether trade represents an opportunity or a threat (48 to 46 percent).

Table 9.2. Education and Views of NAFTA

PIPA 10/99	Good (%)	Bad (%)
Less than high school	40	28
High school graduate	41	35
Some college	44	31
College graduate	52	23
Post graduate	58	21
Gallup 2/00	Good (%)	Bad (%)
High school graduate or less	41	41
Some college	46	42
College graduate	55	36
Post graduate	62	25

Also consistent with the pattern in other questions about trade liberalization, opposition to fast track legislation rose strongly as education level declined. Two-thirds (66 percent) of those who did not graduate from high school opposed fast track legislation, while a bare majority (51 percent) of those with high school or higher opposed such legislation.

This relationship between more education and higher levels of support for trade and NAFTA is consistent with results of other studies. Scheve and Slaughter note, for example, that individuals with higher skill levels (measured by education and income) are not very threatened by trade and thus are less likely to support trade restrictions.[5] Indeed, the PIPA survey found that those with more education also felt that they were less "vulnerable ... to the changes that come with increasing international trade." Those with a high school education or less rated their vulnerability as 5.4 on a scale from 0 to 10, with 10 being most vulnerable; the rating declines with education level, reaching 3.7 for people with an advanced degree.

Age

Responses on NAFTA among different age groups revealed an intriguing pattern: support for NAFTA is strongest among the youngest and oldest groups. As table 9.3 shows, in the PIPA survey, two-thirds of those in the 18–29 age bracket and a plurality of those 65 and over said NAFTA had been good for the United States. On the other hand, those between 30 and 64 were quite divided. Similarly, in the February 2000 Gallup survey, about two in three of those under 30 and a plurality of those 65 and over felt NAFTA had been good; and once again, those between 30 and 64 were divided.

Table 9.3. Age and Views of NAFTA

PIPA 10/99	Good (%)	Bad (%)
18–29	65	15
30–64	37	35
65+	43	32

Gallup 2/00	Good (%)	Bad (%)
18–29	65	25
30–64	42	45
65+	44	35

This result makes sense if one considers that the workers with the most difficulty adjusting to the negative effects of free trade also tend to be middle-aged. They are in mid-career, are more likely to have children at home, have less time and opportunity to learn new skills, and face much more dire economic circumstances if they are laid off. By contrast, those who are younger are likely to have more marketable skills and fewer responsibilities, and those who are retired benefit substantially from lower consumer prices and no longer face the fear of job loss.

Age differences also appear to have some impact on attitudes about international trade more broadly. In general, attitudes tend to grow more negative with age. In the PIPA survey, for example, respondents were asked to rate "the growth of international trade on you personally" on a scale from 0 to 10. On average, those under 30 felt that the growth of international trade had a positive effect on them personally (5.9 of 10), while those 30 and older rated it as having a mildly negative effect on them personally (4.8). In the February 2000 Gallup survey, more than two-thirds of those under 30 viewed foreign trade as an opportunity rather than a threat (69 percent to 29 percent); this proportion declined steadily with each age group, with a slim plurality of those over 65 seeing trade as an opportunity (46 to 41 percent).

Gender

When it comes to attitudes about NAFTA and free trade, gender was also important. The PIPA poll results paint a picture of women as somewhat more skeptical of the benefits of free trade and more sensitized to its costs. When responding to the two arguments about free trade, for example, a solid majority of men said free trade was a good idea (55 to 41 percent), while women were divided (47 percent "good" to 48 percent "bad"). Also, while nearly half of men (49 percent) rated "the growth of international trade" as 6 or higher on the 0-to-10 scale, just 34 percent of women did so.

Though differences on NAFTA were not as pronounced, they do suggest greater uncertainty about trade among women. When asked about NAFTA, a plurality of women (42 percent) said it was good, but that sentiment was stronger among men (47 percent). Importantly, one in four women (25 percent) responded that they did not know whether NAFTA had been good or bad; just 11 percent of men said the same. When asked about NAFTA in the February 2000 Gallup survey, virtually equal proportions of women and men (46 and 47 percent, respectively) said it had been good for the United States. Again, however, women were much more likely than men to say they did not know (19 percent to 10 percent).

RESERVATIONS ABOUT NAFTA

Even though there is general support for NAFTA, that support is quite modest. Indeed, support for the growth of trade in principle—though not overwhelming either—appears substantially stronger relative to that for NAFTA. To understand Americans' lack of enthusiasm, it is necessary to probe their reservations about NAFTA and trade.

Changes to NAFTA

Recent polls have shown that even though more Americans evaluate NAFTA as having been a net benefit for the United States, they nevertheless appear to have some strong reservations. In the May 2000

Epic-MRA poll, as shown in table 9.4, when given three options about their preference for the future of the trade agreement, just 23 percent said they wanted to "continue the NAFTA agreement" as is. A plurality of 42 percent believed NAFTA should be "continued with changes," and 15 percent wanted to "pull out of NAFTA" completely. Thus a rather strong 58 percent majority expressed some dissatisfaction with NAFTA—a finding that has been remarkably consistent since 1998. Even those who said they generally approved of trade agreements with other countries wanted to see changes in NAFTA (43 percent, compared to 37 percent "continue" and 9 percent "pull out").

Table 9.4. Plurality Supporting Changes to NAFTA

Question: This year marks the [Xth] anniversary of NAFTA. After observing how NAFTA has worked between the United States, Mexico, and Canada over the past few years, do you think America should continue the NAFTA agreement, should America pull out of NAFTA, or should it be continued with changes? (Epic-MRA)

| | % Responses | | |
	May 2000	May 1999	May 1998
Continue	23	24	23
Pull out	15	18	16
Continued with changes	42	40	47
Undecided/Don't know	20	18	14

Concern about Jobs

Clearly the biggest concern about NAFTA is its potential impact on jobs. The most recent relevant questions show that pluralities or slight majorities believe NAFTA has meant a net loss of American jobs, not a gain. As revealed by figure 9.4, an October 1996 survey by the Associated Press found that just 21 percent said that NAFTA "makes for more jobs" in the United States, while 47 percent said it makes for fewer jobs here (29 percent said they did not know). A September 1997 Zogby poll that only asked those who said they were familiar with NAFTA (58 percent of the sample) whether they believed that it "has created more jobs or that it has led to a net loss of jobs" found that only 28 percent said NAFTA had led to more jobs, while 44 percent thought it had resulted in a net loss of jobs. In August 1996, a Los Angeles Times poll found that a majority of Americans (52 percent) said the "free trade agreement between Mexico and the United

States"—with no mention of Canada—had "taken jobs away from the American people." Only 6 percent said it had "generated more jobs," and 24 percent said it made no difference one way or the other. Even though views of NAFTA are more positive now than when these polls were taken, it is likely that concern for jobs is still a drag on support.

Figure 9.4. Views of NAFTA's Impact on Jobs, 1996–1997

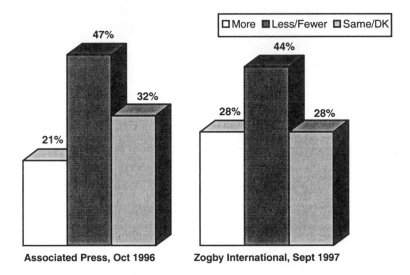

Consistent with the idea that the United States was a net loser of jobs, a majority expressed the view that Mexico was a net gainer. In the October 1996 Associated Press poll, while only 21 percent said NAFTA creates more jobs in the United States, 56 percent thought it creates more jobs in Mexico (just 12 percent said it means fewer jobs there, and 32 percent did not know). Canada was seen as, on balance, having gained jobs by 39 percent. In the same poll, four times as many respondents thought Mexico had been the primary beneficiary of NAFTA as thought the United States had been (49 percent to 12 percent), while 16 percent said both countries had benefited equally. More recent polls have also found concern about job losses to Mexico. In a June 1999 Potomac Associates and Opinion Dynamics poll, 52 percent said imports from Mexico "pose a serious threat to the jobs of American workers" (42 percent said Mexican imports were not a serious threat).

In addition to concern for jobs leaving the United States, a plurality has believed that NAFTA exerts downward pressure on the wages of American workers. In a 1997 poll sponsored by Wisconsin Public Television, 45 percent said they believed free trade agreements like NAFTA have done more to "keep wages down." Twenty-six percent said such agreements have not had much effect, and only 17 percent said they believed they have done more to increase wages. This pattern is similar to one from 1993, when a Gallup/CNN/USA Today poll found that 49 percent thought NAFTA would lower wages, 30 percent thought it would have no effect, and just 11 percent thought it would raise wages. In a September 1993 NBC/Wall Street Journal poll, 54 percent agreed with the assertion that, as a result of NAFTA, "wages in the U.S. will have to fall, so that American companies and workers can compete with Mexico."

Concerns about job and wage pressures due to free trade are heightened in the NAFTA context because Mexico is a relatively low-wage country. As mentioned, in the PIPA poll 64 percent said that if another country is willing to lower its trade barriers to U.S. products, the United States should be willing to lower its trade barriers. But when PIPA followed up that question by asking if the same was true for low-wage countries, about one in four changed their minds. Thus only 50 percent said they would be willing to enter into such an agreement with low-wage countries, while a substantial minority of 39 percent would not.

Even on the question of whether trade in general produces a net gain or net loss of jobs, the public tends to be divided. For example, the 1999 PIPA poll used a series of three questions to address this issue. In two separate questions, respondents were asked whether they believed that exporting products meant the creation of jobs in the United States, and whether they felt importing products meant the loss of jobs. Those who gave the same response to both questions were then asked whether, on balance, "more jobs are lost from imports or more jobs are gained from exports?" Combining all of these answers, respondents were almost exactly divided, with 46 percent saying more were gained and 45 percent saying more were lost. Other polls have found similar results.[6]

In general, Americans show a substantial concern that trade agreements will have a damaging effect on jobs. In an October 1995 Los Angeles Times poll, 63 percent agreed (and 32 percent disagreed) with an affirmative statement saying, "Most American trade agreements with foreign countries are a principal cause of lost jobs and a lower standard of living in this country." Polls that have asked about the effect of trade agreements have found a plurality or a majority saying that the effect has been negative—even when they offered the option of saying that the effect on jobs has been neutral. An April 1997 CNN/Time poll found 42 percent saying trade agreements have mostly "lost jobs for this country," while 41 percent said that they have "done both about equally" and just 7 percent said they had "mostly gained jobs." In an August 1996 Washington Post/Kaiser/Harvard poll, 54 percent said "trade agreements between the U.S. and other countries ... cost the U.S. jobs." Just 17 percent thought they had helped create jobs, and 27 percent said they did not make much difference.

Differential Benefits of NAFTA/Trade

When the American public thinks about NAFTA and trade in general, the perception is that it is a boon for American business but a marginal benefit for average Americans or workers. In various polls, strong majorities of about three in five respondents said that NAFTA would be good for American business, less than half thought it would be good for U.S. consumers, and only about a third thought it would be good for American workers. In February 1996, for example, a Time/CNN poll found 58 percent thought "free trade agreements like NAFTA and GATT are mostly good" for American corporations, and 57 percent thought the same for Wall Street investors. At the same time, only 45 percent felt such agreements to be good for American consumers, and just 31 percent said the same for American workers. Time/CNN and ABC/Washington Post polls taken in 1993 obtained similar results for business and workers, though a slim majority did feel consumers would benefit at that time. In an NBC News/Wall Street Journal poll from September 1993, 55 percent of Americans agreed that "*only* big American corporations will benefit" from NAFTA (emphasis added); 37 percent disagreed.

These attitudes are consistent with the public's views about international trade more broadly. A Gallup poll taken in November 1999 found that 56 percent believed increased trade between the United States and other countries helps American companies, but just 35 percent felt it helps U.S. workers. Several results in the PIPA's October 1999 survey suggest that Americans seem to feel that trade in general benefits primarily the interests of business and the wealthy. When asked in the October 1999 PIPA survey whether, on a scale of 0 to 10, "the growth of international trade" is positive or negative for American business, 61 percent gave a score above 5—far higher than for any other group tested. For American workers, as reflected in figure 9.5, just 25 percent of the public gave a response greater than 5.

Figure 9.5. Assessing the Benefits of International Trade for Workers and Business

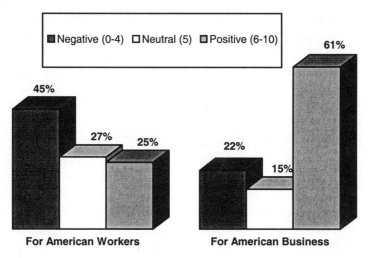

Also in the PIPA poll, U.S. trade policymakers were viewed as adequately considering commercial interests, but an overwhelming majority felt that other sectors of American society got short shrift. Asked about "U.S. government officials who are making decisions about U.S. international trade policy," 54 percent of the respondents said they "consider the concerns of multinational corporations" too much. For "American business," responses were evenly distributed among too much, too little, and about right. However, overwhelming majorities said U.S. trade policymakers give "too little" consideration to "working Americans" (72 percent), to the general public (68 percent), and to "people like you" (73 percent). In keeping with this view, a solid majority (56 percent) said that the growth of international trade has increased the gap between rich and poor in the United States. Only 10 percent felt it had reduced the gap, and 27 percent believed it had not made any difference.

Environmental Impact

Several polls taken during the extensive debate on NAFTA in 1993 found a plurality or majority of Americans expressing the view that NAFTA would have a negative effect on the environment. In September and November 1993, CNN/USA Today polls found majorities (61 percent and 57 percent, respectively) agreeing with the statement, "The environment will suffer, as U.S. businesses move to Mexico to avoid the stricter environmental standards in the U.S." In a November 1993 ABC News/Washington Post poll, 49 percent agreed (and 41 percent disagreed) that NAFTA "will damage Mexico's environment as more factories locate there." Earlier that year, in May, a Time/CNN poll offered respondents three options as to what impact NAFTA would have on "environmental pollution near the border between the United States and Mexico." Forty-three percent said the trade agreement would make it worse, 26 percent said it would have no effect, and 15 percent felt it would make pollution better.

The Clinton administration was successful in negotiating side agreements on labor and the environment, but those have done little to silence critics. As I.M. Destler and Peter Balint have suggested, analysis of the side agreements' effectiveness over the past few years has left environmental groups that supported NAFTA somewhat disappointed, and groups that opposed NAFTA satisfied that their predictions have been affirmed.[7] There are no indications that the public has been satisfied on this front.

REMEDIES AMERICANS SUPPORT

To address the threats to American workers and to the environment posed by NAFTA—and, for that matter, by all trade agreements—there are remedies that a strong majority of Americans support. These include making greater efforts to help American workers adapt to the changes that come from liberalized trade, and incorporating labor standards and environmental standards into the process of trade liberalization. Polls suggest that if such efforts were made, support for trade liberalization could become overwhelming.

Providing Help for Workers

A strong majority believes the U.S. government should do more to help workers cope with the effects of trade. In the 1999 PIPA survey, when given two options, a two-thirds majority (66 percent) agreed that the "federal government should invest in more worker retraining and education to help workers adapt to changes in the economy." Just 31 percent felt that "such efforts just create big government programs that do not work very well." Nearly as many (60 percent) complained that government efforts to help retrain workers who have lost jobs due to international trade have been inadequate. Only 29 percent thought such efforts have been adequate, and only 2 percent believed them to be more than adequate.

Many Americans also felt that making efforts to provide worker retraining for those who lose jobs due to trade would be an effective way to help workers deal with the changes of globalization. Respondents were asked, "How well prepared do you think the average American is for the kind of global economy that will emerge over the next twenty years?" On a scale with 0 for "not at all prepared" and 10 for "extremely well prepared," the mean answer was 4.7. Then, when asked how well prepared the average American would be if "the U.S. substantially increased the money spent on education and retraining for adults," the mean answer jumped to 5.9.

Very striking are indications that, if the government were to make greater efforts to help workers adapt, the public says that what resistance they have to trade liberalization would all but collapse. In the PIPA poll, as shown in figure 9.6, when the possibility of creating government programs to help workers adapt to changes associated with increased trade was spelled out, only 14 percent continued to hold a protectionist view.

Similarly, 87 percent agreed (56 percent strongly) with the statement, "I would favor more free trade if I was confident that we were making major efforts to educate and retrain Americans to be competitive in the global economy." Only 11 percent disagreed.

Standards on Labor and the Environment

In addition to the public's desire for more help for U.S. workers, the public also wants other concerns incorporated into the process of trade talks and ultimately to be made part of trade agreements. Foremost among these are enforcing international labor standards to limit exploitation of foreign workers and unfair competition with domestic industries, and writing environmental standards into trade agreements. Of course, as Destler and Balint note in their work advocating this kind of approach, this thinking represents a direct challenge to traditional trade negotiating practices, which have focused on the elimination of barriers and the establishment of dispute resolution procedures.[8]

Figure 9.6. Support for Trade with Worker Assistance

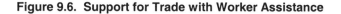

Which of the following three positions comes closest to your point of view?

I favor free trade, and I believe that it IS necessary for the government to have programs to help workers who lose their jobs.
66%

I favor free trade, and I believe that it is NOT necessary for the government to have programs to help workers who lose their jobs.
18%

I do not favor free trade.
14%

Source: PIPA, 10/99

Nevertheless, public support is quite strong. When PIPA presented the outlines of the current debate about whether the process of developing trade agreements should address labor standards and environmental issues, an overwhelming majority (78 percent) said that it should. Similarly, in November 1999, a Zogby poll asked, "When the U.S. enters into free trade agreements with other countries, should there be no conditions placed on the other country or should the U.S. insist the other country meet environmental, job security, and labor condition standards?" Eighty-three percent said the United States should demand such conditions, and just 13 percent disagreed. Also, a 1997 Peter Hart poll found that 72 percent thought it "very important" to include in trade agreements "labor and environmental standards that all countries must agree to meet."

In the 1999 PIPA poll, Americans overwhelmingly supported the view that international labor standards should be incorporated into trade negotiations. Respondents were offered two arguments for, and two against, the idea that countries belonging to a trade agreement "should be required to maintain certain standards for working conditions, such as minimum health and safety standards and the right to organize into unions." The pro arguments were found much more convincing than the con arguments. When, after evaluating the arguments, respondents were asked their conclusion, a near unanimous 93 percent said that countries should be required to maintain such standards.

Interestingly, the pro argument based on moral concerns for foreign workers was the most convincing, with 83 percent endorsing it. Still strong, though, was the more self-interested argument that countries with lower standards have an unfair advantage (74 percent). On the con side, the morally based argument that requiring higher labor standards would "eliminate the jobs of poor people who desperately need the work" was found convincing by just 37 percent. The con argument based on the principle that imposing labor standards is a violation of a country's national sovereignty also fared poorly (41 percent convincing).

Other polls have also found strong support for including environmental standards in trade agreements. When a November 2000 Greenberg Quinlan/Tarrance Group survey presented two arguments, 62 percent chose the one that said, "Future trade agreements should contain safeguards that require the U.S. and other countries to enforce strong environmental protections, even if it limits trade." Only 22 percent chose the alternative, "Expanding trade is critical to the U.S. economy and trade agreements are good for our economy, even if they do not contain strong environmental protections." In an April 2000 Harris poll, an overwhelming 80 percent felt "protecting the environment" should be a major priority for U.S. trade agreements.

Indeed, polling from 1993 indicates that if the public had been confident that environmental and labor standards were incorporated into NAFTA, support would have been substantially higher. A May 1993 Time/CNN poll asked the 43 percent who opposed free trade with Mexico whether they would support it if President Bill Clinton successfully negotiated "additional agreements which would require companies in Mexico to meet higher environmental and labor standards." Forty percent said they would support a trade deal in that case, raising overall approval to 60 percent. As noted, such side agreements were in fact negotiated, but many critics have charged that they have been ineffective.

To put it another way, Americans do not see the growth of trade by itself as an overriding priority, and there is little sense of urgency and willingness to subordinate the goal of increasing trade to other concerns. In the PIPA survey, an overwhelming 88 percent agreed with the following statement: "Increasing international trade is an important goal for the United States, but it should be balanced with other goals, such as protecting workers, the environment, and human rights—even if this may mean slowing the growth of trade and the economy."

Echoing a common critique, President Bush has called demands for including labor standards and environmental protections in trade agreements a "new form of protectionism." The implication seems to be that the real motive is to protect American jobs from foreign imports, not concerns about foreign workers or the environment. However, polls show that in the domestic context, a modest majority of Americans is consistently willing to put a higher priority on the environment than on jobs. Thus at least some of the support for environmental considerations in trade agreements appears to be derived from an intrinsic concern for the environment, not a subterfuge for job protection.

In addition, support for labor standards does seem to be derived from genuine concerns about foreign working conditions, because the majority does not simply support enforcing all possible labor standards but rather emphasizes some more than others. For example, PIPA asked whether the United States should bar products made by children under the age of 15 working under coercive conditions, and an overwhelming 82 percent said that it should and 76 percent said this would apply for products made in factories that are unsafe or unhealthy. When asked whether the United States should bar products from countries where the workers are not allowed to organize, however, only 42 percent were in favor, even though such a condition would be at least as effective for the purpose of simply making it harder for foreign countries to get their products into the United States. This indicates that Americans do care about the other issues that receive strong majorities; they are not merely embracing any measure that would protect jobs.

Other research also shows that support for labor and environmental provisions are not favored simply as a way to limit the growth of trade. In January 2000, for example, a Penn, Schoen, and Berland poll for the Democratic Leadership Council found that 73 percent favored "expand[ing] trade between the U.S. and other nations, including developing countries, while drafting rules of trade that encourage all nations to improve their labor and environmental standards." Just 20 percent favored the alternative, "restrict[ing] trade between the U.S.

and developing countries that have relatively low labor and environmental standards." An April 2000 Harris Interactive survey offered three classifications and asked respondents to choose which best described them. In that case, 37 percent called themselves protectionist, meaning they believe "there should be rules to protect U.S. markets and workers from imports." A slim majority of 51 percent described themselves as fair traders, or "someone who believes in fair trade or trade with some standards for labor and the environment." Another 10 percent believed in free trade "without any restrictions." Thus 61 percent were in favor of some kind of trade liberalization.

ATTITUDES ABOUT EXPANDING NAFTA

Attempts to expand free trade throughout the Western Hemisphere will probably find wan support at best, unless these remedies are pursued. Although some polls indicate modest support for an FTAA in the abstract, attitudes on renewal of trade promotion authority—almost certainly a prerequisite for negotiating the FTAA—are divided and growing more negative.

General Support for FTAA

Although very little polling has been done on the issue, there appears to be general support for expanding free trade to more countries in the Western Hemisphere. As demonstrated by figure 9.7, a Market Strategies survey in August 1998 found that a 67 percent majority supported "negotiating free trade agreements with South American nations," while only 23 percent opposed the idea. In October 1996, when support for NAFTA was at a low point, a bare plurality supported "expanding NAFTA to include free trade with other Latin American countries." Back in December 1994, a year after NAFTA was passed, a slim majority of 52 percent favored and 35 percent opposed "having the U.S. negotiate a similar trade agreement with all the nations of Latin America and South America" (NBC/Wall Street Journal).

These results indicate a modest foundation of public support, but they should be viewed with some skepticism. Americans tend to support the growth of trade in principle; as the issues become more concrete, however, other value concerns may rise to the surface and responses may become more divided and support more conditional on these other issues being addressed. As discussed, attitudes about

NAFTA were much more positive in 1991 and 1992, before it became widely debated in 1993.

Figure 9.7. Support for FTAA or Expansion of NAFTA

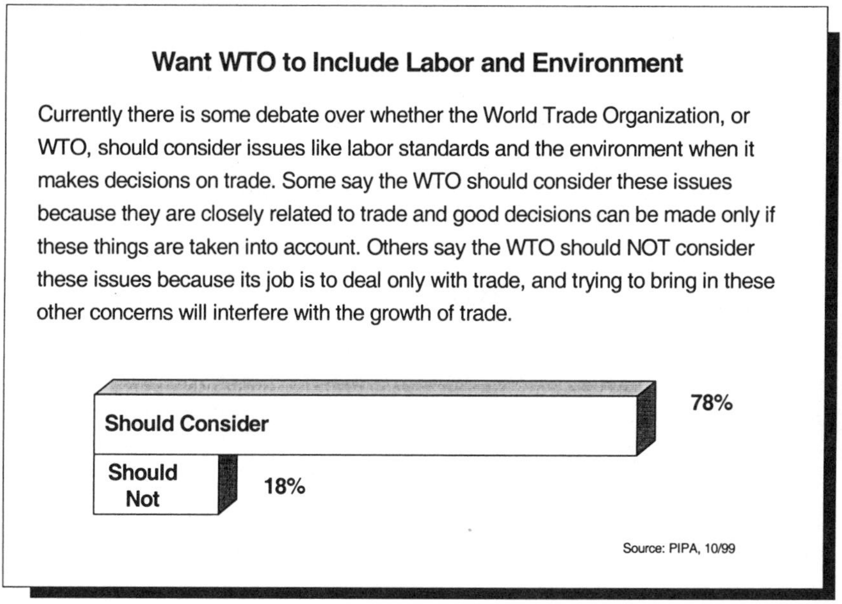

Want WTO to Include Labor and Environment

Currently there is some debate over whether the World Trade Organization, or WTO, should consider issues like labor standards and the environment when it makes decisions on trade. Some say the WTO should consider these issues because they are closely related to trade and good decisions can be made only if these things are taken into account. Others say the WTO should NOT consider these issues because its job is to deal only with trade, and trying to bring in these other concerns will interfere with the growth of trade.

Should Consider — 78%

Should Not — 18%

Source: PIPA, 10/99

Uncertainty over TPA

A key factor in the effort to proceed with FTAA will be renewing trade promotion authority, which lapsed in 1994 under President Clinton. Many in Congress want to deny TPA unless they secure provisions for including labor and environmental standards in future trade agreements.[9] Public attitudes may play a key role in this debate, and politicians will no doubt look to polls to bolster their case.

As of this writing, no polls had used the moniker TPA, but most recent polls show the public mixed on "fast track," with the percentage in favor showing a consistent decline. As shown by table 9.5, several recent polls have posed the same question. As the results indicate, support has dropped from a high of 53 percent in 1998 to just 40 percent in May 2000.

Table 9.5. Declining Support for Fast Track

Question: Presidents since 1974 have had trade negotiating authority known as 'fast track,' which means the trade agreements the President negotiated are considered in Congress within 90 days and put to a simple yes or no vote, without any additions that could upset the agreement. The authority to do this expired in 1994, and President Clinton no longer has such authority. Do you strongly support renewing President Clinton's fast track trade authority, somewhat support, somewhat oppose, or strongly oppose it?

Date	Organization	Support (%)	Oppose (%)	Don't Know/ Refuse (%)
May 00	Epic-MRA	40	39	21
October 99	PIPA	43	55	2
May 99	Epic-MRA	48	41	11
May 98	Epic-MRA	53	39	2
August 97	Penn & Schoen	48	41	11

The lack of support for fast track is striking. For one thing, this question, which puts fast track in historical context and implies that it is business as usual, has done somewhat better than other questions on fast track.[10] Moreover, opposition to fast track is so strong that even a majority of those who support NAFTA are opposed to it. Of those who gave NAFTA a positive evaluation in the 1999 PIPA poll, 56 percent opposed fast track and 44 percent favored it. Seventy-one percent of those who felt NAFTA had been bad were opposed. Awareness of this strongly negative attitude probably prompted pro-trade leaders to eschew the phrase "fast track" in favor of "trade promotion authority." Again, no public polling has yet been done using this new terminology.

It should be noted, in addition, that views on fast track may be in flux. In the PIPA survey, a strong majority of Republicans (77 percent) opposed fast track legislation. A majority of independents (59 percent) were also opposed, yet a plurality (50 percent) of Democrats favored it. It is a good bet that these positions will undergo change during George W. Bush's tenure in the White House. With Bill Clinton's name no longer in the question, Republican support will probably rise; and because Democrats in Congress will likely feel more latitude than Republicans to be critical of fast track, Democratic support will probably drop. What this means for overall public support is not yet clear.

CONCLUSION

Opinion polls reveal that the U.S. public shows modest support for free trade in general, for NAFTA, and for the idea of the FTAA. Yet majorities of the public believe trade can have a negative effect on many American workers, workers in other countries, and the global environment. Thus overall support for trade expansion is lukewarm, and attitudes on TPA (that is, fast track) are cool.

Americans would more strongly support free trade policies if they believed the government was being more responsive to the effects of trade on vulnerable workers at home and to the global environment and workers abroad. It is helpful to think of trade as a train moving down a track. Trade advocates want to accelerate the train, and thus do not want to burden it with labor and environmental baggage. Critics of trade want to throw themselves in front of the train and stop it. The public's goal is not to stop the train but to load it down with these other considerations—and if that does slow the train, most Americans think this is an acceptable cost.

President George W. Bush has made a good rhetorical start in the effort to find consensus, calling trade expansion a "moral imperative" and arguing that it would help clean up the environment and expand worker rights.[11] However, it appears that clear public support will not be won with rhetoric but rather with concrete steps to deal with Americans' concerns about freer trade. Without such efforts, public support for trade expansion will likely remain tepid.

Notes

1. Benjamin I. Page and Robert Y. Shapiro, *The Rational Public* (Chicago: University of Chicago Press, 1992), p. 168.

2. Kenneth F. Scheve and Matthew J. Slaughter, *Globalization and the Perceptions of American Workers* (Washington, D.C.: Institute for International Economics, 2001), p. 44.

3. Ibid., p. 14.

4. Steven Kull, *Americans on Globalization: A Study of US Public Attitudes* (Washington, D.C.: Program on International Policy Attitudes, 2000), pp. 7–8.

5. Scheve and Slaughter, *Globalization,* p. 53.

6. Kull, *Americans on Globalization,* pp. 10–11.

7. I.M. Destler and Peter J. Balint, *The New Politics of American Trade: Trade, Labor and the Environment* (Washington, D.C.: Institute for International Economics, 1999), p. 31.

8. Ibid.

9. Dana Milbank and Paul Blustein, "Bush to Talk Trade at Summit," *Washington Post,* April 20, 2001.

10. Kull, *Americans on Globalization,* pp. 15–16.

11. Marc Lacey, "Bush Chides Critics and Declares Freer Trade a Moral Issue," *New York Times,* May 8, 2001.

Section 4

NAFTA in the Next Ten Years: Issues and Challenges

Section 4 provides an overview of problems that NAFTA will have to confront within the foreseeable future. Some of these issues, like labor rights and environmental protection, are explicitly (but inadequately) addressed in the NAFTA accords. Others, like migration, are excluded. All these concerns form part of the current NAFTA agenda, however, and they are likely to come to a head within the next five to ten years. How NAFTA meets these challenges will be crucial to its economic effectiveness, its level of popular support, and its prospects for meaningful change.

In chapter 10 Graciela Bensusán considers the effects of NAFTA on labor and on opportunities for labor cooperation. Although trade among the three countries has sharply increased, jobs have not grown at the same pace. And despite gains in productivity, wages have tended to stagnate. Organized labor in all countries has focused on labor regulation and unfair labor practices. While Canadian unions forged ties with independent unions in Mexico, the AFL-CIO (opposed to NAFTA from the beginning) connected with the official unions as well. According to Bensusán, the so-called side accord on labor, the North American Agreement on Labor Cooperation (NAALC), has thus far had little effect, especially with regard to harmonization of labor standards. The chapter concludes with policy recommendations, including a guarantee for collective action by workers and unions.

Chapter 11 deals with the environment. Debra Davidson and Ross Mitchell argue forcefully that NAFTA has accomplished little in this area. Reversing the conventional line of causation, they ask not only what effect NAFTA has had on the environment—but how environmental issues will shape the future of NAFTA. Tracing the growth of transnational environmental movements and of local mobilization within the NAFTA countries, Davidson and Mitchell assert that prospects for future economic success will depend largely upon the mitigation of negative side effects and environmental degradation. In their conclusion, the authors recommend that NAFTA consider "green" as well as "brown" environmental issues (that is, conservation as well as anti-pollution measures) and that environmental institutions should be transparent and open to citizen participation. The bad news is that so much remains to be done; the good news is that NAFTA provides a plausible institutional forum for environmental action.

Wayne A. Cornelius next analyzes the impact of NAFTA on Mexico-to-U.S. migration flows. Analyzing trends in recent years, he finds that NAFTA has not thus far reduced the volume of cross-border migration—whether or not it does so in the long run, as many analysts have predicted. On the contrary, continuing wage differentials and rapid growth along Mexico's northern border have actually augmented migration from Mexico to the United States. Targeted development programs for sending areas in Mexico might reduce incentives to migrate in the medium term, and demographic shrinkage in the size of the Mexican workforce might narrow the wage gap over the longer term. In the meantime, political fallout from the terrorist attacks of September 11, 2001, has sharply undermined President Vicente Fox's hope for major migration reform in the United States.

Turning to the question of agriculture, Michelle Veeman, Terrence Veeman, and Ryan Hoskins observe that agricultural labor in continental North America comprises less than 6 percent of the overall workforce. Some areas of agriculture have been significantly affected by trade liberalization; other areas, such as sugar in the United States and the dairy industry in Canada, continue to enjoy protection. Overall, the gains from agricultural trade among the NAFTA partners have been substantial. While bringing benefits to Mexican consumers, however, corn imports into Mexico have destabilized the *ejido* sector. The crop composition of trade reflects the comparative advantages of the member countries: Mexico exports fresh vegetables, wine and beer, and fresh fruits; the United States exports corn, red meat, and soybeans; Canada's product mix is somewhat different, reflecting geography and climate as well as the political arrangements governing agriculture. Predicting that agricultural disputes will continue, the authors express hope that NAFTA will provide a suitable framework for negotiating settlements.

Chapter 14 focuses on a little-noticed practical obstacle to effective economic integration—transportation barriers, which prolong deliveries of goods and accelerate transaction costs. As Barry Prentice and Mark Ojah contend, "The full benefits of NAFTA cannot be obtained until free trade in goods is complemented by free trade in transportation services." Most notably, Mexican transportation networks have lagged far behind Canadian and U.S. transportation grids. And despite recent improvements, especially in rail and marine systems, trucking still carries most of the freight shipped among the NAFTA partners. Increased efficiency will require better roads (costing billions of dollars), improved safety, more competition within the trucking industry—and more consistent regulations among states and provinces within the member countries. Over the objections of powerful vested interests, a coordinated process of deregulation and competition in air, rail, sea, and land transportation has made some modest headway. Harmonized safety standards might provide a constructive first step. Ultimately, Prentice and Ojah envision a "smart" transportation system in the future, one that could use information technology to eliminate the transportation bottlenecks that diminish and delay the benefits of NAFTA trade.

10

NAFTA and Labor: Impacts and Outlooks

Graciela Bensusán

The North American Free Trade Agreement formalized a long process of integration and complementarity between Mexico, Canada, and the United States. Negotiations for the creation of NAFTA were conducted by governments and shaped strongly by the business communities, especially those of Mexico and the United States. Labor played a minor role in the process. As a result, NAFTA came to pay only marginal attention to the need to protect worker rights and wages from the adverse effects of economic globalization.

NAFTA is marked by strong asymmetries. Given its neoliberal underpinnings, however, the treaty contains no effective compensatory mechanisms for reducing these disparities. On the labor front, in particular, there are notable differences between Mexico and its two northern partners—in terms of wages, labor conditions, rules governing unionization, and related issues. This situation generated considerable opposition to the agreement in both Canada and the United States.[1] And it was largely in response to this pressure that a "side accord" on labor was adopted in 1993, along with a parallel accord on environmental protection.

In the course of the treaty negotiations—and in the face of its possible extension to the entire hemisphere—labor unions in the three member countries took divergent positions, pursued different strategies, and displayed differing levels of activism. These were due to various factors, such as state-union relations (subordination versus autonomy) and union types (such as different leadership cultures). The characteristics of the three political systems and of the unions affected the behavior and capacity of labor organizations to influence the regional integration process, and to counteract the adverse effects of the policies stemming from economic restructuring and trade liberalization.

The purpose of this chapter is to discuss the effects of NAFTA on North American labor and unions, and to evaluate the latters' capacity to address challenges resulting from NAFTA-induced trade flows and cross-border investments. I will also analyze the unexploited opportunities for labor union cooperation among the three NAFTA countries, as well as the stance and demands of organized labor in the face of the possible widening and deepening of NAFTA. As such, this chapter seeks to identify the key labor issues within the region that need to be addressed in the near future.

NAFTA EFFECTS

NAFTA's goals for labor were seen as long-term. But even now, evidence accumulated over the past seven years allows us to refute fears about the presumed flight of jobs from Canada and the United States toward Mexico. Indeed, reasoned assessment shows only a limited movement of jobs, especially in light of the impacts of the recent U.S. recession on the Mexican manufacturing sector. And while the treaty has yielded positive results in regard to trade, it has not yet produced substantial benefits for workers—or a reduction in the wage gap between Mexico and its two northern partners.

When the NAFTA negotiations concluded in August 1992, the U.S. government reiterated its ambitious expectation that the expansion of free trade from Alaska to the Yucatán would enhance the competitiveness of American companies throughout the world. In the words of President George H.W. Bush, the agreement would help establish a "level playing field," reactivate economic growth, and create new jobs. Similarly, Mexican president Carlos Salinas de Gortari expressed hope that the accord would result in sustained economic growth with increased employment and improved wages, along with extended phase-out periods for adjustment by less competitive sectors. Canadians took a less optimistic view, partly because of the low level of Canada's trade with Mexico—and partly because of strong opposition to NAFTA from significant sectors and groups (such as unions, environmental organizations, Quebec nationalists, and the Liberal Party).[2]

For Mexico, NAFTA helped increase exports to its North American partners by 93 percent between 1994 and 1998, while its exports to the rest of the world increased by only 22 percent; foreign direct investment (FDI) inflows into Mexico also shot up by more than 150 percent. Moreover, trade among the three NAFTA members has grown by an annual average of 13 percent since the agreement went into effect, which has made Mexico the third most important supplier of goods and services to the United States and the second most important market for U.S. exports. Some 74.3 percent of Mexico's imports originate from the United States, while 87.8 percent of Mexican exports are destined to the U.S. market.[3] In such sectors as electronics and apparel, Mexico has since 1998 been the most important source of imports to the U.S. market. In sum, NAFTA has succeeded in boosting the three members' economic performance, increasing trade flows, and maximizing comparative advantages. While exports have made significant strides, however, the benefits have not been felt across the board at the plant level. Moreover, Mexico has become increasingly vulnerable to U.S. economic cycles.[4]

Employment

Evaluations of NAFTA's impact on job creation are hard-pressed to isolate the effects of the agreement from those produced by economic cycles. However, the benefits appear less spectacular than those obtained on the trade front. Mexico's exporting firms constituted only 5.65 percent of the total employment in the country in 1998, and less than 10 percent of the jobs created between 1993 and 1998 were in the export sector.[5] This suggests that NAFTA has not been able to solve Mexico's massive unemployment problem.

In Canada, unemployment began to rise with the Canada–United States Free Trade Agreement's (CUSFTA) entry into force, and it took its greatest toll on the manufacturing sector. In some cases, the job losses resulted from a flight of industry to the United States and in others, from the closure of uncompetitive companies. Hardest-hit were firms that benefited from high levels of protection before the trade opening, such as apparel and food products. However, jobs were also lost in sectors witnessing export growth, such as electronic machinery. Similarly, the United States experienced a loss in employment due to the reduction of tariff barriers and the internationalization of production in some sectors, such as automotives and apparel. Indeed, these sectors contain the greatest proportions of workers participating in the North American Free Trade Agreement–Transitional Adjustment Assistance (NAFTA-TAA) program designed to provide training for workers displaced by trade or by the flight of jobs, and to reinsert them into the U.S. economy.[6]

In sum, the employment effects have been starkest in sectors most affected by NAFTA. Between 1988 and 1998, employment in the transport equipment sector, and in automotives in particular, remained stable in Canada, but employment fell by 12 percent in the United States and increased by 21 percent in Mexico, which is a major assembler of automotive parts. In the electronics sector, employment declined by 25 percent in Canada and 6.5 percent in the United States while growing by 36 percent in Mexico—principally in the *maquiladora* (in-bond processing) sector, which obtained 98 percent of the new jobs. Finally, employment in the apparel industry went down by 35 percent in the United States and 26 percent in Canada, while increasing by 27 percent in Mexico.[7]

In total, jobs in the manufacturing sector decreased in the three countries as a share of aggregate employment. This may owe both to the global expansion of tertiary sectors and to trade policies and regional integration. The contraction was most notable in Canada, at about 13 percent between 1988 and 1998, followed by the United States at 3.8 percent during the same period. The decline was not significant in Mexico; however, Mexico did experience an important change in the composition of manufacturing employment. The maquiladora industry grew by 117 percent during this period, while the non-maquiladora manufacturing sector shrank.[8]

Sectoral statistics appear to confirm in part the concerns expressed by American and Canadian unions about job losses resulting from NAFTA. However, these losses have not brought notable benefits to Mexican workers or to the Mexican economy. Aside from the fact that NAFTA has failed to provide regular employment for those in the informal sector, the jobs that have emerged—chiefly in the maquiladora sector—tend to be of low quality. Although maquiladora wages have been increasing more rapidly than those in the manufacturing sector as a whole, the average maquiladora wage—as of 1999—equaled only 65 percent of salaries in the manufacturing sector and barely reached the levels attained in 1994.[9] A further consideration relates to the vulnerability of Mexican exports, which respond to fluctuations in the U.S. economy. As a result of the U.S. recession, in fact, Mexico lost more than 260,000 jobs during the five-month period between November 2000 and April 2001.[10]

Wages

The evolution of wages shows that while salaries in the U.S. and Canadian manufacturing sectors have gone up, wages in Mexico have actually declined, particularly in the second half of the 1990s. Between

1994 and 1999, the minimum real wage fell by 24.8 percent in Mexico, while the average real wage in the manufacturing sector declined by 18.4 percent (this trend has, however, turned around since 1999). According to official estimates, using 1993 as the benchmark year, the unit costs in the manufacturing sector fell by 37.31 percent while labor productivity increased by 38.83 percent. This indicates a significant increase in competitiveness in the manufacturing sector after the crisis of 1994 and the devaluation of the peso.[11] This implies that the wage gap between Mexico and the United States widened rather than closed between 1993 and 1999.[12]

Meanwhile, labor productivity in the Mexican manufacturing sector reached higher levels than in the two partner countries (even though it started from lower initial levels). This translated into a greater reduction in the costs of Mexican labor vis-à-vis those in the United States and Canada.[13] These results can be explained in part by the weakness of Mexican unions in ensuring that productivity gains would be matched by wage increases. The reason for such weakness, in turn, may be the absence of an adequate institutional framework to allow for the emergence of truly representative and fully autonomous unions. Thus, although labor unions in both the United States and Canada saw their productivity grow at much greater rates than their wages in the manufacturing sector, the prospects for profitable wages in manufacturing in the two countries are still much brighter than in Mexico.

It has been argued that trade between countries with different levels of development and with different types of labor markets marked by wage inequalities would mean that the less qualified workers in the more developed country would have to compete with the low-skilled labor of the less developed country. The deterioration of wages of U.S. low-income workers seems to confirm this claim. But even though this result has been attributed to trade liberalization, it should be noted that this trend was apparent in the late 1980s. Besides, the pattern has shown signs of a turnaround in the second half of the 1990s, so it is probably not a consequence of NAFTA.[14]

LABOR UNIONS AND REGIONAL INTEGRATION

The positions of organized labor in the United States and Canada on trade agreements underwent significant change during the 1990s. The unions departed from their initial protectionist stance in order to search for viable alternatives that would boost the benefits and lower the costs of trade liberalization and regional integration. With the ex-

ception of those Mexican unions closely tied to the government—
which displayed scant interest in societal efforts to influence the course
of continental integration—the three NAFTA countries have witnessed a recovery of union activism on the trade policy front. This activism has been accompanied by growing links between unions and
social organizations through joint participation in various forums and
movements against the prevailing form of globalization. From Seattle
(in November 1999) to Porto Alegre and Genoa (January and July
2001, respectively), these movements have grown in terms of both the
number of followers and the ability to articulate policy proposals.

In general, the alternative proposals from these groups and movements call for a continental integration project that is more inclusive
and complete. Moreover, they contend that integration should promote the participation of civil society organizations in governmental
decision-making, particularly in regard to the management of social
and labor problems caused by growing international interdependence.

In the beginning of the NAFTA talks, the U.S. and Canadian key
labor organizations—the American Federation of Labor (AFL-CIO)
and the Canadian Labour Congress (CLC)—were determined to oppose NAFTA on the grounds that the wage asymmetries with Mexico
and Mexico's poor enforcement of its labor legislation would induce
companies to move south of the border. In Mexico, by contrast, the
Labor Congress (CT)—closely linked to the Institutional Revolutionary Party (PRI) and the state—expressed unconditional support for
NAFTA. Only some independent unions under the Authentic Labor
Front (FAT), the founding organization of the Mexican Free Trade
Action Network (RMALC) created in 1991, actively questioned
NAFTA due to its lack of mechanisms for the defense of worker
rights.[15] In view of the accelerating pace (and probability) of a democ-
ratic political transition in Mexico, especially after 1994, the stances of
the independent labor unions grouped under the Union of Mexican
Workers (UNT) eventually converged with those of the U.S. and Canadian unions in the call for a new model of regional integration.

During the NAFTA talks, it was clear that the U.S. labor movement
had been weakened by twelve years of Republican administrations
whose policies had seriously undermined the collective rights of workers, as well as by the anti-unionist strategies of American companies.
The AFL-CIO's Industrial Department was the key force in the battle
against the neoliberal version of NAFTA. Its efforts represented a new
kind of unionism geared to making labor a viable force in the processes of regional and global integration.[16] One of the most important

sources of influence was the formation of alliances with other social organizations (environmental, human rights groups, and so on) opposed to NAFTA. This increased the unions' bargaining power and helped gain the support of U.S. public opinion. As such, the new strategy not only improved the standing of unions, but it also altered the balance of power within the AFL-CIO, with the "new unionists" that had led the battle against NAFTA gaining the federation's presidency in 1995.[17] Along with altered strategies, U.S. unions changed their traditionally protectionist postures and opposition to NAFTA in favor of closer ties with the Canadian and Mexican unions. Their goal was to revise the terms of NAFTA in order to strengthen the defense of worker rights. There were also efforts to unionize Mexican workers in the United States. In February 2000, the AFL-CIO took a major new step by proposing a radical change to U.S. immigration policy: an amnesty and equal rights for those who are working illegally in the United States. The purposes of the proposal were to avoid a lowering of U.S. wages and to amplify the ranks of U.S. union members.[18]

In its efforts to alter U.S. trade policy, the AFL-CIO has received its most effective support from its alliance with a diverse array of social organizations in opposition to the Free Trade Area of the Americas (FTAA) process which was set in motion by the 1994 Summit of the Americas. The key union demand is for strong labor regulations that would impede a decline in wages and working conditions as the result of competitive pressures and capital mobility. The efforts appeared to bear fruit: President Clinton's request for fast track authority to pursue the FTAA was not even submitted for a vote in 1997—and was not brought up again during the course of his administration. The failure of fast track was essentially due to the AFL-CIO's weight in the congressional elections of 1998, and also to the systematic resistance by business communities and the Mexican government to substantive modifications of NAFTA or the labor side agreement.[19]

For its part, the Canadian union movement was better positioned in the NAFTA talks thanks to a more favorable legal framework for individual and collective worker rights. Although the political situation at the national level in Canada was no better than in the United States, the fact that the New Democratic Party (NDP), a traditional ally of the CLC, maintained power at the provincial level allowed Canadian unions to avoid major setbacks. Other propitious factors were the public support for the unions' criticism of economic policies with adverse social effects, and widespread reservations about trade integration in general. The Canadian strategy was to create alliances with other organizations opposed to NAFTA and to coordinate their efforts through the Action Canada Network (ACN). In contrast to the United States, Canadian unions were concerned not only about the wage asymmetries but, even more so, about the differences in the policies of unions between the three NAFTA countries. For Canadian unions, the threat stemmed from Mexico and the United States alike, as the latter featured weaker protection of individual and collective worker rights.

The participation of Canadian unions in international information exchanges—as in Fronteras Comunes in 1989—helped them define a clear opposition strategy. Fronteras Comunes carried out studies on the prospective impact of NAFTA on the Mexican economy and on the ties between Mexican and Canadian companies, particularly in the maquiladora sector. During the NAFTA negotiations, the organization gained importance through its efforts to induce Canadian unions to criticize the agreement and to seek alternatives to the neoliberal model of globalization from an international, rather than national, perspective. However, the CLC refused to participate in the NAFTA talks in order not to legitimize what promised to become a weak and ineffective side agreement on labor protection. This prevented the CLC from joining forces with nongovernmental organizations (NGOs) that lobbied for an improvement in the reach and the efficiency of safeguards for workers.[20]

In contrast to their counterparts in Canada and the United States, Mexican unions linked to the government through the Labor Congress, which incorporated the bulk of workers, seconded and supported the Salinas administration's policy line on NAFTA. The key concern of these *oficialista* unions was to ensure that regulations sought by the AFL-CIO would not undermine their privileged position—for example, by demanding transparency and organizational autonomy for unions or the creation of labor tribunals independent of the executive. Thus, even though labor was represented in the Mexican government's advisory committee, it had no influence over NAFTA's terms. Indeed, given the coincidence of these unions' interests with those of the powerful business sector, they were able to limit provisions of the side agreement on labor in order to protect their corporatist privileges.[21]

Meanwhile, a strand of Mexican labor operating under the auspices of the Federation of Goods and Services Unions (FESEBS)—an organization established in 1992 to defend the rights of workers in the privatization of state-owned enterprises—maintained a pragmatic stance toward NAFTA, conditioning its support on the agreement's respect for worker rights and its mechanisms for smoothing its impact on labor. Thus the Mexican Telephone Workers Union (STRM), paralleling the actions of some other FESEBS members, forged interest-based coalitions with employers in efforts to postpone the opening of the telecommunications sector to international competition.[22]

A small vein of Mexican union organizations on the left end of the political spectrum—those with ties to social movements and independent of the government, such as the FAT—assumed a more radical position, openly questioning the government's stance. The FAT launched an intense campaign at the beginning of the NAFTA talks in order to construct a social network that would oppose the integration model as devised by the three governments. It viewed the model as favorable only to the interests of transnational enterprises, and as accentuating asymmetries and the problems of the Mexican economy. The FAT did not oppose NAFTA per se, but rather insisted on the need to regulate social matters surrounding the integration process and to construct ties to U.S. and Canadian union organizations. Working under the RMALC, which helped to unite peasant and other organizations independent of the government, the FAT embarked on an intense campaign to expose the limitations of NAFTA and its side accord. For example, it called for regionwide guarantees of worker rights through the incorporation of social clauses in NAFTA.

Despite its small size, the FAT thus headed, both at home and abroad, the struggle for a new kind of global and regional integration model. This model would promote cooperation between civil society actors and governments in the management of labor and social problems stemming from increased competitive pressures.

The UNT—established in 1997 after the departure of important groups, such as the STRM, from the CT, and the incorporation to the CT of historically independent groups such as FAT—has also become internationally active, taking advantage of Mexico's political opening. Although Mexico's turn toward democracy resulted from a number of factors, NAFTA played a positive role in the process. In particular, the agreement helped pressure the Mexican government to increase the transparency of the electoral process and to provide guarantees of fairness in competition among political parties—the very conditions that unleashed the alternation in power in the Mexican presidency in July 2000. These political trends encouraged a departure from traditional corporatist unionism—one of the pillars of the PRI since the end of the 1930s—in favor of a more genuine representation of workers. To be sure, progress in this area remains limited. On one hand, the old-style unionism of the CT has failed to reform itself through learning from the U.S. and Canadian unions. On the other hand, the alliances formed by UNT unions with labor organizations, social movements, and other groupings in the other two NAFTA countries have, along with growing participation in international forums, served to boost the economic and political power of Mexican unions at a time when the old institutional resources were unable to do so.[23]

In sum, the RMALC has provided a venue for the FAT and other unions in the UNT to participate both in the evaluation of NAFTA and in the creation and development of the Hemispheric Social Alliance. The Alliance is geared toward impeding the creation of the FTAA under the prevailing, limited model of integration, and toward presenting viable alternatives to the FTAA. A document prepared by the RMALC to this effect is the most complete one in the region. The result of joint efforts by hundreds of individuals, social organizations, and unions from both the North and the South, the document calls for a European Union–style continental integration process that is broad in scope and that attaches great importance to the social impact of integration. In particular, it recommends that civil society organizations participate as central interlocutors in the dialogue on globalization in order to diminish the degree of social and economic exclusion.

One chapter in this document discusses labor issues, putting forth mechanisms to guarantee worker rights and to protect the working conditions and living standards of workers and their families in the face of liberalization. One key proposal insists on the right of workers and labor organizations to participate in decision-making on integration on both national and international levels. It also suggests that trade agreements include a clause on worker rights, whose breach would deny a country the benefit of reciprocal tariff reduction. Another suggestion is that compliance with the basic worker rights recognized by the International Labour Organization (ILO) should be enforced directly by the ILO itself; should ILO's recommendations not be followed, the violator would be denied trade preferences.

With regard to migration, the document calls for international subsidies for development projects for countries that are net exporters of labor, and also for the eradication of any type of discrimination. Although the report does not advocate free movement of labor across the continent, it does propose bilateral or subregional agreements among countries featuring intense migratory flows that would harmonize the member states' worker rights and social security regimes.[24]

On October 31–November 1, 1999, on the eve of the fifth FTAA Trade Ministerial, the Inter-American Regional Organization of Workers (ORIT) held a forum on "Workers in the FTAA Process" that summoned the most important labor federations of the Americas. The meeting resulted in demands on the governments to include social, labor, and environmental dimensions in all trade and regional integration negotiations. During the discussions, the AFL-CIO representative called upon the trade ministers to acknowledge the forum as a permanent participant in the FTAA talks. This represented a sharp departure from the AFL-CIO's traditionally protectionist discourse. Organizations united under the Hemispheric Social Alliance endorsed this position, calling for an integration process that would benefit workers around the world. The president of the CLC seconded this position, stressing that unions should insist that their governments include basic worker rights in trade agreements.

Parallel to the labor forum, the Hemispheric Social Alliance met in order to coordinate actions among the social organizations and movements of the Americas. The event was also intended to give the Alliance a sense of permanence, as well as to strengthen its role in the continental integration process. With the help of Canadian officials, the civil society participants succeeded in staging a meeting with the trade ministers, where they called for the opening of more effective channels for the citizens of the Americas to participate in the FTAA process. Although the results were rather slim, holding the meeting per se was an unprecedented milestone in the process of trade negotiation.

PROSPECTS FOR COOPERATION

The adoption of the side accord on labor in 1993—formally known as the North American Agreement on Labor Cooperation (NAALC)— resulted primarily from pressure from U.S. labor unions and, eventually, from the Clinton administration. Despite its low profile, the NAALC has served to set in motion trinational cooperation on labor issues. It has helped pave the way to improved cooperation between social and labor organizations of the three countries in efforts to guarantee the representation of workers' interests and to formulate alternatives to the prevailing models of integration and globalization. Yet NAALC also has serious limitations. These have been exposed by the often-unfruitful attempts to use the agreement to denounce and rectify violations of basic worker rights.

After the approval of the NAALC, efforts were made to improve cooperation between labor movements in the three member countries. For U.S. and Canadian unions, the defense of Mexican workers' living standards became a major issue. The unions came to acknowledge that collective action problems for labor were not limited to Mexico and that the use of the NAALC's provisions required a better understanding of the North American labor regimes. This led to a great many alliances among the unions of North America—which, in turn, fostered the unions' capacity to mobilize and to condemn violations. Besides, groups such as the Sindicato Nacional de Trabajadores Agrícolas of Mexico and the Farm Labor Organizing Committee of the AFL-CIO had cooperative ties that dated back to 1987. These had been forged to counteract U.S. companies' threats to move south if the unions did not moderate their wage claims. Given the improved conditions for capital mobility following the signing of NAFTA, American companies could make even more credible claims about closing operations in the face of rising labor costs—as duly noted in a study by the NAALC's Commission on Labor Cooperation.[25]

Another factor that boosted inter-union cooperation was fear that the NAFTA model of integration would be extended to other countries of the Americas, as was the case with the Canada-Chile Free Trade Agreement. The FTAA, of course, would be the main vehicle for such an extension. Notably, 1998 marked the first visit in fifty years by an important AFL-CIO delegation to Mexico. Led by new AFL-CIO president John Sweeney, the visit resulted in the signing of agreements between the AFL-CIO and the recently formed UNT to cooperate on revising the NAALC and reforming the organization of Mexican workers in the United States. The AFL-CIO subsequently established a Solidarity Center in Mexico. The task of the Center is to follow the labor and union situation in Mexico and to collaborate with Mexican unions on a broad range of activities. The AFL-CIO's position thus differs from that of Canadian unions, which have built ties only with the independent unions in Mexico. The Canadians regard these unions as the most needy for support in efforts to eliminate the simulated forms of labor organization and hiring ("letterhead unions" and "collective contracts of protection") that privilege official unions.[26]

Growing cross-border cooperation involved not only unions but also environmental, human rights, and women's organizations. In particular, unions of the three NAFTA countries (the RMALC in Mexico) joined civil society organizations in efforts to counter the adverse social effects of globalization. Union leaders participated in the protests and efforts to build alternatives to the neoliberal model of globalization at the third World Trade Organization (WTO) ministerial in 1999 in Seattle, the Davos World Economic Forums of 2000 and 2001, and the International Monetary Fund meetings in Washington and Prague. The World Social Forum in Porto Alegre was the scene for the most extensive civil society participation, summoning activists from more than 120 countries, along with numerous academics and politicians. The Declaration of Porto Alegre reflected the predominant view among the participants that the course of globalization should be altered, putting forth proposals for the reduction of poverty and social exclusion. As such, the participants stood in stark contrast to the radical groups that are fully opposed to globalization and that express their views through violence. However, the meager results achieved to date by these moderate forces may increase the appeal of the radical movements in the future.

LIMITS AND RESULTS OF NAALC

Despite its legal standing, the NAALC has achieved very little to date. The modesty of its accomplishments is due to the many differences among NAFTA opponents in the United States (such as the AFL-CIO, NGOs, and Democratic politicians), on the one hand, and the business chambers, Republican lawmakers, and the government of Mexico and its private sector and labor union allies, on the other. It is to be remembered that Mexico's *oficialista* unions opposed the attachment of any conditions to regional free trade.

The lack of political will to harmonize worker rights in North America has been justified with arguments ranging from concerns about national sovereignty to the assertion that NAFTA is a purely commercial accord.[27] The purpose of NAALC, therefore, is not to address regional labor issues but rather to foster national labor regulations in the three member states. Yet the three governments have not only opposed the creation of supranational bodies to oversee the national application of labor laws, but they also reserved the right to establish and modify their respective labor legislations. Domestic authorities thus remain responsible for guaranteeing the "highest labor standards congruent with high quality and productivity."[28] The application of such standards is not, however, guaranteed in the NAFTA region, apart from a few exceptions.

In short, although the NAALC's mandate is very extensive, including guarantees for the effective application of labor laws of each member country, the agreement lacks enforcement mechanisms or ways to promote cooperative resolution of conflicts between labor and employer organizations. Nor is this latter issue addressed in the domestic labor legislations of the three countries.[29] The organ responsible for the implementation of the NAALC's principles is the trinational Labor Commission. But because the Commission consists of a council and a secretariat that respond to the labor ministries of the three countries, there are no guarantees of impartiality—especially when the violators are the governments themselves. Although it is possible to apply trade sanctions in case of breaches, the process is complex and lengthy (three years on average). Furthermore, sanctions can be applied only if the violations involve labor by minors, work safety and health issues, or minimum salary questions; where there is a discernible long-term pattern of omissions or violations; and when all three countries have corresponding regulations (NAALC Article 48). Another restriction concerns the NAALC's reach in Canada, given that the agreement must be ratified by each of the provinces. Only four provinces—Alberta, Manitoba, Quebec, and Prince Edward Island—have ratified thus far. A large part of Canada thus remains outside the agreement.

NAALC's Declaration of Principles is far-reaching.[30] Even so, many key issues—such as union freedoms, collective hiring, and the right to strike (which is frequently not sufficiently guaranteed in the U.S. and Mexican legal frameworks)—cannot even be brought before a committee of "independent" experts. This is a serious deficiency for attempts to promote the representation of workers in deliberations on the costs and benefits of trade opening and on alternative models of regional and hemispheric integration.[31] Complaints or denunciations of violations can result only in a ministerial-level exchange of information.[32]

Although compliance with other principles of the NAALC can be evaluated without the application of sanctions, it is difficult to imagine that nonorganized workers could independently take advantage of the NAALC in efforts to counteract the artificial decline of their salaries and working conditions. The difficulties are exacerbated by the fact that the NAALC does not establish any kind of periodic monitoring mechanisms for compliance with its principles, nor does it guarantee the independence of the committee of experts or the members of the arbitration panel that could recommend the application of sanctions.[33] As a consequence of these limitations, the NAALC's capacity to eradicate "social dumping" or resolve conflicts between different interests (such as between capital and labor or between labor in developing and developed countries) is virtually nil.

Up to the year 2000, the National Administrative Offices (NAOs) located in the NAFTA countries received a total of twenty-one complaints. Some concerned the same cases. A substantial number came forward during the first year of the agreement, which illustrates the initial interest of unions in testing the effectiveness of NAALC. They focused on violations of union rights and the right to form independent collective organizations in the Mexican maquiladora sector. The results were practically zero, even though some of the cases captured the attention of the international press and public opinion. Notably, one case was withdrawn by the complainant—the United Electrical Workers of the United States—as a protest against the inefficiency of the NAALC procedures.[34]

As a result of disillusionment, there were fewer cases in the two years that followed. At this same time, however, the first complaint was lodged against the United States—which meant that Mexico would no longer be the only NAFTA party to be accused. Also, the number of organizations supporting the complaints increased, the detail of the descriptions of the types of violations improved, and the complaints were permitted to include a greater variety of NAALC principles, such as the enforcement of labor safety and health regulations, prevention of professional hazards and illnesses, prohibition against workplace discrimination, and the protection of the rights of migrant workers. All these improvements were the result of the common learning process between organizations in the three NAFTA countries.[35]

Starting in 1997, the NAALC gained dynamism due to the intensification of transnational labor union cooperation and the consequent increase in the number of complaints. Of the twelve complaints presented between 1997 and the end of 1999, five were against the United States, two against Canada, and five against Mexico. Most frequently, the complaints involved breaches of the collective rights of workers; however, the results have not been any better than in the earlier cases. None of the cases came even close to the application of sanctions.

Among the NAFTA countries, Mexico had the most serious problems. Between 1994 and 1999, in fact, Mexico received thirteen complaints, compared with six for the United States and two for Canada. However, the low number of cases presented against Canada owes not only to its better compliance with labor laws, but also to the fact that the NAALC is applicable in only four provinces.

One serious limitation of NAALC is the slow pace of procedures. This implies that violations remain under impunity. According to one analysis, a complaint takes six to eight weeks to be admitted and another twenty-six weeks prior to its first review. From then on, the ministerial-level consultations, if recommended, will last for more than thirty weeks. In other words, the overall process takes a good deal more than a year.[36]

To date, none of the cases has gone beyond the first phase of treatment (ministerial consultations), nor have accused companies voluntarily curbed the violations. These facts illustrate the inability of the NAALC to resolve conflicts between companies and workers, and they also bear witness to the weakness of unionism in the NAFTA region. However, new spaces have been created in the three countries for the construction of cross-national solidarity networks, an improved understanding of the North American labor regimes, and the dissemination of information about labor laws and practices in the region. Violations are now discussed on a regional basis, not just in local arenas.[37] In this sense, one of the NAALC's contributions has been the sharing of experiences and building of organizational skills in the face of strong competitive pressures. These can well develop into durable alliances between unions and nongovernmental organizations in posing a common front to transnational companies and governments of the region.[38]

In terms of intergovernmental cooperation, activities have thus far been limited to comparative studies and seminars on various issues, such as labor market situations and labor legislation, the relationship between income and productivity, and the problems of the process of labor organization[39]—especially the precariousness of collective rights in the world's largest economy.[40] To date, however, there has not been any progress in correcting the existing shortcomings at the national level. Governments have also failed to adopt regional policies or mechanisms to address violations of labor regulations, improve the opportunities for the formation of unions, decrease the wage asymmetries, or resolve some of the most basic issues—such as the migration of Mexican workers to the United States and their illegal status in the U.S. market.

NAALC's meager achievements have given rise to numerous proposals by union and societal organizations to strengthen the agreement through a re-acknowledgment of collective rights, the adoption of faster procedures, and the participation of societal groups in the entities charged with receiving complaints.[41] These efforts were launched in the wake of consultations on the first five years of NAALC's operation. Moreover, a meeting of the three NAFTA labor ministers acknowledged the limitations of the NAALC by suggesting the need to "foster the cooperation mechanisms established in the agreement."

However, whereas Mexico expressed its interest in cooperation on migration issues, the United States was concerned about whether integration would benefit all citizens equally. This impasse revealed that, after five full years of experience with NAALC, even the foremost defenders of the agreement were uncertain as to the best way to revise or strengthen it.[42]

CONCLUSIONS

NAFTA's impact and the NAALC experience show clearly that labor problems cannot be resolved by regional instruments as they stand. The prospects for defending the interests of workers and allowing labor to benefit from integration were largely conditioned by the institutional frameworks and unions existing at the time of the talks. These conclusions indicate a need for profound changes in U.S. and Mexican—and, to a lesser extent, Canadian—domestic legislation in the area of individual and collective rights of workers. Such changes are necessary for the expansion of opportunities and for a more equitable distribution of the costs and benefits of integration. In addition, a new institutional framework should be devised in the three countries to promote cooperation within companies and industries, and to serve as a stepping-stone for greater participation by unions in economic integration and consensus-building on the regional and global levels.

Along with the reform of the national legislation, there should be greater convergence between the different levels of regulation, starting from the strengthening of NAALC's provisions and reach. Similarly, on the global level, common minimum labor standards should be adopted in order to ensure that islands of strong labor protection, such as the European Union, will not succumb before the competitive pressures emanating from other integration schemes such as NAFTA.

Despite its imperfections, in fact, the European experience provides some useful lessons. For example, the North American labor agenda should incorporate a proposal for a supranational model of dealing with labor relations that would make the integration process more inclusive and help address one of the thorniest problems exposed by the NAALC: the absence of guarantees for the collective action of workers through unions. Such a proposal would help establish the following five requirements:

- public guarantees for the existence of strong, independent unions in industry and politics;

- formally approved rules for the establishment of a tripartite system of making decisions, and the extension of any agreements to non-unionized sectors;

- a relatively high ceiling for basic social rights for all workers as in an active welfare state, along with a strong system of collective bargaining;

- coordination between the levels of negotiation and reduction of wage differentials between regions by industries and occupations; and

- agreement at the firm level to allow for the participation of unions and workers in the decisions affecting them through information exchanges, consultations, and collaborative decision-making mechanisms as established by laws.[43]

We are far from meeting these criteria at present.

Over the years since the NAFTA's entry into force, however, unions have improved their ability to set a common agenda in order to foster the collective rights of workers in the NAFTA region. Attesting to this are the convergence between U.S. and Canadian unions after the overhaul of the AFL-CIO, the change in the AFL-CIO's position on the flow of Mexican labor into the United States, the alliances between the three NAFTA countries' unions in defending the collective rights of workers and pushing for a new model of regional integration, and the rise of independent unions in Mexico thanks to the process of democratization. These are promising developments—particularly as the most catastrophic predictions about NAFTA have dissipated, along with the illusions that regional integration would abolish wage asymmetries and other problems. Today's scenario for NAFTA is thus very distinct from that in the beginning of the 1990s, with improved prospects for unions to call for a new integration model.

Yet there are numerous obstacles to creating institutions or adopting labor policies and mechanisms for cooperation between governments and society that would allow for correcting the adverse effects of trade liberalization and the growing interdependence of local, national, and international economies. The most important obstacles are the persistent and marked asymmetries between NAFTA members, the extent of U.S. hegemony throughout the region, and the very character of NAFTA itself. The low profile of labor regulations in the United States and, particularly, the difficulties of U.S. workers to unionize and negotiate collectively tend to undermine the credibility of demands for improved compliance with labor rights in Mexico—and to weaken the prospects for extending the North American labor regulations to the other countries of the continent. Reforms to U.S. labor legislation are thus a central key. In principle they should thus precede, or at least lead, the efforts to foster the rights of workers both regionally and globally; in practice, however, the conditions for this appear absent in the United States. However, it should not be forgotten that the evolution of labor institutions and policies in each country toward a trinational convergence is likely to be a much slower process than macroeconomic policy convergence.[44] Moreover, U.S. domestic and foreign policies contain aspects that limit the prospects for a more complete integration.

Nonetheless, the NAFTA country governments and social actors alike have made important strides toward a regional convergence. For example, the new government in Mexico changed its foreign policy to call for a revision of U.S. migration policies and the creation of development funds for the weakest economy of the NAFTA region. Moreover, the Mexican government has on numerous occasions acknowledged the need to revise the meaning of national sovereignty and to create effective supranational mechanisms to face the complex problems of globalization. As such, it is leaving behind the rigid positions of the PRI regime. Another encouraging sign is the improved capacity of social and union organizations, such as the Hemispheric Social Alliance, to make constructive proposals.

In sum, there are increasing prospects that NAFTA might be revised—or at least amended—and that social forces might exert sufficient pressure to ensure that NAFTA, in its current form, does not become the model for the entire hemisphere. But if the governments fail to assume responsibility for pursuing a more even distribution of benefits within and between the region's countries, for creating mechanisms for social actors to participate in decision-making, for promoting the development of the weakest economy in NAFTA, and for diminishing the adverse effects of integration, NAFTA and FTAA will confront mounting opposition and resistance. And if moderate reformists are ignored, the initiative will pass to the most radical opponents of integration and globalization.

Notes

1. Graciela Bensusán, "Entre candados y dientes: la agenda laboral del TLCAN," *Perfiles Latinoamericanos* 4 (1994).

2. Frederick Mayer, "Juego de dos niveles: las negociaciones del TLCAN," in *Para evaluar al TLCAN*, ed. Arturo Borja (Mexico City: Porrúa, 2001).

3. Juan Carlos Ramírez, "Los efectos del TLCAN sobre el comercio y la industria en México," in *Para evaluar al TLCAN*, ed. Borja, p. 189.

4. Enrique Dussel, "El tratado de libre comercio de Norte América y el desempeño de la economía mexicana" (Mexico City: CEPAL, 2000); Víctor Tockman and Daniel Martínez, "Costo laboral en el sector manufacturero de América Latina," in *Costos laborales y competitividad en América Latina*, ed. Edward Amadeo et al. (Lima: OIT, 1997).

5. Dussel, "El tratado de libre comercio," p. 35.

6. Bruce Campbell et al., "Labour Market Effects under CUSFTA/NAFTA," Employment and Training Papers 29 (Geneva: ILO, 1999), at http://www.ilo-org.

7. Campbell et al., "Labour Market Effects"; and Teresa Rendón and Carlos Salas, "La evolución del empleo," in *Trabajo y trabajadores en el México contemporáneo*, ed. Graciela Bensusán and Teresa Rendón (Mexico City: Porrúa, 2000).

8. Campbell et al., "Labour Market Effects."

9. *Quinto Informe de Gobierno 1999*; Graciela Bensusán and Luis Reygadas, "Relaciones laborales en Chihuahua: un caso de abatimiento artificial de los salarios," *Revista Mexicana de Sociología* 62, no. 2 (2000): 29–57.

10. *Trabajo y Democracia Hoy* 61 (May–June 2001).

11. Enrique de la Garza, *El sindicalismo mexicano ante la transición política* (Mexico City: Cenpros, 2000).

12. During this period Mexican wages declined from $2.10 to $1.90 per hour, while U.S wages rose from $11.70 to $13.80 per hour. Canada experienced a similar trend.

13. Between 1993 and 1999, the unit costs dropped by 40 percent in Mexico—and by only 11.6 percent and 14 percent in the United States and Canada, respectively.

14. Thea Lee, "Comercio y desigualdad," in *Estandares laborales después del TLCAN*, ed. Graciela Bensusán (Mexico City: Plaza y Valdés, 1999); and Lawrence Mishel and Jared Bernstein, "Is the Technology Black Box Empty? An Empirical Examination of the Impact of Technology on Wage Inequality and Employment Structures," Technical Paper 217 (Washington, D.C., Economic Policy Institute, April 1994).

15. Bensusán, "Entre candados y dientes."

16. Ian Robinson, "National Level Analysis, United States of America," Informe Final de Investigación del Proyecto "Estrategias sindicales frente al TLCAN" (Mexico City: Conacyt-Colmex 2000), mimeo.

17. Ibid.

18. Dale Hathaway, "Transnational Support for Labour Organizing in Mexico: Comparative Cases," presented at the international congress of the Latin American Studies Association, Miami, March 2000, p. 20.

19. Víctor Osorio, *Agenda social y libre comercio en las Américas* (Mexico City: RMALC, 1998). It must be noted that the U.S. House of Representatives approved fast track (renamed trade promotion authority) by a vote of 215 to 214 in December 2001.

20. Robinson, "National Level Analysis, Canada."

21. Bensusán, "Entre candados y dientes."

22. Landy Sánchez, "Entre la apertura comercial y la transición política: la estrategia del Sindicato de Telefonistas de la República Mexicana," M.A. thesis, FLACSO-Mexico, 1998.

23. Graciela Bensusán, *El modelo mexicano de regulación laboral* (Mexico City: Plaza y Valdés, 2000).

24. The first draft of the document *Alternatives for the Americas* was prepared at the Peoples' Summit of the Americas in Santiago de Chile in April 1998. Organizers included Common Frontiers (Canada), Development Gap –Alliance for Responsible Trade (the United States), RMALC (Mexico), and Réseau québécois sur l'intégration continentale (RQIC).

25. The 1991 agreement between the United Electrical Workers (UE) and FAT paved the way to numerous meetings and joint activities, setting important precedents for cross-border cooperation. See Stephanie Tréillet and Xavier de la Vega, "Vers des stratégies syndicales transnationales," in *Le syndicalisme dans la mondialisation*, ed. Annei Foquet et al. (Paris: Atelier/Ouvrièr, 2000).

26. In Mexico, there are two ways to undercut the rise or existence of autonomous, truly representative unions: governmental control of union leadership, and "collective contracts of protection" that hamper unionization and measures to seek compensation. See María Xelhuantzi, *La democracia pendiente* (Mexico City: STRM, 2000).

27. For arguments raised in Mexico against an agreement of broad scope and with a power to punish violators of labor rights, see Bensusán, "Entre candados y dientes."

28. NAALC, *Diario Oficial de la Federación* (December 21, 1993).

29. Bensusán, *El modelo mexicano*.

30. The declaration includes the following principles: freedom of association and protection of the right to organize; the right to collective bargaining; the right to strike; prohibition of forced labor; restrictions on work by minors; minimum working conditions; nondiscrimination in hiring practices; equal wages for men and women; prevention of occupational injuries and illnesses; compensation for work-related injuries or illnesses; and protection of migrant workers. See Annex 1 of NAALC.

31. Graciela Bensusán, "Integración regional y cambio institucional: la reforma laboral en América del Norte," in *Estandares laborales*, ed. Bensusán.

32. See Article 22 of NAALC.

33. These committees are to be composed of three members: the chair is to be selected from a list of experts drawn up in collaboration with the International Labour Organization, while the two other members are taken from lists provided by the parties.

34. Bodil Damgaard, "Cooperación laboral transnacional en América del Norte a finales de los noventa," *El Cotidiano* 94 (1999).

35. For a detailed description of such alliances, see Hathaway, "Transnational Support for Labour Organizing."

36. Damgaard, "Cooperación laboral transnacional."

37. Stephen Herzenberg, "El ALCAN y el desarrollo de una alternativa al neoliberalismo," and Lance Compa, "El acuerdo laboral paralelo del TLCAN: un recuento de tres años," both in *Estandares laborales*, ed. Bensusán; and Damgaard, "Cooperación laboral transnacional."

38. Compa, "El acuerdo laboral paralelo," and Hathaway, "Transnational Support for Labour Organizing."

39. Commission for Labor Cooperation, *Plant Closings and Labor Rights* (Dallas, Tex.: Secretariat of the Commission for Labor Cooperation, 1997) was a very important study on this final point. It documented threats made by U.S. companies after NAFTA's entry into force to close down operations as a mechanism to undermine incentives for unionization.

40. Human Rights Watch, *Unfair Advantage* (Washington, D.C.: Human Rights Watch, 2000) maintains that the United States has, paradoxically, failed to protect the rights of U.S. workers while demanding such protection in other countries as a prerequisite for entering trade agreements. Case studies reveal that U.S. laws and practices provide an "unfair advantage" to employers over employees.

41. A summary of the key proposals formulated by the FAT and RMLAC can be found in Bertha Luján, "Los sindicatos frente al TLCAN," in *Estandares laborales*, ed. Bensusán.

42. See RMLAC, *Alternativas*, September–October 1998.

43. Wolfgang Streeck, "Rise and Decline of Corporativism," in Lloyd Ulman et al., *Labor and Integrated Europe* (Washington, D.C.: Brookings Institution, 1993), pp. 89–90.

44. Streeck, "Rise and Decline of Corporativism."

11

Environmental Challenges to International Trade

Debra J. Davidson and Ross E. Mitchell

The nature of the linkages between international trade and environmental well-being has been debated for decades, yet the "greening of trade" is still very far from becoming the rule of the day. To be fair, some progress has been made in trying to draw together the often disparate and highly contentious agenda items of trade and environment. Environmental critics of neoliberal trade policies nonetheless warn of overconsumption, diminishing resource supplies, increasing pollution, and the energy-intensive nature of international trade. These warnings have been overshadowed in the past by the optimistic sentiments touted by certain scholars, government leaders, and corporate interests in support of trade. Trade proponents are confident that individual incomes will improve as a result of trade expansion in less developed regions. They also maintain that rising incomes will lead to increased demand for environmental protection as well as increased capacity to adopt pollution abatement and efficiency technologies.

These debates culminated in one of the most politically charged set of trade agreement negotiations in memory. What was initially expected to be the smooth passage of the North American Free Trade Agreement (NAFTA) dragged out into several months of heated discussions over environmental and labor issues. Environmentalists expressed concern that the lower costs of environmental compliance and lax enforcement in Mexico would encourage businesses to relocate to Mexico,[1] thereby generating "pollution havens" and ultimately encouraging a "race to the bottom" in environmental standards. In contrast, trade supporters suggested that economic growth could be harnessed to the benefit of environmental quality.[2] Environmental regulations were cause for concern, not because of the potential for decline in regulation stringency, but rather because of the potential that they would be inappropriately used to protect domestic producers.[3]

Despite the trade proponents' claims, pressures from environmental and labor concerns led to the establishment of environmental and labor side agreements among NAFTA signatories. The side accords, however, did little to stifle controversy over trade expansion and environmental well-being. This debate has endured largely due to the difficulty of measuring the very complex layers of linkages between trade and environment. Yet voices of concern appear to be growing, both in number and in diversity, and particularly in the case of NAFTA. While touted as the world's greenest trade agreement, NAFTA has not lived up to expectations on the environmental front.

We count ourselves among those critics of current trade regimes who, while not opposed to trade, do question the effectiveness of existing institutional parameters to protect social and environmental well-being. Such protections are necessary, not only because trade liberalization may in certain circumstances place stress on socio-environmental systems, but also because their degradation may strain the long-term sustainability of trade regimes. The longevity of any economic system is dependent upon political and bureaucratic support, a healthy and skilled workforce, and resilient ecosystems capable of providing natural resources and absorbing wastes. Consequently, social and environmental well-being are central trade issues regardless of whether a specific trade regime can be shown directly to have caused social or environmental degradation. To bring trade into a more sustainable system of operation, we must first discard the set of neoliberal assumptions that support the claim that trade liberalization automatically leads to social and environmental improvement.

These assumptions include the enduring belief that there is a positive association between income levels and environmental concern, despite the inconclusive nature of the evidence regarding income elasticity and demand for environmental services.[4] The relationship between support for rainforest protection and personal income, for instance, may be decidedly different from the relationship between income and support for safe drinking water. More recent work on environmental attitudes provides evidence to dispute the relationship between individual economic well-being and environmental attitudes. Second, the notion that improvements in environmental regulations will occur as a result of economic growth must be seriously questioned. Nation-states can be extraordinarily diverse in both political support and institutional capacity for environmental protection; this is true even among developed countries. The political and economic histories of the three NAFTA signatories are sufficiently distinct to generate different opportunities and limitations for environmental protection in each of them. Finally, and most important, reliance on rapid industrialization as a route toward improved social and environmental well-being defies lessons learned over the past two centuries of development. Such strategies are based on inaccurate assumptions that material resource supplies are unlimited, that future environmental conditions can be predicted with certainty, and that the inevitable environmental impacts of industrialization will be reversible once nations acquire sufficient wealth to enter post-industrialization.

This chapter offers an alternative approach to the trade-environment relationship. Instead of attempting to show how NAFTA impacts the environment (a perspective that predominates in the current academic literature), we explore how the environment may impact the future of NAFTA, based on current political and environmental trends—a subtle but significant shift in focus. In the first section, we discuss three aspects of the environment that are likely to pose challenges to NAFTA in the future: the growth of international environmentalism, the social impacts of rapid development and environmental degradation, and the uncertainty of environmental systems.

In the second section, we assess the capacity of NAFTA's existing institutions and policies to respond to such challenges, based on the accord's seven-year history. Sources of information include an extensive review of academic literature, position statements of key environmental organizations, papers submitted to the North American Commission on Environmental Cooperation (NACEC or CEC), media and government documents, and public records of citizen submissions (and subsequent responses) to the CEC. We conclude with a discussion of some measures that may help ensure that trade liberalization and social and environmental well-being in North America go hand in hand.

THREE ENVIRONMENTAL CHALLENGES

The Global Environmental Movement

Regardless of whether one agrees or disagrees with the positions of environmental movement organizations (EMOs), their political power and influence is difficult to ignore. Anyone who has followed NAFTA's history is aware that EMOs will have a significant role to play in its future, if only because they have played a significant role in its past. The reason NAFTA can claim to be the greenest trade agreement in history is precisely because of pressures that EMOs have brought to bear in the international arena.

In short, NAFTA's future will be heavily influenced by the central position of social and environmental issues in global trade politics. This was exemplified by the large-scale protests that occurred during the World Trade Organization (WTO) meetings in Seattle in 1999, the meeting of the Free Trade Area of the Americas (FTAA) negotiators in Quebec City in 2001, and the G-8 Summit in Genoa, Italy, also in 2001. Given the EMOs' strong influence, actions by NAFTA administrators that contribute to a mutually constructive political relationship have the potential to lead to a powerful political alliance. Likewise, EMOs can serve as a valuable source of skills and information for positive environmental change. On the other hand, by ignoring or challenging EMOs, NAFTA administrators can forgo potentially valuable networking opportunities and exacerbate volatile political situations.

Just as economists point out that international trade is not new, international environmental politics likewise has an extended history. In fact, international environmental politics, which contributed to international environmental treaties dating back over a century, appears to predate domestic environmental politics. Nonetheless, EMOs' recent rise in power in international politics may be one of the most significant features of modern society. Several factors have precipitated the EMOs' advance onto the international political stage; these include heightened awareness of global environmental issues, the expansion in size and mandate of the international political apparatus, and the legitimization by scientific institutions of many concerns that EMOs have raised.[5]

As environmental activism has grown in power and influence, general concern for the environment has also become consistently high. This is true even among social actors who are not expected to express such concern. Although early assessments of the modern environmental movement characterized the majority of supporters as members of "post-materialist" or "new class" groups in industrialized countries, this is no longer the case.[6] Recent survey work shows that expressed concern for global environmental issues is just as high in developing countries as in developed countries—and possibly even higher for local environmental issues.[7]

As awareness of the linkages between environment and trade has grown, EMOs have increasingly turned their attention to this connection. This interest crystallized into a formidable force in trade policy after the tuna-dolphin case between the United States and Mexico was submitted to a dispute panel under the rules of the General Agreement on Tariffs and Trade (GATT) in 1991.[8] Ironically, a small number of very visible global trade institutions (International Monetary Fund, WTO, and NAFTA) have by and large provided further impetus for this movement. Without doubt, these institutions serve as centralized targets of political action. Furthermore, given the overlapping impact of trade with several other components of social welfare, EMOs are able to join forces with other movement organizations in the areas of labor, aboriginal, and human rights.

The EMOs' most notable accomplishment, beyond placing the environment on the global political agenda, is their success in guiding debates toward specific issues. This includes trade in products created through environmentally damaging processes; the "Polluter Pays Principle," which establishes that the polluter bears the expense of measures necessary to ensure that the environment is maintained in an acceptable state; and eco-labeling.

In North America, NAFTA proponents were caught off guard by the rapid emergence of organized environmental opposition. Effective collaboration between EMOs and other movement organizations in Canada, Mexico, and the United States ensured that negotiations would not proceed as smoothly as NAFTA negotiators had hoped. Despite the fact that EMOs in all three countries had rarely collaborated in the past, twenty-four major environmental groups from the three countries signed the Declaración de San Ygnacio in April 1991, advocating the inclusion of environmental regulations in NAFTA.

What is perhaps most significant about the EMOs' role in international politics is their staying power. Despite the fact that specific environmental issues suffer from a rather ephemeral "issue attention cycle,"[9] EMOs themselves tend to persist. While the numbers of newly emerging groups may vary, these groups, once formed, tend to remain.[10] International EMOs are also instrumental in networking, linking diverse national and international groups into effective advocacy coalitions.[11]

The breadth of environmental issues and their tendency to overlap with other political issues, particularly social welfare, have prevented the emergence of a single voice for the environmental movement. To some extent, environmental politics have suffered from this lack of coherent identity. Social scientists typically speak of a two-tiered division within the global environmental movement. Although EMOs are far more diverse than this model suggests, such characterizations are useful in understanding recent political actions. At one end of the spectrum are established environmental groups with high national and international memberships that attempt to engage in constructive dialogue with governmental officials. These are known as "reform groups," and they include organizations such as the Worldwide Fund for Nature and the Nature Conservancy. At the other end are "radical groups," which tend to challenge the legitimacy of existing institutions of economic and political power.[12] They include groups such as People's Global Action, a recently formed organization that serves as a forum for local people's movements across the globe. Such groups are often loosely organized in comparison to reform groups, and they are much more likely to use confrontational, direct action movement techniques. The emergence of such radical groups indicates the extent to which the impacts of rapid development have, themselves, served as mobilization mechanisms. Many social groups that might otherwise have nothing in common are finding solidarity in their perceived marginalization in the global economy.

In short, the global environment–trade debate has shifted existing EMOs' focus toward trade issues and catalyzed the emergence of new organizations in direct response to the perceived threats of economic globalization. This two-tiered movement structure was evident in the NAFTA negotiations, in which EMOs split into two camps: those radically opposed to NAFTA and those interested in engagement with the negotiators. President Clinton solidified this split when he pledged that any nongovernmental organizations (NGOs) that wished to play a *constructive* role in the negotiations would have an opportunity for real input.[13] In the end, the NAFTA negotiators entered into dialogue with only seven EMOs, many of them established conservation organizations such as the Audubon Society and the World Wildlife Fund. Not surprisingly, groups that were more critical of NAFTA—large international bodies such as Greenpeace and the Sierra Club, as well as many smaller, less organized radical groups—were left out.

Even though EMOs' tactics and ideologies vary widely, a common mandate on trade-environment linkages is beginning to emerge among them. The main elements of this mandate include at least two concerns: (1) the ability of trade agreements to undermine both national and international efforts at environmental protection; and (2) the general lack of democracy, transparency, and accountability characterizing trade institutions and agreements. These threats to democratic procedures extend to NAFTA's environmental side agreement, an accord initially designed to encourage citizen participation.[14]

The World Wildlife Fund recently joined the National Wildlife Federation, Sierra Club, Enlace Ecológico A.C., the Canadian Environmental Law Association, and several other EMOs in accusing the CEC council of secretly negotiating new rules that would "reduce the ability of citizens to submit effective petitions on enforcement matters."[15] Even some EMOs that were directly involved in the NAFTA negotiations have expressed criticism of NAFTA's environmental record. One of the most contentious items does not concern the environmental side agreement per se, but Chapter 11 of the NAFTA accord, which environmental groups claim allows corporations legally to attack domestic environmental laws. Recently the director of the Sustainable Commerce Program of the World Wildlife Fund—a group that participated in NAFTA's ratification in the United States—said the following of Chapter 11: "To call a country's effort to protect the environment 'an expropriation' is absurd.... It's like saying we should pay polluters every time the government asks them not to pollute."[16] Specific Chapter 11 cases are discussed later in this chapter.

Social Impacts of Environmental Degradation

Industrial development that proceeds without sufficient environmental protection can lead to negative impacts, not only to the natural environment but also to the cultures, economies, and health of local peoples. Few today can deny that poverty and health are environmental issues, and they must be treated accordingly. These impacts substantially challenge the future of NAFTA in two ways. First, the costs of mitigating these impacts are often considerably higher than the costs of prevention. Such expenses can be an extraordinary burden for fiscally strapped countries like Mexico, where basic services like transportation and drinking water are already lacking in many areas. Second, these indirect social impacts reduce labor productivity and represent a direct threat to NAFTA's stated objectives to improve social well-being and promote sustainable development.

If the deleterious social impacts of environmental degradation were distributed in proportion to the benefits of such degradation, then appropriate actions most certainly would have been incorporated into economic policy throughout history. Unfortunately, the deleterious impacts are often concentrated in areas that historically have escaped the attention of national and international polities. This has translated into the persistence of socially and environmentally degrading conditions in regions dependent upon extractive-based industries or in impoverished urban areas characterized by heavy industry.

Many scholars have associated such declines in social and environmental welfare with the degree of participation in international economic exchange, a phenomenon termed "underdevelopment."[17] Even trade proponents warn of the potential for long-term impoverishment when exhaustible materials fuel trade expansion.[18] According to underdevelopment theory, extractive-based industries face an inevitable cost-price squeeze; extraction costs continue to rise while the price of raw materials in the global marketplace remains constant. Because such regions have few economic alternatives, this situation leads to over-exploitation and eventual economic collapse. The environmental impacts of decades of intensive resource extraction leave the land base and local peoples in such poor condition that even a return to subsistence activities is unlikely. Impoverished urban regions can meet a similar fate. In an effort to attract jobs and revenues, such regions often become the sites of locally unwanted land uses, or "LULUs." With weak environmental standards and/or monitoring and enforcement, these regions become sites of concentrated air, soil, and water pollution, threatening both public health and future economic potential.

We do not have to go far to see firsthand examples. The inequitable distribution of the social impacts of environmental degradation can be found throughout the three NAFTA countries. Impoverished urban centers and regions of intensive extractive industries, such as forestry mining operations, bear a disproportionate share of environmental hazards. Hence a realistic assessment of the benefits of trade expansion must include the cumulative impacts of industrialization in regions such as the *maquiladora* (in-bond processing) zone on the U.S.-Mexico border; oil and gas extraction sites in Alberta and British Columbia that are heavily populated by First Nations peoples; and sections of Los Angeles, Mexico City, and southern Ontario that have become sites of hazardous industrial facilities.

An excellent indicator of cumulative social and environmental impacts is the recent increase in both the number and intensity of local environmental mobilizations. What is most notable about the surge in local mobilizations in the past decade is their emergence beyond the borders of wealthy nations—in places like Ecuador, Gambia, Madagascar, and India. Local environmental movements—promoting such causes as NIMBY ("Not In My Backyard"), environmental justice, or ecological democracy—are reactions to perceived inequities in the distribution of environmental costs and benefits.

Such local responses to perceived injustices have emerged in Canada, Mexico, and the United States, and they are increasingly gaining support from established international environmental organizations. Alternatively, they are establishing new collaborative organizations specifically focused on localized environmental threats. The Zapatista movement in Chiapas is one well-known example of a mobilized response to the anticipated local impacts of trade expansion. Other groups, such as the Border Environmental Justice Campaign, have been working with local residents in the U.S.-Mexico border region to respond to local environmental health threats. Still others—the Environmental Health Coalition, the Southwest Network for Economic and Environmental Justice, and the Comité Ciudadano para la Restauración del Cañón del Padre—recently filed a joint petition to push the U.S. Environmental Protection Agency to subpoena ninety-four U.S. companies with subsidiaries in Mexico for information on hazardous materials and waste.[19]

Environmental Uncertainty

Ecological change, besides having social and political implications, also has very real impacts on economic productivity itself. NAFTA's ability to meet the goals of trade liberalization and socioeconomic improvement in North America will be challenged by the depletion of natural resource supplies, lost productivity due to environmental degradation, loss of biodiversity, and global climate change. These phenomena bring high levels of uncertainty to natural resource–based economies in particular. They can also be compounded by the unpredicted social and economic costs of extreme weather events and longer-term climate modifications. A sustainable economic regime must be resilient in the face of such uncertainties. At the same time, it must provide sufficient compensation mechanisms for the marginalized or otherwise neglected segments of society that face potential or actual losses.

The international scientific community has been moving toward consensus on the reality of global climate change (GCC).[20] Although the effects of GCC are difficult to predict, most scientists agree that global climate change will dramatically alter the existing biogeoclimatic characteristics of regions. These changes inevitably affect the types of natural resources that are regionally available. Areas that were historically highly productive in grains or fisheries, for example, may find that conditions are no longer suitable for such products. Industries that are sufficiently adaptable might respond successfully to such fluctuations. Operations characterized by high levels of fixed capital investment in specialized infrastructure, on the other hand, will face difficulties.

Scientists participating in the United Nations Inter-governmental Panel on Climate Change have also noted the potential for increases in the frequency and intensity of extreme weather events.[21] Severe droughts, hurricanes, and other weather phenomena are difficult to predict, and they can be enormously costly in infrastructure and lives. Recent flooding in the U.S. Midwest, Ecuador, and Mexico City took hundreds of lives and destroyed buildings, roads, and crops. Future droughts and pest infestations could contribute to an increase in the occurrence and intensity of forest fires. Aside from the obvious devastation wrought on local communities and the seemingly insurmountable costs of compensation and rebuilding, the economic integration associated with liberalized trade establishes the potential for such localized events to have second-order impacts throughout the NAFTA region.

Even without the added complications introduced by global climate change, the potential for sustainability of natural resource regimes in a global economy remains far from clear. We still lack the scientific knowledge needed to devise management plans that would guarantee the maintenance of ecological health in fisheries, agriculture, forestry, and mining. Compounding the lack of scientific understanding of complex ecological systems is the high variability in the bureaucratic capacity of regulatory institutions to apply what limited knowledge we do possess. Even in the United States, the implementation record for environmental policy is woefully lacking.[22] Moreover, sufficient scientific knowledge and bureaucratic capacity alone would not guarantee improved implementation in all cases; the highly competitive nature of global economies provides far more incentives for maximizing short-term gains than for long-term sustainability of resource supplies.

In addition, because the export economies of both Mexico and Canada are more dependent upon natural resource–based industries than is that of the United States, ecological impacts will likely be concentrated in these two countries. This could potentially place Mexico and Canada in a disadvantaged position relative to their stronger trading partner. The entire region will be affected, however, given that raw materials and agriculture account for a significant proportion of total global merchandise trade in North America.[23] During an October 2000 CEC symposium on "Understanding the Linkages between Trade and the Environment," several presenters addressed NAFTA's potential and actual impacts on fisheries, water, and forestry, in addition to hazardous wastes and industrial pollution. Notably, most indicated significant impacts to these systems. Transportation is another important area that has received inadequate attention within NAFTA. As Barry Prentice and Mark Ojah emphasize in their chapter in this volume, transportation not only affects the environmental quality of North America, but it also is responsible for a significant share of global pollution.

INSTITUTIONAL CAPACITY: CAN NAFTA RESPOND?

Any international governing body with an environmental mandate faces several, often overwhelming difficulties. In this section we highlight four crucial environmental policy challenges. The first major constraint is the complexity intrinsic to trade-related environmental regulations. With five levels of government authority (multilateral, regional, national, subnational, and municipal), the potential for harmonizing environmental regulations, or even agreeing upon minimum standards, is limited. Second, the implementation of any international agreement ultimately is dependent upon the commitment of the according parties, yet signatory nations face vastly divergent levels of political, fiscal, and bureaucratic support at the domestic level. Third, the very same complexity and transboundary nature of global environmental issues that justified their placement on the international governance agenda also place them among the most complicated policy dilemmas imaginable. The scientific uncertainty, multidimensionality, large-scale impact, and regional variation associated with global environmental issues pose formidable challenges to even the most committed policymakers. And fourth, NAFTA has taken on an additional challenge: it is the only trade agreement to partner a developing country with its significantly wealthier neighbors. Thus, in addition to trade expansion and the mitigation of environmental impacts, NAFTA's signatories established policy goals in the areas of development, technology transfer, and politico-economic stability.

NAFTA also stands alone among international trade agreements for the inclusion of an environmental side agreement, and thus it should be well positioned to face many of these challenges. Observers in the social sciences, however, are skeptical of the extent to which this effort has translated into real environmental improvement.[24] Even the authors of a CEC-commissioned report were largely critical of the effectiveness of the environmental side agreement.[25] Furthermore, NAFTA has proven itself to be largely resistant to ongoing pressures for change.

Nonetheless, while the legal power of the environmental side agreement—the North American Agreement on Environmental Cooperation, or NAAEC—may be limited, the actions and potential influence of the institutions established by the NAAEC should not be undermined. The work of the Border Environment Cooperation Commission (BECC) and the North American Development Bank (NADBank), both developed under NAFTA, in financing and enabling needed environmental infrastructure, for example, is commendable. A partial measure of the CEC's success is demonstrated by simply having survived its first seven years as an international organization. In order to understand the extent to which NAFTA can meet the environmental challenges outlined above, the following discussion considers the NAFTA and NAAEC, their administrative institutions, and the mechanisms established by the NAAEC to encourage environmental improvement.

Contradictory Objectives in NAFTA and the NAAEC

The NAFTA preamble explicitly states that the three signatory countries resolve to undertake the NAFTA "in a manner consistent with environmental protection and conservation," to "promote sustainable development," and to "strengthen the development and enforcement of environmental laws and regulations." Nonetheless, protection of the environment goes unmentioned in the register of NAFTA's basic objectives. Rather than deal with environmental and labor issues in the accord itself, negotiators developed separate side agreements to address these issues. Article 3 of the North American Agreement on Environmental Cooperation states that "each party shall ensure its laws and regulations provide for high levels of environmental protection and shall strive to continue to improve those laws and regulations."

Beyond these broad objectives, the NAAEC specifies its parameters of influence. In general, the side agreement establishes a dispute resolution forum and advisory body. It does not establish international environmental policy; rather, it is designed *to encourage the enforcement of domestic environmental law.* Each country maintains the right to set national environmental policies, laws, and regulations, but failure to enforce such laws can lead to repercussions. Even so, the legal "teeth," the sanctions for noncompliance, are quite limited. And even though an assessment of up to US$20 million may be levied against a defendant if an environmental dispute cannot be resolved through the various mechanisms outlined in the side agreement (NAAEC Annex 34), such a charge has yet to be imposed.

Overall, the NAAEC lacks strong sanctions, is restricted to narrowly specified environmental dilemmas, and suffers from ambiguous language. The side agreement has been criticized on other fronts as well. First, it lacks any direct means of encouraging improvements in domestic environmental law. To the contrary, a country that lowers its environmental standards would not incur sanctions, even though the side agreement discourages such downward adjustments. Second, the side agreement does not establish preventive mechanisms, such as the Polluter Pays Principle. In fact, the side agreement's provisions do not apply to polluters since it can only lead to actions against national governing bodies, not private parties. Third, a primary weakness in the side agreement is the exclusion of natural resource policy from its definition of "environmental law." According to Article 45, "'environmental law' does not include any statute or regulation, or provision thereof, the primary purpose of which is managing the commercial harvest or exploitation, or subsistence or aboriginal harvesting, of natural resources." The regulation of natural resource extraction rates and mitigation of impacts remain domestic matters.

One of the greatest weaknesses in NAFTA's ability to address environmental and labor concerns is the failure to include them within the core of the agreement, relegating them instead to their respective side agreements. This immediately establishes the potential for discrepancies between them and/or the prioritization of one agreement over another. This potential has come to light in recent Chapter 11 proceedings. Although governments, not polluting corporations, are the targets of the environmental side agreement, corporations have the right to sue governments under Chapter 11 of NAFTA. Chapter 11 was designed to ensure that a corporation's investment would not be expropriated, but companies have used it to prevent the "expropriation" of their anticipated future profits by the imposition of environmental standards. In 2000, for example, the International Centre for the Settlement of Investment Disputes (ICSID) ordered Mexico to pay US$16.5 million (plus interest) to the California-based company Metalclad after Mexican state and municipal governments refused to permit the company to operate a hazardous waste facility near local residences.[26] In the same year, Methanex, a Canadian corporation, brought a Chapter 11 case against the State of California, arguing that a California measure to phase out the use of methyl tertiary-butyl ether (MTBE) as a gasoline additive in order to prevent water contamination would result in a loss of $970 million in profits to the company.[27] In a third case, in 1998 an Ohio-based waste management firm, SD Myers, filed a complaint against Canada for prohibiting the export of PCB wastes to its facility. In November 2000, Canada was ordered to pay damages.

These Chapter 11 cases have alarmed environmentalists. Some ask, "How is the right of the three NAFTA parties to set their own levels of environmental protection [as per Article 3 of the environmental side agreement] to be respected?"[28] The implication is a reversal of the Polluter Pays Principle: "if the community must pay the polluter, the implicit message is that the polluter owns the environment and can use and pollute it with impunity."[29] Even persons who are optimistic about the ramifications of NAFTA for environmental policy have criticized the secret arbitration procedures of Chapter 11.[30] These criticisms have become so acute that Canada's trade minister recently requested a review of Chapter 11, claiming that it is more investor friendly than originally intended.

CEC Structure

The governing body on environmental issues is the Commission for Environmental Cooperation (CEC). Its core objectives are to advance understanding of the relationship among the environment, the economy, and trade, and to promote an integrated approach to environmental protection.[31] The CEC acknowledges that human activities are intrinsically linked to the environment and that understanding these connections requires nations "to 'think, plan, and act' strategically in terms of ecosystems."[32]

The CEC comprises three components—the Secretariat, the Joint Public Advisory Committee (JPAC), and the CEC Council. The Council, which includes the environment ministers from the three NAFTA member countries, is the primary governing body mandated to offer recommendations to the Free Trade Commission on environment-related matters (Article 10.6) and to provide a forum for discussing NAFTA-related environmental issues (Article 10.1). The Secretariat is primarily designed to provide technical, administrative, and operational support to the Council (Article 11.5) and to develop the CEC's annual report and budget (Article 11.6). The JPAC's fifteen members (five appointees from each country; Article 16.1) advise the Council, especially on the development of factual records associated with the citizen submission process.

Article 14 of the NAAEC establishes the citizen submission mechanism, which enables the public to voice a complaint when any NAFTA country appears to be "failing to enforce" its environmental laws. Any citizen of a NAFTA country can trigger the process by submitting a claim to the CEC, as long as the case is not used to gain a trade advantage. Following a review of the submission, the CEC may investigate the matter and publish a factual record of its findings, subject to approval by the Council. From 1995 to December 2001, the CEC received thirty-one submissions—ten involving Canada, thirteen for Mexico, and eight regarding the United States. At the time of this writing, ten submissions were under review, twenty-one files had been closed, two factual records had been prepared and made public,[33] and the Secretariat had identified five others as warranting further development.

There are at least three points of concern regarding the submission process. First, although intended to be accessible to all citizens, the complaint process can be time-consuming, costly, and require extensive legal and political experience, thus limiting the number of citizens who can submit a complaint. This may explain why most submissions have been filed by nongovernmental organizations, not individual citizens. Second, because the submitter no longer participates in the process after he or she has filed the complaint, public involvement essentially ends at this point. Finally, recent CEC actions may discourage potential submitters; in May 2000, for instance, at the urging of the governments of Canada and Mexico, the CEC Council rescinded its recommendations to investigate matters brought forth in two citizen submissions, one on the impact of Alberta's Oldman River dam on fish habitat, and another on air pollution caused by Quebec hog farms.[34]

THE ROLE OF DOMESTIC POLITICAL STRUCTURES

Policy failures are at least as relevant as market failures to the environmental impacts of trade. Regardless of the support for environmental improvement at the international level, the implementation, monitoring, and enforcement of environmental initiatives must ultimately be assessed at the national level. At the same time, preexisting domestic policies—such as weak, ambiguous, or poor agricultural policies—can exacerbate environmental problems.

The NAFTA countries' political commitment to the NAAEC has proven to be quite fickle.[35] Moreover, the bureaucratic capacities to respond to environmental dilemmas differ markedly among Canada, Mexico, and the United States. To take one indicator, government expenditures per capita in 1996 were US$3,900 in the United States, $3,600 in Canada, and just $500 in Mexico.[36] In the United States, $177 of per capita expenditure went to pollution abatement and control, somewhat more than the $143 per capita spent in Canada; Mexico, by contrast, spent $25 per capita on pollution abatement and control.[37] Lower environmental spending levels could lead to increased environmental degradation, even with tough environmental regulations in place.

Considering that the United States already had a relatively strong federal-level environmental policy apparatus prior to NAFTA, the addition of an international regulatory mechanism did not require any significant changes in bureaucratic structure or financial investment. Thus it is not surprising that the United States exerted the least amount of resistance to the development of the NAAEC. Canada's decentralized political-bureaucratic structure, on the other hand, requires provincial support for the implementation of international initiatives, support that is far from uniform across Canada.

The Mexican case is unique among the NAFTA countries. With the weakest environmental-bureaucratic structure of the three countries, Mexico arguably had the most to gain from international pressures for environmental improvement. Indeed, some observers have suggested that Mexico's environmental policymaking and enforcement improved in the past decade, even during the 1994–1995 financial crisis.[38] The implementation of legislative commitments, however, is still limited by fiscal and bureaucratic capacity. Few Mexican industrial facilities are ever inspected, and only 26 percent of those that are inspected are in full compliance with current environmental law.[39] Although domestic environmental policy does not necessarily figure prominently in the decision-making of all firms, this lax enforcement is purported to be a significant factor in the location decisions of certain environmentally risky businesses in Mexico. Available data support these claims, indicating a continued concentration of hazardous waste generation and management in the U.S.-Mexico border region.[40] A recent survey indicates that 27 percent of maquiladora businesses identified environmental regulations as a primary or important factor in deciding to leave the United States and relocate in Mexico.[41]

FUTURE CHALLENGES TO NAFTA: RESISTANCE OR RESILIENCE?

If, as has been shown elsewhere, global political trends can be brought to bear on the willingness of nation-states to assume environmental responsibility,[42] it stands to reason that international trade agreements can play a significant role in either promoting or constraining this process. In this chapter we have outlined three avenues along which the environment will prove to be a politically, socially, and economically relevant issue in the future of international trade, with the potential to hinder trade policy goals. If NAFTA is successfully to guide the long-term economic development of North America, it must reflect the environment's central role in trade liberalization.

To argue that the environment will pose challenges to NAFTA in the future is not particularly difficult. The real test is to develop environmental safeguards within NAFTA that are appropriate for all three countries. NAFTA's current institutional and legislative bodies make important advances over past trade policies toward addressing environmental concerns. However, further reform is needed. Before we can reach a basis for constructive reform, we must first accept the fact that real social and environmental improvement will require far more engineering than the market can provide.

We conclude with three recommendations. They are not meant to include all potential avenues for reform, but they are intended to offer a constructive point of departure.

- NAFTA and NAAEC must recognize a definition of "environmental policy" that encompasses all components of environmental and ecological management, including, in particular, domestic natural resource policy. The definition of environmental policy currently in use addresses only "brown" issues such as pollution and waste generation. With the exception of certain wildlife issues, the "green" issues—habitat protection, deforestation, desertification, fisheries—are not addressed by the NAAEC. Yet such green issues may hold far more implications for social and economic productivity—and far less reversible impacts. In effect, this renders their exclusion a glaring oversight in terms of ensuring social and environmental well-being during trade liberalization.

- NAFTA and the NAAEC must operate according to democratic principles of transparency, accountability, and public participation. All documents and meetings associated with NAFTA and NAAEC procedures must be as publicly accessible as possible without jeopardizing the privacy or security of interested parties. Lack of transparency gives observers the impression that decisions are being made that will impact their lives but that they have no opportunity to participate. Beyond improving transparency, there is an urgent need to maintain communication venues, not only for established environmental movement organizations, but also for all concerned citizens. Local peoples, the most direct recipients of the impacts of development, must be involved at the time that development is proposed. Individuals and organizations can become embittered, not because they expect the world to change overnight, but because they feel they are not treated with respect and that their concerns are ignored. Providing political avenues for citizens to voice their concerns, and, in turn, providing a substantive explanation of the ways in which those concerns were addressed, would go a long way toward reducing political protest associated with international trade. It could also serve as a conduit for sharing valuable citizen knowledge.

- The harmonization of environmental policy is highly unlikely to materialize in the near future. In fact, harmonization in this area may not even be advisable, given the ecological and political variability across the three NAFTA nations. Nevertheless, economic development projects throughout North America should all be subject to an equally rigorous cumulative effects assessment (CEA) prior to initiation. Current CEA procedures vary tremendously because of differences in domestic political, bureaucratic, and financial capacities. The CEC should establish an independent CEA review body accessible by both scientific institutions and the public, and financed by an international fund to which each country contributes. Prior to undertaking any development with trade implications, a developer would be required to assess the potential cumulative effects of the proposed project according to the criteria and methodology established by the NAFTA CEA review body. An effective CEA mechanism would ensure that social and environmental concerns are addressed prior to development. Potential for social conflict and lost investments would be reduced, thereby minimizing the likelihood of litigation over environmental issues, such as the Chapter 11 cases discussed above. By ensuring that appropriate environmental safeguards are incorporated into economic enterprises at the development stage, a uniform CEA mechanism will also essentially incorporate the intentions of the Polluter Pays Principle. Ultimately, implementing such a preventive mechanism will be less expensive—both financially and environmentally—than attempting to mitigate (or adjudicate) the impacts of poorly planned development projects.

The pace of ecological and environmental decline has not slowed, despite NAFTA's environmental side agreement. Furthermore, in the aftermath of recent terrorist acts in the United States, environmental issues are at risk of falling off national and global political agendas for the foreseeable future. This is a crucial moment in the trajectory toward genuine improvements in social and environmental well-being. Future successes in this area will require strong political will, financial support, and democratic accountability. They will also require consolidating the environmental gains that have been achieved to date under NAFTA and the CEC, gains that are supportive of trinational cooperation and security. Ultimately, our global environment may well depend on our efforts to meet NAFTA's current environmental challenges.

Notes

1. Raymond MacCallum, "Evaluating the Citizen Submission Procedure under the North American Agreement on Environmental Cooperation," *Colorado Journal of Environmental Policy and Law* 8, no. 2 (1997): 395–422.

2. For an excellent example of trade and environmental perspectives during NAFTA's formulation, see Terry L. Anderson, ed., *NAFTA and the Environment* (San Francisco: Pacific Research Institute for Public Policy, 1993).

3. Alan M. Rugman, John Kirton, and Julie Soloway, "NAFTA, Environmental Regulations, and Canadian Competitiveness," *Journal of World Trade* 3, no. 4 (1997): 129–44.

4. John M. Antle and Gregg Heidebrink, "Environment and Development: Theory and International Evidence," *Economic Development and Cultural Change* 43 (1995): 603–24.

5. For good examples, see Deter Rucht, "The Impact of Environmental Movements in Western Societies," in *How Social Movements Matter*, ed. Marco Giugni, Doug McAdam, and Charles Tilly (Minneapolis: University of Minnesota Press, 1999); John Meyer and David John Frank, "The Structuring of a World Environmental Regime, 1870–1990," *International Organization* 51, no. 4 (1997): 623–51; Thomas Princen and Matthias Finger, eds., *Environmental NGOs in World Politics: Linking the Local and the Global* (London: Routledge, 1994).

6. Angela G. Mertig and Riley E. Dunlap, "Environmentalism, New Social Movements, and the New Class: A Cross-National Investigation," *Rural Sociology* 66, no. 1 (2001): 113–36; Rucht, "The Impact of Environmental Movements in Western Societies."

7. Steven R. Brechin, "Objective Problems, Subjective Values, and Global Environmentalism," *Social Science Quarterly* 80, no. 4 (1999): 793–809.

8. Marc Williams and Lucy Ford, "The World Trade Organization, Social Movements, and Global Environmental Management," *Environmental Politics* 8, no. 1 (1999): 268–89.

9. Anthony Downs, "Up and Down with Ecology: The 'Issue Attention Cycle,'" *Public Interest* 28 (Summer 1972): 38–50.

10. Meyer and Frank, "The Structuring of a World Environmental Regime."

11. Williams and Ford, "The World Trade Organization, Social Movements, and Global Environmental Management."

12. Williams and Ford, "The World Trade Organization, Social Movements, and Global Environmental Management"; Michael Dreiling and Brian Wolf, "Environmental Movement Organizations and Political Strategy: Tactical Conflicts over NAFTA," *Organization and Environment* 14, no. 1 (2001): 34–54.

13. Caroline Thomas and Martin Weber, "New Values and International Organizations: Balancing Trade and Environment in the North American Free Trade Agreement," in *Global Trade and Global Social Issues*, ed. Annie Taylor and Caroline Thomas (London: Routledge, 1999).

14. See chapters by Ortiz Mena and Reif in this volume.

15. Posted at www.worldwildlife.org/news/pubs/ceo_statement.pdf.

16. Danielle Knight, "Lawsuits Spark Calls for Changes in NAFTA," posted at http://www.twnside.org.sg/title/spark-cn.htm (June 23, 2000).

17. Stephen G. Bunker, *Underdeveloping the Amazon: Extraction, Unequal Exchange and the Failure of the Modern State* (Chicago: University of Illinois Press, 1985). In a broader sense, of course, the term "underdevelopment" dates back to the 1960s.

18. Diana Tussie, "The Environment and International Trade Negotiations: Open Loops in the Developing World," in *The Environment and International Trade Negotiations: Developing Country Stakes*, ed. Diana Tussie (Ottawa: International Development Research Centre, 2000).

19. Fritz, "Searching for Environmental Justice."

20. Intergovernmental Panel on Climate Change, *Third Assessment Report: Contributions of IPCC Working Groups* (United Nations Environment Programme, 2001).

21. Ibid.

22. David Vogel and Timothy Kessler, "How Compliance Happens and Doesn't Happen Domestically," in *Engaging Countries: Strengthening Compliance*

with International Environmental Accords, ed. Edith Brown Weiss and Harold K. Jacobson (Cambridge, Mass.: MIT Press, 1998).

23. For an account of agricultural trade issues concerning NAFTA, see Veeman, Veeman, and Hoskins, this volume.

24. See, for example, Patricia Marchak, "Environment and Resource Protection: Does NAFTA Make a Difference?" *Organization and Environment* 11, no. 2 (1998): 133–54; Tom Barry, *Zapata's Revenge: Free Trade and the Farm Crisis in Mexico* (Boston: South End, 1995).

25. Commission for Environmental Cooperation, *Report of the Independent Review Committee* (Montreal: CEC, June 1998).

26. Further reference to the Metalclad case can be found in the chapter by Ortiz Mena, this volume.

27. The Methanex suit is still pending as of this writing; see also the chapter by Reif, this volume, for further details.

28. Howard Mann and Konrad von Moltke, *NAFTA's Chapter 11 and the Environment: Addressing the Impacts of the Investor-State Process on the Environment* (Winnipeg, Canada: International Institute for Sustainable Development, 1999).

29. John Moffet and Francois Bregha, "The Role of Law Reform in the Promotion of Sustainable Development," *Journal of Environmental Law and Practice* 6 (1996): 1–22, quote, p. 8.

30. Stephen L. Kass, "NAFTA's Chapter 11: Regulatory Takings Revisited," *New York Law Journal* S-2 (September 11, 2000); Stephen L. Kass and Jean M. McCarroll, "The 'Metalclad' Decision under NAFTA's Chapter 11," *New York Law Journal,* October 27, 2000.

31. Commission for Environmental Cooperation, *North American Agenda for Action 2000–2002: A Three-Year Program for the Commission for Environmental Cooperation* (Montreal: Communications Department of the CEC Secretariat, 2000).

32. Commission for Environmental Cooperation, *Ecological Regions of North America: Toward a Common Perspective* (Montreal: Communications and Public Outreach Department of the CEC Secretariat, 1997), p. 2.

33. A factual record, while important for the potential publicity it may generate, is merely an evaluation and description of matters asserted by the Submitter and the Party. No judgment of wrongdoing is contained in the factual record, and it does not conclude whether a Party is enforcing its laws. As such, it could be conceived of as a "procedural dead-end" because it is not attached to any enforcement mechanism.

34. Barrie McKenna, "Environmental Probes Derailed by NAFTA Nations," *Globe and Mail,* May 18, 2000.

35. Stephen P. Mumme and Pamela Duncan, "The Commission for Environmental Cooperation and Environmental Management in the Americas," *Journal of Interamerican Studies and World Affairs* 39, no. 4 (Winter 1997): 41–58.

36. Organisation for Economic Co-operation and Development, *Towards Sustainable Development: Environmental Indicators* (Paris: OECD, 1998).

37. Ibid.

38. Bryan W. Husted and Jeanne M. Logsdon, "The Impact of NAFTA on Mexico's Environmental Policy," *Growth and Change* 28, no. 1 (1997): 24–48; Tussie, *The Environment and International Trade Negotiations.*

39. Ibid.

40. Marisa Jacott, Cyrus Reed, and Mark Winfield, "The Generation and Management of Hazardous Wastes and Transboundary Hazardous Waste Shipments between Mexico, Canada and the United States, 1990–2000" (Austin, Tex.: Texas Center for Policy Studie s, 2001).

41. Perry Grossman, "Corporate Interest and Trade Liberalization: The North American Free Trade Agreement and Environmental Protection," *Organization and Environment* 13, no. 1 (2000): 61–85.

42. D.J. Frank, A. Hironaka, and E. Schofer, "The Nation -State and the Natural Environment over the Twentieth Century," *American Sociological Review* 65, no. 1 (February 2000): 96–116.

12

Impacts of NAFTA on Mexico-to-U.S. Migration

Wayne A. Cornelius

This chapter reexamines the predictions of theoretical models about the relationship between trade and migration, as well as claims made by government officials on both sides of the border during the debate over NAFTA, in light of the empirical evidence that has accumulated since 1994. It also analyzes the longer-term prospects for reducing Mexico-to-U.S. migration, in the context of Mexico's changing demographic profile and of recent developments in bilateral government-to-government relations.

THE TRADE-MIGRATION LINKAGE, IN THEORY AND POLITICAL ADVOCACY

The standard, neoclassical economics model treats migration and trade as substitutes, in both the short and long run. Trade liberalization is supposed to increase the competitiveness of an emigration country's products and stimulate job creation in its export sector, thereby creating alternatives to emigration. Moreover, deeper trade integration is supposed to accelerate wage convergence between countries with different income levels, also reducing the incentive to migrate from the poor to the rich country. The West European experience is often cited as evidence of this effect. As they were integrated into the European Union (formerly the European Community), poorer southern-tier countries like Spain and Italy quickly caught up with the more prosperous northern-tier nations: "Economic gaps narrowed enough during the six- to ten-year wait for labor mobility that, when Italians and Spaniards were permitted to search freely for jobs throughout the EC, few did."[1] By the mid-1980s, Spain and Italy themselves had become net importers of labor, from the Third World.[2] South Korea is sometimes cited as another example of trade-led migration transition.

In fact, both theoretical modeling and empirical research on various world regions suggest that trade is not always a substitute for international migration. Outcomes are significantly affected by initial economic conditions, the historical period being examined, the source countries for migration, and the time frame for measuring effects.[3] Recognizing the limitations of the standard neoclassical model of the trade/migration relationship, some labor economists have advanced a modified version of it. In that revised model, the long-term effect on migration is to reduce it, but in the short term the employment dislocations in the poor country will cause a spike in emigration, "especially if the countries being integrated have income gaps of five or more, that is, average per capita income in one country is four or five times higher than in the other; if there are established migration networks between them; and if supply-push emigration pressures increase as a result of economic restructuring."[4]

All of these conditions obtain in the case of Mexico-to-U.S. migration: The real-wage differential between the two countries is variously estimated at between 8:1 and 10:1; tens of thousands of mature transborder social networks link U.S.-based migrants with potential migrants in Mexican sending communities; and economic restructuring since 1988 has cost millions of jobs and made it more difficult for small-scale producers to remain viable. In Mexico and other emigration countries that are deregulating, privatizing, and opening their economies to global market forces, large numbers of rural workers, in particular, are likely to be displaced. Thus a country experiencing trade-induced restructuring "is often also awash with internal migrants, some of whom spill over its borders if there is already an established international migration pattern."[5]

This more complex relationship between trade liberalization and international migration is modeled in figure 12.1. The solid line represents the status quo of unwanted or unauthorized migration between sending and receiving countries, in the absence of free trade. The shaded area "A" represents the "migration hump"—the amount of additional migration that will be generated by trade liberalization. Emigration peaks somewhere been five and ten years after the trade liberalization/restructuring process begins. At point "B," about fifteen years from the onset of trade liberalization, we find the same level of migration as there would have been without free trade. Beyond that point, migration continues to fall. Shaded area "C" represents the migration that is prevented by economic integration. Finally, after about twenty years (point "D"), the labor-exporting country becomes a net importer of labor.

Figure 12.1. Hypothesized Relationship between Trade Liberalization and International Migration

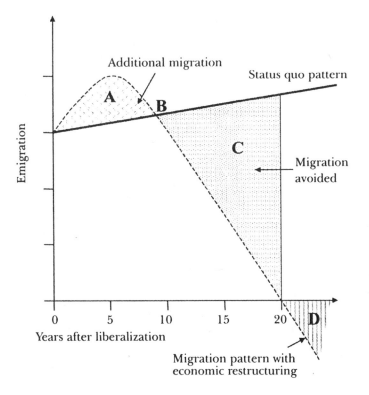

Source: Philip L. Martin, *Trade and Migration: NAFTA and Mexican Agriculture* (Washington, D.C.: Institute of International Economics, 1993), Figure 9.

The amount of time needed to move from point A to points B, C, and D in this model can only be roughly estimated. It is neither dictated by theory nor grounded in North American historical reality.[6] Nevertheless, according to specialists on international trade and migration, this is a reasonable approximation of the path that Mexico is likely to follow under NAFTA. This prediction is also consistent with the analysis and recommendations of the U.S. Commission for the Study of International Migration and Cooperative Economic Development, whose final report was submitted in 1990. The Commission concluded that "expanded trade between the sending countries and the United States is the single most important remedy" for unauthorized immigration from Mexico and other Third World countries. But the Commission also warned that "the economic development process itself tends in the short to medium term to stimulate migration," and it urged U.S. policymakers to stay the course.[7]

Pro-NAFTA political leaders in both Mexico and the United States routinely characterized the agreement as the best possible antidote to illegal immigration, even in the short term. The mantra of President Carlos Salinas de Gortari was that Mexico's goal was "to export goods and not people," and NAFTA was essential to accomplishing it. As he put it in an October 1993 television interview: "Today, Mexicans have to migrate to where jobs are being created, the northern part of our country. With NAFTA, employment opportunities will move toward where the people live, reducing migration drastically, within the country and outside of the country."[8] President Bill Clinton made much the same claim: "If NAFTA passes, you won't have what you have now, which is everybody runs up to the *maquiladora* line, gets a job in a factory, and then runs across the line to get a better job. Instead there will be more uniform growth in investment across [Mexico], and people will be able to work at home with their families. And over the period of the next few years, we will dramatically reduce pressures on illegal immigration from Mexico to the United States."[9]

SHORT-TERM MIGRATION TRENDS

What has actually been happening in Mexico-to-U.S. migration during the period since NAFTA's implementation? As shown in figure 12.2, the volume of unauthorized migration—as measured by apprehensions made by the Border Patrol along the U.S-Mexico border—rose steadily during the second half of the 1990s, to between 1.5 and 1.6 million per year. Border-crossing histories for 4,881 undocumented Mexican household heads show that the probability of being apprehended on any given attempt at clandestine entry increased in the years immediately after concentrated border enforcement operations were launched in El Paso and San Diego, but by 1997–1998 the probability of apprehension was trending downward (see the solid line in figure 12.3). This

decline can be attributed partly to the post-1993 U.S. border enforcement strategy—which has induced a larger proportion of would-be
unauthorized migrants to use the services of professional people-
smugglers ("coyotes")—and to the learning curve: Undocumented migrants soon learned that crossing the border in the heavily fortified San
Diego–Tijuana corridor and, by 1996, anywhere along the California-
Mexico border was likely to result in apprehension. As illegal entry attempts shifted away from California into the Arizona desert and to less
patrolled areas of the Texas-Mexico borderlands (as indicated by the
upward swing in the dashed line at the top of figure 12.3 and in the
dotted line at the bottom), the average overall probability of apprehension declined.[10]

**Figure 12.2. Apprehensions by the U.S. Border Patrol along the
U.S.-Mexico Border, Fiscal Years 1994-2001**

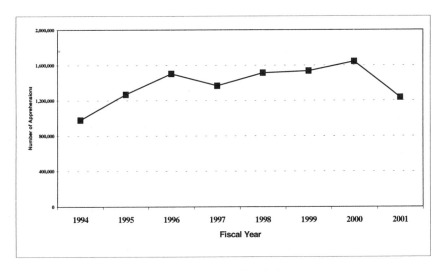

Source: U.S. Immigration and Naturalization Service.

The absolute number of apprehensions dropped by 25 percent in
the 2001 fiscal year, but this decline may well be another unintended
consequence of tougher border enforcement, which does not seem to
be deterring new migrants but *is* keeping undocumented Mexicans in
the United States. By making illegal entry more costly (professional
people-smugglers have raised their fees by 200 to 400 percent, depend-

ing on the corridor of entry) and dangerous (more than 1,700 Mexican migrants died from January 1995 to March 2002 in attempts to enter through hazardous desert and mountainous areas), the U.S. strategy of concentrated border enforcement operations has sharply reduced circular migration that puts the undocumented at risk of being apprehended. Reports from high-emigration communities suggest that only migrants working legally in the United States returned home for the December–January holidays in 2001–2002.[11]

Figure 12.3. Probability of Apprehension (Borderwide) and Percentage of Illegal Border-Crossing Attempts Occurring in Places Other than Tijuana/San Diego and California, 1980–1998

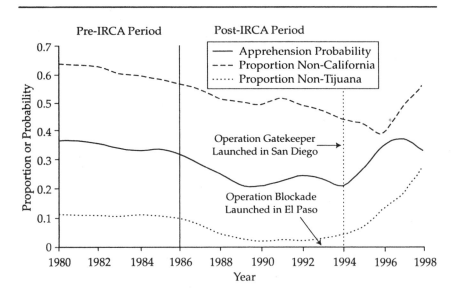

Sources: Data from Mexican Migration Project (University of Pennsylvania); Douglas S. Massey, Jorge Durand, and Nolan J. Malone, *Beyond Smoke and Mirrors: Mexican Immigration in an Era of Economic Integration* (New York: Russell Sage Foundation, 2002), Figure 6.1, p. 107.

Another key indicator of whether Mexico-to-U.S. migration is increasing or decreasing is the representation of Mexican nationals and illegal immigrants in the labor force of certain traditionally immigrant-using industries and occupations in the United States. Data from the National Agricultural Workers Survey conducted annually by the U.S.

Departments of Agriculture and Labor reveal that the percentage of illegal migrants in the U.S. farm labor force rose continuously during the second half of the 1990s.[12] The same pattern obtains in low-level service occupations like housing cleaning, food preparation and food service, and janitorial services. The proportion of Mexican nationals in these occupations also rose sharply during the second half of the decade.[13]

By March 2000, according to the U.S. Census's Current Population Survey, the Mexico-born population living in the United States reached 8.3 million, of whom nearly 3 million were believed to be undocumented. As the new millennium began, an estimated 4 to 5 million Mexico-born workers were employed in the United States, legally and illegally. According to projections by the Mexican government's National Population Council, Mexico-to-U.S. migration will increase from between 366,000 and 379,000 in 2000 to some 381,000 to 412,000 in 2005, and 390,000 to 439,000 in 2010. The range of estimates reflects varying assumptions about GDP growth, unemployment, the U.S.-Mexican wage ratio, and migrant remittances.[14]

WHY NAFTA HAS NOT REDUCED MEXICO-TO-U.S. MIGRATION

These data are consistent with the prediction of the modified trade liberalization/migration model outlined above. In the short term, Mexican migration to the United States has been rising under a liberalized trade regime.[15] Why should this be the case?

NAFTA has not weakened the preexisting incentives and pressures to migrate. First, wage differentials between the United States and Mexico have remained about the same in the post-NAFTA period. The differential remains huge, meaning that a migrant typically can earn as much in one hour in the United States as he or she can make in an entire day in Mexico. As long as daily take-home pay in Mexico averages between US$5 and $6, compared with the $60 to $80 per day that migrants can earn in the United States, with or without papers, the incentive to continue seeking U.S. employment will be overwhelming, especially when the supply of relatively well-paying, low-skilled jobs in the United States is constant or expanding.

On the Mexican side, the job-creating benefits of expanded trade with the United States and Canada have been distributed very unevenly, both geographically and sectorally. Perhaps the most striking consequence of NAFTA to date has been the accelerated bifurcation of the Mexican economy into a booming, export-oriented sector and a far less dynamic sector that still depends on domestic demand.[16] NAFTA has also aggravated regional inequalities in Mexico, especially North/South inequity, by concentrating manufacturing activity more heavily in the northern states. In Mexico's underdeveloped southern states, like Yucatán, there has been a proliferation of assembly plants, but these *maquiladoras* tend to be very small-scale, fragile enterprises that account for only a tiny share of post-1994 foreign direct investment. By 1998 the northern border region was receiving over 30 percent of Mexico's total foreign direct investment.[17] In northern border cities like Tijuana and Mexicali, unemployment rates have been in the 1 to 2 percent range during most of the post-NAFTA period, and employers have frequently complained of labor shortages.[18] Other islands of robust, NAFTA-led industrial production have also emerged, such as Guadalajara, which has been transformed into the "Silicon Valley" of Mexico. However, there has been little diffusion of economic opportunities into the hinterlands of cities that have prospered under NAFTA.

The case of Jalisco State is particularly revealing. Jalisco's exports have increased by 500 percent under NAFTA, GDP per capita has risen significantly, and nearly 400,000 new jobs were created in the state between 1995 and 2000. Jalisco employers have reported labor shortages in both the manufacturing and agricultural sectors.[19] But there is no evidence that migration to the United States from Jalisco has declined under NAFTA, despite the relative abundance of jobs; indeed, Jalisco continues to be the largest exporter of labor to the United States among Mexican states.[20] Many *jaliscienses* have been pushed into the migratory stream by the adverse impacts of NAFTA on small-scale corn farmers and milk producers. There is a substantial body of evidence that free trade has caused severe dislocations in these sectors of Mexico's rural economy. Such impacts were totally predictable, particularly among Mexico's three million corn farmers, given their comparative disadvantage vis-à-vis U.S corn producers in terms of production costs, productivity, and access to infrastructure.[21] NAFTA unloosed a flood of cheap, processed agricultural imports— corn, powdered milk, milk substitutes, and meat—that have depressed the prices received by small Mexican producers.[22] NAFTA also appears to have contributed to a rise in prices for agricultural inputs that these small producers have to purchase.

In Jalisco, large milk processors have begun to require their small-scale suppliers to refrigerate their milk before delivering it to the companies, ostensibly to meet the quality standards of the global marketplace. This has required small dairy farmers to make substantial investments in refrigeration plants. Even so, small-scale producers are losing out because dairy processors continue to prefer the cheaper, imported powdered milk. Mexico today leads the world in powdered-milk imports, importing 40 percent of the milk sold in the domestic market, compared with just 12 percent at the end of the 1980s.[23] Some of these adverse trends affecting small agricultural producers in Jalisco and elsewhere in Mexico antedated NAFTA.[24] But NAFTA has accelerated them and thereby intensified pressure to migrate. Income support programs for extremely poor rural families, like Procampo and Progresa, have not been sufficient to offset these effects.[25]

NAFTA may also have contributed to higher rates of U.S.-bound migration by drawing large numbers of impoverished workers to the northern border states, where the demand for labor in both manufacturing and large-scale commercial agriculture has been stimulated by trade liberalization. For example, working in export-oriented vegetable agriculture in states like Baja California places migrants from southern states like Oaxaca close to the U.S.-Mexico border and gives them access to social networks and information about job opportunities in the United States, thereby lowering the costs and risks of transborder migration. Export-oriented agriculture also provides work for women and children, freeing young male family heads to seek employment in the United States.[26] Similarly, the maquiladora plants in Mexico's largest border cities—most notably Tijuana—have been powerful magnets for migrants from the interior of Mexico in the post-NAFTA period. It has often been argued that such large pools of transient labor in close proximity to the border would inevitably spill over into the U.S. labor market. However, there is little evidence from post-NAFTA surveys of migrant workers, either in Mexican border states or in the United States, that demonstrates such a spill-over effect. Data from several pre-NAFTA survey studies suggest a very low incidence of "stepwise" migration leading from central and southern Mexico to northern border cities and subsequently to U.S. destinations.[27]

LONGER-TERM PROSPECTS FOR REDUCING MIGRATION

NAFTA was clearly oversold as a short-term remedy to unwanted migration, by politicians on both sides of the border. Indeed, NAFTA is unlikely to have much of an effect on the flow of Mexican labor to the United States over the next decade, given the maturation of social networks linking potential migrants with jobs in the United States, the poor quality of many of the jobs being created in Mexico under NAFTA, and the highly skewed spatial distribution of these jobs.

Millions of prospective Mexican migrants are already linked to employers in the United States through relatives living there. Surveys conducted in Mexican sending communities as well as U.S. destinations have found that 70 to 80 percent of Mexican migrants to the United States receive help in finding employment there from U.S.-based relatives.[28] Access to such social networks greatly shortens job-seeking time upon arrival in the United States and reduces almost to zero the probability of not finding employment there. The potent combination of high wages (relative to Mexico) and low uncertainty about employment prospects on the U.S. side of the border is what drives most Mexican migration to the United States, along with the desire for family reunification.

It would be unrealistic to expect the Mexico-to-U.S. "migration hump" to disappear within the next ten years unless the real wage gap between Mexico and the United States has been narrowed drastically—probably by at least half—as a result of NAFTA or some combination of trade integration and successful macroeconomic policies in Mexico. Too many of the jobs being created in Mexico under NAFTA do not pay enough to dissuade young people from going to the United States. Only when Mexico's shrinking labor pool *forces* employers on the Mexican side to raise wages will we see the "migration hump" begin to disappear. The country's demographics are moving in this direction. Taking into account international migration, Mexico's rate of labor force growth is expected to fall from 1.81 percent per annum in 2000 to 1.25 percent in 2005 and 0.78 percent in 2010. In absolute terms, this means that the 897,000 new entrants to the labor force in 2000 will decline to 667,000 in 2005 and to 435,000 in 2010.[29] The projected halving of Mexico's labor force growth will make it more likely that the wage convergence promised by NAFTA advocates will begin to occur by the end of the decade, thereby weakening incentives to migrate. However, recent econometric models suggest that the wages of unskilled Mexican workers may not rise enough, relative to their potential wages as migrants to the United States, to discourage emigration.[30]

A more proactive approach to reducing Mexico-to-U.S. migration in the short to medium term would have to address the severely limited opportunity structure that confronts working-age inhabitants of Mexico's high-emigration regions and communities. According to data compiled by Mexico's National Population Council, the bulk of U.S.-bound migration originates in only 386 of Mexico's 2,400 *municipios* (analogous to U.S. counties).[31] Most of these high-emigration zones are middle-developed municipios concentrated in central and west-central Mexico (see figure 12.4). A well-targeted effort to stimulate creation of better-paying, nonagricultural jobs in these places and incorporate them into the export economy could make a significant dent in Mexico-to-U.S. migration over the next ten to fifteen years. Such an effort would encourage the use of labor-intensive technologies and the development of export capacity.[32] Public infrastructure would need to be upgraded, and training for both employers and workers should be provided. Wages may have to be subsidized during the start-up period (again, the quality of the new jobs created is crucial to discouraging emigration).[33]

Presidents Vicente Fox and George W. Bush recently announced an initiative to encourage joint public-private partnerships aimed at increasing private investment in high-emigration areas of Mexico,[34] but the U.S. government seems to have ruled out large-scale financial support for such development projects ("We're no longer in the business of Marshall Plans," said a senior U.S. official).[35] Indeed, the developmental approach to reducing unwanted migration has always been given short shrift by U.S. policymakers. It is seen as involving too much dependence on Mexican authorities, and the time frame needed to create attractive alternatives to emigration in the source areas exceeds what is tolerable to most U.S. politicians. Even among Mexican officials there seems to be relatively little interest in the developmental approach,[36] which is striking in light of the high priority attached to investment in high-emigration communities by Vicente Fox, both as governor of the state of Guanajuato and in his presidential campaign. Nevertheless, targeted development assistance to sending communities has the potential to create realistic alternatives to migration, especially if it links them firmly to the trade-led sector of the Mexican economy.

CONCLUSION

Managing the migration flow between Mexico and the United States is likely to remain the most intractable issue on the bilateral government-to-government agenda in the next ten years and beyond. Since the terrorist attacks of September 11, 2001, in the United States, what appeared to be an imminent U.S.-Mexican deal on migration has been derailed by resistance in the U.S. Congress, which now conflates anti-terrorism with border enforcement and construes any measure to liberalize immigration policy as a potential threat to national security.

Figure 12.4. Mexican Municipios Classified by Rate of Emigration to the United States, 2000

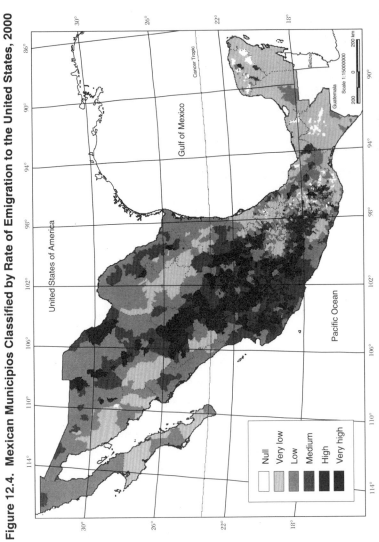

Source: Estimates by Consejo Nacional de Población, based on National Census of Population and Housing, 2000. Adapted from Rodolfo Tuirán, Carlos Fuentes, and Luis Felipe Ramos, "Recent Dynamics of Mexico–United States Migration," *El Mercado de Valores* (Nacional Financiera) 8, no. 4 (July–August 2001), p. 42.

Even before "9/11," however, many U.S. lawmakers were skeptical of the potential benefits to the United States of the "grand bargain" on migration that Presidents Bush and Fox were pursuing so ardently. In Washington, D.C., at the third of three U.S.-Mexico summit meetings devoted largely to this issue during 2001, held just five days before the terrorist attacks, Bush and Fox initialed a detailed framework for a bilateral accord that would have included expanded permanent legal immigration, a new temporary worker program for Mexicans, a limited amnesty ("regularization") for undocumented Mexicans already living in the United States, and a "review" of the current U.S. strategy of concentrated border enforcement operations. The negotiations to achieve such an agreement were suspended immediately after 9/11, and the Fox government's inability to get them back on track in the following year left Mexican officials in a state of complete bewilderment. Foreign Secretary Jorge Castañeda and other members of Fox's team had effectively bet his presidency on getting a migration deal with the United States, and the urgency of consummating a respectable agreement only increased as Fox's domestic policy agenda became mired in disputes with the opposition parties in the Mexican Congress.

Despite the apparent collapse of support for a bilateral migration accord in the United States, Mexican officials continue to frame the issue in terms of the grand vision of North American integration—with unrestricted labor mobility between the United States, Canada, and Mexico—first articulated by Fox during his presidential campaign. They argue that European Union–style unification of the North American labor market is inevitable and should not get lost in the fog of war and terrorism. Such arguments hark back to the early development of NAFTA, when President Carlos Salinas de Gortari actively sought information on how the Europeans had dealt with labor mobility as part of their regional integration process, in hopes of persuading the United States to include the issue in NAFTA negotiations.[37] Free labor mobility was quickly taken off the table when U.S. officials branded it as a certain deal-breaker.

Current realities on the U.S. side make it even less likely that a deepening of NAFTA to permit unrestricted movement of labor will be a politically viable goal in the foreseeable future. Even a "guest-worker" program large enough to make an appreciable dent in illegal Mexican migration to the United States elicits howls of protest from both the left and right of the political spectrum. Labor unions, NGOs advocating immigrant and/or Latino rights, religious groups, and anti-immigration cultural conservatives are united in opposition; only the pro-business, libertarian conservative wing of the Republican Party is supportive. While President Bush sides with the libertarians on this issue, he has chosen not to expend his greatly enhanced political capital after the September 11 attacks to push for a migration deal with Mexico.

Fox's immigration initiative eventually may be revived, albeit in much more modest form, if anti-terrorism efforts prove successful over a sustained period and if robust economic growth in the United States intensifies the demand for Mexican labor. But new rationales for such an agreement will have to be developed and sold to the U.S. public. Fox's initial proposals to end illegal immigration by legalizing the flow and ultimately opening the border "obviously implied that either NAFTA has failed or that it was sold with false arguments.... Both implications hurt the new initiative."[38] Finally, the Mexican government would have to come up with credible new incentives for anti-immigration forces in the United States to get a migration deal. Necessary (but not necessarily sufficient) incentives would include a serious commitment to patrol the Mexican side of the southwestern border, with a view toward interdiction of U.S.-bound economic migrants (not just warning them of the hazards of illegal entry), and a sustained crackdown on "third-country" illegal migration via Mexico's southern border. Obstructing the movement of Mexican citizens within Mexican territory would raise major constitutional issues (Mexico's 1917 Constitution guarantees freedom of migration), and doing the U.S. Border Patrol's dirty work on Mexican soil would invite strong criticism both at home and abroad. In short, Mexico's options for securing greater legal access for its citizens to the U.S. labor market remain quite limited, and NAFTA, if anything, is a troublesome reminder of past promises not kept.

Notes

1. Philip Martin, B. Lindsay Lowell, and J. Edward Taylor, "Migration Outcomes of Guest Worker and Free Trade Regimes: The Case of Mexico - U.S. Migration," in *Managing Migration: Time for a New International Regime?* ed. Bimal Ghosh (Oxford: Oxford University Press, 2000), p. 148.

2. See the chapters on Spain and Italy in Wayne A. Cornelius, Philip L. Martin, and James F. Hollifield, eds., *Controlling Immigration: A Global Perspective* (Stanford, Calif.: Stanford University Press, 1995).

3. Riccardo Faini, Jaime de Melo, and Klaus F. Zimmermann, eds., *Migration: The Controversies and the Evidence* (Cambridge: Cambridge University Press,

1999); and Michael Vogler and Ralph Rotte, "The Effects of Development on Migration: Theoretical Issues and New Empirical Evidence," *Journal of Population Economics* 13, no. 3 (2000): 485–508.

4. Philip L. Martin and J. Edward Taylor, "Managing Migration: The Role of Economic Policies," in *Global Migrants, Global Refugees,* ed. Aristide Zolberg and Peter M. Benda (New York: Berghahn Books, 2001), p. 96.

5. Ibid., p. 107.

6. West European experience suggests that if wage differentials between poor and rich countries with a free trade area can be reduced to 4:1 or 5:1 and robust economic growth in countries of emigration creates expectations of continued narrowing of the gap, economically motivated transborder migration will virtually cease. See Philip L. Martin, *Trade and Migration: NAFTA and Agriculture* (Washington, D.C.: Institute for International Economics, 1993).

7. U.S. Commission for the Study of International Migration and Cooperative Economic Development, *Unauthorized Migration: An Economic Development Response* (Washington, D.C., 1990), pp. xv–xvi.

8. Quoted in Robert Manning, *Five Years after NAFTA: Rhetoric and Reality of Mexican Immigration in the 21st Century* (Washington, D.C.: Center for Immigration Studies, 2000), p. 10.

9. Ibid.

10. Douglas S. Massey, Jorge Durand, and Nolan J. Malone, *Beyond Smoke and Mirrors: Mexican Immigration in an Era of Economic Integration* (New York: Russell Sage Foundation, 2002), pp. 107–11.

11. See Wayne A. Cornelius, "Death at the Border: Efficacy and Unintended Consequences of U.S. Immigration Policy," *Population and Development Review* 27, no. 4 (December 2001): 661–85; Alfredo Corchado, "Immigrants Caught in Job Trap," *Dallas Morning News,* March 20, 2002.

12. Belinda T. Reyes and Hans Johnson, "Holding the Line? The Effect of Border Enforcement on Unauthorized Immigration: Preliminary Report" (San Francisco, Calif.: Public Policy Institute of California, August 2000).

13. Ibid.

14. Consejo Nacional de Población, *Migración México–Estados Unidos: presente y futuro* (Mexico City: CONAPO, 2000), table 7, p. 60; and Rodolfo Tuirán, Carlos Fuentes, and Luis Felipe Ramos, "Recent Dynamics of Mexico–United States Migration," *El Mercado de Valores* (Nacional Financiera) 8, no. 4 (July–August 2001): 22–45.

15. It should be noted that illegal Mexico-to-U.S. migration would have increased in 1995–1996, regardless of any dislocations resulting from NAFTA, because of the December 1994 peso devaluation crisis and the deep recession it caused in Mexico. Hundreds of thousands of jobs were lost in this recession, and creation of new jobs virtually ceased until mid-1996.

16. See Enrique Dussel Peters, *Polarizing Mexico: The Impact of Liberalization Strategy* (Boulder, Colo.: Lynne Rienner, 2000).

17. F. Aguayo and Carlos Salas, "Restructuración regional y dinámica del empleo en México, 1980–1998," *Territorio y Sociedad* (El Colegio de Sonora), forthcoming.

18. See Gordon H. Hanson, "North American Economic Integration and Industry Location," *Oxford Review of Economic Policy* 14 (1998): 30–44; Gordon H. Hanson, "Regional Adjustment to Trade Liberalization," *Regional Science and Urban Economics* 28 (1998): 419–44; Gordon H. Hanson and Ann Harrison, "Trade, Technology, and Wage Inequality in Mexico," *Industrial and Labor Relations Review* 52 (1999): 271–88.

19. For further evidence that Jalisco's regional economy has been one of NAFTA's brightest success stories, in the terms just mentioned, see Carlos Alba, this volume, and Enrique Dussel Peters, "Effects of Export-led Growth on the Structure of Mexican Industrial Production," in *U.S.-Mexican Economic Integration: NAFTA at the Grassroots*, ed. John Bailey, U.S.-Mexico Policy Report No. 11 (Austin, Tex.: Lyndon B. Johnson School of Public Affairs, University of Texas at Austin, 2001).

20. Comprehensive data on the regional origins of recent Mexican migrants to the United States can be found in *Binational Study of Migration between Mexico and the United States: Final Report* (Washington, D.C. and Mexico City: U.S. Commission on Immigration Reform and Mexican Ministry of Foreign Relations, 1997); Jorge Durand, Douglas S. Massey, and Rene M. Zenteno, "Mexican Immigration to the United States: Continuities and Changes," *Latin American Research Review* 36, no. 1 (2001): 107–26; Enrico Marcelli and Wayne A. Cornelius, "The Changing Profile of Mexican Migrants to the United States: New Evidence from California and Mexico," *Latin American Research Review* 36, no. 3 (2001): 105–31.

21. See Veeman, Veeman, and Hoskins, this volume, and James R. Markusen and Steven Kahniser, "Liberalisation and Incentives for Labour Migration: Theory with Applications to NAFTA," in *Migration: The Controversies and the Evidence*, ed. Faini, de Melo, and Zimmermann, pp. 284–90.

22. The flood of corn imports has accelerated under the government of Vicente Fox, which in June 2001 drastically reduced tariffs on imports of U.S. corn that exceed the annual quota of 3 million metric tons established by NAFTA, on the grounds that tight supplies of Mexican-produced corn were pushing up consumer prices for tortillas, milk, and meat (*El Financiero*, June 30, 2001).

23. Guadalupe Rodríguez Gómez, "A Matter of Quality: Power and Change among Dairy Farmers in Los Altos de Jalisco," in *Strategies for Resource Management in Rural Mexico*, ed. Guadalupe Rodríguez Gómez and Richard Snyder (La Jolla, Calif.: Center for U.S.-Mexican Studies, University of California, San Diego, 2000).

24. See, for example, Francis Mestries, "Migración internacional y agricultura campesina en Zacatecas," in *Campo y ciudad en una era de transición*, ed. Mario Bassols (Mexico City: Departamento de Sociología, Universidad Autónoma

Metropolitana–Unidad Iztapalapa, 1994). As Luis Rubio has pointed out, it is difficult to separate the adverse consequences of NAFTA from the general effects of trade liberalization since Mexico's entry into the GATT in 1986. Most small-scale producers lump them together and blame NAFTA for their economic woes (Luis Rubio, "El TLC en el desarrollo de México," in *Políticas económicas del México contemporáneo,* ed. Luis Rubio [Mexico City: Consejo Nacional para la Cultura y las Artes/Fondo de Cultura Económica, 2001], pp. 259–60). This tendency was evident in one rural Jalisco community studied in January 1995, where 68 percent of the residents believed that they had already been harmed by NAFTA, in the form of depressed prices for their milk, meat, and corn and/or higher prices for agricultural inputs. See Wayne A. Cornelius, "Ejido Reform: Stimulus or Alternative to Migration?" in *The Transformation of Rural Mexico,* ed. Wayne A. Cornelius and David Myhre (La Jolla: Center for U.S.-Mexican Studies, University of California, San Diego, 1998), p. 243.

25. Cf. J. Edward Taylor, Antonio Yúnez-Naude, and George Dyer-Leal, "Agricultural Price Policy, Employment, and Migration in a Diversified Rural Economy: A Village-Town CGE Analysis from Mexico," *American Journal of Agricultural Economics* 81, no. 3 (August 1999): 653–62.

26. Carol Zabin and Sallie Hughes, "Economic Integration and Labor Flows: Stage Migration in Farm Labor Markets in Mexico and the United States," *International Migration Review* 29, no. 2 (Summer 1995): 395–422; Antonieta Barrón Pérez, "Cambios en las relaciones salariales en los mercados de trabajo rurales en México," *Investigación Económica* 60, no. 234 (October–December 2000): 17–32.

27. This evidence is summarized in Wayne A. Cornelius and Philip L. Martin, "The Uncertain Connection: Free Trade and Rural Mexican Migration to the United States," *International Migration Review* 27, no. 3 (Fall 1993): 484–512.

28. Tuirán, Fuentes, and Ramos, "Recent Dynamics of Mexico–United States Migration," p. 30; and Wayne A. Cornelius, "The Structural Embeddedness of Demand for Mexican Immigrant Labor: New Evidence from California," in *Crossings: Mexican Immigration in Interdisciplinary Perspective,* ed. Marcelo Suárez-Orozco (Cambridge, Mass.: Harvard University Press, 1998), p. 126.

29. CONAPO, *Migración México–Estados Unidos,* p. 42. A team of Mexican and U.S. scholars predicted in 1997 that the rate of job creation in Mexico would match the labor force growth rate by 2005 or 2006 (*Binational Study of Migration between Mexico and the United States*), but this projection assumed a sustained GDP growth rate in Mexico of at least 4 percent, which may not be attainable in the foreseeable future.

30. Markusen and Kahniser, "Liberalisation and Incentives for Labour Migration." Even in the urban sector, recent real wage trends in Mexico do not augur well. While cities in northern Mexico made significant wage and employment progress during this period of recovery from the economic crisis of

1994–1995, in southern cities the percentage of economicall y active residents who earn less than one minimum wage and who are unemployed actually increased between 1995 and 1999 (see Claudio G. Jones Tamayo, "La s o-ciedad, la economía y las políticas del empleo en México," in *Políticas económi-cas del México contemporáneo,* ed. Luis Rubio, pp. 362–66).

31. Melba Pria, "Mexican Economic Development Initiatives Targeted at Migrant-Sending Communities," testimony presented at a joint hearing of the California State Assembly Select Committee on California -Mexico Affairs and Subcommittee on International Trade, Long Beach, California, May 3, 2002.

32. Only 10 percent of Mexico's manufacturing firms have succeeded in exporting anything on a consistent basis in the post -NAFTA period (Rubio, "El TLC en el desarrollo de México," p. 260).

33. For supporting data from three high-emigration communities in west-central Mexico, see Wayne A. Cornelius, "Labor Migration to the United States: Development Outcomes and Alternatives in Mexican Sending Co m-munities," in *Regional and Sectoral Development in Mexico as Alternatives to Migra-tion,* ed. Sergio Díaz-Briquets and Sidney Weintraub (Boulder, Colo.: Westview , 1991).

34. Ginger Thompson, "U.S.-Mexico Relations: Alliance Meets Bound a-ries," *New York Times,* March 23, 2002.

35. Esther Schrader, "Mexican Development Aid Not in the Offing, U.S. Says," *Los Angeles Times,* September 1, 2001.

36. See Marc Rosenblum, "Moving Beyond the Policy of No Policy: Em i-gration from Mexico and Central America," paper presented at the Research Seminar of the Center fo r U.S.-Mexican Studies, University of California, San Diego, May 22, 2002.

37. Salinas recalls and reaffirms this thinking in his memoirs. See Carlos Sa-linas de Gortari, *México: un paso difícil a la modernidad* (Barcelona: Plaza and Janés, 2000), pp. 92, 224–26.

38. David R. Ayón, Center for the Study of Los Angeles, Loyola Mar y-mount University, Los Angeles, California, unpublished memorandum, May 2002.

13

NAFTA and Agriculture: Challenges for Trade and Policy

Michele M. Veeman, Terrence S. Veeman, and Ryan Hoskins

This chapter focuses on the implications for agriculture of the North American Free Trade Agreement (NAFTA). The three nations comprising continental North America encompass populations nearing 400 million people, an aggregate workforce of nearly 200 million, and an agricultural workforce that has dwindled to some 11.5 million. Urbanization and a decline over time in the sectoral contribution of agriculture to the economy overall have been consistent trends in the development of each NAFTA partner, as is the case for virtually all countries. Perhaps because of this tendency in the relative role of agriculture in the process of economic growth and development, agriculture received relatively little attention in the public debate over ratification of NAFTA. Similarly, outside of the agricultural sector itself, there has been relatively little discussion of NAFTA's impact on the agricultural industries of the three nations. Yet a focus on agriculture reveals some important similarities and differences in the three nations and in their capacity to benefit from freer trade, particularly in the case of Mexico.

One of our objectives is to provide a general overview of the changes that have occurred in North American agriculture since the introduction of freer trade in agricultural goods. Associated with this, we also consider the influence of NAFTA on agricultural trade relative to the role of the multilateral trade agreement of the General Agreement on Tariffs and Trade (GATT) and the World Trade Organization (WTO). Assessment of the influence of trade liberalization on agriculture must recognize the considerably different structure of agriculture in Mexico, as compared to Canada and the United States. Consequently, a second objective of this chapter is to explore the factors underlying these differences. We address three principal questions: What are some of the changes that have occurred in Mexico, in particular, as freer agricultural trade has occurred? Are member nations adjusting their agricultural production increasingly to exploit their comparative advantages? What restrictions prevent further adjustment of agricultural production and associated trade flows? In our concluding remarks, we outline some challenges for future agricultural trade both within NAFTA and in the global community.

AGRICULTURE IN GATT/WTO AND NAFTA

Prior to the Uruguay Round (UR) negotiations of the GATT (1986–1994), agriculture had effectively been insulated from international efforts to move toward freer world trade. The increasing budgetary costs associated with subsidization of agriculture in most rich nations became less tolerable to many national governments in the 1980s and early 1990s. Recognition of domestic and international distortions associated with very high levels of protection of primary agriculture became more widespread as the Organisation for Economic Co-operation and Development (OECD) spearheaded efforts to measure the levels of support to agriculture and the economic distortions associated with many nations' farm policies.

Efforts to bring agriculture into the GATT led to the affiliation of a varied group of the world's midsize agricultural exporting nations, including Australia, New Zealand, and Canada, among others, which became known as the Cairns Group. This coalition undertook the role of a concerted third voice in multilateral negotiations, as a means to counteract the likelihood of a bilateral outcome of the UR for agriculture that would largely reflect the interests and negotiating strengths of two major economic superpowers, the United States and the European Union. Bringing agriculture into the GATT contributed to the length of the much-protracted UR negotiations. These efforts eventually met with success in late 1994 in the form of the UR Agreement on Agriculture, which is now administered by the WTO. The outcome of the Agreement on Agriculture provided for only a partial and relatively modest liberalization of international agricultural trade. Even so, this represented the first comprehensive inclusion of agriculture in the rules-based system of the GATT.

A number of the provisions of the UR Agreement on Agriculture were presaged by the agreement that came into effect through NAFTA on January 1, 1994, and by the precursor Canada–United States Free Trade Agreement (CUSFTA), which became effective in 1989. As outlined below, other features of the provisions of CUSFTA/NAFTA are complementary to the provisions of the GATT/WTO for agriculture. Specifically, the CUSFTA/NAFTA provisions included the replacement of major nontariff barriers to agricultural trade by equivalent tariffs, as well as the commitment to reduce these and other agricultural tariffs within specified time periods. Most Canada-U.S. tariffs were eliminated by January 1998. Most tariffs on agricultural trade with Mexico will be eliminated by the year 2008. However, in the negotiations for CUSFTA and subsequently for NAFTA, trade liberalization for commodities produced by some highly protected sectors was viewed to be politically unpalatable in Canada and the United States; these sectors were largely exempted from such provisions for freer agricultural trade. For Canada, the exceptions were essentially the supply-managed dairy and feather (poultry, eggs, turkeys, and hatching eggs) industries. For the United States, the exceptions included sugar, sugar products, dairy, cotton, and peanuts. "Snap back" provisions for tariff reinstatement if imports were to surge were also provided for other commodities, mainly for seasonal fruits and vegetables. Subsequently, limitations to agricultural trade liberalization for most of the "sensitive" Canadian and U.S. agricultural products became entrenched through the tariff-rate quota system that was adopted in the UR negotiations.[1]

The CUSFTA also made some agricultural trade–liberalizing actions conditional on the relative levels of various domestic subsidies provided for particular agricultural products (specifically for grains), presaging efforts to achieve commitments to reductions in domestic support in the UR Agreement on Agriculture. The negotiations of CUSFTA stimulated a change in Canada's previous system of applying rail-freight subsidies for grains and oilseeds shipped to export points (these subsidies were phased out from 1995), and the text of the NAFTA gives general support to the reduction of export subsidies through GATT. Questions of market access, domestic support, and export subsidies for agriculture, which are focal points of Chapter 7 of NAFTA (Agriculture and Sanitary and Phytosanitary Measures), were all issues of major concern in the UR negotiations. The CUSFTA and NAFTA placed considerable emphasis on the development of principles to apply to sanitary and phytosanitary (SPS) measures for agricultural trade. Guidelines for SPS procedures under NAFTA specify that these must be scientifically based, nondiscriminatory, and consistently and transparently applied in the least trade-restrictive manner. The negotiations of the UR built on these various provisions of NAFTA for agriculture.

Another component of CUSFTA/NAFTA that has had considerable significance for agriculture relates to dispute settlement procedures. Canada had hoped to achieve an agreement that would do away with the unilateral trade remedy legislation of antidumping and countervailing actions, two forms of administrative protection that have frequently been applied to agricultural trade. Canada was not successful in achieving this. However, a system of dispute settlement procedures was introduced in the CUSFTA (Chapter 19) that uses binational appeal panels to review whether the procedures followed by agencies in national trade remedy interventions are correctly applied. Provision was also made for dispute settlement procedures relative to CUSFTA itself (Chapter 20). These provisions were carried forward into NAFTA, an extension that required significant changes in Mexico's legal system.[2] The considerable strengthening of the WTO's dispute settlement provisions that was achieved in the Uruguay Round yielded dispute provisions that differ from those of CUSFTA/NAFTA and that provide a complementary mechanism for appealing inappropriate trade interventions.

The CUSFTA/NAFTA dispute settlement procedures have been invoked—through panels constituted under provisions of both Chapter 19 and Chapter 20—in contentious cases of application of countervailing and antidumping duties for agricultural products. Examples of countervail appeals are the Canadian requests for panel assessments of the series of determinations on U.S. countervailing duties on pork and swine imported from Canada. The United States has also been involved in disputes over its sugar exports to Canada, Mexican exports of cut flowers to the United States, and Mexican antidumping duties against high-fructose corn syrup.[3] The dispute settlement provisions of NAFTA are credited with improving the precision with which national countervail legislation is applied.[4]

The ability to appeal trade interventions through the provisions of NAFTA and GATT/WTO, as well as the need to apply SPS procedures in a nondiscriminatory manner, were among the reasons given for the 1997 U.S. agreement to that country's limited importation of Hass avocados from Mexico, despite strong opposition from avocado growers in Florida and California. U.S. avocado imports from Mexico had essentially been banned on phytosanitary grounds from 1914 until the 1997 agreement, which specifies a very rigorous system of SPS requirements for the importation and shipment, in specified winter months (November through February), of Hass avocados. Avocados are accepted only from farms that follow specific SPS guidelines and that are located in a specified region—Michoacán, a state in southwest Mexico which is free of coddling moth. Specific practices of grove management, pest monitoring, packing, inspection, and shipping are required, and U.S. shipment destinations are restricted to nineteen northeastern states.[5] The establishment of intergovernmental standing committees on various technical issues related to trade—such as on SPS issues—is also credited with providing a venue for resolving disputes before these move to investigation or litigation.[6]

ECONOMIC ROLES OF AGRICULTURE IN CANADA, THE UNITED STATES, AND MEXICO

The structure and role of agriculture are much different in Mexico than in Canada and the United States. These differences reflect Mexico's considerably different level of economic development, as well as the very different nature of agricultural policies that have prevailed in these three nations. The sectoral role of agriculture in Canada and the United States has been considerably influenced by the process of economic development that these nations have enjoyed. Growth in agriculture, evident in the rapid adoption of new technology, was aided by early policies to invest in public research and extension activities directed at the development of farming. Growth in the general economy, resulting in increasing real wages of workers relative to the cost of capital goods, tended to encourage the substitution of capital-intensive technology for labor. Economic growth, translated into increasing levels of income, stimulated demand for goods other than food, since once basic food needs are met, demand for food tends to grow at a slower rate than demand for non-food goods and services in a growing economy (a feature that is known as Engel's Law). Labor movement out of agriculture—stimulated by the growth in labor productivity, accompanied by the substitution of machinery for labor and also by the slower growth of demand for food—was aided by job opportunities associated with growth in industry and an associated trend to urbanization.

The pace of structural change within North American nations is clearly most advanced in the United States, followed quite closely by Canada. Structural change is less advanced in Mexico, where over eight million workers are still involved in primary agriculture. For the United

Table 13.1. Declining Roles of Agriculture in Mexico, Canada, and the United States, 1960–1999

	Agriculture as Share of Total Labor Force				Agriculture as Share of GDP		
	México (%)	Canada (%)	U.S. (%)		México (%)	Canada (%)	U.S. (%)
1960	54	13	6	1960	16	5	4
1970	44	8	4	1970	12	4	3
1980	36	7	3	1980	8	5	3
1990	28	3	3	1990	8	3	3
1995	25	3	2	1995	8	2	2
1996	24	3	2	1996	7	2	2
1997	23	3	2	1997	5	2	2
1998	23	3	2	1998	5	2	2
1999	22	2	2	1999	N.A.	N.A.	N.A.

Source: Food and Agricultural Organization statistics (www.fao.org), and World Bank, Development Report, various issues.
N.A. = Not available.

States and Canada, the process of structural adjustment to the mechanization of agriculture had largely been accomplished by the 1960s. Since then there have been small but steady decreases in the proportional contribution of agriculture to the economy, reflecting the economic adjustments outlined above. As table 13.1 demonstrates, agricultural labor declined from 13 percent to 2 percent of the total labor force for Canada between 1960 and 1999. For the United States, labor employed in agriculture declined from 6 percent to 2 percent in this period. Agricultural output has increased in both nations but at a slower rate than for the economy as a whole. Thus Canada's agricultural sector accounted for 5 percent of gross domestic product (GDP) in 1960 and only 2 percent in 1999, while for the United States these figures were 4 percent in 1960 and 2 percent in 1999. For Mexico, on the other hand, agriculture contributed 5 percent of GDP in 1999, and some 22 percent of the labor force was involved in this sector. This is an indication of two important features: agricultural labor productivity and the incomes earned in agriculture are both much lower than is the case, on average, for the rest of the Mexican economy. The standard of living of rural people in each of the three nations also reflects significant off-farm income; even in Mexico, roughly half the income of the small-scale communal farm sector, composed of *ejido* households, comes from off-farm sources.[7]

The processes of economic and agricultural development have resulted, in both the United States and Canada, in the evolution of the relatively large-scale, capital-intensive, cost-efficient, family-based farming operations that account for the largest proportion of agricultural output in both nations. An increasing proportion of smaller-scale, part-time, and limited-resource farmers also continue, but they contribute a relatively small and decreasing proportion of agricultural output in both Canada and the United States. As discussed above, these types of structural change are consequences of the process of economic growth. Even so, the adjustments of labor transfers from agriculture have not been painless; many farmers who might have preferred to continue in agriculture have been forced out by cost-price pressures that have arisen from the process of structural adjustment associated with economic growth. The process of structural adjustment for agriculture has been aided in both nations by a range of public policies, including support for research, education, communications, and transportation infrastructure. Farm policies have been directed to overcoming inefficiencies in financial, information, and risk markets. In contrast, the recent pace of structural adjustments for agriculture in

Mexico has been much more rapid, and the agricultural sector has been the recipient of much less support to roads, communication, and other infrastructure.

Structural adjustment in Canada and the United States has led to some regional differences in the type and structure of agriculture, but these are relatively minor compared to the marked regional differences in agricultural adjustment and modernization in Mexico. Structural adjustment in Mexico is characterized by "double dualism." Dualism refers to a mode of development in which one sector applies modern technology, achieves high productivity, and competes in international markets, while another sector is dominated by subsistence production, typically oriented to home consumption and local markets, which leads to low levels of income. The term "double dualism" has been coined for Mexico to reflect these types of pronounced differences, not only between the industrial sector and the agricultural sector but also within the agricultural sector itself.[8]

Some regions of Mexico, mostly in the north, exhibited enormous growth in agricultural productivity for at least two decades following World War II; these productivity gains were based on large investments in irrigation and mechanization and the introduction of fertilizers. In central and southern Mexico, however, large segments of agricultural land are characterized by small plots, limited capital investment, subsistence production, and income supplementation by seasonal work on commercial farms. Between 1940 and 1960, crop output in the relatively capital-intensive north and Pacific-north regions of Mexico grew at rates between 8 and 11 percent per year, while crop output in the relatively labor-intensive central region rose at a little over 3 percent annually.[9]

Mexico's agricultural growth model dates from the Mexican Revolution of 1910–1917. The goal of land reform was central to the new revolutionary government. Large landholdings were broken into small, communal properties known as ejidos, a concept subsequently enshrined in Mexico's Constitution. By 1940, approximately half of the existing cultivated land had been redistributed to peasant groups. Much land reform was directed to the central and southern agricultural regions, where rural poverty was most extreme. The policy of land reform redressed major inequalities in land ownership, but the eijdo system provided these farmers with only use rights to their small plots, rather than the rights to rent, buy, or sell land, foreclosing opportunities for structural adjustment in this sector that could allow transition to larger scales of farming associated with more modern farming methods. The 1992 amendment to Article 27 of the Mexican Constitution legalized land rental and provided for a process that may allow ejidos to move to a private property regime. However, land records are still being sorted out.[10]

In contrast, the genesis of land distribution and the basis of agricultural development in the relatively unpopulated and arid north and Pacific-north regions of Mexico date from the 1940s. Bruce Johnson and Peter Kilby point out that policymakers became aware that the large amounts of unused, sparsely populated land in these regions, if provided with sufficient investment in irrigation, had the potential to be highly productive in wheat and cotton, which at that time had strong market prospects in both the United States and Mexico. The World Bank offered generous loan rates, and technical support came from U.S. firms already cultivating similar land.[11] One of the goals of these initiatives was to stimulate agricultural exports as a means to increase foreign exchange receipts, enabling importation of capital equipment to aid industrial development through a policy of import substitution. Agricultural exports did indeed grow. In 1940, Mexico's commodity exports were largely based on energy, with agriculture accounting for only 20 percent of exports. By 1950, agricultural exports accounted for 52 percent of commodity exports; coffee and cotton were major exports for Mexico, followed by sugar and meat. By the 1970s, Mexico's exports of fresh and frozen fruits and vegetables, specifically tomatoes and strawberries, had become significant. By 2000, fresh vegetables had become Mexico's leading agricultural export.

The effects of agricultural dualism were marked by the mid-1960s; they could be seen, for example, by comparing production of wheat, then a relatively new crop for Mexico, and maize (corn), the traditional staple-food crop. By 1964, 72 percent of wheat production was concentrated in the north, with production methods using mechanization, large-scale plots, irrigated land, and new wheat varieties. Maize production, in contrast, was spread across Mexico; more than two million farm households were estimated to be involved in maize cultivation, compared to fewer than 50,000 farmers growing wheat. The average wheat farm measured between 15 and 20 hectares, compared to only 2 hectares for a maize farm.[12] Corn production in the United States, on large plots and using modern machinery and fertilizers, continues to be much more efficient and less expensive than the small-scale, labor-intensive production of Mexico. By the late 1990s, the average maize yield per hectare in Mexico was about 2.4 metric tons, while the average yield in the United States was about 8 metric tons. It has been estimated that only 2.5 million hectares of Mexico's 9 million hectares of maize are commercially viable.[13]

An extensive system of state involvement in Mexico's agricultural and food marketing, distribution, and pricing had been established by the 1980s. The debt crisis of 1982 forced a reassessment of Mexico's policies of protection, state control, and industry-based import substitution, and Mexico began the process of moving toward a more outward-looking policy from about 1984. NAFTA can be viewed as only one component in the process of moving from a state-dominated protectionist economic system to a more market-oriented and less-interventionist economy. In regard to agriculture, domestic support to basic commodities like grain and milk had involved systems of support prices that exceeded market prices; consumer price subsidies were applied for maize tortillas, a crucial component of rural and urban diets, as well as for milk; some farm inputs were subsidized; and imports were licensed. Mexico moved to reduce subsidies to agriculture and to food consumption, phased out the extensive system of state-trading (through the agency known as CONASUPO), and replaced its system of farm support prices with a limited program of income subsidy and technical support introduced through the Procampo agency.[14] Mexico's liberalization of agricultural trade has actually proceeded faster than provided for by its NAFTA commitments. These allowed for a fifteen-year transition for maize, with provision for over-quota tariffs through a tariff rate quota (TRQ) system. However, Mexico has allowed higher import levels of duty-free corn than was required according to its NAFTA commitments.[15]

Although food subsidies have been phased out, limited food assistance programs have been introduced, targeted by geographic and household criteria. These appear to have little impact on poverty, however, due to the limited level of benefits and the relatively low numbers of eligible households.[16] An innovative income support program targeted at poverty-level families with small children—Progresa—was introduced in 1997, but it currently reaches a very small proportion of families in poverty.[17] All in all, the policies of which NAFTA is a part have contributed to Mexico's economic growth, but this process has been accompanied by increased income inequality and little or no improvement in the level of absolute poverty within Mexican society.[18] Increasing income inequality applies across both individuals and regions; the highest incidence of poverty is concentrated in the rural sector and in southern and southeastern Mexico. Overall, changes in domestic policy reforms in Mexico, as in the other two NAFTA partners, are believed to have had greater impacts on agricultural output, employment, and trade than has NAFTA itself.

NAFTA AND AGRICULTURE: TRADE PATTERNS AND SOME IMPLICATIONS

In keeping with broad trends, trade in agriculture has grown among the NAFTA member nations since the agreement took effect in 1994. As shown in table 13.2, the United States is the dominant agricultural trading partner, and an increased concentration of trade with the United States is seen for both Canada and Mexico. As revealed in table 13.3, increases in agricultural trade have matched the increases in total merchandise trade during the 1990s. Several factors may be associated with the pattern of increased agricultural and other trade among the NAFTA partners. Changes in national policies for agriculture, changes in the policies for and the characteristics of the three economies, cross-border economic integration, and the reductions in trade barriers that are associated with NAFTA and GATT may all have contributed to this pattern. From the inception of NAFTA until 2001, the United States experienced strong economic growth, Mexico suffered through a peso crisis, and Canada's dollar was relatively weak. Each of these macroeconomic influences may have had as much or more influence on trade than NAFTA itself.

Mexico-U.S. Agricultural Trade under NAFTA

Agricultural exports from the United States to Mexico grew by some 43 percent between 1994 and 2000, from US$4.6 billion to $6.5 billion. Exports from Mexico to the United States grew from US$2.9 billion to $4.7 billion, an increase of 65 percent. Mexico had a deficit in its balance of agricultural trade with the United States in 2000 of some $1.5 billion.[19]

The major agricultural export items (and their associated values, expressed in U.S dollars) that were shipped from Mexico to the United States in 2000 were:

- fresh vegetables: $1.4 billion,
- wine and beer: $757 million,
- fresh fruits: $578 million,
- live animals: $407 million, and
- processed fruits and vegetables: $400 million.

Table 13.2. Agricultural Imports and Exports: Mexico, Canada, and the United States, 1960–1999

	Value of Agricultural Imports (US$ million)				Value of Agricultural Exports (US$ million)		
	Mexico	Canada	U.S.		Mexico	Canada	U.S.
1960	86	806	3,836	1960	457	1,260	5,187
1970	221	1,261	6,301	1970	694	1,815	7,507
1980	3,168	4,899	18,410	1980	1,833	7,071	42,921
1990	4,989	7,346	27,088	1990	2,936	9,181	45,210
1995	5,333	9,079	33,839	1995	5,717	12,788	62,259
1996	7,549	9,522	37,892	1996	5,622	14,702	66,255
1997	7,764	10,515	41,067	1997	6,292	15,191	62,544
1998	8,493	10,845	41,864	1998	6,864	15,393	57,351
1999	8,752	10,844	43,251	1999	7,006	14,683	52,704

Source: Food and Agricultural Organization statistics (www.fao.org).

Table 13.3. Agricultural Trade as Share of Total Trade, 1990–1998

	U.S. Exports to Mexico (%)	U.S. Imports from Mexico (%)	U.S. Exports to Canada (%)	U.S. Imports from Canada (%)
1990	9.0	8.7	5.0	3.5
1993	8.7	6.8	5.3	4.2
1994	9.0	5.8	4.9	4.1
1995	7.6	6.2	4.6	3.9
1996	9.6	5.2	4.6	4.3
1997	7.3	4.8	4.5	4.4
1998	7.8	5.0	4.6	4.5

Source: Derived from Food and Agricultural Organization statistics.

Mexico's ability to supply out-of-season vegetables to its northern neighbors contributes to the large increase in exports for this group of products, especially since 1994. Mexico's fresh vegetable exports have grown by some 60 percent. Fresh tomato exports from Mexico to the United States have particularly increased, but not as much as might have been expected, due to trade disputes. An 83 percent growth in tomato exports from 1993 to 1998 reflected consumers' preferences for new varieties of extended shelf-life tomatoes produced in Sinaloa and Baja California. By 1998, tomatoes accounted for 22 percent (US$567 million) of total Mexican fresh fruit and vegetable exports to the United States. Imported Mexican tomatoes were less expensive than tomatoes from Florida and California. The original NAFTA TRQ scenario was for U.S. import restrictions to fall to zero by 2004. However, Florida producers accused Mexico of dumping in 1995 and 1996, a claim that was rejected by the U.S. International Trade Commission. Florida agencies then emphasized rigorous inspection of Mexican tomato imports for sanitary violations. Ultimately, a trade suspension agreement was entered into, which stipulated that Mexico would not sell tomatoes at less than specified prices.[20]

Cantaloupe exports from Mexico have grown considerably, increasing by 126 percent between 1993 and 1999. Sugar exports from Mexico to the United States have grown somewhat, but this has occurred in the context of limited liberalization by the United States. The pattern of increased Mexican exports of fresh fruits and vegetables was certainly not influenced solely by trade liberalization; consumer preferences have also changed markedly. For example, the average annual consumption of cantaloupe in the United States in 1980 was 5.8 pounds per person; the figure had doubled to 11.8 pounds per person by 2000.

The leading groups of agricultural goods exported from the United States to Mexico in 2000, and their associated values expressed in U.S. dollars, were:

- corn: $973 million,
- red meat: $876 million,
- soybeans: $678 million,
- cotton: $476 million,
- processed fruits and vegetables: $250 million, and
- poultry meat: $250 million.

Bulk commodities accounted for 39 percent of U.S. agricultural exports to Mexico in 2000. The fastest-growing U.S. exports to Mexico include corn (these imports exceeded TRQ levels for almost every year between 1993 and 1997), pork, and cattle.

U.S.-Canada Agricultural Trade under NAFTA

Agricultural goods exported from the United States to Canada grew by 37 percent in value between 1994 and 2000; their value, again in U.S. dollars, grew from $5.6 billion to $7.6 billion. Agricultural exports from Canada to the United States grew 47 percent, from $5.3 billion to $7.8 billion. Over this period, the balance of U.S. agricultural trade with Canada moved from a small surplus to a deficit of some $500 million.

The largest groups of agricultural goods exported from the United States to Canada in 2000 were:

- fresh vegetables: $869 million,
- fresh fruits: $639 million,
- snack foods: $617 million,
- processed fruits and vegetables: $434 million, and
- fresh and frozen red meats: $349 million.

Nearly 72 percent of U.S. exports to Canada were consumer-oriented food goods, as opposed to bulk agricultural commodities or intermediate goods, significantly more than for U.S. exports to Mexico. Agricultural items exported from the United States to Canada that showed the highest growth rates included beef, cotton, and fresh fruits and vegetables.

The largest groups of agricultural exports from Canada to the United States in 2000, again cited in U.S. dollars, were:

- red meats: $1.6 billion,
- live animals: $1.1 billion,
- snack foods: $1.1 billion,
- processed fruits and vegetables: $552 million, and
- fresh vegetables: $412 million.

Wheat exports from Canada to the United States increased considerably in 1994, by 70 percent from the year before, and although volatile, they have remained at higher levels than in previous years.

Canada-Mexico Agricultural Trade under NAFTA

Agricultural trade between Mexico and Canada is on a much smaller scale than is the case for each nation's trade with the United States. Expressed in Canadian dollars, Canadian agricultural exports to Mexico grew 112 percent, from $213 million to $452 million, between 1994 and 2000. Meanwhile, Mexican exports to Canada grew from $217 million to $398 million, an increase of 83 percent. Agricultural trade between these two nations has remained relatively balanced throughout this period.[21]

Until recently Canadian exports to Mexico had been dominated by oilseeds. These exports, mostly canola, grew from $147 million in 1994 to $245 million in 1999. Meat and meat products exports to Mexico from Canada have expanded at a very rapid rate in recent years, growing from $12 million in 1998 to $166 million (accounting for 37 percent of total exports) in 2000, a twelve-fold increase. Pork and beef were the major meat products that led this meat trade growth. Wheat was another significant Canadian export to Mexico in 2000, valued at $36 million.

Mexican exports of agricultural products to Canada have been concentrated in fruits and vegetables. Expressed in Canadian dollars, Mexico's vegetable and vegetable preparation exports to Canada grew from $71 million in 1994 to $124 million in 2000, accounting for roughly 32 percent of Mexico's total agricultural exports to Canada throughout the period. Fresh fruits accounted for $58 million of exports to Canada in 1994, and these reached $104 million in 2000, continuing to account for 27 percent of total Mexican agricultural exports to Canada.

Changes in Agricultural Trade Patterns

Standard economic reasoning regarding the likely patterns of agricultural trade that might be associated with NAFTA suggests that because Mexico is endowed with a large, relatively unskilled labor force, more liberalized trade could lead to increased production and exportation of agricultural goods that tend to require labor-intensive production processes, as has occurred with the appreciable increases in fresh fruit and vegetable exports from that nation. Canada and the United States—with greater access to capital, relatively large endowments of land, and educated labor forces—have emerged as low-cost world exporters of grains and livestock, and both nations tend to export these products to Mexico. These features of the NAFTA agricultural trade patterns that have occurred since 1994 seem to be consistent with apparent patterns of comparative advantage within subsectors of agriculture in the three nations. Strawberries, melons, avocados, and out-of-season fruits are major exports from Mexico. Maize (corn) is a major export from the United States to Mexico. Even so, there are some evident distortions associated with the remaining pockets of agricultural protection that persist in Canada and the United States. One of the most glaring may well be sugar; Mexico's ability to export sugar to the United States is severely constrained.

Another point of interest is the tendency for increasing trade in complementary goods between the NAFTA partners. Intra-industry trade is not readily explained by standard textbook theories of international trade. However, this trade pattern is consistent with the observation that intra-industry trade is often evident within nations, as shown in patterns of trade within Canada. In the context of the large geographical areas that constitute the North American continent and the reduction in transaction costs of cross-border trading that have occurred since 1994, it is not surprising that north-south trade patterns have emerged that are consistent with efforts to minimize transportation costs, including backhaul, or that cater to short-term regional differences in supply and demand. These features reflect the fact that it is sometimes more cost efficient to buy and sell in markets relatively close to the site of production, whether or not they are within the same country. When tariffs exist, or when there are incompatibilities in transport infrastructure or other sources of cross-border frictions that contribute to cross-border transaction costs, this form of trade is discouraged; but when tariffs are lowered or eliminated, as with NAFTA, it can evolve rapidly.

This dynamic seems to explain the increasing extent of intra-industry trade between the United States and Canada that is occurring in grains and feed, livestock and animal products, and oilseeds and oilseed products. For instance, pork products produced in western Canada are exported and sold to U.S. West Coast consumers, while U.S. pork production can be sold into the eastern Canadian market. The ability for cross-border trade to accommodate local or regional circumstances explains the surge in cattle exports from Mexico to the United States that occurred in 1995. Mexican ranchers, facing a severe drought, were able to ship cattle for slaughter in the United States, an option that would not have existed prior to NAFTA, due to tariffs and other impediments to cross border-trade.[22]

NAFTA, WTO, AND AGRICULTURE: CHALLENGES FOR THE FUTURE

Cross-Border Trade Dispute Problems

One facet of the increasing concentration of agricultural trade between the three nations has been increased trade tensions, typically seen as U.S.-Mexico or U.S.-Canada trade problems and disputes. Some of these were noted in preceding sections, as with the administered agreements that limit tomatoes exported from Mexico to the United States and the agreement on Mexico's avocado exports to the United States. Trade disputes frequently seem to have flared up as changes in trade patterns stimulated regionally based pressures from special interest groups. From the viewpoint of Canada and Mexico, these often seem to reflect the relative ease with which U.S. special interest groups can call for countervailing and antidumping procedures. Other trade frictions arise from continued protection for politically sensitive sectors (especially for U.S. sugar, relative to Mexico) and higher levels of transfers and support to farming in the United States (as for grains, relative to western Canadian grain growers). Occasional overzealous border holdups under the guise of SPS regulations have been an irritation. Points of tension associated with agricultural trade for the United States include its opposition to the Canadian Wheat Board as a single-desk exporter and the continuation of Canadian supply management programs as the means of maintaining high levels of protection for the politically sensitive dairy sector and for poultry/eggs. However, differences in farm policies exist in the three nations, and some of these seem likely to continue.

Sugar and high-fructose corn syrup (HFCS) have been a particularly contentious agricultural trade issue for Mexico and the United States. Mexican sugar production increased significantly soon after NAFTA was implemented. In 1994, production stood at 3.8 metric tons, raw value; in 1998 this grew to nearly 5.5 million tons, raw value. U.S. sugar producers do not want imports of excess Mexican product, but Mexican producers are eager to export to the United States. This issue is complicated further since both the Mexican government and U.S. sugar producers are not eager to see U.S. HFCS exports to Mexico increase. HFCS is an excellent substitute for sugar in cola production, a burgeoning industry in Mexico. Further, Mexico continues to have extensive government involvement in the sugar industry, with a government-controlled bank holding a large amount of sugar industry debt. Regulation of sugar and HFCS exports were initially encompassed in the NAFTA agreement, but the Mexican and U.S. governments subsequently signed a side agreement that Mexico could export certain quantities in excess of domestic consumption. Debate surrounds whether consumption of HFCS is to be counted in this calculation. The agreement has been contested by both governments, resulting in calls by each for antidumping investigations through NAFTA and the WTO.[23]

Transportation of Agricultural Products

Transportation bottlenecks have become a serious impediment in agricultural trade between the United States and Mexico, causing considerable delays at border crossing points. In addition, transportation infrastructure is a problem in some areas of Mexico; this is pronounced in the south. Mexico has some modern toll highways, but the high cost of using them is reported to deter standard commercial traffic.[24] Transportation delays are a particular problem for perishable agricultural products because these must be delivered rapidly from producers' fields to market. More than 45 percent of agricultural trade products that cross the U.S.-Mexico border are perishable; this is the case for about 75 percent of northbound agricultural products and some 25 percent of southbound products. These products include fresh and frozen fruits and vegetables, as well as chilled or frozen dairy, livestock, and poultry products.[25] Since fresh fruits and vegetables are among the fastest-growing products exported from Mexico to the United States, and because these products face a high level of inspection that reflects SPS requirements, border holdups can be onerous and costly for Mexican producers and shippers.

Much of the bottleneck problem has been related to the United States' failure to allow Mexican trucks to cross the border freely, a provision that was to apply eventually under NAFTA. The moratorium on licensing new Mexican carriers to operate in the United States, in effect since 1982, continued through 2001 despite the finding of a NAFTA panel early that year that refusal to provide access to all Mexican trucking firms was unjustified. The United States has continued to bar reciprocal truck crossing, based on concerns regarding safety problems such as overweight Mexican trucks and their lack of operational logs. As a result, trucks have not been able to simply drive across the border; instead, they must deliver their trailers to the border and use hired short-haul trucks to pull these across the border, to then be re-attached to long-haul trucks on the other side of the border.

Moreover, trucks are subject to the same intensive investigations for drugs and illegal immigrants that apply to other vehicles crossing the border. Inadequate crossing infrastructure is also a problem.[26] Consequently, border crossing can take up to twenty-three hours. In effect, this represents a tax on cross-border trade between Mexico and the United States, which can affect Mexican products that are trucked further north to Canada as well. This is expensive in terms of both shipment times and deteriorated product. Efforts to reduce the burden of cross-border bottlenecks are leading to more modernized inspection methods and procedures, but the lack of transportation infrastructure and other issues noted above are a considerable current problem.

The terrorist attacks of September 11, 2001, focused attention on national security, led to concerns of border holdups for traded goods, and stimulated discussion about the political and practical feasibility of measures to harmonize customs and immigration policies. This has been a particular concern at the U.S.-Canada border, which had been less rigorously policed than the U.S.-Mexico border. In the three months following the terrorist attack, Canada and the United States entered into agreements to develop joint customs and immigration databases and related information, as well as to develop more uniform visa policies. Immigration and customs procedures have traditionally been considered hallmarks of national sovereignty; consequently, there has been some political resistance in Canada to U.S. pressures to adopt common policies. Nonetheless, convergence of these policies seems likely. An IPSOS-Reid poll in early October 2001 found a high degree of support among the Canadian public for collaboration with the

United States in border-related security procedures that would stream-line cross-border movement of people and traded goods. Cross-border security issues and their impacts on trade are likely to be a continuing issue of concern, both nationally and internationally, for each of the NAFTA partners.

Labor and Agriculture

The question of whether the NAFTA provisions might be extended to freer labor movement between NAFTA partners continues to be con-troversial, particularly for the United States and Mexico.[27] Migrant farm labor constitutes a particularly difficult problem. Agriculture em-ploys a large proportion of Mexico's population, especially in the poorer southern states, where alternative employment is in short sup-ply and poverty levels are high. A large proportion of hired farmwork-ers in Mexico are migrant laborers, for whom part-time work in agri-culture and in a variety of other sectors reflects the lack of other jobs and the highly seasonal nature of farm employment. Some 2.3 million farmworkers were hired for pay in 1998, according to an official Mexi-can employment survey.[28] (The balance of recorded Mexican farm la-bor was reported to be unpaid family labor.) The market for hired farmworkers in the United States also fluctuates seasonally. Some 890,000 hired farmworkers were reportedly employed in this relatively low-paid occupation in 1980, according to the National Statistics Ser-vice of the U.S. Department of Agriculture. Many of these farmwork-ers were born outside the United States, mostly in Mexico, and many of them are illegal migrants.[29]

Julián Castro Rea has suggested one approach that may relieve this situation—a temporary worker program, such as the one Canada and Mexico have operated since 1974 for agricultural labor.[30] The possibil-ity of granting amnesty status to illegal Mexican migrants currently re-siding in the United States became the subject of serious political con-sideration in early 2001, but it was sidelined later that year by pressing concerns regarding border security following the September 11 terror-ist attacks.

Canada's Seasonal Agricultural Workers Program (SAWP), which currently operates in the provinces of Ontario, Quebec, Manitoba, and Alberta, allows for the organized movement of foreign workers to meet temporary seasonal labor needs of Canadian farm operators and the food industry; SAWP wages are specified to be comparable to those of domestic Canadian farmworkers. Currently SAWP also involves employer-paid accommodation, subsidized international airfare, and health and medical benefits. This is a tiny program relative to Mexico's agricultural labor force, with somewhat fewer than 17,000 foreign workers in Canada under SAWP auspices in 2001; more than 9,000 of these were Mexican. In April 2001, Canada and Mexico signed a letter of intent to extend SAWP, both by region and by sector.

Extending Agricultural Trade Liberalization

Globally, agricultural trade liberalization is far from complete. The next step of substantive agricultural trade liberalization will require an effective round of WTO negotiations. However, there are significant challenges to the achievement of a substantive agreement from such agricultural negotiations.

Tariff-rate quotas introduced in the UR Agreement on Agriculture have legitimized some very high tariffs for many farm products in the international arena. Agricultural export subsidies were also legitimized in the UR, and these are substantial for some nations/commodities. Domestic support to the farm sector, recognized to impinge on other nations through lower world prices and reduced market access, is appreciable and increasing in some nations, including the United States. In Canada, which has largely removed domestic support to agriculture except through supply management, there are pressures to increase government transfers to agriculture.

Other challenges face the SPS agreement. Technical barriers, trademarks, and labeling issues are likely to be difficult to deal with for agriculture and food. Agricultural/food biotechnology has emerged as an important social and economic issue that is likely to strain the SPS and dispute settlement procedures of the WTO and to contribute to the backlash against globalization.

The influence of Third World nations is expected to be crucial in getting the WTO agricultural discussions and negotiations under way. Their support will require that they be given more access to the benefits of trade liberalization in goods that have continued to receive protection in high-income nations. Will the United States and the European Union, as major economic players, take the lead to secure the support of low-income nations for further trade negotiations through providing sufficient concessions/benefits to them by reducing trade barriers for textiles and sugar, or through other means? To date, a positive answer to this question is not evident.

What is the scope for extensions of NAFTA versus WTO in providing more potential benefits for consumers and for the farm and food sectors of the three partners? Expanding the geographic focus of NAFTA through a Free Trade Area of the Americas is one approach. Emphasis on reducing major remaining trade barriers for agriculture and on reducing the extent of trade disputes through changes in trade remedy or competition legislation could arguably be more likely to be achieved through a multilateral approach, as through WTO. However, as the experience of NAFTA and the UR shows, following both approaches simultaneously can be complementary.

Even so, there are some irritations and problems relating to agriculture within NAFTA. These include continuing pockets of agricultural protectionism in the United States and Canada, and transport bottlenecks. For Mexico, the focus of agricultural export growth has been the more prosperous north. Adjustment costs associated with imports of corn have tended to be concentrated in the agrarian south.

CONCLUSION

NAFTA is generally credited with having stimulated cross-border agricultural trade within North America, although this increase also reflects other changes in policy and in the economic environment. The resulting changes in the role of agriculture in the economy are particularly evident for Mexico. Economists' expectations regarding the effects of trade liberalization overall, prior to NAFTA, tended to suggest that gains from trade in Canada and the United States might be relatively modest compared to the situation for Mexico. In essence, this type of projection mirrored expectations that one of the easiest ways to aid the transfer of modern technology from rich nations to poor nations is through economic integration and that smaller economies may benefit most from expansion of markets and division of labor—that is, from increased specialization.

Has this happened with agricultural trade? Assessments of the impacts of NAFTA on agricultural trade have focused on changes in trade patterns.[31] Agricultural trade has tended to increase among all partners since the CUSFTA and NAFTA came into effect. Some of these changes seem to build on comparative advantages of each nation in agriculture. Some areas of trade are limited by national protectionist policies, as for sugar in the United States and dairy in Canada. Intra-industry trade is increasing, suggesting that a degree of regional economic integration is occurring across borders. Some national policies and deficiencies in infrastructure limit this regional economic integration.

We conclude that adjustments for agriculture that are associated with Mexico's move from an inward-looking protected economy toward a more open economy have had relatively high costs for some segments of Mexico's agrarian population. In this context it appears that migratory workers or those with non-farm incomes were best able to adapt to the recent economic reforms.

The ultimate goal of trade is to improve total social welfare. Trade liberalization often can involve concentrated economic losses, while gains may be widely distributed. Corn imports into Mexico, for instance, have had destabilizing effects on *ejidatarios* while providing Mexican corn consumers, overall, with cheaper, more stable corn prices in the longer term. Over time this allows consumers to improve their nutrition and make other consumption choices. However, achievement of the full benefits of the opportunities for agricultural modernization offered by NAFTA has been hampered by a lack of infrastructure to support agricultural development, particularly in Mexico's less prosperous, more agrarian southeastern and southern states.

Effective approaches to reduce poverty require aggressive efforts to reduce inequities in access to education and economic opportunities.[32] Policies to reduce the human costs of illegal migration from Mexico to the United States may also help in the shorter term.[33] Overall, the benefits and opportunities from freer trade within North America have been significant, and they are far from being exhausted.

Notes

1. Fuller discussions of the agricultural issues associated with the GATT/WTO and with NAFTA are in Michele Veeman, "Canada's Agricultural Trade Policy: Choices and Challenges," *Canadian Journal of Agricultural Economics* 46 (1998): 371–77, and Michele Veeman, "Changes in Canadian Agricultural Marketing and Trade Policy: The Impacts of New Rules and New Institutions," *Review of Marketing and Agricultural Economics* 64, no. 3 (1996): 227–39.

2. This point is noted by Sylvia Ostrey, "Regional versus Multilateral Trade Strategies," *ISUMA: Canadian Journal of Policy Research* 1, no. 1 (2000): 45–56.

3. A listing of agricultural trade disputes is given in U.S. Department of Agriculture, Economic Research Service (USDA, ERS), "NAFTA: The Record to Date," *Agricultural Outlook,* September 1999.

4. See Veeman, "Changes in Canadian Agricultural Marketing and Trade Policy."

5. U.S. Department of Agriculture, Animal and Plant Health Inspection Service (USDA, APHIS), "Systems Approach for Importing Mexican Avoc a-dos," January 1997.

6. USDA, ERS, "NAFTA: Situation and Outlook," WRS -99-1, 1999.

7. Benjamin Davis, Alain de Janvry, Elisabeth Sadoulet, and Todd Diehl, "Policy Reforms and Poverty in the Mexican Ejido Sector," in *Policy Harmoni-zation and Adjustment in the North American Agricultural and Food Industry*, ed. R.M.A. Loyns, R. Knutson, K. Mielke, and A. Yúnez -Naude (Proceedings of the Fifth Agricultural and Food Policy Systems Information Workshop, Texas A&M University, University of Guelph, and El Colegio de Mexico, February 2000).

8. Bruce Johnson and Peter Kilby, *Agriculture and Structural Transformation: Economic Strategies in Late-Developing Nations* (New York: Oxford University Press, 1971).

9. Ibid.

10. The process is complicated by the fact that, in some instances, land had reportedly been granted to several people. Useful discussions of Mexico's land reform policies are given by Davis et al., "Policy Reforms and Poverty." An informative overview is also provided by *The Economist*, A Survey of Mex-ico, October 28, 2000.

11. Johnson and Kilby, *Agriculture and Structural Transformation*.

12. Ibid.

13. The yield data cited are from the Food and Agricultural Organization, *Production Yearbook*. An estimate that only 2.5 of 9 million hectares of maize are commercially viable is cited by Robert Randolph, "Plowed Under," *Busi-ness Mexico*, March 1999.

14. The elimination of the gene ral subsidy for tortillas at the end of 1998 was associated with the closure of CONASUPO. This and other components of agricultural and food policy reform are summarized in Organisation for Ec o-nomic Co-operation and Development, *Agricultural Policies in OECD Countries: Monitoring and Evaluation 2000* (Paris: OECD, 2000).

15. This point is noted in Mary E. Burfisher, Sherman Robinson, and Karen Thierfelder, "The Impact of NAFTA on the United States," *Journal of Economic Perspectives* 15, no. 1 (Winter 2001): 125–44.

16. An assessment of these programs is given by Craig Gundersen, Mara Yanex, Constanza Valdez, and Betsey Kuhn, "A Comparison of Food Assi s-tance Programs in Mexico and the United States," USDA Food Assistance and Nutrition Research Report No. 6 (Washi ngton, D.C., 2000).

17. Nora Lustig, "Life Is Not Easy: Mexico's Quest for Stability and Growth," *Journal of Economic Perspectives* 13, no. 1 (2001): 85–106.

18. For further discussion of this issue, see ibid.; Davis et al., "Policy R e-forms and Poverty in the Mexican Ejido Sector"; and Julián Castro Rea, "The

North American Challenge: A Mexican Perspective*,*" *ISUMA: Canadian Journal of Policy Research* 1, no. 1 (2000): 24–30.

19. The figures cited for Mexico-U.S. and U.S.-Canada agricultural trade are based on trade data from the United States Department of Agriculture Foreign Agricultural Service. Values cited in these instances are in U.S. dollars.

20. An outline of this issue is given in USDA, ERS, "NAFTA Commodity Supplement," Market and Trade Economics Division, Economic Research Service, WRS-99-1A, March 2000.

21. The data for Canada-Mexico trade noted in this section are from Statistics Canada; the cited values are in Canadian dollars. In 1994, one Canadian dollar equaled 0.732 U.S. dollar; by 2000, it had fallen to 0.673 U.S. dollar.

22. See USDA, ERS, "NAFTA: The Record to Date."

23. A discussion of this issue is given by Stephen Haley and Nydia Suárez, "U.S.-Mexico Sweetener Trade Mired in Dispute," *Agricultural Outlook* (Washington: USDA, ERS), September 1999.

24. USDA, ERS, "Special Article: Transportation Bottlenecks Shape U.S.-Mexico Food and Agricultural Trade," *Agricultural Outlook,* September 2000.

25. Ibid.

26. Ibid. An overview of political pressures applied by the U.S. trucking and insurance industries to maintain opposition to lifting the moratorium on the issuance of U.S. trucking permits to Mexican truckers by the U.S. Department of Transport is given in Bradley Condon and Tapen Sinha, "An Analysis of an Alliance: NAFTA Trucking and the US Insurance Industry," *Estey Centre Journal of International Law and Trade Policy* 2, no. 1 (2001): 235–45.

27. For an overview, see Rea, "The North American Challenge."

28. Information on employment of hired farmworkers for both Mexico and the United States cited here is from USDA, ERS, "Hired Farm Labour: Comparing the U.S. and Mexico," *Agricultural Outlook,* January–February 2001, pp. 14–21.

29. Ibid., p. 14.

30. Rea, "The North American Challenge." Details of "Canada-Mexico Letter of Intent to Extend the Seasonal Agricultural Workers Program" and a companion "Letter of Intent on Social and Human Development" are given in news releases of Human Resources Development Canada, available at http://hrdc/drhc.gc.ca (December 2001).

31. For example, see USDA, ERS, "NAFTA: Situation and Outlook."

32. Lustig, "Life Is Not Easy."

33. Rea, "The North American Challenge," and Cornelius, this volume.

14

Transportation: Bottlenecks and Possibilities

Barry E. Prentice and Mark Ojah

Shared social, political, and economic characteristics have fostered a unique relationship of closeness between Canada and the United States. Conversely, Mexico's culture, language, political atmosphere, and economic development create more than a mere geographical separation between Mexico and its northern neighbors. Having evolved in a relatively closed market, Mexican transportation networks were far below the standards of Canada and the United States prior to the North American Free Trade Agreement (NAFTA). Whereas Canadian and U.S. transportation systems are mature and well integrated, transportation networks in Mexico are still under development and in the process of integration with broader North American systems. The isolation and developmental disparity of NAFTA's southernmost signatory is being ameliorated by free trade.

If the rapid transportation growth observed in the first few years of NAFTA is to be extended over the next ten years, many issues and challenges will have to be addressed. Harmonization of regulations, compatibility of infrastructure, and integration of business processes are crucial to the growth of North American trade and transportation in the new millennium. This chapter begins with a snapshot of NAFTA's trade progress and trends in North American transportation. The modal shares of air, road, rail, and marine transport are examined with respect to NAFTA trade and changes in their organizational structure. Subsequently, the remaining impediments to north-south transportation are considered with a view to the coming decade. We conclude with some examples of regulatory and technological change that are likely to affect transportation between the NAFTA countries.

NAFTA TRADE AND TRANSPORTATION

As emphasized throughout this volume, trade between Canada, the United States, and Mexico has grown rapidly since implementation of NAFTA in 1994. While the largest volume of trade is between the United States and Canada, trade with Mexico exhibited the fastest growth rate over the past ten years. At the current level of trade growth, Mexico will soon overtake Canada as the United States' primary trade partner. From 1991 to 2000, Canadian exports to Mexico grew 392 percent, while U.S. exports to Mexico rose 333 percent. Mexican exports to the United States and Canada grew by 437 percent and 468 percent, respectively. By way of comparison, Canadian interprovincial trade grew at the meager rate of 4.7 percent per year between 1992 and 1998.

The rapid expansion of trade in North America during the 1990s has focused attention on the development of north-south transportation links. Despite large increases in freight volumes, modal shares of transportation have remained relatively constant. The charts in figure 14.1 show modal shares (by value) for North American transportation in 1996.

With the exception of Canadian exports to Mexico that rely more heavily on the marine mode, North American freight transportation is dominated by trucking. More than two-thirds of U.S.-Mexico trade and over half of U.S.-Canada trade are transported by truck.[1] The location of Canada and Mexico at the extremities of the North American land mass contributes to the more intense utilization of low-cost, long-haul modes of transportation such as rail and ocean shipping in these markets. Canadian resource-based exports are highly dependent on rail. Similarly, marine exports from Canada to Mexico and from Mexico to the United States are significant, but they comprise only a small portion of U.S. export values to its NAFTA neighbors. Although air cargo's share of North American trade is relatively small, it is one of the fastest-growing sectors in transportation.

Rise of Air Cargo

Code-sharing, carrier alliances, and bilateral air transport agreements have enhanced the international movement of air cargo. Swift development in the Mexican economy and heightened transportation demands for high-value, time-sensitive freight transportation in the United States and Canada have helped promote rapid growth in the

Figure 14.1. Value of Trade by Mode of Transportation, 1996

Canadian Exports to United States

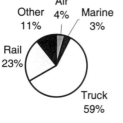

Canadian Exports to Mexico, 1996

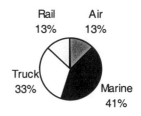

U.S. Exports to Canada

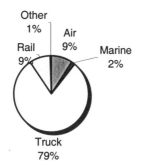

U.S. Exports to Mexico

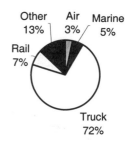

Mexican Exports to United States

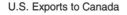
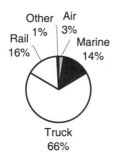

Mexican Exports to Canada

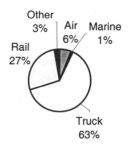

Source: North American Transportation in Figures, 2000.

North American air cargo sector. In addition to the expansion of passenger services, integrated package carriers like Federal Express and UPS are contributing to increased volumes of NAFTA air freight. Cargo airports such as the Alliance Airport near Fort Worth, Texas, are changing the way industry views the role of air freight in international trade. In North America, the air and trucking sectors are both competitors and collaborators in the time-sensitive freight market.

Dominance of Trucking

The emergence of tightly integrated just-in-time inventory strategies in North American manufacturing and processing was made possible by fast, reliable trucking services. But the dominance of trucking in North America varies widely across markets and cargo classes. The disparity between trucking's share of northbound and southbound Canada-U.S. freight movements is due to the greater quantity of manufactured goods and fabricated materials moving into Canada and the significant amount of bulk freight moving southbound. The volume of truck-borne trade between the United States and Mexico is distorted by the *maquiladora* industry that has sprung up along the U.S.-Mexico border. More than one million Mexicans are now employed in these in-bond processing plants, an increase of 150 percent since 1990.[2] Trucks move U.S. semi-processed goods and parts across the border to Mexico for assembly and re-export to the United States. Accurate data on this "ricochet" trade are not available, but it represents a significant portion of recent growth in NAFTA trucking.

The United States has one of the best-developed highway systems in the world. The quality and coverage of the U.S. highway network have enabled trucking to increase its dominance of transportation despite ongoing service improvements in the rail and marine sectors. In Mexico, the historically inefficient and unreliable state-run rail service has made trucking the overwhelming choice for freight transportation. In 1999, trucking hauled 87 percent of Mexican land cargo by weight, versus only 13 percent for rail.[3] Surprisingly, this represents an improvement for rail compared to previous years. Positive developments in the rail sector and the continued absence of significant single-line, cross-border trucking activity between the United States and Mexico have provided a window of opportunity for rail to gain market share.

Rail Consolidation and Realignment

The rail sector in North America has undergone major changes since the introduction of NAFTA. The proliferation of service agreements, alliances, and joint ventures has boosted investment, expanded network coverage, streamlined the movement of international freight, and standardized service levels. North American rail consolidation in the 1990s began with the Canadian Pacific Railway's (CPR) acquisition of the Soo Line. Canada's oldest transcontinental railroad has since forged numerous haulage agreements with the Canadian National Railway (CN) and several U.S. carriers. Almost one-third of CPR's track now lies in the U.S. Midwest and Northeast.

The CPR's chief competitor, Canadian National, was privatized in 1995. This brought about efficiency and productivity gains that have transformed CN into one of North America's most efficient railways and positioned it to reclaim market share from trucking. In 1999, the railway successfully grafted a north-south corridor onto its east-west network through its merger with the Illinois Central Railroad. In 2001, CN's north-south network was completed through the acquisition of the short-line Wisconsin Central Railroad. Today, over half of CN's revenue is generated from cross-border or domestic U.S. traffic.[4] This underscores the international character of the North American rail industry induced by NAFTA.

Major U.S. rail consolidation began with the Burlington Northern–Santa Fe (BNSF) merger in 1995. In 1996, the Union Pacific Railroad acquired the Southern Pacific Railroad, creating North America's largest railway. This takeover was followed by the problematic division of Conrail between Norfolk Southern and CSX in 1999, which created massive service disruptions and led many stakeholders to question the value and wisdom of permitting future Class 1 mergers.[5] In 2001, Canadian Pacific Limited decided to divest its holdings into five separate companies. Analysts predicted that this move was a precursor to the Canadian Pacific Railway being swallowed by one of North America's larger Class 1 railroads.

Given the failure of the proposed CN-BNSF merger in 2000 and the establishment of stringent U.S. and Canadian regulations governing future rail consolidation, doomsday predictions of a North American rail industry controlled by just two carriers is premature. The moratorium on major rail mergers in the United States has expired, but pressure by governments and shipper groups to preserve rail competition in North America has made the likelihood of Class 1 mergers in the near future uncertain. Some industry experts believe that the North American rail industry is experiencing a temporary lull or cooling-off period that will be followed by further consolidation.

Privatization of the Mexican National Railway in 1997 and 1998 permitted foreign companies to bid on fifty-year leases for the Mexican railway's three regional systems: the Northeast, Pacific North, and Southeast networks. The first system to be privatized was the high-density Northeast network that carries over 60 percent of all U.S.-Mexico rail freight. This railway, TFM, was won by a joint venture between the Kansas City Southern Railway and the Mexican transportation and logistics giant, TMM. The winning bidder for the Pacific North concession was Ferromex, a joint venture between 26-percent stakeholder Union Pacific Railroad and the Mexican conglomerate Grupo México. Mexico's struggling Southeast railroad, Ferrosur, was the last to be privatized and has had a minimal impact on North American transportation and trade.

The capital influx enjoyed by Mexico's new private railroads has dramatically improved productivity and efficiency, and has stimulated modernization in Mexican rail. TFM reduced its operating ratio from over 85 in 1998 to below 70 in 2000, making it one of North America's most efficient railroads.[6] Ferromex has also capitalized on privatization; its freight volumes are up by over 45 percent since 1997.[7]

Rail's brighter future in Mexico and North America is a function of service quality. Despite offering lower rates, Mexican rail traditionally lost customers to trucking because of the unreliability of its service. With greater service consistency, improved integration, and the advent of competitive double-stack and refrigerated container services, North American railroads are now better positioned to compete for traffic that is able to move by either truck or rail. In the next decade, both rail and trucking should experience growth, but worsening highway and border congestion may negatively affect trucking's market share. The emergence of a more efficient, streamlined rail sector offering diversified, customer-oriented services may enable rail to regain market share from trucking. This will depend, in part, on sustaining high levels of capital investment in the rail industry, which grew until 1998 but has since declined.

Ocean Shipping

If one considers the extensive overland transportation networks linking Canada, the United States, and Mexico, it is not surprising that

North American trade in manufactured goods occurs primarily via land modes. Bulk commodities such as petroleum and grain, on the other hand, rely heavily on maritime transport. The benefits conferred by port privatization in Mexico and the ongoing infrastructure and efficiency improvements made at ports throughout North America have enhanced the competitiveness of this mode. For example, ocean shipping is currently 10 to 15 percent cheaper than rail for grain and oilseed shipments from the United States to Mexico City.[8] As figure 14.2 indicates for bulk grain exports, the combined market share gains realized by rail and truck in the early 1990s have declined in the face of improvements in the marine mode in the latter half of the decade.

Figure 14.2. U.S. Overland Grain Exports as a Share of Total U.S. Grain Exports (Overland and Marine) to Mexico

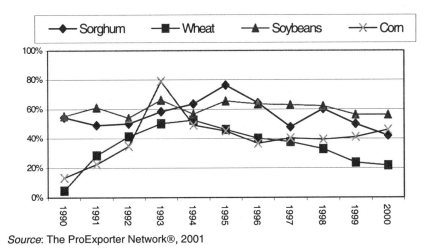

Source: The ProExporter Network®, 2001

Greater port efficiency has been particularly important to the realization of advantages generated by larger ships. As part of the Mexican government's National Development Plan in the 1990s, the country's ports were privatized along with its rail system. The result has been increased capital investments, intensified competition among service providers, and improved port productivity and throughput. At major Mexican ports such as Manzanillo, Lázaro Cárdenas, Veracruz, and Tampico/Altamira, Post-Panamax cranes and fully mechanized bulk receiving terminals are replacing rudimentary infrastructure and facilities of the past. Veracruz is dredging its harbor to a depth of 40 feet to accommodate 65,000-ton Panamax vessels (harbor depth presently limits ship sizes to 45,000 deadweight tons). This may make distant Canadian and American ports more competitive with U.S. Gulf ports for grain exports to Mexico. Larger ship sizes and port modernization are bolstering NAFTA maritime trade, but they are also placing new demands on landside infrastructure and transportation.

Post-Panamax containerships capable of carrying between 4,000 and 6,500 TEUs were brought into service during the 1980s and 1990s.[9] As these vessels become even larger and faster, they achieve economies of size, and per-unit transportation costs fall. Shipping lines employing massive containerships on trans-Pacific routes now offer rates and transit times from the Pacific Northwest to the Mexican port of Manzanillo that are comparable to international trucking services. Mexican importers of apples from Washington State and British Columbia, for example, have found that refrigerated container service via the marine mode is cost effective, reduces product damage, and takes only slightly longer than trucking. On container movements between Long Beach and Manzanillo, ocean shipping now offers a substantial price advantage over both trucking and rail.[10]

The intermodal nature of most maritime movements leaves shipping vulnerable to developments in the rail and trucking industries. Congestion and insufficient landside access are becoming critical problems for ports, intermodal terminals, customs inspections facilities, and the like. With increased volumes of trade moving over all modes, transportation providers and their clients risk being caught up in a spiral of congestion that has the potential to undermine the overall reliability of the intermodal system and its capacity to accommodate further growth.

BARRIERS TO TRANSPORTATION IN NORTH AMERICA

Infrastructure

Trade growth between Canada, the United States, and Mexico has heightened concerns about the ability of North America's transportation infrastructure to cope with increases in traffic volumes. Port infrastructure has already been discussed in this vein. Many container facilities at large North American ports will handle multiples of their current volumes within the next ten to fifteen years. Equipment and technological adaptation is a necessary part of the solution to this problem, but the powerful Longshoreman's Union may have the last say in how quickly these changes are implemented. This highlights the importance of integrated transportation solutions that account for the broad range of factors contributing to the efficient movement of freight.

Another area of concern is highway infrastructure. The age of Canada's primary road network and the growing volume of international truck traffic it supports underscore the urgency of stepped-up investment. In 1997, an update of the Canadian National Highway Policy estimated that $16 billion in improvements would be necessary just to meet the minimal engineering standards on Canada's National Highway System.[11] Some analysts believe that this figure is now approaching $20 billion. Failure to address highway infrastructure needs in Canada is an increasingly important barrier to north-south transportation and trade in North America. Further procrastination will result in critical damage and the necessity for reconstruction instead of less costly repair and maintenance.

Mexico has an excellent network of divided toll highways, but many stretches charge among the highest toll rates in the world and are prohibitively expensive for truck traffic. This has kept trucks on the country's decaying network of public roads, which follow longer, meandering routes roughly parallel to the toll roads. The crumbling network of public road infrastructure in Mexico is prone to delays, congestion, and accidents, all of which fortify existing barriers to trade.

Highway funding in the United States since the implementation of NAFTA has encouraged the development of north-south trade corridors and given priority to investment in infrastructure that promotes trade. Figure 14.3 shows three of the many highway corridors—the West Coast, CANAMEX, and the Mid-Continent Trade Corridor—that have emerged over the past decade as important Canada-U.S.-Mexico trade routes.[12]

Trade corridors are garnering more attention due to the NAFTA-induced realignment of transportation activities. All three countries have realized the economic benefit of investing in the development and expansion of NAFTA transportation infrastructure and facilities. But accommodation of growing international trade volumes in the new millennium will require greater commitment by all three NAFTA signatories. The current dominance of trucking in North American transportation is likely to be challenged by rail and ocean shipping. Governments and industry stakeholders will have to work together to create transportation services that are more seamless across modes and international boundaries. Sub-jurisdictions of provincial and state governments will need to adopt some common regulations to facilitate highway transport. This topic is discussed further in the following section.

Figure 14.3. Selected North American Highway Corridors

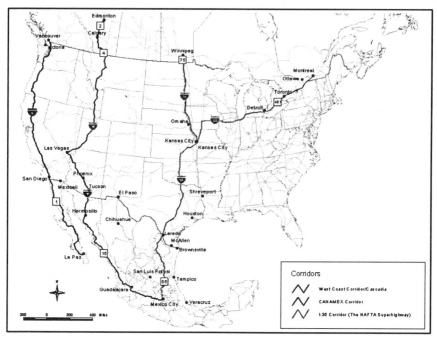

Source: ICF Consulting, 2001.

Regulation

A recently published report on worldwide trade and economic liberalization showed that although Mexico remains a more closed economy than the United States or Canada, it registered the world's largest increase in trade openness between 1980 and 1997.[13] Notwithstanding this improvement, freight movements between Mexico, Canada, and the United States continue to be hampered by transportation regulations and economic protectionism that pose costly barriers to trade. In theory, higher transportation costs imposed by these inefficiencies operate identically to the customs duties abolished by NAFTA.

All NAFTA countries impose cabotage restrictions that are designed to protect national transportation industries by prohibiting foreign carriers from exploiting a country's domestic transportation market.[14] These regulations reduce efficiency in transportation and impede the movement of people and freight. Restrictions on the activity of foreign steamships, trucking companies, and airlines can be detrimental to shippers and the movement of international freight. By limiting foreign competition, cabotage restrictions also serve to relieve pressure on domestic carriers to improve service levels, operational efficiencies, and transportation rates.

Many of the negative effects of cabotage restrictions are evident in Canada's air industry, where Air Canada's dominance is well protected against American encroachment. The 2001 review of the Canada Transportation Act recommended that the Canadian government consider altering legislation to rectify this problem. It also suggested that Canada, the United States, and Mexico work toward the creation of a common NAFTA air market. While it is unlikely that this will happen in the short term, recent progress toward reducing regulatory barriers in the North American air market is an encouraging sign.

Passenger carriers flying between Canada and the United States benefited from industry deregulation in the 1990s and implementation of an "open skies" agreement in 1995. Under this bilateral agreement, U.S. and Canadian passenger carriers are permitted to fly continuous routes serving more than one point in the foreign country, so long as they do not take on revenue traffic between the two points (cabotage). The Canada-U.S. open skies agreement is a notable advance in passenger market liberalization, but it has not been extended to dedicated air cargo carriers.

Mexico has yet to sign a major air traffic liberalization agreement with either the United States or Canada. Concerns that Mexican airlines are not prepared to compete head to head with U.S. and Canadian carriers may postpone the signing of open skies agreements with Mexico for several more years.

In the trucking industry, customs regulations on vehicles dissuade foreign carriers from serving markets where international backhauls are scarce. Canadian truckers, for example, are reluctant to take loads deep into the southern United States due to cabotage regulations. If a Canadian trucker could not find an international load back to Canada from Texas, he or she would be forced to drive north empty until a suitable Canada-bound shipment was found. Without a significant commercial presence in the United States, backhaul freight can be difficult to secure. For trucking firms serving transborder markets, cabotage restrictions can severely compromise the efficiency and competitiveness of their service. If service is provided and backhauls are inaccessible due to cabotage restrictions, the higher transportation costs are eventually passed on to the shipper.

Given the predominant role of trucking in NAFTA trade, a massive barrier to efficient transportation of freight to and from Mexico has been the absence of cross-border trucking activities between the United States and Mexico. Under the original terms set out in NAFTA, trucks from both countries were to be given access to states on either side of the international boundary in 1995. By 2000, reciprocal nation-wide access was to be granted. The U.S. government has prevented enactment of these provisions. Safety concerns were cited as the primary justification for blocking the opening of the border to Mexican trucks. Old, overweight Mexican vehicles with noncompliant braking systems and overworked drivers were said to be unfit for U.S. roads because they posed a safety risk to the American public. However, it is widely accepted that the threat of layoffs in the U.S. trucking industry due to competition from cheaper Mexican services was the primary underlying reason for the U.S. government's refusal to open the border to Mexican trucks.

In February 2001, the Bush administration indicated that it would comply with an arbitration panel decision stipulating that the United States must allow entry to Mexican trucks. Despite the widespread trumpeting of this decision, practical changes to the complex trailer transfer process between the United States and Mexico have not oc-curred. Currently, U.S. and Canadian trailers destined for Mexico must be dropped off on the U.S. side of the border, pulled across the inter-national boundary by a drayage tractor, and then picked up and hauled to final destination by a Mexican trucking company. The reverse proc-ess is required for northbound movements.

Nearly half of the thousands of trucks crossing the U.S.-Mexico border every day move empty, exacerbating congestion and environ-mental problems and driving up costs and delays. A "real" opening of the border could occur sometime soon, but lobbying pressure and threats by the Teamsters and other powerful unions in the United States make the timetable for implementation uncertain. Large interna-tional carriers such as Celadon and J.B. Hunt are preparing to engage in direct, international service similar to what has been permitted for years between Canada and the United States, but several issues will likely continue to impede the direct, single-carrier trucking of freight between the United States and Mexico on a large scale.

Trade imbalances and limited international backhaul opportunities may discourage large-scale cross-border trucking once the U.S.-Mexico border has been opened. Mexico City, Guadalajara, and other popu-lous centers in southern Mexico suffer from trade deficits that make export loads to the United States scarce. Similar problems exist in major urban areas in Texas, where inbound traffic far exceeds the level of exports. The differing sulfur content of diesel fuel in Mexico complicates deep runs by U.S. and Canadian truckers into Mexican territory. Variations in the level of sulfur in diesel fuel can affect truck ignition systems, engine performance, maintenance scheduling, and the selection of motor oil.[15]

High insurance rates for foreign carriers and disparate Mexican legal processes for traffic violations and accidents are potentially serious obstacles to cross-border trucking. Attorneys specializing in this issue have warned of the dangers of foreign carriers operating under laws and regulations with which they may be unfamiliar. The lack of an established domestic sales presence is an additional barrier confronted by many foreign trucking firms trying to break into another country's market. Some industry sources have suggested that as few as a dozen Mexican trucking firms will have the wherewithal to compete in the U.S. market.

Incompatible vehicle-weight limits are additional impediments to north-south long-haul trucking in North America. Weight regulations on roads vary by province and state along all routes between Canada and Mexico (see table 14.1). This mosaic of truck weight limits is further complicated by incompatible regulations regarding truck configurations. Northern U.S. states commonly permit heavier vehicles, while southern states allow higher cube trailers. Many of the heavier, long-combination trucks that are popular in Canada and Mexico are prohibited on U.S. highways. This requires non-U.S. firms to dedicate separate fleets of trucks for transborder movements or forgo full utilization of their assets.

The administration of customs-regulation and border-crossing congestion is another source of inefficiency in North American transportation. Even if Mexican and U.S. trucks are permitted to deliver into one another's territory, trucking firms may be reluctant to tie up new, expensive long-haul tractors in the lengthy lineups that tend to form at major border crossings such as Laredo, El Paso, and Nogales.

Customs regulation problems are most prevalent at the U.S.-Mexico border, but they also create significant nontariff barriers to trade between Canada and the United States. CN's CEO, Paul Tellier, claims that cumbersome U.S. customs procedures result in a total annual delay equivalent to 425 years for drivers crossing the U.S.-Canada border. On the rail side, customs-induced service and scheduling disruptions can affect as many as forty trains per day in busy cross-border rail corridors.[16]

Table 14.1. Vehicle Weight Limits in Mid-Continent Corridor Jurisdictions

Highway Routing	Weight Limits (kgs)	
	Tractor Semi-Trucks	Double Trailer
75 Manitoba	46,560	62,500
I–29 North Dakota	36,287	47,855
I–29 South Dakota	36,287	56,700
I–26 Iowa	36,287	
I–29/I–35 Missouri	36,287	
I–35 Kansas	38,783	38,783
I–35 Oklahoma	40,824	40,824
I–35 Texas	36,287	
85 Mexico	48,500	66,500
54 Mexico	48,500	66,500

Source: Barry Prentice and Bill Wilson, "Future Transportation Developments in the U.S./Canada/Mexico Grain-Livestock Subsector under NAFTA and WTO," *Economic Harmonization in the Canadian/U.S./Mexican Grain-Livestock Subsector*, ed. R.M.A. Loyns et al. (College Station: Texas A&M University, 1998).

Tellier and others are pushing for changes in NAFTA customs processes. These include systems harmonization and automation, standardization of reporting requirements, greater use of pre-clearance and in-bond inspection regimes, and, ultimately, a phasing out of intra-NAFTA customs facilities. These facilities would be replaced by a North American customs perimeter for all offshore freight destined for the continent. While some of Tellier's suggestions are already in the planning and pilot study stages, others (particularly the final objective) may prove overly optimistic even in the long term.

The United States' struggle to combat the narcotics trade, international money laundering, and the illegal immigration of some 300,000 Mexicans per year has contributed to the creation of stringent customs regulations at the U.S.-Mexico frontier. American drug officials estimate that 55 to 60 percent of the cocaine entering the United States comes from Mexico.[17] Across the Rio Grande, Mexican authorities have legitimate concerns about illegal firearms and contraband coming from the United States. With nearly one million civilian crossings and up to 10,000 truck crossings per day at the Laredo–Nuevo Laredo border point alone, officials on both sides of the 2,000-mile boundary have their work cut out for them. In an attempt to ensure that its customs officials do not abuse their authority, the Mexican government has put in place a series of redundant procedures and checks. For some products, more than a dozen documents and two independent customs revisions are required for clearance.

Under Mexican law, documents filed by customs brokers must be 100 percent accurate 100 percent of the time. Customs brokers face harsh fines or incarceration for errors and discrepancies in freight documentation. The meticulous checking and rechecking of cargo by customs brokers and Mexican customs officials causes frequent and sometimes lengthy border delays that preempt efficient international transportation and logistics. Even so, Mexico's president, Vicente Fox, has vowed to crack down on customs fraud and corruption. In May 2001, forty-three midlevel customs officials were fired for "loss of trust." This lot of dismissals came only months after a mass firing of over 90 percent of Mexico's regional customs directors and fifty leaders of the Mexican customs police force.[18] Despite these thorough housecleaning efforts, the complicated and time-consuming customs procedures for freight transportation between Mexico and the United States/Canada are likely to be long-lived.

The intensive inspection protocol brought about by the aforementioned problems has negated some of the benefits conferred by improved border-crossing infrastructure and regulation harmonization and automation. The U.S. Department of Agriculture (USDA) estimates that the current truck crossing process at Laredo–Nuevo Laredo (the principal U.S.-Mexico overland gateway) takes between four and twenty-three hours. Clearance times for trucks at the busiest Canada-U.S. border crossings usually take only minutes. According to a study conducted by Texas A&M International University, overland transit times between Chicago and Monterrey could be reduced by up to 40 percent if border delays were removed. The idling of thousands of trucks per day in border lineups several miles long is the equivalent of a tariff charge on traders. In addition to imposing delays and monetary costs on shippers, border congestion takes a heavy toll on the environment. A modal shift away from trucking may benefit the flow of trade in North America and lessen the environmental impact of transportation activities, but this also depends on the development of truck and rail emissions technology.

LOOKING AHEAD: THE NEXT TEN YEARS

Space does not permit us to adequately address all the potential changes affecting transportation in NAFTA during the coming decade.

Instead, some examples of likely trends in regulation and technology are presented.

Freer Trade in Transportation

Expansion of North American trade under NAFTA has nurtured the creation of north-south transportation networks and focused attention on removing regulatory barriers that obstruct the movement of freight. Partial foreign ownership of Mexican railroads, which resulted from privatization of the Mexican rail network in the 1990s, is indicative of the increasing openness of North American transportation markets. Laborious and time-consuming customs requirements for U.S.-Mexico rail movements are now being replaced by streamlined pre-clearance and in-bond customs procedures, which have helped move traffic through the border expeditiously.

All parties appear to be committed to the further dismantling of barriers to trade and transportation and to the continued reduction and harmonization of regulation. While the Mexican, Canadian, and U.S. governments are unlikely to relinquish all control over foreign competition, their direct involvement in transportation is shifting from economic regulation to safety regulation. Attempts in the North American trucking industry to liberalize market access, establish standard safety and operational regulations, and expedite the border crossings are examples of this trend. President Bush's decision to comply with an arbitration panel decision to allow trucking between the United States and Mexico signified the political opening of the U.S.-Mexico border to trucking. However, a real opening of the border to trucking has not yet occurred.

Over the long term, cross-border trucking could precipitate consolidation in the Mexican trucking industry, which is largely comprised of smaller firms and owner operators that may be unable to compete under the new market conditions. One should not underestimate the role of Mexican carriers though. Like the Mexican rail industry, the Mexican trucking industry has retooled itself in recent years. Although many independent Mexican truckers continue to use older equipment, many midsize and large trucking firms in Mexico use modern equipment comparable to that of Canadian and American firms. Whereas Canada and the United States have experienced years of chronic driver shortages, Mexico has a large, youthful labor force that would be eager to earn wages well below those of U.S. or Canadian truckers.

Environmental Issues

Governments have often addressed transportation and the environment as separate issues. In the 1990s, environmental issues relating to transportation gained a higher profile as scientists presented compelling evidence linking global warming to human activity. The United States and Canada have signed various international treaties and agreements aimed at curtailing greenhouse gas emissions.[19] Over the next ten years, the Canadian, U.S., and Mexican governments may employ transportation policy as a means of promoting greater use of the more fuel-efficient modes of transportation such as rail and ocean shipping.

Environmental legislation will support the adoption of emissions control technologies and alternative fuel systems for trucks. The costs of creating widespread alternative fuel distribution systems, however, are a significant barrier to conversion. As a result, they are likely to be installed first along strategic transportation corridors, such as the NAFTA trade routes.

Environmental changes brought about by polluting activities could instigate modifications in North American transportation. Climate changes attributed to global warming are the suggested cause for record low water levels on the Great Lakes. Continuation of such trends would adversely affect shipping on the Great Lakes–St. Lawrence Seaway system which, ironically, is one of the most environmentally friendly means of moving freight into and out of North America's heartland.

One North American port that stands to benefit if global warming trends continue is the Port of Churchill on Hudson's Bay. Historically, the development of Churchill into a major port has been constrained by its short shipping season. Outside of the July-to-November ice-free period, shipping costs are prohibitively expensive due to high insurance rates charged by international underwriters. Warmer northern summers are extending Churchill's shipping season and providing leverage to the port's owners in their negotiations with international underwriters for more reasonable off-season insurance rates.

Some climate forecasts estimate that if the current rate of warming persists, the Port of Churchill will be free of ice year-round by the end of this century. The port's advantages as an international grain-shipping seaport stem from proximity to North American major grain-producing regions. The Port of Churchill offers low transportation costs to Mexico and other world markets and deep-sea berths that accommodate vessels of up to 57,000 deadweight tons.[20] Large volumes of Canadian and U.S. wheat exports to Mexico could eventually flow north through the Port of Churchill, rather than south to the Mississippi delta ports.

Intelligent Transportation Systems

Technological advances in electronics and communications systems are already shaping North American transportation. Intelligent transportation systems (ITS), which utilize diverse technologies to enhance the efficiency and safety of transportation activities, are a key component of the technological revolution taking place in transportation. ITS technologies include automated traffic control and signal management systems, electronic toll collection systems, vehicle X-ray and weigh-in-motion devices, electronic data interchange systems, and vehicle-to-roadside communications systems. These technologies can reduce transportation costs and barriers for the private sector and government. Less congestion and improved traffic safety save time, reduce infrastructure needs, and diminish environmental pollution.

Experts suggest that the world market for intelligent transportation systems could quadruple in the next ten years. Sophisticated ITS equipment has already been installed at border crossings between Canada and the United States. Since the late 1990s, a border clearance prototype system called NATAP (North American Trade Automation Prototype) has been used at the busy Niagara Falls commercial crossing between Buffalo, New York, and Fort Erie, Ontario. The system is based on the electronic submission and processing of vehicle, driver, and customs information via on-board computers, special transponders, and the Internet. Customs inspectors review the documentation before vehicles reach the border and determine (through random and target examination protocol) if vehicles are stopped for inspection or proceed unimpeded.

NATAP's seamless design is the beginning of a new era for customs regulation in North America. Weigh-in-motion and instantaneous vehicle X-ray technologies are being developed to work in conjunction with this technology. In the near future, a Canadian operational version of NATAP called the Customs Self-Assessment system (CSA) will be employed for larger carriers operating all across the Canada-U.S. border. The goal is to fine-tune this technology and make it available to smaller carriers, and eventually to trucking companies operating throughout NAFTA territory.

RoadRailer Technology

Trade growth has led to the swift development of intermodal transportation in North America. Trucking will continue to begin and end most freight movements, but a growing combination of modes is employed on the long-haul portion of transportation routes. A transportation technology that holds promise for the new decade and beyond is the RoadRailer service. RoadRailer units are standard 53-foot highway trailers that have special coupling and suspension mechanisms that enable them to link up to sets of rail wheels (bogies) and ride like suspended trailer railcars over the rail. Up to 110 RoadRailer units can be assembled into one train and pulled to the destination ramp by locomotives. There the trailers are separated from the rail bogies and hauled to final destination by standard tractors. Unlike trailer-on-flatcar (TOFC) movements, RoadRailer units do not require gantry cranes or flatcars for assembly or breakdown.

Shippers load the units like normal highway trailers and benefit from slack-free air-ride cargo suspension over the rail. Exploitation of both the truck and rail modes reduces energy consumption and pollution, lessens traffic congestion and road maintenance, and lowers transportation costs. Since its inauguration in the 1980s, RoadRailer technology has evolved and service has expanded to dry freight and reefer markets in the United States, Canada, and Mexico. The rapid proliferation of RoadRailer services throughout the continent may result in this technology taking on a greater role in the transportation of North American trade in the twenty-first century.

Container Hub Ports

The expansion of intermodalism has been a driving force in the flourishing containerized freight sector. Standardized shipping containers are more efficient and versatile than truck trailers because they can be double-stacked on railcars, transported by the thousands via containerships, and set onto truck chassis and flatbeds. The imminent withdrawal of many older, inefficient break bulk and general cargo ships from service will fuel growth in North American container traffic.

Containership size has more than doubled in the last fifteen years and is now nearing 10,000 TEUs. The justification for building ever-larger ships lies in the economies of size that they generate. The relationship between containership size and transportation costs is illustrated in figure 14.4. Savings accruing to the new generation of containerships make it viable to containerize lower-value commodities like grains and oilseeds, which have traditionally been transported in bulk vessels.

Figure 14.4. Containership Size vs. Transportation Costs (per TEU Mile)

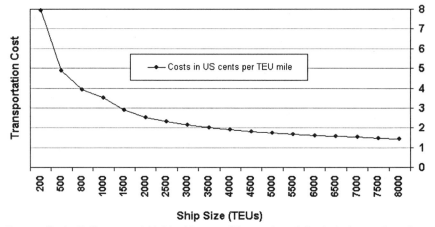

Ship Size (TEUs)

Source: Kevin Cullinane and Mahim Khanna, "Economies of Scale in Large Container Ships," *Journal of Transport Economics and Policy* 33, no. 2 (May 1999).

The sheer size of mega containerships limits their potential ports of call. Ports aspiring to attract these vessels must be situated relatively close to large population centers and handle sufficient volumes to permit the consolidation of large amounts of freight. Other requirements to justify service include a highly productive and reasonably priced labor supply, a deep-water harbor with wide navigation channels, and extensive landside infrastructure with large container storage areas, Post-Panamax cranes, and well-developed intermodal links.[21]

Smaller, less efficient ports will become feeders to the large hubs with the aforementioned characteristics. This emergence of hubs is of concern to ports in northern Mexico such as Altamira and Tampico, which face stiff competition from their immense neighbors to the north, New Orleans and Houston/Galveston. On the North American Atlantic and Gulf coasts, ports such as Halifax, Baltimore, New York, Charleston, New Orleans, Houston/Galveston, and Veracruz will likely strengthen their position as container hubs over the next decade. Likewise, prominent Pacific ports such as Manzanillo, Long Beach,

Los Angeles, Oakland, Seattle, and Vancouver will vie for international container traffic. At the present time, about 60 percent of NAFTA trade is carried by trucks. Coastwise container services could compete for part of this traffic, but they are more likely to grow their own market in the lower value, non–time-sensitive freight.

CONCLUSION

The success of NAFTA in expanding trade speaks to the merit of reducing artificial barriers. The removal of customs duties has stimulated exchange between the three countries, but it has also highlighted impediments to trade that are either not part of this agreement or that remain unimplemented. Transportation issues have become more visible as regulation and logistics costs emerge as the most prominent remaining barriers to trade. The full benefits of NAFTA cannot be obtained until free trade in goods is complemented by free trade in transportation services.

NAFTA has increased the demand for transportation infrastructure and services while promoting greater integration of the Canadian, U.S., and Mexican transportation systems. Safety regulation in the three countries is converging, and economic regulation is being phased out and replaced by free competition. The former, however, is progressing more rapidly than the latter.

Transportation received scant attention in NAFTA, and to the degree that it did (such as cross-border trucking), reforms have been delayed. Thus far, governments and private industry have been more successful in removing infrastructure bottlenecks than regulatory barriers.

North-south transportation corridors are becoming as important as traditional east-west trade routes. Carrier mergers, joint ventures, and alliances are streamlining the movement of cross-border NAFTA freight. Service levels for shippers across the continent are becoming standardized in the core industrial areas, and to a lesser extent in the periphery. Consolidation has also affected competition in transportation. Like most mature markets, the industrial structure is becoming segregated into very large and very small carriers, with mounting pressure on the existence of midsize carriers.

The future of transportation in NAFTA is a function of technological as well as regulatory change. Applications of electronics and information systems promise to reduce costs and assist integration. Similarly, advances in intermodal transport will shape the future of marine and land shipments. Perhaps the greatest unknown is how society will adapt to the challenges posed by the environment. Trade is crucial to our economic well-being, but the transport that makes such trade possible is also responsible for a significant share of global pollution. Undoubtedly, efforts to mitigate the environmental impacts of transportation will shape the system, its costs, and ultimately the potential of NAFTA to integrate the North American economies.

Notes

1. Some caution should be used in the interpretation of these data. A 20-ton truckload of computers could have the same value as a 10,000-ton unit train shipment of grain. If these trade data were expressed in terms of volume, the shares of rail and marine would increase significantly.

2. "Special Report on the U.S.-Mexico Border: Between Here and There," *The Economist*, July 7, 2001.

3. William C. Vantuono, "Cross-Border Bonanza," *Railway Age*, October 2000.

4. Canadian National Railway, "Canadian National's Paul Tellier Urges Level Playing Field, Better Customs Procedures to Help Railroads Reduce Highway Congestion at Canada–United States Border Points," 2001.

5. Major railroads in Canada and the United States are referred to as Class 1 railroads. These include Union Pacific, Burlington Northern–Santa Fe, Norfolk Southern, CSX, Canadian National, and Canadian Pacific.

6. Transportación Ferroviaria Mexicana (TFM), *3er Informe a Nuestros Clientes* (June 24, 2000). A railroad's operating ratio is the ratio of its operating expenses to revenues.

7. Ferromex, company information brochure, 2000.

8. William Hall, "Developing Other Transportation Links: The Maritime Case," *Proceedings of the Transportation Bottlenecks in the U.S.-Mexico Food System*, January 2001.

9. Post-Panamax vessels are ocean-going vessels that are too large to pass through the Panama Canal. TEU (twenty-foot equivalent unit) is the standard abbreviation for a twenty-foot shipping container.

10. Hall, "Other Transportation Links."

11. The National Highway System is 24,460 kilometers of roads connecting Canada's major cities, ports, airports, and international border crossings.

12. The Winnipeg to Mexico City route of the Mid-Continent Trade Corridor is also referred to as the NAFTA Superhighway.

13. James Gwartney and Robert Lawson, *Economic Freedom of the World, 2001 Annual Report* (Vancouver: Fraser Institute, 2001).

14. Cabotage restrictions most often take the form of customs duties on the vehicle or prohibitions on the employment of nonresident drivers.

15. Daniel J. McCosh, "Infrastructure Could Delay Open Border to Mexican Trucks," *Journal of Commerce Online,* February 15, 2001; Jim Giermanski, "NAFTA: Continue Interlining or Operate Both Sides of the Border?" *Proceedings of the Transportation Research Forum,* November 1994.

16. Canadian National Railway, "Canadian National's Paul Tellier Urges Level Playing Field."

17. Peter H. Smith, "Semiorganized International Crime: Drug Trafficking in Mexico," in *Transnational Crime in the Americas,* ed. Tom Farer (New York: Routledge, 1999).

18. Daniel J. McCosh, "Mexican Customs Cleans House Again," *Journal of Commerce Online,* May 4, 2001.

19. Commitment to these accords faltered when the United States decided not to honor previously agreed to provisions of the 1997 Kyoto Protocol on greenhouse gas reductions. This illustrates the limitations of such agreements when confronted with economic priorities.

20. OmniTRAX, at http://www.omnitrax.com, 2001.

21. Michael C. Ircha, "Changes in Marine Technology Impact on Canadian Ports," *Proceedings of the Canadian Transportation Research Forum,* June 2000.

Section 5

NAFTA in the Longer Term: Prospects for Institutional Development

Section 5 explores prospects for long-term institutional development of NAFTA. Essays focus on fundamental revisions of NAFTA itself—what is often referred to as its "deepening"—and on its possible extension to Central and South America, what is generally called "widening." Taken together, these chapters address one central question: what are the chances for major reform?

Rolf Mirus and Nataliya Rylska open the discussion by presenting a hypothetical array of institutional options. As they observe, preferential trade agreements (PTAs) can take many forms—ranging from a free trade area (FTA), such as NAFTA, to a common market or even to an economic union, such as the European Union. In particular, the authors focus on key differences between FTAs and customs unions (CUs). The distinctive feature of an FTA, where each country has its own external tariff regarding nonmembers, is the provision for rules of origin; the distinctive feature of a customs union, by contrast, is the common external tariff. Analyzing the political and economic implications of these two arrangements, Mirus and Rylska maintain that CUs offer special advantages and that, as a result of their dynamics, they are more likely to promote continuing trade liberalization. Transformation of NAFTA into a CU implies a relatively deep level of integration, they acknowledge, and this would require substantial political leadership. They nonetheless conclude that it would be highly desirable—as a next step in the evolution of NAFTA, and possibly as the final step.

In chapter 16 Constance Smith examines alternative forms of currency coordination—another key facet of deepening. Her analysis reveals a rather broad menu of options. It includes: continuation of the status quo, in which each NAFTA member has its own national currency and exchange-rate regime; creation of a common currency, as in the case of the euro; adoption by all parties of an existing currency, presumably via "dollarization"; or, as a less drastic measure, pegging exchange rates against a single currency (presumably, again, the U.S. dollar). Expanding trade and investment within NAFTA have increased pressures for closer currency coordination among the member countries. This would reduce (or eliminate) variation in exchange rates, the costs of currency exchange, and hedging against exchange rates. It would stimulate trade by simplifying price comparisons, and also lower inflation and interest rates. Despite such economic benefits, Smith says, currency union would imply a loss of monetary control for Canada and Mexico. Popular concerns about political sovereignty might thus result in a moderate form of currency management and exchange rate coordination.

In chapter 17, Robert Pastor considers lessons that might be drawn from the European Union's determined efforts to reduce economic and social disparities among and within its member countries. Noting that the EU's programs for regional development and social cohesion have met with resounding success—with spectacular results in the case of Ireland—Pastor asserts that NAFTA should undertake a similar effort. Disparities between Mexico and the other two NAFTA countries (and within Mexico itself) present serious obstacles to full realization of NAFTA's potential. A North American Development Fund could help address this problem. While there would no doubt be political resistance to such an idea, the European experience offers yet another hint: make lower-income regions in the richer countries eligible for small but symbolic levels of support.

Yet another key question for NAFTA concerns the possibility of erecting a supranational authority to guide broad policy and to resolve conflicts among member countries. Antonio Ortiz Mena examines and evaluates the dispute settlement mechanisms (DSMs) that exist within NAFTA. Analyzing cases to date, he concludes that the DSMs have performed acceptably well. The greatest challenges concern the investor-state provisions and, to a lesser degree, the general DSM. Calling for greater transparency, Ortiz Mena proposes modest changes in the short term and more far-reaching changes that may be necessary and viable in the medium and longer term. And in his view, NAFTA's institutions should complement those of the World Trade Organization (WTO) and a prospective Free Trade Area of the Americas (FTAA).

In chapter 19 Linda Reif explores another dimension of this theme, pointing out that—especially with the prospect of FTAA—conflicts may be brought before a variety of forums: NAFTA (regional), FTAA (hemispheric), or WTO (multilateral). Choice of forum complicates the dispute settlement process. For now, all three NAFTA countries belong to WTO, so governments can bring cases before either institution. Reif examines a whole series of considerations behind the choice of forum, as governments seek the most advantageous venue available. She points out that under NAFTA, unlike the WTO, dispute settlement mechanisms are open to private parties. Moreover, NAFTA's Chapter 11 on investment has produced some controversial decisions. This precedent may well influence the investment clause that might be contained in a potential FTAA.

To conclude the volume, Peter H. Smith analyzes prospects for "widening"—that is, for moving from NAFTA toward FTAA. The picture is not as simple as it might seem. Different countries have different interests: not everyone wants FTAA, and not everyone wants the same kind of FTAA. Focusing on patterns of interstate bargaining, Smith utilizes elementary game theory to uncover differing paths and diverse outcomes. Finding only one practical route to an FTAA, Smith concludes that the initiative rests with the United States. A Free Trade Area of the Americas will be desirable, however, only if it meets key concerns of Latin American countries and addresses problems of poverty and inequality.

15

Should NAFTA Become a Customs Union?

Rolf Mirus and Nataliya Rylska

The Canada–United States Free Trade Agreement (CUSFTA) anchored the Canada-U.S. trading relationship on a stronger, more open, and rule-based approach. The conclusion of the North American Free Trade Agreement (NAFTA) represented an opportunity to include Mexico in the relationship, to resolve specific irritants between Canada and the United States, and to ensure that Canada remained an attractive location for foreign direct investment (FDI). The formation of NAFTA, then, illustrates the motivation for forming preferential trade agreements (PTAs)—to ensure market access, to attract FDI, to improve efficiency through competition and specialization, and to apply a cooperative approach to commercial policy.

At the same time, NAFTA and other PTAs—like the EU, CARICOM, MERCOSUR, CETA, ASEAN, and GCC[1]—reflect the difficulty of moving trade liberalization forward at the multilateral level. Some liberalization among a few partners becomes preferable to the agonizingly slow progress at the level of the World Trade Organization (WTO). By improving growth prospects for their members, PTAs also bring the benefits of increased exports for nonmember countries, and that is why the WTO sanctions their formation. The drawback is that PTAs tend to divert trade from more efficient outside sources of supply to the now favored member-country producers.

The question arises whether PTAs should be seen as welcome *building blocks* toward an improvement of the multilateral trading system, or as *stumbling blocks* to WTO-sponsored efforts toward this end. It is too early to judge which of these views will turn out to be more correct. Nevertheless, because the issue of increasing economic integration is likely to occupy significant space in policy debates in many countries, a better understanding of some key distinctions between different forms of PTAs is clearly needed.

This chapter reviews the various forms of economic integration— in particular, the distinctions between a free trade agreement (FTA) such as NAFTA and a customs union (CU) like the one that preceded the present European Union (EU). Based on the economics literature, we show the benefits that can be expected to derive from a PTA, highlighting the key differences in this regard between FTAs and CUs. Concluding that the economic benefits of a CU outweigh those of an FTA, we discuss the implications of moving from the latter to the former.

While faster multilateral trade liberalization would be the best economic outcome, progress at the WTO level appears stalled. We argue that establishment of a North American Customs Union (NACU) may be a desirable next (and possibly final) step in the evolution of the continent's economic integration.

ECONOMIC INTEGRATION

Economic theory shows free trade on a worldwide basis as the best outcome, inasmuch as it allows specialization and exchange to take place globally, thus leading to greater world output and welfare. PTAs among a subset of countries are therefore a second-best solution. They create trade among their members as trade barriers fall, and they divert trade from efficient nonmember producers to members because of their privileged market access. It should be noted that PTAs can take a variety of forms. These range from low-level integration by means of FTAs or CUs to higher levels of integration, such as a common market, economic (and monetary) union, or even economic and political union. A PTA also refers to two or more countries forming a union with lower tariffs (and other trade barriers) for goods and services from member countries. FTAs eliminate tariffs on goods from members entirely, and CUs are FTAs with a common external tariff (CET).

More specifically, economic integration proceeds by agreements to:

- abolish tariffs and import quotas among members (FTAs and sectoral FTAs);
- establish common external tariffs and quotas (CUs);
- allow free movement of goods, services, and workers (common market);

- harmonize competition, structural, fiscal, monetary, and social policies (economic union); and

- unify economic policies and establish supranational institutions (economic and political union).

Thus three progressively higher levels of integration can be distinguished. The first level entails modest integration by means of an agreement to apply symmetric preferential treatment of imports and assign supporting functions and instruments to jointly operated institutions. Examples would be NAFTA's commitment to eliminate tariffs among its members, its dispute settlement provisions, and the various working groups and committees that serve to facilitate trade and investment among the three partners. In the case of a CU, the agreement would additionally involve a common external tariff applicable to nonmembers, which, in turn, requires an understanding regarding how to apportion collected tariff revenue among the partners.

The second level of economic integration would be the harmonization of instruments over which the parties retain control, and through which, due to different national approaches, obstacles to a common market exist. This could be the case in the area of migration of workers, competition policy, and production standards. One example of such harmonization is the European Single Act. Among other provisions, this act applied the "principle of mutual recognition" to product standards. More cooperation and supranational institutions, such as a joint tribunal on competition policy, are also characteristic of this second level.

The third and highest level of economic integration adds coordination of national policies and the creation of further supranational bodies that entail not only economic but, increasingly, political integration. Examples here are the creation of a common currency and central bank, and even a supranational parliament as in the case of the EU.

Free Trade Area

This is the preferred option for countries embarking on economic integration and for those unwilling or unable to engage in higher levels of integration. An FTA can be limited to particular sectors, thus retaining a high degree of control at the national level and preventing exposure to competition for other sectors. The authority to decide how third countries are to be treated remains unaffected (independent trade policy) in an FTA. However, rules of origin (ROO) have to be agreed upon among members so as to determine which products can be transferred duty-free. In the case of NAFTA, a product has to have been substantially transformed so that a change in tariff classification has occurred, or it must have 50 percent (62.5 percent for cars) member-country content[2] to qualify for duty-free treatment. There are extensive and complex provisions on how such content is arrived at and what documentation is necessary at the border. If there were no such ROO, third-country products could be landed in the lower duty jurisdiction and then transferred duty-free to the higher tariff member, thereby circumventing its tariff. As a result, in an FTA, border controls are necessary for commerce among members, and arguments over interpretation of ROO can lead to delays and disputes. These restrictive effects of ROO have led one eminent economist to observe: "It is reported that Canadian producers have on occasion chosen to pay the relevant duties rather than incur costs of proving origin."[3]

Customs Union

When two or more countries agree to remove (essentially) all restrictions on mutual trade and set up a common system of tariffs and import quotas vis-à-vis nonmembers, the result is referred to as a CU. The adoption of a common external tariff and joint quotas necessitates closer cooperation with respect to the sharing of customs revenues collected on nonmember imports. Rules of origin are no longer necessary; when a common external tariff exists, imports into the CU area face the same tariff in each CU member country. Hence there is no incentive for transshipment of imports between members. The CET effectively creates "destination neutrality" for imports into the CU.

Both FTAs and CUs imply that the member countries remain nation-states, yet when viewed in the historical context there are some subtle differences between the agreements. The German Zollverein and the European Community for Coal and Steel are examples of successful CUs. The Zollverein preceded the formation of Germany in 1870 and thus holds fewer lessons for today. The European Community for Coal and Steel, a sectoral CU created in 1951, was not expected to be a precursor to eventual European political union. Nevertheless, it was recognized at the time that free trade, and the consequent rationalization and specialization of production in coal and steel products, would require a supranational body to regulate pricing practices and commercial policies. This historical precedent therefore suggests that a successful CU implies a common competition policy. Subsequently, the European Common Market naturally adopted and extended this competition policy.

A common competition policy would replace the need for, and the application of, trade remedy laws among the CU members. Predatory pricing (dumping) would be dealt with by the common competition watchdog, and Article 19 of the GATT/WTO could be relied upon to obtain temporary relief from import surges that threaten an industry's survival.

That said, the key feature of a CU remains the CET. Derivative issues are a matter of negotiation and will determine the CU's level of success.

Common Market

A common market (CM) can be considered the first stage of deep economic integration. Free mobility of the key participants in the process of production is its characteristic. In addition to goods and services, capital and people move freely inside a common market. The benefits expected consist of further gains in efficiency through a more appropriate allocation of resources: capital moves to where skills are, and people move to where opportunities beckon.

In addition to the common external tariff that defines a CU, in order to ensure the viability of a common market, uniform regulations have to be worked out among the members regarding the movement of people and capital. This is a major task that requires, at least over time, agreement on qualifications and certifications of workers from different member countries.

For a common market to become effective, therefore, cooperation in decision-making is required in yet more areas. Nontariff barriers have to be dismantled, structural adjustment policies have to be jointly reassessed, distribution policies will face harmonization pressures, and fiscal and monetary policies, as a dynamic consequence or by design, will show greater convergence. This convergence results from the increased economic interdependence among the members, and it necessitates that greater consideration be given to the effects of national policies on the welfare of CM partners.

Economic Union

The next step in deep economic integration—economic union—adds harmonized fiscal, monetary, and labor market policies to the common market. Tax and monetary policies affect where a business locates; and because labor market policies affect migration patterns and production costs, these will have to be streamlined among members. There will be no room for different national transportation, regional, or industrial policies because these distort competition among firms from different member countries.

To achieve such a union, it is necessary to form supranational institutions that legislate the rules of commerce for the entire area, leaving the administration to national bodies but with recourse to supranational administrative tribunals to ensure uniform application of these rules. In an economic union, supranational commercial law replaces national law.

For example, the European Union's regional adjustment policy provides infrastructure funds to regions within the EU that have 75 percent or less of the average income level in the EU, with a budget of 0.45 percent of the EU's gross domestic product (GDP). This illustrates the degree of cooperation that an economic union requires.

An economic union is made more effective, furthermore, by a common currency. When there is no uncertainty about exchange rates among members, location decisions and trade patterns will follow efficiency considerations, and borrowing costs will not be affected by an exchange risk premium on a particular member country's currency.

At this level of integration, pressures for uniform taxation policies will increase even if agreement on these may prove elusive, as shown in the case of Europe. The final outcome of economic union may well be a political confederation with unified economic policies. Economic union will stop short of political union if no supranational bodies regarding defense and foreign policy are created.

Shades of Gray

In practice, we observe FTAs and CUs with varying degrees of supranational cooperation or sovereignty abdication. A case in point is the issue of contingent protection—specifically, the imposition of antidumping or countervailing duties and safeguard provisions in case of an import surge.

Obviously the mere existence of such provisions represents a barrier to trade, but producer lobbies tend to be strongly opposed to withdrawing such protection when an FTA is formed. This is the likely reason that most FTAs are characterized by the continued application of trade remedy provisions among partners.

Yet this need not be so. Partners in an FTA and a CU could agree to exempt each other's firms from the application of contingent protection. The Canada-Chile FTA is an example of such cooperation, demonstrating that the distinction between FTAs and CUs cannot be drawn neatly when it comes to competition policy. It is conceivable for both NAFTA and a North American Customs Union to agree to subject member-country firms to each other's antitrust bodies. This would mean that Canadian exporters would be scrutinized for anti-competitive practices (like dumping) by the Federal Trade Commission, rather than by the International Trade Administration (a unit of the U.S. Department of Commerce) and the International Trade Commission (ITC).[4]

CUSTOMS UNION VERSUS FREE TRADE AREA

Each of these two forms of economic integration has a distinguishing characteristic with significant implications. For an FTA, each country has its own external tariff, and the ROO is the distinctive feature. For a CU, the distinctive characteristic is the common external tariff applicable to third countries.

Economic Effects of Rules of Origin

As already discussed, ROO have the purpose of preventing trade deflection—goods or services entering the member country with the lowest tariff for the purpose of transshipment. A number of negative effects are ascribed to ROO in the literature on economic integration.

- ROO create incentives for producers to purchase higher-cost inputs from member countries to satisfy the origin requirements, thus adding to trade diversion.

- ROO lend themselves to lobbying by interest groups. Interest groups may seek protection from foreign competitors by demanding stringent ROO that favor component suppliers from member countries over competing firms from third countries.

- With different input prices in different member countries (due to different tariff schedules), producers face different input costs, thus distorting production.

- ROO tend to be complex. Thus their application results in additional costs and bureaucratic surveillance.

Different criteria—"substantial transformation," "change in tariff heading" (CTH), "value-added," or "specified process"—are possible, and each brings its own set of complexities.

The criterion of substantial transformation of a product is rooted in common law and is decided by the courts in the case of a challenge. On the surface the CTH criterion is more objective "but in fact requires specification of what level of tariff headings to be updated with changes in technology."[5] The value-added criterion poses difficulties because it requires agreement on accounting methods and audits. Finally, process criteria must be specified for each individual product. As a result, interpretation is subjective, and there is substantial room for discretion in implementation. The NAFTA contains two hundred pages of fine print regarding the ROO.

Anne Krueger relates that even where the intent of ROO is not protectionist, they have a significant cost for producers and administrators.[6] In Europe, EFTA producers reported costs of 3 to 5 percent of the delivered cost of goods solely for providing ROO documentation, though this estimate dates back to the mid-1980s when tariffs were higher.

Economic Effects of the Common External Tariff

The effects of the negotiated CET can be summarized as follows:

- Because negotiations are carried out at the government-to-government level, this reduces incentives for individual lobbies. Once established, a common external tariff remains nonnegotiable. On the other hand, internal pressures—as in the well-known "prisoner's dilemma"—could result in a higher CET.

- Given the inability to influence the (re)negotiation of the CET, efforts to increase nontariff barriers may be observed. Common commercial and trade policies would limit such efforts.

- There is administrative simplicity in a CET that makes it easy to implement, and it creates predictability.

- The fact that input costs will not differ among members solely as a result of tariffs will promote efficiency and competition.

Based on these differences, Krueger has shown that an FTA does not lead to more net trade creation than a CU for the same partners, provided the CU takes into account the levels of higher- and lower-tariff countries and settles on an average CET for each commodity.[7]

An FTA also will not be more welfare-enhancing than a CU for the same members, if the CET is set below the level of the high-cost country. In that case, trade is created when the high-cost country cuts production in the wake of tariff cuts. By contrast, an FTA would retain the tariff and create less trade.

Together with the trade-diversion (protectionist) effect of ROO, this implies more trade creation and less trade diversion for a CU. Hence the conclusion that the potential welfare effects of a CU outweigh those of an FTA.[8]

While borders and separate customs procedures continue under an FTA, a CU approximates a larger single market. In negotiations with third countries, this lessens the power of interest groups compared to an FTA, and it makes for more pronounced scale economies and pro-competitive effects. Nonmembers of a PTA will behave in more conciliatory fashion toward an emerging CU than toward an emerging FTA, because the risks of confrontation with a larger economic unit (market) with a common external tariff act as a strong deterrent.

Furthermore, a sufficiently large CU will influence the prices of internationally traded goods, forcing outside countries to accept the prices prevailing inside the CU. Thus the outside countries will export to the CU at prices that include the CET and transport costs, bestowing an element of monopsony power to the CU. This effect is much less clear for an FTA of similar composition. Therefore, on balance, the economic benefits of a CU outweigh those of an FTA.

Political Implications

FTAs are a limited form of integration. By design, little sovereignty is compromised, in both economic and political terms. The institutional agreements for an FTA are not extensive; a secretariat as a monitoring device and a forum for ongoing dialogue among members are all that is necessary.

The existence of ROO mitigates against expansion of an FTA inasmuch as new members need to negotiate new ROO. Each new application for entry provides an opportunity for lobbyists to renegotiate existing ROO, slowing down the process of enlargement in comparison with the given CET of a CU.

In addition, if a country has membership in two or more FTAs (for example, NAFTA and the emerging FTA of APEC), different ROO for different FTAs create administrative complexity and customs disputes. It is difficult to envision the emergence of a single market in the face of such complicated access conditions. By contrast, a CU, by definition, represents tariff unification. While FTAs mean a continuing administrative presence at internal borders for the purpose of documentation monitoring, CUs foster the borderless movement of goods among members.

As a result, the political economy of FTAs is less conducive than that of CUs to further trade liberalization, and the ROO of the former create opacity, complexity, and lobbying room for protection. A CU, in turn, requires cooperation in arriving at a CET and agreement on a sharing rule for the customs revenue that is actually raised. For future trade negotiations, a CU demands a harmonized trade policy, and that means an additional loss of sovereignty.

The question then arises as to how much more sovereignty will have to be ceded to arrive at a CU compared to an FTA. The initial negotiations for either an FTA or a CU are not that different in substance; agreement has to be reached on the schedule of implementing free trade among the partners. Adding on the negotiation to unify tariffs toward outsiders is the extra complication for a CU. The number of partners and the differences of national tariff codes will determine the complexity of these discussions. At present, WTO obligations dictate that existing schedules are not raised to facilitate a compromise with respect to the CET. For this reason, the deliberations for a CU will be more complex. Just as revenue-sharing agreements exist within countries, we observe formula-based voting and international reserve allocation at the supranational level—at the International Monetary Fund, for example. It is not inconceivable, therefore, that an allocation of tariff revenue can be found that mimics international practice elsewhere.[9] Whether or not such an agreement represents a significant loss of sovereignty is a matter for debate.

As mentioned above, one consequence of a CU is that future trade liberalization at the WTO level will force member countries to coordinate their negotiating position closely with one another. A common stance is necessary for a CU, and this need for a coordinated approach represents an additional loss of sovereignty compared to an FTA.

The foregoing explains why it is politically easier to arrive at an FTA than a CU. Trade creation, an economic gain, is viewed as a loss by domestic industry and by other lobbying groups. Hence they oppose it. Trade diversion occurs at the expense of external producers; hence it does not elicit a negative response. And since free movement of workers is an extremely sensitive issue anywhere, a higher degree of integration tends to prompt stronger political resistance.

Political feasibility favors an FTA over a CU. The fact that FTAs have a higher potential for trade diversion and no greater potential for trade creation than CUs implies that FTAs are less likely to encounter political resistance. A CET is difficult to arrive at; indeed, it took the European Union thirty years to overcome national quotas on clothing, footwear, and steel imports. Substantial political will and preparation have to be nurtured for a CU formation. This is made more important by the fact that the economic gains from any PTA tend to be longer term, whereas the adjustment costs tend to occur right away. Not surprisingly, we rarely observe successful economic integration at a level higher than the FTA. By May 1998, 162 PTAs had been declared to the WTO. Of these, only 19 were CUs.[10]

Other Implications

Environmental and Labor Standards

There appear to be no differences between FTAs and CUs regarding environmental and labor standards. Both FTAs and CUs can have subcommittees that work toward mutually acceptable standards. NAFTA explicitly recognizes that certain of its provisions are overruled by obligations that members may have from international agreements such as the Convention on International Trade in Endangered Species (1973), the Montreal Protocol (1987, 1990) on ozone layer depletion, and the Basel Convention (1989) on transborder movement of hazardous wastes. A CU could have similar clauses.

Neither an FTA nor a CU would force harmonization of national environmental standards toward a "more lax" common level. In either form of PTA, arguments arising from standards issues can be handled by the joint dispute settlement mechanism. Environmental and labor standards are therefore a matter of negotiation for a CU just as for an FTA. For example, NAFTA led to a side agreement on workplace conditions and safety because of concerns about enforcement of existing rules in Mexico. This is also conceivable for a CU of members at different stages of economic development. Given that nations tend to resist ceding sovereignty in these areas, commissions with supranational power have not emerged in NAFTA. A CU would not be different in this respect.

Other PTA Commitments

An interesting complexity arises when a country is party to several FTAs, which is the case for Canada (NAFTA, FTA with Chile), Mexico (NAFTA, FTA with the EU), and the United States (NAFTA, FTA with Israel). Can a CU be formed out of NAFTA under such circumstances?

The existence of overlapping FTAs has indeed led to what Jagdish Bhagwati calls a "spaghetti bowl" of tariff rates, with countries levying different rates of duty on a product depending solely on its origin.[11] Even abstracting from the varying tariff levels during the transition to free trade, a world with several overlapping FTAs has become a reality, moving us away from the ideal of the (one) "most favored nation" (MFN) tariff. This development creates a significant practical obstacle to moving from an FTA to a CU; it makes it necessary to agree to a new set of ROO while doing away with an old set.

Concretely in the case of NAFTA, the establishment of a CU for North America would require:

- negotiation of a CET for the NAFTA members that applies to all nonmembers except imports from the EU into Mexico;

- dissolution of existing NAFTA ROO; and

- acceptance by the United States and Canada of the ROO applicable to trade between the European Union and Mexico; similarly for the ROO between Canada and Chile, and between the United States and Israel.

FROM NAFTA TO A NORTH AMERICAN CUSTOMS UNION?

It therefore emerges that a CU brings more economic benefits—and political costs—than an FTA for the same partner grouping. The economic benefits are the following:

- more positive scale and competition effects;

- increased market and negotiation power vis-à-vis outsiders;

- diminished role for lobbyists (protection seekers);

- simplified transborder trade among members; and

- simplified accession for new members due to the CET.

The political costs are:

- more complex negotiations (CET, tariff revenue allocation); and

- deeper integration, hence more harmonization pressure (for example, the need for a common external trade policy stance).

If a CU brings more economic benefits than an FTA for the same partner grouping, what are the steps that can or must be taken to move from an FTA to a CU? Are these steps worth the political costs? No steps would be necessary if multilateral liberalization occurred at a reasonable and predictable pace. In that event, an FTA would gradually become a CU with zero tariffs as the CET. Our first choice, therefore, would be rapid progress in multilateral trade liberalization. Given that the next round of WTO-sponsored negotiations does not look promising at present, it is worth considering the CU option.

Given the current North American context, a North American Customs Union (NACU) would not be intended as a stepping-stone to a higher-order integration, such as a common market or economic and/or political union. In our view, there is no consensus for that degree of integration. Rather, a more modest objective would be to further reduce trade barriers while maintaining independent commercial, taxation, foreign, and monetary policies. In order to achieve a CU along these lines, an agreement would be required to phase out ROO while phasing in a common external tariff and the attendant uniform customs administration.

As for expanding NAFTA or NACU, this could occur under one of two principles—open regionalism or unanimous regionalism. In the former, membership would be open to all applicants willing to abide by the rules of the group; in the latter, new entrants would require the unanimous consent of existing members. Current discussions of a Free Trade Area of the Americas (FTAA) and the expansion of the European Union are grappling with these principles. The CET of a CU would make accession easier inasmuch as negotiations over ROO would be unnecessary.

A CU as a step up from an FTA would involve special working groups in each member state to implement the CET. Common administrative authorities would be necessary to monitor compliance to timelines and schedules agreed upon by the members. Additionally, procedures would be essential for exceptions from agreed rules, for other special authorities, and for financing.

In addition to a uniform customs code, administrative procedures and information systems would have to be agreed upon. As already mentioned, a revenue-sharing rule would become necessary as well. There is also the complication of Mexico's FTA with the European Union, which requires acceptance by Canada and the United States of the ROO in that agreement. To date, little is known about these ROO.

These steps would require considerable political will, but they should face less opposition than the original FTA—for the simple reason that most of the adjustment costs were already incurred when the FTA was formed. Similarly, the previous FTA will already have brought harmonization pressures regarding sectoral, regional, and labor market policies. The experience with the FTA dispute settlement and other joint institutions should prove beneficial.

As regards fair trade rules (antidumping and countervailing duty rules) and competition policy, a move from an FTA to a CU would not bring new challenges. With experience accumulating, moving to a CU may or may not lead to a common market or monetary union, depending on the post-CU integration dynamics. Our reading of the current North American situation is that integration beyond a basic CU is not politically feasible.

CONCLUSION

In summary, a CU means deeper economic and political integration. On economic grounds, deeper is better, as simplified and more harmonized border procedures facilitate trade, common product standards enable longer production runs, and a common competition policy serves to unify the market. The price to be paid for these benefits is reduced national autonomy, a cost that is more difficult to assess. Some harmonization has already occurred without causing much anguish. For example, in 1992 Canada adopted U.S. auto emission standards, thus avoiding separate production lines for cars to be exported. In light of the significant dependence on the U.S. market, Canada's self-interest suggests that closer economic integration be explored to safeguard and enhance market access.

Still, the relatively modest step from an FTA to a CU is more readily urged than undertaken. It requires substantial political leadership. In comparison to the political courage that was necessary to implement the European Union CU, MERCOSUR, or the European Union–Turkey CU, however, the commitment required for a North American Customs Union does not appear that great. These CUs resulted from a strong common purpose, based on geopolitical events (wars, rivalry, the threat of isolation) as well as common economic interests. Yet even these CUs emerged on the basis of an evolutionary process that started with much less ambitious sectoral agreements such as the European Coal and Steel Community.

Seen in this light, a North American evolution from Auto-Pact FTA/NAFTA to NACU seems plausible. However, trade negotiations can take governments away from other pressing problems, and trade professionals are in short supply. Should the multilateral negotiations become stalled, it appears realistic and worthwhile to pursue NACU. What is needed now is a thorough analysis of the economic impact that ROO entail and the political decisions necessary to move to a common external tariff for NACU, as well as the scrutiny of Mexico's rules of origin vis-à-vis the European Union.

Notes

1. See the list of acronyms in this volume.

2. This content is based on the "net cost" test. This method is mandatory for automotive products. Usually exporters can choose between "net cost" and "transaction value" tests. For the latter, 60 percent is the threshold level. It refers to the f.o.b. price less the value of non-originating components.

3. A.O. Krueger, "Free Trade Arrangements versus Customs Unions," NBER Working Paper No. W5084, April 1995 (published in *Journal of Development Economics* 54, no.1 [October 1997]).

4. In our view this would be highly desirable. According to Messerlin and Schöne, more than 90 percent of antidumping cases would not have led to antitrust proceedings on competition grounds, let alone for predation. Whether such a change is achievable is another matter, of course. See P. Messerlin, "Reforming the Rules of Antidumping Policies," in *Towards a New Global Framework for High-Technology Competition*, ed. Horst Siebert (Institut für Weltwirtschaft an der Universität Kiel Symposia and Conference Proceedings, Mohr, Tübingen, 1997), and R. Schöne, "Alternatives to Anti-Dumping from an Antitrust Perspective," Ph.D. dissertation, University of St. Gallen, Switzerland, 1996.

5. A.O. Krueger, "Problems with Overlapping Free Trade Areas," in *Regionalism versus Multilateral Trade*, ed. T. Ito and A.O. Krueger (Chicago: University of Chicago Press, 1997), p. 15.

6. Ibid.

7. Krueger, "Free Trade Arrangements versus Customs Unions."

8. This argument assumes that FTAs and CUs are welfare enhancing, for the group and each participating country. Economic theory allows for welfare-reducing CUs and FTAs, for the group and for individual countries.

9. In the EU, tariff revenue is allocated to the central budget. Value-added tax collections on imports are allocated according to the planned destination of the goods in question.

10. *Trade Blocs*, A World Bank Policy Research Report (Oxford: Oxford University Press, 2000).

11. J. Bhagwati, "U.S. Trade Policy: The Infatuation with Free Trade Areas," in *The Dangerous Drift to Preferential Trade Agreements*, ed. J. Bhagwati and A.O. Krueger (Washington, D.C.: American Enterprise Institute for Public Policy Research, 1995).

Appendix: A Primer on ROO

In "NAFTA Rules of Origin and Automotive Content Requirements," Peter Morici explains the essential role of rules of origin (ROO) for an arrangement that extends preferential tariff treatment. This primer pulls together a few of the key points that have relevance in the current context.[i]

1. If the PTA is a CU, no ROO are necessary for intra-CU trade. A CU has a common external tariff, which means that imports into the CU are "destination-neutral."

2. When the PTA is an FTA in which members maintain different national tariff schedules, ROO serve the purpose of preventing:

    a) transshipment of imports from low- to high-tariff members to circumvent higher duties, and

    b) light processing or assembly (screwdriver plants) by foreign suppliers in the low-tariff jurisdiction for sale in the high-tariff jurisdiction. ROO ensure that only "genuine" products of countries entitled to preferential treatment receive this benefit.

3. As multilateral trade liberalization progresses, the world gradually approaches a CU with a common external tariff of zero—at which point ROO become superfluous.

4. For industrialized countries in the WTO, there is no ROO issue, as they grant and receive the MFN tariff.

5. On one hand, an FTA needs ROO in order to ascertain "qualifying" imports. On the other hand, member countries can use ROO as an industrial subsidy by making their details strict and administration onerous.

6. An example of why NAFTA needs ROO is the fact that Canada, through its (now discontinued) duty remission program, lowered to zero the tariff on imported engines for Japanese producers building plants in Canada. The duty remission program therefore encouraged automotive FDI, but it also enabled Japanese producers to export cars to the United States duty-free, circumventing the U.S. tariff on imported engines.

7. An example of how NAFTA is using the ROO as a subsidy to thread, fiber, and clothing producers is the "thread-forward" rule for textile and apparel imports.

   Beyond a certain quota of duty-free imports (that do not fulfill the ROO), garment imports must be made from North American thread in order to qualify for duty-free access. Such a requirement obviously increases the demand for North American thread and cloth, creating cascading distortions with effects on costs and prices that are not transparent.

   Basically, consumers end up subsidizing the industries involved. This effect is also quite pronounced in the processed-food industry, where ROO prevent the transformation of imported fresh fruits and vegetables into frozen or canned products as a subsidy to domestic farmers.

   Similarly, imported sugar, milk, or peanuts used in processed foods are denied duty-free status by ROO in order to protect North American producers of these commodities.

8. Strict ROO may even have perverse effects. Morici presents the following situation: the 50 percent net-cost rule of NAFTA could induce Mexican producers of, for example, baby carriages to purchase mostly Asian parts and absorb the (then) 4.4 and 12.5 percent U.S. and Canadian duties because the additional cost of using U.S. or Canadian parts exceeds the cost of the tariff.

   As tariffs are coming down in the wake of the WTO's Uruguay Round, this perverse outcome becomes even more likely: lower U.S. and Canadian tariffs provide more incentive for importing Asian components.

---

i. Peter Morici, "NAFTA Rules of Origin and Automotive Content Requirements," in *Assessing NAFTA: A Trinational Analysis*, ed. S. Globerman and M. Walker (Vancouver, B.C.: Fraser Institute, 1993).

16

Dollarization and Its Alternatives: Currency Arrangements under NAFTA

Constance Smith

A century ago, most countries were on the gold standard, so currency values were fixed through the link with gold. Two world wars and the Great Depression of the 1930s led to controls on the international movement of capital and goods. Only in the last decade have international capital flows reached a level of free movement comparable to that prevailing at the end of the nineteenth century. Coincident with the recent liberalization of international capital flows has been an expansion in the number of countries sharing the same currency, either in a currency union or by the formal adoption of the currency of another country.[1] The most significant currency union is the euro zone, with twelve European member countries. Other countries where a currency union or similar type of currency arrangement is now being seriously debated include all the European countries that are not yet part of the European Monetary Union, Australia and New Zealand, the countries of the Economic Community of West African States, and most countries in North and South America.

The debate on a currency union for North America has been spurred, at least in part, by the growth of international flows of goods and capital since the signing of the North American Free Trade Agreement (NAFTA). Technological advances in transportation and communication, and government promotion of international investment and trade, suggest that the trend toward greater North American economic integration is likely to continue. Therefore, it is important to consider the benefits and the costs of a correspondingly closer monetary arrangement among Mexico, Canada, and the United States. This chapter will focus on a North American currency union because it is the most extreme form of exchange rate fixity. As such, it provides the greatest contrast with the current system of floating exchange rates. Also, recent empirical evidence suggests that an intermediate form of fixed exchange rate, such as an exchange rate "peg" (a conventional fixed exchange rate of the Bretton Woods type), is not likely to be sustainable in countries with open international capital flows.

Currency union would mean that Mexico, Canada, and the United States together adopt a new common currency.[2] An alternative method to achieve a common currency in North America is for Mexico and Canada to unilaterally "dollarize," that is, to adopt the U.S. dollar as the legal means of payment. Currency union and dollarization both result in the use of a single currency across North America, so for the most part the distinction between the two is not important. However, these two different institutional arrangements have different implications for central bank governance and seigniorage revenues, which will be discussed in a later section.

The next section outlines the chief benefits of a North American currency union. Some of the costs arising from the loss of monetary control in a currency union are then assessed. The special concerns of the United States, Mexico, and Canada are examined. The chapter concludes with a comparison of the merits of currency union relative to a pegged exchange rate and dollarization.

THE BENEFITS OF A NORTH AMERICAN CURRENCY UNION

There are two types of benefits that would follow from a North American currency union. The gain in terms of expanded trade flows is generally considered the most important of these. A second significant benefit follows from the impact of a reduction in inflation and exchange rate uncertainty on capital markets.

The Impact of a Currency Union on Trade

A single currency in North America would simplify price comparisons across the union. This increase in price transparency is likely to promote trade, with all the benefits that follow. For consumers, the elimination of exchange rate uncertainty would allow customers to choose between suppliers in Mexico, Canada, and the United States without worrying that a foreign supplier's price advantage will be wiped out by a change in the exchange rate. Prices would also be expected to fall overall, as customers could easily compare prices across suppliers from all three countries. Furthermore, the price transparency of a single currency makes it more difficult for firms to price discriminate and segment national markets. As a consequence, competition in North America as a whole would be expected to converge to the level in the U.S. market, a market that has some of the lowest prices and strongest competition in the world.

For producers, the reduction in price uncertainty, as a result of a currency union, would be expected to increase the exports of firms that might not have ventured into foreign markets because of the costs associated with learning about and dealing with exchange rate fluctuations. In Europe, in anticipation of the introduction of the euro, Salomon Brothers estimated that currency fluctuations (and the costs of dealing with them) deterred fully a third of small and midsize German companies from venturing abroad. In France, a study of small companies in the Paris region found that nearly half expect to start selling in new markets as a result of the single currency's introduction.[3]

A related benefit of a currency union is the reduction in foreign exchange transactions costs and the costs of hedging against future exchange rate changes with forward or derivative contracts. A study for the European Commission estimated the benefit from the elimination of these transactions costs by replacing the fourteen independent currencies of the European Union with the euro to be 0.4 percent of gross domestic product (GDP) each year.[4] Lucas and Reid calculate this cost for Canada to be US$1.27 billion annually, or approximately 0.2 percent of Canadian GDP.[5]

Empirical studies indicate that the use of a single currency promotes international trade. More importantly, Frankel and Rose show that the increase in trade, in turn, stimulates national output.[6] Using data for 180 countries over the 1970–1995 period, they find that belonging to a currency union or a currency board arrangement increases trade by the partners in question more than threefold. Using a somewhat different methodology, Rose and van Wincoop estimate that dollarization in Mexico would lead to an increase in trade with the United States of 53 percent, and dollarization in Canada would lead to an increase in trade with the United States of 38 percent.[7] These numbers are large; as a comparison, McCallum finds that Canadian provinces trade twenty-two times as much with other Canadian provinces than with U.S. states, after controlling for distance and size.[8] Using data from after the implementation of the Canada–United States Free Trade Agreement (CUSFTA), Helliwell finds the number is still large, on the order of twelve times.[9] These results suggest that a common currency would lead to greatly expanded trade between Mexico, Canada, and the United States, although country-specific characteristics would probably still cause trade between countries to be less than trade within a single country.

A major issue in the debate in Canada over free trade with the United States was the need for Canadian firms to have access to a large export market to gain economies of scale in production. A North American currency union should lead to increased international price transparency and an expansion of potential buyers. This would facilitate the greater exploitation of scale economies based on national comparative advantage. In the same way that gains from specialization were anticipated following the introduction of NAFTA, the existence of scale economies should increase productivity in all three countries. In particular, productivity gains would be expected in Mexico and Canada, where currency fluctuations may deter small and midsize firms from exporting.

The Impact of a Currency Union on Financial Markets

Countries in a currency union all share the same monetary policy and, as a consequence, experience approximately the same inflation rate. Figure 16.1 shows that the inflation rate in Mexico has historically been much higher than in the United States. In the last five years Mexico had an average inflation rate of 19 percent, compared to 2.5 percent in the United States. Therefore, there could be a significant advantage for Mexico if currency union led to an inflation rate similar to the U.S. rate. By making the commitment to join a currency union with the United States, Mexico would gain a credibility boost in terms of its commitment to lower inflation, since an independent monetary policy would no longer be an option. This credibility effect is sometimes referred to as the gain "from tying one's hands" or "burning one's bridges."

A significant advantage of lower inflation is lower interest rates. Interest rates incorporate the expected inflation premium that investors require to compensate them for the expected loss in the real value of their nominal investment over the life of an investment. The expected inflation gains were striking for Italy, which saw its interest rates shift down quickly to near German rates after the lira was fixed to the euro. According to Rudi Dornbusch, lower inflation in Mexico may also lead to a deepening of financial markets. He argues that with a low and stable inflation rate and a stable currency, economic horizons lengthen, which is conducive to investment and risk-taking, and ultimately to growth.[10]

For Canada, the inflation credibility gain would be smaller, given that Canada already has a relatively low and stable inflation rate that is similar to the rate in the United States, as indicated in figure 16.1. Nevertheless, Grubel argues that interest rates in Canada would drop by one percentage point if Canada and the United States were in a currency union, since a single currency would eliminate the premium that is required as long as investors believe currency depreciation is a possibility.[11] Lucas and Reid provide a more conservative 0.6 percent estimate of the currency risk premium.[12]

Figure 16.1. Annual Inflation Rates in Mexico, Canada, and the United States (percentages)

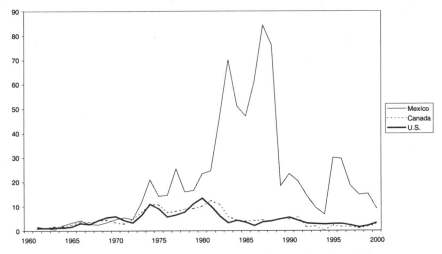

Sources: International Financial Statistics and Statistics Canada Cansim database.

THE COSTS OF A CURRENCY UNION: THE LOSS OF MONETARY POLICY FLEXIBILITY

The Exchange Rate and Output Stabilization

A defining characteristic of a currency union, or any type of fixed exchange rate system, is that member countries surrender monetary policy independence. As a consequence, monetary policy cannot be used to stabilize output and inflation in response to domestic economic downturns or booms. Because each country may have a different economic situation and objectives, Milton Friedman advocates floating exchange rates, which allow "the pursuit by each nation of domestic economic stability according to its own lights."[13]

In Canada, the former governor of the Bank of Canada, Gordon Thiessen, claims that Canada's floating exchange rate has helped insulate the economy by acting as a "shock absorber." He points to the Asian crisis of 1997–1998, when the U.S. dollar prices of primary commodities decreased by about 20 percent. The Canadian dollar fell by about 12 percent over the same period, so the Canadian dollar prices of commodities (which represent approximately 30 percent of Canada's exports) declined by less than the world price, thereby cushioning the negative impact on Canadian primary good exporters. Further, the low value of the Canadian dollar provided an incentive to Canadian producers and exporters of non-commodity goods and services to expand their sales abroad. As a consequence, the negative effects were spread out across the economy and "were less pronounced overall than they might otherwise have been." [14]

The stabilizing feature of a floating exchange rate is more advantageous the greater is the difference in the impact of shocks between a country and its trading partners. For Canada, exports of commodities have become much less important than they were in the 1970s, but Canada remains a net commodity exporter. In contrast, the United States, Canada's largest trading partner, is a commodity importer.

Critics of floating exchange rates point to a number of problems with the view that exchange rate movements can effectively stabilize the economy. It has been recognized, at least since Robert Mundell's 1961 article on optimal currency areas,[15] that the diverse nature of the Canadian economy makes a satisfactory exchange rate policy difficult to implement. For example, a fall in the world price of commodities may lead to a fall in demand and a recession in western Canada. A currency depreciation would raise foreign demand and increase the domestic currency price of exports, and this limits the extent of the recession. However, a currency depreciation also increases the Canadian dollar value of revenues from other export sectors, such as manufactured goods, and exacerbates price inflation in eastern manufacturing regions.

Another problem with stabilizing demand through currency depreciation is the negative impact on living standards. This initial effect is obvious since currency depreciation means goods and assets are sold abroad more cheaply, while imports are more expensive. Thomas

Courchene and Richard Harris argue that there may also be an impact on productivity.[16] This effect comes through the higher price of imported capital equipment. Further, a currency depreciation provides a disincentive for the introduction of productivity improvements since it raises the price of competing imported goods.[17] There may also be greater costs if the market comes to view the central bank as allowing the currency to fall in value in response to negative economic shocks while not allowing it to rise with positive shocks.[18] Michael Porter argues that, in the longer term, the expectation of a lower exchange rate leads firms toward a dependency on price competition and toward competing in price-sensitive and cost-sensitive market segments where competitive advantage is less sustainable.[19]

A final factor to note is that a currency depreciation helps promote exports through a reduction in the price of the home country's products, but only at the expense of other countries, because it raises the relative price of foreign countries' output. This type of "competitive" depreciation can be a major source of international friction. Alberto Giovannini argues that an important reason for moving to the single currency in Europe was to prevent national governments from exploiting monetary policy for temporary advantage at the expense of their neighbors.[20] The competitive devaluations of the 1930s motivated the framers of the Bretton Woods fixed exchange rate system to design a regime that would promote international monetary cooperation and limit the need for currency valuation changes.

The Effectiveness of the Exchange Rate in Output Stabilization

The empirical evidence to date does not provide a consensus on whether a flexible exchange rate regime helps stabilize national output by serving, in effect, as a shock absorber. This unclear result is probably due partly to the inherent difficulty in assessing the influence on output of one factor, the exchange rate regime, given that there are so many factors that may be important determinants of output. A recent study by Christian Broda finds that flexible exchange rate regimes are more effective at buffering developing country economies from terms-of-trade shocks. Using a post–Bretton Woods sample of seventy-four developing countries, he finds that in countries with a floating exchange rate regime, a fall in the terms of trade causes a larger change in the real exchange rate and higher inflation, but a smaller decline in output.[21]

In the case of Canadian monetary and exchange rate policy, while Thiessen claims exchange rate changes have helped to stabilize incomes,[22] Courchene and Harris disagree. They note that the Canadian dollar has experienced a downward trend in the 1990s, but neither commodity export prices nor overall Canadian export prices have shown a similar downward trend. Also, they argue that the tight monetary policy of the late 1980s did nothing to help Canada make the structural adjustments necessitated by the introduction of the Canada–United States Free Trade Agreement.[23] Another observer of Canadian monetary policy, Canadian-born Nobel Laureate Robert Mundell claims that the zero inflation policy announced in early 1987 was a huge mistake at a time when the United States was maintaining an inflation rate of 4 percent. Because there was no serious dialogue between the Bank of Canada and the Canadian public about the implications of this policy, expectations were not correctly adjusted to a policy that would have required (assuming equal growth rates in the United States and Canada) increases in Canadian wage rates that were 4 percentage points less than the increase in U.S. wage rates, as well as Canadian bond yields that were 4 percentage points less than U.S. bond yields. Mundell argues that it was this exercise of an independent Canadian monetary policy that led to two-digit unemployment at a time when the U.S. unemployment rate was falling below 5 percent.[24]

An observer of Mexican monetary and exchange rate policy, Rudi Dornbusch, argues that exchange rate policy has hindered more than helped stabilize Mexican income. He notes that for the last twenty-five years (which include both the floating rate period since 1995 and the earlier period when the peso was pegged to the U.S. dollar) the currency collapsed every six years, shortly after each new president took office. He adds that, "Far from being used as a stabilization device, the exchange rate has been the very focus of economic instability and dismal macroeconomic performance."[25]

Canadian and Mexican monetary and exchange rate policies have, with hindsight, involved many mistakes, but it is important to consider as well the monetary policy of the United States, which would be the largest country in the monetary union and, thus, would play a key role in the determination of monetary policy. Longtime observer of U.S. monetary policy Milton Friedman notes that, "The history of U.S. monetary policy since the establishment of the Fed has many more periods of poor than of good policy."[26] Although recent U.S. monetary policy has maintained relatively low inflation and strong output growth, monetary management is inherently very difficult. As a consequence, there will always be some uncertainty about whether the monetary policy of a North American currency union would be more stabilizing than the monetary policies of the three individual member countries.

The Implications of Technological Change for Floating Currencies

In recent years, technological and regulatory changes have altered the ability of central banks to conduct independent monetary policy and, thereby, to stabilize national income. To control prices and the exchange rate, central banks use their power over the domestic money supply, which in most countries is the only legal means of payment. Recent technological advances, such as electronic banking and credit cards, along with reductions in required reserves on bank deposits, have shrunk the size of high-powered money and, arguably, the effectiveness of monetary policy. As a consequence, a floating exchange rate is not necessarily associated with significant monetary policy independence.

In Canada and Mexico, as elsewhere in the world, it has become simpler for multinational corporations to make transfers between their branches or subsidiaries, using whatever currency is most convenient. As well, reductions in restrictions on holding foreign currency deposits have facilitated the coexistence of different currencies in one country. In Argentina, approximately 70 percent of transactions are conducted in U.S. dollars, even though the legal currency is the Argentine peso. There has been a movement toward the use of the euro in Switzerland, a country that conducts about 70 percent of its trade with the European Union (but itself is a not a member country).

As a consequence of globalization and technological change, it is easier to switch out of the domestic currency if individuals and firms are unhappy with the domestic monetary standard—because, for example, a high domestic inflation rate creates uncertainty about the domestic currency's value. International Monetary Fund economist Paul Masson predicts that, in future, payments may be made increasingly out of the control of governments, and currency use may be dictated more by private choice.[27] This type of change would be expected to lead to greater competition between monies and a move toward fewer currencies. For firms operating in Mexico and Canada, greater private-sector use of the U.S. dollar might be expected (since the United States is the dominant trading partner for both countries) even if both countries retain their floating exchange rate systems.

CONSIDERATIONS FOR THE UNITED STATES, MEXICO, AND CANADA

For each of the three signatories to NAFTA, there are specific factors that are important in a debate on currency union.

Specific Considerations for the United States

As discussed above, currency union would be expected to lead to an increase in trade among the NAFTA countries. For this reason, the gains in the United States are likely to be similar to the gains from trade that followed the North American and Canada-U.S. trade agreements. In addition, there is potential for a currency union to lead to an increase in financial stability in the region, and this could benefit U.S. investors. For example, greater financial stability would reduce the possibility of a repeat of the currency crisis in Mexico in 1994–1995, when U.S. investors in Mexico put pressure on the U.S. government for a financial aid package.[28]

Another implication of a North American currency union is that it would rule out the use of "competitive" devaluations by Canada and Mexico. Canada and Mexico are two of the largest trading partners of the United States. They account for 36 percent of U.S. merchandise exports (23.5 percent are destined for Canada, and 12.5 percent go to Mexico) and 29 percent of U.S. merchandise imports (19 percent are from Canada, and 10 percent are from Mexico).[29] In recent years, U.S. policymakers have been less preoccupied with the large U.S. trade deficit. However, in the 1970s and 1980s, concern about U.S. trade deficits was a significant policy issue. Paul Krugman argues that an important reason the United States favored the NAFTA was the belief that it would help reduce the U.S. trade deficit with Mexico.[30] Therefore, it is certainly possible that the pursuit of independent exchange rate policies by Canada and Mexico could become a trade irritant for the United States in the future.

Currency union in North America would require that the U.S. Federal Reserve adopt new governing rules to accommodate Mexico and Canada. Fred Bergsten, the director of the Washington, D.C.–based Institute for International Economics, states that if Canada and Mexico decided to adopt the U.S. dollar, there would probably be a noticeable impact on U.S. monetary conditions that would require an adjustment in the conduct of U.S. monetary policy. In this event, he notes that, "we would have to contemplate accepting those countries as new Federal Reserve districts and giving them seats on the Fed's Open Market Committee."[31] However, given that the United States represents 68 percent of the three-country population and its economy produces 89 percent of the GDP, it seems probable that whatever governing arrangements were chosen, the United States would have the dominant role in the conduct of monetary policy in the union.

Specific Considerations for Mexico

One of the gains in joining a currency union is the reduction in currency conversion costs that firms must bear in order to trade internationally. This gain is larger the greater is the amount of trade (and potential trade) between countries. Most of Mexico's trade is with the United States: 88 percent of Mexico's merchandise exports go to the United States, and 74 percent of its merchandise imports come from that country. This trade is also large relative to total output in the economy. Merchandise exports to the United States in 1999 were equal in value to approximately 25 percent of Mexican GDP.[32]

Mexico currently maintains a floating exchange rate, but until the currency crisis in 1994–1995, the value of the peso was pegged to the U.S. dollar (although the pegged level changed periodically). The governor of the Bank of Mexico, Guillermo Ortiz, said in 1999 that Mexico's experience with a floating exchange rate was generally positive. He noted that the floating rate had not impeded efforts to significantly lower inflation rates, foreign investment flows had held reasonably steady, and the floating regime had allowed Mexico to weather the Asian, Russian, and Brazilian shocks "in a very satisfactory fashion."[33]

The current Mexican president, Vicente Fox, elected in 2000, has stated that he is in favor of a currency union with the United States, although he felt this change would require considerable time.[34] The chief reason currency union would be difficult at the moment is the wide divergence between the inflation rates in Mexico and the United States, as shown in figure 16.1. As this figure indicates, the trend in Mexico is toward lower inflation rates. However, a currency union is only likely to be feasible when markets and governments in Mexico become accustomed to a low inflation environment. Union before this would potentially lead to serious imbalances in the Mexican economy.

Specific Considerations for Canada

Canada has more experience with a floating exchange rate than most countries. It maintained a floating exchange rate from September 1950 to May 1962, when most currencies in the world were fixed to the U.S. dollar. The Canadian dollar began to float again on May 31, 1970, before the general breakdown of the Bretton Woods system in 1973. Nevertheless, the inflation rate in Canada has closely followed the rate in the United States (as indicated in figure 16.1), as has Canadian monetary policy. This historical similarity between the monetary policies of the two countries means that it would probably be relatively easy for consumers, firms, and governments in Canada to adapt to a currency union with the United States.

For Canada, the benefits of a currency union with the United States have increased as a result of the large expansion in trade that followed the Canada–United States Free Trade Agreement. Between 1988 and 2000, Canada's exports of goods and services to the United States, as a share of total exports, increased from 71 percent to 82 percent. Even more dramatic has been the increase in exports of goods and services to the United States as a ratio of GDP, which rose from 19 percent to 37 percent during the same period.[35] International trade has also grown relative to trade within Canada. In 1992, the ratio of international exports to inter-provincial exports of goods and services was 1.42. By 1999 this ratio had increased to 2.19.[36] Since 82 percent of Canada's exports are destined for the United States, these numbers indicate that, as Courchene and Harris state, "north-south trade clearly exceeds east-west trade in the aggregate."[37] Given that the benefits of a currency union increase with the amount of trade, the benefits to Canada could be large, and the current trends suggest that these benefits may increase in the future.

In Canada, a potential concern with a currency union is whether it would necessarily lead to greater coordination with U.S. fiscal and other government policies. Although fiscal policies would have to be consistent with monetary policy (in that the federal government could no longer finance a fiscal deficit through money creation), evidence from other countries suggests that monetary union does not require a fiscal union. Even in the euro zone, while there exist some specific European Union programs to transfer funds between countries (mainly as agricultural transfers), there are no plans to introduce transfers with the purpose of stabilizing incomes to compensate for the loss of monetary policy flexibility. Furthermore, under the Bretton Woods system, fiscal convergence was not envisaged, and a fixed exchange rate was not viewed as a hindrance to the introduction of social welfare programs, such as Medicare in Canada in the 1960s. Finally, the Canadian and U.S. economies are already closely linked, and the pressure to harmonize (corporate income tax rates, for example) is likely to continue regardless of whether Canada maintains a floating exchange rate or joins a currency union with the United States.

CURRENCY UNION VERSUS OTHER TYPES OF FIXED EXCHANGE RATE REGIMES

A currency union is similar to any fixed exchange rate system to the extent that, whenever exchange rates are not variable, price comparisons are simplified and exchange rate uncertainty is reduced. Given that a currency union represents the strongest form of exchange rate fixity, it is useful to consider the merits of a currency union relative to the other major fixed exchange rate alternatives: pegged exchange rates and dollarization.

Currency Union versus a Pegged Exchange Rate

An obvious advantage of a currency union relative to a pegged, or simple fixed exchange rate, system is lower currency trading transactions costs. As noted earlier, a single currency circulates within a currency union, so the costs of changing currencies and hedging against possible future exchange rate changes are eliminated. With a fixed exchange rate, as with a floating exchange rate, these costs persist, although the hedging costs will be smaller the smaller is the perceived probability that the currency will be devalued.

The other advantage of a currency union over a fixed exchange rate is that, because it is more costly to set up, it is a more credible commitment. In the early 1990s, the market did not view as credible the simple fixed exchange rate with the German mark of the British pound and the Italian lira. The contractionary monetary policy and high interest rates in Germany at that time, plus the slow growth in Europe, led financial markets to speculate (correctly) that the pound and lira fixed exchange rates with the mark would be abandoned. However, since the formation of the currency union between the twelve countries in the euro currency zone in January 1999, speculative capital movements in the zone have disappeared.

Speculative attacks on a currency can be limited somewhat by controls on international capital, which were widespread during the Bretton Woods period of fixed exchange rates. However, as far back as 1950, the decision in Canada to let the Canadian dollar float was prompted by the view that restrictions on international capital flows were untenable in a country so dependent on foreign capital.[38] The experience of the 1990s in Europe and elsewhere led the International Monetary Fund's first deputy managing director, Stanley Fischer, to conclude that an exchange rate peg is not sustainable in a country with free capital flows.[39] Given that Mexico, the United States, and Canada allow the free flow of international capital,[40] a fixed exchange rate system is unlikely to be viable in the longer term. [41]

Currency Union versus Dollarization

A North American currency union would be governed taking into account the input of all three member countries.[42] With dollarization, Canada and Mexico would have no influence on the conduct of U.S. monetary policy. For this reason, a policy of dollarization may be less acceptable from a political standpoint. However, Drummond, Lévesque, and Alexander argue that dollarization is the only viable fixed exchange rate regime for Canada since a pegged rate is not sustainable and the United States is not interested in a currency union.[43] Dollarization is also worth considering because "market dollarization," where private-sector agents increasingly conduct their affairs in U.S. dollars, may become more important if higher trade flows lead to greater use of the U.S. dollar in Mexico and Canada.[44] The implications of dollarization, other than the obvious one of no input into monetary policy decisions, include the loss of seigniorage revenues; the question of what institution will act as a "lender of last resort," a role usually fulfilled by the national central bank; and the less credible commitment to a fixed exchange rate.

Seigniorage revenues exist because people give up real resources in exchange for currency, while the cost to the central bank of printing money is near zero. In a currency union all members share the seigniorage revenues.[45] By contrast, under dollarization, individuals in Mexico and Canada would have to give up real resources (through exports to the United States) to acquire U.S. dollars. Lucas and Reid estimate that the cost of the loss of seigniorage revenue from unilateral adoption of the U.S. dollar as legal currency in Canada would be approximately 0.4 of 1 percent of GDP.[46] This cost is not trivial. As an indication of its size, it is of the same order of magnitude as estimates of the reduction in exchange rate conversion and hedging costs that would follow from a currency union.[47]

Dollarization would also raise the question of which institution would assume the role of "lender of last resort" for the banking system. In Mexico, the governor of the central bank takes the view that dollarization requires a very strong financial system with ample liquidity and credit lines from abroad if it is to function without a lender of last resort.[48] In a country that issues its own currency, the central bank has the ability to issue money, and this is sometimes viewed as enhancing confidence in the banking system in the case of a crisis. However, Dornbusch argues that in a banking crisis real resources are required, where good credit (not money) must replace bad credit to restore confidence. He notes that this is intrinsically a role of the Treasury or for the world capital market, rather than for the central bank.[49] Thus the domestic government could act as a lender of last resort even if it did not have the ability to print money.

A final difference between dollarization and a currency union is that the cost of dollarization is lower than the cost of setting up a currency union. Thus there is less policy commitment to the regime. As a consequence, the credibility impact on inflation expectations and interest rates is weaker.

CONCLUSION

The general trend toward fewer currencies in the world and the expansion of trade between the NAFTA countries are likely to increase pressure for closer currency arrangements among the United States, Canada, and Mexico. As outlined above, the benefits of a currency union rise with the amount of trade since currency union eliminates exchange rate variation and the costs of currency exchange and exchange rate hedging. Moreover, the main cost of a currency union—the loss of monetary control—is expected to continue to decline over time due to regulatory and technological changes. These changes have reduced high-powered money, which has made independent monetary policy control more difficult and has made it easier for domestic transactions to be conducted in foreign currencies, such as U.S. dollars.

One consideration that has not yet been addressed, but that may limit enthusiasm for a North American currency union, is the cultural attachment to a national currency. The importance of this is difficult to measure, but experience in Europe suggests that this attachment declines the weaker is a currency. For example, polls indicate that there was significant reluctance in Germany to give up the mark but much enthusiasm in Italy to adopt the euro. In Canada, McCallum notes that the desire to maintain the Canadian dollar may be less strong in Quebec than in other parts of the country.[50] In fact, currency union with the United States is even favored by the current Quebec government, which advocates political independence for Quebec and is eager to limit its ties to the rest of Canada.

Even if the governments of the United States, Mexico, and Canada decide that a currency union is in the best interests of their three countries, public opinion would be expected to play a role in determining whether a common currency is actually adopted. In Europe, several countries, including France and Ireland, held a national referendum on the Maastricht Treaty, which included the provisions for a currency union. In Denmark, Sweden, and the United Kingdom, which are all members of the European Union but not members of the euro zone, the ruling parties stated that, once they decide that it is in the country's best interest to adopt the euro, they would put the question to a national referendum.[51]

A democratic vote in favor of currency union makes the decision to join legitimate. As a consequence, if a government is under pressure to devalue during an economic downturn, public support for the currency union would motivate policymakers to keep the country within the union and to utilize other instruments of stabilization. Therefore, a significant advantage of a positive referendum result is that it strengthens the credibility of the currency union.

Notes

1. In the ten years between 1990 and 1999, the number of countries that had no national currency because they are part of a currency union, have dollarized by formally adopting the currency of another country, or have a currency board, mushroomed from three to forty-five. These countries incorporate approximately one-quarter of all IMF member countries. See Stanley Fischer, "Distinguished Lecture on Economics in Government—Exchange Rate Regimes: Is the Bipolar View Correct?" *Journal of Economic Perspectives* 15, no. 2 (Spring 2001): 3–24. Since 1999, Greece has joined the euro zone countries, and Ecuador and El Salvador have chosen to dollarize.

2. Herbert G. Grubel has proposed that this North American currency be called the "amero." Grubel, *The Case for the Amero: The Economics and Politics of a North American Monetary Union* (Vancouver, B.C.: Fraser Institute, 1999).

3. "When the Walls Come Down," *The Economist*, July 5, 1997, pp. 61–63.

4. Commission of the European Communities, "One Market, One Money: An Evaluation of the Potential Benefits and Costs of Forming an Economic and Monetary Union," *European Economy*, October 1990.

5. R.F. Lucas and B. Reid, "The Choice of Efficient Monetary Arrangements in the Post Meech Lake Era," *Canadian Public Policy* 17, no. 4 (1991): 417–33.

6. Frankel and Rose find that every one percent increase in trade (relative to GDP) raises income per capita by at least one-third of a percent over a twenty-year period. Jeffrey A. Frankel and Andrew K. Rose, *An Estimate of the Effect of Common Currencies on Trade and Income* (Cambridge, Mass.: John F. Kennedy School of Government, Harvard University, April 2001).

7. Andrew K. Rose and Eric van Wincoop, "National Money as a Barrier to International Trade: The Real Case for Currency Union," *American Economic Review* 91, no. 2 (May 2001): 386–90.

8. John McCallum, "National Borders Matter: Canada-U.S. Regional Trade Patterns," *American Economic Review* 85, no. 3 (June 1995): 615–23.

9. John Helliwell, "Do National Borders Matter for Quebec's Trade?" *Canadian Journal of Economics* 29, no. 3 (August 1996): 507–22.

10. Rudi Dornbusch, "Fewer Monies, Better Monies," *American Economic Review* 91, no. 2 (May 2001): 238–42.

11. Grubel, *The Case for the Amero*, p. 63.

12. Lucas and Reid, "The Choice of Efficient Monetary Arrangements in the Post Meech Lake Era."

13. Milton Friedman, "The Case for Flexible Exchange Rates," *Essays in Positive Economics* (Chicago: University of Chicago Press, 1953), p. 158.

14. Gordon Thiessen, "The Conduct of Monetary Policy When You Live Next Door to a Large Neighbour," remarks to the Canadian Society of New York, March 9, 2000 (Ottawa: Bank of Canada, 2000).

15. Robert A. Mundell, "A Theory of Optimum Currency Areas," *American Economic Review* 51, no. 4 (September 1961): 657–65.

16. Thomas J. Courchene and Richard G. Harris, *From Fixing to Monetary Union: Options for North American Currency Integration* (Toronto: C.D. Howe Institute, June 1999), p. 8.

17. This argument is similar to that of Michael Porter, who claims that while in a static world a reduction in factor cost arising from a currency depreciation would benefit industry, in a dynamic world, artificially intervening to keep down the value of the currency "removes pressures for innovation and upgrading.... Instead of improving quality, introducing more sophisticated new models, and lowering manufacturing costs through automation, firms breathe a sigh of relief and collect profits." Michael Porter, *The Competitive Advantage of Nations* (New York: Free Press, 1990), p. 641.

18. For example, Jeffrey Rubin suggests that this is the case for the Canadian dollar. Rubin, "Heading for 60 Cents," *Monthly Indicators* (CIBC World Markets), November 2000.

19. Porter, *The Competitive Advantage of Nations*, pp. 352, 641.

20. Alberto Giovannini, "Letters," *The Economist*, July 11, 1992.

21. Broda finds that after a 10 percent fall in the terms of trade, in the short run real output falls by over 2 percent in the average country with a pegged exchange rate, compared to less than half a percent in countries with a floating exchange rate. Christian Broda, "Coping with Terms of Trade Shocks: Pegs versus Floats," *American Economic Review* 91, no. 2 (May 2001): 376–80.

22. Thiessen, "The Conduct of Monetary Policy When You Live Next Door to a Large Neighbour."

23. Courchene and Harris, *From Fixing to Monetary Union*.

24. Robert Mundell, "Canada's Dollar: To Fix or Not," *National Post*, December 12, 2000.

25. Dornbusch, "Fewer Monies, Better Monies," p. 241.

26. Milton Friedman, "Canada's Dollar: To Fix or Not," *National Post*, December 12, 2000.

27. See the discussion in the *IMF Survey*, " Economic Forum" (Washington, D.C.: IMF, December 11, 2000): 391–93.

28. Under pressure from market participants in the United States in 1994–1995, the U.S. government offered Mexico a financing package of $40 billion. See Arminio Fraga, "From Halifax to Lyons: What Has Been Done about Crisis Management?" *Essays in International Finance* (Princeton University) 200 (1996): 46–55.

29. These figures are from the International Monetary Fund's *Direction of Trade Statistics*, 1999.

30. Paul Krugman, "Book Review of *NAFTA: An Assessment* by Gary Clyde Hufbauer and Jeffrey J. Schott," *Journal of Economic Literature* 33, no. 2 (June 1995): 849–51.

31. Fred Bergsten, *Dollarization in Emerging-Market Economies and Its Policy Implications for the United States* (Washington, D.C.: Institute for International Economics, 1999), p. 6.

32. Based on data from the International Monetary Fund's *Direction of Trade Statistics* and *International Financial Statistics*.

33. Sheila Meehan, "Economic Forum: Participants Debate Benefits and Challenges of Dollarization for Latin American Economies," *IMF Survey* 28, no. 14 (July 19, 1999): 238–40.

34. Fox's comments were made during a visit to Ottawa in 2000. See Roy Culperer, introductory remarks at the conference "Dollarization in the Western Hemisphere," Ottawa, North-South Institute, October 4, 2000.

35. If trade in services is excluded, exports of goods rose from 17 to 34 percent as a ratio of GDP between 1988 and 2000 (*Statistics Canada*).

36. See *Statistics Canada.*

37. Courchene and Harris, *From Fixing to Monetary Union*, p. 11.

38. James Powell, *A History of the Canadian Dollar* (Ottawa: Bank of Canada, 1999).

39. Fischer, "Distinguished Lecture on Economics in Government."

40. Mexico maintains some controls on international flows of capital, but Minushkin and Ortiz Mena argue that these controls have little effect. Susan Minushkin and Antonio Ortiz Mena, *The Institutional Structure of Financial and Monetary Integration in the Americas* (Mexico City: Centro de Investigación y Docencia Económicas, 2001).

41. Another type of fixed exchange rate system, a currency board, provides a stronger exchange rate fix than a simple peg, but because it is very similar to a standard fixed exchange rate, it will not be considered here.

42. There are few precedents as to how the separate countries should provide input to guide the conduct of the central bank. The appropriate governing system for the European Central Bank remains controversial, especially with respect to the role of new member countries. For a discussion of some of the issues related to governance of a North American monetary authority, see Willem H. Buiter, "The EMU and the NAMU: What Is the Case for North American Monetary Union?" *Canadian Public Policy* 25, no. 3 (1999): 285–305.

43. Don Drummond, Marc Lévesque, and Craig Alexander, *The Penny Drops* (Toronto: TD Economics, April 2001).

44. While there has long been limited use of U.S. dollars in the Canadian economy, Courchene and Harris (*From Fixing to Monetary Union*, p. 21) warn this trend may accelerate and "it would be a major mistake on the part of Canada's monetary authorities to assign a zero probability to a dollarization scenario."

45. In the euro zone, Article 33(1.b) of the Protocols and Declarations annexed to the Maastricht Treaty provides for the transfer of the European Central Bank's net profits (except for a maximum of 20 percent transferred to the general reserve fund) to the shareholders (the national central banks) in proportion to their paid-up shares. Article 29 states that the share allocation is 50 percent based on population and 50 percent based on country GDP.

46. Lucas and Reid, "The Choice of Efficient Monetary Arrangements in the Post Meech Lake Era." These authors calculate the cost to be approximately US$2.5 billion in 1991.

47. The seigniorage lost by a country is gained by the United States. In 1999, U.S. Senator Connie Mack proposed a bill to rebate back 85 percent of the seigniorage a country loses to the United States as a result of dollarization.

48. Meehan, "Economic Forum."

49. Dornbusch, "Fewer Monies, Better Monies."

50. John McCallum, "North American Integration and Dollarization: North America Is Not Europe," speech at Kalamazoo College, Kalamazoo, Michigan, May 11, 2001.

51. Sweden and the United Kingdom have not yet had a referendum. In Denmark, even though all major political parties advocated adop tion of the euro, on September 28, 2000, the proposal to replace the krone with the euro was defeated by a vote of 53 percent to 47 percent. Danish politicians have indicated that there may be another vote on the issue in the future.

17

A Regional Development Policy for North America: Adapting the European Union Model

Robert A. Pastor

The United States, Canada, and Mexico negotiated the North American Free Trade Agreement (NAFTA) as if their countries were of equal size and economic weight. That unrealistic assumption permitted agreement on a single, rule-based formula for eliminating trade and investment barriers, and in the long term that is probably the best approach. However, as John Maynard Keynes reminded us, we live in the short and medium term, and in that time frame, NAFTA's problem is that it ignores the uneven economic development, the different vulnerabilities, and the wide disparities among the three countries. The failure to take these differences into account has meant that the burden of financial problems, such as the "peso crisis" of 1994, has fallen disproportionately on the weaker parties. It has also meant that the three countries did not have the capacity to anticipate, coordinate, or plan for new shocks or take advantage of opportunities.

Soon after he won Mexico's presidential election on July 2, 2000, Vicente Fox proposed a common market to replace the free trade area, and he also volunteered the idea of a compensation fund for the poorest country. He invited President George W. Bush to his home in February 2001 and persuaded him to endorse the "Guanajuato Proposal." A key part of this proposal said:

> After consultation with our Canadian partners, we will strive to consolidate a North American economic community whose benefits reach the lesser-developed areas of the region and extend to the most vulnerable social groups in our countries.[1]

This idea represents a very different approach to North America than the one envisaged in NAFTA, and it remains to be seen which of the two visions will prevail. Fox and his foreign minister, Jorge Castañeda, consciously modeled the proposal on Europe's program to reduce disparities in income between rich and poor countries. During the last forty years, Europe experimented with many approaches to this problem, and it has had considerable success. The question for NAFTA is whether there are valuable lessons to be drawn from the European Union's experience that could be adapted for NAFTA.

In this chapter, I will begin with a brief comparison of the European Union (EU) and NAFTA. I will then review and evaluate the EU's regional and cohesion policies and suggest the lessons that can be drawn from their experience that might be pertinent to NAFTA. Recognizing the differences between the two entities, I will seek to adapt these lessons to North America and propose a plan for reducing disparities.

THE EUROPEAN COMMUNITY AND NAFTA

The establishment of the European Coal and Steel Community in 1951 consciously sought "a broader and deeper community among peoples long divided by bloody conflicts." Since that auspicious beginning, Europe has become increasingly integrated economically, socially, and politically. In 1957, France, Germany, Italy, Belgium, Netherlands, and Luxembourg signed the Treaty of Rome "to lay the foundation for an ever closer union." In 1986, the twelve members of the European Community (EC) signed the Single European Act, which declared their intent to speak with "one voice," and in 1992 they established the European Union to forge a common citizenship, a single currency, and a united foreign and defense policy.[2]

Since its beginning, the EC established as one of its key objectives the need to "reduce the differences between the various regions and the backwardness of the less favored regions." With the first enlargement in 1973 to include the United Kingdom, Denmark, and Ireland, the United Kingdom pressed for a more concerted approach to help the poorer regions, and George Thomson, a British commissioner, was given responsibility to oversee EC regional policy. The subsequent enlargement to include Greece (1981) and Spain and Portugal (1986) led to a significant restructuring and infusion of aid to these countries and Ireland. The EU's model involves a "recognition that wide disparities are intolerable in a community, if the term has any meaning at all."[3] To join the EU, new members have to meet precise standards with regard both to economic and social policies and to democracy and civil liberties.

The North American Free Trade Agreement was born of different soil. It aspired to be nothing more than an area where goods, services, and capital should be traded freely while labor's movements should be restricted. Until Fox raised the idea of a common market, no other leader in the three countries had even broached a preliminary step—a Customs Union with a common external tariff. NAFTA is also silent on an issue—disparities among members—about which the EU is preoccupied, even though the income and employment gaps are far wider in North America than in Europe.

The goals of NAFTA, as specified in the preamble of the agreement, speak of strengthening "the special bonds of friendship and cooperation among their nations" (not their peoples); of expanding and securing markets; of establishing rules consistent with the General Agreement on Tariffs and Trade (GATT); and of preserving each nation's "flexibility to safeguard the public welfare."[4] The two-volume treaty aims to reduce trade and investment barriers and to establish a framework for resolving disputes, but not to create a community of people of North America or to promote the well-being of all the people. After his inauguration in January 1993, President Bill Clinton insisted on adding two side agreements, on labor and the environment, respectively, and establishing commissions whose purpose was to encourage each government to fulfill its promises in each area. The style of NAFTA's governance is laissez-faire, reactive, and legalistic: problems are defined by plaintiffs and settled by litigation. There is no mechanism for defining problems in a proactive way or addressing them from a continental perspective.

To understand the relevance of the EU's experience for NAFTA, we need to begin with a more focused comparison between the two entities. In terms of gross product and population, the two entities are comparable. From 1960 to 1999, the EU's gross product expanded from less than US$200 billion to $8.3 trillion as its membership expanded from seven to fifteen states (see table 17.1). In comparison, the gross product of the three countries of North America grew in that same period from US$565 billion to $9.8 trillion. But the aggregate size of the two economies masks the unevenness of their memberships. In 1960 the U.S. gross domestic product (GDP) was two and one-half times larger than that of all seven EC countries. At the end of the twentieth century, U.S. GDP exceeded all fifteen EU countries by

Table 17.1. Gross Domestic Product of Europe and North America, 1960–1999 (in millions of current dollars)

Group or Country	1960	1970	1980	1990	1999	1999 as Share of World GDP (%)
EC/EU total	196,509	482,433	2,844,712	5,574,100	8,277,649	27
Germany[1]	72,765	188,612	819,206	1,522,710	2,081,200	7
France	61,318	141,525	666,090	1,002,400	1,410,260	
United Kingdom	71,864	120,670	534,240	921,120	1,373,610	
Italy	39,550	93,258	446,432	954,680	1,149,960	
Spain	11,220	37,026	209,346	481,260	562,245	
Netherlands	11,297	31,577	170,044	241,050	384,766	
Belgium	11,016	26,520	120,760	181,800	245,706	
Sweden	13,195	32,872	120,872	151,740	226,388	
Austria	6,363	13,524	83,184	140,880	208,949	
Denmark	6,500	15,795	64,730	88,050	174,363	
Finland	4,752	11,255	53,665	84,650	126,130	
Greece	4,080	10,206	50,410	99,600	123,934	
Portugal	2,934	6,399	29,420	116,160	107,716	
Ireland	2,642	3,975	17,712	46,560	84,861	
Luxembourg	563	961	5,498	8,340	17,561	
NAFTA total	565,410	1,096,359	3,260,853	5,934,746	9,795,870	32
United States	513,316	981,745	2,706,294	5,135,000	8,708,870	29
Canada	40,626	81,564	267,550	503,820	612,049	
Mexico	12,744	33,050	196,042	295,926	474,951	
World	1,346,474	2,917,900	10,704,486	21,354,000	30,212,000	

Sources: World Bank, World Development Indicators CD-ROM, 1999; United Nations, Compendium of Social Statistics, 1980 and 1998; World Bank, World Development Indicators Database, http://www.worldbank.org/data/query.html; and Alan Heston and Robert Summers, Penn World Tables, http://datacentre.chass.utoronto.ca:5680/pwt/pwt.html.

EC = European Community.

EU = European Union.

NAFTA = North American Free Trade Area, North American Free Trade Agreement.

[1] Data include statistics on the former West Germany only, except for 1999.

$500 billion, and Canada and Mexico added another trillion dollars. A similar distribution is evident by comparing population, with the United States having 10 million more people than the seven EC countries in 1960 and all of NAFTA exceeding the fifteen countries of the EU by 26 million people in 1999.[5]

In contrast to NAFTA, which is dominated by a single state, the EU is composed of four strong states—Germany, France, United Kingdom, and Italy—followed by numerous middle powers and then some very small states. The most powerful state, Germany, has about one-fourth of the EU's gross product and 7 percent of the world's product. The center and power of North America is the United States, with almost 90 percent of the region's gross product and 29 percent of the world's product.

Beyond the sheer difference in weight among the three countries of North America, the disparity in incomes between Mexico and its two northern neighbors is probably the most significant dimension of asymmetry. The per capita gross domestic product of the United States, Canada, and Mexico, respectively, in 1960 was $2,836, $2,257, and $354. The average for all of North America was $2,406, with the United States representing 118 percent of the average and Mexico, 15 percent. Nearly four decades later, the differences between the three countries had hardly improved. The U.S. per capita GDP was 7.9 times higher than Mexico's in 1960 and 6.5 times higher in 1999. In comparison, the gaps within Europe were much more modest. In 1999, Germany's per capita GDP was 2.4 times that of Portugal, the EU's poorest country.

There are differences also in the way that Europeans and Americans view income disparities and the possible instruments for alleviating them that might shed some light on the political philosophies of the two entities. Only 29 percent of Americans believe that "it is the responsibility of government to reduce the differences in income between people," whereas 61 percent of (West) Germans, 64 percent of British, and 81 percent of Italians believe their governments have such a responsibility.[6] One might draw the conclusion that this variation explains why the European Union has a "regional policy" for narrowing disparities and NAFTA does not, except that other data blur this fine point. For example, 94 percent of Americans believe that "our society should do what is necessary to make sure that everyone has an equal opportunity to succeed."[7] And the U.S. government does invest in a wide range of programs aimed to give children an equal start and also to compensate for unemployment, old age, and ill health. The

United States spends much more than Europe on health and education, but the United States spends more privately and the EU, publicly. In addition, the United States has an efficient mechanism through the Federal Reserve banking system and via the progressive income tax and the earned-income tax credit for mitigating inequalities between regions and economic classes.[8] Through the tax system, the wealthiest 8 percent of the U.S. population (earning above $100,000) pays nearly two-thirds of all taxes, and the poorer 60 percent pay about 12 percent of total taxes.[9]

In Canada, two provinces—Ontario and Quebec—account for about two-thirds of the country's gross domestic product, and provincial per capita incomes vary a great deal. Like the United States, Canada has multiple policies to reduce the disparities between individuals and provinces. Canada's Department of Regional Industrial Expansion (DRIE) invests in depressed regions and encourages businesses to do the same. Its average annual expenditure of $235 million between 1968 and 1973 doubled during the next eight years. These funds, however, were roughly 2.5 to 6 percent of total fiscal transfers during the same periods. Recognizing the diminished effect of DRIE, Parliament abolished the agency in the late 1980s and replaced it with smaller regional offices. By 1993, due to the growing impact of freer trade with the United States, Canada undertook a different approach—promoting the free movement of goods, capital, and labor and harmonizing government regulations among the provinces.[10] Without the government's transfers, the people in Newfoundland earn about two-thirds of the per capita income of those living in Ontario. After the government's corrective measures are incorporated in the data, provincial per capita income varies by 14 percent below and 16 percent above the national average. In 1995 in the Atlantic provinces, for example, government programs succeeded in raising the average provincial per capita income from 71 to 77 percent of that in Ontario.[11]

The differences among the states of Mexico are far wider, and the capacity of the government to reduce those disparities is less. In 1995, about half of domestic production (48.6 percent) was concentrated in Mexico City and the states of Nuevo León, México, and Jalisco; and twenty-five of the thirty-two states accounted for less than 3 percent each of total production.[12] Per capita income in the southern states of Chiapas, Guerrero, and Oaxaca is 62 percent less than per capita income in the northeast, and health and education statistics mirror that difference.[13] Since government expenditures as a percent of GDP in Mexico are about one-third of the corresponding values for the United

States and Canada, the Mexican government's capacity to equalize inequalities is weak.

It is not surprising, therefore, that the income ratio between the three richest states or provinces and the three poorest states/provinces is roughly twice as large in Mexico as in its two northern neighbors (see table 17.2). This poses a serious problem for Mexico, but also, as we shall see, for all of North America.

Table 17.2. Income Ratio of Three Richest to Three Poorest States/ Provinces in North America, 1997

Canada	United States	Mexico
2.1	1.9	4.1

Sources: Canada (www.statcan.ca/english/Pgdb/Economy/Economic/econ50.htm); Instituto Nacional de Estadística, Geografía e Informática, "Gross Domestic Product at Constant Prices, 2000" (www.inegi.gob.mx/difusion/ingles/portadai.html); for the United States, see www.census.gov/hhes/income/income99/99tabled.html.

In summary, income disparities are far wider in North America than in Europe. The United States and Canada have provisions for mitigating the disparity, but Mexico does not have any capacity to do so, and the region as a whole has not developed a redistributive mechanism to compensate the weaker countries.

EUROPE'S REGIONAL POLICIES

The Treaty of Rome included references to two instruments that would define Europe's initial approach to the problem of reducing disparities within the European Community. The European Investment Bank (EIB) would make loans in lagging regions, and the European Social Fund (ESF) would provide funds for vocational training and for facilitating movement by workers into other areas or jobs. The European Agricultural Fund (different from the Common Agricultural Policy, or CAP) began providing grants to farmers in 1968 to help them modernize their equipment and operations and, in subsequent years, to develop rural areas. Until 1973, most of the resources were funneled into southern Italy.

The first institution that focused exclusively on the problem of regional disparities was the European Regional Development Fund (ERDF), which was established in 1975 after the EU was enlarged to include the United Kingdom, Ireland, and Denmark. The ERDF's purpose was "to help to redress the main regional imbalances in the Community."[14] Roughly 85 percent of the ERDF-funded projects in the 1970s and 1980s were for infrastructure, and 91 percent of ERDF funds went to the poorest regions in five countries—France, Germany, Italy, Greece, and the United Kingdom. Member governments co-financed the projects. The budget increased eightfold in the first ten years of the program (1975–1984), but that only amounted to one-eighth of what was spent for the Common Agricultural Policy.

The enlargements of the 1980s (Greece, Spain, and Portugal) coincided with the leadership of Jacques Delors, president of the European Commission, who used the moment to transform the mandate, programs, and amount of funds devoted to the task. The Single European Act of 1986, which he shepherded to eliminate roughly three hundred intra-EU barriers by 1992, included a new concept and a more precise set of goals under the title of "Economic and Social Cohesion" (Article 130A-E):

> In order to promote its overall harmonious development, the Community shall develop and pursue its actions leading to the strengthening of its economic and social cohesion. In particular, the Community shall aim aid at reducing disparities between the levels of development of the various regions and the backwardness of the least favored regions, including rural areas.[15]

The premise of the European Community was that its people shared fundamental interests, and, therefore, progress should be measured in terms of lifting the entire community in a fair and equitable manner. "Imbalances," the EC's *Report on Cohesion* writes, "do not just imply a poorer quality of life for the most disadvantaged regions ... [but also] an under-utilisation of human potential and a failure to take advantage of economic opportunities which could benefit the Union as a whole."[16] The operational definition of "economic cohesion" was convergence of basic incomes, rates of employment, and competitiveness. "Social cohesion" could be measured in universal systems of social protection and mutual support. This would mean a reduction of the incidence of poverty as well as improvements in productivity and the quality of life. Under the "Delors I" plan, adopted by the EC in 1988 for a five-year plan (1989–1993), the budget for structural funds for the poorer countries doubled in real terms, to 60 billion ECUs over five years, in 1992 reaching almost 30 percent of the total budget and about 0.3 percent of EC gross domestic product.

The end of the Cold War and the negotiations for the Maastricht Treaty led to Delors II (a six-year plan, 1994–1999), which boosted funding for cohesion by 50 percent, up to 0.46 percent of EU GDP. The Maastricht Treaty also created two more cohesion instruments: the Cohesion Fund for the four poorest countries (Ireland, Greece, Spain, and Portugal) and the European Investment Fund for the poorer regions. The Cohesion Fund would also be used to help poorer countries achieve the standards ("national convergence criteria") necessary for them to qualify for the economic and monetary union. In addition, a new Committee of the Regions (Article 198-C) was established to permit Europe's regions to have direct representation in Brussels.

The proliferation of funds necessitated some reorganization. The EU allotted 15.5 billion euros for the Cohesion Fund's four poorer countries for grants for projects between 1993 and 1999, rising from an annual level of 795 million euros in 1993 to 2,769 million in 1999. This, however, represented only about 10 percent of money allocated to the "structural funds," which in 1995 referred to the following four previously established funds: the European Regional Development Fund (which represented 50 percent of total structural funds), European Social Fund (30 percent of the total), Agriculture (17 percent), and Fisheries (3 percent). The structural funds were also grants and amounted to 170 billion ECUs during the 1994–1999 period, or about one-third of total Community spending. The total budget for 2000–2006 amounts to 195 billion euros (at 1999 prices). This represents 1.27 percent of the EU's GDP in 1999 (table 17.3).[17]

The structural funds aim at six different targets or areas. They are: regions where development is lagging (70 percent of total structural funds); regions suffering from industrial decline (11 percent); long-term and youth employment (5 percent); training for workers (5 percent); adjustment in agricultural (rural) and fisheries sectors (9 percent); and adjustment for sparsely populated areas (0.5 percent).[18]

The process of deciding on the distribution of the funds is complex, shaped by a multi-tiered political process.[19] First, the structural funds are distributed to more than half the regions in the EU, given that every state has poor regions. This means that the biggest donors are among the largest recipients. Other than Spain, the two countries that have received the most in structural funds since 1989 are Italy and Germany, which received 61.9 billion and 58.1 billion euros, respec-

Table 17.3. EU Structural and Cohesion Funds, 1992–2006

Funds	Share of Total Fund (%)	Date Established	Objective	Funds 1992–93 (billions of EUR)	Funds 1994–99[1,2] (billions of EUR)	Funds 2000–06[2,3] (billions of EUR)	Total, 1992–2006
Structural Funds	100	1995[4]		26.7	170.0	195.0	391.7
European Regional Development Fund	50	1975	Economic development	11.1	85.0	97.5	193.6
European Social Fund	30	1957	Training, wage subsidies	9.7	51.0	58.5	119.2
European Agricultural Guidance and Guarantee Fund	17	1957	Agriculture	5.9	28.9	33.2	68.0
Financial Instrument for Fisheries	3	1993	Fisheries		5.1	5.9	11.0
Cohesion Funds	100	1993	Poor-country development	N.A.	15.5	18.0	33.5
European Investment Bank[5]	100	1958	Economic development	17.7[6]	133.1	N.A.	

Sources: European Union, http://www.europa.eu.int/comm/regional_policy.htm; Simon Hix, *The Political System of the European Union* (New York: St. Martin's Press, 1999); and European Investment Bank Web site, http://www.eib.org/loans.htm.

N.A. = Not available.

[1] For the Cohesion Funds, figures are for 1993–99.

[2] Amounts for each subfund are estimates based on the percentage of the total Structural Fund budget they usually receive.

[3] Projected.

[4] The four funds listed below were consolidated under Structural Funds in 1995.

[5] Figures are for loans.

[6] Number is for 1993 only.

tively. France received 36.3 billion euros in structural funds, and the United Kingdom, 33.8 billion (table 17.3). Second, the objectives are sufficiently diverse that most states are eligible for some aid. Third, the Cohesion Fund, which delivers grants directly to central governments, was the product of a bargain that the Spanish prime minister struck at Maastricht. In exchange for receiving what would grow to the single largest amount of funds—111.6 billion euros from 1989—Spain agreed to sign the treaty. Cohesion funds are spent on the environment, infrastructure, and research and development in the four countries whose per capita GDP is less than 90 percent of the EU average (Spain, Portugal, Greece, and Ireland). The overall amount allotted to each state is decided by all the states. The EC Commission, in collaboration with the subnational governments, then decides on the specific projects.[20]

The European Investment Bank has made loans for regional development to all member states, and the amounts are significant. In 1999 the Bank approved loans of 27.8 billion euros and in 2000, for 30.7 billion euros,[21] but these loans are not considered part of the structural or cohesion funds. The EU claims that the total allocated for structural and cohesion funds amounted cumulatively to 6.5 percent of annual EU GDP during the 1989–1999 decade. In comparison, Marshall Plan aid from 1948 to 1951 amounted cumulatively to 4 percent of annual U.S. GDP.[22]

The comparison is a bit deceptive on both statistical and substantive grounds. First, the EU aid was a ten-year total, and the Marshall Plan was for four years, though the denominator in both cases is the GDP in just the first year of the program. Second, the EU transferred the funds to itself, often to the same countries.

Nonetheless, in an age when foreign aid has been declining precipitously, the EU transfers represent a significant effort. In just the period from 1992 and programmed through 2006, the EU would have transferred roughly 425.2 billion euros (table 17.3). What motivated the EU? First, equity and solidarity are goals that are mandated in the EU treaties. Second, if regions endured a shock or even a slow decline, the rest of Europe felt the negative consequences and therefore had an incentive to buffer the downturns in the poorer countries. Fiscal transfers spread the burden of adjustment and assisted the adversely affected countries. Third, growth in the poorer countries often translated readily into fast-growing markets for the goods of the richer countries. And fourth, lest we forget, is politics. One study found that the transfers serve to shore up political support in the poorer areas where the

EU is unpopular or the government is weak.[23] With each enlargement, the stronger countries in the EU felt it necessary to offer increasing funds to the poorer applicants. Some view the side payments as necessary for the stronger countries to secure the wider market.[24]

EVALUATING THE EU'S REGIONAL POLICY

In 1996, in its first *Cohesion Report,* the European Commission focused its analysis on the four poorer "cohesion" countries. It found the evidence mixed as to whether the disparities in income and employment between the richer and poorer states had narrowed, but by the sixth report, issued in February 1999, the Commission declared: "The evidence is now unambiguous: the GDP, or output, per head of poorer regions is converging toward the EU average." From 1986 to 1999, the per capita GDP in the four Cohesion countries rose from 65 percent of the EU average to 78 percent. As for the regions, per capita GDP in the ten poorest regions increased from 41 to 50 percent of the EU average, and of the twenty-five poorest regions, from 52 to 59 percent.[25]

Although the disparities in income declined, the unemployment picture did not improve.[26] Growth is unlikely to solve this problem, but the good news is that the poorer regions experienced a relatively greater improvement in productivity as indicated by the reduction of the gap in income.

Another way of looking at the unemployment problem is to realize that the poorer regions, particularly those in the poorest states, had historically high levels of underemployment, and their safety nets, if they had any at all, were flimsy. As these poorer states were integrated into the EU, new investments tended to be more capital- and technology-intensive, meaning that jobs were created but they were fewer and better than those from previous investments. At the same time, the countries approved social legislation to assist the jobless.

Although all four Cohesion countries (Ireland, Spain, Portugal, and Greece) have made substantial progress since entering the EU, an analysis of the differences in their rates of growth might be a useful vehicle for assessing the relative effectiveness of the EU's regional policies. Ireland has been the most successful. Although burdened with a weak infrastructure and educational system, Ireland took quick advantage of the EU and achieved the highest growth rates of any member state.[27] Its per capita GDP rose from only 61 percent of the EU average in 1986 to 96.5 percent one decade later. In 1999, Ireland's per capita GDP had reached 105.1 percent of the EU average.[28] The growth was not evenly distributed within Ireland. Most of it was concentrated in the eastern part of the country, particularly in the service sector around Dublin.

Ireland received significant resources from the EU. For the decade beginning in 1989, Ireland received 10.2 billion euros in both structural and cohesion funds, and the government matched that amount as counterpart investments. (Another 6 billion euros are programmed for the next six years.)[29] In addition, it received $10.4 billion of private investment linked to the projects funded by the EU, for a total of 31 billion euros. The EU transferred resources that were equivalent to 2.8 percent of Ireland's GDP. National counterpart funding raised the total investment to 5 percent of GDP.[30] This undoubtedly provided a significant boost to Ireland's development. Of the 10.2 billion euro grants, about 35 percent went to education and training, 25 percent to infrastructure (roads, rails, ports), and the rest to small and medium-sized enterprises (SMEs) and environmental projects. Technical advice was also important in helping Irish government officials fashion an outward-oriented development strategy and in persuading the central government to give greater attention to the views of the officials at lower levels than they had ever done before.[31]

The Economic and Social Research Institute in Dublin did a rather intensive analysis and evaluation of the EU's programs in Ireland and concluded that "no single factor can explain the economic turnaround," but it identified three mutually reinforcing variables: the gradual accumulation of human capital, fiscal control and the maintenance of wage competitiveness, and a sharp increase in EU structural funds. These funds began to arrive in 1989 just when there was a substantial backlog of projects and urgent infrastructural needs. "Without the support of the structural funds," the report concludes, "congestion in public infrastructure and constraints in third-level education would have limited the recovery."[32] Using several different models, the Institute concluded that the combined effect in the period 1995–1999 was to raise the level of GNP by 3 to 4 percent above the level it would have been without the EU funding.[33]

Ireland's trajectory was astonishing, but the other three poor countries—Spain, Portugal, and Greece—also made progress. All three governments slowly opened their economies and began to emerge from their authoritarian, protectionist shells in the early 1960s. As tariffs declined, foreign investment arrived, and the result was that all three countries witnessed important economic growth and an increase in real wages during the 1963–1973 decade: 6.4 percent in Spain, 6.8 percent in Portugal, and 7 percent in Greece.[34]

Spain's per capita GDP rose from 70 percent of the EC average in 1986 to nearly 80 percent in 1999. Like Ireland, Spain's growth was uneven, with the most prosperous areas in Madrid and Catalonia reaching the EC average by 1996.[35] The scale of EU transfers to Spain tripled between the two periods (1989–1993 and 1994–1999), and transfers are programmed to continue at a high rate until 2006. By that time, Spain will have received 111.6 billion euros—about the same as the other three Cohesion countries combined, and double the next highest recipient. Adding both the national counterpart funding and the private-sector financing for the EU projects, the total amount of resources mobilized by the EU constituted about 1.5 percent of Spain's average annual GDP in 1989 and 3.4 percent in the years 1994 to 1999.[36] The investments were concentrated in infrastructure (primarily roads), but attention and resources were also devoted to telecommunications. Within five years of Spain's entry into the EU, foreign businesses tripled their direct investment in that country, giving rise to suggestions that Spain was "turning into the continent's Sun Belt."[37]

During the last decade Portugal grew faster than Spain and the EU as a whole, but it started from a lower base. Its GDP per capita increased from 55 percent of the EC average in 1986 to 72 percent in 1999. With a weaker economy, Portugal's development has been more unbalanced. Most of the country has remained poor, but average incomes in its two urbanized regions—Lisbon and Norte—now approach the EU average.[38] The Community's investment of 46.3 billion euros, beginning in 1989 and projected to continue until 2006, supported the transformation of the economy. This amounts to about 4 percent of Portugal's GDP (at the 1994 level) or 7.2 percent when the central government and private-sector funding are included. As in Spain, the EU emphasis on infrastructure was key to Portugal's development. During the last decade, the EU financed and constructed or improved nearly 4,000 kilometers of roads, or almost half of all the roads in Portugal. It also constructed or improved 640 kilometers of railroad and expanded and digitalized almost the entire telephone network.[39] Also, as in Spain and Ireland, foreign investment played a pivotal role, mobilizing new development and introducing modern technology and higher-valued jobs.[40]

Greece, the poorest state in the European Union, initially made the least progress after its entry into the EU following a decade of chronic fiscal and current account deficits. In 1994, Greece's budget deficit was 12.1 percent of GDP, but the country sharply reduced the deficit and the economy began to grow. Per capita GDP rose from 60 percent of the EU average in 1986 to 69 percent in 1999. As Greece's trade barriers dropped and its macroeconomic policies improved, the income gap between Athens and the rest of the country began to widen, much the same pattern as found in the other Cohesion countries.[41]

Notwithstanding the Greek government's flawed economic policies, the EU nearly doubled its aid in the second period, so that from 1989 to 2006 the EU will have transferred 51 billion euros to Greece. Together with national and private funds, the total amount represented 4.5 percent of the average annual GDP in the 1989–1993 period and a substantial 7.2 percent for 1994–1999. Repeated and credible reports of corruption impeded Greek development, but the EU helped the government address the problem in order to expedite crucial projects on infrastructure (roads and subways) and telecommunications.

To what extent did these funds contribute to growth in the four Cohesion countries and to the reduction of income disparities? Perhaps the most comprehensive and incisive study of the effect of regional and cohesion policies was done by Robert Leonardi, the Jean Monnet Lecturer in European Union Politics and Policy at the London School of Economics. He, like others, found significant convergence among the states. Using regression analyses, he tested various explanatory variables, including distance from the core countries, foreign investment, level of industrialization, unemployment, and EC funding. The best predictors of convergence were distance from the core countries and EC spending. Structural and cohesion aid, he concluded, "made a substantial contribution to economic investment and overall GDP in the three nations. [It] acted as a significant stimulus to the national economies, explaining in part the surge of these countries toward convergence."[42]

As to why Greece did not do as well as the other three Cohesion countries, Leonardi identified several factors. Greece joined the EC at a time of a European-wide recession; and its weak infrastructure and notoriously corrupt administration led foreign investors to "remain aloof."[43] Leonardi also found the gap between developed and underdeveloped regions to have narrowed, and he explained this by "significant upward movement of the bottom regions."[44]

Leonardi did not assess whether structural funds or the single market were more important in explaining the convergence of the poorer states. The Organisation for Economic Co-operation and Development did such a study in 1994, and it concluded that it was "difficult to find strong evidence [that] the single market program has yet had sizeable effects on aggregate output." The OECD estimated that it had improved GDP by perhaps 1.5 percent.[45] That is not exactly a trivial contribution, but it also does not compare to the kind of contribution to GDP that Leonardi attributes to the structural funds. But the OECD study suffered from the same problem that others, including Leonardi, have had: how to answer the counter-factual—what would have happened in the absence of the single market.

Of the structural funds, which policies and projects were most effective? In a study of the regional policies and projects, Rainer Martin concluded that investments in two areas—infrastructure and human capital—were most effective.[46] The EU has emphasized these two areas, but it has also scattered funds into projects in other areas, such as environmental protection, regulatory policies, new initiatives to provide low-interest loans to small and midsize businesses, and technical assistance.

LESSONS FROM THE EU'S EXPERIENCE

Let us extract the lessons from the European Union that may be relevant to NAFTA.

- *A Declaration of Goals.* From the beginning, European leaders set goals of solidarity and community—a sense that the peoples of Europe would cooperate in new ways to bring peace and well-being to all. These goals provided general guidance to member states but did not aid them in defining specific policies. The lesson is that a clear statement of goals is necessary but not sufficient to construct a community of nations.

- *Institutions at Sunset.* The EU established many supranational institutions. Most of them are needed to implement EU laws, but some exist because it is too hard to eliminate them, and many have expanded their activities because no one has stopped them. Clearly, one could identify a golden mean between the excessive institutionalism of the EU and the under-institutionalized NAFTA. The lesson is that policymakers should incorporate a "sunset" provision into every institution or funding mechanism, lest each assume a permanence that would diminish the capacity to reduce disparities.

- *The Promise of Convergence.* The spectacular reduction in the income gap between the richer and poorer countries of Europe in a relatively short period of time (since 1986) offers hope that regional trading schemes could be an effective vehicle for lifting middle-income countries. Among the many factors responsible for narrowing the gap were the establishment of a single market, foreign investment, and the massive aid programs from the EU. An analysis of the difference in growth rates among the four Cohesion countries leads to the inescapable conclusion that national policy is a fourth and crucial determinant. There is a consensus that all four factors contributed to the reduction of disparities, despite some disagreement as to which one is most important. The lesson is to use the first three factors to induce the recipient government to adopt the appropriate economic policies that would make best use of the resources.

- *The Best Projects for Regional Assistance.* The EU has funded almost every imaginable kind of project through many channels, but most analysts believe that the most effective projects were aimed at infrastructure and higher-level education.

- *The Perils of Convergence—Volatility.* Although convergence did occur between richer and poorer countries, the poorer ones did not follow a straight path upward. Rather, the Cohesion countries outperformed the EU average in boom years and did worse than the EU average during recessions.[47] The opportunities and the dangers of integration are much more serious for the weaker countries than for the more advanced ones. Another study by Rainer Martin also found greater volatility among the weaker partners of an integration effort.[48] The lesson is that the richer countries need to find ways to cushion the swings that the poorer economies suffer. Macroeconomic policy coordination and financial arrangements should be undertaken to protect the poorer countries from foreign exchange crises.

- *Growing Inequality.* In many cases, rapid integration tended to coincide with accelerating inequality among the regions in the poorer country. More often, this is not because the poor became poorer but because the prosperous regions—the ones tied to the EU by both exports and inward flows of investment—sped ahead. The poorer regions grew more slowly or just halted their growth. The lesson is that a supranational agency needs to monitor the progress within each member state.

- *Funds for the Affluent.* More than half of all the structural funds go to poor regions in the rich countries, and several of the richer countries (notably France and Denmark) obtain large subsidies from the Common Agricultural Policy, which is half of the EU budget. ("Regional policies" take 30 percent of the budget.)[49] Given the greater difficulty of narrowing differences among regions than among states, it would be a more efficient use of resources to concentrate the funds in the poorer states. Given that the presence of EU projects in the richer countries gives their people a sense of community, some symbolic projects should remain in these nations. The lesson is to concentrate the money where it is most needed.

- *Emigration.* As the disparities between rich and poor countries were reduced, migration was significantly reduced.

GAPS AND DISPARITIES WITHIN NAFTA

When Europe decided on enlargement in the 1970s and 1980s, concerns were raised about the effect on the poorer countries. The differences between the economies in Europe were quite small as compared to North America. Therefore, let us briefly assess the effect of NAFTA on its weaker members.

It was a sad but potent coincidence that shortly after the Canada–United States Free Trade Agreement (CUSFTA) came into effect in 1991, Canada suffered its worst recession since the 1930s. More than 450,000 jobs were lost, dissatisfaction with free trade increased, the value of the Canadian dollar fell, and the Progressive Conservative Party lost all but two seats in a humiliating defeat in the 1993 elections. The CUSFTA did not cause the recession, nor did it lead to the defeat of the Conservative Party, but the treaty was affected by the same factors that caused these two outcomes—tight monetary and fiscal policies, overvaluation of the Canadian dollar, recession in the United States, and the introduction in Canada of the unpopular Goods and Services Tax (GST).

The Canadian debacle was not as bad as the peso shock. In 1995 the Mexican economy declined 6.2 percent, the most precipitous drop since 1932. Because of NAFTA and the expansion of an export-oriented manufacturing sector, the impact of the contraction of the economy was very uneven. Exports grew, but the domestic side of the economy, which represented 70 percent of GDP, declined by 14 percent.[50] Even though manufacturing grew by 29.5 percent from 1993 to 1998 and manufacturing exports expanded by 154 percent during that period (from US$41.6 billion to $105.9 billion), the number of jobs for skilled and unskilled workers actually declined and their wages suffered. Skilled workers, according to Mexico's National Institute of Statistics, Geography, and Informatics (INEGI), saw a decline in real wages during this period of 13.2 percent, and 17.1 percent for unskilled workers.[51] NAFTA, as we have noted, did not cause this crisis in Mexico, except in the sense that the lowering of investment barriers might have given Wall Street more encouragement than was deserved, but the absence of a foreign exchange safety net made the currency problem an unmitigated crisis.

There is some evidence that NAFTA has contributed to Mexico's regional disparities, which were already quite marked. About half of all domestic production is concentrated in Mexico City and the states of México, Jalisco (Guadalajara), and Nuevo León (Monterrey). Twenty-five of thirty-two states account for less than 3 percent of total domestic production. After the 1994 crisis, the disparities between regions became even more pronounced. Per capita income in the southern states of Chiapas, Guerrero, and Oaxaca is 62 percent of the per capita income of Nuevo León—roughly proportional to Southern Europe's income in relation to the EU average. An analysis of the eight regions of Mexico conducted by the National Confederation of Chambers of Industry (CONCAMIN), using data from INEGI, concluded that the social and economic gap between the regions has widened since NAFTA. CONCAMIN called on the Mexican government to develop regional policies and plans,[52] but the government did not respond, in part because austerity measures have reduced government spending to about 16 percent of GDP, by far the lowest of any OECD nation. (In comparison, Argentina's government spends about 20 percent of GDP; the United States, about 40 percent; and Canada, above that.)[53]

Another analysis of NAFTA's geographical impact on Mexico found that the trade accord "expanded the gap between southern and northern states."[54] That study, by Rafael Tamayo-Flores, did not clearly identify the reason that the gap expanded, and Tamayo-Flores's research in Oaxaca found considerable growth in that state, albeit not in areas stimulated by NAFTA's liberalization. Oaxaca grew, though not at the pace of some of the northern states. Tamayo-Flores also notes that the railroad and road networks were not developed in the southern states, reinforcing the power of the richer states.

Income inequalities in Mexico are far more severe. The World Bank estimates that two out of every three Mexicans are poor, and one in three is extremely poor. The 1994 crisis reversed the 10 percent reduction in poverty that Mexico had achieved over the previous decade.[55]

Canada's trade dependence (trade/GDP) also increased substantially, from 37.7 percent in 1965 to about 60 percent in 1993[56] and, including services, to 83 percent in 1999.[57] The expansion of trade not only heightened dependence on the U.S. market (from 75 percent in 1990 to 86 percent in 1999), but it also widened disparities between Canadian provinces. Newfoundland has been dependent on a declining fishing industry, and its per capita income is only about two-thirds of Ontario's. Unlike Mexico, however, Canada has an extensive system of transfer payments (welfare, social security, federal tax transfers to provincial governments) and regional policies (development grants and subsidies) that together have had a significant effect on narrowing the differences in income and employment opportunities between the provinces.[58] In Canada, the problem of volatility is increasingly focused on the Canadian dollar, and the question is whether a unified currency with the United States would mitigate the swings.

Like Canada, the United States has an elaborate system of federal transfers that reduces the differences between the states. In addition, labor mobility is very high in the United States, as is evident by the large movement of people in the last two decades to the south and southwest and the economic growth in those areas.[59] Both federal transfers and labor movement smooth the disparities among regions.

From the early 1970s until 1993, the gap between rich and poor in the United States widened, and questions were raised as to whether this was a consequence of increased dependence on trade. Most studies attributed the widening gap to technological improvements and to disparities in education. Recent data impugn the thesis that trade widened the gap between rich and poor. As trade began to soar between 1993 and 1998, the income gap began to close. Family incomes in the lowest quintile rose at a 2.7 percent annual rate, slightly faster than the 2.4 percent rate recorded by the top quintile. Similar evidence can be found in the broad-based growth in earnings since 1994. Moreover, of the new jobs created in the 1990s, 81 percent were in industries or occupations that paid wages above the median. Finally, the proportion of Americans living in poverty declined from 15.1 percent in 1993 to 12.7 percent in 1998.[60]

Thus the evidence on the diverging effects of integration is mixed, but it is not inconsistent with what was learned from Europe. The strongest economic power in North America experienced the least effect. The weaker countries suffered the most volatility, although this was due at least as much, if not more, to mistaken macroeconomic policies. The weakest country experienced the widest disparities in income among classes and regions. The Canadian and U.S. systems of income transfers among regions mitigate these disparities and lift the countries as a whole, but Mexico does not yet have the fiscal system that could permit such transfers, and there is no regional mechanism.

A REGIONAL DEVELOPMENT POLICY FOR NAFTA

What makes NAFTA unique is the integration of a developing country with two more advanced ones. So the issue for North America is how to assure that the integration is successful and becomes a model worth emulating by other areas. Can a framework of policy coordination be established to anticipate and solve problems before they become sources of tension? Can it help governments view future opportunities with sufficient clarity that they would quickly marshal their resources to seize the chance?

In contemplating a "regional policy" for North America, let us recall the lessons from the EU. There is a clear need for a North American Development Fund, and Mexico is at the stage that the Iberian countries were when they joined the EU. The fund should focus on infrastructure and education in the poorer regions of Mexico. It should multiply existing resources and serve to encourage sensible macroeconomic policies. Finally, the program should have a sunset provision.

When the EU first decided on a regional policy, its funds were scarce. But with each enlargement, the EU expanded the amount of resources to the point that the sheer magnitude—about 2 to 3 percent of GDP of the receiving country—helped lift some of them. It is not hard to judge the reaction in the U.S. Congress if the president requested an aid program to Mexico that amounted to 2 percent of its GDP—roughly $9.4 billion—each year for the next five. The American people and Congress are unlikely to consider such a request at this time, regardless of how good an investment it would be. The president needs to frame the issue and help Americans understand the vital interests at stake. Americans have always risen to a challenge when their leaders have explained it clearly. There is no national interest greater for the United States than to help lift all of North America to a new level of prosperity and social justice. The amount of investment is small compared to the return. After all, of every additional dollar of imports that Mexico buys, the United States sells about 80 cents. The United States profits from Mexico's prosperity.

Nevertheless, it might take some time to build a consensus for a partnership strategy. Even if the president tried to win congressional approval, Congress would undoubtedly saddle the new program with so many conditions that it would undermine the very partnership that should be the premise and purpose of the structural funds. Therefore, let me propose an intermediate option as the three countries' leaders begin constructing a relationship that will make such a program seem a wholly natural extension of their summits and of a new North America.

Since the establishment of the World Bank, Mexico has been its third largest loan recipient, with 169 loans totaling $30 billion. Only India, which received $52 billion, and China, with $33 billion, obtained more. In June 1999 the World Bank's Board decided to direct US$5.2 billion to Mexico during the following two years to improve social conditions for the poor, strengthen public-sector reforms, and reinforce macroeconomic stability. Mexico has also received more loans from the Inter-American Development Bank (IDB)—160 loans totaling $12.2 billion—than any other country.[61] These loans have gone to a wide range of projects, but none of them has addressed the question of how the funds could best facilitate the integration of North America.

If Mexico, the United States, and Canada all agreed to devote some portion, perhaps half, of the loans from these two institutions during the next ten years to answering the question of integration, the two banks would probably respond positively. This is especially likely given that the precedent—integrating a developing country into a regional agreement with industrialized countries—is so important for the world.

A cost-benefit analysis of various sectoral plans might show how a relatively small amount of investment would yield a high rate of return for all three countries, particularly because the private sector would play a large role. Under those circumstances, all three countries might devote a substantial amount of call-in capital or foreign aid to implement the plan—building better roads and bridges across the borders and into central and southern Mexico, modernizing railways, and so on. It would be neither necessary nor desirable to establish a new bureaucracy to undertake these projects. A special coordinating office in the World Bank could work with the IDB and other institutions to mobilize the funds, supervise the bidding, and oversee the projects. Perhaps the tasks could be assumed by the North American Development Bank (NADBank).

The donors—the United States and, to a lesser degree, Canada— would need to be persuaded that such an investment would alleviate their concerns about Mexico and advance their interests. If a plan can integrate the various interests of the United States—stemming the flows of drugs and illegal immigrants, expanding trade and development—then the prospects for supporting such a venture would increase.

One effective way to reduce geographical disparities within Mexico while reducing pressures for out-migration would be to improve the road system from the U.S. border to the center and southern parts of Mexico. Thanks to foreign investment, the northern border economy is booming and attracting labor from the poorer parts of the country. However, in many cases workers stay on the Mexican side of the border only long enough to learn how to cross into the United States, where they can earn a lot more. U.S. firms do not like to invest in the border area because of the region's pollution and the inefficiencies associated with high turnover rates, but they do so, nevertheless, because roads from the border to central Mexico are very poor.[62]

If roads were built or improved from the border to the center of the country, investors would locate in the interior, for three reasons. First, the center and south of Mexico—including the states of Guanajuato, Michoacán, Oaxaca, and Zacatecas—have the highest unemployment rates. In fact, these are the principal sources of immigrants to the border and to the United States. Second, the wage level is much lower in these areas, and the workers are no less educated than those on the border. Indeed, they are often the same workers. Finally, the region is not the polluted, cramped border. The Mexican government has incentive systems to encourage investors to locate in these areas, but the problem is a lack of infrastructure—roads, electricity, and so on. If such infrastructure were built, investors would come, immigration levels would decline, and so would disparities in income.

Vicente Fox has already proposed a Puebla-Panama Corridor to connect Puebla, a city southeast of Mexico City, with the countries of Central America. He has gained the support of the international development banks to help Mexico build roads and infrastructure to connect the ten poorest southern and eastern states of his country to Central America. Many of these Mexican areas have few or no roads, and so such a development project would have a profound effect on the region, and even more so if those roads were connected to new ones coming from the border.

While much of the infrastructure will be built in Mexico, the United States and Canada also have considerable infrastructure problems. The increase in trade has slowed border-bound traffic in Texas, and traffic congestion has led to a rise in the number of vehicle accidents. The U.S. Congress allocated $700 million for NAFTA-related highway and infrastructure improvements, but apparently only a small portion was allocated for Texas.[63]

In terms of forging a regional identity, a case could be made that some "North American" projects should be built in Canada and the United States and advertised, following the EU example, as North American Community Projects. Historically, one reason that the United States has had so much difficulty sustaining public support for foreign aid or for international organizations is that the projects and the offices that manage them are outside of the public's view. That could be corrected if there were projects and offices in the United States as well as in the two other countries, which are also the nations most visited by Americans. As in Europe, it would be wise for these funds to be relatively small and symbolic.

A regional development policy is essential to help Mexico move onto the First World integration train. Lacking such a policy, Mexico is likely to experience greater volatility in its economics and politics, with devastating consequences for itself and its neighbors. To successfully integrate North America, it is hard to conceive of a better or more efficient investment.

Notes

Adapted from Robert A. Pastor, *Toward a North American Community: Lessons from the Old World for the New* (Washington, D.C.: Institute for International Economics, 2001). Used with permission.

1. "Towards a Partnership for Prosperity: The Guanajuato Proposal," a Joint Communique, February 16, 2001, at www.presidencia/gob.mex./?P=42 &Orden=Leer&Tipo=Pe&Art=548.

2. Brent F. Nelsen and Alexander C.G. Stubb, eds., *The European Union: Readings on the Theory and Practice of European Integration*, 2d ed. (Boulder, Colo.: Lynne Rienner, 1998), pp. 13–15, 45–47, 69–70.

3. European Commission, *First Report on Economic and Social Cohesion, 1996* (Luxembourg: Office for Official Publications of the European Commission, 1996), p. 13.

4. *The North American Free Trade Agreement between the Government of the United States, the Government of Canada, and the Government of the United Mexican States* (Washington, D.C.: U.S. Government Printing Office, 1992), p. iii.

5. World Bank, *World Development Indicators Database*, at www.worldbank.org/dataquery.html.

6. Opinion survey is cited by Derek Bok, *State of the Nation* (Cambridge, Mass.: Harvard University Press, 1998), p. 157.

7. Ibid.

8. For a summary and analysis of the redistribution of fiscal transfers each year, see www.nemw.org/fedspending.htm; and for a good summary of the distinctiveness of the states and regions in the United States, see "America's States and Regions: How Similar? Where Different? Sectionalism at Century's End," *The Public Perspective: A Roper Center Review of Public Opinion and Polling* 9, no. 4 (June/July 1998).

9. Data provided by the U.S. Treasury Department and the House Ways and Means Committee, published in the *New York Times*, July 26, 1999, p. A11.

10. Michael Howlett, Alex Netherton, and M. Ramesh, *The Political Economy of North America: An Introduction*, 2d ed. (New York: Oxford University Press, 1999), pp. 309–11.

11. Ibid., pp. 106–108.

12. Mauricio A. González Gómez, "Crisis and Economic Change in Mexico," in *Mexico under Zedillo*, ed. Susan Kaufman Purcell and Luis Rubio (Boulder, Colo.: Lynne Rienner, 1998), p. 55.

13. Elvia Gutiérrez, "Disturbing Trend Haunts Economic Development: Regional Disparities Are Alarming," *El Financiero International*, May 31, 1999.

14. Rainer Martin, *Regional Policy in the European Union: Economic Foundations and Reality* (Brussels: Centre for European Policy Studies, 1998), pp. 81–83.

15. European Commission, *First Report on Economic and Social Cohesion, 1996*, p. 13.

16. Ibid.

17. For the data, see http://europa.eu.int/comm/regional_policy/activity/index_en.htm.

18. European Commission, *First Report on Economic and Social Cohesion, 1996*, p. 9.

19. For a description of the structural funds and the political process by which the funds are allocated, see Andrew Evans, *The EU Structural Funds* (New York: Oxford University Press, 1999).

20. For a political analysis of the decision-making that led to the various Structural and Cohesion funds and how they are allocated, see Gary Marks, "Exploring and Explaining Variation in EU Cohesion Policy," in *Cohesion Policy and European Integration: Building Multilevel Governance*, ed. Liesbet Hooghe (Oxford: Oxford University Press, 1996), p. 396.

21. For data and background on the European Investment Bank, see: http://eib.eu.int/.

22. European Commission, *First Report on Economic and Social Cohesion, 1996*, p. 9.

23. Clifford J. Carrubba, "Net Financial Transfers in the European Union: Who Gets What and Why?" *Journal of Politics* 59, no. 2 (May 1997): 469–96.

24. This contrasts with the case of Mexico and most of Latin America, which evidently believe that they gain more from entry to a free trade area with the United States than does Washington.

25. European Commission, *Regional Policy and Cohesion: Sixth Periodic Report on the Social and Economic Situation and Development of the Regions of the European Union* (Luxembourg, February 1999), pp. i, 9.

26. Ibid., p. i.

27. European Commission, *The Impact of Structural Policies on Economic and Social Cohesion in the Union, 1989–99* (Luxembourg: Office for Official Publications of the European Communities, 1997), p. 71.

28. European Commission, *Regional Policy and Cohesion: Sixth Periodic Report*, p. 9.

29. Ibid., table 3.2.

30. European Commission, *The Impact of Structural Policies*, pp. 73–75.

31. Brigid Laffan, "Ireland: A Region without Regions—The Odd Man Out?" in *Cohesion Policy and European Integration*, ed. Liesbet Hooghe, pp. 320–41.

32. Patrick Honohan, ed., *EU Structural Funds in Ireland: A Mid-Term Evaluation of the CSF, 1994–99* (Dublin: The Economic and Social Research Institute, 1997), pp. xv–xxi.

33. Ibid., p. xviii.

34. See Otto Holman, *Integrating Southern Europe: EC Expansion and the Transnationalization of Spain* (New York: Routledge, 1996).

35. European Commission, *Regional Policy and Cohesion: Sixth Periodic Report*, p. 10.

36. European Commission, *The Impact of Structural Policies*, p. 45.

37. Stephen Greenhouse, "With Spain in Common Market, New Prosperity and Employment," *New York Times*, January 15, 1989; Alan Riding, "Spain

Aims for a Competitive Edge in a Unified Europe," *New York Times,* June 14, 1992.

38. European Commission, *Regional Policy and Cohesion: Sixth Periodic Report,* p. 10.

39. European Commission, *The Impact of Structural Policies,* pp. 111–21.

40. Peter Gumbel, "Portugal: A Recovery That East Europe Can Emulate," *Wall Street Journal,* May 1, 1992.

41. European Commission, *Regional Policy and Cohesion: Sixth Periodic Report,* pp. 10–11.

42. Robert Leonardi, *Convergence, Cohesion, and Integration in the European Union* (New York: St. Martin's Press, 1995), pp. 133, 170–76; see chapter 3 for methodology.

43. Ibid., pp. 134–36.

44. Ibid., p. 116. Leonardi looks closely at the southern Italian case and believes that the lack of convergence is due to excessive government involvement and a lack of a market economy (chapter 5).

45. Cited by Loukas Tsoukalis, *The New European Economy Revisited* (New York: Oxford University Press, 1997), pp. 75–76.

46. Martin, *Regional Policy in the European Union,* pp. 66–72.

47. European Commission, *Regional Policy and Cohesion: Sixth Periodic Report,* p. 9.

48. Martin, *Regional Policy in the European Union,* pp. 53–61.

49. See Tsoukalis, *The New European Economy Revisited,* pp. 202–22.

50. For an excellent analysis of the impact of the 1994 crisis, see González Gómez, "Crisis and Economic Change in Mexico."

51. Tom Philpott, "Boom and Gloom: Manufacturing Rises as Wages Fall," *El Financiero International,* June 14, 1999.

52. González Gómez, "Crisis and Economic Change," pp. 55–56; Gutiérrez, "Disturbing Trend Haunts Economic Development," p. 15.

53. Tom Philpott, "Cash Strapped: Tax System Flounders in Neglect," *El Financiero International,* July 5, 1999.

54. Rafael Tamayo-Flores, "The Differential Impact of International Integration on Local Economies: How Are Lagging Mexican Regions Performing?" Documento de Trabajo AP-77 (Mexico City: Centro de Investigación y Docencia Económicas, 2000), p. 21.

55. World Bank, *Government Programs and Poverty in Mexico,* June 2, 1999.

56. Gary C. Hufbauer and Jeffrey J. Schott, *North American Economic Integration: 25 Years Backward and Forward* (Ottawa: Industry Canada, 1998), table 2.

57. Department of Foreign Affairs and International Trade of Canada, *Opening Doors to the World: Canada's Market Access Priorities, 2000* (Ottawa, 2000).

58. See Howlett, Netherton, and Ramesh, *The Political Economy of Canada,* pp. 107–108, particularly table 4 on "Provincial Per Capita Incomes and

Transfers," and pp. 309–11 on the government's regional development measures.

59. In one year, about 16 percent of Americans (43 million) move from one home to another. This trend has remained relatively constant since the 1950s. Most move within the same state, although 6.4 million move to a different state. U.S. Department of Commerce Bureau of the Census, "Moving Rate among Americans," January 19, 2000, at www.census.gov/Press-Release.

60. *Economic Report of the President 2000* (Washington, D.C.: U.S. Government Printing Office, February 2000), pp. 26–28.

61. The figures from the World Bank and the Inter-American Development Bank are from their Web sites.

62. For a more detailed discussion of road and transportation systems, see the chapter by Prentice and Ojah in this volume.

63. Robert Bryce, "A Texas-Size Tie-Up: Traffic from Trade Agreement Has Created a Lone Star Nightmare on Interstate 35," *U.S. News and World Report*, October 25, 1999.

18

Dispute Settlement under NAFTA

Antonio Ortiz Mena L.N.

When the North American Free Trade Agreement (NAFTA) went into effect in January 1994, all three parties hailed the treaty's dispute settlement mechanisms (DSMs) as a major achievement. Canada and Mexico touted Chapter 19 provisions for the settlement of subsidy and dumping disputes, while the United States highlighted the gains it made through Mexico's acceptance of a mechanism to settle investor-state disputes.[1] NAFTA's general DSM, contained in Chapter 20, is also an important element of the dispute settlement system. A track record of more than seven years allows us to ascertain whether NAFTA's DSMs are up to the task for the challenges they will face in the new millennium. This chapter addresses two central questions: How have NAFTA's DSMs performed? What changes to NAFTA's DSMs are desirable and politically feasible to help them successfully face the challenges that lie ahead?

I argue that NAFTA's DSMs have performed acceptably well, that some changes are necessary, especially in the area of transparency, and that the greatest challenges are faced by the investor-state DSM and, to a lesser degree, by the general DSM. I propose some relatively limited changes that are politically viable in the short term, as well as some more far-reaching changes that may be both necessary and viable in the medium and long term.

The next section provides a brief overview of NAFTA's dispute settlement provisions. Then follows a section in which I assess their performance. This discussion is followed, in turn, by a section containing suggestions for institutional developments that would improve DSM performance.

NAFTA'S DISPUTE-SETTLEMENT MECHANISMS

NAFTA is an atypical agreement. Unlike most preferential trade agreements, which tend to contain a single general DSM, NAFTA incorporates several specialized DSMs.[2] Along with Chapter 20 (the general DSM), NAFTA includes Chapter 11, which covers investor-state disputes, and Chapter 19, which deals with subsidy and dumping disputes.[3]

NAFTA can be seen as a comprehensive, precise free trade agreement that incorporates two types of rules.[4] The first are rules that will only be in force temporarily. These would cover instruments such as tariffs covering cross-border trade in goods; most tariffs, except those in a few sensitive sectors, will be eliminated by January 2004. The second type encompasses rules that are permanent in nature; when the transition period has concluded and the liberalization of trade and investment flows has been accomplished, these rules will remain in force to manage economic interaction among the countries of North America. Foremost among them are rules of origin and dispute settlement mechanisms. The latter are of paramount importance; they contribute to meeting liberalization commitments during the transition period, and they will serve for the foreseeable future as the main channel for resolving trade and investment conflicts in this trade bloc of 400 million persons, a combined GDP of approximately US$9.5 trillion, and intra-regional exports in excess of US$600 billion.

NAFTA also differs from other trade agreements in that it was basically a "one shot" deal. It reflects a very delicate balance of economic and political interests, and it could well unravel if it is opened for renegotiation. In contrast, other trade agreements, such as MERCOSUR,[5] were intended to take shape over a series of steps, allowing for gradual institutional evolution.[6] Barring very strong pressures from pro-integration forces or anti-integration activists, the DSMs of NAFTA are here to stay in their present form for the foreseeable future.

Chapter 11: Investor-State Disputes

Section B of NAFTA's Chapter 11, which contains the provisions for investor-state disputes, is similar to the DSMs of many bilateral investment treaties (BITs). The basic logic is to allow NAFTA investors to bypass the local courts of a host government through access to binding international arbitration under ICSID or UNCITRAL rules.[7] Under both sets of rules, the awards rendered by arbitration tribunals are enforceable by domestic courts, making this mechanism the most rule-oriented one in NAFTA. The parties are entitled, but not required, to make the awards public.[8]

Chapter 19: Subsidies and Dumping Disputes

From a Canadian perspective, Chapter 19 of NAFTA built on one of the raisons d'être of the original bilateral Canada–United States Free Trade Agreement (CUSFTA). The Canadians wanted to privilege competition policy instead of relying on antidumping legislation—or, if that was not possible, to agree on a common subsidy and dumping regime. They had to settle for a third option, by which binational panels would review the interpretation and application of each country's laws on the matter.[9]

The solution was quite novel. Formally, the system is an inter-state DSM, as is usually the case in preferential trade agreements, but in practice it is "a government-initiated procedure in a system that is really a private party system."[10] The litigants are typically affected importers or exporters, together with the pertinent authorities from each country. Panel decisions are binding and, if need be, enforceable through sanctioned retaliation. NAFTA's Chapter 19 superseded the CUSFTA's bilateral provisions in this area.

Articles 1903, 1904, and 1905 constitute the core elements of Chapter 19's DSM provisions. Article 1903 entitles a party to request that an amendment to a second party's legislation on subsidies or dumping be referred to a panel for a declaratory opinion on whether it is consistent with the provisions of the GATT (now WTO) and NAFTA. Article 1904 provides for the establishment of panels to review final antidumping and countervailing duty determinations made by local authorities in each country. A final panel decision must be made within 315 days after the panel is requested, and interim timelines within that 315-day period are also stipulated. Article 1904 also provides an Extraordinary Challenge Procedure to address cases in which a party alleges that there has been gross misconduct on the part of the panel. The matter is referred to a committee of judges or former judges who can affirm, vacate, or remand the original panel decision. Finally, Article 1905 provides an additional safeguard for the proper functioning of the panel system, whereby a three-member special committee may review whether a party's domestic law has interfered with panel proceedings.[11]

Chapter 20: General DSM

The general DSM governs issues pertaining to the application and interpretation of NAFTA, except for issues covered by Chapters 11 and 19. The NAFTA Free Trade Commission, which acts on the basis of consensus and comprises cabinet-level officials, plays a significant role in Chapter 20 proceedings. The basic thrust behind these proceedings is to keep disputes from reaching the panel stage by providing consultations, good offices, conciliation, and mediation through the Commission.[12]

The first stage of dispute settlement provides a party with the opportunity to request consultations. If the matter is not resolved within forty-five days, the party may request a meeting of the Commission. If after an additional thirty days the matter has not been resolved through good offices, conciliation, or mediation, the party may request the establishment of an arbitration panel. Once established, a panel must present its initial report to the Commission within ninety days, followed by a final report thirty days later. The findings contained in the final report are regarded as recommendations (not binding decisions), but it is expected that the party found in violation will not implement (or will remove) the nonconforming measure or otherwise provide compensation. Sanctioned retaliation is retained as an option to ensure compliance.

DISPUTES UNDER NAFTA, 1994–2000

Chapter 11: Investor-State Disputes

Two things stand out when analyzing investor-state disputes under NAFTA.[13] First, such disputes appear to be the most controversial, and, second and somewhat paradoxically, there is a relative dearth of information on the cases reviewed under Chapter 11. Unlike Chapter 19 and Chapter 20 cases, which NAFTA's Secretariat records and makes available to the public through its official Web site, there is no official trilateral source for NAFTA Chapter 11 disputes.[14]

One way to assess the effectiveness of Chapter 11's DSM is to look at changes in the volume and source of investment flows into Mexico before and after NAFTA's entry into force.[15] Although a number of factors determine foreign direct investment (FDI) flows, and the Chapter 11 DSM would help attract FDI only if accompanied by substantive liberalization,[16] investors do want transparent and stable rules before committing substantial resources, and dispute settlement is a key element in giving investors greater certainty.[17]

From this perspective, the DSM has been a great success. By 1993 Mexico had received an accumulated total of US$25.3 billion in FDI; by 2000 the amount had risen to US$110.2 billion. Notably, there was no drop in FDI flows even after disputes began to emerge, which may reflect satisfaction with NAFTA's FDI regime.

Another way to assess the performance of the Chapter 11 DSM is to determine whether proceedings have been efficient and impartial.[18] Regarding efficiency, one would need to establish the counterfactual— how long the same proceedings would have taken in a domestic court. Although it is not possible to do this, it is clear that some cases were very lengthy, including the three-year Metalclad case (ARB (AF)/97/1) and the Azinian case (ARB (AF)/97/2), which lasted over two years.[19]

Regarding impartiality, the rules of procedure followed in Chapter 11 (UNCITRAL or ICSID) are well established and generally regarded as adequate; panelists have typically been outstanding jurists, and plaintiffs and defendants have both abided by the rulings. It is also likely that the weaker party would be at an immediate disadvantage under direct negotiations, so the impartiality rendered by the mechanism is especially important for a country like Mexico.[20]

Foreign investors seem to have few reservations regarding the Chapter 11 DSM, and this is not too surprising. In their assessment of NAFTA, Hufbauer and Schott argue that the investment DSM rules:

> are so well drafted that NAFTA critics have argued that comparable enforcement procedures should be applied to the labor and environmental areas.... NAFTA marks the first time that a developing country has accorded to foreign investors from developed countries the more favo rable of either national treatment or MFN treatment, has adopted rigorous dispute settlement procedures, and has accepted comprehensive constraints on its use of performance re-quirements.... We regard the NAFTA agreement on i nvestment as far superior to that produced in the Uruguay Round on TRIMS.[21]

Other groups have voiced radically different viewpoints, and opposition to the Chapter 11 DSM has made for strange bedfellows. For example, Bernardo Sepúlveda, Mexico's foreign minister from 1982 to 1988 and representing the views of the traditional foreign policy establishment in Mexico, has been loudly critical. He argues that the Chapter 11 DSM constitutes an unwarranted intrusion into strictly sovereign affairs of states and the operations of the domestic judicial system, and he asserts further that a better alternative would have been to shore up Mexico's flawed judicial system rather than bypass it.[22] In contrast, critics in environmental and labor rights advocacy groups argue that the DSM is an instrument used by multinational corporations to ride roughshod over labor and environmental rights in secrecy-shrouded moves against host governments.[23]

The issues regarding the Chapter 11 DSM and the contending parties' positions are clear-cut. Foreign investors are largely satisfied; if anything, they want labor and environmental issues to intrude even less than they do now. The Canadian government wants to clarify the scope of Chapter 11's substantive procedures regarding environmental issues so as to gain greater leeway in imposing its own health and environmental regulations. Following a challenge to the results of Chapter 11 arbitration proceedings in the Metalclad case (a British Columbia court upheld the award in favor of Metalclad but reduced the amount of damages to be paid by the Mexican government),[24] the Canadian government proposed negotiating a letter of agreement whereby the three NAFTA signatories would clarify the scope of Chapter 11 so that legitimate measures undertaken by host governments to protect health and environmental polices and conditions are not undermined by the dispute settlement proceedings. In July 2001 the NAFTA Free Trade Commission issued notes of interpretation on certain Chapter 11 provisions, but these did not placate NAFTA's critics.[25]

From a substantive perspective, critics want to ensure the protection of labor and, especially, environmental rights when dealing with investment disputes. And from a procedural perspective, they are demanding greater openness and accountability. These contending positions will represent one of the greatest challenges for NAFTA in upcoming years. In the next section I assess whether it would be possible to make certain changes to Chapter 11 procedures and if this would avert an exacerbation of political tensions over investment disputes.

Chapter 19: Subsidies and Dumping Disputes

The vast majority (approximately 88 percent) of NAFTA disputes that have reached the panel stage under Chapters 11, 19, and 20 fall under Chapter 19. Of all Chapter 19 cases, 89 percent refer to dumping and related issues, and only 11 percent to subsidies. The majority of complaints (78 percent) have been filed against U.S. authorities, and disputes have centered on just a few areas—metallurgy (46 percent), manufactures (22 percent), foods and agricultural products (16 percent), construction (13 percent), and chemicals (3 percent). Despite the relatively large number of Chapter 19 cases, as compared to Chapter 11 and Chapter 20 cases, their incidence is relatively rare if seen from the perspective of overall trade flows.

During the CUSFTA negotiations, Canadian business groups insisted on the need to deal with U.S. contingent protection. The chairman of Dupont Canada argued as follows:

> Unless we can negotiate increased and assured access to the U.S. market, Canadian industry will be unable to take the risks involved in making the substantial investments required to operate on a North American basis. Whether the strategy chosen to take advantage of the U.S. potential is specialization, rationalization, or whatever, secure access to the American market is mandatory.[26]

Secure access means not only low tariffs but also, and above all, eliminating or at least reducing the threat of unilateral action by the United States through the use of contingent protection. Mexican business groups expressed similar concerns during the NAFTA negotiations and also insisted on the need to have a "fair" dispute settlement system that would effectively deal with the unilateral imposition of antidumping and countervailing duties by the United States.[27]

The certainty that Chapter 19 provides has played a significant part in favoring a substantial increase in intra-regional trade flows, as shown in figure I.3 in the introduction to this volume. Trade flows have continued to increase despite the Chapter 19 disputes that have arisen.

Chapter 19 proceedings seem not to have aroused the animosity of labor and environmental NGOs. The criticisms have been of a highly technical nature and have been levied by issue experts. Concerns have focused, not on making significant changes to Chapter 19 proceedings, but on issues such as the alleged misinterpretation of NAFTA rules in case MEX-94-1904-02 (cut-to-length steel);[28] panelists' need to recuse themselves in the middle of lengthy proceedings; and the need to strengthen domestic institutions, such as Mexico's Tribunal Fiscal de la Federación, that deal with dumping and subsidies issues.[29]

Approximately 90 percent of Chapter 19 cases have been decided by unanimous rulings, and although decisions have usually not been rendered within the stipulated 315-day limit, there have been no major complaints in this regard.[30] In addition, until mid-2000 the Extraordinary Challenge Procedure had been used only once,[31] suggesting that all parties are thus far pleased with the functioning of the panel system.[32]

Although it has not yet been necessary to apply Article 1905, which was designed to address Mexico's *amparo* proceedings, the *amparo* law still poses a potential threat to the correct functioning of Chapter 19. Unless the Mexican Congress amends the draft prepared by the Supreme Court,[33] thereby reducing the scope and coverage of *amparo* proceedings vis-à-vis Chapter 19 panels, the new law could seriously complicate the correct operation of Chapter 19 proceedings regarding Mexico and would undermine confidence in the system.

Chapter 20: General DSM

The negotiation of NAFTA Chapter 20 was less contentious than the debates involving Chapters 11 and 19.[34] Mexico strongly supported having binding panel decisions instead of recommendations, but the United States rejected this proposal.

NAFTA's general DSM has been called into action much less frequently than its Chapter 11 and Chapter 19 counterparts, especially if we consider only the disputes that reach the panel stage. Many disputes did arise, but these did not reach the panel stage because they were resolved through consultations, good offices, conciliation, and/or mediation. Several features stand out in the Chapter 20 cases that reached the panel stage.[35] First, the United States has always been involved, as either defendant or plaintiff; there have been no cases between Mexico and Canada, and all cases have been initiated either by Mexico (75 percent) or by the United States (25 percent). Second, the vast majority of cases involve trade in goods (69 percent). Services account for another 19 percent of cases.[36]

In terms of compliance with time limits, Chapter 20 proceedings are found wanting. The main reason for these systematic delays is difficulty in agreeing on panelist selection. A final roster, which should have been in place when NAFTA was implemented in 1994,[37] had still not been agreed upon by late 2000. The long delays of the panel process have sometimes exacerbated political and economic tensions instead of easing them, which, of course, is the stated aim of this highly flexible mechanism. Two instances in which tensions worsened over the course of the panel process are the case involving Mexico and the

United States over Mexican sugar exports[38] and the Mexico-U.S. dispute over trucking (USA-98-2008-01).

Another problem has been full compliance with panel recommendations. In the case of broomcorn brooms (USA-97-2008-01), the panel made its recommendation in favor of the plaintiff in January 1998, but it was not until December of that year that the United States removed the safeguards. Although Mexico did not invoke its right to suspend benefits until the United States complied, future delays in abiding by panel recommendations could result in the use of sanctioned retaliation. This would be a costly result for both parties[39] and one that would delegitimize panel recommendations, which are aimed first and foremost at securing the removal of inconsistent measures— not at compensation, and even less at sanctioned retaliation in the face of sustained noncompliance.

THE NEED FOR AND FEASIBILITY OF INSTITUTIONAL DEVELOPMENT IN NAFTA

Before presenting specific suggestions regarding the operation of the three DSMs examined in this chapter, it is advisable to mention some general issues. The first involves the evaluation criteria for DSM performance. The preceding brief evaluation of DSM performance referred to the guidelines—number of cases submitted and compliance with timelines and panel rulings—by which these mechanisms are typically assessed.[40] An assumption underlying this approach is that a frequently used DSM is an "effective" one insofar as the parties involved comply with panel decisions or recommendations. Yet, strictly speaking, the best DSM is one that is never used because the simple threat of its use is sufficient to ensure that all parties comply with their treaty commitments. Indeed, the frequency with which DSMs are used may reflect situations of incomplete and imperfect information.[41] Resorting to DSMs, like labor strikes, may be an expensive way to reveal information.

Another way of looking at this issue would be the following: the best indicator of superlative performance on the part of NAFTA's DSMs would be if the DSMs had never been used and trade and investment had proceeded apace. A less propitious scenario would be one in which the DSMs were used infrequently and all parties abided by panel decisions or recommendations. While determining what represents "frequent" or "infrequent" use is not a simple endeavor, I venture that the ratio of trade and investment flows to disputes is low, and the use of the DSMs can thus be regarded as "infrequent." And given the increasing economic interaction throughout the 1994–2000 period, they can also be regarded as "effective."

Second, certain issues must be borne in mind when proposing modifications to the DSMs. Like the classic dilemma regarding the trade-off between efficiency and representativeness in the design of domestic political systems,[42] the trade-off with a DSM is between increasing access to a great number of actors[43] and furthering "transparency" in general, on the one hand, and, on the other, favoring expedient solutions, which, at an extreme, would be ensured by granting full authority to a single individual. Procuring greater representativeness would, however, increase the probability that there would be less resistance to the goodwill acceptance—and implementation—of panel decisions.

Providing flexibility would likewise facilitate the implementation of panel decisions in the vast majority of cases. When for domestic political reasons it would prove very costly to implement a panel decision, the first party may have other ways of making compensation to the second party. If this were not possible, there might be a serious backlash against the "intrusion" of "international bodies" into "domestic" affairs.[44]

Third, by its very nature, NAFTA makes institutional adjustments difficult. As noted earlier, NAFTA was a "one-shot" deal; it does not provide for substantial institutional evolution. Nevertheless, under the faculties granted to the Free Trade Commission—which include overseeing the "further elaboration" of the Agreement (Article 2001:2b) and taking "such other action in the exercise of its functions as the Parties may agree" (Article 2001:2e)—it may be possible to make some modifications to current practices without legislative approval. Proposing modifications that require legislative approval may be politically unfeasible. It would also set a dangerous precedent; suggesting that relatively new international agreements can easily be opened for renegotiation would impair these agreements' aim of enhancing certainty and predictability.[45]

Chapter 11: Investor-State Disputes

In my view, the greatest challenges to the NAFTA DSM in upcoming years will involve the investor-state mechanism. Several steps can and should be taken to shore up the system, so that it satisfies both supporters and critics and can weather the political environment. Preemptive modifications will prove more fruitful than ex-post changes after a crisis.[46] The biggest risk for the adequate functioning of Chapter 11 would be to do nothing.

The primary criticism coming from Mexico's traditional foreign policy establishment has become moot, at least for the time being. Mexico, like many other developing countries, has continued to enter a number of trade agreements that include an investor-state DSM; it has even negotiated a significant number of BITs.[47]

The points raised by labor and environmental rights advocates will have to be addressed, and they include both procedural and substantive issues. A primary procedural concern is the lack of transparency in the process, but this concern actually comprises two separate issues. The first pertains to the arbitration proceedings themselves; the second, to information on cases and rulings. Regarding the procedural questions, I see no reason—or possibility—to amend dispute settlement proceedings as they are currently carried out under ICSID or UNCITRAL rules, given that the relative secrecy of the proceedings is the very characteristic that allows the system to function. If some substantive concerns were addressed, there would likely be less insistence on procedural changes.

Regarding the dissemination of information on cases and rulings, the current situation is untenable. The parties are not legally bound to make awards public, although they can do so at their discretion.[48] The Canadian and U.S. governments are already doing this,[49] and information is also available through various formal and informal channels.[50] The flat refusal on the part of Mexico to make this information public exacerbates concerns about the secrecy of the procedures themselves, and it casts suspicion on the system as a whole. NAFTA's Secretariat already releases information on Chapter 19 and Chapter 20 disputes, and it could also provide (with the necessary disclaimers) information on Chapter 11 disputes on its Web site.

Environmental matters are among the most salient substantive concerns; it will be increasingly difficult to ignore them when investment-related disputes arise. Indeed, the Ministerial Declaration of the Free Trade Area of the Americas (FTAA) process stated that protecting labor and environmental rights would be of paramount importance.[51]

An issue that must be addressed resulted from the British Columbia court decision on the Metalclad case. Dissenting views regarding the scope of Chapter 11's substantive provisions (Section A) not only generate uncertainty, but they also provide fertile ground for protests by environmental groups. One solution could be for the Free Trade Commission to signal its intent to give priority to environmental matters when interpreting the scope of Chapter 11.[52]

Chapter 19: Subsidies and Dumping Disputes

Although Chapter 19 disputes constitute the vast majority of cases submitted under NAFTA's three main DSMs, the Chapter 19 process seems to be working acceptably well. Nevertheless, the continuing predominance of antidumping disputes speaks to the need for efforts to reduce their incidence or, at minimum, their disruptive effects. One minor change could be to amend current Mexican law so that reimbursements for duties paid by exporters under a preliminary investigation would either be avoided or be made in a more timely manner.[53] Likewise, greater coordination of macroeconomic policies (or, rather, unilateral actions on Mexico's part as it pursues stability) would reduce the need to resort to antidumping measures, given that wide swings in exchange rates greatly increase the pressure to use antidumping actions.

A more complicated matter regards the *amparo* proceedings. The use of Article 1905 could be interpreted as an unwarranted intrusion into Mexico's domestic legal proceedings. To avoid this situation, care must be taken to ensure that the new *amparo* law does not interfere with the correct functioning of Chapter 19. This will require intensive congressional lobbying on the part of Mexico's economic minister, but the situation does not look promising given that the United States has frequently failed to comply fully and promptly with Chapter 20 panel recommendations that favor Mexico.[54] A quid pro quo regarding U.S. compliance with Chapter 20 recommendations may be required before the Mexican Congress agrees to limit the scope of the new *amparo* law.

A more far-reaching alternative would be to include sectors in which antidumping actions are relatively rare in a list of exempt sectors. In this way, only the most contentious sectors—such as intermediate and capital goods, and agricultural items—would remain subject to antidumping actions. The excluded sectors could then be governed by each country's competition policies, the basic commitments set out in NAFTA Chapter 15, and, especially, the activities of the Working Group on Trade and Competition set up under Article 1504.

This approach could serve as the basis of a long-term goal: eliminating antidumping policies among the members of NAFTA and replacing them with competition policies. This was proposed by placing them with competition policies. This was proposed by Canada during the bilateral negotiations of the CUSFTA[55] and by Mexico during the NAFTA negotiations,[56] but the United States refused to support the proposals. This approach may prove more feasible once the fifteen-year transition period of full tariff elimination has run its course. By that time, most adjustment costs would have been absorbed by uncompetitive industries, so there would be no rationale for continuing to protect them. In any case, given the role of Chapter 19 proceedings in curtailing the abuse of unfair trade law, these industries would no longer be able to request antidumping protection from their government.

Canada has already accepted the application of competition instead of antidumping policies in its free trade agreement with Chile, and that approach may be valuable when thinking about NAFTA's long-term institutional evolution. Nevertheless, this is a very complex and specialized area, and it will require further research.[57]

Finally, one issue to address in the longer term is jurisprudence, the aims being to avoid the potentially dangerous precedent of obtaining different rulings in similar cases and, more generally, to avoid unnecessary case submission in the first place.[58]

Chapter 20: General DSM

Even though there have been relatively few Chapter 20 cases, I suggest that the flexible nature of this process has become more of a liability than an asset. Given that NAFTA has been in operation since 1994, it is probably fair to assume that most politically sensitive issues regarding the interpretation and application of the agreement have already come to the fore. Many of these issues have been addressed under the flexible mechanism, but there have been inordinate delays at the pre-panel stage and, when a panel is requested, in agreeing on the panel's composition. By opting not to turn up the political heat, parties involved in disputes have ended up with festering problems.

Although the parties have abided, by and large, by panel recommendations, they have not done so promptly (consider, for example, the case of broomcorn brooms) or in a manner that satisfies the other party, and this outcome may result in recourse to sanctioned retaliation.[59] At this stage in NAFTA's development, it would be well worth the effort for the parties to reach an understanding regarding the application of Chapter 20. They could, for instance, commit to expediting the pre-panel stages of dispute settlement and to complying fully with panel recommendations, thereby avoiding the need for sanctioned retaliation.[60]

CONCLUSIONS

NAFTA's DSMs were designed to address the challenges the trade accord would face in its operation. Now the mechanisms themselves are facing challenges. Their functioning—and the functioning of the agreement as a whole—will depend in part on remedying their short-comings, whether through some of the actions suggested above or some other corrective measures.

I noted at the outset the importance of providing more information on Chapter 11 cases. The same could be said of Chapter 19 and Chapter 20 cases. Information is available on Chapter 19 cases, but it is not always up to date. Little information is available regarding issues that are under examination in Chapter 20's pre-panel stages. Providing complete, timely, and clear information on NAFTA disputes would substantially offset criticisms of lack of transparency.

To fulfill this dissemination function, the NAFTA Secretariat would likely require increased resources, both human and financial. Perhaps NADBank funds could be secured for this purpose. The Secretariat could also play a more salient role in the annual Free Trade Commission meetings. It could, for instance, prepare detailed reports on DSM performance, which could be made public. These reports could also include the viewpoints of business organizations, NGOs, and other social interest groups, making them feel part of the NAFTA process and helping all groups find "middle ground"[61] and avoid confrontation.

Another challenge facing the DSMs lies outside NAFTA: these mechanisms must be able to respond to developments in other areas, especially the new round of WTO trade negotiations[62] and the FTAA process. NAFTA's institutions must complement those in other venues at the same time that they remain at the fore of the integration process. They must not become obsolete or, worse, irrelevant. A specific issue to be addressed is the potential duplication of dispute settlement forums.[63] The GATT was addressed in Chapter 20 but not in Chapter 19. NAFTA must be adjusted to avoid a similar situation in the future, and care must be taken in this regard in light of new commitments under the WTO and FTAA.

Thus both internal and external developments will challenge the NAFTA institutions. The best way to deal with these challenges will be through creative and proactive engagement, rather than through hesitant actions in response to political crises.

Notes

I would like to thank César Hernández and Gustavo Vega Cánovas for their comments on a previous draft of this essay. All shortcomings and om issions are solely the responsibility of the author. Carlos Echeverría and A lfonso Martínez provided valuable research assistance.

1. Hermann Von Bertrab, *Negotiating NAFTA: A Mexican Envoy's Account* (Westport, Conn.: Praeger, 1997), and Maxwell A. Cameron and Brian Tomlin, *The Making of NAFTA: How the Deal Was Done* (Ithaca, N.Y.: Cornell University Press, 2000).

2. See James McCall Smith, "The Politics of Dispute Settlement Design," *International Organization* 54, no. 1 (Winter 2000): 137–80, and Antonio Ortiz Mena L.N., "The Politics of Institutional Choice: International Trade and Dispute Settlement" (Ph.D. dissertation, University of California, San Diego, 2001).

3. NAFTA also provides for a separate roster of experts for financial se rvices disputes (which are conducted under Chapter 20 provisions), and there are specialized dispute settlement provisions for labor and environmental issues. The latter two issues are taken up in this volume in the chapters by Bensusán and by Davidson and Mitchell, respective ly. There are some excellent summaries of the three main NAFTA DSMs; only a brief overview is presented here, in order to focus the discussion on their performance and possible institutional evolution. Those wishing to consult NAFTA's legal text can do so at the NAFTA Secretariat Web site: www.nafta-sec-alena.org/english/index.htm. The site also provides a summary and timeline of dispute settlement provisions. A very good, succinct overview is to be found in Gi lbert L. Winham, "Dispute Settlement in NAFTA and the FTA," in *Assessing NAFTA: A Trinational Analysis*, ed. Steven Globerman and M ichael Walker (Vancouver, B.C.: Fraser Institute, 1993). For more thorough coverage, see Jeffrey P. Bialos and Deborah E. Siegel, "Dispute Resolution under NAFTA: The Newer and Improved Model," *International Lawyer* 27, no. 3 (Fall 1993): 603–22. Those wishing to delve more deeply into the intricacies of the Cha pter 11 DSM can refer to the following: Daniel M. Price, "An Overview of the NAFTA Investment Chapter: Substantive R ules and Investor-State Dispute Settlement," *International Lawyer* 27, no. 3 (Fall 1993): 727–36; Richard C. Levin and Susan Erickson Marin, "NAFTA Chapter 11: Investment and I nvestment Disputes," *NAFTA: Law and Business Review of the Americas* 2, no. 3 (Summer 1996): 82–115; and Gary N. Horlick and Alicia R. Marti, "NAFTA Chapter 11B: A Private Right of Action to Enforce Market Access Through Investments," *Journal of International Arbitration* 14, no. 1 (March 1997): 43–54.

Regarding Chapter 19, see Homer E. Moyer, Jr., "Chapter 19 of the NAFTA: Binational Panels as the Trade Courts of Last Resort," *International Lawyer* 27, no. 3 (Fall 1993): 707–26; and Beatriz Leycegui, William B.P. Robson, and S. Dahlia Stein, eds., *Trading Punches: Trade Remedy Law and Disputes under NAFTA* (Washington, D.C.: National Planning Association, 1995). For Chapter 20, refer to Fernando Serrano Migallón, "El Mecanismo de Solución de Controversias en el Tratado de Libre Comercio de América del Norte," in *Resolución de controversias comerciales en América del Norte*, ed. Jorge Witker V. (Mexico City: Universidad Nacional Autónoma de México, 1997); and Beatriz Leycegui, "Acordar para disentir: la solución de controversias en el Tratado de Libre Comercio de América del Norte," in *¿Socios naturales? Cinco años del Tratado de Libre Comercio de América del Norte*, ed. Rafael Fernández de Castro and Beatriz Leycegui (Mexico City: Instituto Tecnológico Autónomo de México/Miguel Ángel Porrúa, 2000).

4. For a discussion of "obligation," "precision," and "delegation" aspects of the legalization of international relations, see Kenneth W. Abbott, Robert O. Keohane, Andrew Moravcsik, and Anne-Marie Slaughter, "The Concept of Legalization," *International Organization* 54, no. 3 (Summer 2001): 401–19.

5. MERCOSUR is the Common Market of the South, comprising Argentina, Brazil, Paraguay, and Uruguay.

6. One need only compare NAFTA's legal text with the Treaty of Asunción, which establishes MERCOSUR, to have an immediate grasp of differences in design. MERCOSUR's legal and institutional structure has evolved through a series of protocols, such as the Brasilia Protocol on dispute settlement. For an overview of MERCOSUR's institutional structure, see Luiz Olavo Baptista, *O MERCOSUL: Suas Instituçoes e Ordenamento Jurídico* (São Paulo: LTR, 1998).

7. ICSID is the World Bank's International Centre for Settlement of Investment Disputes; UNCITRAL is the United Nations Commission on International Trade Law.

8. NAFTA Annex 1137-4.

9. Michael Hart (with Bill Dymond and Colin Robertson), *Decision at Midnight: Inside the Canada-US Free Trade Negotiations* (Vancouver, B.C.: University of British Columbia Press, 1994).

10. Debra Steger, "Analysis of the Dispute Settlement Provisions: A Canadian Perspective," in *Assessing the Canada-U.S. Free Trade Agreement*, ed. Murray G. Smith and Frank Stone (Halifax, Nova Scotia: Institute for Research on Public Policy, 1987), p. 94.

11. Article 1905 is designed to deal with *amparo* proceedings. There is no exact equivalent to the *amparo* in Anglo-Saxon legislation. It is "a general constitutional guarantee protecting one's civil rights against violation by public authorities, a writ issued against final judgment in certain cases when no other ordinary recourse is available." See Luis Miguel Díaz and Ben Lenhart, *Diccio-*

nario de términos jurídicos español-inglés. English-Spanish (Mexico City: Themis, 1992): 37. Under Mexican law, individuals and corporations can seek an *amparo* against laws or "acts of authority" if they deem their interests to ha ve been unjustly affected by such acts. Judicial proceedings and *amparo* trials are extremely lengthy and cumbersome, and can quite effectively disrupt the i n-tended effects of public policy decisions.

12. There is an Advisory Committee on Private Commercial Disputes ascribed to the Commission, and the Commission is entitled to call on technical advisers. For an overview of alternative dispute resolution (consultations, good offices, conciliation, and mediation), see J.G. Merrills, *International Dispute Settlement* (London: Sweet and Maxwell, 1984); and Peter Behrens, "Alte r-native Methods of Dispute Settlement in International Economic Relations," in *Adjudication of International Trade Disputes in International and National Economic Law*, ed. Ernst-Ulrich Petersmann and Gunther Jaenicke (Fribourg, Switze r-land: University Press Fribourg, 1992).

13. The list of cases used as the basis for this analysis is not reproduced herein. It can be obtained directly from the author at antonio.ortiz@cide.edu.

14. NAFTA's Secretariat provides information on Chapter 19 and Chapter 20 cases at www.nafta-sec-alena.org/english/index.htm. Chapter 11 cases are not reported by the Secretariat, but the Canadian Foreign Ministry provides some information about them at http://www.dfait-maeci.gc.ca/tna-nac/ NAFTA-e.asp—as does the U.S. Department of State at www.state.gov/ s/l/c3439.htm. An unofficial source for Chapter 11 cases is www.naftaclaims. com. UNCITRAL's Web site (www.uncitral.org) does not contain a listing of cases.

15. Canada-U.S. FDI flows are not contemplated in this analysis because they were already affected by the earlier bilateral free trade agreement, and more to the point, neither party was unduly concerned about threats to their investments in the other party. They did not see the need to include an investor-state DSM in their bilateral deal.

16. For an overview of FDI flow determinants, see Kenneth A. Froot, ed., *Foreign Direct Investment: National Bureau of Economic Research Project Report* (Chicago: University of Chicago Press, 1994). A recent UNCTAD report co n-cludes that, in general, the effects of BITs on investment flows are modest; see *Bilateral Investment Treaties in the Mid-1990s* (New York: United Nations, 1998), pp. 105–22.

17. These concerns are greater when there are trade-related asset-specific investments involved. See Beth V. Yarbrough and Robert M. Yarbrough, *Cooperation and Governance in International Trade: The Strategic Organizational Approach* (Princeton, N.J.: Princeton University Press, 1992).

18. I am indebted to César Hernández for suggesting this approach and providing the relevant information.

19. See "Inversión extranjera directa en México," Power Point presentation made by Mexico's Ministry of the Economy, available at its Web site: www.economia.gob.mx.

20. I am indebted to Gustavo Vega for bringing up this point.

21. Gary Clyde Hufbauer and Jeffrey J. Schott, *NAFTA: An Assessment* (Washington, D.C.: Institute for International Economics, 1993): 81–84.

22. Bernardo Sepúlveda Amor, "Orden jurídico y soberanía n acional: el TLC y las reivindicaciones de la jurisdicción mexicana," *Este País* 68 (November 1996): 40–46.

23. See, for example, "NAFTA's Powerful Little Secret," *New York Times*, March 11, 2001, and "Sovereign Corporations," *The Nation*, April 30, 2001.

24. For an overview of the Metalclad case, see Arturo Borja, "The New Federalism in Mexico and Foreign Economic Policy: An Alternative Two - Level Analysis of the Metalclad Case," *Latin American Politics and Society* (formerly *Journal of Interamerican Studies and World Affairs*), forthcoming. In May 2001, a British Columbia court ruled that the panel that decided the Metalclad case had interpreted the rights of the plaintiff too broadly, and thus reduced the amount of damages to be paid by the Mexican government to M etalclad. In addition, the ruling was regarded as opening the door for government a r-guments on expropriation of foreign investments based on health and safety concerns. See "Company Wins Ruling against Mexico, but 'In Name Only,'" *The News* (Mexico City), May 5, 2001; "Landmark Decision Empowers Health, Safety Concerns over Corporate Trade Rights," *The News*, May 6, 2001; and "B.C. Court Affirms Metalclad Ruling," *Financial Post* (Canada), May 5, 2001.

25. See Howard Mann and Konrad Von Moltke, *NAFTA's Chapter 11 and the Environment: Addressing the Impact of the Investor State Process on the Environment* (Winnipeg, Manitoba: International Institute for Sustainable Development, 1999). The notes of interpretation issued by the Free Trade Commission are available at www.dfait-maeci.gc.ca/tna-nac/NAFTA-interp-e.asp.

26. Cited in Hart, *Decision at Midnight*, p. 77.

27. Von Bertrab, *Negotiating NAFTA;* Cameron and Tomlin, *The Making of NAFTA*; Ortiz Mena L.N., "The Politics of Institutional Choice," pp. 75 – 122.

28. J.C. Thomas and Sergio López Ayllon, "NAFTA Dispute Settlement and Mexico: Interpreting Treaties and Reconciling Common and Civil Law Systems in a Free Trade Area," in *Canadian Yearbook of International Law*, vol. 33 (Vancouver, B.C.: University of British Columbia P ress, 1995).

29. Leycegui, "Acordar para disentir."

30. The average time for sixty-nine cases from January 1994 to August 2000 was fifteen months with Canada as defendant, nineteen months with Mexico as defendant, and thirteen months with the United States a s defendant. See Gustavo Vega, "Resolución de controversias en materia de prácticas

desleales de comercio en el TLCAN: la experiencia del Capítulo XIX," in *Las prácticas desleales de comercio en el proceso de integración comercial en el continente americano: la experiencia de América del Norte y Chile*, ed. Sergio López Ayllon and Gustavo Vega Cánovas (Mexico City: SECOFI/Instituto de Investigaciones Jurídicas, Universidad Nacional Autónoma de México, 2001). Vega argues that the problems that generated delays in the Mexican case have largely been taken care of, and that the system is functioning well overall. See also Gustavo Vega Cánovas, "Liberación del comercio y regulación supranacional del antidumping: el Capítulo XIX del TLCAN," *Foro Internacional* 39, no. 4 (October–December 1999): 527–44.

31. On March 23, 2000, the United States requested the initiation of the Extraordinary Challenge Procedure to oversee a case involving exports of gray Portland cement and clinker from Mexico (ECC-2000-1904-01 USA).

32. Not all analysts concur with this assessment. Gilbert Gagné ("North American Free Trade, Canada, and U.S. Trade Remedies: An Analysis after Ten Years," *World Economy* 23, no. 1 [2000]: 77–91) argues that Canada has enhanced, but not secured, its access to the U.S. market. He notes shortcomings such as delays in the panel review process, the maintenance of U.S. trade remedy law and the ability to modify it in restrictive ways, the persistence of harassment tactics by the United States which frequently lead to compromises in order to avoid costly litigation, and the possibly greater incidence of antidumping actions by the United States in times of economic hardship. He is especially critical of the results of the softwood lumber and wheat cases. Part of his criticism lies in the fact that not all panel rulings have been in favor of Canada when it has been the plaintiff, so in his view this translates only into enhanced access.

I submit that if all rulings had been in favor of Canada, this would indeed reflect a worrisome pattern of incorrect application of antidumping law by U.S. authorities, but this has not been the case. Gagné misses the point, made by Judith Goldstein ("International Law and Domestic Institutions: Reconciling North American 'Unfair' Trade Law," *International Organization* 50, no. 4 [Autumn 1996]: 385–99) that it is not necessary for a matter to reach the panel stage to ensure greater objectivity and fairness in the application of antidumping law by U.S. authorities. Likewise, while it certainly would have been preferable to have either common competition law or at least common antidumping law, other countries would be very glad to have the privilege that is now only accorded to Canada and Mexico. Lastly, Chapter 19 provisions also mandate that changes to domestic antidumping law must be consistent with GATT and NAFTA provisions on the matter (Article 1903), although it is true that a panel reviewing such a case may only issue a declaratory opinion.

33. Suprema Corte de Justicia, *Proyecto de Ley de Amparo Reglamentaria de los Artículos 103 y 107 de la Constitución Política de los Estados Unidos Mexicanos* (Mexico City: Suprema Corte de Justicia, 2000).

34. Cameron and Tomlin, *The Making of NAFTA*, Ortiz Mena L.N., "The Politics of Institutional Choice."

35. The NAFTA Secretariat does not provide information on cases that did not reach the panel stage. Some information on these cases is available in Leycegui, "Acordar para disentir."

36. This latter statistic refers to the 1994–1998 period. See Leycegui, "Acordar para disentir," p. 562.

37. Leycegui, "Acordar para disentir."

38. As of early 2001, this case had not been reported on the NAFTA S e-cretariat Web page. On August 1, 2000, Mexico asked the Free Trade Co m-mission to establish a panel to resolve the issue given that the governments had been unable to reach an agreement through negotiations since 1993. See Secretaría de Comercio y Fomento Industrial, "México solicita el establec i-miento de un panel que analice el tema del acceso del azúcar a EE.UU." (Di-rección de Comunicación Social, press release, August 1, 2000).

39. Richard D. Farmer, "Costs of Economic Sanctions to the Sender," *World Economy* 23, no. 1 (2000): 93–117.

40. See, for example, Fernández de Castro and Leycegui, eds., *¿Socios naturales?*, and A. Imtiaz Hussain, "¿Un puente sobre aguas turbulentas? Los páneles binacionales en el TLCAN y las prácticas comerciales desleales en América del Norte," in *Para evaluar al TLCAN*, ed. Arturo Borja (Mexico City: TEC/Miguel Ángel Porrúa, 2001).

41. This argument is related to the notion of "backwards induction" in games of complete and perfect information used by game theorists. See David A. Kreps, *A Course in Microeconomic Theory* (Princeton, N.J.: Princeton University Press, 1990), and James D. Morrow, *Game Theory for Political Scientists* (Princeton, N.J.: Princeton University Press, 1994). I am indebted to David A. Lake for making this point.

42. See Matthew S. Shugart and John M. Carey, *Presidents and Assemblies: Constitutional Design and Electoral Dynamics* (New York: Cambridge University Press, 1992).

43. Technically this would translate into private rights of action.

44. Judith Goldstein makes a similar argument, criticizing the rather inflexible nature of DSM proceedings under the WTO. See Goldstein, "I n-ternational Institutions and Domestic Politics: GATT, WTO and the Libe r-alization of International Trade," presented at the Graduate School of Inte r-national Relations and Pacific Studies, University of California, San Diego, November 22, 1996. Her reasoning is a dev elopment of the "embedded libe r-alism" argument developed by John G. Ruggie in "International Regimes, Transactions, and Change: Embedded Liberalism in the Postwar Economic

Order," in *International Regimes*, ed. Stephen D. Krasner (Ithaca, N.Y.: Cornell University Press, 1993).

45. It would also be important to carry out such modifications in an open and transparent manner, for otherwise the end result might be counter‐productive.

46. This was precisely the uncomfortable situation in which the WTO found itself after the December 1999 protests in Seattle.

47. See Susan Minushkin and Antonio Ortiz Mena L.N., "The Institutional Structure of Financial and Monetary Integration in the Americas," CIDE Working Paper EI 73 (2001). The issue does remain highly contentious at the multilateral level. See Yoshi Kodama, "Dispute Settlement under the Draft Multilateral Agreement on Investment," *Journal of International Arbitration* 16, no. 3 (1999): 45–87.

48. Chapter 11 Rules of Procedure allow investors to publish the award when the defendant has been Canada or the United States, but the provisions are ambiguous in the Mexican case. The Metalclad panel stated that ICSID rules do not forbid the dispute to be heard in public, and the Methanex panel (UNCITRAL 7/99) clarified that UNCITRAL rules permit petitions from third parties under the precept of *amicus curiae* if the panel deems it pertinent. I am indebted to Gustavo Vega for bringing this to my attention.

49. See www.dfait-maeci.gc.ca/tna-nac/NAFTA-es.asp.

50. An important informal source is www.naftaclaims.com. In addition, references frequently appear in specialized publications, such as *Inside U.S. Trade*.

51. The way to do so has not been agreed upon, but it will be difficult to simply simulate that issues are being taken care of. The Declaration states, "We reiterate that the negotiation of the FTAA will continue to take into account the broad social and economic agenda contained in the Miami and Santiago Declarations and Plans of Action with a view to contributing to raising living standards, improving the working conditions of all people in the Americas and better protecting the environment." See www.sice.oas.org/ftaa/baires/minis/bamin_e.asp.

52. This would entail applying Article 1131:2 (Governing Law) in the interpretation of Article 1141:1 (Environmental Measures), and would not require a renegotiation of Chapter 11. Article 1131:2 states that "An interpretation by the Commission of a provision of this Agreement shall be binding on a Tribunal established under this section." Article 1141:1 states that "Nothing in this Chapter shall be construed to prevent a Party from adopting, maintaining or enforcing any measure otherwise consistent with this Chapter that it considers appropriate to ensure that investment activity in its territory is undertaken in a manner sensitive to environmental concerns." I am indebted to César Hernández for drawing this to my attention. The notes of interpretation issued in July 2001 do not follow this approach; see note 25.

53. For an overview of the Mexican antidumping regulatory framework, see Beatriz Leycegui, "A Legal Analysis of Mexico's Antidumping and Cou n-tervailing Duty Regulatory Network," in *Trading Punches*, ed. Leycegui, Robson, and Stein.

54. For example, in the broomcorn brooms and trucking d isputes.

55. Hart, *Decision at Midnight.*

56. Cameron and Tomlin, *The Making of NAFTA.*

57. For a discussion of possible reforms of antidumping laws in North Americas, see Michel Hart, ed., *Finding Middle Ground: Reforming the Antidumping Laws in North America* (Ottawa: Centre for Trade Policy and Law, 1997).

58. See the comments on "backwards induction" made above. Regarding jurisprudence, it is not necessary to formally provide for it. "Persuasive" precedents are established in cases where panel decisions have b een unanimous. In addition, providing for full-time panelists (which would not require the establishment of a permanent arbitration body) would also greatly co n-tribute toward this end.

59. Case USA-98-2008-01 on cross-border trucking services ended with a unanimous panel decision in favor of Mexico in February 2001, and U.S. a u-thorities received a recommendation to comply with NAFTA commi tments on the matter. The preliminary guidelines that the U.S. Department of Tran s-portation subsequently emitted were not well regarded by the Mexican go v-ernment, which argued that they still discriminated against Mexican trucks and drivers. If the issue is not resolved before final guidelines enter into force, there is a possibility that the Mexican government will resort to sanctioned retaliation.

60. While Mexico provides for binding panel decisions in the general DSM of its free trade agreements with Latin American countries, the DSM of the Canada-Chile free trade agreement is still of a very flexible nature and does not provide for binding decisions. During NAFTA negotiations, the United States objected to Mexico's proposal providing for binding decisions under Chapter 20. See Ortiz Mena L.N., "The Politics of Institutional Choice."

61. This expression is borrowed from Hart, *Finding Middle Ground.*

62. A new round of multilateral trade negotiations was held in Qatar in November 2001.

63. See Reif, this volume.

19

NAFTA, WTO, and FTAA: Choice of Forum in Dispute Resolution

Linda C. Reif

Canada, Mexico and the United States—the three parties to the North American Free Trade Agreement (NAFTA)[1] and the accompanying environmental and labor agreements[2]—are also parties to a growing number of multilateral and bilateral trade and investment treaties. These agreements range from the Marrakesh Agreement Establishing the World Trade Organization (WTO Agreement),[3] with all three states being WTO members, to a growing number of free trade agreements and bilateral investment treaties that each of the NAFTA parties has entered into with other states in the Western Hemisphere and beyond.[4] In addition, the Free Trade Area of the Americas (FTAA) negotiating process may result in a free trade agreement that includes all Western Hemisphere states except Cuba.[5]

From an inter-state perspective, if a trade or investment dispute arises between two of the NAFTA partners, more than one treaty with its substantive rights and obligations may be applicable, and, consequently, different dispute resolution mechanisms may also be available. At present, the only other trade and investment treaty that involves all three NAFTA states is the WTO Agreement. However, if an FTAA is established in the future, and assuming that all three NAFTA states sign the FTAA individually, then the NAFTA parties will have a third treaty regime applicable to their trade/investment relations. Currently, if a trade/investment dispute arises between NAFTA parties, they have to decide whether to resort to the WTO or the NAFTA treaty regime—depending on the nature of the dispute, the relevant legal rights and obligations of each treaty, and the different characteristics of the inter-state dispute resolution mechanisms in each agreement. This determination will become even more complex if a third treaty alternative—the FTAA—is added to the equation.

From the perspective of nongovernmental organizations (NGOs) and business in the NAFTA states, there are also differences between the WTO and NAFTA in terms of the standing of private actors to access and participate in dispute resolution processes. An FTAA may also contain dispute resolution mechanisms open to private actors. Thus the issue of choice of forum may also become relevant for NAFTA civil society complaints.

In this chapter I explore the differences, interaction, and resultant possibility of forum shopping between NAFTA, the WTO, and a potential FTAA from the perspective of a NAFTA state. I also examine the differences between the agreements in terms of private actor access to and participation in dispute settlement processes, and the implications this entails. I examine differentials in the WTO and NAFTA in terms of substantive coverage, dispute resolution procedures, and the standing of states and non-state actors to access dispute resolution mechanisms. In particular, I explore how this can result in "forum shopping" by governments and in the heavy use of dispute resolution mechanisms that are open to non-state entities. The FTAA negotiating text is also reviewed in the light of these issues.

NAFTA AND THE WTO

The WTO entered into force on January 1, 1995, the product of the 1986–1994 Uruguay Round of multilateral trade negotiations.[6] This international organization incorporates a number of multilateral trade agreements that cover trade in goods, trade in services, trade-related investment measures (TRIMS), and trade-related intellectual property (TRIPs). The General Agreement on Tariffs and Trade (GATT) has been incorporated within the WTO (as GATT 1994) and remains the core agreement governing trade in goods.

NAFTA entered into force on January 1, 1994, the result of about three years of negotiations and closely based on the earlier 1989 Canada–United States Free Trade Agreement (CUSFTA).[7] NAFTA as a free trade agreement between three of the GATT/WTO members is regulated by the WTO/GATT, and many GATT/WTO rules are incorporated into NAFTA by reference or because the NAFTA drafters followed the GATT legal doctrine relatively closely in structuring other NAFTA obligations.[8] NAFTA is a "free trade agreement plus," covering trade in goods, but also government procurement, trade in services (including financial services), investment, competition policy, intellectual property, and temporary entry for business persons. Given the overlapping time frames in the drafting of the WTO Agreement and NAFTA, "both negotiations borrowed heavily from the innovations and lessons of the other" and "[w]hen the results of the two do overlap, NAFTA usually provides for greater and quicker strides toward complete market access."[9]

While a comprehensive comparison of the similarities and differences between the WTO Agreement and NAFTA is beyond the scope of this essay, some of the differences in substantive content between the two treaties can be highlighted. For example, NAFTA's Chapter 6 on trade in energy goods is much more detailed and tighter on nontariff barriers than corresponding provisions in the GATT/WTO. NAFTA expressly provides for the paramountcy of trade controls in listed environmental treaties in the event of a conflict between NAFTA and these treaties, and it has a number of other provisions that expressly address the environment.[10] Mexico has taken a number of exemptions to its trade and investment obligations under NAFTA beyond those also taken by Canada and the United States.[11] NAFTA does not contain any substantive law on subsidies and dumping, whereas the WTO Agreement contains substantive rights and obligations in these two areas of contingent protection.[12] NAFTA has an ambiguous exemption for cultural industry matters carried forward from the CUSFTA, whereas the WTO Agreement does not contain a similar blanket carve-out, although the WTO rights and obligations will differ depending on whether the cultural matter is classified as trade in goods or services, or trade-related intellectual property rights.[13] NAFTA's Chapter 11 on investment is much more extensive and stronger in its controls on government action compared to the WTO TRIMS Agreement. NAFTA's Chapter 12 on services contains specific obligations on government and takes an "opt-out" approach to service-sector coverage, in contrast to the more general obligations and the "opt-in" approach of the WTO General Agreement on Trade in Services (GATS). NAFTA has a chapter on temporary entry of businesspersons, while the WTO does not have substantive provisions on this subject. There can also be slight differences in legal rights and obligations between NAFTA and the WTO depending on the exact wording used in a clause—which may make all the difference in the resolution of a legal dispute.

WTO and NAFTA Dispute Settlement Mechanisms

One landmark achievement of the Uruguay Round of trade negotiations was the reform of the WTO dispute settlement system in the Dispute Settlement Understanding (DSU).[14] Under the GATT, the dispute resolution system had been a blend of the diplomatic and legal aspects of dispute resolution, dispute resolution procedures were split up between the GATT and the Tokyo Round agreements, the disputing parties were able to block the adoption of panel reports by the Council (and thus deny them legal effect), and the losing party could easily delay the implementation of the report.[15] With the advent of the WTO and its DSU, an integrated dispute resolution system was created, with many more legalistic and rule-oriented elements.[16] For example, an Appellate Body was created to hear appeals of the panel reports on "issues of law covered in the panel report and legal interpretations developed by the panel."[17] Also, the WTO panelists are individuals from neutral third-party states, and the Appellate Body members are completely independent.[18] Further, it is now extremely difficult for a panel or Appellate Body report not to be adopted by the Dispute Settlement Body (DSB)—and thereby receive formal legal status—because of the creation of a "reverse consensus" process (that is, a consensus among all the members not to adopt the report must be obtained).[19] If an adopted final report is not implemented by the losing party, WTO-authorized compensation for, or trade retaliation by, the aggrieved party are the final sanctions. However, the WTO dispute settlement system, like its GATT predecessor, is purely an inter-state dispute settlement mechanism. Non-state actors do not have rights and obligations under the WTO Agreement, and they do not have any standing to bring complaints to the WTO dispute settlement system.

In contrast, NAFTA contains a number of dispute settlement mechanisms that are accessible to different actors, cover different subject matter, and refer to different systems of law. Further, the results have different levels of legal force. The main mechanisms are:

Chapter 20

- Inter-state disputes over NAFTA, not open to private actors.
- Application of the NAFTA and other international law.
- Political forms of dispute settlement with no integral legally binding force.
- "Arbitral" panels are misnamed as they do not result in legally binding decisions.

Chapter 19

- Disputes between NAFTA parties; private actors (such as exporters) have the right to appear and be represented before binational panel.
- Application of the domestic law of the importing NAFTA state to review the administrative action.
- Binational panel review: legally binding but limited to upholding decision of domestic authority or instructing it to act in accordance with panel's determination.
- Extraordinary challenge committee to review binational panel determination if panelist misconduct, conflict of interest, or procedural irregularities alleged.

Chapter 11

- Disputes between a NAFTA state and a private investor of another NAFTA party.
- Application of NAFTA Chapter 11 substantive law, other NAFTA principles, and other international law.
- International arbitration results in a legally binding award enforceable in domestic courts.

Specialized Chapters with Dispute Resolution Provisions

- Chapter 14 on financial service disputes adapts Chapter 20 dispute settlement system.
- Chapters 8 (emergency action), 10 (government procurement), and 17 (intellectual property) require the NAFTA states to have domestic legal procedures for disputes or enforcement.

North American Agreement on Environmental Cooperation (NAAEC)

- Covers improving substance and enforcement of domestic environment laws.
- Inter-state dispute mechanism (specified failure of state to enforce environmental law).
- Citizen submission procedure (specified failure of state to enforce environmental law).

North American Agreement on Labor Cooperation (NAALC)

- Covers improving substance and enforcement of specified domestic labor laws.
- Inter-state dispute mechanism (specified failure of state to enforce certain labor laws)—no formal citizen submission procedure, but private actors can complain to National Administrative Office.

The Chapter 20 inter-state dispute settlement mechanism is the NAFTA counterpart to the WTO DSU. A comparison between the WTO dispute settlement system and the NAFTA inter-state dispute settlement mechanism in Chapter 20 finds both similarities and differences.[20] Chapter 20 provides for an escalating series of dispute settlement methods, starting with consultations, followed by the NAFTA trade ministers (the Commission) using nonbinding forms of dispute settlement and, if the matter still has not been resolved, moving on to use of an arbitral panel where the majority of panelists come from the disputing states.[21] However, despite its title, the arbitral panel does not produce a legally binding decision. Rather, the panel provides determinations and recommendations in its final report. The report is then returned to the disputing governments, who "shall agree on the resolution of the dispute which *normally shall conform* with the determinations and recommendations of the panel." This essentially gives the NAFTA states the freedom to depart from the panel's report in reaching a final agreement on the matter.[22] There is no appellate review of panel reports. If the disputing states do not reach agreement on implementation of the panel report, compensation for, or trade retaliation by, the aggrieved state are the final sanctions. Thus the Chapter 20 inter-state mechanism is more political and less legalistic compared to the WTO DSU system. But like the WTO DSU, private parties do not have access to the NAFTA Chapter 20 system.

NAFTA Chapter 19 provides for a binational panel review of the final decisions of domestic tribunals in subsidies and dumping cases as an optional replacement for domestic judicial review.[23] The law applied by a binational panel is the specialized domestic law on review of administrative action that would have been applied by a court in the importing state. It is not an appeal of the tribunal decision, and the panel can only uphold the final determination or remand it for action not inconsistent with its determination.[24] There is no substantive law on subsidies and antidumping in NAFTA Chapter 19. Only involved NAFTA parties are empowered to initiate cases under this Chapter, but private actors who would have had the right to appear in the domestic review process (such as an exporter exporting into the NAFTA state taking the action) have the right to appear and be represented by counsel before the panel.[25]

NAFTA Chapter 11, on investment, provides for arbitration as a dispute resolution mechanism between a NAFTA state and the investor of another NAFTA party.[26] The investors—private individuals and companies—have the right to launch an arbitral claim against the host NAFTA state if they believe that the government has violated one or more of its extensive Chapter 11 obligations concerning the treatment of the foreign investment.[27] The arbitral award is legally binding. Failure to comply can lead to a Chapter 20 proceeding, and the award can be enforced in the domestic courts.[28] There is no appeal of these awards, but in very limited situations an international tribunal or domestic court can set aside or refuse to enforce the award.[29]

Finally, the NAFTA side agreements on environmental and labor cooperation (NAAEC and NAALC) address the strengthening of the content and enforcement of the NAFTA states' *domestic* environmental and labor laws.[30] Each provides for an inter-state dispute settlement procedure. If a NAFTA state shows a "persistent pattern of failure ... to effectively enforce" environmental or specified labor law that is trade related, another NAFTA party can launch a complaint under the appropriate agreement.[31] The NAAEC contains a separate citizen submission process, permitting persons and NGOs to complain to the NAAEC Secretariat that a NAFTA state "is failing to effectively enforce its environmental law."[32] However, it is relatively toothless; if internal administrative and political bodies consider that the complaint warrants further action, a factual record *may* be prepared. That is, there is no provision requiring the preparation of a factual record and no power to determine whether the state has violated environmental laws. The NAALC is also weak with respect to private party complaints. Private actors (such as trade unions, for example) can complain to the National Administrative Offices (NAOs) that another NAFTA state is not enforcing a variety of labor laws, and this may lead to hearings and the preparation of a nonbinding report by the Evaluation Committee of Experts (ECE).[33]

Inter-State Disputes: Forum Shopping between NAFTA and WTO

Given that there are both overlaps and differences in substantive content between NAFTA and the WTO, and that there are differences between the inter-state dispute settlement processes in the two treaties, when a NAFTA state perceives that another party has acted in a manner that may be in breach of both NAFTA and the WTO Agreement, it is to be expected that the aggrieved party will choose the forum for dispute settlement that it perceives is going to be most advantageous to it.[34] This can be called "forum shopping" or "choice of forum."[35]

In the case of disputes between WTO members that raise allegations of violation of the WTO Agreement or nullification and impairment of benefits, "they shall have recourse to, and abide by, the rules and procedures of this Understanding."[36] The WTO DSU makes no mention of or allowance for the dispute settlement mechanisms in regional or bilateral economic integration agreements. However, there is no WTO provision to prevent parties to an FTA (such as NAFTA) from resolving FTA disputes under the FTA's dispute resolution mechanism. In contrast, choice of forum is expressly permitted by NAFTA Article 2005(1), which states that when a dispute arising between NAFTA parties raises legal issues under both the WTO and the NAFTA, the complainant can choose either the WTO or the NAFTA inter-state dispute settlement system (with a few listed exceptions where the dispute has to be decided under NAFTA Chapter 20).[37]

David Gantz states that disputes between NAFTA parties may be characterized according to three types: (1) there is no effective choice of forum—that is, the nature of the dispute raises legal issues under only one agreement; (2) there is an apparent choice of forum, with factors "in some instances dictating one forum over the other"; and (3) there are parallel forums available—that is, the same subject matter raises different legal issues, allowing one complaint to go to NAFTA and the other to the WTO.[38] Parallel forums are more likely to exist in subsidies and dumping cases given that NAFTA only covers review of the administrative decisions of domestic tribunals, whereas the WTO contains substantive obligations on the nature of subsidies and dumping. Where there is a choice of forum, "such decisions will be made on a case-by-case basis, and influenced by legal, political, and practical considerations, as well as which NAFTA Party is the complainant."[39]

Gantz has categorized the factors influencing forum choice between the WTO and the NAFTA as follows: (1) legal requirements controlling choice of forum—that is, given the subject matter or the wording of a treaty, some disputes must be brought under either NAFTA or the WTO; (2) substantive law advantages to bringing a complaint under either the WTO or NAFTA; (3) different inter-state procedures in the WTO DSU and NAFTA Chapter 20 may influence the complainant's choice of one or the other in a particular case; and (4) political considerations.[40] In Gantz's view, forum choice does not exist in all circumstances, but NAFTA states do exercise this choice when it is present.[41] With respect to procedural concerns, Loungnarath and Stehly have argued that the creation of the WTO DSU has resulted in NAFTA Chapter 20 losing its procedural advantages; that the more adjudicative DSU will be more attractive to states involved with a politically and economically stronger state in a dispute (Canada and Mexico vis-à-vis the United States, for example); and that relatively stronger states will be attracted to regimes with more diplomatic forms of settlement (such as the case of the United States and NAFTA Chapter 20).[42]

As of July 2001, NAFTA parties had called for a number of consultations under Chapter 20, but only three disputes had resulted in an arbitral panel report.[43] The panel reports arose out of the following disputes: (1) the United States against Canada over the "tariffication" of Canada's imports of agricultural products to replace nontariff import restrictions pursuant to their WTO obligations, (2) Mexico against the United States over a safeguard action on broomcorn brooms; and (3) Mexico against the United States over U.S. restrictions on Mexican cross-border truck services.[44]

The Canada-U.S. dispute over the tariffication of agricultural products was a case in which there was no effective choice of forum. The WTO Agreement on Agriculture required members to change nontariff barriers to tariffs, which would then be reduced over time. The United States had to bring a NAFTA Chapter 20 case because it was the only agreement in which they could argue that Canada could not legally implement its WTO obligations given NAFTA's tariff elimination obligations.[45] In the *Broomcorn Brooms* case, the United States had launched a domestic combined global and bilateral safeguard action against this product under both WTO- and NAFTA-governed procedures, which resulted in tariffs being imposed on Mexican brooms under the multilateral regime. However, Mexico requested a NAFTA Chapter 20 panel, arguing that both the WTO and NAFTA had been violated. The panel avoided the issue of whether it had jurisdiction to decide if, in fact, GATT/WTO Agreement provisions had been violated by applying NAFTA Chapter 8 on safeguard actions (the GATT/WTO and NAFTA provisions were basically identical in content).[46] In this case, Mexico could have selected either the WTO DSU or NAFTA Chapter 20, especially since the original measure was not taken pursuant to NAFTA.[47] It is not entirely clear why the Mexican government selected NAFTA in *Broomcorn Brooms*, given that the substantive provisions are not materially different, but it has been suggested that the desire to avoid a multilateral WTO "precedent" may have been a factor.[48]

In the *Cross-Border Trucking* case, there was no real choice of forum because the interpretation of NAFTA temporary reservations to trucking services obligations were in issue.[49] With respect to other legal arguments, the NAFTA also contained more extensive provisions on services and investment compared to the WTO Agreement.

To date, there have been no panel reports arising out of the interstate dispute settlement mechanisms in the NAFTA side agreements. Nevertheless, in this area of enforcement of domestic environmental and labor laws, there is no choice of forum possibility because there is no counterpart mechanism in the WTO.

Looking at WTO disputes as of July 2001, three U.S.-Canada disputes, one Canada-U.S. dispute, and one U.S.-Mexico dispute had been taken to the panel/Appellate Body level. They were *Certain Measures Concerning Periodicals* (United States v. Canada);[50] *Term of Patent Protection* (United States v. Canada);[51] *Measures Affecting the Importation of Milk and the Exportation of Dairy Products* (United States and New Zealand v. Canada);[52] *Measures Treating Export Restraints as Subsidies* (Canada v. United States);[53] and *Anti-Dumping Investigation of High Fructose Corn Syrup from the U.S.* (United States v. Mexico).[54]

In the *Periodicals* case, the United States complained that a series of Canadian import restrictions and postal rates imposed on U.S. split-run periodicals (periodicals where the original U.S. content is used, along with Canadian advertising) violated a number of Canada's obligations under the WTO Agreement. The panel and Appellate Body reports went against Canada on all points, with the Appellate Body characterizing the measures against split-run periodicals as measures applied to goods—with the stronger GATT 1994 applying—rather than services.[55] The United States could have brought its case under NAFTA, but the cultural industries protection provision provided a possible exemption for Canada—albeit in an unclear fashion and in terms that would have given the United States the right to impose trade retaliation against Canada if the Canadian measures would have been found to violate NAFTA but for the exemption.[56]

The U.S. government did have a choice in the *Periodicals* case to use either NAFTA Chapter 20 or the WTO DSU to resolve the issue. Although there is no public statement as to why it chose the WTO, there are a number of substantive, procedural, and political factors that likely influenced the choice of forum.[57] The lack of exemptions for cultural industries under GATT 1994, combined with the easier factual argument to describe a magazine as a good rather than a service, and the more legalistic WTO DSU compared to NAFTA Chapter 20 were factors that the U.S. government would have taken into account in making its choice. Also, the NAFTA cultural "exemption" would have enabled Canada to maintain its measures against split-run periodicals. However, if the measures had been found by a NAFTA panel to have violated other NAFTA obligations, the U.S. government would have been able to impose trade sanctions against Canada.[58]

Further, a U.S. win at the WTO would send strong signals to other WTO members about their measures protecting the cultural sector, and Canada's use of the cultural exception (in NAFTA) could have robbed the United States of a clear victory in the dispute. Canada's commitment to the smooth functioning of the WTO dispute settlement provisions, which precluded any risk that Canada would not abide by an adverse panel decision, meant that the WTO was the preferred forum to litigate the dispute.[59]

In the *Patent Protection* case, the United States complained about Canada's patent legislation. The legislation had been amended to provide for a twenty-year period of protection from filing date for patents, to accord with Canada's international obligations. But it applied a seventeen-year period from date of patent issue to applications filed before October 1, 1989. Both the panel and the Appellate Body found that Canada had violated its obligations under the WTO TRIPs Agreement. In this case, both the WTO TRIPs Agreement and NAFTA Chapter 17 contain provisions on the length of patent protection, but the NAFTA expressly allows for seventeen years from date of grant period, while the TRIPs Agreement provides for twenty years from filing date period.[60] Thus, in terms of forum choice, a U.S. complaint under the WTO was much more likely to be advantageous in substantive terms. In addition, the more legalistic procedural provisions of the WTO DSU compared to NAFTA Chapter 20 may also have been influential.

In the third case, on *Dairy Products*, the United States complained that Canada had granted export subsidies on milk exports and restricted imports of milk, contrary to its WTO obligations under a number of agreements.[61] NAFTA does not contain any substantive obligations on subsidies, although it does contain legal obligations on import restrictions. The WTO, in contrast, contains legal obligations on both subsidies and import restrictions. Thus the *Dairy Products* case is one in which there was no possible choice of forum; the United States had to use the WTO Agreement in order to attack the substantive merits of the Canadian subsidies regime.

Similarly, in *Measures Treating Export Restraints as Subsidies,* the Canadian government did not have a choice of forum. In this case connected with the ongoing bilateral Canada-U.S. softwood lumber dispute, Canada was contesting the treatment of export restraints under U.S. subsidies law. Given that substantive law on subsidization was in issue, GATT/WTO was the only venue in which such an argument could be made.[62] In the U.S.-Mexico complaint on *Anti-Dumping Investigation of High Fructose Corn Syrup from the U.S.,* the consistency of Mexico's final antidumping measure with its substantive obligations under the WTO Anti-Dumping Agreement and GATT 1994 Article VI was examined. In contrast, this is an example of action taken in parallel forums because the United States was simultaneously conducting a NAFTA Chapter 19 case against Mexico on the same domestic antidumping process, but based on the concept of quasi-judicial review of administrative action. That is, different legal issues and concepts were at play.[63]

Thus, in four of the eight NAFTA and WTO cases discussed here, there was no effective choice of forum (NAFTA: *Agricultural Products, Cross-Border Trucking;* WTO: *Dairy Products, Export Restraints on Subsidies*). In the other four cases, where there was a choice or parallel forums were used (NAFTA: *Broomcorn Brooms;* WTO: *Periodicals, Patent Protection;* parallel forums: *Corn Syrup*), it appeared that substantive, procedural, and political issues were influential in the decision whether to resort to the WTO DSU or NAFTA Chapter 20. However, Loungnarath and Stehly's proposition—that due to the relative power imbalance, weaker states such as Canada and Mexico will tend to opt for the WTO DSU, while presumably the stronger United States will prefer the diplomatic mechanism in NAFTA Chapter 20—has not been clearly demonstrated by the NAFTA and WTO cases discussed. In the one case that Canada has launched against the United States—in the WTO—it was not possible to use NAFTA Chapter 20 because of the subject matter at issue (and Canada did pursue three complaints against the United States under the CUSFTA). Mexico has brought more cases against the United States under NAFTA, although in most instances there was no choice of forum or there were parallel forums. And the United States is opting for the WTO more than would be anticipated pursuant to such an argument. Rather, the choice-of-forum considerations discussed earlier appear to be the decisive factors.

Private Actors' Access to Dispute Settlement Mechanisms under WTO and NAFTA

Trade and investment agreements have different attitudes to the standing that is accorded private parties to access and use dispute resolution mechanisms, and to the direct applicability of treaty rights and obligations to private parties.[64] The WTO Agreement does not grant any substantive rights to private parties or give them access to any dispute settlement mechanism; it is purely an inter-state agreement. NAFTA has some dispute settlement procedures open to private parties. NAFTA Chapter 11 contains government obligations that are enforceable by private investors, and certain private actors can appear in Chapter 19 hearings. However, these private actors represent the business sector—primarily exporters and investors. In contrast, broader civil society concerns can only be expressed through the NAFTA side agreements on labor and the environment, which focus on domestic law, not international trade and investment law, and which contain extremely weak dispute settlement procedures accessible to private actors.

However, the NAFTA experience to date shows that where a trade agreement does provide for private party standing in dispute settlement systems, private actors will maximize the opportunity. Also, private party access to dispute settlement mechanisms may result in interpretations of the agreement that are unexpected, at least to the state parties. There have been numerous Chapter 19 cases that have been perceived as relatively uncontroversial.[65] In contrast, investors' aggressive use of the NAFTA Chapter 11 arbitral process has been controversial and worrisome for both the NAFTA governments and a wide cross-section of NGOs and civil society. By mid-2001, sixteen Chapter 11 claims had been launched by investors against the Canadian, Mexican, and U.S. governments. These claims attack domestic measures that are not directly aimed at foreign investment (on, for example, environment, postal system practices, size of jury damages award).[66] This unforeseen development has produced tensions between NAFTA Chapter 11 and the environmental side agreement, and between the interests of business and civil society. There are concerns that it will have a chilling effect, limiting the NAFTA governments' ability to legislate.[67] Several of the arbitral awards finding against the government are being reviewed by domestic courts in attempts by the losing governments to prevent the awards from being enforced.[68] The Canadian government has also stated that it will not sign an FTAA that includes a chapter equivalent to that of NAFTA Chapter 11.[69]

Regarding the NAFTA side agreements, environmental NGOs have made frequent complaints under the NAAEC citizen submission procedure, but the weak and political nature of the process has resulted in the preparation of only a few factual records to date.[70] Similarly, although there have been many applications by private actors under the NAALC since 1994, any resulting reports are not legally binding and no complaints have resulted in sanctions.[71]

THE FTAA: NEGOTIATING PROCESS AND FORUM SHOPPING

The concept of a Free Trade Area of the Americas (FTAA) was launched at the 1994 Miami Summit of the Americas. An FTAA would join thirty-four Western Hemisphere states in a free trade agreement to be concluded no later than 2005.[72] After preliminary meetings, formal FTAA negotiations were launched at the second Summit of the Americas in Santiago, Chile, in 1998.[73] Early on, there were a number of alternative ideas concerning the structure of the FTAA: accession to NAFTA by the other states, convergence of the many existing subregional agreements, bipolar amalgamation of regional integration centered around NAFTA and MERCOSUR (or a potential South American Free Trade Agreement), or the drafting of a completely new treaty that states could sign individually or as part of a subregional group.[74]

One overarching requirement—given that all the FTAA negotiating states except for the Bahamas are WTO members—is that an FTAA must be WTO consistent. Another is that the different development levels of the FTAA states be accounted for.[75] It has also been agreed that the FTAA will be "a single undertaking comprising mutual rights and obligations," that any FTAA can coexist with subregional and bilateral agreements (to the extent that the rights and obligations in these agreements are not covered by or go beyond those in the FTAA), and that states can join the FTAA individually or as part of one of these trade agreements.[76]

At the third Summit of the Americas, held in Quebec City in April 2001, the heads of state/government set January 1, 2005, as the deadline to complete negotiation of the FTAA, and the end of 2005 as the deadline for the treaty's entry into force.[77]

The FTAA 2001 draft negotiating text makes it evident that the FTAA will be a new treaty.[78] Although the draft text is heavily bracketed, indicating that many provisions have not been definitely defined, it is clear that many legal concepts have been taken from the WTO Agreement and NAFTA. The draft text's chapter on inter-state dispute settlement is a mix of NAFTA Chapter 20 and WTO DSU concepts, with an escalating series of diplomatic forms of dispute settlement followed by a neutral panel procedure and a standing Appellate Body.[79] The inter-state dispute settlement chapter also contains a complex "choice of forum" clause.[80] It allows states to choose between the FTAA and the WTO for disputes arising under both agreements. The clause is undecided about disputes arising under both the FTAA and a subregional trade agreement (such as NAFTA) to which all disputing states are parties. The alternatives are either a choice between the two forums or use of the dispute settlement mechanism in the subregional agreement.[81]

The draft text's chapter on investment, which presents international arbitration as the means for the settlement of investment disputes between states and investors of other FTAA states, is based closely on NAFTA Chapter 11.[82] The chapter on subsidies and dumping, which contains substantive and procedural rules, contemplates sending disputes over the implementation of this chapter to the FTAA inter-state dispute settlement chapter.[83] The possible negotiation of an international mechanism to replace domestic judicial or other review of domestic administrative action on subsidies and dumping, and the renunciation by FTAA states of the use of antidumping measures in reciprocal trade, are other bracketed clauses in this chapter.[84]

There are no side agreements on labor or environmental protection, and the FTAA draft text does not appear to contain any mechanisms for private parties to complain about labor and environmental law enforcement matters. However, the FTAA draft chapter on investment contemplates greater leeway for governmental environmental and labor measures.[85]

CONCLUSION

This chapter has illustrated the possibilities of choice of forum for inter-state dispute settlement between the WTO and NAFTA. Each time there is an international trade or investment dispute between NAFTA states, officials in the complaining government have to carefully examine the dispute and the contents of the WTO and NAFTA to advise on which venue will be the most advantageous for bringing a complaint. The NAFTA dispute settlement mechanisms that are open to private parties have been heavily used; Chapter 11 (on investment), in particular, has resulted in some contentious awards that are legally binding on the states concerned.

There are still barriers to successful negotiation of the FTAA, including the absence of agreement on many clauses of the treaty and the need for the U.S. administration to obtain trade promotion authority to sign an agreement without Congress picking apart the contents. However, if an FTAA comes about and if the NAFTA member states sign it individually, a third agreement will be added to the possibilities for forum shopping based on substantive and procedural differences. A well-drafted and comprehensive "choice of forum" clause in the FTAA inter-state dispute settlement chapter can reduce, but probably cannot eliminate, choice of forum issues between the FTAA and NAFTA or the WTO. FTAA negotiators should ensure that such a clause is present in a finalized FTAA. In any event, forum shopping between NAFTA and the WTO will continue.

Private investors' heavy use of the NAFTA Chapter 11 dispute settlement mechanism may make some FTAA states leery of agreeing to the FTAA draft investment chapter as it now stands.[86] If the investment chapter is carried through into a final agreement, private investors in NAFTA states may also face choice of forum questions between NAFTA Chapter 11 and the FTAA chapter, especially where there are differences between the treaties in substantive obligations on the host state. The FTAA draft investment chapter does not contain a choice of forum clause that prevents forum shopping, although there is an attempt to avoid parallel actions.[87] Although it appears that the FTAA states are currently unwilling to consider side agreements on domestic environmental and labor protection, the existing NAFTA side agreements are quite weak when it comes to private party roles in dispute resolution. While there may be a legitimate hesitation to re-create inter-state dispute settlement processes, creating the same private-actor access provisions in FTAA side agreements should not be feared.

Notes

1. North American Free Trade Agreement, *International Legal Materials* 32 (1993): 296–456 and 605–799 (in force January 1, 1994).

2. North American Agreement on Environmental Cooperation, *International Legal Materials* 32 (1993): 1480–98 (in force January 1, 1994); North American Agreement on Labor Cooperation, *International Legal Materials* 32 (1993): 1499–1518 (in force January 1, 1994).

3. Marrakesh Agreement Establishing the World Trade Organization, *International Legal Materials* 33 (1994): 1141–1272 (in force January 1, 1995) [hereinafter WTO Agreement].

4. Canada has bilateral free trade agreements (FTAs) with Israel, Chile, and Costa Rica, and environmental and labor side agreements with Chile and Costa Rica. It is negotiating FTAs with Guatemala, Honduras, El Salvador, the Commonwealth Caribbean, Singapore, and the European Free Trade Association. See Canada-Chile Free Trade Agreement, *International Legal Materials* 36 (1997): 1079–1192 (in force July 5, 1997). Canada has bilateral investment treaties (BITs) with states in Latin America and the Caribbean. Mexico has bilateral FTAs with the European Union, Chile, Uruguay, Argentina, Peru, Bolivia, Israel, and the Central American states. The United States has BITs with various states in the region and bilateral FTAs with Israel and Jordan (the latter signed, but not in force), and it is negotiating FTAs with Chile and Singapore.

5. Antigua and Barbuda, Argentina, the Bahamas, Barbados, Belize, Bolivia, Brazil, Canada, Chile, Colombia, Costa Rica, Dominica, the Dominican Republic, Ecuador, El Salvador, Grenada, Guatemala, Guyana, Haiti, Honduras, Jamaica, Mexico, Nicaragua, Panama, Paraguay, Peru, St. Vincent and the Grenadines, St. Lucia, St. Kitts and Nevis, Suriname, Trinidad and Tobago, Uruguay, the United States, and Venezuela.

6. WTO Agreement. See, for example, Ernst-Ulrich Petersmann and Meinhard Hilf, eds., *The New GATT Round of Multilateral Trade Negotiations: Legal and Economic Problems* (Deventer: Kluwer, 1988); Paolo Mengozzi, ed., *International Trade Law on the 50th Anniversary of the Multilateral Trade System* (Milano: Dott. A. Giuffrè Editore, S.p.A., 1999).

7. The CUSFTA has been suspended while NAFTA is in force, except for certain CUSFTA provisions that have been incorporated into NAFTA.

8. GATT 1994 Art. XXIV, Uruguay Round Understanding on the Interpretation of Art. XXIV. NAFTA Art. 101 states that NAFTA is consistent with GATT Art. XXIV. A review of the tariff phase-out and the elimination or reduction of many nontariff barriers leads to the conclusion that this statement is justified. See, for example, Paul De Maret et al., eds., *Regionalism and Multilateralism after the Uruguay Round: Convergence, Divergence and Interaction* (Brussels: European Interuniversity Press, 1997).

9. Peter S. Watson, Joseph E. Flynn, and Chad C. Conwell, *Completing the World Trading System: Proposals for a Millennium Round* (The Hague: Kluwer Law International, 1999), p. 141.

10. For example, NAFTA Art. 104, Chap. 9 on technical standards, Arts. 1114, 2005(4), and 2015.

11. For example, export taxes/controls on food products (NAFTA Annexes 314–315), exemptions from NAFTA Chap. 6 on energy (NAFTA Annexes 602.3, 603.6, 607).

12. NAFTA Chap. 19 provides only for binational panel review of the parties' existing domestic subsidies and dumping law and changes to domestic
law. The WTO Agreement contains substantive law on subsidies and dumping in the GATT 1994, the Agreement on Subsidies and Countervailing
Measures, the Agreement on Implementation of Article VI of the GATT
1994 (antidumping), and the Agreement on Agriculture.

13. NAFTA Art. 2106 and Annex 2106 incorporate CUSFTA provisions
on cultural industries. In the WTO, GATT 1994 and Uruguay Round Agreements in Annex 1A cover trade in goods and trade-related investment, the
General Agreement on Trade in Services (GATS) in Annex 1B covers trade
in services, and the Agreement on Trade-Related Aspects of Intellectual
Property (TRIPs) in Annex 1C covers intellectual property issues.

14. Understanding on Rules and Procedures Governing the Settlement of
Disputes, WTO Agreement Annex 2 [hereinafter DSU], based on GATT
1994, Arts. XXII–XXIII.

15. See Robert E. Hudec, *The GATT Legal System and World Trade Diplomacy*,
2d ed. (Salem: Butterworth Legal Publishers, 1990); Meinhard Hilf, "Settlement of Disputes in International Economic Organizations: Comparative
Analysis and Proposals for Strengthening the GATT Dispute Settlement Procedures," in *The New GATT Round of Multilateral Trade Negotiations*, p. 285.

16. See, for example, James Cameron and Karen Campbell, eds., *Dispute
Resolution in the World Trade Organization* (London: Cameron May, 1998); Ernst-
Ulrich Petersmann, *International Trade Law and the GATT/WTO Dispute Settle-
ment System* (London: Kluwer Law International, 1997).

17. DSU Art. 17.6.

18. DSU Arts. 8.3, 17.3. Gabrielle Marceau, "NAFTA and WTO Dispute
Settlement Rules: A Thematic Comparison," *Journal of World Trade* 31, no. 2
(1997): 25–81, p. 31.

19. DSU Arts.16.4, 17.4. Panel and Appellate Body reports are not integrally legally binding.

20. See Vilaysoun Loungnarath and Céline Stehly, "The General Dispute
Settlement Mechanism in the North American Free Trade Agreement and the
World Trade Organization System: Is North American Regionalism Really
Preferable to Multilateralism?" *Journal of World Trade* 34, no. 1 (2000): 39–71;
Patrick Specht, "The Dispute Settlement Systems of WTO and NAFTA —
Analysis and Comparison," *Georgia Journal of International and Comparative Law*
27 (1998): 57–138; Marceau, "NAFTA and WTO Dispute Settlement Rules."

21. NAFTA Arts. 2006 (consultations), 2007 (Commission may use good
offices, conciliation, mediation, or "such other dispute resolution procedures"
or make recommendations to the parties), 2008 (request for arbitral panel).
To increase panelist neutrality, each disputing state selects the panelists from
the other disputing state from a roster, NAFTA Art. 2011(1).

22. NAFTA Art. 2018(1) (emphasis added). See Loungnarath and Stehly,
"The General Dispute Settlement Mechanism," p. 45. But it has been argued

that "even a non-binding panel report has a certain influence on the disputing parties" (Specht, "The Dispute Settlement Systems of WTO and NAFTA," pp. 103–104).

23. See Eric J. Pan, "Assessing the NAFTA Chapter 19 Binational Panel System: An Experiment in International Adjudication," *Harvard International Law Journal* 40 (1999): 379–449.

24. NAFTA Art. 1908(4).

25. NAFTA Arts. 1904(2), (7) and 1911.

26. NAFTA Chap. 11, Sec. B.

27. Depending on the NAFTA states involved, the arbitration may be brought under ICSID Convention Rules, ICSID Additio nal Facility Rules, or UNCITRAL International Arbitration Rules, NAFTA Art. 1120.

28. NAFTA Art. 1136(1)–(2), (5), (6).

29. The ICSID Convention provides for an annulment procedure for pr o-cedural irregularities or corruption of an arbitrator. With UNCITRAL arbitra-tions, a losing party can apply to a court in a NAFTA state arguing that d o-mestic law incorporating the New York Convention on the Recognition and Enforcement of Foreign Arbitral Awards or the UNCITRAL Model Law on International Commercial Arbitration permits the court to set aside or refuse to enforce the award if there were procedural irregularities in the pro cess, or on public policy or nonarbitrability grounds.

30. Armand L.C. de Mestral, "The Significance of the NAFTA Side Agreements on Environmental and Labor Cooperation," *Arizona Journal of International and Comparative Law* 15 (1998): 169.

31. NAAEC Arts. 22–24, 33; NAALC Arts. 22–23, 27–29, 38. Whereas the environmental laws covered are extensive, the NAALC inter -state dispute mechanism is limited to occupational health and safety, child labor, and minimum wage standards.

32. NAAEC Arts. 14–15.

33. NAALC Arts.15, 20–26; Human Rights Watch, *Trading Away Rights: The Unfulfilled Promise of NAFTA's Labor Side Agreement* (April 16, 2001), at http://www.hrw.org (of the twenty-three complaints filed since 1994, none has resulted in sanctions against the alleged law vi olator).

34. See David A. Gantz, "Dispute Settlement under the NAFTA and the WTO: Choice of Forum Opportunities and Risks for the NAFTA P arties," *American University International Law Review* 14 (1999): 1025–1106; Stefan Ohl-hoff and Hannes L. Schloemann, "Rational Allocation of Disputes and 'Co n-stitutionalisation': Forum Choice as an Issue of Competence," in *Dispute Reso-lution in the World Trade Organization,* ed. Cameron and Campbell, p. 302. Pan ("Assessing the NAFTA Chapter 19 Binational Panel System," p. 392) has also raised the possibility of forum shopping occurring between NAFTA Chap. 19 panel review and domestic judicial review in the event that the Chap. 19 panels' interpretation of domestic law on review of administrative

action begins to diverge from that applied by the domestic courts in the NAFTA states.

35. The term "forum shopping" comes from private international law where it is used to describe the behavior of a plaintiff in a civil case with elements attached to more than one country in deciding which of the relevant states is the most advantageous place to launch a civil action based on legal and other factors, such as favorable substantive law, statute of limitations, likelihood of high damages awards, and expenses of litigation.

36. DSU Art. 23(1).

37. The exceptions are: Arts. 2005(2) (third party involvement, failing agreement NAFTA normally will be used), 2005(3) (dispute involves NAFTA Art. 104 environment treaties, respondent requests NAFTA) and 2005(4) (disputes in Chaps. 7, Sec. B, and 9 on health/environment, respondent requests NAFTA). Also, Art. 2005(6) specifies that once dispute settlement proceedings are launched under either NAFTA or GATT/WTO, the forum selected shall be used to the exclusion of the other.

38. Gantz, "Dispute Settlement under the NAFTA and the WTO," pp. 1091, 1096.

39. Ibid., p. 1097.

40. Ibid., pp. 1098–1105.

41. Ibid., p. 1106.

42. Loungnarath and Stehly, "The General Dispute Settlement Mechanism," pp. 39–40, 42, 67–68.

43. While the subject matter of consultations is also relevant to the issue of forum shopping, the scope of this essay is confined to disputes that passed to the formal panel stage. Cf. Gantz, "Dispute Settlement under the NAFTA and the WTO."

44. *Tariffs Applied by Canada to Certain U.S.-Origin Agricultural Products*, CDA-95-2008-1, U.S.A. v. Canada (December 2, 1996); *U.S. Safeguard Action Taken on Broomcorn Brooms from Mexico*, USA-97-2008-01, Mexico v. U.S.A. (January 30, 1998); *Cross-Border Trucking Services and Investment*, USA-98-2008-01, Mexico v. U.S.A. (February 6, 2001).

45. The panel interpreted NAFTA Chap. 7 on agriculture to incorporate GATT as an evolving system of law—that is, including WTO obligations and that these prevailed over the NAFTA Chap. 3 tariff elimination provisions. Ibid.; Gantz, "Dispute Settlement under the NAFTA and the WTO," pp. 1061, 1092.

46. Gantz, "Dispute Settlement under the NAFTA and the WTO," p. 1070. This should be contrasted with the practice of many NAFTA Chap. 20 (and predecessor CUSFTA) panels that have used GATT/WTO legal principles as persuasive guidance in the interpretation of the NAFTA/CUSFTA.

47. Loungnarath and Stehly, "The General Dispute Settlement Mechanism," p. 62 n 99.

48. Gantz, "Dispute Settlement under the NAFTA and the WTO," p. 1071. Technically, there is no system of precedent in cases decided under international law, but in practice international tribunals and panels often follow prior decisions.

49. The panel construed these reservations narrowly and decided that the moratorium had ended, no other NAFTA provisions were applicable, and the United States was in violation of its NAFTA obligations. See *Cross-Border Trucking*, USA-98-2008-01, Mexico v. U.S.A.

50. Panel Report (WT/DS31/R, March 14, 1997); Appellate Body Report (WT/DS31/AB/R, June 30, 1997).

51. Panel Report (WT/DS170/R, May 5, 2000); Appellate Body Report (WT/DS170/AB/R, September 18, 2000); Arbitration under DSU Art. 21.3(c) (WT/DS170/10, February 28, 2001).

52. Panel Report (WT/DS103R, WT/DS113R, May 17, 1999); Appellate Body Report (WT/DS103/AB/R, WT/DS113/AB/R, October 13, 1999); Recourse to DSU Art. 21.5 by New Zealand and the U.S. (WT/DS103/RW, WT/DS113/RW, July 11, 2001).

53. Panel Report (WT/DS194/R, June 29, 2001).

54. Panel Report (WT/DS132/R, January 28, 2000); Recourse to DSU Art. 21.5 by the U.S. (WT/DS132/RW, June 22, 2001).

55. The Canadian argument was that the measures applied to advertising so that trade in services was involved, with the result that the GATS should have applied; and because Canada had excluded advertising services from its GATS commitments, Canada would not have violated its GATS/WTO obligations.

56. NAFTA Art. 2106, Annex 2106, incorporating CUSFTA provisions on cultural industries; Art. 2107 definition of cultural industries includes periodicals and magazines. Cf. Gantz, "Dispute Settlement under the NAFTA and the WTO," p. 1092; Gantz is of the opinion that there was no choice of forum in this case.

57. Stephen de Boer, "Trading Culture: The Canada-U.S. Magazine Dispute," in *Dispute Resolution in the World Trade Organization*, ed. Cameron and Campbell, pp. 239–40.

58. NAFTA Art. 2106, Annex 2106; de Boer, "Trading Culture."

59. De Boer, "Trading Culture," p. 240.

60. NAFTA Art. 1709(12); WTO TRIPs Agreement Art. 33.

61. GATT 1994, Agreement on Agriculture, Subsidies Agreement, Import Licensing Agreement. New Zealand later also brought a case against Canada on the export subsidies issue, and the cases were heard jointly.

62. Using the GATT 1994 and the Uruguay Round Agreement on Subsidies and Countervailing Measures; "Something for Both Parties in Canada-U.S. Softwood Lumber Dispute," *Bridges Weekly Trade News Digest* 5, no. 26 (July 17, 2001): 11.

63. *Imports of High-Fructose Corn Syrup Originating in the USA*, MEX-USA-98-1904-01 (active); Gantz, "Dispute Settlement under the NAFTA and the WTO," pp. 1091, 1095–96.

64. See Andrea K. Schneider, "Getting Along: The Evolution of Dispute Settlement Regimes in International Trade Organizations," *Michigan Journal of International Law* 20 (1999): 697–774.

65. By July 2001 there had been seventy-four NAFTA Chap. 19 applications, although not all have gone to the binational panel stage. There were also numerous cases under the CUSFTA, although a few were controve rsial.

66. By July 2001 there were five final arbitral awards, and several claims had been settled or terminated. See www.worldbank.org/icsid, www.dfait-maeci.gc.ca, and http://www.naftaclaims.c om.

67. Anthony DePalma, "Nafta's Powerful Little Secret," *New York Times*, March 11, 2001, at www.nytimes.com.

68. The Canadian government has applied to the Federal Court of Canada to set aside the arbitral award in the S.D. Myers case. In the Metalclad C orporation v. Mexico arbitration, the Mexican government applied to the British Columbia courts to have the award set aside (the arbitration was held in Va n-couver). The British Columbia Supreme Court set aside the award in part, deciding that the tribunal had exceeded its jurisdiction in interpreting several of the Chap. 11 arguments, *The United Mexican States* v. *Metalclad Corporation* (2001) B.C.S.C. 664 (B.C. Supreme Court). See note 29, above, and the r elated text.

69. M. MacKinnon, "Canada Seeks Review o f NAFTA's Chapter 11," *Globe and Mail*, December 13, 2000.

70. By July 19, 2001, thirty-one citizen submissions had been made since 1995 (ten against Canada, thirteen against Mexico, and eight against the United States); two factual records had been prepare d and made public, and a third was being prepared. See www.cec.org.

71. Human Rights Watch, *Trading Away Rights*.

72. I Summit of the Americas, Declaration of Principles and Plan of A ction, *International Legal Materials* 34 (1995): 808–38. See J. Steven Jarreau, "Negotiating Trade Liberalization in the Western Hemisphere: The Free Trade Area of the Americas," *Temple International and Comparative Law Journal* 13 (1999): 57–86; Frank J. Garcia, "'Americas Agreements': An Interim Stage in Building the Free Trade Area of the Americas," *Columbia Journal of Transnational Law* 35 (1997): 63–130; Frank J. Garcia, "Decisonmaking and Dispute Resolution in the Free Trade Area of the Americas: An Essay in Trade Go vernance," *Michigan Journal of International Law* 18 (1997): 357–97; Richard L. Bernal, "Regional Trade Arrangements and the Establishment of a Free Trade Area of the Americas," *Law and Policy in International Business* 27 (1996): 945–62; Frank J. Garcia, "NAFTA and the Creation of the FTAA: A Critique of Piecemeal Accession," *Virginia Journal of International Law* 35 (1995): 539–86.

73. I Summit of the Americas, Plan of Action; II Summit of the Americas, Declaration of Santiago, *International Legal Materials* 37 (1998): 950–75.

74. Garcia, "'Americas Agreements,'" pp. 67–68; Garcia, "NAFTA and the Creation of the FTAA," pp. 540–44, 549; Bernal, "Regional Trade Arrangements," pp. 950–55; and P.H. Smith, this volume. See MERCOSUR (Argentina, Brazil, Paraguay, and Uruguay are members; Chile and Bolivia are associate members); CARICOM/Caribbean Common Market (thirteen former British territories, Haiti, and Suriname); Central American Common Market (Costa Rica, Guatemala, El Salvador, Honduras, and Nicaragua); Andean Community/Common Market (Bolivia, Colombia, Ecuador, Peru, and Venezuela); Group of Three FTA (Mexico, Venezuela, Colombia). Further, Chile and Mexico have each entered into numerous bilateral FTAs.

75. I Summit of the Americas, Declaration of Principles; Summit of the Americas Trade Ministerial, San José Ministerial Declaration (March 19, 1998), Paras. 5–6, 9, Annex 1; Declaration of Santiago.

76. For example, Summit of the Americas Trade Ministerial, Belo Horizonte Ministerial Declaration (May 16, 1997), Para. 5(b), (d); San José Ministerial Declaration, Para. 9, Annex I; Declaration of Santiago.

77. http://www.globeandmail.comIII Summit of the Americas, Declaration of Quebec City (April 22, 2001); www/americascanada.org/eventsummit/declarations/declara-e.asp (Venezuela reserved its position). See also Summit of the Americas Trade Ministerial, Buenos Aires Ministerial Declaration (April 7, 2001), at www.alca-ftaa.org. The Declaration reiterated that the FTAA should be WTO consistent, constitute a single undertaking, and take into account the different size and development levels of the FTAA states.

78. FTAA Draft Negotiating Text (July 3, 2001), at www.alca-ftaa.org. Since most of the other subregional trade agreements are designed to be customs unions or common markets, their inter-state dispute settlement mechanisms will not be so influential. See San José Ministerial Declaration, Annex II (the dispute settlement mechanism will be established taking into account inter alia the WTO DSU).

79. FTAA Draft Negotiating Text, "Chapter on Dispute Settlement," Arts. 6–45.

80. Ibid., Art. 5.

81. There are also bracketed provisions for the use of the FTAA mechanism in disputes (1) among parties to a subregional agreement when the matter is exclusively governed by the FTAA, and (2) among parties to a subregional agreement and FTAA states who are not parties to the agreement.

82. FTAA Draft Negotiating Text, "Chapter on Investment."

83. FTAA Draft Negotiating Text, "Chapter on Subsidies, Anti-Dumping and Countervailing Duties," Art. 17.

84. Ibid., Arts. 17.2 and 19.

85. FTAA Draft Negotiating Text, "Chapter on Investment," Arts. 12, 18 – 19.

86. About twenty-seven of the thirty-four FTAA states (excluding, for example, Canada and Mexico) are already ICSID Convention contracting parties, with the result that they have already consented on a multilateral basis to international arbitration for investment disputes with foreign investors whose national state is an ICSID party.

87. FTAA Draft Negotiating Text, "Chapter on Investment," Art. 8(2)(b).

20

From NAFTA to FTAA? Paths toward Hemispheric Integration

Peter H. Smith

Will the Western Hemisphere succeed in building a free trade area? This possibility has been at the forefront of the inter-American agenda ever since 1990, when President George Bush *père* launched the Enterprise for the Americas Initiative and offered his vision of a free trade zone "stretching from the port of Anchorage to the Tierra del Fuego." Approval of NAFTA lent further credence to the idea. Presidents Bush and later Bill Clinton both announced that the process of NAFTA expansion would begin with Chile. In December 1993 then vice president Al Gore expressed his hope for "a Western Hemisphere community of democracies" that would consolidate political and economic harmony throughout the region, with NAFTA as "a starting point." Eager to gain access to this privileged circle, Latin American leaders came to regard a hemispheric free trade area (FTA) as a key part of their development strategy. Expectations were soon running high.

An unprecedented series of summit gatherings sustained the momentum. In December 1994 thirty-four heads of state (minus Fidel Castro) gathered in Miami and proclaimed their intention of forming a Free Trade Area of the Americas (FTAA) by the year 2005. This goal has since been ratified in two subsequent summits—one in Santiago de Chile, in 1998, and another in Quebec City, in 2001. Notably, too, the conclave in Quebec led to adoption of a "democracy clause" which asserted that "any unconstitutional alteration or interruption of the democratic order in a state of the hemisphere constitutes an insurmountable obstacle to the participation of that state's government in the Summit of the Americas process." The Plan of Action from Quebec was comprehensive and ambitious—with more than 260 action items[1]—and prospects for implementation were uncertain.[2] Through it all, the basic questions still lingered: Will FTAA come into effect? How? What might it look like?[3]

This chapter explores these questions through a schematic examination of bargaining processes among nations of the Western Hemisphere—in other words, of what has come to be known as patterns of inter-state bargaining. The analysis is based on three interrelated premises. One is the simple recognition that the actual content of "free trade areas" can vary substantially—from light commercial accords (known in their most innocuous form as Economic Complementarity Agreements) to dense arrangements with explicit provisions not only for trade but also for investment, procurement, dispute resolution, and a host of other "trade-related" issues. Second is the idea that different nations are likely to have different interests—some might want a light agreement, others might want a dense agreement, still others might not want any agreement at all. Third is the proposition that the actual outcome of free trade negotiations is likely to depend on the process of inter-state bargaining.

The first section of the essay begins with an analysis of the distinct but overlapping modes of integration recently and currently at work within the hemisphere. The second identifies the priorities and preferences of key states in the region. Building upon these arguments, section three employs a game-theoretic model of interaction among key actors in order to arrive at possible outcomes. Its purpose is not so much to anticipate or "predict" precise results of the bargaining process; rather, it is to illustrate the underlying logic of negotiations. And even at an abstract level, the exercise demonstrates the crucial importance of the sequence and substance of moves by the principal players. Contrary to much official rhetoric, a hemispheric free trade area is neither predetermined nor God-given. Where you go depends upon the path you take.[4]

ROUTES TO INTEGRATION

The 1990s gave rise to unabashed enthusiasm about the benefits of "free trade" throughout the Americas—not only in Washington, but also in Ottawa and in capital cities of Latin America. Economic liberalization would benefit both producers (by expanding markets) and consumers (by lowering prices). It would enhance efficiency, promote competitiveness, and strengthen the region's position in the rapidly changing global economy. As country after country followed the dictates of "the Washington consensus" and cast off the protectionist legacies of import-substitution industrialization (ISI), the principal question became not *whether* to pursue hemispheric economic integration but *how*.

The answer has never been crystal-clear. In fact, the availability of routes toward hemispheric integration (read: economic integration with the United States) has undergone significant and sometimes bewildering change over the past decade.

Accession to NAFTA

The initial option was to join NAFTA. As more and more countries demonstrated will and capacity to comply with the terms of the NAFTA accord, it was thought, the "North American" free trade area would gradually expand into Central and South America. Eventually it would embrace all countries of the hemisphere (even a post-Castro Cuba), and it would become a de facto FTAA. Given the comprehensive nature of NAFTA itself, the FTAA that emerged from this process would be an extremely "dense" form of free trade agreement.

Institutional and political impediments nonetheless proved to be daunting. In final form, NAFTA did not establish criteria for admission. In a deliberately uninformative accession clause, the treaty simply held that new countries may join NAFTA "subject to such terms and conditions as may be agreed" by the member countries, and "following approval in accordance with applicable approval procedures in each country." This vague language meant that member countries—Canada, Mexico, and the United States—retained the right to establish arbitrary or impossible accession criteria if they so chose.

Any expansion of NAFTA would have to be in the interests of all the member states, as well as in the interests of the applicants. In this respect the interests of NAFTA partners appeared to be ambiguous. Still adjusting to its own bilateral FTA with the United States, which had prompted deep discord and strident debates, Canada seemed unlikely in the mid-1990s to welcome the rapid accession of Latin American countries. The United States might regard expansion of NAFTA as a means of consolidating economic and political influence—and of gaining access to new markets—but it would have to balance these advantages against potentially negative impacts on relations with Europe and Japan. Especially telling was the case of Mexico, which presumably wanted to be the *only* NAFTA-approved site for foreign investment in Latin America—and which would therefore resist new accessions (which would also dilute Mexico's political status as a unique interlocutor between Latin America and the United States). Decisions on accession would have to be unanimous at any rate, which meant that each of the three member countries possessed a veto.

Second, the prospect of joining NAFTA posed substantial dilemmas for many countries of Latin America. One issue was potential trade diversion. This risk seemed substantial for countries in the Southern Cone, which had major commercial partners outside the hemisphere. Another issue was NAFTA itself. This is a highly specialized treaty, adorned with special provisions and festooned with supplementary agreements on environmental and labor issues. It is a cumbersome instrument. What nonmember candidates have really wanted (at various times) are bilateral FTAs with the United States, straightforward and simple accords that would certify the signatories as secure and desirable sites for foreign investment and guarantee access to the U.S. consumer market. NAFTA was both more and less than Latin America wanted.

In any event, this option proved illusory. Not a single country gained admission to NAFTA. The key case in point was Chile, which was explicitly invited by the three NAFTA members to initiate negotiations for accession at the Miami summit of 1994—only to have the process collapse. Moreover, the list of viable candidates turned out to be very short—Argentina and Colombia fell by the wayside for different reasons, leaving only Costa Rica as a perpetual favorite.[5] Then the whole scheme collapsed in late 1997, when the U.S. Congress refused to renew fast track negotiating authority for the Clinton administration.

FTAA Negotiations

A second route to hemispheric integration emerged from the Miami "Summit of the Americas" in late 1994, where participants unanimously agreed on the ideal of a "Free Trade Area of the Americas." What happened in fact was that signatories designated the year 2005 as a deadline for the conclusion of *negotiations* for a free trade area, with implementation to follow in subsequent years. This was an ambiguous result. Advocates hailed the agreement for its high-minded principles and ambitious goals. Skeptics lamented its vagueness and its drawn-out timetable, which meant that official talks could drag on for a decade or more.

Miami also created confusion. While launching the FTAA process, NAFTA members invited Chile to commence negotiations on accession. This was apparently intended as a sign of good faith and as a commitment to tangible progress in what was then the near future. The practical result of the FTAA initiative, however, was to sow uncertainty about the feasibility of NAFTA accession. To a considerable extent, the lure of FTAA has closed the door to NAFTA.

Progress has been uneven over the years. Not surprisingly, President Clinton's inability to win congressional approval for fast track authorization in 1997 cast a long, dark shadow over hemispheric planning and negotiation. (Under fast track legislation, the U.S. Congress would have to approve or reject commercial treaties in their entirety, without introducing potentially crippling amendments.) Even so, the FTAA process has spawned a host of task forces and committee meetings. Ministers have met on a regular basis. And the ultimate pressure has continued to come from summit gatherings, in which heads of state have reaffirmed their commitment to the goal of hemispheric free trade.

The FTAA process differs sharply from NAFTA accession. All thirty-four participating countries have a role to play in the FTAA negotiations. Some are more influential than others, but all can take part. And while it can be expected that the United States would exercise paramount influence, it does not command an explicit veto; nor does Canada or Mexico, which would not necessarily enjoy special status because of membership in NAFTA. In fact, there is no clear rule for making decisions: at the rhetorical level, the emphasis appears to be on unanimity; at the operational level, it seems likely that the more powerful actors will strike bargains of their own. In general, however, the FTAA process seems fluid, flexible, and uncertain—not to say capricious.

Civil society has also been invited to make substantive contributions. And rather than aiming at a specific target (such as the provisions of NAFTA), the FTAA discussions tend to be expansive and open-ended. Such open-ended inclusiveness carries obvious risks. One is delay. Another is the temptation—even the likelihood—of least-common-denominator solutions.

North-South Coupling

Within the FTAA process, different states have different ideas about how the trade area should evolve. The most significant variation has come from Brazil, which has sought to reaffirm its position as a subregional hegemon and hemispheric power. Already the dominant country within MERCOSUR (the Common Market of the South), Brazil officially launched in April 1994 its proposal for a South American Free Trade Area, or SAFTA. Its declared goal is to create a free trade zone for "substantially all trade" throughout the continent—thus capitalizing on the experience of MERCOSUR, embracing neighboring countries, and building negotiating power for dealing with the United States.[6]

There is a political purpose as well. SAFTA would confirm Brazil's historic claim to leadership of South America, and it would give Brazil the role of representing the entire continent in FTAA negotiations with the United States. In effect, Brazil and the United States—leaders of South and North America, respectively—would settle the terms of hemispheric integration in tandem, more or less as equals. This would comply with a long-standing aspiration of Brazilian foreign policy. It would leave the terms of the North-South coupling open to negotiation: however "deep" the integration might be *within* the two regions, the linkage *between* the two regions could be quite another thing.

Prospects for SAFTA have waxed and waned. With prodding from Brazil, MERCOSUR reached agreements with Chile, Bolivia, and the Andean Community. The Brazilian financial crisis of 1999 brought this scheme to a temporary halt. It was revived the following year, when President Fernando Henrique Cardoso hosted a summit meeting of all South American presidents in the capital city of Brasília. Participants dealt with a broad range of issues—including democracy and drug trafficking—and pledged to strengthen economic relations. MERCOSUR and the Andean Community proposed to forge an FTA agreement by January 2002; it was hoped that Chile would become a full member of MERCOSUR; and, equally important, the governments agreed to coordinate negotiating positions in the FTAA process. As asserted in the final communiqué, the path to FTAA should be "based on the consolidation of subregional processes," not just on preferences of individual states.[7] And as Cardoso said in his closing statement, "South America will be one of the crucial elements in the building of a gradual integration at the hemispheric level and in the strengthening of our interface with the international economy." Not surprisingly, the stress upon South America—rather than Latin America—caused considerable discomfiture in Mexico, which was eventually invited to attend as an observer.

So Brazil is willing to consider the prospect of an FTAA, but it wants to play a major role in shaping the negotiating process and determining its outcome. In this context, Brazil has two major concerns:

one is maintaining its large (and long-protected) industrial sector, based in the city of São Paulo; the other is gaining access to the U.S. market—especially for steel, textiles, sugar, and frozen orange juice. It has been estimated, in fact, that U.S. subsidies and nontariff barriers cost Brazil as much as US$10 billion per year. To be acceptable to Brazil, FTAA must meet these two concerns. As the president of the Brazilian Rural Society has proclaimed, "I am in favor of free trade, but not in favor of getting ripped off." Foreign Minister Celso Lafer has bluntly stated that "The FTAA is an option, not destiny." In response to the U.S. government's imposition of new tariffs on imported steel in March 2002, Brazilian senator Paulo Hartung bristled: "There is already a prejudice in [the Brazilian] Congress about the FTAA, and a lack of confidence in relation to free trade.... The exacerbation of protectionism in the United States transforms these uncertainties into certainties and will oblige the Brazilian government to treat the FTAA in a different way."[8] And as the Brazilian ambassador to the United States has put it, with diplomatic delicacy: "Brazil believes that, for the FTAA to become a reality, it must be perceived as a two-way street by all the countries of the hemisphere, large and small, developed and developing. A zero-sum approach would kill the dream of a free trade area extending from Alaska to Tierra del Fuego."[9]

Apparently in deference to such concerns, Brazil and the United States have been designated as co-chairs for the final phase of FTAA negotiations—from late 2002 through to 2005. To a degree, this appears to enshrine the idea of North-South coupling. Whether this happens in practice is yet another matter.

Bilaterals with the United States

Still another option emerged at the turn of the century—bilateral free trade negotiations with the United States. In its waning days, the Clinton administration announced that it would open free trade discussions with Chile. Within its first year in office, the George W. Bush *fils* administration concluded its support for an IMF bailout of Argentina by declaring its intent to pursue "four-plus-one" trade negotiations with MERCOSUR. The Argentine situation deteriorated sharply at the end of 2001, the United States withdrew its support, and the trade negotiations went on hold. (Paradoxically, one consequence of the Argentine collapse was to strengthen that country's links to Brazil, since devaluation of the peso brought their exchange rate policies into much closer alignment. MERCOSUR thus became more cohesive as a bargaining unit but lost luster as an economic partner.) In the aftermath of this debacle, President Bush proclaimed in January 2002 that the United States would open free trade talks with countries of Central America.

These developments added still more confusion to the process of hemispheric integration. Tacitly at least, the initiation of bilateral (or minilateral) talks underscored frustration with—or the failure of—previously existing paths to regional integration. They left the content of the talks entirely open: the U.S.-Chile negotiations appeared to be heading toward a free trade agreement, as might be expected of U.S.–Central America talks as well, but there were no such signals for the "four-plus-one" conversations. There was no reason to assume that either agreement would resemble NAFTA or provide a blueprint for FTAA.

These undertakings further reaffirmed the power of the United States. These would not be conversations among equals. They would be highly asymmetrical negotiations (the U.S. economy is approximately 175 times larger than that of Central America, 140 times larger than Chile's, and 11 times larger than all of MERCOSUR's). Moreover, these initiatives have raised the possibility—long feared by Latin America and Canada—that the United States might eventually attempt to construct a "hub-and-spoke" network of economic arrangements throughout the hemisphere, with itself at the center—and in the commanding position. Several years ago, when NAFTA accession was still a major possibility, Sidney Weintraub warned of dangers in the bilateral approach:

> Using the bilateral and not the NAFTA accession route would, I am convinced, be a disaster for U.S. and hemispheric trade policy. If the United States concluded a bilateral agreement with Chile, Canada has said it would do the same to link the two spokes to the U.S. hub. Canada might well go further and sign bilateral agreements more broadly; in other words, there is a danger of competitive bilateralism in the name of economic integration. [10]

At bottom, these various routes—NAFTA accession, FTAA negotiations, North-South coupling, bilateral treaties—have not only opened different pathways toward hemispheric integration. They have also represented different levels or types of integration. By definition, expansion of NAFTA offered a "deep" form of integration. None of the others is so well defined. It seems reasonable to suppose that an open-ended FTAA process with active participants would lead to a relatively "light" or shallow form of integration. A more contained form of FTAA, achieved through North-South coupling, would perhaps be deep in some areas and shallow in others. Bilateral or minilateral discussions with the United States could yield almost anything, depending on the preferences of U.S. negotiators and policymakers; it is not at all clear that they would result in full-fledged free trade agreements or move in the direction of hemispheric integration.

At this writing, it seems reasonable to imagine six distinct scenarios for hemispheric trade.

- One is prolongation of the status quo, with a three-member NAFTA as the only formal trade accord connecting Latin America to the United States.

- A second possibility might be called "NAFTA-plus"—that is, a scenario under which NAFTA would undergo limited expansion to include three or four other countries of Latin America. The process would begin with Chile and then move on to other countries. (In theory, this might also be achieved through NAFTA-compatible bilateral arrangements with the United States, although this seems unlikely in practice.)

- A third possibility envisions the achievement of an FTAA through successive and eventually inclusive accessions to NAFTA, in which case the resulting extent of hemispheric integration would be relatively deep.

- An alternative path might entail a "docking" arrangement between NAFTA and either MERCOCUR or SAFTA—in other words, between the United States and Brazil.

- Yet another route would be the FTAA process itself, negotiated among all thirty-four countries, in which case the eventual degree of integration would probably be relatively shallow.

- Still another variation could be an incomplete or partial FTAA—a broad agreement accepted by most but not all countries of the hemisphere. In practice, the most important—and probable—holdout would be Brazil.

This broad range of plausible outcomes serves to emphasize the level of uncertainty surrounding the negotiating processes. The path to hemispheric integration is strewn with unintentional as well as intentional outcomes.

INTERESTS AND PREFERENCES

What is clear, however, is that different countries want different things. It could be surmised that, as the dominant power in the region, the United States would seek the deepest possible form of integration. Smaller countries, such as Chile, would prefer lighter forms— agreements that would provide them with "seals of good housekeeping" for attracting foreign investment, but without binding restrictions on environmental and labor practices. For its part, Brazil wants an agreement to be fairly comprehensive with regard to trade—effectively prohibiting U.S. nontariff barriers and discriminatory practices against Brazilian goods, including subsidies and antidumping measures—but not very intrusive in other areas of economic activity.[11]

Interests follow a different alignment with regard to rules. In general, smaller and weaker economies would want to establish a "rule-based" process for decision-making. This would have the inestimable advantage of leveling the playing field, since large and small countries would all have to abide by uniform rules. This impetus could even lead to a stated preference for some kind of supranational regulatory authority. The United States, by contrast, is likely to prefer weak rules, leaving dispute resolution to one-on-one negotiations among members—a process in which the United States could use its weight and influence to maximum advantage.

Moreover, it is essential to understand that processes of regional integration involve political (and geopolitical) interests as well as economic motivations. Participating nations seek political goals. This has been abundantly clear in the case of the European Union (EU), which drew strength at its outset from twin motivations: entanglement of Germany and containment of the Soviet Union. A political agenda has been equally apparent, if somewhat less visible, in the case of NAFTA.[12] Political goals will also have to undergird FTAA. Without strong political motivation, there will be no lasting integration.

These and other considerations translate into different preferences for different routes toward hemispheric economic integration. Table 20.1 displays the rank-order preferences for different nations as of late 2000/early 2001. These are based on first-hand observation, numerous conversations, and evaluations by an informal panel of judges. Choices include: the status quo (that is, with NAFTA in its current form and without FTAA); accession to NAFTA; North-South coupling, as espoused by Brazil; and the FTAA process, with thirty-four countries simultaneously involved in the negotiations.[13] Bilateral discussions with the United States are not included here, since they bear such a tenuous relationship to the hemispheric project.

Table 20.1. Rank-Order Preferences for Hemispheric Integration[1]

	Status Quo	NAFTA Accession	North-South Coupling	FTAA Process
Principal Actors				
Mexico	1	2	3	4
Brazil	2	4	1	3
Canada	3	2	4	1
United States$_{WH}$[2]	3	2	4	1
United States$_{CON}$[3]	1	2	4	3
Other Candidates				
Argentina	4	1	3	2
Chile	4	2	3	1
Central America and Caribbean	4	1–2	3	1–2
Andean Community	4	3	2	1

[1] 1 = first choice, 2 = second choice,… 4 = last choice.

[2] United States$_{WH}$ = U.S. White House.

[3] United States$_{CON}$ = U.S. Congress.

As presented in the table, Mexico's first choice would be the status quo, which would leave Mexico as the sole Latin American country to have formal and privileged access to the United States and Canada through NAFTA. Its second choice would be for accession to NAFTA, which would allow Mexico to control the process through the exercise of its virtual veto on expansion. North-South coupling would be a distant third; in this situation Mexico would act as a partner in the coalition of the "North" but as a junior partner with only modest influence. Last would be the FTAA process, in which Mexico would be only one of thirty-plus countries, without any privileged status.

Brazil, by contrast, has been avidly espousing the process of North-South coupling, which would clearly be its first choice. Second might be the status quo, in which Brazil would remain the dominant power in MERCOSUR and perhaps all of South America. Its third choice would be the FTAA process; here Brazil would be only one of thirty-four countries, but it would be the second-largest participant in the negotiations. From the standpoint of Brasília, accession to NAFTA would be the least desirable of all: it would require acceptance of provisions on labor and the environment, it would give the United States and Canada access to all elements of the Brazilian economy, and it would put Brazil in the position of being a supplicant—to Mexico, as well as to Canada and the United States.

Priorities for Canada are somewhat ambiguous. Government spokespersons fervently proclaim that Canada's leading preference—especially in the wake of the Quebec summit—is for the FTAA process. This could support Canada's increasingly active diplomacy throughout the region, elevate its position in the eyes of Latin America, and provide additional access to consumer markets and investment opportunities. Its second choice would be for NAFTA accession, which would enable Canada to strengthen ties to some countries of Latin America (the most desirable partners, in fact) while also managing to exercise a veto on admissions (for this reason, some Canadian analysts argue that NAFTA accession should really be the country's number-one preference). The status quo would be third, leaving Canada as a member of NAFTA. North-South coupling would probably be the last choice, since it would leave Canada largely on the sidelines in bilateral negotiations between Brazil and the United States.

The United States also reveals ambivalence. There are elements within the U.S. government that are deeply committed to the FTAA process. For U.S. business, a workable FTAA could open markets and expand new opportunities. And in negotiations with other world powers, specifically the EU and China and Japan, FTAA could provide the United States with considerable bargaining power. But the question is not merely whether hemispheric integration would be "good" for the United States. The question is whether the anticipated gains *above and beyond the benefits already provided by NAFTA* are substantial enough to generate a major effort on the part of Washington. Here the evidence is not entirely conclusive. Latin America accounts for only 15 to 17 percent of U.S. trade. More than half of that share (55 percent) is with Mexico alone, which has passed Japan to become the number two trading partner for the United States. Within the Americas, U.S. commercial interests focus mainly on Canada and Mexico, not on Latin America as a whole.

As shown by recent history, it tends to be the executive branch—under Bill Clinton, as well as under Bush father and son—that supports the FTAA process. Current President George W. Bush made this clear during his campaign and also during the Quebec summit. The second choice for the White House would be NAFTA accession, regarded (correctly) as a slower and less efficient means of integrating the hemisphere. Third would be the status quo. And fourth, in my estimation, is the idea of North-South coupling, in which the United States would have to grant inordinate leverage to Brazil.

The U.S. Congress has a different array of priorities. Most Democrats seem to favor the status quo—or, more accurately, they oppose any expansion of NAFTA or FTAA negotiations. This stance has taken the form of opposition to "trade promotion authority"—formerly known as fast track, under which Congress would have to vote for or against commercial agreements without amendment. The second choice for Congress might be NAFTA accession, precisely because it is slow and cumbersome, and because each new membership would require legislative approval. Third, for Congress, might be the FTAA process, which is likely to be supported by Republicans. And fourth would be the prospect of North-South coupling, which is not receiving a great deal of legislative attention at the moment.

These five actors—Mexico, Brazil, Canada, the U.S. White House, and the U.S. Congress—are likely to have a major influence on the process of hemispheric integration. And for all its imperfections and approximations, table 20.1 makes one fundamental point: there is no single route toward hemispheric integration that receives unanimous support. The FTAA process is favored perhaps by the White House and by Canada, but not by the U.S. Congress or Brazil or Mexico. NAFTA accession is a second-best choice for all actors except for Brazil, for which it would be the least favorite option. North-South coupling receives strong support only from Brazil.

Table 20.1 also demonstrates the power of the status quo, which is favored by both Mexico and the U.S. Congress. This fact has serious implications, since both of these parties possess a veto over NAFTA expansion—and the U.S. Congress can by itself veto FTAA negotiations (either by withholding fast track authority at the beginning or by refusing to ratify a proposed agreement at the end). If exercised, these vetoes would lead to only one result: preservation of the status quo.[14]

In sum, this analysis helps explain the intractability of the negotiation process. Key actors are not unanimous on where they want to go or on how they want to get there.

Aside from these major players, other countries of Latin America have one overriding interest: to find a workable means of integration with North America, especially with the United States. As displayed in table 20.1, all other nations (or groups)—Argentina, Chile, the Andean Community, Central America, and the Caribbean—want to change the status quo. That is to say, they want to avoid exclusion from ongoing processes of integration.

- Argentina has often proclaimed that its number-one aspiration would be to join NAFTA; its second-place preference would be FTAA negotiations. North-South coupling would be a bitter pill, since it would leave Argentina at the virtual mercy of longtime rival Brazil, but it would be better than nothing at all. And in the wake of the country's disastrous collapse in 2001–2002, Buenos Aires may have little choice.

- Chile, in contrast, has expressed reluctance about joining NAFTA, especially because of its denseness and its provisions on labor and the environment. (Largely for that reason, it has been happy to pursue bilateral negotiations with the United States alone.) NAFTA accession would be its second choice, and North-South coupling third.

- With slightly differing permutations, the Andean Community, Central America, and the Caribbean all want the same things— integration via FTAA, in which small countries could play a substantial role, or via NAFTA or even via North-South coupling. Anything would be better than the status quo.

Herein lies a bitter irony. The countries that want FTAA most are the smallest and weakest in the hemisphere—the ones that will have least impact on the outcome. For decisive action to take place, the major actors will have to resolve their differences.

Let me introduce some caveats. This is a highly schematic representation of complex realities. Moreover, the interests of a nation-state— or, better said, the *perceptions* of state interests—are subject to change over time. Revisions and redefinitions of interests can come about in response to (1) shifts in social and political coalitions, (2) changes in government (that is, from one party to another), (3) the appearance of new alternatives, or (4) alterations in the international environment—in particular, the emergence of common threats or re-arrangements of power. Thus the U.S. Congress switched from a more or less receptive attitude toward NAFTA expansion in the mid-1990s (1993–1997) to undisguised hostility (1997 to mid-2001); the White House changed from tepid endorsement of FTAA under Clinton to fervent advocacy under George W. Bush, although the president's attention was directed elsewhere in the aftermath of September 11; Canada has changed its first-choice preference from NAFTA expansion to the FTAA process; and Chile, repeatedly frustrated in its good-faith efforts to join NAFTA, has thrown its support toward FTAA (and sees its bilateral negotiations with the United States as enhancing that objective).

Moreover, the definition (and perception) of interests is highly contingent. Even if preferences are firm, voting can be strategic—that is, parties might forgo their preferences in one arena in hopes of gaining larger benefits in another arena. And preferences can come in combinations. For example, Mexico might soften its resistance to FTAA if the resulting accord were extremely shallow—a kind of "FTA lite"—one that would pose no challenge to Mexico's unique economic relationship with North America and the United States. (By the same token, Mexico would be increasingly receptive to FTAA in the event that NAFTA were substantially "deepened," as suggested by several other essays in this volume; the crucial factor is the *difference* between NAFTA and FTAA, since that is the marker of Mexico's special status.) Under these conditions, an FTAA could serve Mexico's geopolitical goal of reestablishing itself as a leader of Latin America. There is a point, of course, at which an FTAA could become so shallow as to have only symbolic meaning.

MODES OF BARGAINING

We now turn to modes of interaction among key actors in the integration process. In keeping with basic elements of game theory, the idea is to examine a series of contingent choices by key actors—contingent, that is, upon the choices made by other actors. This will provide a sense of the underlying dynamics of the bargaining process and, as a result, help identify the most plausible routes to FTAA.

In the interests of parsimony (and with apologies to Canada), the model has only four principal actors: the U.S. Congress, the U.S. White

House, Brazil, and "Spanish America"—a composite construction representing Spanish-speaking Latin America (but minus Mexico, which is already a member of NAFTA). Of course, these are analytical constructs—there is no such real-world unit as Spanish America. At the same time, it is not necessary for countries in this category to belong to some kind of political federation, or even to coordinate policies in a deliberate fashion; if their interests converge in such a way that sovereign decisions all move in the same direction, then the resulting behavior is essentially the same. The model also conflates the preference structure for Spanish America as follows: FTAA is the first choice; NAFTA accession is second; North-South coupling, third; and status quo is last. Preference structures for the other three actors are unchanged from table 20.1.

Table 20.2. Rank-Order Preferences for Hemispheric Integration, Reduced and Simplified

	Status Quo	NAFTA Accession	North-South Coupling	FTAA Process
United States (USA$_{CON}$)[1]	1	2	4	3
United States (USA$_{WH}$)[2]	3	2	4	1
Brazil (BRA)	2	4	1	3
Spanish America (SPAM)	4	2	3	1

[1] USA$_{CON}$ = U.S. Congress.
[2] USA$_{WH}$ = U.S. White House.

Beyond these options, there can be unintentional outcomes as well. One has been referred to as "NAFTA-plus," a modest process of NAFTA accession to include three or four countries, which would no doubt regard it as a positive development. But for those countries excluded from such an expansion—no doubt the majority—this would be a thoroughly disagreeable scenario, tantamount to perpetuation of the status quo, if not even worse, so it is considered as equivalent to a fourth-place choice. The other possible outcome is a "partial FTAA," imagined here as a relatively inclusive arrangement with a small number of abstentions. For Spanish American countries included in the scheme (SPAM$_{IN}$), it would be highly desirable; for the excluded countries (SPAM$_{OUT}$), it would be a negative outcome. And even for Brazil, the most important and likely holdout, the payoff would be as undesirable as NAFTA accession. For the U.S. White House, a partial FTAA would be less positive than a comprehensive arrangement but better than nothing at all—so this outcome would stand between the second- and third-place choices displayed in table 20.2.

The analysis traces sequential patterns of moves by participant actors. We here examine three such iterations, each beginning in a different fashion. Key questions are: Who moves first and in what direction? Who comes next and with what move? Who and what follows? And, perhaps most important, where is each sequence likely to lead? What are the predictable outcomes?

As displayed below, Iteration 1 (figure 20.1) involves three actors— Brazil, Spanish America, and the U.S. Congress—and reflects real-world situations as of the mid-1990s. The first move belongs to the U.S. Congress, on whether to approve and extend NAFTA or not. In fact, Congress chose to ratify NAFTA and, at least until it stood against fast track renewal in 1997, appeared to keep the door open to additional accession by members of SPAM (Chile being the conspicuous example).[15]

Reality came to a halt at this point. Let us nonetheless construct some counterfactual hypotheses. If this iteration had continued, it would have given the next move to SPAM. Had there been a genuine opportunity to accede to NAFTA, all the available evidence (and the preferences in table 20.2) suggests that SPAM would have chosen to cooperate. Had Spanish America chosen otherwise, the outcome would have been the status quo. As things turned out, Spanish America was unable to cooperate—in effect, the NAFTA invitation was withdrawn—and the status quo was the empirical result.

Had SPAM supported NAFTA accession, though, the next move would have gone to Brazil. Faced with a choice of joining NAFTA or being isolated from it, Brazil might have revised its preferences and elected to accede, in which case hemispheric integration would have been achieved through NAFTA expansion. As shown by the payoff matrix, Spanish America and the U.S. Congress would each have attained their second-place preference, while Brazil would have settled for its last-place choice. Were Brazil to decline, in keeping with the expectations in tables 20.1 and 20.2, the outcome would have been a variation of what we have called NAFTA-plus: an expanded NAFTA but without Brazil.

Figure 20.1. Iteration 1: Brazil, SPAM, USA_{CON} (1994–1997), First Move United States

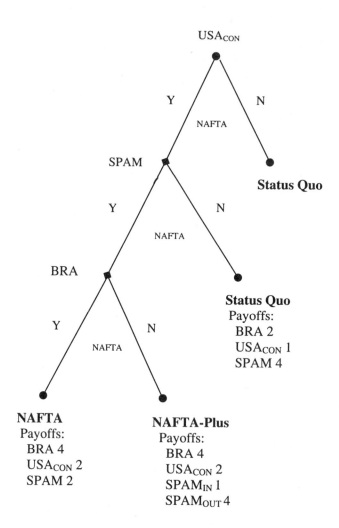

SPAM_{IN} = Spanish American countries included in NAFTA expansion.
SPAM_{OUT} = Spanish American countries excluded from NAFTA expansion.

With its definitive opposition to fast track authority in late 1997, the U.S. Congress effectively voted "no" on NAFTA expansion. For the next several years, that handed the initiative to Brazil.

In reflection of this situation, Iteration 2 (figure 20.2) involves the same three actors—Brazil, Spanish America, and the U.S. Congress—and begins with a move by Brazil in favor of North-South coupling. This represents Brazil's first-place choice, as argued above, and it corresponds to the campaign to build SAFTA. Moving down the left-hand side of the tree, the next step would go to Spanish America (SPAM)—which could either cooperate with Brazil (by joining or supporting SAFTA) or defect (by refusing to comply). If SPAM were to cooperate—since it would rather have North-South coupling than the status quo—the initiative would then pass on to the U.S. Congress, either in the form of fast track authorization for a North-South negotiation or ratification of a treaty. If Congress were to go along, which seems uncertain, the result would be North-South coupling with payoffs as follows: Brazil would get its first choice, Spanish America its third choice, and Congress would settle for its last-place choice. But this is not what the preference structures in table 20.2 anticipate. Instead, they suggest that that Congress would veto the North-South proposal in one way or another. There would be no North-South coupling, and the end result would be the status quo.

The right-hand side of the tree reflects these dynamics in another way. If Brazil were to give up on North-South coupling, this would result in the status quo. Under these circumstances, it would have been conceivable for the U.S. Congress to promote NAFTA expansion—and thus replicate the left-hand side of Iteration 1 with potential outcomes being a NAFTA expansion, NAFTA-plus, and the status quo. But Congress did not make this move, choosing instead to oppose fast track authorization, effectively ceding the next initiative to the White House.

This brings us to Iteration 3 (figure 20.3), which bears some resemblance to the real-world situation in the present moment. The first move belongs to the U.S. White House, which has declared its intent to press vigorously for FTAA. If the Bush II administration is able to make a meaningful move in this direction—by extracting trade promotion authority from the U.S. Congress[16] *and* moving forward with diplomatic negotiations—this would be a significant step. As of this writing, there are signs that the Bush team is proposing to do precisely that.[17]

Figure 20.2. Iteration 2: Brazil, SPAM, USA$_{CON}$ (1998–2000), First Move Brazil

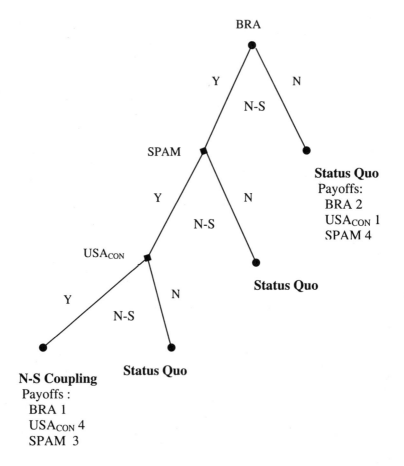

BRA

Y   N

N-S

SPAM

Y   N

N-S

Status Quo
Payoffs:
BRA 2
USA$_{CON}$ 1
SPAM 4

USA$_{CON}$

Y   N

N-S

Status Quo

N-S Coupling
Payoffs :
BRA 1
USA$_{CON}$ 4
SPAM 3

Status Quo

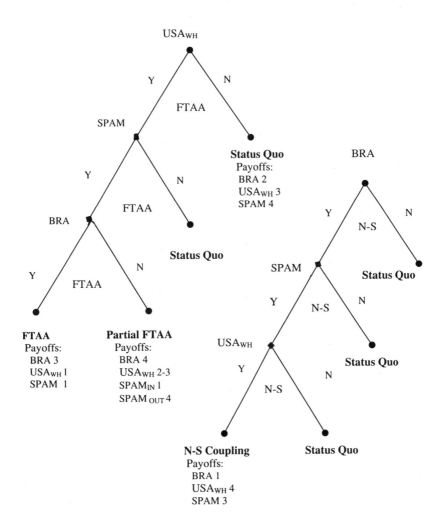

**Figure 20.3. Iteration 3: Brazil, SPAM, USA_WH (2001– ?),
First Move United States**

USA_WH

Y   N

FTAA

SPAM

Y   N

FTAA

BRA

Y   N

FTAA

FTAA
Payoffs:
BRA 3
USA_WH 1
SPAM 1

Partial FTAA
Payoffs:
BRA 4
USA_WH 2-3
SPAM_IN 1
SPAM _OUT 4

Status Quo
Payoffs:
BRA 2
USA_WH 3
SPAM 4

Status Quo

BRA

Y   N
N-S

SPAM   **Status Quo**

Y   N
N-S

USA_WH   **Status Quo**

Y   N
N-S

N-S Coupling
Payoffs:
BRA 1
USA_WH 4
SPAM 3

Status Quo

SPAM_IN = Spanish American countries included in FTAA.
SPAM_OUT = Spanish American countries excluded from FTAA.

The next move might then go to Spanish America, which, given its preference structure, would be certain to cooperate. Indeed, the recent flurry of U.S. bilateral proposals—for talks with Chile, MERCOSUR, and Central America—seems calculated to curry favor and support from Spanish America. This would leave the next move to Brazil, which would have the choice of cooperation or defection—in effect, inclusion or exclusion. If Brazil were to go along, this would lead to FTAA, with payoffs as follows: Spanish America and the White House would each get their first-place choice, while Brazil would settle for third. If Brazil were to refuse, we would then end up with a "partial FTAA"—a free trade agreement that would be different in content from NAFTA and that would include virtually all countries of Latin America except Brazil. $SPAM_{IN}$ would obtain its first-place choice, $SPAM_{OUT}$ would be forced into its last-place choice, the U.S. White House would have to accept an incomplete integration scheme, and Brazil would settle for exclusion. According to the preference structure, though, Brazil would favor FTAA over the lonesome prospect of hemispheric isolation.

The right-hand side of this diagram brings us back to prior starting points. If the White House is unable to make a serious move in the direction of FTAA, the initiative would move to Brazil—which would once again promote North-South coupling. In a replay of Iteration 2, this would give Spanish America the next move in North-South coupling: it could defect, thus perpetuating the status quo, or cooperate, giving the next move to the White House. If the White House (and Congress) were to accede, the outcome would be North-South coupling: Brazil would get its first choice, SPAM its third choice, and the White House its last choice. If the White House were to refuse, as seems likely in view of its preferences, the result would be the status quo.

CONCLUSIONS

Despite their abstract quality, these models yield significant conclusions. One relates to predicted outcomes. Ever since the withdrawal of fast track authorization by the U.S. Congress, hemispheric integration via NAFTA accession—as outlined in Iteration 1—has become a non-option. According to all three models, one of the most recurrent possible outcomes is continuation of the status quo. (This is the prediction for seven out of twelve separate results.) There has been nothing inevitable about FTAA.

As sketched out in Iteration 3, in fact, there appears to be only one plausible route toward a Free Trade Area of the Americas. This has a clear implication for U.S. policy. The White House should make a strong move in support of FTAA—by obtaining fast track authority, by proclaiming its support for hemispheric integration, and by enlisting support from Spanish America. If all these steps were taken by the time that the United States and Brazil assume the co-chairmanship of the FTAA negotiations, Brazil would be expected to cooperate— especially if negotiations are conducted in such a way as to have the appearance, at least, of North-South coupling.[18] Given the array of interests and preferences, there is no other way to get there.

Caveats on methodology offer warning signs on policy. First, it is entirely possible that preferences for key actors might change. Presidential elections in Brazil and other countries could elevate FTAA skeptics or opponents to pinnacles of national power (as almost happened in Peru). Political fallout from the terrorist attacks of September 2001 might lead to isolationist feelings throughout the United States. And economic downturns throughout the hemisphere could promote nationalist sentiments and beggar-thy-neighbor outlooks among peoples and governments of the Americas.

Second, three-player games have the benefits of elegance and parsimony, but they can obscure practical complexity. In actual fact, the United States and other major actors in the FTAA process will have to deal with dozens or even scores of participants in the course of the negotiations (as one colleague thundered in response to an early presentation of this essay, "There is no such thing as Spanish America!"). And at the other extreme, it is conceivable that Latin American countries could form a unified bloc in confronting the United States— which would lead to a two-player game, making it impossible for Washington (or anyone else) to play Brazil and Spanish America against one another.

Third, the game-theoretic models implicitly assume that all participant actors are able to make their moves according to their preferences—in other words, with a reasonable degree of independence. Some would argue that this condition does not hold. In the post–Cold War environment, radical analysts (from both left and right) could plausibly claim that Latin American countries simply do not command sufficient resources to resist the United States: what Washington wants, Washington gets. Under such circumstances, the only question is how much pressure the United States is willing to apply in order to achieve the kind of hemispheric integration that it wants. This viewpoint has some merit, but I believe that it is an exaggeration: U.S. hegemony does not mean total U.S. domination.[19] Moreover, the preference structures for Latin America tacitly consider U.S. power as a contributing factor in the construction of priorities.

Ultimately, concerns of this kind raise fundamental questions about the substance of FTAA. Will it be a good thing? Not necessarily. In my personal view, FTAA will not be such a positive development if it fails to address social and political realities and becomes yet another instrument for the exercise of U.S. power in the hemisphere. FTAA could be genuinely beneficial, however, if it were to meet key criteria:

- if it addresses Latin America's legitimate concerns on agriculture, including Brazilian complaints about subsidies and antidumping;

- if it provides a way to address long-standing issues of poverty and inequality throughout the region;

- if it levels the playing field for dispute resolution and related matters through multilateral mechanisms and rule-based criteria;

- and if, in the long run, it promotes economic integration on a global scale, rather than forging an autonomous bloc that the United States can use as a weapon in disputes with other countries and regions of the world.[20]

These goals can be achieved only if the United States listens, really listens, to the voice of the governments and peoples of Latin America.

Therein lies the challenge. *Carpe diem.*

Notes

I wish to thank Matthew McCubbins for guidance on methodology, Chrisje Aardening and Kati Suominen for research assistance, and Felipe de la Balze for helpful comments on an earlier draft of this essay.

1. See 43-page "Plan of Action."

2. See Richard Feinberg and Robin Rosenberg, "The Quebec Summit: Tear Gas, Trade, and Democracy," *North-South Center Update* (May 2001). For background, also see Richard Feinberg, *Summitry in the Americas: A Progress Report* (Washington, D.C.: Institute of International Economics, 1997), and

Richard Feinberg and Robin Rosenberg, eds., *Civil Society and the Summit of the Americas: The 1998 Santiago Summit* (Miami: North-South Center Press, 1999).

3. True to form, Fidel Castro responded to the Quebec accords with a stinging rebuke: "For Cuba," he declared, "it is clear that the so -called Free Trade Agreement of the Americas in its conditions, time frame, strategy, objectives and procedures imposed by the United States, inexorably leads to the annexation of Latin America by the United States.... The worst, the saddest, the most cynical and hypocritical [fact] is that this monstrous path is being attempted without consulting the people. That is all the democracy that the empire and its lackeys can conceive of." In David Gonzalez, "On Free Trade, Castro Sees U.S. Guile and Latin Dupes," *New York Times*, May 2, 2001.

4. Scholarly treatments of FTAA processes are conspicuous by scarcity. Leading examples include chapters by Carol Wise and Stephan Haggard in *The Post-NAFTA Political Economy: Mexico and the Western Hemisphere*, ed. Carol Wise (University Park: Pennsylvania State University Press, 1998); Victor Bulmer-Thomas and Sheila Page, "Trade Relations in the Americas: MERCOSUR, the Free Trade Area of the Americas and the European Union," in *The United States and Latin America: The New Agenda*, ed. Victor Bulmer-Thomas and James Dunkerley (Cambridge, Mass.: Harvard University Press, 1999); Roberto Bouzas, "Trade and Investment Issues in the Americas," in *The Future of Inter-American Relations*, ed. Jorge I. Domínguez (New York: Routledge, 2000); Pedro da Motta Veiga, "Os países do Mercosul frente às negoci acões comerciais: um exercicio de elaboracão de cenários" (Buenos Aires: FLACSO, November 2000); and papers presented by Richard Stahler -Sholk and others at a meeting of the International Studies Association (Chicago, February 2001).

5. See Carol Wise, "The Trade Scenario for Other Latin American Reformers in the NAFTA Era," in *The Post-NAFTA Political Economy*, ed. Wise, pp. 294–97.

6. Negotiations with the European Union are also intended to enhance bargaining power vis-à-vis the United States. See Victor Bulmer-Thomas, "The European Union and MERCOSUR: Prospects for a Free Trade Agreement," *Journal of Interamerican Studies and World Affairs* 42, no. 1 (March 2000).

7. "The Brasília Communiqué," Meeting of the Presidents of South America, September 1, 2000.

8. Quoted in Matthew Flynn, "Free Trade According to U.S.," Americas Program Commentary (Silver City, N.M.: Interhemispheric Resource Center, March 11, 2002), at www.americaspolicy.org.

9. Rubens A. Barbosa, "A View from Brazil," *Washington Quarterly* 24, no. 2 (Spring 2001): 149–57, quote p. 152. In addition, the U.S. farm bill of May 2002—which increased agricultural subsidies by nearly 80 percent—drew stinging attacks from Europe and Latin America. "As a result of the increase in farm subsidies," said Brazilian minister of agriculture Marcus Pratini de Moraes, "negotiations for the creation of FTAA are now nonviable."

10. Sidney Weintraub, *NAFTA: What Comes Next?* (Washington, D.C.: Center for Strategic and International Studies, 1994), p. 96.

11. Brazil became a major target of antidumping measures during the 1990s. See José Tavares de Araujo, Jr., Carla Macario, and Karsten Steinfatt, "Antidumping in the Americas" (Santiago: CEPAL/ECLAC, March 2001).

12. See Peter H. Smith, *Talons of the Eagle: Dynamics of U.S.–Latin American Relations* (New York: Oxford University Press, 2000), pp. 259–66.

13. For an earlier version of this table, see Peter H. Smith, "Whither Hemispheric Integration?" *Business Economics* 34, no. 3 (July 1999): 38–46, especially p. 44.

14. It is entirely possible that Mexico, under Vicente Fox, might waive its veto rights on NAFTA accession—for the sake of foreign policy goals in relation to either Latin America or the United States.

15. As Carol Wise has reported, "Chile was still considered by U.S. trade-policy makers to be a contender for NAFTA entry right up until the definitive failure of the Clinton administration to obtain the necessary fast track negotiating authority in late 1997." Wise, "The Trade Scenario for Other Latin American Reformers," pp. 295–96.

16. The White House finally obtained trade promotion authority (TPA) in July–August 2002. The U.S. House of Representatives approved the measure by the razor-thin margin of 215 to 212; the Senate then voted in favor by 64 to 34.

17. See op-ed piece entitled "Countering Terror with Trade" by U.S. Trade Representative Robert Zoellick, *Washington Post*, September 20, 2001. In the wake of the terrorist attacks of September 11, he wrote, "Congress now needs to send an unmistakable signal to the world that the United States is committed to global leadership of openness.... And most important, Congress needs to enact U.S. trade promotion authority so America can negotiate agreements that advance the cause of openness, development and growth."

18. Depending in part on the outcome of Brazil's presidential election in October 2002, since prominent candidates have expressed opposition to FTAA.

19. See Smith, *Talons of the Eagle*, especially chap. 9.

20. See Jagdish Bhagwati, Pravin Krishna, and Arvind Panagariya, eds., *Trading Blocs: Alternative Approaches to Analyzing Preferential Trade Agreements* (Cambridge, Mass.: MIT Press, 1999).

About the Contributors

Carlos Alba Vega is professor of international relations at El Colegio de México. He earned his doctorate from the École des Hautes Études en Sciences Sociales in Paris. Dr. Alba has published numerous books and articles on matters related to Mexican economics, society, and politics. These works give special attention to small-scale industry and the informal sector, the regional impact of the Mexican crisis, industrial history and development, relations between the business community and the state, the effects of globalization, and the dynamics and consequences of economic liberalization and NAFTA in Mexico.

Leigh Anderson is associate professor at the Daniel J. Evans School of Public Affairs at the University of Washington. Anderson is an economist with research and teaching interests in international economic development, particularly microfinance, and trade and environmental policy. Within these areas she has published articles in *World Development*, the *Journal of Economic History*, and the *International Review of Law and Economics*.

Graciela Bensusán is professor at the Universidad Autónoma Metropolitana (UAM) in Xochimilco and a researcher at the Facultad Latinoamericana de Ciencias Sociales (FLACSO) in Mexico City. An expert on social policy and labor organizations, Bensusán has written and coauthored several books, including *Negociación y conflicto laboral en México* (1991); *Las relaciones laborales y el Tratado de Libre Comercio* (1992); *Integración regional y relaciones sindicales en América del Norte* (1996); and *Modelo mexicano de regulación laboral* (2000). She holds a Ph.D. in political science from the Universidad Nacional Autónoma de México (UNAM) and is a member of Mexico's Sistema Nacional de Investigadores.

Robert J. Brym is professor of sociology at the University of Toronto. His main areas of research are political sociology, race and ethnic relations, and the sociology of culture. His major works include *Intellectuals and Politics* (1980); *From Culture to Power: The Sociology of English Canada* (1989); *The Jews of Moscow, Kiev, and Minsk* (1994); *New Society*

(3d ed., 2001), and *Sociology: Your Compass for a New World* (forthcoming 2003). He has served as editor of the *Canadian Review of Sociology and Anthropology* (Montreal), *Current Sociology* (London), and *East European Jewish Affairs* (London).

Edward J. Chambers is director of the Western Centre for Economic Research at the University of Alberta. After teaching at the University of Montana and the University of Washington, he joined the University of Alberta to serve as Dean of the Faculty of Business. Dr. Chambers has published extensively in the fields of business fluctuations and regional economics. His present research interests focus on western Canada's economic position in the international economy, and on the effects of structural adjustment on resource requirements and allocations within the region.

Wayne A. Cornelius is Gildred Professor of Political Science and International Relations, Director of the Center for Comparative Immigration Studies, and Director of the Center for U.S.-Mexican Studies at the University of California, San Diego. Cornelius specializes in comparative studies of the political economy of immigration and immigration policy in advanced industrial nations, Mexican politics, and U.S.-Mexican relations. His books include *Controlling Immigration: A Global Perspective* (1994); *Subnational Politics and Democratization in Mexico* (1998); and *The International Migration of the Highly Skilled: Demand, Supply, and Development Consequences for Sending and Receiving Countries* (coeditor, 2001).

Debra J. Davidson is assistant professor of environmental sociology in the departments of Rural Economy and Renewable Resources at the University of Alberta. Her primary areas of research and teaching include: environmental governance systems, environmental risk and justice, and social conflicts over natural resource issues. A Ph.D. from the University of Wisconsin–Madison, she has written articles on resource management, environmental policy, and implementation of the Endangered Species Act in the United States.

James B. Gerber is professor of economics at San Diego State University and a research fellow at the San Diego Dialogue, University of California, San Diego. His most recent book publications include *International Economics* (2001) and *North American Economic Integration: Theory and Practice* (1999). Dr. Gerber has taught in Canada and Mexico and is currently involved in the study of trade patterns in Chile and the rest of South America. His areas of expertise include international economics, U.S. economic history, economic integration, and Latin America.

Raúl Hinojosa-Ojeda is research director at the North American Integration and Development Center and assistant professor of international and regional development in the School of Public Policy and Social Research at the University of California, Los Angeles. He is the author of numerous articles and books on the political economy of regional integration, including trade, investment, and migration relations between the United States, Mexico, Latin American, and the Pacific Rim. He is coeditor of *Labor Market Interdependence between the United States and Mexico* (1992) and *Convergence and Divergence between NAFTA, Chile, and MERCOSUR: Overcoming Dilemmas of North and South American Economic Integration* (1997). He has been a visiting scholar at the Inter-American Development Bank, the World Bank, and academic institutions in Mexico and the United States.

Ryan Hoskins completed his B.A. in Combined Honours Economics and History from the University of Alberta in 2001; his academic interest has focused on the economic development of Latin America, especially with respect to trade. In the summer of 2000 and again in 2001, he worked as a research assistant for Michele Veeman and Terry Veeman. He has also worked as a policy researcher at the Alberta Legislature. He intends to pursue a Master's degree program that will advance his interest in public policy.

Steven Kull is director of the Center on Policy Attitudes and professor at the School of Public Affairs, University of Maryland. His most recent book, coauthored with I.M. Destler, is *Misreading the Public: The Myth of a New Isolationism* (1999). A frequent consultant to governments and international organizations, he has published articles in *Foreign Policy*, the *Public Opinion Quarterly*, the *Washington Post*, and the *Christian Science Monitor*. He has written extensively on U.S. and Soviet attitudes during and after the Cold War, including *Burying Lenin: The Revolution in Soviet Ideology and Foreign Policy*.

Robert K. McCleery is professor of economics at the Monterey Institute of International Studies. His research focuses on Mexican and Southeast Asian development, trade policy and economic integration in Asia and the Americas, and international political economy issues.

He has held faculty positions at the East-West Center in Honolulu, Kobe University in Japan, and Claremont McKenna College in Los Angeles, as well as short-term consulting positions with the United Nations, the Asian Development Bank, the Institute for Developing Economies (Tokyo), and the U.S. Department of Commerce. Recent publications include "The Dynamics of Integration in the Americas," in *Regionalism, Multilateralism and the Politics of Global Trade,* edited by D. Barry and R. Keith (1999).

Rolf Mirus is professor of international business at the University of Alberta's School of Business. A native of Germany, he holds a Ph.D. in economics from the University of Minnesota. His research has focused on the underground economy, countertrade, and commercial policy. He is coeditor of a forthcoming book, *The Economics of Barter and Countertrade,* and the author of articles in the *Journal of Finance,* the *Journal of International Money, Canadian Public Policy,* and other prominent journals.

Ross E. Mitchell is a Ph.D. candidate in the Department of Rural Economy at the University of Alberta. His research interests focus on environmental sociology, natural resource management, community development, and ecotourism. His is currently working on forest-dependent communities in Oaxaca, Mexico, with partial funding from the International Research Development Centre in Ottawa.

Alejandro Moreno teaches at the Instituto Tecnológico Autónomo de México (ITAM) and directs the public opinion research unit at the newspaper *Reforma* in Mexico City. He holds a Ph.D. in political science from the University of Michigan, Ann Arbor. He is the author of *Political Cleavages: Issues, Parties and the Consolidation of Democracy,* and co-author of *Human Values and Beliefs: A Cross-Cultural Sourcebook.*

Neil Nevitte is professor of political science at the University of Toronto. His areas of expertise include statistics, research methodology, and public opinion and voting. He has published fourteen books including, recently, *Value Change and Governance* (forthcoming 2002), *Anatomy of a Liberal Victory* (forthcoming 2002), *Unsteady State* (2000), *Political Value Change in Western Democracies* (1998), and *The Decline of Deference* (1996), as well as more than fifty articles and book chapters. Nevitte is the principal investigator of the World Values Surveys (Canada) and co-investigator of the 1997 and 2000 Canadian Election Study research team. He has previously taught at Harvard University and the University of Calgary.

Kenneth Norrie is Provost at McMaster University and former Dean of the Faculty of Arts at the University of Alberta. He was seconded to the Royal Commission on the Economic Union and Development Prospects for Canada (the Macdonald Commission) in 1983–1985 and served as a visiting economist at the Canadian Government's Department of Finance in 1990–1991. He is the author or coauthor of five monographs, including *A History of the Canadian Economy* (2d ed., 1996) with Douglas Owram. He has published articles in *The Canadian Journal of Economics, Journal of Economic History, Canadian Public Policy, Agricultural History, Canadian Papers in Rural History, Canadian Journal of Political Science, Economy and History, Journal of Canadian Studies, Explorations in Economic History,* and *Publius: the Journal of Federalism.*

Mark Ojah is a research associate at the Texas Transportation Institute in College Station, Texas. His current research focuses on the development of improved stakeholder coordination systems at major commercial ports of entry along the U.S.–Mexico border. Prior to joining TTI, he was a research affiliate at the University of Manitoba Transport Institute in Winnipeg, Canada, where he examined the impact of NAFTA on Mexican and North American transportation networks. Mr. Ojah is a graduate of the University of Manitoba's C.Log program in Transportation and Logistics.

Antonio Ortiz Mena L.N. is researcher and lecturer in international studies at the Centro de Investigación y Docencia Económicas (CIDE) in Mexico City. He earned an M.A. in Latin American Studies from the University of London and a Ph.D. in political science from the University of California, San Diego. He also worked for the NAFTA Negotiation Office of the Mexican government. His research interests are in the field of international political economy, especially regional integration and economic governance.

Douglas Owram is Vice-President (Academic) and professor of history at the University of Alberta. His specialties include the nineteenth and twentieth centuries, international relations, and the Canadian economy as well as social and intellectual history. His research has resulted in the publication of seven books and numerous articles. His most recent work has focused on the youth of Canada after World War II, from the 1940s through the tumultuous 1960s.

Robert A. Pastor is Vice President of International Affairs and Professor of International Relations at American University, where he is establishing and directing a Center on North American Studies and a Center for Democracy and Election Management. From 1985 to 1998, Dr. Pastor was Fellow and Founding Director of the Latin American and Caribbean Program, the Democracy Program, and the China Elections Project at the Carter Center, and until 2002 he was also professor of political science at Emory University. His recent books include *Toward a North American Community: Lessons from the Old World for the New* (2001) and *Exiting the Whirlpool: US Foreign Policy toward Latin America and the Caribbean* (2001).

Barry E. Prentice is director of the Transport Institute and associate professor of transportation economics and logistics at the University of Manitoba. His major research and teaching interests include logistics, transportation economics, agribusiness marketing, and trade policy, and he has authored or coauthored more than one hundred research reports, journal articles, and contributions to books. In 1999, National Transportation Week named him Manitoba Transportation Person of the Year. He is Associate Editor of the *Journal of Transportation Research Forum* and Honourary President of the Canadian Institute for Traffic and Transportation.

Linda C. Reif is professor in the Faculty of Law at the University of Alberta. She has written on international trade and investment law, international environmental law, and international human rights law in Canada, the United States, Japan, and Europe. She serves on editorial boards of both the *Canadian Yearbook of International Law* and *Global Governance*. She is on the roster of environmental experts under the Canada-Chile Agreement on Environmental Cooperation and on the roster for NAFTA Chapter 20 disputes.

Nataliya Rylska, a native of the Ukraine, holds a Ph.D. in economics from the Institute of Economics in Kiev and an MBA from the University of Alberta. She is currently pursuing graduate studies in financial economics and has been a research associate of the Western Centre for Economic Research at the University of Alberta.

Constance Smith is professor of economics at the University of Alberta. She has been Economist at the Bank of Canada and Visiting Scholar at the Australian National University. Her research interests include the macroeconomic effects of tariffs, the impact of government debt on sovereign debt credit ratings, and the importance of country and currency risk in exchange rate determination.

Peter H. Smith is professor of political science and Simón Bolívar Professor of Latin American Studies at the University of California, San Diego. His most recent publications include the coauthored *Modern Latin America* (5th rev. ed., 2001) and *Talons of the Eagle: Dynamics of U.S.-Latin American Relations* (2d rev. ed., 2000). He is also editor of *The Challenge of Integration: Europe and the Americas* (1993) and coeditor of *Cooperation or Rivalry? Regional Integration in the Americas and the Pacific Rim* (1996).

José Luis Valdés Ugalde is director of the Centro de Investigaciones sobre América del Norte (CISAN) at the Universidad Nacional Autónoma de México (UNAM). He holds a doctorate in international relations from the London School of Economics. His publications include *The Mirror of the Hemispheric Past: The United States and Latin America; NAFTA and Mexico, the Future of Democracy and Economic Development;* and, most recently, *Análisis de los efectos del Tratado de Libre Comercio de América del Norte en la economía mexicana: una visión sectorial a cinco años de distancia* (2000). He has held visiting appointments at Pennsylvania State University, the London School of Economics, the University of Westminster, and Kings College.

Michele M. Veeman is professor of Agricultural and Resource Economics in the Department of Rural Economy at the University of Alberta and was chair of that department from 1992 to 2002. She holds a Master's degree from Adelaide University, South Australia, and a Ph.D. from the University of California, Berkeley. Her research and publications focus on agricultural and food product markets, trade and policy, and the regulation of markets for primary products. She is Fellow and previous President of the Canadian Agricultural Economics Society.

Terrence S. Veeman is a professor in the departments of Economics and Rural Economy of the University of Alberta. He was educated at the University of Saskatchewan, Oxford University (where he was a Rhodes Scholar), and the University of California, Berkeley. His re-

search and publications focus on agricultural and forest productivity, sustainable development, water policy, and grain export demand. He has served as president of the Canadian Agricultural Economics Society, co-leader of the Socio-Economic Sustainability Theme of the Sustainable Forest Management Network of Centres of Excellence in Canada, and as the Network's interim program leader.

Phillip S. Warf is a research associate at the Center on Policy Attitudes and its Program on International Policy Attitudes (a program of the University of Maryland) in Washington, D.C. Mr. Warf has an extensive background in U.S. and international politics and survey research. He has implemented survey research projects for political campaigns, corporations, and advocacy organizations in the United States, Europe, the Middle East, Africa, and Latin America